TRAINERS

JUMPS STATISTICS 2005–2006

Edited by Ashley Rumney

Published in 2006 by Raceform Ltd
Compton, Newbury, Berkshire RG20 6NL
Raceform Ltd is a wholly-owned subsidiary of Trinity Mirror plc

A catalogue record of this book is available from the British Library.

ISBN 1-905153-19-8

Cover designed by Tracey Scarlett
Interiors designed by Fiona Pike
Data programming by Dan Dipol

Printed and bound in Great Britain by William Clowes Ltd, Beccles, Suffolk

CONTENTS

WINNING TRAINERS

Jumps statistics for the 2005-2006 season for winning British-based trainers, including overseas runners. Trainers with less than ten winners are shown with abbreviated statistics.

Winning horses preceded by an asterisk joined the stable during the course of the season; an asterisk following the horse's name denotes a switch to another trainer during the season. Horses that have changed ownership within the yard are shown with statistics for each owner. Names may be abbreviated due to the pressure of space.

N W ALEXANDER

KINNESTON, PERTH & KINROSS

	No. of Hrs	Races Run	1st	2nd	3rd	Unpl	Per cent	£1 Level Stake
NH Flat	4	5	0	0	0	5	0.0	-5.00
Hurdles	8	22	0	2	1	19	0.0	-22.00
Chases	6	16	1	1	1	13	6.3	-5.00
Totals	**11**	**43**	**1**	**3**	**2**	**37**	**2.3**	**-32.00**
04-05	7	32	1	4	6	21	3.1	-23.50
03-04	7	25	4	1	0	20	16.0	+13.33

JOCKEYS

	W-R	Per cent	£1 Level Stake
Brian Harding	1-4	25.0	+7.00

COURSE RECORD

	Total W-R	Non-Hndcps Hurdles	Chases	Hndcps Hurdles	Chases	NH Flat	Per cent	£1 Level Stake
Ayr	1-23	0-7	0-0	0-4	1-9	0-3	4.3	-12.00

WINNING HORSES

Horse	Races Run	1st	2nd	3rd	£
Fountain Brig	6	1	1	1	4959
Total winning prize-money					**£4959**
Favourites	0-2		0.0%		-2.00

R ALLAN

CORNHILL-ON-TWEED, NORTHUMBERLAND

	No. of Hrs	Races Run	1st	2nd	3rd	Unpl	Per cent	£1 Level Stake
NH Flat	2	3	0	0	0	3	0.0	-3.00
Hurdles	8	34	2	3	1	28	5.9	-6.00
Chases	0	0	0	0	0	0	0.0	0.00
Totals	**9**	**37**	**2**	**3**	**1**	**31**	**5.4**	**-9.00**
04-05	9	46	1	1	3	41	2.2	-41.00
03-04	14	49	2	5	4	38	4.1	-34.50

JOCKEYS

	W-R	Per cent	£1 Level Stake
G Lee	1-2	50.0	+13.00
Tony Dobbin	1-7	14.3	+6.00

COURSE RECORD

	Total W-R	Non-Hndcps Hurdles	Chases	Hndcps Hurdles	Chases	NH Flat	Per cent	£1 Level Stake
Kelso	2-9	0-2	0-0	2-7	0-0	0-0	22.2	+19.00

WINNING HORSES

Horse		Races Run	1st	2nd	3rd	£
Acceleration		9	2	0	1	8831
Total winning prize-money						**£8831**
Favourites	0-1		0.0%			-1.00

R H ALNER

DROOP, DORSET

	No. of Hrs	Races Run	1st	2nd	3rd	Unpl	Per cent	£1 Level Stake
NH Flat	8	12	0	1	1	10	0.0	-12.00
Hurdles	46	152	16	18	18	100	10.5	-64.64
Chases	46	188	22	25	20	121	11.7	-17.49
Totals	**80**	**352**	**38**	**44**	**39**	**231**	**10.8**	**-94.13**
04-05	68	342	40	45	50	207	11.7	-28.98
03-04	65	287	28	34	42	183	9.8	-124.67

BY MONTH

NH Flat	W-R	Per cent	£1 Level Stake	Hurdles	W-R	Per cent	£1 Level Stake
May	0-0	0.0	0.00	May	1-9	11.1	-6.38
June	0-0	0.0	0.00	June	0-4	0.0	-4.00
July	0-0	0.0	0.00	July	1-4	25.0	+7.00
August	0-0	0.0	0.00	August	0-4	0.0	-4.00
September	0-0	0.0	0.00	September	0-3	0.0	3.00
October	0-1	0.0	-1.00	October	1-16	6.3	-10.00
November	0-0	0.0	0.00	November	3-21	14.3	-8.63
December	0-2	0.0	-2.00	December	4-21	19.0	+12.50
January	0-4	0.0	-4.00	January	0-17	0.0	-17.00
February	0-2	0.0	-2.00	February	0-18	0.0	-18.00
March	0-1	0.0	-1.00	March	3-16	18.8	-9.88
April	0-2	0.0	-2.00	April	3-19	15.8	-3.25

Chases	W-R	Per cent	£1 Level Stake	Totals	W-R	Per cent	£1 Level Stake
May	2-7	28.6	-1.17	May	3-16	18.8	-7.55
June	0-2	0.0	-2.00	June	0-6	0.0	-6.00
July	0-3	0.0	-3.00	July	1-7	14.3	+4.00
August	0-4	0.0	-4.00	August	0-8	0.0	8.00
September	0-5	0.0	-5.00	September	0-8	0.0	-8.00
October	1-17	5.9	-13.75	October	2-34	5.9	-24.75
November	3-31	9.7	+1.00	November	6-52	11.5	-7.63
December	3-24	12.5	-12.00	December	7-47	14.9	-1.50
January	4-30	13.3	+0.48	January	4-51	7.8	-20.52
February	2-23	8.7	+1.50	February	2-43	4.7	-18.50
March	4-23	17.4	+5.25	March	7-40	17.5	-5.63
April	3-19	15.8	+15.20	April	6-40	15.0	+9.95

DISTANCE

Hurdles	W-R	Per cent	£1 Level Stake	Chases	W-R	Per cent	£1 Level Stake
2m-2m3f	5-71	7.0	-47.76	2m-2m3f	7-42	16.7	-17.30
2m4f-2m7f	10-58	17.2	-14.88	2m4f-2m7f	10-60	16.7	+42.31
3m+	1-23	4.3	-2.00	3m+	5-86	5.8	-42.50

TYPE OF RACE

Non-Handicaps	W-R	Per cent	£1 Level Stake	Handicaps	W-R	Per cent	£1 Level Stake
Nov Hrdls	3-55	5.5	-46.50	Nov Hrdls	3-13	23.1	+1.25
Hrdls	2-17	11.8	-14.14	Hrdls	8-63	12.7	-1.25
Nov Chs	10-35	28.6	+41.01	Nov Chs	4-23	17.4	-5.25
Chases	1-9	11.1	0.00	Chases	7-121	5.8	-53.25
Sell/Claim	0-2	0.0	-2.00	Sell/Claim	0-0	0.0	0.00

RACE CLASS / FIRST TIME OUT

Race Class	W-R	Per cent	£1 Level Stake	First Time Out	W-R	Per cent	£1 Level Stake
Class 1	3-28	10.7	-15.02	Bumpers	0-8	0.0	-8.00
Class 2	2-17	11.8	+7.00	Hurdles	5-36	13.9	-14.25
Class 3	11-133	8.3	-13.30	Chases	7-36	19.4	+37.08
Class 4	21-154	13.6	-54.64				
Class 5	0-9	0.0	-9.00	Totals	12-80	15.0	+14.83
Class 6	1-11	9.1	-9.17				

JOCKEYS

	W-R	Per cent	£1 Level Stake
Andrew Thornton	21-170	12.4	-68.82
Robert Walford	9-95	9.5	-11.75
Daryl Jacob	6-37	16.2	+19.83
Tom Scudamore	1-4	25.0	+11.00
Timmy Murphy	1-7	14.3	-5.38

COURSE RECORD

	Total W-R	Non-Hndcps Hurdles	Chases	Hndcps Hurdles	Chases	NH Flat	Per cent	£1 Level Stake
Wincanton	5-37	2-12	1-2	0-6	2-15	0-2	13.5	+0.38
Taunton	4-24	1-7	0-0	1-5	2-11	0-1	16.7	+18.37
Southwell	3-6	0-0	0-0	1-1	2-5	0-0	50.0	+7.50
Chepstow	3-24	0-6	0-1	0-6	3-11	0-0	12.5	-9.75
Exeter	3-54	0-8	1-11	2-11	0-21	0-3	5.6	-35.25
Leicester	2-8	0-3	1-2	1-1	0-2	0-0	25.0	+15.50
Warwick	2-9	1-3	0-0	1-3	0-3	0-0	22.2	-4.50
Lingfield	2-11	0-2	0-3	2-4	0-2	0-0	18.2	+1.00
Nton Abbot	2-11	0-2	1-1	1-3	0-4	0-1	18.2	+15.00
Fontwell	2-23	0-7	1-2	1-5	0-8	0-1	8.7	-18.25
Bangor	1-3	0-0	1-1	0-1	0-1	0-0	33.3	-0.80
Hereford	1-3	0-0	1-1	0-1	0-1	0-0	33.3	+0.25
Windsor	1-3	0-0	1-1	0-1	0-1	0-0	33.3	-0.75
Haydock	1-7	0-1	1-1	0-1	0-4	0-0	14.3	+2.00
Ludlow	1-7	0-2	0-0	0-0	1-5	0-0	14.3	+6.00
Cheltenham	1-8	0-0	1-5	0-2	0-1	0-0	12.5	-6.27
Folkestone	1-9	0-2	1-3	0-0	0-3	0-1	11.1	-7.17
Worcester	1-14	1-6	0-1	0-1	0-6	0-0	7.1	-11.38
Uttoxeter	1-19	0-5	0-0	0-5	1-9	0-0	5.3	-2.00
Plumpton	1-22	0-7	0-3	1-4	0-6	0-2	4.5	-14.00

WINNING HORSES

Horse	Races Run	1st	2nd	3rd	£
Kingscliff	5	1	2	0	85530
The Listener	5	3	0	0	52239
Trust Fund	7	1	0	1	12045
No Visibility	6	1	0	1	7807
Matthew Muroto	8	2	2	1	12230
My World	5	2	1	0	12036
Magot De Grugy	6	3	1	0	14085
Fox In The Box	6	1	0	0	6350
Toulouse	7	2	0	2	10426
Mort De Rire	2	1	0	1	6263
Even More	12	1	1	2	5530
Motcombe	7	2	1	0	10702
Keepers Mead	10	1	2	2	5465
Manawanui	7	1	2	2	5205
Diletia	4	1	0	0	5159
Roman Court	6	1	0	1	4880
Room To Room Gold	5	1	0	0	4784
Miko De Beauchene	7	1	2	2	4782
Avas Delight	1	1	0	0	4755
Free Gift	5	1	1	1	4216
Novacella	7	3	0	0	10878
Up The Pub	8	1	2	0	4060
Rowlands Dream	5	1	2	0	3904
Bowleaze	3	1	0	0	3570
Brigadier Benson	5	1	0	2	3562
Macmar	7	1	2	1	3426
Rare Gold	3	1	2	0	3253
Trade Off	1	1	0	0	2737
Total winning prize-money					**£309879**
Favourites	16-39		41.0%		3.37

M APPLEBY

SHREWLEY, WARWICKS

	No. of Hrs	Races Run	1st	2nd	3rd	Unpl	Per cent	£1 Level Stake
NH Flat	1	1	0	0	0	1	0.0	-1.00
Hurdles	12	56	1	1	2	52	1.8	-52.75
Chases	2	9	0	0	0	9	0.0	-9.00
Totals	14	66	1	1	2	62	1.5	-62.75
04-05	12	35	0	0	2	33	0.0	-35.00
03-04	9	37	1	3	1	32	2.7	-29.00

JOCKEYS

	W-R	Per cent	£1 Level Stake
Richard Spate	1-19	5.3	-15.75

COURSE RECORD

	Total W-R	Non-Hndcps Hurdles Chases	Hndcps Hurdles Chases	NH Flat	Per cent	£1 Level Stake
Leicester	1-5	1-3 0-1	0-1 0-0	0-0	20.0	-1.75

WINNING HORSES

Horse	Races Run	1st	2nd	3rd	£
*Blackthorn	6	1	1	0	2823
Total winning prize-money					**£2823**
Favourites	0-1		0.0%		-1.00

P G ATKINSON

YAFFORTH, N YORKS

	No. of Hrs	Races Run	1st	2nd	3rd	Unpl	Per cent	£1 Level Stake
NH Flat	1	2	0	0	0	2	0.0	-2.00
Hurdles	0	0	0	0	0	0	0.0	0.00
Chases	2	15	1	1	0	12	6.7	-9.00
Totals	3	17	1	1	0	14	5.9	-11.00
04-05	3	15	1	3	1	10	6.7	-9.00
03-04	1	3	0	0	0	3	0.0	-3.00

JOCKEYS

	W-R	Per cent	£1 Level Stake
Mark Bradburne	1-3	33.3	+3.00

COURSE RECORD

	Total W-R	Non-Hndcps Hurdles Chases	Hndcps Hurdles Chases	NH Flat	Per cent	£1 Level Stake
Kelso	1-1	0-0 0-0	0-0 1-1	0-0	100.0	+5.00

WINNING HORSES

Horse	Races Run	1st	2nd	3rd	£
Go Nomadic	3	1	1	0	4706
Total winning prize-money					**£4706**
Favourites	0-0		0.0%		0.00

JEAN-RENE AUVRAY

UPPER LAMBOURN, BERKS

	No. of Hrs	Races Run	1st	2nd	3rd	Unpl	Per cent	£1 Level Stake
NH Flat	2	4	0	0	1	3	0.0	-4.00
Hurdles	7	24	2	4	1	17	8.3	+12.00
Chases	2	7	0	1	1	5	0.0	-7.00
Totals	9	35	2	5	3	25	5.7	+1.00
04-05	8	26	0	3	6	17	0.0	-26.00
03-04	8	32	8	2	6	16	25.0	+38.75

JOCKEYS

	W-R	Per cent	£1 Level Stake
Dave Crosse	2-17	11.8	+19.00

COURSE RECORD

	Total W-R	Non-Hndcps Hurdles Chases	Hndcps Hurdles Chases	NH Flat	Per cent	£1 Level Stake
Nton Abbot	1-1	0-0 0-0	1-1 0-0	0-0	100.0	+25.00
Uttoxeter	1-3	0-0 0-0	1-3 0-0	0-0	33.3	+7.00

WINNING HORSES

Horse	Races Run	1st	2nd	3rd	£
Irishkawa Bellevue	9	2	2	0	8371
Total winning prize-money					**£8371**
Favourites	0-3		0.0%		-3.00

N G AYLIFFE

WINSFORD, SOMERSET

	No. of Hrs	Races Run	1st	2nd	3rd	Unpl	Per cent	£1 Level Stake
NH Flat	0	0	0	0	0	0	0.0	0.00
Hurdles	6	22	1	1	1	19	4.5	-1.00
Chases	1	4	0	0	1	3	0.0	-4.00
Totals	6	26	1	1	2	22	3.8	-5.00
04-05	6	30	1	1	1	27	3.3	+37.00
03-04	8	24	0	0	2	22	0.0	-24.00

JOCKEYS

	W-R	Per cent	£1 Level Stake
Andrew Tinkler	1-2	50.0	+19.00

COURSE RECORD

	Total W-R	Non-Hndcps Hurdles Chases	Hndcps Hurdles Chases	NH Flat	Per cent	£1 Level Stake
Worcester	1-4	1-4 0-0	0-0 0-0	0-0	25.0	+17.00

WINNING HORSES

Horse	Races Run	1st	2nd	3rd	£
Fairly High	2	1	0	0	3770
Total winning prize-money					**£3770**
Favourites	0-1		0.0%		-1.00

N M BABBAGE

BROCKHAMPTON, GLOUCS

	No. of Hrs	Races Run	1st	2nd	3rd	Unpl	Per cent	£1 Level Stake
NH Flat	2	4	0	0	0	4	0.0	-4.00
Hurdles	8	16	0	1	1	14	0.0	-16.00

	No. of Hrs	Races Run	1st	2nd	3rd	Unpl	Per cent	£1 Level Stake
Chases	2	9	1	1	0	7	11.1	-2.00
Totals	11	29	1	2	1	25	3.4	-22.00
04-05	11	25	1	2	3	19	4.0	-16.00
03-04	12	29	2	2	3	22	6.9	-15.50

JOCKEYS

	W-R	Per cent	£1 Level Stake
T J Phelan	1-19	5.3	-12.00

COURSE RECORD

	Total W-R	Non-Hndcps Hurdles	Chases	Hndcps Hurdles	Chases	NH Flat	Per cent	£1 Level Stake
Towcester	1-7	0-3	0-0	0-1	1-2	0-1	14.3	0.00

WINNING HORSES

Horse	Races Run	1st	2nd	3rd	£
Lord Broadway	6	1	1	0	5070
Total winning prize-money					**£5070**
Favourites	0-0		0.0%		0.00

K C BAILEY

PRESTON CAPES, NORTHANTS

	No. of Hrs	Races Run	1st	2nd	3rd	Unpl	Per cent	£1 Level Stake
NH Flat	8	12	0	1	0	11	0.0	-12.00
Hurdles	27	82	1	13	5	63	1.2	-77.00
Chases	22	67	5	11	5	46	7.5	+4.00
Totals	41	161	6	25	10	120	3.7	-85.00
04-05	48	133	6	15	9	103	4.5	-76.75
03-04	57	236	24	24	38	150	10.2	-34.42

JOCKEYS

	W-R	Per cent	£1 Level Stake
John McNamara	4-98	4.1	-57.50
Tom Scudamore	2-14	14.3	+21.50

COURSE RECORD

	Total W-R	Non-Hndcps Hurdles	Chases	Hndcps Hurdles	Chases	NH Flat	Per cent	£1 Level Stake
Towcester	3-20	0-4	1-5	0-3	2-7	0-1	15.0	+28.50
Stratford	1-2	0-1	0-0	1-1	0-0	0-0	50.0	+3.00
Uttoxeter	1-9	0-6	0-0	0-1	1-2	0-0	11.1	-3.50
Huntingdon	1-15	0-2	0-2	0-7	1-3	0-1	6.7	+2.00

WINNING HORSES

Horse	Races Run	1st	2nd	3rd	£
King Of Gothland	4	1	1	0	5478
Terivic	8	1	2	1	5400
Glen Thyne	9	2	0	1	8323
Front Rank	6	1	0	0	4340
Malko De Beaumont	6	1	1	0	4229
Total winning prize-money					**£27770**
Favourites	0-8		0.0%		-8.00

MRS CAROLINE BAILEY

HOLDENBY, NORTHANTS

	No. of Hrs	Races Run	1st	2nd	3rd	Unpl	Per cent	£1 Level Stake
NH Flat	0	0	0	0	0	0	0.0	0.00
Hurdles	0	0	0	0	0	0	0.0	0.00
Chases	7	18	3	2	1	12	16.7	-6.25
Totals	7	18	3	2	1	12	16.7	-6.25
04-05	3	6	2	2	0	2	33.3	+5.75
03-04	2	2	0	1	0	1	0.0	-2.00

JOCKEYS

	W-R	Per cent	£1 Level Stake
Mr R Cope	3-15	20.0	-3.25

COURSE RECORD

	Total W-R	Non-Hndcps Hurdles	Chases	Hndcps Hurdles	Chases	NH Flat	Per cent	£1 Level Stake
Towcester	2-3	0-0	2-3	0-0	0-0	0-0	66.7	+3.75
Wetherby	1-1	0-0	1-1	0-0	0-0	0-0	100.0	+4.00

WINNING HORSES

Horse	Races Run	1st	2nd	3rd	£
Denvale	6	2	0	1	2186
My Best Buddy	2	1	0	0	1874
Total winning prize-money					**£4060**
Favourites	0-2		0.0%		-2.00

R T BAIMBRIDGE

HERRINGSWELL, SUFF

	No. of Hrs	Races Run	1st	2nd	3rd	Unpl	Per cent	£1 Level Stake
NH Flat	0	0	0	0	0	0	0.0	0.00
Hurdles	0	0	0	0	0	0	0.0	0.00
Chases	1	1	1	0	0	0	100.0	+2.25
Totals	1	1	1	0	0	0	100.0	+2.25

JOCKEYS

	W-R	Per cent	£1 Level Stake
Mr J M Pritchard	1-1	100.0	+2.25

COURSE RECORD

	Total W-R	Non-Hndcps Hurdles	Chases	Hndcps Hurdles	Chases	NH Flat	Per cent	£1 Level Stake
Huntingdon	1-1	0-0	1-1	0-0	0-0	0-0	100.0	+2.25

WINNING HORSES

Horse	Races Run	1st	2nd	3rd	£
Martin Ossie	1	1	0	0	3367
Total winning prize-money					£3367
Favourites	0-0		0.0%		0.00

A M BALDING

KINGSCLERE, HANTS

	No. of Hrs	Races Run	1st	2nd	3rd	Unpl	Per cent	£1 Level Stake
NH Flat	1	1	0	0	0	1	0.0	-1.00
Hurdles	5	17	2	3	0	12	11.8	+0.88
Chases	3	6	0	0	0	6	0.0	-6.00
Totals	9	24	2	3	0	19	8.3	-6.12
04-05	9	35	10	4	5	16	28.6	+16.50
03-04	8	29	8	5	1	15	27.6	+19.33

JOCKEYS

	W-R	Per cent	£1 Level Stake
Mr T Greenall	1-3	33.3	+12.00
A P McCoy	1-5	20.0	-2.13

COURSE RECORD

	Total W-R	Non-Hndcps Hurdles	Chases	Hndcps Hurdles	Chases	NH Flat	Per cent	£1 Level Stake
Ludlow	1-2	1-1	0-0	0-1	0-0	0-0	50.0	+0.88
Wincanton	1-4	1-2	0-1	0-1	0-0	0-0	25.0	+11.00

WINNING HORSES

Horse	Races Run	1st	2nd	3rd	£
Briareus	4	1	1	0	39914
Rosecliff	5	1	2	0	3904
Total winning prize-money					£43818
Favourites	1-3		33.3%		-0.13

R BARBER

BEAMINSTER, DORSET

	No. of Hrs	Races Run	1st	2nd	3rd	Unpl	Per cent	£1 Level Stake
NH Flat	0	0	0	0	0	0	0.0	0.00
Hurdles	0	0	0	0	0	0	0.0	0.00
Chases	6	6	1	1	1	3	16.7	-0.50
Totals	6	6	1	1	1	3	16.7	-0.50
04-05	7	11	3	2	1	5	27.3	-2.33
03-04	6	11	5	0	1	5	45.5	+12.58

JOCKEYS

	W-R	Per cent	£1 Level Stake
Miss R A Green	1-1	100.0	+4.50

COURSE RECORD

	Total W-R	Non-Hndcps Hurdles	Chases	Hndcps Hurdles	Chases	NH Flat	Per cent	£1 Level Stake
Stratford	1-2	0-0	1-2	0-0	0-0	0-0	50.0	+3.50

WINNING HORSES

Horse	Races Run	1st	2nd	3rd	£
*Tales Of Bounty	1	1	0	0	3582
Total winning prize-money					£3582
Favourites	0-2		0.0%		-2.00

SIR JOHN BARLOW BT

BRINDLEY, CHESHIRE

	No. of Hrs	Races Run	1st	2nd	3rd	Unpl	Per cent	£1 Level Stake
NH Flat	0	0	0	0	0	0	0.0	0.00
Hurdles	4	6	0	0	0	6	0.0	-6.00
Chases	3	10	1	1	1	7	10.0	+3.00
Totals	5	16	1	1	1	13	6.3	-3.00
04-05	5	15	0	1	1	13	0.0	-15.00
03-04	3	8	1	0	0	7	12.5	-5.25

JOCKEYS

	W-R	Per cent	£1 Level Stake
Richard McGrath	1-10	10.0	+3.00

COURSE RECORD

	Total W-R	Non-Hndcps Hurdles	Chases	Hndcps Hurdles	Chases	NH Flat	Per cent	£1 Level Stake
Aintree	1-6	0-0	0-0	0-3	1-3	0-0	16.7	+7.00

WINNING HORSES

Horse	Races Run	1st	2nd	3rd	£
Ilverain	6	1	1	1	5928
Total winning prize-money					£5928
Favourites	0-0		0.0%		0.00

M A BARNES

FARLAM, CUMBRIA

	No. of Hrs	Races Run	1st	2nd	3rd	Unpl	Per cent	£1 Level Stake
NH Flat	3	7	0	0	0	7	0.0	-7.00
Hurdles	19	88	5	8	7	68	5.7	-31.75
Chases	5	10	0	0	0	10	0.0	-10.00
Totals	22	105	5	8	7	85	4.8	-48.75

04-05	23	80	5	1	1	73	6.3	-2.75
03-04	23	85	3	3	6	73	3.5	-57.50

JOCKEYS

	W-R	Per cent	£1 Level Stake
Ben Orde-Powlett	3-46	6.5	-26.50
G Lee	1-4	25.0	-1.25
Miss Angela Barnes	1-6	16.7	+28.00

COURSE RECORD

	Total W-R	Non-Hndcps Hurdles	Chases	Hndcps Hurdles	Chases	NH Flat	Per cent	£1 Level Stake
Newcastle	2-4	0-1	0-0	2-3	0-0	0-0	50.0	+34.00
Sedgefield	2-16	0-7	0-2	2-6	0-1	0-0	12.5	-0.50
Hexham	1-17	0-6	0-1	1-8	0-0	0-2	5.9	-14.25

WINNING HORSES

Horse	Races Run	1st	2nd	3rd	£
Torkinking	7	2	0	1	9123
Pikestaff	10	2	0	1	5938
Winds Supreme	5	1	0	0	2082
Total winning prize-money					**£17143**
Favourites	1-2		**50.0%**		**2.00**

R E BARR

SEAMER, N YORKS

	No. of Hrs	Races Run	1st	2nd	3rd	Unpl	Per cent	£1 Level Stake
NH Flat	0	0	0	0	0	0	0.0	0.00
Hurdles	5	22	1	1	1	19	4.5	-12.00
Chases	1	4	0	1	0	3	0.0	-4.00
Totals	6	26	1	2	1	22	3.8	-16.00
04-05	5	28	1	3	3	21	3.6	-15.00
03-04	9	45	2	3	3	37	4.4	-23.00

JOCKEYS

	W-R	Per cent	£1 Level Stake
Phil Kinsella	1-22	4.5	-12.00

COURSE RECORD

	Total W-R	Non-Hndcps Hurdles	Chases	Hndcps Hurdles	Chases	NH Flat	Per cent	£1 Level Stake
Sedgefield	1-7	0-3	0-0	1-3	0-1	0-0	14.3	+3.00

WINNING HORSES

Horse	Races Run	1st	2nd	3rd	£
In Good Faith	11	1	1	0	6721
Total winning prize-money					**£6721**
Favourites	0-0		**0.0%**		**0.00**

R BASTIMAN

COWTHORPE, N YORKS

	No. of Hrs	Races Run	1st	2nd	3rd	Unpl	Per cent	£1 Level Stake
NH Flat	0	0	0	0	0	0	0.0	0.00
Hurdles	3	12	2	1	1	8	16.7	-4.42
Chases	1	2	0	1	0	1	0.0	-2.00
Totals	4	14	2	2	1	9	14.3	-6.42
04-05	7	31	3	2	1	25	9.7	-0.50
03-04	8	21	1	0	2	18	4.8	+5.00

JOCKEYS

	W-R	Per cent	£1 Level Stake
Jim Crowley	1-3	33.3	+1.33
G Lee	1-4	25.0	-0.75

COURSE RECORD

	Total W-R	Non-Hndcps Hurdles	Chases	Hndcps Hurdles	Chases	NH Flat	Per cent	£1 Level Stake
Sedgefield	1-2	0-0	0-0	1-2	0-0	0-0	50.0	+1.25
Mrket Rsn	1-3	0-0	0-0	1-2	0-1	0-0	33.3	+1.33

WINNING HORSES

Horse	Races Run	1st	2nd	3rd	£
Wally Wonder	7	2	1	1	5669
Total winning prize-money					**£5669**
Favourites	2-3		**66.7%**		**4.58**

A J BATEMAN

MINEHEAD, SOMERSET

	No. of Hrs	Races Run	1st	2nd	3rd	Unpl	Per cent	£1 Level Stake
NH Flat	0	0	0	0	0	0	0.0	0.00
Hurdles	0	0	0	0	0	0	0.0	0.00
Chases	1	1	1	0	0	0	100.0	+6.50
Totals	1	1	1	0	0	0	100.0	+6.50
04-05	1	2	1	1	0	0	50.0	+2.00

JOCKEYS

	W-R	Per cent	£1 Level Stake
T J O'Brien	1-1	100.0	+6.50

COURSE RECORD

	Total W-R	Non-Hndcps Hurdles	Chases	Hndcps Hurdles	Chases	NH Flat	Per cent	£1 Level Stake
Stratford	1-1	0-0	1-1	0-0	0-0	0-0	100.0	+6.50

WINNING HORSES

Horse	Races Run	1st	2nd	3rd	£
Lord Beau	1	1	0	0	12479
Total winning prize-money					**£12479**
Favourites	**0-0**		**0.0%**		**0.00**

B P J BAUGH

AUDLEY, STAFFS

	No. of Hrs	Races Run	1st	2nd	3rd	Unpl	Per cent	£1 Level Stake
NH Flat	0	0	0	0	0	0	0.0	0.00
Hurdles	9	28	1	0	2	25	3.6	+39.00
Chases	3	7	0	1	0	6	0.0	-7.00
Totals	10	35	1	1	2	31	2.9	+32.00
04-05	6	19	0	0	0	19	0.0	-19.00
03-04	12	19	0	0	1	18	0.0	-19.00

JOCKEYS

	W-R	Per cent	£1 Level Stake
T J Phelan	1-5	20.0	+62.00

COURSE RECORD

	Total W-R	Non-Hndcps Hurdles	Chases	Hndcps Hurdles	Chases	NH Flat	Per cent	£1 Level Stake
Exeter	1-1	0-0	0-0	1-1	0-0	0-0	100.0	+66.00

WINNING HORSES

Horse	Races Run	1st	2nd	3rd	£
Island Warrior	10	1	0	0	3084
Total winning prize-money					**£3084**
Favourites	**0-0**		**0.0%**		**0.00**

C C BEALBY

BARROWBY, LINCS

	No. of Hrs	Races Run	1st	2nd	3rd	Unpl	Per cent	£1 Level Stake
NH Flat	9	15	1	0	0	14	6.7	-2.00
Hurdles	23	67	5	12	6	44	7.5	-19.50
Chases	19	50	5	4	6	35	10.0	-27.13
Totals	39	132	11	16	12	93	8.3	-48.63
04-05	23	105	9	19	16	61	8.6	-5.25
03-04	28	100	6	12	6	76	6.0	+26.75

BY MONTH

NH Flat	W-R	Per cent	£1 Level Stake	Hurdles	W-R	Per cent	£1 Level Stake
May	0-1	0.0	-1.00	May	0-0	0.0	0.00
June	0-0	0.0	0.00	June	0-1	0.0	-1.00
July	0-0	0.0	0.00	July	0-2	0.0	-2.00
August	0-0	0.0	0.00	August	0-1	0.0	-1.00
September	0-1	0.0	-1.00	September	1-5	20.0	+2.50
October	0-1	0.0	-1.00	October	1-13	7.7	-2.00
November	0-2	0.0	-2.00	November	0-8	0.0	-8.00
December	0-3	0.0	-3.00	December	1-10	10.0	-2.50
January	1-3	33.3	+10.00	January	0-5	0.0	-5.00
February	0-1	0.0	-1.00	February	0-6	0.0	-6.00
March	0-2	0.0	-2.00	March	2-10	20.0	+11.50
April	0-1	0.0	-1.00	April	0-6	0.0	-6.00

Chases	W-R	Per cent	£1 Level Stake	Totals	W-R	Per cent	£1 Level Stake
May	0-2	0.0	-2.00	May	0-3	0.0	-3.00
June	0-0	0.0	0.00	June	0-1	0.0	-1.00
July	0-0	0.0	0.00	July	0-2	0.0	-2.00
August	0-0	0.0	0.00	August	0-1	0.0	-1.00
September	0-1	0.0	-1.00	September	1-7	14.3	+0.50
October	1-6	16.7	-1.50	October	2-20	10.0	-4.50
November	2-11	18.2	-1.00	November	2-21	9.5	-11.00
December	0-9	0.0	-9.00	December	1-22	4.5	-14.50
January	1-6	16.7	-0.50	January	2-14	14.3	+4.50
February	1-7	14.3	-4.13	February	1-14	7.1	-11.13
March	0-2	0.0	-2.00	March	2-14	14.3	+7.50
April	0-6	0.0	-6.00	April	0-13	0.0	13.00

DISTANCE

Hurdles	W-R	Per cent	£1 Level Stake	Chases	W-R	Per cent	£1 Level Stake
2m-2m3f	1-33	3.0	22.00	2m-2m3f	0-6	0.0	-6.00
2m4f-2m7f	2-23	8.7	+1.50	2m4f-2m7f	1-22	4.5	-15.50
3m+	2-11	18.2	+1.00	3m+	4-22	18.2	-5.63

TYPE OF RACE

Non-Handicaps	W-R	Per cent	£1 Level Stake	Handicaps	W-R	Per cent	£1 Level Stake
Nov Hrdls	1-20	5.0	-12.50	Nov Hrdls	1-9	11.1	+8.00
Hrdls	0-6	0.0	-6.00	Hrdls	3-26	11.5	-3.00
Nov Chs	3-14	21.4	+0.88	Nov Chs	1-10	10.0	-5.50
Chases	0-0	0.0	0.00	Chases	1-26	3.8	-22.50
Sell/Claim	0-3	0.0	-3.00	Sell/Claim	0-3	0.0	-3.00

RACE CLASS

	W-R	Per cent	£1 Level Stake
Class 1	0-1	0.0	-1.00
Class 2	0-3	0.0	-3.00
Class 3	3-28	10.7	+1.00
Class 4	7-72	9.7	-30.63
Class 5	1-15	6.7	-2.00
Class 6	0-13	0.0	-13.00

FIRST TIME OUT

	W-R	Per cent	£1 Level Stake
Bumpers	1-9	11.1	+4.00
Hurdles	1-16	6.3	-8.50
Chases	2-14	14.3	-3.00
Totals	4-39	10.3	-7.50

JOCKEYS

	W-R	Per cent	£1 Level Stake
Noel Fehily	7-42	16.7	+4.38
Tom Messenger	2-28	7.1	-12.50

Wayne Hutchinson	1-8	12.5	+9.00
Lee Vickers	1-17	5.9	-12.50

COURSE RECORD

	Total W-R	Non-Hndcps Hurdles	Chases	Hndcps Hurdles	Chases	NH Flat	Per cent	£1 Level Stake
Fakenham	4-20	0-3	2-2	1-4	0-7	1-4	20.0	+12.38
Uttoxeter	2-19	1-6	0-1	1-4	0-6	0-2	10.5	-4.00
Mrket Rsn	2-25	0-5	0-1	1-11	1-5	0-3	8.0	-4.50
Wetherby	1-6	0-2	0-0	0-2	1-1	0-1	16.7	-1.50
Sedgefield	1-8	0-3	0-1	1-3	0-1	0-0	12.5	-3.50
Huntingdon	1-11	0-1	1-2	0-5	0-2	0-1	9.1	-4.50

WINNING HORSES

Horse	Races Run	1st	2nd	3rd	£
Extra Smooth	5	1	1	0	11060
Thistlecraft	6	1	0	2	6506
Un Autre Espere	8	1	2	0	5836
Wicked Nice Fella	5	1	0	0	5452
Moustique De L'Isle	10	3	1	2	11922
Eskimo Pie	6	1	1	3	4099
Blame The Ref	2	1	0	0	3833
Thedublinpublican	5	1	0	1	2979
Golden Parachute	2	1	0	0	2912
Total winning prize-money					**£54599**
Favourites	1-7	14.3%			**-3.50**

MRS ANTONIA BEALBY

BARROWBY, LINCS

	No. of Hrs	Races Run	1st	2nd	3rd	Unpl	Per cent	£1 Level Stake
NH Flat	0	0	0	0	0	0	0.0	0.00
Hurdles	0	0	0	0	0	0	0.0	0.00
Chases	2	4	2	2	0	0	50.0	+4.50
Totals	2	4	2	2	0	0	50.0	+4.50
04-05	1	1	0	1	0	0	0.0	-1.00

JOCKEYS

	W-R	Per cent	£1 Level Stake
Mr M Briggs	2-4	50.0	+4.50

COURSE RECORD

	Total W-R	Non-Hndcps Hurdles	Chases	Hndcps Hurdles	Chases	NH Flat	Per cent	£1 Level Stake
Mrket Rsn	1-1	0-0	1-1	0-0	0-0	0-0	100.0	+3.50
Fakenham	1-2	0-0	1-2	0-0	0-0	0-0	50.0	+2.00

WINNING HORSES

Horse	Races Run	1st	2nd	3rd	£
*Sea Ferry	3	2	1	0	3398
Total winning prize-money					**£3398**
Favourites	0-0	0.0%			**0.00**

P BEAUMONT

STEARSBY, N YORKS

	No. of Hrs	Races Run	1st	2nd	3rd	Unpl	Per cent	£1 Level Stake
NH Flat	11	23	0	0	3	20	0.0	-23.00
Hurdles	16	43	2	6	3	32	4.7	-25.00
Chases	12	47	4	4	5	34	8.5	+11.50
Totals	29	113	6	10	11	86	5.3	-36.50
04-05	32	134	12	21	8	93	9.0	-45.00
03-04	34	159	8	14	18	119	5.0	-91.84

JOCKEYS

	W-R	Per cent	£1 Level Stake
Russ Garritty	5-54	9.3	-11.50
Tom Siddall	1-7	14.3	+27.00

COURSE RECORD

	Total W-R	Non-Hndcps Hurdles	Chases	Hndcps Hurdles	Chases	NH Flat	Per cent	£1 Level Stake
Newcastle	2-7	0-1	0-0	1-2	1-3	0-1	28.6	+5.00
Kelso	2-15	0-8	1-1	0-2	1-4	0-0	13.3	+2.50
Southwell	1-3	0-0	0-0	0-0	1-2	0-1	33.3	+31.00
Doncaster	1-4	1-2	0-1	0-0	0-1	0-0	25.0	+9.00

WINNING HORSES

Horse	Races Run	1st	2nd	3rd	£
Cloudless Dawn	7	1	2	1	5127
Lord Rodney	7	1	0	0	4880
Profowens	6	1	1	0	4554
Mr Prickle	6	1	1	1	3904
Moor Spirit	5	1	0	0	3708
Seymar Lad	8	1	2	0	3253
Total winning prize-money					**£25426**
Favourites	2-8	25.0%			**4.00**

S B BELL

SWINHOE, NORTHUMBERLAND

	No. of Hrs	Races Run	1st	2nd	3rd	Unpl	Per cent	£1 Level Stake
NH Flat	2	2	0	0	0	2	0.0	-2.00
Hurdles	4	7	0	0	0	7	0.0	-7.00
Chases	2	10	1	0	1	8	10.0	-4.00
Totals	7	19	1	0	1	17	5.3	-13.00
04-05	5	19	2	0	2	15	10.5	0.00
03-04	2	2	0	1	0	1	0.0	-2.00

JOCKEYS

	W-R	Per cent	£1 Level Stake
Mark Bradburne	1-2	50.0	+4.00

COURSE RECORD

	Total W-R	Non-Hndcps Hurdles	Chases	Hndcps Hurdles	Chases	NH Flat	Per cent	£1 Level Stake
Kelso	1-5	0-1	0-0	0-2	1-2	0-0	20.0	+1.00

WINNING HORSES

Horse	Races Run	1st	2nd	3rd	£
Diamond Cottage	7	1	0	0	4732
Total winning prize-money					£4732
Favourites	0-1		0.0%		-1.00

A BERRY

COCKERHAM, LANCS

	No. of Hrs	Races Run	1st	2nd	3rd	Unpl	Per cent	£1 Level Stake
NH Flat	0	0	0	0	0	0	0.0	0.00
Hurdles	4	10	1	0	0	9	10.0	-4.50
Chases	1	1	0	0	0	1	0.0	-1.00
Totals	4	11	1	0	0	10	9.1	-5.50
04-05	2	6	2	0	0	4	33.3	+2.50
03-04	5	14	2	1	0	11	14.3	+4.00

JOCKEYS

	W-R	Per cent	£1 Level Stake
Keith Mercer	1-1	100.0	+4.50

COURSE RECORD

	Total W-R	Non-Hndcps Hurdles	Chases	Hndcps Hurdles	Chases	NH Flat	Per cent	£1 Level Stake
Cartmel	1-6	0-2	0-1	1-3	0-0	0-0	16.7	-0.50

WINNING HORSES

Horse	Races Run	1st	2nd	3rd	£
Peter's Imp	7	1	0	0	2723
Total winning prize-money					£2723
Favourites	1-1		100.0%		4.50

N E BERRY

LLANISHEN, MONMOUTHS

	No. of Hrs	Races Run	1st	2nd	3rd	Unpl	Per cent	£1 Level Stake
NH Flat	2	2	0	0	0	2	0.0	-2.00
Hurdles	6	24	2	1	2	19	8.3	+4.00
Chases	1	4	0	1	1	2	0.0	-4.00
Totals	8	30	2	2	3	23	6.7	-2.00
04-05	8	16	1	2	1	12	6.3	-12.50
03-04	2	2	0	0	0	2	0.0	-2.00

JOCKEYS

	W-R	Per cent	£1 Level Stake
Tom Malone	1-2	50.0	+11.00
Mr G Barfoot-Saunt	1-2	50.0	+13.00

COURSE RECORD

	Total W-R	Non-Hndcps Hurdles	Chases	Hndcps Hurdles	Chases	NH Flat	Per cent	£1 Level Stake
Towcester	2-2	0-0	0-0	2-2	0-0	0-0	100.0	+26.00

WINNING HORSES

Horse	Races Run	1st	2nd	3rd	£
*Ask The Umpire	12	2	1	1	5734
Total winning prize-money					£5734
Favourites	0-0		0.0%		0.00

J R BEST

HUCKING, KENT

	No. of Hrs	Races Run	1st	2nd	3rd	Unpl	Per cent	£1 Level Stake
NH Flat	1	1	0	0	0	1	0.0	-1.00
Hurdles	5	13	4	1	1	7	30.8	+4.00
Chases	4	9	0	0	2	7	0.0	-9.00
Totals	8	23	4	1	3	15	17.4	-6.00
04-05	11	42	0	3	3	36	0.0	-42.00
03-04	10	42	5	2	11	24	11.9	+1.75

JOCKEYS

	W-R	Per cent	£1 Level Stake
Dave Crosse	4-17	23.5	0.00

COURSE RECORD

	Total W-R	Non-Hndcps Hurdles	Chases	Hndcps Hurdles	Chases	NH Flat	Per cent	£1 Level Stake
Stratford	2-2	0-0	0-0	2-2	0-0	0-0	100.0	+6.50
Fakenham	1-1	0-0	0-0	1-1	0-0	0-0	100.0	+5.00
Hereford	1-1	0-0	0-0	1-1	0-0	0-0	100.0	+1.50

WINNING HORSES

Horse	Races Run	1st	2nd	3rd	£
Charlie's Double	7	4	1	1	17440
Total winning prize-money					£17440
Favourites	2-3		66.7%		3.50

JIM BEST

LEWES, E SUSSEX

	No. of Hrs	Races Run	1st	2nd	3rd	Unpl	Per cent	£1 Level Stake
NH Flat	0	0	0	0	0	0	0.0	0.00
Hurdles	7	24	4	4	3	13	16.7	+5.00
Chases	1	5	2	1	0	2	40.0	+11.00
Totals	**7**	**29**	**6**	**5**	**3**	**15**	**20.7**	**+16.00**
04-05	4	10	0	0	0	10	0.0	-10.00

JOCKEYS

	W-R	Per cent	£1 Level Stake
Jamie Moore	2-7	28.6	+9.00
Christopher Murray	2-11	18.2	-3.00
William Kennedy	1-3	33.3	+12.00
Robert Lucey-Butler	1-6	16.7	0.00

COURSE RECORD

	Total W-R	Non-Hndcps Hurdles	Chases	Hndcps Hurdles	Chases	NH Flat	Per cent	£1 Level Stake
Plumpton	3-4	1-1	0-0	2-3	0-0	0-0	75.0	+20.00
Fontwell	2-5	0-1	0-0	0-1	2-3	0-0	40.0	+11.00
Huntingdon	1-2	0-0	0-0	1-1	0-1	0-0	50.0	+3.00

WINNING HORSES

Horse	Races Run	1st	2nd	3rd	£
Misbehaviour	5	2	2	0	7807
Brendar	4	1	0	0	3904
River Amora	7	2	1	0	5815
Dance With Wolves	2	1	0	0	2741
Total winning prize-money					**£20267**
Favourites	1-1		100.0%		2.00

R N BEVIS

THREAPWOOD, CHESHIRE

	No. of Hrs	Races Run	1st	2nd	3rd	Unpl	Per cent	£1 Level Stake
NH Flat	1	2	0	0	0	2	0.0	-2.00
Hurdles	5	10	2	2	1	5	20.0	+4.50
Chases	1	2	0	0	0	2	0.0	-2.00
Totals	**5**	**14**	**2**	**2**	**1**	**9**	**14.3**	**+0.50**
04-05	6	20	0	0	0	20	0.0	-20.00
03-04	9	14	1	1	0	12	7.1	+37.00

JOCKEYS

	W-R	Per cent	£1 Level Stake
Stephen Craine	1-1	100.0	+5.00
Mr G Tumelty	1-6	16.7	+2.50

COURSE RECORD

	Total W-R	Non-Hndcps Hurdles	Chases	Hndcps Hurdles	Chases	NH Flat	Per cent	£1 Level Stake
Towcester	1-1	0-0	0-0	1-1	0-0	0-0	100.0	+7.50
Warwick	1-1	0-0	0-0	1-1	0-0	0-0	100.0	+5.00

WINNING HORSES

Horse	Races Run	1st	2nd	3rd	£
Elegant Clutter	3	2	0	1	7690
Total winning prize-money					**£7690**
Favourites	1-1		100.0%		5.00

G T BEWLEY

HAWICK, BORDERS

	No. of Hrs	Races Run	1st	2nd	3rd	Unpl	Per cent	£1 Level Stake
NH Flat	0	0	0	0	0	0	0.0	0.00
Hurdles	0	0	0	0	0	0	0.0	0.00
Chases	1	1	1	0	0	0	100.0	+8.00
Totals	**1**	**1**	**1**	**0**	**0**	**0**	**100.0**	**+8.00**
04-05	1	5	2	0	0	3	40.0	+6.10
03-04	1	5	0	1	0	4	0.0	-5.00

JOCKEYS

	W-R	Per cent	£1 Level Stake
Ewan Whillans	1-1	100.0	+8.00

COURSE RECORD

	Total W-R	Non-Hndcps Hurdles	Chases	Hndcps Hurdles	Chases	NH Flat	Per cent	£1 Level Stake
Kelso	1-1	0-0	1-1	0-0	0-0	0-0	100.0	+8.00

WINNING HORSES

Horse	Races Run	1st	2nd	3rd	£
Geordies Express	1	1	0	0	3042
Total winning prize-money					**£3042**
Favourites	0-0		0.0%		0.00

M BIDDICK

BODMIN, CORNWALL

	No. of Hrs	Races Run	1st	2nd	3rd	Unpl	Per cent	£1 Level Stake
NH Flat	0	0	0	0	0	0	0.0	0.00
Hurdles	0	0	0	0	0	0	0.0	0.00
Chases	1	7	2	1	0	4	28.6	-2.20
Totals	**1**	**7**	**2**	**1**	**0**	**4**	**28.6**	**-2.20**
04-05	1	1	0	0	0	1	0.0	-1.00
03-04	1	4	2	1	1	0	50.0	+2.00

JOCKEYS

	W-R	Per cent	£1 Level Stake
Mr W Biddick	2-7	28.6	-2.20

COURSE RECORD

	Total W-R	Non-Hndcps Hurdles Chases	Hndcps Hurdles Chases	NH Flat	Per cent	£1 Level Stake
Leicester	1-1	0-0 1-1	0-0 0-0	0-0	100.0	+2.00
Wincanton	1-1	0-0 1-1	0-0 0-0	0-0	100.0	+0.80

WINNING HORSES

Horse	Races Run	1st	2nd	3rd	£
Raregem	7	2	1	0	4739
Total winning prize-money					£4739
Favourites	2-2		100.0%		2.00

K BISHOP

SPAXTON, SOMERSET

	No. of Hrs	Races Run	1st	2nd	3rd	Unpl	Per cent	£1 Level Stake
NH Flat	2	3	0	0	0	3	0.0	-3.00
Hurdles	17	46	4	1	3	38	8.7	+113.00
Chases	15	48	3	6	9	30	6.3	-11.67
Totals	28	97	7	7	12	71	7.2	+98.33
04-05	27	113	11	16	7	79	9.7	-61.22
03-04	23	76	8	4	5	59	10.5	+57.53

JOCKEYS

	W-R	Per cent	£1 Level Stake
John McNamara	2-13	15.4	+39.00
P J Brennan	2-15	13.3	+101.00
Marcus Foley	1-2	50.0	+15.00
Wayne Hutchinson	1-8	12.5	-2.00
R J Greene	1-23	4.3	-18.67

COURSE RECORD

	Total W-R	Non-Hndcps Hurdles Chases	Hndcps Hurdles Chases	NH Flat	Per cent	£1 Level Stake
Nton Abbot	3-11	2-5 0-1	0-3 1-2	0-0	27.3	+120.33
Exeter	2-21	1-3 0-2	1-6 0-10	0-0	9.5	+11.00
Leicester	1-2	0-0 0-0	0-0 1-2	0-0	50.0	+13.00
Worcester	1-10	0-3 0-0	0-1 1-4	0-2	10.0	+7.00

WINNING HORSES

Horse	Races Run	1st	2nd	3rd	£
Gumley Gale	8	1	1	2	6134
Dare Too Dream	5	1	0	0	5836
Monger Lane	5	2	0	0	9325

Sacrifice	4	1	0	0	4212
*Gortumblo	3	1	0	0	3058
Dancing Hill	5	1	0	1	2625
Total winning prize-money					**£31190**
Favourites	0-5		0.0%		-5.00

MISS L A BLACKFORD

TIVERTON, DEVON

	No. of Hrs	Races Run	1st	2nd	3rd	Unpl	Per cent	£1 Level Stake
NH Flat	0	0	0	0	0	0	0.0	0.00
Hurdles	0	0	0	0	0	0	0.0	0.00
Chases	2	4	1	0	0	3	25.0	+30.00
Totals	2	4	1	0	0	3	25.0	+30.00
04-05	2	2	0	0	0	2	0.0	-2.00
03-04	3	4	0	0	0	4	0.0	-4.00

JOCKEYS

	W-R	Per cent	£1 Level Stake
Mr A Charles-Jones	1-1	100.0	+33.00

COURSE RECORD

	Total W-R	Non-Hndcps Hurdles Chases	Hndcps Hurdles Chases	NH Flat	Per cent	£1 Level Stake
Nton Abbot	1-1	0-0 1-1	0-0 0-0	0-0	100.0	+33.00

WINNING HORSES

Horse	Races Run	1st	2nd	3rd	£
*River Dante	3	1	0	0	1055
Total winning prize-money					**£1055**
Favourites	0-0		0.0%		0.00

P A BLOCKLEY

COEDKERNEW, NEWPORT

	No. of Hrs	Races Run	1st	2nd	3rd	Unpl	Per cent	£1 Level Stake
NH Flat	3	7	1	0	0	6	14.3	+8.00
Hurdles	16	43	1	2	0	40	2.3	-14.00
Chases	2	5	0	0	1	4	0.0	-5.00
Totals	19	55	2	2	1	50	3.6	-11.00
04-05	9	18	0	1	3	14	0.0	-18.00
03-04	13	32	4	1	2	25	12.5	+0.50

JOCKEYS

	W-R	Per cent	£1 Level Stake
Miss Faye Bramley	1-8	12.5	+21.00
Angharad Frieze	1-13	7.7	+2.00

COURSE RECORD

	Total W-R	Non-Hndcps Hurdles	Chases	Hndcps Hurdles	Chases	NH Flat	Per cent	£1 Level Stake
Hereford	1-4	0-1	0-0	0-1	0-1	1-1	25.0	+11.00
Exeter	1-7	0-2	0-0	1-4	0-0	0-1	14.3	+22.00

WINNING HORSES

Horse		Races Run	1st	2nd	3rd	£
Kings Rock		5	1	1	0	3415
Surfboard		8	1	0	0	2079
Total winning prize-money						**£5494**
Favourites	0-1		**0.0%**			**-1.00**

SIMON BLOSS

BIBURY, GLOUCS

	No. of Hrs	Races Run	1st	2nd	3rd	Unpl	Per cent	£1 Level Stake
NH Flat	0	0	0	0	0	0	0.0	0.00
Hurdles	0	0	0	0	0	0	0.0	0.00
Chases	1	2	1	0	0	1	50.0	+0.75
Totals	1	2	1	0	0	1	50.0	+0.75
04-05	2	3	1	0	0	2	33.3	+0.50
03-04	1	3	0	0	0	3	0.0	-3.00

JOKEYS

	W-R	Per cent	£1 Level Stake
Mr N Phillips	1-2	50.0	+0.75

COURSE RECORD

	Total W-R	Non-Hndcps Hurdles	Chases	Hndcps Hurdles	Chases	NH Flat	Per cent	£1 Level Stake
Chepstow	1-1	0-0	1-1	0-0	0-0	0-0	100.0	+1.75

WINNING HORSES

Horse		Races Run	1st	2nd	3rd	£
Camden Carrig		2	1	0	0	1124
Total winning prize-money						**£1124**
Favourites	1-1		**100.0%**			**1.75**

MRS L BORRADAILE

BEAMINSTER, DORSET

	No. of Hrs	Races Run	1st	2nd	3rd	Unpl	Per cent	£1 Level Stake
NH Flat	0	0	0	0	0	0	0.0	0.00
Hurdles	0	0	0	0	0	0	0.0	0.00
Chases	1	4	1	0	0	3	25.0	+2.00
Totals	1	4	1	0	0	3	25.0	+2.00
04-05	1	5	3	0	0	2	60.0	+23.25

JOCKEYS

	W-R	Per cent	£1 Level Stake
Mr J Snowden	1-3	33.3	+3.00

COURSE RECORD

	Total W-R	Non-Hndcps Hurdles	Chases	Hndcps Hurdles	Chases	NH Flat	Per cent	£1 Level Stake
Haydock	1-1	0-0	1-1	0-0	0-0	0-0	100.0	+5.00

WINNING HORSES

Horse		Races Run	1st	2nd	3rd	£
Cobreces		4	1	0	0	7183
Total winning prize-money						**£7183**
Favourites	0-1		**0.0%**			**-1.00**

M R BOSLEY

LOCKERIDGE, WILTS

	No. of Hrs	Races Run	1st	2nd	3rd	Unpl	Per cent	£1 Level Stake
NH Flat	4	8	1	0	0	7	12.5	-1.00
Hurdles	8	27	0	1	3	22	0.0	-27.00
Chases	1	1	0	0	0	1	0.0	-1.00
Totals	11	36	1	1	3	30	2.8	-29.00
04-05	11	22	1	1	1	19	4.5	-1.00
03-04	7	24	1	0	3	20	4.2	-18.00

JOCKEYS

	W-R	Per cent	£1 Level Stake
Sean Curran	1-22	4.5	-15.00

COURSE RECORD

	Total W-R	Non-Hndcps Hurdles	Chases	Hndcps Hurdles	Chases	NH Flat	Per cent	£1 Level Stake
Towcester	1-1	0-0	0-0	0-0	0-0	1-1	100.0	+6.00

WINNING HORSES

Horse		Races Run	1st	2nd	3rd	£
Castlemainevillage		2	1	0	0	2324
Total winning prize-money						**£2324**
Favourites	0-0		**0.0%**			**0.00**

P BOWEN

LITTLE NEWCASTLE, PEMBROKES

	No. of Hrs	Races Run	1st	2nd	3rd	Unpl	Per cent	£1 Level Stake
NH Flat	16	26	3	5	3	15	11.5	-12.75
Hurdles	62	181	21	18	21	120	11.6	-64.47
Chases	25	107	17	14	9	67	15.9	-35.41

Totals	82	314	41	37	33	202	13.1	-112.63
04-05	45	205	41	26	25	113	20.0	+10.11
03-04	32	128	39	16	10	63	30.5	+60.07

	W-R	Per cent	£1 Level Stake				
Class 3	14-83	16.9	-23.93		Chases	5-15	33.3	+1.48
Class 4	17-141	12.1	-46.92					
Class 5	1-9	11.1	-3.00		Totals	13-82	15.9	-24.65
Class 6	3-25	12.0	-11.75					

BY MONTH

NH Flat	W-R	Per cent	£1 Level Stake	Hurdles	W-R	Per cent	£1 Level Stake
May	0-1	0.0	-1.00	May	3-19	15.8	-8.22
June	1-4	25.0	-1.00	June	3-20	15.0	-11.88
July	1-2	50.0	+1.75	July	1-14	7.1	-8.00
August	0-2	0.0	-2.00	August	5-20	25.0	+1.13
September	0-1	0.0	-1.00	September	2-9	22.2	+1.00
October	0-5	0.0	-5.00	October	0-6	0.0	-6.00
November	0-4	0.0	-4.00	November	2-19	10.5	+18.00
December	0-2	0.0	-2.00	December	0-19	0.0	-19.00
January	1-1	100.0	+5.50	January	2-18	11.1	-10.00
February	0-0	0.0	0.00	February	2-13	15.4	3.00
March	0-1	0.0	-1.00	March	0-9	0.0	-9.00
April	0-3	0.0	-3.00	April	1-15	6.7	-9.50

Chases	W-R	Per cent	£1 Level Stake	Totals	W-R	Per cent	£1 Level Stake
May	3-8	37.5	+0.48	May	6-28	21.4	-8.74
June	2-9	22.2	-2.71	June	6-33	18.2	-15.59
July	2-10	20.0	0.00	July	4-26	15.4	-6.25
August	3-10	30.0	+1.00	August	8-32	25.0	+0.13
September	1-3	33.3	-1.09	September	3-13	23.1	-1.09
October	0-8	0.0	-8.00	October	0-19	0.0	-19.00
November	1-13	7.7	-8.67	November	3-36	8.3	+5.33
December	1-12	8.3	-7.67	December	1-33	3.0	-28.67
January	1-8	12.5	-1.00	January	4-27	14.8	-5.50
February	1-8	12.5	+1.00	February	3-21	14.3	-2.00
March	0-4	0.0	-4.00	March	0-14	0.0	-14.00
April	2-14	14.3	-4.75	April	3-32	9.4	-17.25

DISTANCE

Hurdles	W-R	Per cent	£1 Level Stake	Chases	W-R	Per cent	£1 Level Stake
2m-2m3f	10-80	12.5	-8.43	2m-2m3f	0-7	0.0	-7.00
2m4f-2m7f	5-68	7.4	-47.17	2m4f-2m7f	7-37	18.9	-12.61
3m+	6-33	18.2	-8.88	3m+	10-63	15.9	-15.80

TYPE OF RACE

Non-Handicaps	W-R	Per cent	£1 Level Stake	Handicaps	W-R	Per cent	£1 Level Stake
Nov Hrdls	8-51	15.7	-14.38	Nov Hrdls	0-11	0.0	-11.00
Hrdls	3-29	10.3	-23.22	Hrdls	9-79	11.4	-10.88
Nov Chs	7-25	28.0	-2.08	Nov Chs	1-10	10.0	-7.25
Chases	0-9	0.0	-9.00	Chases	9-63	14.3	-17.08
Sell/Claim	0-7	0.0	-7.00	Sell/Claim	1-3	33.3	+3.00

RACE CLASS / FIRST TIME OUT

Race Class	W-R	Per cent	£1 Level Stake	First Time Out	W-R	Per cent	£1 Level Stake
Class 1	0-26	0.0	-26.00	Bumpers	3-16	18.8	-2.75
Class 2	6-30	20.0	-1.04	Hurdles	5-51	9.8	-23.38

JOCKEYS

	W-R	Per cent	£1 Level Stake
Richard Johnson	16-58	27.6	+11.24
A P McCoy	10-56	17.9	-26.46
Tom Greenway	4-17	23.5	+25.50
Tom Malone	2-9	22.2	+7.00
Tony Dobbin	2-18	11.1	-10.00
Mr P Sheldrake	1-1	100.0	+4.50
Jason Maguire	1-2	50.0	+4.00
S Durack	1-5	20.0	-1.75
P J Brennan	1-6	16.7	-0.50
Mick Fitzgerald	1-8	12.5	3.00
T J O'Brien	1-14	7.1	-7.50
Christian Williams	1-32	3.1	-27.67

COURSE RECORD

	Total W-R	Non-Hndcps Hurdles	Chases	Hndcps Hurdles	Chases	NH Flat	Per cent	£1 Level Stake
Perth	7-11	2-4	2-2	1-2	2-2	0-1	63.6	+13.20
Worcester	7-45	0-9	2-4	4-16	1-10	0-6	15.6	-11.63
Kelso	3-7	2-2	0-1	0-3	1-1	0-0	42.9	-0.22
Nton Abbot	3-17	2-6	0-0	0-5	1-5	0-1	17.6	-8.63
Uttoxeter	3-20	0-6	0-1	2-8	0-1	1-4	15.0	-0.25
Catterick	2-5	0-1	0-1	1-1	0-1	1-1	40.0	+4.00
Plumpton	2-5	1-2	0-0	0-1	1-2	0-0	40.0	+7.50
Fontwell	2-6	0-1	0-0	0-2	2-3	0-0	33.3	+1.58
Mrket Rsn	2-17	0-3	2-2	0-6	0-5	0-1	11.8	-11.50
Huntingdon	2-19	1-4	0-1	1-6	0-7	0-1	10.5	+18.00
Sandown	1-3	0-0	0-1	0-0	1-2	0-0	33.3	+6.00
Southwell	1-3	1-1	0-1	0-1	0-0	0-0	33.3	+0.25
Sedgefield	1-4	0-1	1-1	0-1	0-1	0-0	25.0	-2.27
Lingfield	1-7	1-2	0-1	0-2	0-2	0-0	14.3	-2.00
Wetherby	1-8	0-1	0-2	0-2	1-3	0-0	12.5	-3.67
Aintree	1-9	0-0	0-1	0-2	0-4	1-2	11.1	-6.00
Bangor	1-10	0-3	0-1	1-4	0-1	0-1	10.0	-4.00
Ludlow	1-16	1-9	0-0	0-3	0-2	0-2	6.3	-11.00

WINNING HORSES

Horse	Races Run	1st	2nd	3rd	£
Dunbrody Millar	11	3	3	0	50987
Yes Sir	11	3	1	1	39052
Ballycassidy	11	3	0	2	49421
Mckelvey	9	2	3	1	16208
Celtic Boy	9	4	0	1	23816
Mr Ed	5	1	2	0	6773
Swansea Bay	7	1	0	3	6014
Touch Closer	4	2	0	1	9419
*Decisive	2	2	0	0	9009
Qabas	5	1	1	0	5236
Zipalong Lad	7	2	1	1	9759

*Sunday City	6	2	2	0	8263
Burren Moonshine	5	1	0	1	4997
Robber	5	1	1	0	4677
Rebelle	4	1	1	0	4154
Lawyer Des Ormeaux	5	2	0	2	4134
It's Definite	10	1	0	0	4124
Splash Out Again	3	1	0	0	4037
Adventurist	7	1	1	1	3904
Irish Wolf	7	2	0	2	6707
Faddad	2	1	0	0	3094
Tommy Spar	7	1	1	1	3087
Zumrah	5	1	1	2	2261
Mumbles Head	4	1	2	0	2056
Ericas Charm	7	1	0	0	1981
Total winning prize-money					**£283170**
Favourites	15-74		20.3%		-36.68

	No. of Hrs	Races Run	1st	2nd	3rd	Unpl	Per cent	£1 Level Stake
04-05	2	4	0	0	0	4	0.0	-4.00
03-04	5	9	1	1	0	7	11.1	-5.00

JOCKEYS

	W-R	Per cent	£1 Level Stake
Stephen Craine	1-2	50.0	+15.00
Philip Hide	1-3	33.3	+5.50

COURSE RECORD

	Total W-R	Non-Hndcps Hurdles	Chases	Hndcps Hurdles	Chases	NH Flat	Per cent	£1 Level Stake
Folkestone	1-2	0-1	0-0	1-1	0-0	0-0	50.0	+15.00
Plumpton	1-2	1-2	0-0	0-0	0-0	0-0	50.0	+6.50

WINNING HORSES

Horse	Races Run	1st	2nd	3rd	£
Paddy Boy	7	1	1	0	3248
*Barking Mad	2	1	0	0	2576
Total winning prize-money					**£5824**
Favourites	0-314		0.0%		-314.00

MRS A J BOWLBY

KINGSTON LISLE, OXON

	No. of Hrs	Races Run	1st	2nd	3rd	Unpl	Per cent	£1 Level Stake
NH Flat	1	2	0	0	0	2	0.0	-2.00
Hurdles	5	14	1	0	0	13	7.1	+7.00
Chases	0	0	0	0	0	0	0.0	0.00
Totals	5	16	1	0	0	15	6.3	+5.00
04-05	6	18	1	1	1	15	5.6	-12.00
03-04	3	9	1	1	1	6	11.1	-3.00

JOCKEYS

	W-R	Per cent	£1 Level Stake
Andrew Tinkler	1-10	10.0	+11.00

COURSE RECORD

	Total W-R	Non-Hndcps Hurdles	Chases	Hndcps Hurdles	Chases	NH Flat	Per cent	£1 Level Stake
Worcester	1-2	0-1	0-0	1-1	0-0	0-0	50.0	+19.00

WINNING HORSES

Horse	Races Run	1st	2nd	3rd	£
Lady Racquet	1	1	0	0	5083
Total winning prize-money					**£5083**
Favourites	0-0		0.0%		0.00

J R BOYLE

EPSOM, SURREY

	No. of Hrs	Races Run	1st	2nd	3rd	Unpl	Per cent	£1 Level Stake
NH Flat	0	0	0	0	0	0	0.0	0.00
Hurdles	4	15	2	1	1	11	13.3	+10.50
Chases	0	0	0	0	0	0	0.0	0.00
Totals	4	15	2	1	1	11	13.3	+10.50

MRS S C BRADBURNE

CUNNOQUHIE, FIFE

	No. of Hrs	Races Run	1st	2nd	3rd	Unpl	Per cent	£1 Level Stake
NH Flat	3	6	0	1	0	5	0.0	-6.00
Hurdles	17	84	6	8	6	64	7.1	-53.00
Chases	10	63	5	5	7	46	7.9	-13.25
Totals	21	153	11	14	13	115	7.2	-72.25
04-05	21	107	5	17	19	66	4.7	-73.25
03-04	13	103	10	18	23	52	9.7	-34.50

BY MONTH

NH Flat	W-R	Per cent	£1 Level Stake	Hurdles	W-R	Per cent	£1 Level Stake
May	0-1	0.0	-1.00	May	2-11	18.2	0.00
June	0-0	0.0	0.00	June	1-5	20.0	-1.50
July	0-0	0.0	0.00	July	0-4	0.0	-4.00
August	0-0	0.0	0.00	August	0-4	0.0	-4.00
September	0-1	0.0	-1.00	September	0-1	0.0	-1.00
October	0-0	0.0	0.00	October	0-9	0.0	-9.00
November	0-0	0.0	0.00	November	0-14	0.0	-14.00
December	0-0	0.0	0.00	December	0-5	0.0	-5.00
January	0-1	0.0	-1.00	January	0-9	0.0	-9.00
February	0-1	0.0	-1.00	February	0-6	0.0	-6.00
March	0-1	0.0	-1.00	March	2-4	50.0	+9.50
April	0-1	0.0	-1.00	April	1-12	8.3	-9.00

Chases	W-R	Per cent	£1 Level Stake	Totals	W-R	Per cent	£1 Level Stake
May	2-2	100.0	+5.25	May	4-14	28.6	+4.25
June	0-1	0.0	-1.00	June	1-6	16.7	-2.50
July	0-0	0.0	0.00	July	0-4	0.0	-4.00
August	0-0	0.0	0.00	August	0-4	0.0	-4.00

September	0-2	0.0	-2.00	September	0-4	0.0	-4.00
October	1-5	20.0	+0.50	October	1-14	7.1	-8.50
November	1-12	8.3	+14.00	November	1-26	3.8	0.00
December	0-6	0.0	-6.00	December	0-11	0.0	-11.00
January	0-10	0.0	-10.00	January	0-20	0.0	-20.00
February	0-7	0.0	-7.00	February	0-14	0.0	-14.00
March	1-6	16.7	+5.00	March	3-11	27.3	+13.50
April	0-12	0.0	-12.00	April	1-25	4.0	-22.00

DISTANCE

Hurdles	W-R	Per cent	£1 Level Stake	Chases	W-R	Per cent	£1 Level Stake
2m-2m3f	1-26	3.8	-23.00	2m-2m3f	1-9	11.1	-3.50
2m4f-2m7f	2-35	5.7	-26.50	2m4f-2m7f	0-17	0.0	-17.00
3m+	3-23	13.0	-3.50	3m+	4-37	10.8	+7.25

TYPE OF RACE

Non-Handicaps	W-R	Per cent	£1 Level Stake	Handicaps	W-R	Per cent	£1 Level Stake
Nov Hrdls	1-24	4.2	-20.50	Nov Hrdls	2-6	33.3	+7.50
Hrdls	2-14	14.3	-5.00	Hrdls	1-39	2.6	-34.00
Nov Chs	1-15	6.7	-9.50	Nov Chs	0-12	0.0	-12.00
Chases	0-0	0.0	0.00	Chases	4-36	11.1	+8.25
Sell/Claim	0-0	0.0	0.00	Sell/Claim	0-1	0.0	-1.00

RACE CLASS / FIRST TIME OUT

	W-R	Per cent	£1 Level Stake		W-R	Per cent	£1 Level Stake
Class 1	0-0	0.0	0.00	Bumpers	0-3	0.0	-3.00
Class 2	0-3	0.0	-3.00	Hurdles	3-14	21.4	0.00
Class 3	1-41	2.4	-35.50	Chases	1-4	25.0	0.00
Class 4	10-97	10.3	-21.75				
Class 5	0-6	0.0	-6.00	Totals	4-21	19.0	-3.00
Class 6	0-6	0.0	-6.00				

JOCKEYS

	W-R	Per cent	£1 Level Stake
Mark Bradburne	6-61	9.8	-34.25
Wilson Renwick	4-28	14.3	+20.00
Owyn Nelmes	1-17	5.9	-11.00

COURSE RECORD

	Total W-R	Non-Hndcps Hurdles	Chases	Hndcps Hurdles	Chases	NH Flat	Per cent	£1 Level Stake
Ayr	3-24	0-7	0-3	2-6	1-8	0-0	12.5	+0.50
Kelso	3-32	1-8	1-7	0-8	1-8	0-1	9.4	-19.50
Hexham	2-9	1-3	0-0	0-1	1-5	0-0	22.2	+0.25
Perth	2-32	1-8	0-0	1-15	0-6	0-3	6.3	-23.50
Newcastle	1-13	0-1	0-1	0-1	1-10	0-0	7.7	+13.00

WINNING HORSES

Horse	Races Run	1st	2nd	3rd	£
Ta Ta For Now	10	1	0	0	6825
South Bronx	7	1	2	0	5421

Bodfari Signet	13	1	2	0	5109
Almire Du Lia	10	2	0	0	8159
Powerlove	7	1	1	1	4554
Tandava	8	2	2	0	8307
Kirkside Pleasure	6	1	0	1	4229
Arctic Lagoon	10	2	0	2	6003
Total winning prize-money					**£48607**
Favourites	3-9		33.3%		2.25

C BRADER

MELTON MOWBRAY, LEICS

	No. of Hrs	Races Run	1st	2nd	3rd	Unpl	Per cent	£1 Level Stake
NH Flat	0	0	0	0	0	0	0.0	0.00
Hurdles	0	0	0	0	0	0	0.0	0.00
Chases	1	2	1	0	0	1	50.0	+5.50
Totals	1	2	1	0	0	1	50.0	+5.50

JOCKEYS

	W-R	Per cent	£1 Level Stake
Mr R Wakeham	1-2	50.0	+5.50

COURSE RECORD

	Total W-R	Non-Hndcps Hurdles	Chases	Hndcps Hurdles	Chases	NH Flat	Per cent	£1 Level Stake
Catterick	1-1	0-0	1-1	0-0	0-0	0-0	100.0	+6.50

WINNING HORSES

Horse	Races Run	1st	2nd	3rd	£
*Skew Whip	2	1	0	0	1562
Total winning prize-money					**£1562**
Favourites	0-0		0.0%		0.00

J M BRADLEY

SEDBURY, GLOUCS

	No. of Hrs	Races Run	1st	2nd	3rd	Unpl	Per cent	£1 Level Stake
NH Flat	1	2	0	1	0	1	0.0	-2.00
Hurdles	9	27	1	1	2	23	3.7	-17.00
Chases	1	5	0	0	1	4	0.0	-5.00
Totals	10	34	1	2	3	28	2.9	-24.00
04-05	6	12	0	0	0	12	0.0	-12.00
03-04	21	46	4	0	2	40	8.7	-1.75

JOCKEYS

	W-R	Per cent	£1 Level Stake
Warren Marston	1-15	6.7	-5.00

COURSE RECORD

	Total W-R	Non-Hndcps Hurdles	Chases	Hndcps Hurdles	Chases	NH Flat	Per cent	£1 Level Stake
Hereford	1-3	1-3	0-0	0-0	0-0	0-0	33.3	+7.00

WINNING HORSES

Horse	Races Run	1st	2nd	3rd	£
Davy's Luck	4	1	0	0	3920
Total winning prize-money					**£3920**
Favourites	0-1		0.0%		-1.00

M BRADSTOCK

LETCOMBE BASSETT, OXON

	No. of Hrs	Races Run	1st	2nd	3rd	Unpl	Per cent	£1 Level Stake
NH Flat	3	5	0	0	0	5	0.0	-5.00
Hurdles	6	21	1	3	0	17	4.8	0.00
Chases	3	9	1	3	0	5	11.1	7.43
Totals	11	35	2	6	0	27	5.7	-12.43
04-05	13	34	5	5	3	21	14.7	-0.13
03-04	17	47	9	5	5	28	19.1	+33.00

JOCKEYS

	W-R	Per cent	£1 Level Stake
Matthew Batchelor	2-20	10.0	+2.57

COURSE RECORD

	Total W-R	Non-Hndcps Hurdles	Chases	Hndcps Hurdles	Chases	NH Flat	Per cent	£1 Level Stake
Ludlow	1-3	0-0	1-1	0-1	0-1	0-0	33.3	-1.43
Uttoxeter	1-3	0-0	0-0	1-3	0-0	0-0	33.3	+18.00

WINNING HORSES

Horse	Races Run	1st	2nd	3rd	£
Nonantais	7	1	1	0	15399
Cossack Dancer	6	1	3	0	6263
Total winning prize-money					**£21662**
Favourites	1-1		100.0%		0.57

MISS M BRAGG

BUCKFASTLEIGH, DEVON

	No. of Hrs	Races Run	1st	2nd	3rd	Unpl	Per cent	£1 Level Stake
NH Flat	2	2	0	0	0	2	0.0	-2.00
Hurdles	3	8	1	1	0	6	12.5	+59.00
Chases	0	0	0	0	0	0	0.0	0.00
Totals	5	10	1	1	0	8	10.0	+57.00
04-05	8	20	0	0	2	18	0.0	-20.00
03-04	11	25	0	0	1	24	0.0	-25.00

JOCKEYS

	W-R	Per cent	£1 Level Stake
David Dennis	1-1	100.0	+66.00

COURSE RECORD

	Total W-R	Non-Hndcps Hurdles	Chases	Hndcps Hurdles	Chases	NH Flat	Per cent	£1 Level Stake
Wincanton	1-2	0-1	0-0	1-1	0-0	0-0	50.0	+65.00

WINNING HORSES

Horse	Races Run	1st	2nd	3rd	£
Festival Flyer	2	1	1	0	2741
Total winning prize-money					**£2741**
Favourites	0-0		0.0%		0.00

O BRENNAN

WORKSOP, NOTTS

	No. of Hrs	Races Run	1st	2nd	3rd	Unpl	Per cent	£1 Level Stake
NH Flat	12	22	0	0	4	18	0.0	-22.00
Hurdles	12	39	4	3	4	28	10.3	-6.77
Chases	10	33	3	4	2	24	9.1	-15.67
Totals	28	94	7	7	10	70	7.4	-44.44
04-05	22	75	4	7	11	53	5.3	-43.00
03-04	21	59	6	4	6	43	10.2	+83.50

JOCKEYS

	W-R	Per cent	£1 Level Stake
Jamie Moore	4-18	22.2	+17.23
John McNamara	2-11	18.2	-3.17
Tom Doyle	1-8	12.5	-1.50

COURSE RECORD

	Total W-R	Non-Hndcps Hurdles	Chases	Hndcps Hurdles	Chases	NH Flat	Per cent	£1 Level Stake
Fakenham	4-20	2-4	0-2	0-1	2-9	0-4	20.0	-2.27
Worcester	1-6	0-1	0-0	1-2	0-1	0-2	16.7	+15.00
Towcester	1-7	0-4	0-0	0-1	1-1	0-1	14.3	-2.67
Wetherby	1-7	0-2	0-0	1-1	0-2	0-2	14.3	-0.50

WINNING HORSES

Horse	Races Run	1st	2nd	3rd	£
Swift Swallow	4	2	1	0	12090
Common Girl	10	2	0	2	9516
Gale Star	4	1	1	0	4202
Tipp Top	9	2	0	2	7612
Total winning prize-money					**£33420**
Favourites	2-4		50.0%		1.23

MISS LUCY BRIDGES

SHAFTESBURY, DORSET

	No. of Hrs	Races Run	1st	2nd	3rd	Unpl	Per cent	£1 Level Stake
NH Flat	0	0	0	0	0	0	0.0	0.00
Hurdles	4	17	1	0	0	16	5.9	+17.00
Chases	2	6	0	0	1	5	0.0	-6.00
Totals	**6**	**23**	**1**	**0**	**1**	**21**	**4.3**	**+11.00**

JOCKEYS

	W-R	Per cent	£1 Level Stake
Miss Lucy Bridges	1-18	5.6	+16.00

COURSE RECORD

	Total W-R	Non-Hndcps Hurdles Chases		Hndcps Hurdles Chases		NH Flat	Per cent	£1 Level Stake
Wincanton	1-2	1-2	0-0	0-0	0-0	0-0	50.0	+32.00

WINNING HORSES

Horse	Races Run	1st	2nd	3rd	£
Nero West	5	1	0	0	4229
Total winning prize-money					**£4229**
Favourites	0-0		0.0%		0.00

R S BROOKHOUSE

WIXFORD, WARWICKS

	No. of Hrs	Races Run	1st	2nd	3rd	Unpl	Per cent	£1 Level Stake
NH Flat	1	3	1	0	0	2	33.3	+23.00
Hurdles	9	38	5	3	2	28	13.2	+67.00
Chases	3	3	0	0	0	3	0.0	-3.00
Totals	**10**	**44**	**6**	**3**	**2**	**33**	**13.6**	**+87.00**
04-05	9	57	2	7	4	44	3.5	-29.00
03-04	8	31	0	1	2	28	0.0	-31.00

JOCKEYS

	W-R	Per cent	£1 Level Stake
John McNamara	6-28	21.4	+103.00

COURSE RECORD

	Total W-R	Non-Hndcps Hurdles Chases		Hndcps Hurdles Chases		NH Flat	Per cent	£1 Level Stake
Wetherby	2-2	1-1	0-0	0-0	0-0	1-1	100.0	+65.00
Uttoxeter	2-3	0-1	0-0	2-2	0-0	0-0	66.7	+33.00
Aintree	1-3	1-2	0-0	0-1	0-0	0-0	33.3	+14.00
Stratford	1-4	0-0	0-0	1-4	0-0	0-0	25.0	+7.00

WINNING HORSES

Horse	Races Run	1st	2nd	3rd	£
Herne Bay	7	2	1	0	8197
Three Lions	7	1	0	1	4261
Whispered Promises	7	2	1	0	7943
She's The Lady	3	1	0	0	2686
Total winning prize-money					**£23087**
Favourites	0-0		0.0%		0.00

MRS A E BROOKS

TOWCESTER, NORTHAMPTONSHIRE

	No. of Hrs	Races Run	1st	2nd	3rd	Unpl	Per cent	£1 Level Stake
NH Flat	0	0	0	0	0	0	0.0	0.00
Hurdles	5	10	2	1	1	6	20.0	+18.00
Chases	1	1	0	0	0	1	0.0	1.00
Totals	**5**	**11**	**2**	**1**	**1**	**7**	**18.2**	**+17.00**
04-05	2	2	0	0	0	2	0.0	-2.00

JOCKEYS

	W-R	Per cent	£1 Level Stake
James Diment	1-4	25.0	+15.00
Mr R J Barrett	1-6	16.7	+3.00

COURSE RECORD

	Total W-R	Non-Hndcps Hurdles Chases		Hndcps Hurdles Chases		NH Flat	Per cent	£1 Level Stake
Towcester	1-2	0-0	0-0	1-2	0-0	0-0	50.0	+7.00
Hereford	1-3	0-1	0-0	1-2	0-0	0-0	33.3	+16.00

WINNING HORSES

Horse	Races Run	1st	2nd	3rd	£
Franco	5	1	1	1	5211
*The Small Farmer	3	1	0	0	2928
Total winning prize-money					**£8139**
Favourites	0-1		0.0%		-1.00

S A BROOKSHAW

WOLLERTON, SHROPSHIRE

	No. of Hrs	Races Run	1st	2nd	3rd	Unpl	Per cent	£1 Level Stake
NH Flat	5	10	0	0	0	10	0.0	-10.00
Hurdles	9	25	1	1	1	22	4.0	-12.00
Chases	7	38	2	3	6	27	5.3	-30.00
Totals	**16**	**73**	**3**	**4**	**7**	**59**	**4.1**	**-52.00**
04-05	11	54	4	7	1	42	7.4	-15.00
03-04	14	83	10	11	12	50	12.0	+60.94

JOCKEYS

	W-R	Per cent	£1 Level Stake
Phil Kinsella	1-1	100.0	+12.00
Tony Dobbin	1-6	16.7	-1.50
Joseph Byrne	1-12	8.3	-8.50

COURSE RECORD

	Total W-R	Non-Hndcps Hurdles Chases	Hndcps Hurdles Chases	NH Flat	Per cent	£1 Level Stake
Leicester	1-1	0-0 0-0	0-0 1-1	0-0	100.0	+3.50
Haydock	1-12	0-3 0-0	1-2 0-5	0-2	8.3	+1.00
Hereford	1-12	0-1 0-0	0-2 1-7	0-2	8.3	-8.50

WINNING HORSES

Horse	Races Run	1st	2nd	3rd	£
*Glimmer Of Light	1	1	0	0	9759
Cassia Heights	10	1	0	2	5582
Silver Samuel	4	1	1	0	4794
Total winning prize-money					**£20135**
Favourites	1-2		50.0%		1.50

I A BROWN

GREAT EDSTONE, N YORKS

	No. of Hrs	Races Run	1st	2nd	3rd	Unpl	Per cent	£1 Level Stake
NH Flat	0	0	0	0	0	0	0.0	0.00
Hurdles	3	17	1	0	3	13	5.9	-10.50
Chases	0	0	0	0	0	0	0.0	0.00
Totals	**3**	**17**	**1**	**0**	**3**	**13**	**5.9**	**-10.50**
04-05	3	22	1	2	0	19	4.5	-9.00
03-04	6	12	0	0	0	12	0.0	-12.00

JOCKEYS

	W-R	Per cent	£1 Level Stake
Dave Crosse	1-2	50.0	+4.50

COURSE RECORD

	Total W-R	Non-Hndcps Hurdles Chases	Hndcps Hurdles Chases	NH Flat	Per cent	£1 Level Stake
Sedgefield	1-6	0-2 0-0	1-4 0-0	0-0	16.7	+0.50

WINNING HORSES

Horse	Races Run	1st	2nd	3rd	£
Fortune's Fool	9	1	0	2	2681
Total winning prize-money					**£2681**
Favourites	0-2		0.0%		-2.00

R H BUCKLER

MELPLASH, DORSET

	No. of Hrs	Races Run	1st	2nd	3rd	Unpl	Per cent	£1 Level Stake
NH Flat	6	12	0	1	3	8	0.0	-12.00
Hurdles	24	55	1	11	5	38	1.8	-49.50
Chases	20	96	8	8	8	71	8.3	-37.25
Totals	**36**	**163**	**9**	**20**	**16**	**117**	**5.5**	**-98.75**
04-05	34	168	15	20	16	117	8.9	-34.27
03-04	33	166	14	19	19	114	8.4	-49.33

JOCKEYS

	W-R	Per cent	£1 Level Stake
Benjamin Hitchcott	5-99	5.1	-64.25
Robert Thornton	2-8	25.0	+1.00
Sam Thomas	1-3	33.3	+1.50
Paul Davey	1-13	7.7	+3.00

COURSE RECORD

	Total W-R	Non-Hndcps Hurdles Chases	Hndcps Hurdles Chases	NH Flat	Per cent	£1 Level Stake
Plumpton	2-16	0-1 0-2	0-2 2-9	0-2	12.5	-2.50
Wincanton	2-23	0-6 0-0	0-2 2-12	0-3	8.7	0.00
Taunton	1-4	0-0 0-2	0-1 1-1	0-0	25.0	+1.50
Leicester	1-6	1-1 0-2	0-1 0-2	0-0	16.7	-0.50
Uttoxeter	1-6	0-0 1-2	0-0 0-4	0-0	16.7	-2.75
Chepstow	1-12	0-2 0-1	0-2 1-7	0-0	8.3	-2.00
Fontwell	1-16	0-3 0-2	0-4 1-7	0-0	6.3	-12.50

WINNING HORSES

Horse	Races Run	1st	2nd	3rd	£
I Hear Thunder	8	2	0	0	33338
Clyffe Hanger	2	1	0	1	6996
He's The Gaffer	9	2	1	0	9971
He's The Guv'Nor	8	1	3	1	5143
Elfkirk	6	1	1	0	5080
Five Alley	12	1	3	3	3682
Taksina	12	1	0	2	0
Total winning prize-money					**£64210**
Favourites	1-5		20.0%		-1.75

D BURCHELL

BRIERY HILL, BLAENAU GWENT

	No. of Hrs	Races Run	1st	2nd	3rd	Unpl	Per cent	£1 Level Stake
NH Flat	1	2	0	0	0	2	0.0	-2.00
Hurdles	22	134	8	13	10	103	6.0	-10.00
Chases	6	29	1	1	6	21	3.4	-19.00
Totals	**28**	**165**	**9**	**14**	**16**	**126**	**5.5**	**-31.00**

04-05	37	158	14	15	23	106	8.9	+21.67
03-04	19	86	8	9	11	58	9.3	-18.50

JOCKEYS

	W-R	Per cent	£1 Level Stake
Lee Stephens	3-34	8.8	-10.00
William Kennedy	2-17	11.8	+30.00
Tom Messenger	1-3	33.3	+18.00
Antony Evans	1-5	20.0	+12.00
T J O'Brien	1-6	16.7	+9.00
Adrian Scholes	1-13	7.7	-3.00

COURSE RECORD

	Total W-R	Non-Hndcps Hurdles	Chases	Hndcps Hurdles	Chases	NH Flat	Per cent	£1 Level Stake
Hereford	2-22	0-2	0-0	2-12	0-8	0-0	9.1	-8.00
Leicester	1-2	0-0	0-0	1-1	0-1	0-0	50.0	+39.00
Newcastle	1-2	0-0	0-0	1-2	0-0	0-0	50.0	+13.00
Southwell	1-2	0-0	0-0	1-2	0-0	0-0	50.0	+4.00
Uttoxeter	1-10	0-2	0-0	0-6	1-2	0-0	10.0	0.00
Taunton	1-11	0-2	0-0	1-7	0-2	0-0	9.1	+6.00
Worcester	1-23	1-9	0-0	0-9	0-4	0-1	4.3	-13.00
Chepstow	1-26	0-9	0-0	1-14	0-3	0-0	3.8	-5.00

WINNING HORSES

Horse	Races Run	1st	2nd	3rd	£
Marrel	11	2	0	0	9591
Nick's Choice	17	1	1	1	5205
Flahive's First	12	1	0	1	5174
Kilns Pearl	4	2	0	0	8297
Titian Flame	13	1	1	1	3904
*Slalom	7	1	1	2	3562
West End Wonder	7	1	1	1	3471
Total winning prize-money					£39204
Favourites	0-8		0.0%		-8.00

K J BURKE

BOURTON-ON-THE-WATER, GLOUCS

	No. of Hrs	Races Run	1st	2nd	3rd	Unpl	Per cent	£1 Level Stake
NH Flat	1	2	0	0	0	2	0.0	2.00
Hurdles	11	25	0	0	1	24	0.0	-25.00
Chases	6	16	2	0	2	12	12.5	+100.00
Totals	14	43	2	0	3	38	4.7	+73.00
04-05	5	9	0	0	1	8	0.0	-9.00
03-04	3	6	0	0	0	5	0.0	-6.00

JOCKEYS

	W-R	Per cent	£1 Level Stake
Colin Bolger	1-1	100.0	+14.00
Mr Matthew Smith	1-2	50.0	+99.00

COURSE RECORD

	Total W-R	Non-Hndcps Hurdles	Chases	Hndcps Hurdles	Chases	NH Flat	Per cent	£1 Level Stake
Sedgefield	1-2	0-1	1-1	0-0	0-0	0-0	50.0	+99.00
Uttoxeter	1-4	0-2	0-0	0-0	1-1	0-1	25.0	+11.00

WINNING HORSES

Horse	Races Run	1st	2nd	3rd	£
Sarahs Quay	11	2	0	3	21426
Total winning prize-money					£21426
Favourites	0-0		0.0%		0.00

MRS O BUSH

CULLOMPTON, DEVON

	No. of Hrs	Races Run	1st	2nd	3rd	Unpl	Per cent	£1 Level Stake
NH Flat	0	0	0	0	0	0	0.0	0.00
Hurdles	0	0	0	0	0	0	0.0	0.00
Chases	2	7	1	2	0	4	14.3	-4.00
Totals	2	7	1	2	0	4	14.3	-4.00
04-05	3	7	1	1	3	2	14.3	+14.00
03-04	4	9	1	2	1	5	11.1	-7.64

JOCKEYS

	W-R	Per cent	£1 Level Stake
Miss P Gundry	1-5	20.0	-2.00

COURSE RECORD

	Total W-R	Non-Hndcps Hurdles	Chases	Hndcps Hurdles	Chases	NH Flat	Per cent	£1 Level Stake
Huntingdon	1-1	0-0	1-1	0-0	0-0	0-0	100.0	+2.00

WINNING HORSES

Horse	Races Run	1st	2nd	3rd	£
Vinnie Boy	5	1	1	0	1596
Total winning prize-money					£1596
Favourites	1-1		100.0%		2.00

P BUTLER

EAST CHILTINGTON, E SUSSEX

	No. of Hrs	Races Run	1st	2nd	3rd	Unpl	Per cent	£1 Level Stake
NH Flat	1	2	0	0	0	2	0.0	-2.00
Hurdles	9	39	1	2	2	34	2.6	-22.00
Chases	2	3	0	0	0	3	0.0	-3.00
Totals	9	44	1	2	2	39	2.3	-27.00
04-05	8	55	3	1	4	47	5.5	-2.00
03-04	14	40	1	3	1	35	2.5	-35.50

JOCKEYS

	W-R	Per cent	£1 Level Stake
Richard Gordon	1-2	50.0	+15.00

COURSE RECORD

	Total W-R	Non-Hndcps Hurdles	Chases	Hndcps Hurdles	Chases	NH Flat	Per cent	£1 Level Stake
Fontwell	1-11	0-3	0-1	1-7	0-0	0-0	9.1	+6.00

WINNING HORSES

Horse	Races Run	1st	2nd	3rd	£
Geography	11	1	0	1	2277
Total winning prize-money					£2277
Favourites	0-0		0.0%		0.00

G A BUTLER

BLEWBURY, OXON

	No. of Hrs	Races Run	1st	2nd	3rd	Unpl	Per cent	£1 Level Stake
NH Flat	0	0	0	0	0	0	0.0	0.00
Hurdles	3	3	1	0	0	2	33.3	+12.00
Chases	0	0	0	0	0	0	0.0	0.00
Totals	**3**	**3**	**1**	**0**	**0**	**2**	**33.3**	**+12.00**

JOCKEYS

	W-R	Per cent	£1 Level Stake
Steven Crawford	1-2	50.0	+13.00

COURSE RECORD

	Total W-R	Non-Hndcps Hurdles	Chases	Hndcps Hurdles	Chases	NH Flat	Per cent	£1 Level Stake
Worcester	1-1	1-1	0-0	0-0	0-0	0-0	100.0	+14.00

WINNING HORSES

Horse	Races Run	1st	2nd	3rd	£
Compton Drake	1	1	0	0	3445
Total winning prize-money					£3445
Favourites	0-0		0.0%		0.00

T BUTT

JEDBURGH, BORDERS

	No. of Hrs	Races Run	1st	2nd	3rd	Unpl	Per cent	£1 Level Stake
NH Flat	0	0	0	0	0	0	0.0	0.00
Hurdles	2	14	1	2	1	10	7.1	-6.00
Chases	2	8	1	0	0	7	12.5	-2.00
Totals	**4**	**22**	**2**	**2**	**1**	**17**	**9.1**	**-8.00**

04-05	2	3	0	1	0	2	0.0	-3.00
03-04	3	7	1	0	0	6	14.3	-3.25

JOCKEYS

	W-R	Per cent	£1 Level Stake
Mr M Ellwood	1-3	33.3	+3.00
Dougie Costello	1-11	9.1	-3.00

COURSE RECORD

	Total W-R	Non-Hndcps Hurdles	Chases	Hndcps Hurdles	Chases	NH Flat	Per cent	£1 Level Stake
Hexham	1-2	0-0	1-2	0-0	0-0	0-0	50.0	+4.00
Perth	1-3	1-1	0-1	0-1	0-0	0-0	33.3	+5.00

WINNING HORSES

Horse	Races Run	1st	2nd	3rd	£
*Lethem Air	9	1	2	1	5205
Highland Brig	7	1	0	0	1249
Total winning prize-money					£6454
Favourites	0-0		0.0%		0.00

MISS J A CAMACHO

NORTON, N YORKS

	No. of Hrs	Races Run	1st	2nd	3rd	Unpl	Per cent	£1 Level Stake
NH Flat	2	2	0	2	0	0	0.0	-2.00
Hurdles	2	6	1	0	0	5	16.7	-1.00
Chases	0	0	0	0	0	0	0.0	0.00
Totals	**3**	**8**	**1**	**2**	**0**	**5**	**12.5**	**-3.00**
04-05	1	4	0	0	0	4	0.0	-4.00
03-04	1	3	0	1	1	1	0.0	-3.00

JOCKEYS

	W-R	Per cent	£1 Level Stake
G Lee	1-3	33.3	+2.00

COURSE RECORD

	Total W-R	Non-Hndcps Hurdles	Chases	Hndcps Hurdles	Chases	NH Flat	Per cent	£1 Level Stake
Mrket Rsn	1-2	1-1	0-0	0-0	0-0	0-1	50.0	+3.00

WINNING HORSES

Horse	Races Run	1st	2nd	3rd	£
Lago D'Oro	3	1	1	0	4433
Total winning prize-money					£4433
Favourites	0-1		0.0%		-1.00

MISS H CAMPBELL

TILTON ON THE HILL, LEICS

	No. of Hrs	Races Run	1st	2nd	3rd	Unpl	Per cent	£1 Level Stake
NH Flat	0	0	0	0	0	0	0.0	0.00
Hurdles	0	0	0	0	0	0	0.0	0.00
Chases	1	2	1	0	0	1	50.0	+7.00
Totals	1	2	1	0	0	1	50.0	+7.00

JOCKEYS

	W-R	Per cent	£1 Level Stake
Mr J Docker	1-2	50.0	+7.00

COURSE RECORD

	Total W-R	Non-Hndcps Hurdles	Chases	Hndcps Hurdles	Chases	NH Flat	Per cent	£1 Level Stake
Mrket Rsn	1-1	0-0	1-1	0-0	0 0	0-0	100.0	+8.00

WINNING HORSES

Horse	Races Run	1st	2nd	3rd	£
*Bedtime Boys	2	1	0	0	1648
Total winning prize-money					£1648
Favourites	0-0		0.0%		0.00

JENNIE CANDLISH

BASFORD GREEN, STAFFS

	No. of Hrs	Races Run	1st	2nd	3rd	Unpl	Per cent	£1 Level Stake
NH Flat	4	7	2	0	1	4	28.6	+32.00
Hurdles	22	64	5	0	5	54	7.8	-8.00
Chases	3	8	0	0	0	8	0.0	-8.00
Totals	25	79	7	0	6	66	8.9	+16.00
04-05	25	94	9	6	6	73	9.6	-35.17
03-04	24	89	2	5	8	74	2.2	-72.50

JOCKEYS

	W-R	Per cent	£1 Level Stake
Alan O'Keeffe	4-48	8.3	-12.00
John McNamara	2-5	40.0	+35.00
Joseph Byrne	1-21	4.8	-2.00

COURSE RECORD

	Total W-R	Non-Hndcps Hurdles	Chases	Hndcps Hurdles	Chases	NH Flat	Per cent	£1 Level Stake
Uttoxeter	3-14	1-4	0-0	1-6	0-2	1-2	21.4	+34.50
Carlisle	1-3	0-1	0-0	0-1	0-0	1-1	33.3	+7.00
Perth	1-3	1-1	0-0	0-0	0-2	0-0	33.3	+8.00
Sedgefield	1-4	0-0	0-0	1-1	0-3	0-0	25.0	+15.00
Worcester	1-7	0-1	0-0	1-6	0-0	0-0	14.3	-0.50

WINNING HORSES

Horse	Races Run	1st	2nd	3rd	£
Downing Street	5	3	0	1	14531
Greencard Golf	10	1	0	2	3458
Suprendre Espere	6	2	0	0	4742
Harbour Breeze	1	1	0	0	1713
Total winning prize-money					£24444
Favourites	0-0		0.0%		0.00

J G CANN

CULLOMPTON, DEVON

	No. of Hrs	Races Run	1st	2nd	3rd	Unpl	Per cent	£1 Level Stake
NH Flat	3	6	1	2	1	2	16.7	+11.00
Hurdles	1	3	0	0	0	3	0.0	-3.00
Chases	4	15	2	2	2	9	13.3	-8.50
Totals	7	24	3	4	3	14	12.5	-0.50
04-05	4	19	2	5	5	7	10.5	-11.50
03-04	3	10	2	5	1	2	20.0	+8.00

JOCKEYS

	W-R	Per cent	£1 Level Stake
Miss P Gundry	2-12	16.7	-5.50
T J O'Brien	1-6	16.7	+11.00

COURSE RECORD

	Total W-R	Non-Hndcps Hurdles	Chases	Hndcps Hurdles	Chases	NH Flat	Per cent	£1 Level Stake
Towcester	1-1	0-0	0-0	0-0	0-0	1-1	100.0	+16.00
Plumpton	1-3	0-0	1-1	0-0	0-0	0-2	33.3	-1.50
Stratford	1-3	0-0	1-1	0-0	0-1	0-1	33.3	+2.00

WINNING HORSES

Horse	Races Run	1st	2nd	3rd	£
Mrs Be	6	2	0	1	23401
Solid As A Rock	2	1	0	1	2602
Total winning prize-money					£26003
Favourites	2-5		40.0%		1.50

D E CANTILLON

NEWMARKET, SUFFOLK

	No. of Hrs	Races Run	1st	2nd	3rd	Unpl	Per cent	£1 Level Stake
NH Flat	1	2	0	0	0	2	0.0	-2.00
Hurdles	7	15	2	4	1	8	13.3	-5.75
Chases	4	10	0	1	2	7	0.0	-10.00
Totals	10	27	2	5	3	17	7.4	-17.75

04-05	9	21	3	4	2	12	14.3	-12.25
03-04	5	11	3	1	1	6	27.3	-6.82

JOCKEYS

	W-R	Per cent	£1 Level Stake
Miss P Buckley	1-4	25.0	-0.75
Paul Moloney	1-11	9.1	-5.00

COURSE RECORD

	Total W-R	Non-Hndcps Hurdles	Chases	Hndcps Hurdles	Chases	NH Flat	Per cent	£1 Level Stake
Worcester	1-4	1-3	0-0	0-0	0-1	0-0	25.0	+2.00
Huntingdon	1-6	0-3	0-1	1-1	0-1	0-0	16.7	-2.75

WINNING HORSES

Horse	Races Run	1st	2nd	3rd	£
Sharaab	5	1	1	0	3388
Garnett	2	1	1	0	2702
Total winning prize-money					**£6090**
Favourites	1-2		**50.0%**		1.25

D CARROLL

WARTHILL, N YORKS

	No. of Hrs	Races Run	1st	2nd	3rd	Unpl	Per cent	£1 Level Stake
NH Flat	1	1	0	0	0	1	0.0	-1.00
Hurdles	9	22	1	1	0	20	4.5	-7.00
Chases	0	0	0	0	0	0	0.0	0.00
Totals	10	23	1	1	0	21	4.3	-8.00
04-05	7	18	1	2	2	13	5.6	-11.00
03-04	4	13	2	2	0	9	15.4	+1.00

JOCKEYS

	W-R	Per cent	£1 Level Stake
William Kennedy	1-2	50.0	+13.00

COURSE RECORD

	Total W-R	Non-Hndcps Hurdles	Chases	Hndcps Hurdles	Chases	NH Flat	Per cent	£1 Level Stake
Bangor	1-1	1-1	0-0	0-0	0-0	0-0	100.0	+14.00

WINNING HORSES

Horse	Races Run	1st	2nd	3rd	£
Mezereon	1	1	0	0	2878
Total winning prize-money					**£2878**
Favourites	0-0		**0.0%**		0.00

A W CARROLL

CROPTHORNE, WORCS

	No. of Hrs	Races Run	1st	2nd	3rd	Unpl	Per cent	£1 Level Stake
NH Flat	3	3	0	0	0	3	0.0	-3.00
Hurdles	39	128	11	9	11	97	8.6	-16.29
Chases	14	42	3	5	3	31	7.1	-14.50
Totals	44	173	14	14	14	131	8.1	-33.79
04-05	36	127	20	9	11	87	15.7	+3.08
03-04	32	129	6	18	13	92	4.7	-104.30

BY MONTH

NH Flat	W-R	Per cent	£1 Level Stake	Hurdles	W-R	Per cent	£1 Level Stake
May	0-1	0.0	-1.00	May	0-2	0.0	-2.00
June	0-0	0.0	0.00	June	0-5	0.0	-5.00
July	0-0	0.0	0.00	July	0-3	0.0	-3.00
August	0-0	0.0	0.00	August	2-7	28.6	+10.50
September	0-0	0.0	0.00	September	1-4	25.0	+5.00
October	0-0	0.0	0.00	October	2-17	11.8	-9.50
November	0-1	0.0	-1.00	November	1-24	4.2	-20.50
December	0-0	0.0	0.00	December	1-16	6.3	-10.00
January	0-0	0.0	0.00	January	1-14	7.1	+37.00
February	0-0	0.0	0.00	February	2-15	13.3	-0.67
March	0-1	0.0	-1.00	March	1-11	9.1	-8.13
April	0-0	0.0	0.00	April	0-10	0.0	-10.00

Chases	W-R	Per cent	£1 Level Stake	Totals	W-R	Per cent	£1 Level Stake
May	1-4	25.0	+7.00	May	1-7	14.3	+4.00
June	1-5	20.0	+0.50	June	1-10	10.0	-4.50
July	0-2	0.0	-2.00	July	0-5	0.0	-5.00
August	0-1	0.0	-1.00	August	2-8	25.0	+9.50
September	0-0	0.0	0.00	September	1-4	25.0	+5.00
October	0-3	0.0	-3.00	October	2-20	10.0	-12.50
November	0-1	0.0	-1.00	November	1-26	3.8	-22.50
December	0-0	0.0	0.00	December	1-16	6.3	-10.00
January	0-6	0.0	-6.00	January	1-20	5.0	+31.00
February	0-3	0.0	-3.00	February	2-18	11.1	-3.67
March	0-6	0.0	-6.00	March	1-18	5.6	-15.13
April	1-11	9.1	0.00	April	1-21	4.8	-10.00

DISTANCE

Hurdles	W-R	Per cent	£1 Level Stake	Chases	W-R	Per cent	£1 Level Stake
2m-2m3f	8-90	8.9	-5.29	2m-2m3f	1-19	5.3	-8.00
2m4f-2m7f	2-30	6.7	-9.00	2m4f-2m7f	1-17	5.9	-11.50
3m+	1-8	12.5	-2.00	3m+	1-6	16.7	+5.00

TYPE OF RACE

Non-Handicaps	W-R	Per cent	£1 Level Stake	Handicaps	W-R	Per cent	£1 Level Stake
Nov Hrdls	1-36	2.8	+15.00	Nov Hrdls	1-19	5.3	-13.00
Hrdls	0-5	0.0	-5.00	Hrdls	7-47	14.9	-7.29

Nov Chs	0-6	0.0	-6.00	Nov Chs	1-10	10.0	+1.00
Chases	0-1	0.0	-1.00	Chases	2-25	8.0	-8.50
Sell/Claim	2-12	16.7	+3.00	Sell/Claim	0-10	0.0	-10.00

RACE CLASS / FIRST TIME OUT

	W-R	Per cent	£1 Level Stake		W-R	Per cent	£1 Level Stake
Class 1	0-2	0.0	-2.00	Bumpers	0-3	0.0	-3.00
Class 2	0-6	0.0	-6.00	Hurdles	1-33	3.0	-27.50
Class 3	7-62	11.3	+40.00	Chases	1-8	12.5	+3.00
Class 4	5-77	6.5	-54.79				
Class 5	2-24	8.3	-9.00	Totals	2-44	4.5	-27.50
Class 6	0-2	0.0	-2.00				

JOCKEYS

	W-R	Per cent	£1 Level Stake
Wayne Hutchinson	7-66	10.6	+31.50
Timmy Murphy	2-8	25.0	0.00
Mr J Snowden	1-1	100.0	+1.88
Mr G Tumelty	1-3	33.3	+0.50
Carl Llewellyn	1-8	12.5	+3.00
Willie McCarthy	1-8	12.5	-3.67
Noel Fehily	1-25	4.0	-13.00

COURSE RECORD

	Total W-R	Non-Hndcps Hurdles	Chases	Hndcps Hurdles	Chases	NH Flat	Per cent	£1 Level Stake
Sandown	3-13	1-4	0-0	2-7	0-2	0-0	23.1	+45.21
Huntingdon	2-12	0-3	0-0	2-7	0-2	0-0	16.7	-4.00
Towcester	2-13	1-6	0-1	0-3	1-7	0-1	15.4	+3.00
Ludlow	2-19	1-5	0-1	0-5	1-8	0-0	10.5	+2.00
Mrket Rsn	1-3	0-0	0-0	0-1	1-2	0-0	33.3	+2.50
Uttoxeter	1-5	0-2	0-0	1-3	0-0	0-0	20.0	+4.00
Taunton	1-6	0-1	0-0	1-4	0-1	0-0	16.7	-2.50
Wetherby	1-10	0-3	0-0	1-5	0-1	0-1	10.0	-4.00
Worcester	1-13	0-0	0-0	1-8	0-5	0-0	7.7	-1.00

WINNING HORSES

Horse	Races Run	1st	2nd	3rd	£
Moving Earth	4	1	0	1	8096
Kind Sir	10	1	2	0	7474
Burundi	5	2	0	0	12058
Quasimodo	6	1	0	0	6506
*Mexican Pete	4	2	1	0	9781
Mokum	10	1	1	0	6338
Danse Macabre	7	2	1	1	8900
*Meadow Hawk	4	1	1	0	3868
Banningham Blaze	4	1	0	0	2891
Spectested	3	1	0	0	2799
Ambersong	6	1	0	2	2602
Total winning prize-money					£71313
Favourites	3-12		25.0%		-3.13

B I CASE

EDGCOTE, NORTHANTS

	No. of Hrs	Races Run	1st	2nd	3rd	Unpl	Per cent	£1 Level Stake
NH Flat	4	6	1	0	1	4	16.7	+5.00
Hurdles	7	17	2	0	2	13	11.8	+13.00
Chases	4	12	0	1	2	9	0.0	-12.00
Totals	12	35	3	1	5	26	8.6	+6.00
04-05	13	54	3	10	5	36	5.6	-39.00
03-04	10	44	1	3	7	33	2.3	-33.00

JOCKEYS

	W-R	Per cent	£1 Level Stake
Mark Nicolls	2-11	18.2	+15.00
Sam Stronge	1-2	50.0	+13.00

COURSE RECORD

	Total W-R	Non-Hndcps Hurdles	Chases	Hndcps Hurdles	Chases	NH Flat	Per cent	£1 Level Stake
Warwick	1-2	0-0	0-0	0-1	0-0	1-1	50.0	+9.00
Hereford	1-3	0-0	0-1	1-2	0-0	0-0	33.3	+12.00
Huntingdon	1-7	0-1	0-0	1-2	0-2	0-2	14.3	+8.00

WINNING HORSES

Horse	Races Run	1st	2nd	3rd	£
True Mariner	10	2	0	2	6394
Ring Back	3	1	0	1	2056
Total winning prize-money					£8450
Favourites	0-1		0.0%		-1.00

J M CASTLE

LONG CRENDON, BUCKS

	No. of Hrs	Races Run	1st	2nd	3rd	Unpl	Per cent	£1 Level Stake
NH Flat	0	0	0	0	0	0	0.0	0.00
Hurdles	1	1	0	0	0	1	0.0	-1.00
Chases	1	9	1	0	0	8	11.1	+25.00
Totals	1	10	1	0	0	9	10.0	+24.00
04-05	1	6	0	0	0	6	0.0	-6.00
03-04	1	5	0	0	0	5	0.0	-5.00

JOCKEYS

	W-R	Per cent	£1 Level Stake
Mr N Pearce	1-3	33.3	+31.00

COURSE RECORD

	Total W-R	Non-Hndcps Hurdles	Chases	Hndcps Hurdles	Chases	NH Flat	Per cent	£1 Level Stake
Towcester	1-3	0-0	1-2	0-0	0-1	0-0	33.3	+31.00

WINNING HORSES

Horse	Races Run	1st	2nd	3rd	£
Monty Be Quick	10	1	0	0	3553
Total winning prize-money					£3553
Favourites	0-0		0.0%		0.00

P R CHAMINGS

BAUGHURST, HANTS

	No. of Hrs	Races Run	1st	2nd	3rd	Unpl	Per cent	£1 Level Stake
NH Flat	3	5	0	0	2	3	0.0	-5.00
Hurdles	5	8	1	0	0	7	12.5	+2.00
Chases	1	1	0	0	0	1	0.0	-1.00
Totals	9	14	1	0	2	11	7.1	-4.00
04-05	11	39	5	3	6	25	12.8	-16.43
03-04	8	37	4	7	4	22	10.8	-9.50

JOCKEYS

	W-R	Per cent	£1 Level Stake
P J Brennan	1-1	100.0	+9.00

COURSE RECORD

	Total W-R	Non-Hndcps Hurdles	Chases	Hndcps Hurdles	Chases	NH Flat	Per cent	£1 Level Stake
Newbury	1-2	1-1	0-0	0-0	0-0	0-1	50.0	+8.00

WINNING HORSES

Horse	Races Run	1st	2nd	3rd	£
Midas Way	1	1	0	0	3904
Total winning prize-money					£3904
Favourites	0-0		0.0%		0.00

NOEL T CHANCE

UPPER LAMBOURN, BERKS

	No. of Hrs	Races Run	1st	2nd	3rd	Unpl	Per cent	£1 Level Stake
NH Flat	11	23	2	5	4	12	8.7	-14.00
Hurdles	14	40	6	10	8	16	15.0	-1.06
Chases	9	20	3	1	3	13	15.0	+3.00
Totals	29	83	11	16	15	41	13.3	-12.06
04-05	37	100	20	14	11	55	20.0	-34.92
03-04	32	95	17	13	15	50	17.9	-16.79

BY MONTH

NH Flat	W-R	Per cent	£1 Level Stake	Hurdles	W-R	Per cent	£1 Level Stake
May	0-0	0.0	0.00	May	0-2	0.0	-2.00
June	0-0	0.0	0.00	June	0-0	0.0	0.00
July	0-0	0.0	0.00	July	0-0	0.0	0.00
August	0-0	0.0	0.00	August	0-0	0.0	0.00
September	0-0	0.0	0.00	September	0-0	0.0	0.00
October	0-2	0.0	-2.00	October	0-0	0.0	0.00
November	0-4	0.0	-4.00	November	0-1	0.0	-1.00
December	1-3	33.3	+1.00	December	1-3	33.3	+3.00
January	0-3	0.0	-3.00	January	1-11	9.1	-6.00
February	0-1	0.0	-1.00	February	1-9	11.1	-3.00
March	0-4	0.0	-4.00	March	1-7	14.3	+8.00
April	1-6	16.7	-1.00	April	2-7	28.6	-0.06

Chases	W-R	Per cent	£1 Level Stake	Totals	W-R	Per cent	£1 Level Stake
May	0-2	0.0	-2.00	May	0-4	0.0	-4.00
June	0-1	0.0	-1.00	June	0-1	0.0	-1.00
July	0-0	0.0	0.00	July	0-0	0.0	0.00
August	0-0	0.0	0.00	August	0-0	0.0	0.00
September	1-1	100.0	+7.50	September	1-1	100.0	+7.50
October	0-2	0.0	-2.00	October	0-4	0.0	-4.00
November	1-3	33.3	+1.50	November	1-8	12.5	-3.50
December	0-1	0.0	-1.00	December	2-7	28.6	+3.00
January	0-4	0.0	4.00	January	1-18	5.6	-13.00
February	0-0	0.0	0.00	February	1-10	10.0	-4.00
March	0-2	0.0	-2.00	March	1-13	7.7	+2.00
April	1-4	25.0	+6.00	April	4-17	23.5	+4.94

DISTANCE

Hurdles	W-R	Per cent	£1 Level Stake	Chases	W-R	Per cent	£1 Level Stake
2m-2m3f	3-16	18.8	+10.50	2m-2m3f	2-11	18.2	+3.50
2m4f-2m7f	0-18	0.0	-18.00	2m4f-2m7f	1-8	12.5	+0.50
3m+	3-6	50.0	+6.44	3m+	0-1	0.0	-1.00

TYPE OF RACE

Non-Handicaps	W-R	Per cent	£1 Level Stake	Handicaps	W-R	Per cent	£1 Level Stake
Nov Hrdls	2-15	13.3	-7.56	Nov Hrdls	1-4	25.0	+11.00
Hrdls	0-4	0.0	-4.00	Hrdls	3-17	17.6	-0.50
Nov Chs	0-3	0.0	-3.00	Nov Chs	1-7	14.3	+1.50
Chases	1-4	25.0	+6.00	Chases	1-6	16.7	-1.50
Sell/Claim	0-0	0.0	0.00	Sell/Claim	0-0	0.0	0.00

RACE CLASS

	W-R	Per cent	£1 Level Stake
Class 1	1-5	20.0	+5.00
Class 2	0-5	0.0	-5.00
Class 3	1-21	4.8	-16.00
Class 4	7-29	24.1	+17.94
Class 5	0-2	0.0	-2.00
Class 6	2-21	9.5	-12.00

FIRST TIME OUT

	W-R	Per cent	£1 Level Stake
Bumpers	2-11	18.2	-2.00
Hurdles	2-11	18.2	-3.56
Chases	1-7	14.3	+1.50
Totals	5-29	17.2	-4.06

JOCKEYS

	W-R	Per cent	£1 Level Stake
William Kennedy	6-41	14.6	-7.50

Tom Doyle	2-22	9.1	-6.00
A P McCoy	1-1	100.0	+4.00
John Kington	1-2	50.0	+13.00
Brian Crowley	1-9	11.1	-7.56

COURSE RECORD

	Total W-R	Non-Hndcps Hurdles	Chases	Hndcps Hurdles	Chases	NH Flat	Per cent	£1 Level Stake
Warwick	3-8	0-2	0-1	2-3	0-0	1-2	37.5	+7.00
Haydock	1-1	0-0	0-0	0-0	0-0	1-1	100.0	+4.00
Nton Abbot	1-1	0-0	0-0	1-1	0-0	0-0	100.0	+4.50
Bangor	1-2	1-1	0-0	0-0	0-1	0-0	50.0	-0.56
Mrket Rsn	1-2	1-1	0-0	0-1	0-0	0-0	50.0	+4.00
Sandown	1-2	0-0	1-1	0-1	0-0	0-0	50.0	+8.00
Hereford	1-4	0-3	0-0	0-0	1-1	0-0	25.0	+0.50
Plumpton	1-5	0-3	0-0	0-0	1-2	0-0	20.0	+3.50
Newbury	1-6	0-0	0-0	1 2	0-1	0-3	16.7	+9.00

WINNING HORSES

Horse	Races Run	1st	2nd	3rd	£
River City	4	1	1	0	57020
Passenger Omar	4	2	0	1	8474
Gaelic Flight	4	1	0	1	4554
Direct Flight	7	1	1	1	4444
Slew Charm	4	1	2	1	4229
Make It A Double	1	1	0	0	4124
Corporate Player	1	1	0	0	3390
New Mischief	5	1	0	2	3220
Aux Le Bahnn	1	1	0	0	2001
Little Bit Of Hush	1	1	0	0	1713
Total winning prize-money					**£93169**
Favourites	2-15		13.3%		-9.56

M C CHAPMAN

MARKET RASEN, LINCS

	No. of Hrs	Races Run	1st	2nd	3rd	Unpl	Per cent	£1 Level Stake
NH Flat	1	2	0	0	0	2	0.0	-2.00
Hurdles	19	85	1	4	3	77	1.2	-80.50
Chases	9	41	0	2	0	39	0.0	-41.00
Totals	20	128	1	6	3	110	0.0	-123.50
04-05	16	113	6	10	11	86	5.3	-38.50
03-04	22	101	8	10	10	73	7.9	-24.50

JOCKEYS

	W-R	Per cent	£1 Level Stake
Lee Vickers	1-5	20.0	-0.50

COURSE RECORD

	Total W-R	Non-Hndcps Hurdles	Chases	Hndcps Hurdles	Chases	NH Flat	Per cent	£1 Level Stake
Fakenham	1-20	0-4	0-2	1-9	0-5	0-0	5.0	-15.50

WINNING HORSES

Horse	Races Run	1st	2nd	3rd	£
Siegfrieds Night	18	1	1	0	4554
Total winning prize-money					**£4554**
Favourites	0-0		0.0%		0.00

J I A CHARLTON

STOCKSFIELD, NORTHUMBERLAND

	No. of Hrs	Races Run	1st	2nd	3rd	Unpl	Per cent	£1 Level Stake
NH Flat	11	25	1	7	1	16	4.0	-19.50
Hurdles	10	37	2	3	6	26	5.4	-19.50
Chases	3	15	3	1	0	11	20.0	+19.08
Totals	20	77	6	11	7	53	7.8	-19.92
04-05	16	65	2	6	9	48	3.1	-51.50
03-04	15	58	4	10	7	37	6.9	-23.67

JOCKEYS

	W-R	Per cent	£1 Level Stake
G Lee	3-6	50.0	+11.08
Michal Kohl	2-43	4.7	-8.50
P Robson	1-16	6.3	-10.50

COURSE RECORD

	Total W-R	Non-Hndcps Hurdles	Chases	Hndcps Hurdles	Chases	NH Flat	Per cent	£1 Level Stake
Musselbgh	2-10	0-1	0-1	0-1	2-5	0-2	20.0	+19.75
Kelso	2-16	0-8	0-1	1-4	1-2	0-1	12.5	-3.17
Newcastle	1-4	1-4	0-0	0-0	0-0	0-0	25.0	+5.00
Perth	1-7	0-2	0-1	0-0	0-1	1-3	14.3	-1.50

WINNING HORSES

Horse	Races Run	1st	2nd	3rd	£
Snowy	7	2	1	0	10477
Tobesure	7	1	0	1	3679
No Kidding	5	1	0	0	3253
Rathowen	7	1	1	2	3083
Lunar Eclipse	3	1	2	0	2226
Total winning prize-money					**£22718**
Favourites	1-5		20.0%		-1.25

S B CLARK

SUTTON-ON-THE-FOREST, N YORKS

	No. of Hrs	Races Run	1st	2nd	3rd	Unpl	Per cent	£1 Level Stake
NH Flat	0	0	0	0	0	0	0.0	0.00
Hurdles	10	57	2	5	3	47	3.5	-36.50
Chases	2	4	0	0	0	4	0.0	-4.00
Totals	10	61	2	5	3	51	3.3	-40.50

04-05	2	14	0	0	2	12	0.0	-14.00
03-04	4	15	1	1	2	11	6.7	+19.00

JOCKEYS

	W-R	Per cent	£1 Level Stake
Miss Rachel Clark	1-7	14.3	+8.00
Colm Sharkey	1-24	4.2	-18.50

COURSE RECORD

	Total W-R	Non-Hndcps Hurdles	Chases	Hndcps Hurdles	Chases	NH Flat	Per cent	£1 Level Stake
Wetherby	1-2	0-1	0-0	1-1	0-0	0-0	50.0	+13.00
Mrket Rsn	1-18	0-4	0-0	1-12	0-2	0-0	5.6	-12.50

WINNING HORSES

Horse	Races Run	1st	2nd	3rd	£
Lone Soldier	16	2	1	1	4900
Total winning prize-money					**£4900**
Favourites	0-1		0.0%		-1.00

P L CLINTON

DOVERIDGE, DERBYS

	No. of Hrs	Races Run	1st	2nd	3rd	Unpl	Per cent	£1 Level Stake
NH Flat	1	1	0	0	0	1	0.0	-1.00
Hurdles	5	21	1	1	0	19	4.8	-9.00
Chases	0	0	0	0	0	0	0.0	0.00
Totals	6	22	1	1	0	20	4.5	-10.00
04-05	7	14	3	0	0	11	21.4	-5.19
03-04	2	5	0	0	0	5	0.0	-5.00

JOCKEYS

	W-R	Per cent	£1 Level Stake
Miss S Sharratt	1-1	100.0	+11.00

COURSE RECORD

	Total W-R	Non-Hndcps Hurdles	Chases	Hndcps Hurdles	Chases	NH Flat	Per cent	£1 Level Stake
Leicester	1-2	0-1	0-0	1-1	0-0	0-0	50.0	+10.00

WINNING HORSES

Horse	Races Run	1st	2nd	3rd	£
Imperial Royale	8	1	1	0	3803
Total winning prize-money					**£3803**
Favourites	0-0		0.0%		0.00

E R CLOUGH

NARBERTH, PEMBROKES

	No. of Hrs	Races Run	1st	2nd	3rd	Unpl	Per cent	£1 Level Stake
NH Flat	0	0	0	0	0	0	0.0	0.00
Hurdles	0	0	0	0	0	0	0.0	0.00
Chases	2	3	1	0	0	2	33.3	+12.00
Totals	2	3	1	0	0	2	33.3	+12.00
04-05	1	1	0	1	0	0	0.0	-1.00
03-04	3	6	1	0	1	4	16.7	-2.25

JOCKEYS

	W-R	Per cent	£1 Level Stake
Daryl Jacob	1-1	100.0	+14.00

COURSE RECORD

	Total W-R	Non-Hndcps Hurdles	Chases	Hndcps Hurdles	Chases	NH Flat	Per cent	£1 Level Stake
Ludlow	1-2	0-0	1-2	0-0	0-0	0-0	50.0	+13.00

WINNING HORSES

Horse	Races Run	1st	2nd	3rd	£
Longstone Boy	2	1	0	0	2713
Total winning prize-money					**£2713**
Favourites	0-0		0.0%		0.00

K F CLUTTERBUCK

EXNING, SUFFOLK

	No. of Hrs	Races Run	1st	2nd	3rd	Unpl	Per cent	£1 Level Stake
NH Flat	4	7	0	0	1	6	0.0	-7.00
Hurdles	6	14	2	1	0	11	14.3	+93.00
Chases	3	11	1	2	0	8	9.1	+15.00
Totals	11	32	3	3	1	25	9.4	+101.00
04-05	10	32	3	1	1	27	9.4	+116.00
03-04	7	26	3	2	0	21	11.5	-15.18

JOCKEYS

	W-R	Per cent	£1 Level Stake
Shane Walsh	3-21	14.3	+112.00

COURSE RECORD

	Total W-R	Non-Hndcps Hurdles	Chases	Hndcps Hurdles	Chases	NH Flat	Per cent	£1 Level Stake
Fontwell	1-3	1-2	0-0	0-0	0-0	0-1	33.3	+98.00
Worcester	1-4	0-1	0-0	0-0	1-3	0-0	25.0	+22.00
Fakenham	1-12	0-2	0-0	1-5	0-2	0-3	8.3	-6.00

WINNING HORSES

Horse	Races Run	1st	2nd	3rd	£
Bayadere	7	2	0	0	5864
Clydeoneeyed	4	1	1	0	2597
Total winning prize-money					**£8461**
Favourites	0-0		0.0%		0.00

M V COGLAN

CROOK, CO DURHAM

	No. of Hrs	Races Run	1st	2nd	3rd	Unpl	Per cent	£1 Level Stake
NH Flat	0	0	0	0	0	0	0.0	0.00
Hurdles	0	0	0	0	0	0	0.0	0.00
Chases	2	7	2	0	1	4	28.6	+9.00
Totals	2	7	2	0	1	4	28.6	+9.00
04-05	1	7	0	0	1	6	0.0	-7.00
03-04	1	1	0	0	0	1	0.0	-1.00

JOCKEYS

	W-R	Per cent	£1 Level Stake
Mr S W Byrne	1-3	33.3	+2.00
Tom Messenger	1-3	33.3	+8.00

COURSE RECORD

	Total W-R	Non-Hndcps Hurdles	Chases	Hndcps Hurdles	Chases	NH Flat	Per cent	£1 Level Stake
Perth	1-1	0-0	1-1	0-0	0-0	0-0	100.0	+10.00
Musselbgh	1-2	0-0	1-2	0-0	0-0	0-0	50.0	+3.00

WINNING HORSES

Horse	Races Run	1st	2nd	3rd	£
Jupiter's Fancy	6	2	0	1	4721
Total winning prize-money					**£4721**
Favourites	0-0		0.0%		0.00

W S COLTHERD

SELKIRK, BORDERS

	No. of Hrs	Races Run	1st	2nd	3rd	Unpl	Per cent	£1 Level Stake
NH Flat	2	3	0	0	1	2	0.0	-3.00
Hurdles	9	49	4	2	3	40	8.2	+40.50
Chases	5	18	2	1	3	12	11.1	+2.00
Totals	14	70	6	3	7	54	8.6	+39.50
04-05	11	58	1	4	5	48	1.7	-54.25
03-04	10	45	6	8	4	27	13.3	+14.50

JOCKEYS

	W-R	Per cent	£1 Level Stake
Richard McGrath	3-7	42.9	+74.50
Miss P Robson	1-2	50.0	+6.00
G Lee	1-10	10.0	-1.00
David O'Meara	1-21	4.8	-10.00

COURSE RECORD

	Total W-R	Non-Hndcps Hurdles	Chases	Hndcps Hurdles	Chases	NH Flat	Per cent	£1 Level Stake
Hexham	4-17	1-5	0-0	2-5	1-6	0-1	23.5	+74.50
Perth	2-17	0-0	0-2	1-8	1-5	0-2	11.8	+1.00

WINNING HORSES

Horse	Races Run	1st	2nd	3rd	£
Risky Way	11	2	1	3	11109
Royal Glen	14	3	0	0	12876
Casterflo	5	1	1	1	2716
Total winning prize-money					**£26701**
Favourites	0-2		0.0%		-2.00

M J COOMBE

FLEET, DORSET

	No. of Hrs	Races Run	1st	2nd	3rd	Unpl	Per cent	£1 Level Stake
NH Flat	2	2	1	0	0	1	50.0	+4.50
Hurdles	2	3	0	1	0	2	0.0	-3.00
Chases	2	9	0	2	1	6	0.0	-9.00
Totals	5	14	1	3	1	9	7.1	-7.50
04-05	2	3	0	1	0	2	0.0	-3.00
03-04	2	4	0	0	0	4	0.0	-4.00

JOCKEYS

	W-R	Per cent	£1 Level Stake
Mrs M Roberts	1-5	20.0	+1.50

COURSE RECORD

	Total W-R	Non-Hndcps Hurdles	Chases	Hndcps Hurdles	Chases	NH Flat	Per cent	£1 Level Stake
Worcester	1-1	0-0	0-0	0-0	0-0	1-1	100.0	+5.50

WINNING HORSES

Horse	Races Run	1st	2nd	3rd	£
Go On Ahead	1	1	0	0	1713
Total winning prize-money					**£1713**
Favourites	0-0		0.0%		0.00

L CORCORAN

KINGSBRIDGE, DEVON

	No. of Hrs	Races Run	1st	2nd	3rd	Unpl	Per cent	£1 Level Stake
NH Flat	3	4	1	1	0	2	25.0	+7.00
Hurdles	13	34	3	3	4	24	8.8	+30.50
Chases	4	6	0	0	0	6	0.0	-6.00
Totals	16	44	4	4	4	32	9.1	+31.50
04-05	2	4	0	0	0	4	0.0	-4.00
03-04	2	2	0	0	0	2	0.0	-2.00

JOCKEYS

	W-R	Per cent	£1 Level Stake
T J O'Brien	2-3	66.7	+17.50
Howie Ephgrave	2-36	5.6	+19.00

COURSE RECORD

	Total W-R	Non-Hndcps Hurdles	Chases	Hndcps Hurdles	Chases	NH Flat	Per cent	£1 Level Stake
Fontwell	2-4	0-2	0-0	1-1	0-0	1-1	50.0	+41.00
Stratford	1-2	1-1	0-0	0-0	0-0	0-1	50.0	+7.50
Taunton	1-6	1-3	0-1	0-2	0-0	0-0	16.7	+15.00

WINNING HORSES

Horse	Races Run	1st	2nd	3rd	£
Fait Le Jojo	7	1	0	2	9031
Magical Legend	6	2	2	1	8765
Anemix	4	1	2	0	4554
Total winning prize-money					£22350
Favourites	0-1		0.0%		-1.00

P CORNFORTH

KNARESBOROUGH, N YORKS

	No. of Hrs	Races Run	1st	2nd	3rd	Unpl	Per cent	£1 Level Stake
NH Flat	0	0	0	0	0	0	0.0	0.00
Hurdles	0	0	0	0	0	0	0.0	0.00
Chases	1	2	1	0	0	1	50.0	+3.00
Totals	1	2	1	0	0	1	50.0	+3.00
04-05	1	2	0	1	0	1	0.0	-2.00
03-04	1	3	0	2	0	1	0.0	-3.00

JOCKEYS

	W-R	Per cent	£1 Level Stake
Mr P Cornforth	1-2	50.0	+3.00

COURSE RECORD

	Total W-R	Non-Hndcps Hurdles	Chases	Hndcps Hurdles	Chases	NH Flat	Per cent	£1 Level Stake
Cartmel	1-1	0-0	1-1	0-0	0-0	0-0	100.0	+4.00

WINNING HORSES

Horse	Races Run	1st	2nd	3rd	£
Buddy Girie	2	1	0	0	1495
Total winning prize-money					£1495
Favourites	0-0		0.0%		0.00

J R CORNWALL

LONG CLAWSON, LEICS

	No. of Hrs	Races Run	1st	2nd	3rd	Unpl	Per cent	£1 Level Stake
NH Flat	0	0	0	0	0	0	0.0	0.00
Hurdles	6	11	0	0	0	11	0.0	-11.00
Chases	11	82	5	6	11	60	6.1	-26.50
Totals	12	93	5	6	11	71	5.4	-37.50
04-05	14	107	7	7	15	78	6.5	-54.13
03-04	10	80	10	8	14	48	12.5	+14.00

JOCKEYS

	W-R	Per cent	£1 Level Stake
Adam Pogson	2-30	6.7	-19.50
Richard Hobson	2-32	6.3	+9.00
Mark Nicolls	1-17	5.9	-13.00

COURSE RECORD

	Total W-R	Non-Hndcps Hurdles	Chases	Hndcps Hurdles	Chases	NH Flat	Per cent	£1 Level Stake
Mrket Rsn	2-21	0-3	1-2	0-2	1-14	0-0	9.5	+20.00
Towcester	1-11	0-0	0-0	0-0	1-11	0-0	9.1	-6.50
Fakenham	1-12	0-1	0-2	0-1	1-8	0-0	8.3	-8.00
Leicester	1-15	0-0	0-4	0-1	1-10	0-0	6.7	-9.00

WINNING HORSES

Horse	Races Run	1st	2nd	3rd	£
Strong Magic	13	2	1	1	13739
Kercabellec	16	1	3	4	5139
*Log On Intersky	8	1	0	1	4071
Runaway Bishop	16	1	2	3	3809
Total winning prize-money					£26758
Favourites	1-1		100.0%		3.50

MRS T CORRIGAN-CLARK

SCARBOROUGH, N YORKS

	No. of Hrs	Races Run	1st	2nd	3rd	Unpl	Per cent	£1 Level Stake
NH Flat	0	0	0	0	0	0	0.0	0.00
Hurdles	0	0	0	0	0	0	0.0	0.00
Chases	1	5	2	1	1	1	40.0	+5.25
Totals	**1**	**5**	**2**	**1**	**1**	**1**	**40.0**	**+5.25**
04-05	1	5	0	1	1	3	0.0	-5.00
03-04	1	3	0	0	2	1	0.0	-3.00

JOCKEYS

	W-R	Per cent	£1 Level Stake
Mr C Mulhall	2-5	40.0	+5.25

COURSE RECORD

	Total W-R	Non-Hndcps Hurdles	Chases	Hndcps Hurdles	Chases	NH Flat	Per cent	£1 Level Stake
Hexham	2-2	0-0	2-2	0-0	0-0	0-0	100.0	+8.25

WINNING HORSES

Horse	Races Run	1st	2nd	3rd	£
Imps Way	5	2	1	1	3776
Total winning prize-money					**£3776**
Favourites	0-0		0.0%		0.00

C G COX

LAMBOURN, BERKS

	No. of Hrs	Races Run	1st	2nd	3rd	Unpl	Per cent	£1 Level Stake
NH Flat	4	8	1	1	1	5	12.5	0.00
Hurdles	1	2	0	0	0	2	0.0	-2.00
Chases	1	5	0	1	0	4	0.0	-5.00
Totals	**G**	**15**	**1**	**2**	**1**	**11**	**6.7**	**-7.00**
04-05	4	11	1	2	0	8	9.1	-7.25
03-04	5	25	4	1	1	19	16.0	+59.50

JOCKEYS

	W-R	Per cent	£1 Level Stake
Mark Bradburne	1-12	8.3	-4.00

COURSE RECORD

	Total W-R	Non-Hndcps Hurdles	Chases	Hndcps Hurdles	Chases	NH Flat	Per cent	£1 Level Stake
Newbury	1-3	0-0	0-0	0-0	0-0	1-3	33.3	+5.00

WINNING HORSES

Horse	Races Run	1st	2nd	3rd	£
Inherent	4	1	0	1	2686
Total winning prize-money					**£2686**
Favourites	0-2		0.0%		-2.00

A CROOK

MIDDLEHAM MOOR, N YORKS

	No. of Hrs	Races Run	1st	2nd	3rd	Unpl	Per cent	£1 Level Stake
NH Flat	4	6	1	0	0	5	16.7	+5.00
Hurdles	12	47	1	5	4	37	2.1	-26.00
Chases	9	38	2	4	2	30	5.3	-13.00
Totals	**17**	**91**	**4**	**9**	**6**	**72**	**4.4**	**-34.00**
04-05	10	40	2	2	6	30	5.0	-28.00
03-04	18	83	3	6	3	71	3.6	-67.33

JOCKEYS

	W-R	Per cent	£1 Level Stake
Mr T Greenall	2-6	33.3	+26.00
Patrick McDonald	1-3	33.3	+14.00
Dougie Costello	1-6	16.7	+2.00

COURSE RECORD

	Total W-R	Non-Hndcps Hurdles	Chases	Hndcps Hurdles	Chases	NH Flat	Per cent	£1 Level Stake
Hexham	1-4	0-1	0-0	0-0	1-1	0-2	25.0	+13.00
Carlisle	1-6	1-2	0-2	0-0	0-2	0-0	16.7	+15.00
Wetherby	1-9	0-3	0-1	0-4	0-0	1-1	11.1	+2.00
Sedgefield	1-13	0-2	0-5	0-1	1-5	0-0	7.7	-5.00

WINNING HORSES

Horse	Races Run	1st	2nd	3rd	£
*Ornella Speed	1	1	0	0	6610
Matmata De Tendron	10	1	2	1	4384
Jontys'Lass	11	2	2	2	5920
Total winning prize-money					**£16914**
Favourites	0-1		0.0%		-1.00

A M CROW

BONJEDWARD, BORDERS

	No. of Hrs	Races Run	1st	2nd	3rd	Unpl	Per cent	£1 Level Stake
NH Flat	6	12	1	1	0	10	8.3	+89.00
Hurdles	6	26	2	1	3	20	7.7	-18.63
Chases	3	11	0	2	2	7	0.0	-11.00
Totals	**12**	**49**	**3**	**4**	**5**	**37**	**6.1**	**+59.37**

04-05	7	21	2	1	2	16	9.5	-12.75
03-04	6	17	1	0	0	16	5.9	-9.00

JOCKEYS

	W-R	Per cent	£1 Level Stake
Declan McGann	3-47	6.4	+61.38

COURSE RECORD

	Total W-R	Non-Hndcps Hurdles	Chases	Hndcps Hurdles	Chases	NH Flat	Per cent	£1 Level Stake
Mrket Rsn	1-5	1-2	0-0	0-0	0-1	0-2	20.0	-2.13
Ayr	1-6	0-2	0-0	0-1	0-0	1-3	16.7	+95.00
Wetherby	1-6	1-2	0-1	0-2	0-0	0-1	16.7	-1.50

WINNING HORSES

Horse	Races Run	1st	2nd	3rd	£
Relix	8	2	0	0	8190
Phardessa	1	1	0	0	3253
Total winning prize-money					£11443
Favourites	1-3	33.3%			-0.13

MRS EDWARD CROW

SHREWSBURY, SHROPSHIRE

	No. of Hrs	Races Run	1st	2nd	3rd	Unpl	Per cent	£1 Level Stake
NH Flat	0	0	0	0	0	0	0.0	0.00
Hurdles	0	0	0	0	0	0	0.0	0.00
Chases	4	9	2	1	1	5	22.2	-2.00
Totals	4	9	2	1	1	5	22.2	-2.00
04-05	3	10	1	4	0	5	10.0	-6.50
03-04	3	4	0	1	1	2	0.0	-4.00

JOCKEYS

	W-R	Per cent	£1 Level Stake
Mr C P Huxley	1-1	100.0	+4.00
Mr R Burton	1-5	20.0	-3.00

COURSE RECORD

	Total W-R	Non-Hndcps Hurdles	Chases	Hndcps Hurdles	Chases	NH Flat	Per cent	£1 Level Stake
Bangor	1-2	0-0	1-2	0-0	0-0	0-0	50.0	+3.00
Ludlow	1-4	0-0	1-4	0-0	0-0	0-0	25.0	-2.00

WINNING HORSES

Horse	Races Run	1st	2nd	3rd	£
An Capall Dubh	6	2	1	1	4877
Total winning prize-money					£4877
Favourites	1-3	33.3%			-1.00

P D CUNDELL

COMPTON, BERKS

	No. of Hrs	Races Run	1st	2nd	3rd	Unpl	Per cent	£1 Level Stake
NH Flat	0	0	0	0	0	0	0.0	0.00
Hurdles	2	2	0	0	0	2	0.0	-2.00
Chases	3	8	1	0	0	7	12.5	0.00
Totals	5	10	1	0	0	9	10.0	-2.00
04-05	3	11	3	1	0	7	27.3	-2.88
03-04	9	16	2	3	2	9	12.5	-8.25

JOCKEYS

	W-R	Per cent	£1 Level Stake
Andrew Tinkler	1-6	16.7	+2.00

COURSE RECORD

	Total W-R	Non-Hndcps Hurdles	Chases	Hndcps Hurdles	Chases	NH Flat	Per cent	£1 Level Stake
Southwell	1-1	0-0	1-1	0-0	0-0	0-0	100.0	+7.00

WINNING HORSES

Horse	Races Run	1st	2nd	3rd	£
Nawow	3	1	0	0	4310
Total winning prize-money					£4310
Favourites	0-1	0.0%			-1.00

B J CURLEY

NEWMARKET, SUFFOLK

	No. of Hrs	Races Run	1st	2nd	3rd	Unpl	Per cent	£1 Level Stake
NH Flat	0	0	0	0	0	0	0.0	0.00
Hurdles	4	13	1	0	1	11	7.7	-9.25
Chases	1	1	0	0	0	1	0.0	-1.00
Totals	4	14	1	0	1	12	7.1	-10.25
04-05	6	16	2	2	0	12	12.5	-8.75
03-04	7	20	1	2	2	15	5.0	-16.75

JOCKEYS

	W-R	Per cent	£1 Level Stake
Paul Moloney	1-13	7.7	-9.25

COURSE RECORD

	Total W-R	Non-Hndcps Hurdles	Chases	Hndcps Hurdles	Chases	NH Flat	Per cent	£1 Level Stake
Wetherby	1-1	0-0	0-0	1-1	0-0	0-0	100.0	+2.75

WINNING HORSES

Horse	Races Run	1st	2nd	3rd	£
Cristoforo	2	1	0	0	3486

Total winning prize-money			£3486
Favourites	0-1	0.0%	-1.00

R CURTIS

LAMBOURN, BERKS

	No. of Hrs	Races Run	1st	2nd	3rd	Unpl	Per cent	£1 Level Stake
NH Flat	5	9	0	1	0	8	0.0	-9.00
Hurdles	11	39	3	2	2	32	7.7	-24.50
Chases	3	7	0	0	0	7	0.0	-7.00
Totals	18	55	3	3	2	47	5.5	-40.50
04-05	11	39	0	0	4	35	0.0	-39.00
03-04	9	37	4	4	1	28	10.8	-19.13

JOCKEYS

	W-R	Per cent	£1 Level Stake
Tom Doyle	2-18	11.1	-10.00
Dave Crosse	1-8	12.5	-1.50

COURSE RECORD

	Total W-R	Non-Hndcps Hurdles	Chases	Hndcps Hurdles	Chases	NH Flat	Per cent	£1 Level Stake
Stratford	1-1	0-0	0-0	1-1	0-0	0-0	100.0	+5.50
Worcester	1-5	1-1	0-0	0-2	0-0	0-2	20.0	0.00
Fontwell	1-8	1-1	0-0	0-4	0-2	0-1	12.5	5.00

WINNING HORSES

Horse	Races Run	1st	2nd	3rd	£
Tech Eagle	8	2	2	1	6181
Coppermalt	6	1	0	0	2704
Total winning prize-money					£8885
Favourites	1-1		100.0%		2.00

P T DALTON

BRETBY, DERBYS

	No. of Hrs	Races Run	1st	2nd	3rd	Unpl	Per cent	£1 Level Stake
NH Flat	3	6	0	2	1	3	0.0	-6.00
Hurdles	3	7	0	0	0	7	0.0	-7.00
Chases	3	18	1	3	3	11	5.6	-15.25
Totals	8	31	1	5	4	21	3.2	-28.25
04-05	10	30	2	2	2	24	6.7	-19.50
03-04	14	54	1	3	2	48	1.9	-45.00

JOCKEYS

	W-R	Per cent	£1 Level Stake
Tom Doyle	1-7	14.3	-4.25

COURSE RECORD

	Total W-R	Non-Hndcps Hurdles	Chases	Hndcps Hurdles	Chases	NH Flat	Per cent	£1 Level Stake
Mrket Rsn	1-1	0-0	0-0	0-0	1-1	0-0	100.0	+1.75

WINNING HORSES

Horse	Races Run	1st	2nd	3rd	£
Avadi	10	1	2	1	3172
Total winning prize-money					£3172
Favourites	1-2		50.0%		0.75

HEATHER DALTON

NORTON, SHROPSHIRE

	No. of Hrs	Races Run	1st	2nd	3rd	Unpl	Per cent	£1 Level Stake
NH Flat	12	20	2	1	2	15	10.0	-2.50
Hurdles	36	89	11	7	6	65	12.4	+47.25
Chases	12	45	10	1	4	30	22.2	+25.83
Totals	50	154	23	9	12	110	14.9	+70.58
04-05	50	150	18	15	20	97	12.0	+9.56
03-04	53	153	17	11	23	102	11.1	-33.77

BY MONTH

NH Flat	W-R	Per cent	£1 Level Stake	Hurdles	W-R	Per cent	£1 Level Stake
May	0-3	0.0	-3.00	May	1-9	11.1	+4.00
June	0-0	0.0	0.00	June	0-4	0.0	-4.00
July	0-0	0.0	0.00	July	0-4	0.0	-4.00
August	0-0	0.0	0.00	August	0-3	0.0	-3.00
September	0-0	0.0	0.00	September	0-3	0.0	-3.00
October	1-3	33.3	+3.50	October	3-7	42.9	+10.00
November	0-1	0.0	-1.00	November	0-7	0.0	-7.00
December	1-2	50.0	+9.00	December	0-11	0.0	-11.00
January	0-4	0.0	-4.00	January	3-13	23.1	+73.00
February	0-2	0.0	-2.00	February	0-7	0.0	-7.00
March	0-3	0.0	-3.00	March	2-10	20.0	-1.75
April	0-2	0.0	-2.00	April	2-11	18.2	+1.00

Chases	W-R	Per cent	£1 Level Stake	Totals	W-R	Per cent	£1 Level Stake
May	0-2	0.0	-2.00	May	1-14	7.1	-1.00
June	0-0	0.0	0.00	June	0-4	0.0	-4.00
July	0-3	0.0	-3.00	July	0-7	0.0	-7.00
August	1-3	33.3	+12.00	August	1-6	16.7	+9.00
September	1-2	50.0	+1.50	September	1-5	20.0	-1.50
October	5-11	45.5	+8.32	October	9-21	42.9	+21.82
November	0-5	0.0	-5.00	November	0-13	0.0	-13.00
December	1-5	20.0	+4.00	December	2-18	11.1	+2.00
January	0-5	0.0	-5.00	January	3-22	13.6	+64.00
February	0-4	0.0	-4.00	February	0-13	0.0	-13.00
March	0-0	0.0	0.00	March	2-13	15.4	-4.75
April	2-5	40.0	+19.00	April	4-18	22.2	+18.00

DISTANCE

Hurdles	W-R	Per cent	£1 Level Stake	Chases	W-R	Per cent	£1 Level Stake
2m-2m3f	2-49	4.1	-38.75	2m-2m3f	1-11	9.1	+2.00
2m4f-2m7f	4-19	21.1	+35.50	2m4f-2m7f	3-18	16.7	-6.18
3m+	5-21	23.8	+50.50	3m+	6-16	37.5	+30.00

TYPE OF RACE

Non-Handicaps	W-R	Per cent	£1 Level Stake	Handicaps	W-R	Per cent	£1 Level Stake
Nov Hrdls	2-31	6.5	+15.50	Nov Hrdls	1-9	11.1	-1.00
Hrdls	3-15	20.0	+43.50	Hrdls	3-25	12.0	-12.00
Nov Chs	2-4	50.0	+1.70	Nov Chs	0-1	0.0	-1.00
Chases	0-0	0.0	0.00	Chases	8-39	20.5	+26.13
Sell/Claim	1-2	50.0	+0.75	Sell/Claim	1-8	12.5	-0.50

RACE CLASS / FIRST TIME OUT

	W-R	Per cent	£1 Level Stake		W-R	Per cent	£1 Level Stake
Class 1	0-1	0.0	-1.00	Bumpers	2-12	16.7	+5.50
Class 2	0-4	0.0	-4.00	Hurdles	5-30	16.7	+41.00
Class 3	6-32	18.8	+10.50	Chases	0-8	0.0	-8.00
Class 4	12-84	14.3	+59.32				
Class 5	3-16	18.8	+5.25	Totals	7-50	14.0	+38.50
Class 6	2-17	11.8	+0.50				

JOCKEYS

	W-R	Per cent	£1 Level Stake
Paddy Merrigan	6-48	12.5	-9.30
Paul O'Neill	3-10	30.0	+0.13
Jodie Mogford	3-10	30.0	+19.00
T J Phelan	3-13	23.1	+43.50
Alan O'Keeffe	2-5	40.0	+13.50
Richard Johnson	2-8	25.0	+38.50
Jim Crowley	2-16	12.5	-9.25
Andrew Tinkler	1-5	20.0	+6.00
A P McCoy	1-6	16.7	+1.50

COURSE RECORD

	Total W-R	Non-Hndcps Hurdles	Chases	Hndcps Hurdles	Chases	NH Flat	Per cent	£1 Level Stake
Aintree	2-2	0-0	0-0	2-2	0-0	0-0	100.0	+10.00
Fakenham	2-6	0-3	0-0	0-0	2-3	0-0	33.3	+10.00
Mrket Rsn	2-7	0-2	0-0	1-2	0-2	1-1	28.6	+4.50
Taunton	2-7	0-1	0-0	0-1	2-5	0-0	28.6	+8.63
Hereford	2-9	1-3	0-0	0-2	1-3	0-1	22.2	+36.00
Ludlow	2-9	2-3	0-0	0-3	0-2	0-1	22.2	+34.75
Bangor	2-10	0-3	0-0	0-3	2-4	0-0	20.0	+8.50
Carlisle	1-1	0-0	1-1	0-0	0-0	0-0	100.0	+2.50
Plumpton	1-4	0-1	0-0	0-1	1-2	0-0	25.0	+7.00
Sedgefield	1-4	0-1	0-0	1-2	0-1	0-0	25.0	0.00
Wetherby	1-5	0-1	1-2	0-1	0-0	0-1	20.0	-2.80
Perth	1-6	1-2	0-0	0-1	0-2	0-1	16.7	-1.50
Exeter	1-7	1-2	0-1	0-1	0-0	0-3	14.3	-1.50
Towcester	1-7	0-1	0-1	0-1	0-1	1-3	14.3	+4.00
Uttoxeter	1-8	1-3	0-0	0-2	0-3	0-0	12.5	+5.00
Worcester	1-14	0-4	0-0	1-5	0-2	0-3	7.1	-6.50

WINNING HORSES

Horse	Races Run	1st	2nd	3rd	£
Jorobaden	3	2	0	0	14430
Terre De Java	6	1	1	0	7807
Model Son	4	2	0	0	10286
Nite Fox	3	2	0	0	10219
Reverse Swing	10	3	0	2	13298
All Things Equal	1	1	0	0	5205
Hehasalife	7	2	0	0	9224
Fearless Mel	6	2	0	0	8479
Before Dark	5	2	1	1	7157
Atlantic Jane	2	1	0	0	3904
Test Of Friendship	3	1	0	0	3492
Joe Brown	6	1	1	1	3383
Broke Road	6	1	0	0	2928
Victor Daly	2	1	0	0	2521
Not For Diamonds	3	1	0	0	1974
Total winning prize-money					**£104307**
Favourites	6-14		42.9%		4.57

H D DALY

STANTON LACY, SHROPSHIRE

	No. of Hrs	Races Run	1st	2nd	3rd	Unpl	Per cent	£1 Level Stake
NH Flat	27	35	2	2	4	27	5.7	-22.00
Hurdles	38	116	15	20	6	75	12.9	-28.88
Chases	26	121	18	14	13	76	14.9	-52.73
Totals	75	272	35	36	23	178	12.9	-103.61
04-05	68	239	32	30	33	144	13.4	-58.61
03-04	60	214	44	30	29	111	20.6	+6.51

BY MONTH

NH Flat	W-R	Per cent	£1 Level Stake	Hurdles	W-R	Per cent	£1 Level Stake
May	1-3	33.3	+6.00	May	0-5	0.0	-5.00
June	0-0	0.0	0.00	June	0-3	0.0	-3.00
July	0-0	0.0	0.00	July	0-1	0.0	-1.00
August	0-0	0.0	0.00	August	0-0	0.0	0.00
September	0-0	0.0	0.00	September	0-0	0.0	0.00
October	0-0	0.0	0.00	October	0-3	0.0	-3.00
November	0-3	0.0	-3.00	November	1-17	5.9	-14.75
December	0-4	0.0	-4.00	December	5-20	25.0	+20.00
January	0-2	0.0	-2.00	January	3-17	17.6	+7.83
February	1-1	100.0	+3.00	February	2-12	16.7	-6.13
March	0-10	0.0	-10.00	March	2-17	11.8	-13.59
April	0-12	0.0	-12.00	April	2-21	9.5	-10.25

Chases	W-R	Per cent	£1 Level Stake	Totals	W-R	Per cent	£1 Level Stake
May	0-11	0.0	-11.00	May	1-19	5.3	-10.00
June	0-6	0.0	-6.00	June	0-9	0.0	-9.00

July	0-2	0.0	-2.00	July	0-3	0.0	-3.00
August	0-3	0.0	-3.00	August	0-3	0.0	-3.00
September	0-1	0.0	-1.00	September	0-1	0.0	-1.00
October	0-5	0.0	-5.00	October	0-8	0.0	-8.00
November	3-17	17.6	-5.15	November	4-37	10.8	-22.90
December	4-16	25.0	+1.23	December	9-40	22.5	+17.23
January	3-18	16.7	-8.92	January	6-37	16.2	-3.09
February	4-10	40.0	+5.38	February	7-23	30.4	+2.25
March	2-13	15.4	-2.50	March	4-40	10.0	-26.09
April	2-19	10.5	-14.76	April	4-52	7.7	-37.01

DISTANCE

Hurdles	W-R	Per cent	£1 Level Stake	Chases	W-R	Per cent	£1 Level Stake
2m-2m3f	8-61	13.1	-1.79	2m-2m3f	7-31	22.6	-6.05
2m4f-2m7f	5-37	13.5	-14.75	2m4f-2m7f	5-35	14.3	-18.17
3m+	2-18	11.1	-12.34	3m+	6-55	10.9	-28.50

TYPE OF RACE

Non-Handicaps	W-R	Per cent	£1 Level Stake	Handicaps	W-R	Per cent	£1 Level Stake
Nov Hrdls	7-51	13.7	-22.97	Nov Hrdls	1-14	7.1	-6.50
Hrdls	3-22	13.6	+9.25	Hrdls	4-27	14.8	-6.67
Nov Chs	10-39	25.6	-8.35	Nov Chs	2-7	28.6	+2.75
Chases	0-7	0.0	-7.00	Chases	6-68	8.8	-40.13
Sell/Claim	0-1	0.0	-1.00	Sell/Claim	0-0	0.0	0.00

RACE CLASS

	W-R	Per cent	£1 Level Stake
Class 1	1-19	5.3	-15.25
Class 2	2-19	10.5	-10.67
Class 3	18-94	19.1	-25.28
Class 4	12-99	12.1	-24.41
Class 5	1-10	10.0	-6.00
Class 6	1-31	3.2	-22.00

FIRST TIME OUT

	W-R	Per cent	£1 Level Stake
Bumpers	2-27	7.4	-14.00
Hurdles	2-24	8.3	-8.75
Chases	4-24	16.7	-9.53
Totals	8-75	10.7	-32.28

JOCKEYS

	W-R	Per cent	£1 Level Stake
Richard Johnson	24-94	25.5	+3.82
Mark Bradburne	8-107	7.5	-53.93
Tom Greenway	2-14	14.3	-2.50
Wayne Hutchinson	1-1	100.0	+5.00

COURSE RECORD

	Total W-R	Non-Hndcps Hurdles	Non-Hndcps Chases	Hndcps Hurdles	Hndcps Chases	NH Flat	Per cent	£1 Level Stake
Warwick	7-21	3-7	0-3	2-3	2-5	0-3	33.3	+15.38
Exeter	4-8	1-2	0-2	2-3	0-0	1-1	50.0	+9.24
Ludlow	3-25	0-4	2-5	0-4	1-10	0-2	12.0	-16.75
Doncaster	2-2	0-0	0-0	1-1	1-1	0-0	100.0	+9.50
Leicester	2-8	0-3	2-3	0-1	0-1	0-0	25.0	-3.52
Mrket Rsn	2-10	1-3	1-3	0-0	0-3	0-1	20.0	+13.10
Huntingdon	2-12	0-2	1-3	0-1	1-3	0-3	16.7	-5.00
Hereford	2-16	0-8	1-1	0-4	1-3	0-0	12.5	-5.50
Perth	1-3	0-0	1-2	0-0	0-1	0-0	33.3	-1.39
Southwell	1-3	0-0	1-1	0-0	0-2	0-0	33.3	-1.17
Fakenham	1-4	0-1	1-2	0-0	0-1	0-0	25.0	+3.00
Stratford	1-7	1-1	0-1	0-2	0-3	0-0	14.3	-5.50
Aintree	1-8	1-2	0-1	0-0	0-4	0-1	12.5	-4.25
Chepstow	1-11	1-7	0-1	0-1	0-2	0-0	9.1	-7.50
Newbury	1-11	0-0	0-1	0-3	1-7	0-0	9.1	-4.50
Haydock	1-12	0-2	0-1	0-1	1-4	0-4	8.3	-5.50
Worcester	1-13	0-3	0-3	0-2	0-3	1-2	7.7	-4.00
Towcester	1-15	1-6	0-1	0-2	0-1	0-5	6.7	-12.75
Cheltenham	1-17	1-3	0-5	0-3	0-6	0-0	5.9	-10.50

WINNING HORSES

Horse	Races Run	1st	2nd	3rd	£
Mighty Man	6	2	2	1	53301
Green Tango	7	3	1	0	25781
Briery Fox	5	1	2	0	8073
King Bee	5	2	0	1	13337
Alderburn	6	2	0	0	12742
Von Origny	6	2	1	0	13646
Billyvoddan	6	2	0	1	15014
Lindsay	5	3	0	0	17528
Opera De Coeur	4	3	0	0	15973
Saafend Rocket	12	1	2	2	6721
Down's Folly	6	2	2	0	11109
Coursing Run	5	1	0	0	6506
Jaunty Times	6	2	1	0	10696
In Accord	5	3	0	0	11795
Martha's Kinsman	6	1	3	2	4097
Kayceecee	8	1	1	0	4554
Principe Azzurro	5	1	2	0	4229
Sherwoods Folly	2	1	0	0	2261
Waterloo Son	6	1	2	0	2213
Nocivo	2	1	0	0	1897
Total winning prize-money					**£242076**
Favourites	**11-37**		**29.7%**		**-8.07**

P DANDO

CARDIFF

	No of Hrs	Races Run	1st	2nd	3rd	Unpl	Per cent	£1 Level Stake
NH Flat	*0*	*0*	*0*	*0*	*0*	*0*	*0.0*	*0.00*
Hurdles	*0*	*0*	*0*	*0*	*0*	*0*	*0.0*	*0.00*
Chases	*1*	*6*	*3*	*2*	*0*	*1*	*50.0*	*+27.00*
Totals	**1**	**6**	**3**	**2**	**0**	**1**	**50.0**	**+27.00**
03-04	*1*	*1*	*0*	*0*	*0*	*1*	*0.0*	*-1.00*

JOCKEYS

	W-R	Per cent	£1 Level Stake
Mr P Sheldrake	2-4	50.0	+21.50
Mr Rhys Hughes	1-2	50.0	+5.50

COURSE RECORD

	Total W-R	Non-Hndcps Hurdles	Chases	Hndcps Hurdles	Chases	NH Flat	Per cent	£1 Level Stake
Leicester	2-3	0-0	2-3	0-0	0-0	0-0	66.7	+22.50
Hereford	1-1	0-0	1-1	0-0	0-0	0-0	100.0	+6.50

WINNING HORSES

Horse	Races Run	1st	2nd	3rd	£
Bill Haze	6	3	2	0	6178
Total winning prize-money					**£6178**
Favourites	0-1		0.0%		-1.00

V R A DARTNALL

BRAYFORD, DEVON

	No. of Hrs	Races Run	1st	2nd	3rd	Unpl	Per cent	£1 Level Stake
NH Flat	9	10	2	2	2	4	20.0	-3.50
Hurdles	21	55	11	3	7	34	20.0	+36.25
Chases	7	17	4	1	2	10	23.5	+0.75
Totals	27	82	17	6	11	48	20.7	+33.50
04-05	21	67	7	2	11	47	10.4	-3.88
03-04	15	39	7	9	5	18	17.9	-4.77

BY MONTH

NH Flat	W-R	Per cent	£1 Level Stake	Hurdles	W-R	Per cent	£1 Level Stake
May	0-0	0.0	0.00	May	0-1	0.0	-1.00
June	0-0	0.0	0.00	June	1-2	50.0	+6.00
July	0-0	0.0	0.00	July	0-0	0.0	0.00
August	0-0	0.0	0.00	August	1-1	100.0	+3.50
September	0-0	0.0	0.00	September	0-1	0.0	-1.00
October	0-1	0.0	-1.00	October	0-5	0.0	-5.00
November	1-2	50.0	+1.75	November	3-10	30.0	+14.00
December	0-1	0.0	-1.00	December	3-5	60.0	+8.25
January	0-0	0.0	0.00	January	0-8	0.0	-8.00
February	0-2	0.0	-2.00	February	2-7	28.6	+27.00
March	0-2	0.0	-2.00	March	0-7	0.0	-7.00
April	1-2	50.0	+0.75	April	1-8	12.5	-0.50

Chases	W-R	Per cent	£1 Level Stake	Totals	W-R	Per cent	£1 Level Stake
May	0-1	0.0	-1.00	May	0-2	0.0	-2.00
June	0-0	0.0	0.00	June	1-2	50.0	+6.00
July	0-0	0.0	0.00	July	0-0	0.0	0.00
August	0-0	0.0	0.00	August	1-1	100.0	+3.50
September	0-0	0.0	0.00	September	0-1	0.0	-1.00
October	1-4	25.0	-0.75	October	1-10	10.0	-6.75
November	1-2	50.0	+1.75	November	5-14	35.7	+17.50
December	0-3	0.0	-3.00	December	3-9	33.3	+4.25
January	0-1	0.0	-1.00	January	0-9	0.0	-9.00
February	0-0	0.0	0.00	February	2-9	22.2	+25.00
March	0-2	0.0	-2.00	March	0-11	0.0	-11.00
April	2-4	50.0	+6.75	April	4-14	28.6	+7.00

DISTANCE

Hurdles	W-R	Per cent	£1 Level Stake	Chases	W-R	Per cent	£1 Level Stake
2m-2m3f	3-23	13.0	-3.00	2m-2m3f	1-1	100.0	+2.25
2m4f-2m7f	7-24	29.2	+45.25	2m4f-2m7f	2-10	20.0	-2.50
3m+	1-8	12.5	-6.00	3m+	1-6	16.7	+1.00

TYPE OF RACE

Non-Handicaps	W-R	Per cent	£1 Level Stake	Handicaps	W-R	Per cent	£1 Level Stake
Nov Hrdls	4-20	20.0	+18.25	Nov Hrdls	2-4	50.0	+18.00
Hrdls	0-3	0.0	-3.00	Hrdls	5-28	17.9	+3.00
Nov Chs	2-7	28.6	+0.50	Nov Chs	0-1	0.0	-1.00
Chases	0-0	0.0	0.00	Chases	2-9	22.2	+1.25
Sell/Claim	0-0	0.0	0.00	Sell/Claim	0-0	0.0	0.00

RACE CLASS

	W-R	Per cent	£1 Level Stake
Class 1	0-7	0.0	-7.00
Class 2	0-7	0.0	-7.00
Class 3	1-18	5.6	-1.00
Class 4	13-39	33.3	+46.00
Class 5	1-2	50.0	+5.00
Class 6	2-9	22.2	-2.50

FIRST TIME OUT

	W-R	Per cent	£1 Level Stake
Bumpers	2-9	22.2	-7.50
Hurdles	4-15	26.7	+31.50
Chases	0-3	0.0	-3.00
Totals	6-27	22.2	+26.00

JOCKEYS

	W-R	Per cent	£1 Level Stake
Liam Heard	3-8	37.5	+8.25
Mr J J Doyle	3-14	21.4	+9.00
P J Brennan	2-6	33.3	+14.00
Andrew Thornton	2-8	25.0	+16.75
A P McCoy	1-1	100.0	+1.75
T J Phelan	1-1	100.0	+3.50
J Culloty	1-2	50.0	+6.00
Noel Fehily	1-2	50.0	0.00
Jamie Goldstein	1-2	50.0	+3.00
Richard Johnson	1-4	25.0	-0.75
Mick Fitzgerald	1-5	20.0	+1.00

COURSE RECORD

	Total W-R	Non-Hndcps Hurdles	Chases	Hndcps Hurdles	Chases	NH Flat	Per cent	£1 Level Stake
Uttoxeter	4-8	2-2	1-1	0-1	1-2	0-2	50.0	+3.25
Fontwell	4-9	1-1	0-1	1-4	1-2	1-1	44.4	+18.75
Taunton	2-4	0-1	1-2	1-1	0-0	0-0	50.0	+7.25
Nton Abbot	1-1	0-0	0-0	1-1	0-0	0-0	100.0	+7.00
Windsor	1-2	0-0	0-1	1-1	0-0	0-0	50.0	+4.00
Worcester	1-2	0-0	0-0	1-1	0-0	0-0	50.0	+2.50
Aintree	1-3	0-1	0-0	1-1	0-1	0-0	33.3	+14.00
Plumpton	1-3	0-0	0-0	1-2	0-0	0-1	33.3	+2.00
Sandown	1-4	0-0	0-0	0-2	0-1	1-1	25.0	-0.25
Wincanton	1-8	1-5	0-0	0-2	0-0	0-1	12.5	+13.00

WINNING HORSES

Horse	Races Run	1st	2nd	3rd	£
Vingis Park	7	3	0	1	16269
Philomena	2	1	0	0	5205
*Polished	7	2	1	1	7391
Mount Clerigo	7	1	1	1	4313
Businessmoney Jake	8	3	0	1	10907
Hollywood	2	1	0	1	3904
Karanja	5	1	2	0	3443
Silkwood Top	3	1	0	1	3438
Norton Sapphire	1	1	0	0	3381
Russian Lord	3	1	0	0	3253
Here's Johnny	3	1	0	1	2247
Benetwood	1	1	0	0	1627
Total winning prize-money					**£65378**
Favourites	8-18		44.4%		10.25

T G DASCOMBE

LAMBOURN, BERKS

	No. of Hrs	Races Run	1st	2nd	3rd	Unpl	Per cent	£1 Level Stake
NH Flat	0	0	0	0	0	0	0.0	0.00
Hurdles	1	3	2	0	0	1	66.7	+9.50
Chases	0	0	0	0	0	0	0.0	0.00
Totals	1	3	2	0	0	1	66.7	+9.50

JOCKEYS

	W-R	Per cent	£1 Level Stake
Jim Crowley	2-3	66.7	+9.50

COURSE RECORD

	Total W-R	Non-Hndcps Hurdles	Chases	Hndcps Hurdles	Chases	NH Flat	Per cent	£1 Level Stake
Ludlow	2-2	1-1	0-0	1-1	0-0	0-0	100.0	+10.50

WINNING HORSES

Horse	Races Run	1st	2nd	3rd	£
*Political Intrigue	3	2	0	0	10492
Total winning prize-money					**£10492**
Favourites	0-0		0.0%		0.00

W DAVIES

LEOMINSTER, H'FORDS

	No. of Hrs	Races Run	1st	2nd	3rd	Unpl	Per cent	£1 Level Stake
NH Flat	0	0	0	0	0	0	0.0	0.00
Hurdles	3	11	0	0	1	10	0.0	-11.00

Chases	1	3	1	0	0	2	33.3	+18.00
Totals	3	14	1	0	1	12	7.1	+7.00
04-05	5	11	0	1	1	9	0.0	-11.00
03-04	2	16	0	0	1	15	0.0	-16.00

JOCKEYS

	W-R	Per cent	£1 Level Stake
Derek Laverty	1-8	12.5	+13.00

COURSE RECORD

	Total W-R	Non-Hndcps Hurdles	Chases	Hndcps Hurdles	Chases	NH Flat	Per cent	£1 Level Stake
Chepstow	1-1	0-0	1-1	0-0	0-0	0-0	100.0	+20.00

WINNING HORSES

Horse	Races Run	1st	2nd	3rd	£
Arceye	4	1	0	0	4229
Total winning prize-money					**£4229**
Favourites	0-0		0.0%		0.00

MISS J S DAVIS

CODRINGTON, S GLOUCS

	No. of Hrs	Races Run	1st	2nd	3rd	Unpl	Per cent	£1 Level Stake
NH Flat	1	1	0	0	0	1	0.0	-1.00
Hurdles	12	35	2	0	2	31	5.7	+29.00
Chases	7	15	1	0	3	11	6.7	+19.00
Totals	14	51	3	0	5	43	5.9	+47.00
04-05	12	43	2	1	0	40	4.7	-3.50
03-04	8	23	0	1	2	20	0.0	-23.00

JOCKEYS

	W-R	Per cent	£1 Level Stake
Sean Curran	2-11	18.2	+36.00
Charlie Poste	1-2	50.0	+49.00

COURSE RECORD

	Total W-R	Non-Hndcps Hurdles	Chases	Hndcps Hurdles	Chases	NH Flat	Per cent	£1 Level Stake
Worcester	1-1	0-0	0-0	0-0	1-1	0-0	100.0	+33.00
Wincanton	1-5	0-1	0-0	1-3	0-1	0-0	20.0	+46.00
Ludlow	1-6	0-1	0-0	1-4	0-1	0-0	16.7	+7.00

WINNING HORSES

Horse	Races Run	1st	2nd	3rd	£
Pure Magic	8	2	0	0	8458
Meehan	4	1	0	2	3904
Total winning prize-money					**£12362**
Favourites	0-0		0.0%		0.00

MISS Z C DAVISON

HAMMERWOOD, E SUSSEX

	No. of Hrs	Races Run	1st	2nd	3rd	Unpl	Per cent	£1 Level Stake
NH Flat	4	6	0	0	0	6	0.0	-6.00
Hurdles	8	29	2	1	3	23	6.9	+5.00
Chases	5	13	0	1	4	8	0.0	-13.00
Totals	12	48	2	2	7	37	4.2	-14.00
04-05	11	45	1	1	7	36	2.2	-32.00
03-04	14	49	2	3	3	41	4.1	-25.00

JOCKEYS

	W-R	Per cent	£1 Level Stake
Robert Lucey-Butler	2-38	5.3	-4.00

COURSE RECORD

	Total W-R	Non-Hndcps Hurdles	Chases	Hndcps Hurdles	Chases	NH Flat	Per cent	£1 Level Stake
Folkestone	1-5	0-1	0-0	1-2	0-2	0-0	20.0	+3.00
Fontwell	1-13	0-4	0-1	1-6	0-1	0-1	7.7	+13.00

WINNING HORSES

Horse	Races Run	1st	2nd	3rd	£
Roman Rampage	6	1	0	1	2741
Distant Romance	7	1	0	0	2394
Total winning prize-money					**£5135**
Favourites	0-0		0.0%		0.00

MRS SARAH L DENT

BILLINGHAM, CO DURHAM

	No. of Hrs	Races Run	1st	2nd	3rd	Unpl	Per cent	£1 Level Stake
NH Flat	0	0	0	0	0	0	0.0	0.00
Hurdles	0	0	0	0	0	0	0.0	0.00
Chases	1	2	1	0	1	0	50.0	+0.20
Totals	1	2	1	0	1	0	50.0	+0.20
04-05	2	4	0	0	0	4	0.0	-4.00
03-04	3	6	0	2	0	4	0.0	-6.00

JOCKEYS

	W-R	Per cent	£1 Level Stake
Mr R Abrahams	1-2	50.0	+0.20

COURSE RECORD

	Total W-R	Non-Hndcps Hurdles	Chases	Hndcps Hurdles	Chases	NH Flat	Per cent	£1 Level Stake
Mrket Rsn	1-1	0-0	1-1	0-0	0-0	0-0	100.0	+1.20

WINNING HORSES

Horse	Races Run	1st	2nd	3rd	£
*Royal Snoopy	2	1	0	1	1282
Total winning prize-money					**£1282**
Favourites	1-1		100.0%		1.20

A R DICKEN

WEST BARNS, E LOTHIAN

	No. of Hrs	Races Run	1st	2nd	3rd	Unpl	Per cent	£1 Level Stake
NH Flat	2	4	0	0	0	4	0.0	-4.00
Hurdles	4	21	2	0	2	17	9.5	+1.50
Chases	1	9	0	0	3	6	0.0	-9.00
Totals	7	34	2	0	5	27	5.9	-11.50
04-05	8	29	0	2	1	26	0.0	-29.00
03-04	9	26	0	0	2	24	0.0	-26.00

JOCKEYS

	W-R	Per cent	£1 Level Stake
Patrick McDonald	2-5	40.0	+17.50

COURSE RECORD

	Total W-R	Non-Hndcps Hurdles	Chases	Hndcps Hurdles	Chases	NH Flat	Per cent	£1 Level Stake
Musselbgh	1-3	0-2	0-0	1-1	0-0	0-0	33.3	+14.00
Newcastle	1-4	0-1	0-0	1-2	0-1	0-0	25.0	+1.50

WINNING HORSES

Horse	Races Run	1st	2nd	3rd	£
Silver Seeker	8	2	0	1	4823
Total winning prize-money					**£4823**
Favourites	0-0		0.0%		0.00

R DICKIN

ATHERSTONE ON STOUR, WARWICKS

	No. of Hrs	Races Run	1st	2nd	3rd	Unpl	Per cent	£1 Level Stake
NH Flat	6	8	0	0	0	8	0.0	-8.00
Hurdles	33	73	3	5	4	61	4.1	+27.00
Chases	27	115	8	11	11	85	7.0	-34.50
Totals	46	196	11	16	15	154	5.6	-15.50
04-05	39	195	15	16	21	143	7.7	-86.15
03-04	47	196	18	21	20	137	9.2	-89.63

BY MONTH

NH Flat	W-R	Per cent	£1 Level Stake	Hurdles	W-R	Per cent	£1 Level Stake
May	0-0	0.0	0.00	May	1-10	10.0	+57.00

	W-R	Per cent	£1 Level Stake		W-R	Per cent	£1 Level Stake
June	0-1	0.0	-1.00	June	1-5	20.0	+21.00
July	0-0	0.0	0.00	July	0-1	0.0	-1.00
August	0-1	0.0	-1.00	August	0-2	0.0	-2.00
September	0-0	0.0	0.00	September	0-1	0.0	-1.00
October	0-0	0.0	0.00	October	0-2	0.0	-2.00
November	0-1	0.0	-1.00	November	1-8	12.5	-1.00
December	0-1	0.0	-1.00	December	0-7	0.0	-7.00
January	0-2	0.0	-2.00	January	0-7	0.0	-7.00
February	0-0	0.0	0.00	February	0-12	0.0	-12.00
March	0-0	0.0	0.00	March	0-7	0.0	-7.00
April	0-2	0.0	-2.00	April	0-11	0.0	-11.00

Chases	W-R	Per cent	£1 Level Stake	Totals	W-R	Per cent	£1 Level Stake
May	0-15	0.0	-15.00	May	1-25	4.0	+42.00
June	0-8	0.0	-8.00	June	1-14	7.1	+12.00
July	0-5	0.0	-5.00	July	0-6	0.0	-6.00
August	1-6	16.7	+7.00	August	1-9	11.1	+4.00
September	0-2	0.0	-2.00	September	0-3	0.0	-3.00
October	1-7	14.3	-3.50	October	1-9	11.1	-5.50
November	2-13	15.4	+4.00	November	3-22	13.6	+2.00
December	0-4	0.0	-4.00	December	0-12	0.0	-12.00
January	0-9	0.0	-9.00	January	0-18	0.0	-18.00
February	1-16	6.3	-1.00	February	1-28	3.6	-13.00
March	0-10	0.0	-10.00	March	0-17	0.0	-17.00
April	3-20	15.0	+12.00	April	3-33	9.1	-1.00

	W-R	Per cent	£1 Level Stake
Henry Oliver	3-20	15.0	+12.00
John Pritchard	2-34	5.9	+7.00
Tom Malone	1-5	20.0	+1.00

COURSE RECORD

	Total W-R	Non-Hndcps Hurdles	Non-Hndcps Chases	Hndcps Hurdles	Hndcps Chases	NH Flat	Per cent	£1 Level Stake
Chepstow	2-11	0-3	0-0	0-2	2-5	0-1	18.2	+4.00
Leicester	2-15	0-1	0-4	0-0	2-10	0-0	13.3	+6.00
Mrket Rsn	2-15	0-2	0-2	0-3	2-8	0-0	13.3	+15.00
Warwick	2-19	0-3	0-0	0-7	2-9	0-0	10.5	-4.50
Worcester	1-19	0-5	0-1	1-4	0-8	0-1	5.3	+7.00
Hereford	1-23	1-6	0-1	0-4	0-11	0-1	4.3	-16.00
Towcester	1-39	1-10	0-2	0-8	0-19	0-0	2.6	+28.00

WINNING HORSES

Horse	Races Run	1st	2nd	3rd	£
Regal Term	5	1	1	0	6506
Channahrlie	11	1	1	2	4866
Sissinghurst Storm	10	2	2	2	7157
Nautic	1	1	0	0	4115
*Miss Pebbles	7	1	0	2	3865
Romany Dream	17	2	4	2	7488
Jacarado	9	1	1	1	3578
Blue Hawk	4	1	0	0	3517
Lrins Lass	10	1	0	0	3343
Total winning prize-money					£44435
Favourites	1-8		12.5%		-3.00

DISTANCE

Hurdles	W-R	Per cent	£1 Level Stake	Chases	W-R	Per cent	£1 Level Stake
2m-2m3f	2-48	4.2	+26.00	2m-2m3f	2-35	5.7	-20.50
2m4f-2m7f	1-14	7.1	+12.00	2m4f-2m7f	4-41	9.8	+10.00
3m+	0-11	0.0	-11.00	3m+	2-39	5.1	-24.00

TYPE OF RACE

Non-Handicaps	W-R	Per cent	£1 Level Stake	Handicaps	W-R	Per cent	£1 Level Stake
Nov Hrdls	1-23	4.3	+44.00	Nov Hrdls	0-5	0.0	-5.00
Hrdls	1-14	7.1	-7.00	Hrdls	1-27	3.7	-1.00
Nov Chs	0-6	0.0	-6.00	Nov Chs	1-18	5.6	-1.00
Chases	0-3	0.0	-3.00	Chases	7-87	8.0	-23.50
Sell/Claim	0-2	0.0	-2.00	Sell/Claim	0-3	0.0	-3.00

RACE CLASS

	W-R	Per cent	£1 Level Stake	FIRST TIME OUT	W-R	Per cent	£1 Level Stake
Class 1	0-0	0.0	0.00	Bumpers	0-6	0.0	-6.00
Class 2	0-1	0.0	-1.00	Hurdles	2-25	8.0	+49.00
Class 3	1-36	2.8	-19.00	Chases	0-15	0.0	-15.00
Class 4	8-127	6.3	+11.50				
Class 5	2-24	8.3	+1.00	Totals	2-46	4.3	+28.00
Class 6	0-8	0.0	-8.00				

JOCKEYS

	W-R	Per cent	£1 Level Stake
Wayne Hutchinson	5-66	7.6	+35.50

M DODS

DENTON, CO DURHAM

	No. of Hrs	Races Run	1st	2nd	3rd	Unpl	Per cent	£1 Level Stake
NH Flat	1	1	0	0	0	1	0.0	-1.00
Hurdles	2	7	1	2	1	3	14.3	+8.00
Chases	1	2	0	0	0	2	0.0	-2.00
Totals	4	10	1	2	1	6	10.0	+5.00
04-05	3	11	0	2	1	8	0.0	-11.00
03-04	9	22	3	3	2	14	13.6	-2.50

JOCKEYS

	W-R	Per cent	£1 Level Stake
Brian Harding	1-7	14.3	+8.00

COURSE RECORD

	Total W-R	Non-Hndcps Hurdles	Non-Hndcps Chases	Hndcps Hurdles	Hndcps Chases	NH Flat	Per cent	£1 Level Stake
Haydock	1-1	1-1	0-0	0-0	0-0	0-0	100.0	+14.00

WINNING HORSES

Horse	Races Run	1st	2nd	3rd	£
Spring Breeze	4	1	1	1	5148

Total winning prize-money			£5148
Favourites	0-0	0.0%	0.00

C R DORE

WEST PINCHBECK, LINCS

	No. of Hrs	Races Run	1st	2nd	3rd	Unpl	Per cent	£1 Level Stake
NH Flat	1	1	0	0	0	1	0.0	-1.00
Hurdles	6	18	2	0	1	15	11.1	+26.75
Chases	1	2	0	0	0	2	0.0	-2.00
Totals	6	21	2	0	1	18	9.5	+23.75
04-05	9	41	2	3	5	31	4.9	-32.00
03-04	8	60	9	8	8	35	15.0	+12.19

JOCKEYS

	W-R	Per cent	£1 Level Stake
Noel Fehily	1 4	25.0	+37.00
Andrew Thornton	1-4	25.0	-0.25

COURSE RECORD

	Total W-R	Non-Hndcps Hurdles	Chases	Hndcps Hurdles	Chases	NH Flat	Per cent	£1 Level Stake
Southwell	1-2	1-2	0-0	0-0	0-0	0-0	50.0	+1.75
Huntingdon	1-3	1-3	0-0	0-0	0-0	0-0	33.3	+38.00

WINNING HORSES

Horse	Races Run	1st	2nd	3rd	£
Dishdasha	5	1	0	0	3452
Ela Re	4	1	0	0	2632
Total winning prize-money					£6084
Favourites	1-1		100.0%		2.75

S DOW

EPSOM, SURREY

	No. of Hrs	Races Run	1st	2nd	3rd	Unpl	Per cent	£1 Level Stake
NH Flat	0	0	0	0	0	0	0.0	0.00
Hurdles	5	13	1	0	0	12	7.7	-10.25
Chases	1	4	0	1	1	2	0.0	-4.00
Totals	6	17	1	1	1	14	5.9	-14.25
04-05	8	23	4	2	1	16	17.4	-5.77
03-04	9	22	3	1	1	17	13.6	-8.50

JOCKEYS

	W-R	Per cent	£1 Level Stake
Leighton Aspell	1-6	16.7	-3.25

COURSE RECORD

	Total W-R	Non-Hndcps Hurdles	Chases	Hndcps Hurdles	Chases	NH Flat	Per cent	£1 Level Stake
Fontwell	1-4	0-3	0-0	1-1	0-0	0-0	25.0	-1.25

WINNING HORSES

Horse	Races Run	1st	2nd	3rd	£
Vengeance	5	1	0	0	2928
Total winning prize-money					£2928
Favourites	142-142		100.0%		248.50

C J DOWN

MUTTERTON, DEVON

	No. of Hrs	Races Run	1st	2nd	3rd	Unpl	Per cent	£1 Level Stake
NH Flat	14	26	3	0	2	21	11.5	-4.00
Hurdles	25	85	2	9	11	63	2.4	-76.00
Chases	6	16	2	1	1	12	12.5	+2.00
Totals	41	127	7	10	14	96	5.5	-78.00
04-05	48	148	8	18	11	111	5.4	-66.00
03-04	42	148	10	15	14	109	6.8	-29.75

JOCKEYS

	W-R	Per cent	£1 Level Stake
Philip Hide	2-14	14.3	+5.00
R Walsh	1-1	100.0	+7.00
Chris Honour	1-4	25.0	+1.00
James Davies	1-4	25.0	+4.00
Shane Walsh	1-16	6.3	-11.50
Mark Bradburne	1-19	5.3	-14.50

COURSE RECORD

	Total W-R	Non-Hndcps Hurdles	Chases	Hndcps Hurdles	Chases	NH Flat	Per cent	£1 Level Stake
Fontwell	2-12	0-4	0-0	0-6	1-1	1-1	16.7	+1.00
Aintree	1-1	0-0	0-0	0-0	0-0	1-1	100.0	+7.00
Taunton	1-4	0-0	0-1	0-0	0-1	1-2	25.0	+5.00
Plumpton	1-6	1-3	0-0	0-3	0-0	0-0	16.7	-1.50
Hereford	1-12	0-7	0-0	0-2	1-2	0-1	8.3	-2.00
Worcester	1-21	1-7	0-1	0-2	0-4	0-7	4.8	-16.50

WINNING HORSES

Horse	Races Run	1st	2nd	3rd	£
Rhacophorus	3	2	0	0	18819
Native Daisy	3	1	0	0	5398
Team Captain	3	1	0	0	4576
Aspra	5	1	0	1	3332
*Josear	14	1	1	6	3262
Supreme Cara	4	1	0	1	1627

Total winning prize-money			£37014
Favourites	0-3	0.0%	-3.00

C DREW
RAMPTON, CAMBS

	No. of Hrs	Races Run	1st	2nd	3rd	Unpl	Per cent	£1 Level Stake
NH Flat	1	2	1	0	0	1	50.0	+8.00
Hurdles	0	0	0	0	0	0	0.0	0.00
Chases	0	0	0	0	0	0	0.0	0.00
Totals	1	2	1	0	0	1	50.0	+8.00
04-05	1	2	0	0	0	2	0.0	-2.00
03-04	1	2	0	0	0	2	0.0	-2.00

JOCKEYS

	W-R	Per cent	£1 Level Stake
Adam Pogson	1-2	50.0	+8.00

COURSE RECORD

	Total W-R	Non-Hndcps Hurdles	Chases	Hndcps Hurdles	Chases	NH Flat	Per cent	£1 Level Stake
Stratford	1-1	0-0	0-0	0-0	0-0	1-1	100.0	+9.00

WINNING HORSES

Horse	Races Run	1st	2nd	3rd	£
Tickers Way	2	1	0	0	3107
Total winning prize-money					£3107
Favourites	0-0		0.0%		0.00

MRS A DUFFIELD
CONSTABLE BURTON, N YORKS

	No. of Hrs	Races Run	1st	2nd	3rd	Unpl	Per cent	£1 Level Stake
NH Flat	1	1	0	0	0	1	0.0	-1.00
Hurdles	6	23	5	3	4	11	21.7	+2.75
Chases	2	2	0	0	0	2	0.0	-2.00
Totals	7	26	5	3	4	14	19.2	-0.25
04-05	5	29	2	7	3	17	6.9	-17.38
03-04	8	29	1	1	2	23	3.4	-22.00

JOCKEYS

	W-R	Per cent	£1 Level Stake
Keith Mercer	3-15	20.0	+2.50
Joe Tizzard	2-4	50.0	+4.25

COURSE RECORD

	Total W-R	Non-Hndcps Hurdles	Chases	Hndcps Hurdles	Chases	NH Flat	Per cent	£1 Level Stake
Perth	3-3	2-2	0-0	1-1	0-0	0-0	100.0	+14.50
Bangor	1-1	0-0	0-0	1-1	0-0	0-0	100.0	+4.00

Haydock	1-1	1-1	0-0	0-0	0-0	0-0	100.0	+2.25

WINNING HORSES

Horse	Races Run	1st	2nd	3rd	£
Prairie Sun	3	1	0	1	10332
Finland	5	1	0	2	4836
Constable Burton	4	2	1	0	8073
Noble House	4	1	1	0	3155
Total winning prize-money					£26396
Favourites	3-7		42.9%		4.25

B W DUKE
LAMBOURN, BERKS

	No. of Hrs	Races Run	1st	2nd	3rd	Unpl	Per cent	£1 Level Stake
NH Flat	4	4	0	0	0	4	0.0	-4.00
Hurdles	11	36	1	3	3	29	2.8	-23.00
Chases	1	3	0	0	1	2	0.0	-3.00
Totals	14	43	1	3	4	35	2.3	-30.00
04-05	9	52	4	2	3	43	7.7	+60.50
03-04	5	26	5	3	1	17	19.2	+197.00

JOCKEYS

	W-R	Per cent	£1 Level Stake
A P McCoy	1-3	33.3	+10.00

COURSE RECORD

	Total W-R	Non-Hndcps Hurdles	Chases	Hndcps Hurdles	Chases	NH Flat	Per cent	£1 Level Stake
Nton Abbot	1-3	0-2	0-0	1-1	0-0	0-0	33.3	+10.00

WINNING HORSES

Horse	Races Run	1st	2nd	3rd	£
Taranai	6	1	0	1	2716
Total winning prize-money					£2716
Favourites	0-2		0.0%		-2.00

J M DUN
HERIOT, BORDERS

	No. of Hrs	Races Run	1st	2nd	3rd	Unpl	Per cent	£1 Level Stake
NH Flat	0	0	0	0	0	0	0.0	0.00
Hurdles	2	7	2	0	1	4	28.6	+22.00
Chases	0	0	0	0	0	0	0.0	0.00
Totals	2	7	2	0	1	4	28.6	+22.00
04-05	1	3	0	0	2	1	0.0	-3.00

JOCKEYS

	W-R	Per cent	£1 Level Stake
Peter Buchanan	2-4	50.0	+25.00

COURSE RECORD

	Total W-R	Non-Hndcps Hurdles	Chases	Hndcps Hurdles	Chases	NH Flat	Per cent	£1 Level Stake
Kelso	2-5	0-2	0-0	2-3	0-0	0-0	40.0	+24.00

WINNING HORSES

Horse	Races Run	1st	2nd	3rd	£
River Alder	5	2	0	1	20161
Total winning prize-money					£20161
Favourites	0-0		0.0%		0.00

MRS P N DUTFIELD

AXMOUTH, DEVON

	No. of Hrs	Races Run	1st	2nd	3rd	Unpl	Per cent	£1 Level Stake
NH Flat	1	4	0	0	0	4	0.0	-4.00
Hurdles	7	20	2	3	1	14	10.0	-6.67
Chases	1	2	0	0	0	2	0.0	-2.00
Totals	9	26	2	3	1	20	7.7	-12.67
04-05	13	51	1	4	2	44	2.0	-43.00
03-04	11	32	1	3	3	25	3.1	-17.00

JOCKEYS

	W-R	Per cent	£1 Level Stake
Angharad Frieze	1-5	20.0	-0.67
Richard Young	1-10	10.0	-1.00

COURSE RECORD

	Total W-R	Non-Hndcps Hurdles	Chases	Hndcps Hurdles	Chases	NH Flat	Per cent	£1 Level Stake
Huntingdon	2-5	2-4	0-0	0-0	0-0	0-1	40.0	+8.33

WINNING HORSES

Horse	Races Run	1st	2nd	3rd	£
Voir Dire	2	1	0	0	4466
Surface To Air	4	1	1	1	3253
Total winning prize-money					£7719
Favourites	0-0		0.0%		0.00

MISS C DYSON

LOWER BENTLEY, WORCS

	No. of Hrs	Races Run	1st	2nd	3rd	Unpl	Per cent	£1 Level Stake
NH Flat	3	7	0	0	0	7	0.0	-7.00
Hurdles	8	20	0	1	2	17	0.0	-20.00
Chases	1	6	2	0	1	3	33.3	+18.50
Totals	10	33	2	1	3	27	6.1	-8.50
04-05	7	25	1	0	0	24	4.0	-17.00
03-04	6	24	1	2	3	18	4.2	-13.00

JOCKEYS

	W-R	Per cent	£1 Level Stake
Miss C Dyson	2-33	6.1	-8.50

COURSE RECORD

	Total W-R	Non-Hndcps Hurdles	Chases	Hndcps Hurdles	Chases	NH Flat	Per cent	£1 Level Stake
Ludlow	1-3	0-0	0-0	0-0	1-1	0-2	33.3	+4.50
Huntingdon	1-7	0-1	0-0	0-1	1-3	0-2	14.3	+10.00

WINNING HORSES

Horse	Races Run	1st	2nd	3rd	£
Regal Vision	9	2	0	2	7079
Total winning prize-money					£7079
Favourites	0-0		0.0%		0.00

SIMON EARLE

SUTTON VENY, WILTS

	No. of Hrs	Races Run	1st	2nd	3rd	Unpl	Per cent	£1 Level Stake
NH Flat	3	5	1	1	1	2	20.0	-1.75
Hurdles	6	11	1	1	0	9	9.1	-8.90
Chases	2	5	0	2	0	3	0.0	-5.00
Totals	10	21	2	4	1	14	9.5	-15.65
04-05	8	25	5	4	2	14	20.0	+18.88
03-04	5	17	1	2	1	13	5.9	-12.50

JOCKEYS

	W-R	Per cent	£1 Level Stake
Liam Heard	1-2	50.0	+0.10
Mick Fitzgerald	1-5	20.0	-1.75

COURSE RECORD

	Total W-R	Non-Hndcps Hurdles	Chases	Hndcps Hurdles	Chases	NH Flat	Per cent	£1 Level Stake
Plumpton	1-1	0-0	0-0	1-1	0-0	0-0	100.0	+1.10
Worcester	1-2	0-0	0-0	0-0	0-0	1-2	50.0	+1.25

WINNING HORSES

Horse	Races Run	1st	2nd	3rd	£
Saucy Night	4	1	1	0	2681
Tihui Two	2	1	1	0	1873
Total winning prize-money					£4554
Favourites	1-4		25.0%		-1.90

M W EASTERBY

SHERIFF HUTTON, N YORKS

	No. of Hrs	Races Run	1st	2nd	3rd	Unpl	Per cent	£1 Level Stake
NH Flat	29	44	3	7	7	27	6.8	-27.25
Hurdles	38	115	4	8	10	92	3.5	-51.50
Chases	13	48	5	4	4	34	10.4	+28.50
Totals	**61**	**207**	**12**	**19**	**21**	**153**	**5.8**	**-50.25**
04-05	*61*	*217*	*19*	*31*	*22*	*145*	*8.8*	*-116.63*
03-04	*56*	*184*	*24*	*28*	*18*	*114*	*13.0*	*+12.21*

BY MONTH

NH Flat	W-R	Per cent	£1 Level Stake	Hurdles	W-R	Per cent	£1 Level Stake
May	0-0	0.0	0.00	May	0-11	0.0	-11.00
June	1-3	33.3	-0.25	June	0-0	0.0	0.00
July	0-0	0.0	0.00	July	0-3	0.0	-3.00
August	0-0	0.0	0.00	August	0-3	0.0	-3.00
September	0-6	0.0	-6.00	September	0-3	0.0	-3.00
October	0-6	0.0	-6.00	October	1-7	14.3	+6.00
November	0-4	0.0	-4.00	November	0-23	0.0	-23.00
December	0-3	0.0	-3.00	December	0-21	0.0	-21.00
January	1-6	16.7	+0.50	January	1-15	6.7	-8.50
February	0-5	0.0	-5.00	February	1-11	9.1	-8.00
March	1-6	16.7	+1.50	March	1-10	10.0	+31.00
April	0-5	0.0	-5.00	April	0-8	0.0	-8.00

Chases	W-R	Per cent	£1 Level Stake	Totals	W-R	Per cent	£1 Level Stake
May	0-2	0.0	-2.00	May	0-13	0.0	-13.00
June	0-0	0.0	0.00	June	1-3	33.3	-0.25
July	0-0	0.0	0.00	July	0-3	0.0	-3.00
August	0-3	0.0	-3.00	August	0-6	0.0	-6.00
September	0-1	0.0	-1.00	September	0-10	0.0	-10.00
October	0-5	0.0	-5.00	October	1-18	5.6	-5.00
November	1-5	20.0	+29.00	November	1-32	3.1	+2.00
December	2-10	20.0	+18.00	December	2-34	5.9	-6.00
January	1-7	14.3	0.00	January	3-28	10.7	-8.00
February	0-4	0.0	-4.00	February	1-20	5.0	-17.00
March	1-7	14.3	+0.50	March	3-23	13.0	+33.00
April	0-4	0.0	-4.00	April	0-17	0.0	-17.00

DISTANCE

Hurdles	W-R	Per cent	£1 Level Stake	Chases	W-R	Per cent	£1 Level Stake
2m-2m3f	3-83	3.6	-32.50	2m-2m3f	1-23	4.3	-2.00
2m4f-2m7f	1-27	3.7	-14.00	2m4f-2m7f	0-9	0.0	-9.00
3m+	0-5	0.0	-5.00	3m+	4-16	25.0	+39.50

TYPE OF RACE

Non-Handicaps	W-R	Per cent	£1 Level Stake	Handicaps	W-R	Per cent	£1 Level Stake
Nov Hrdls	2-54	3.7	-10.00	Nov Hrdls	1-10	10.0	+3.00
Hrdls	1-10	10.0	-3.50	Hrdls	0-29	0.0	-29.00
Nov Chs	0-9	0.0	-9.00	Nov Chs	1-11	9.1	+10.00
Chases	0-3	0.0	-3.00	Chases	4-25	16.0	+30.50
Sell/Claim	0-2	0.0	-2.00	Sell/Claim	0-10	0.0	-10.00

RACE CLASS

	W-R	Per cent	£1 Level Stake
Class 1	0-1	0.0	-1.00
Class 2	0-3	0.0	-3.00
Class 3	0-41	0.0	-41.00
Class 4	9-102	8.8	+38.00
Class 5	0-18	0.0	-18.00
Class 6	3-42	7.1	-25.25

FIRST TIME OUT

	W-R	Per cent	£1 Level Stake
Bumpers	1-29	3.4	-22.50
Hurdles	1-24	4.2	-11.00
Chases	0-8	0.0	-8.00
Totals	2-61	3.3	-41.50

JOCKEYS

	W-R	Per cent	£1 Level Stake
Mr T Greenall	7-123	5.7	-62.75
Michael McAlister	4-7	57.1	+48.50
Wilson Renwick	1-13	7.7	+28.00

COURSE RECORD

	Total W-R	Non-Hndcps Hurdles	Non-Hndcps Chases	Hndcps Hurdles	Hndcps Chases	NH Flat	Per cent	£1 Level Stake
Sedgefield	4-17	1-4	0-3	0-1	3-6	0-3	23.5	+34.00
Newcastle	2-10	1-8	0-0	0-0	1-1	1-1	20.0	+3.00
Kelso	2-11	0-5	0-0	0-2	1-3	1-1	18.2	+17.50
Mrket Rsn	2-38	1-13	0-1	0-10	1-3	0-11	5.3	+10.50
Carlisle	1-5	0-0	0-1	1-1	0-0	0-3	20.0	+8.00
Hexham	1-11	0-4	0-0	0-2	1-4		9.1	-8.25

WINNING HORSES

Horse	Races Run	1st	2nd	3rd	£
Bang And Blame	13	4	0	0	18277
One Five Eight	6	1	0	0	3969
Saucy King	1	1	0	0	3416
*Turbo	5	1	0	2	3253
Woodford Consult	6	1	0	0	2928
Commanche Sioux	7	1	0	0	2741
Spitfire Sortie	3	1	0	0	1713
The Gleaner	2	1	0	1	1713
Bluecoat	5	1	2	1	1519
Total winning prize-money					**£39529**
Favourites	2-314		0.4%		-508.25

T D EASTERBY

GREAT HABTON, N YORKS

	No. of Hrs	Races Run	1st	2nd	3rd	Unpl	Per cent	£1 Level Stake
NH Flat	7	12	2	0	1	9	16.7	+6.00
Hurdles	17	50	2	10	4	34	4.0	-28.50
Chases	11	57	7	5	10	35	12.3	-13.25
Totals	**32**	**119**	**11**	**15**	**15**	**78**	**9.2**	**-35.75**
04-05	*34*	*154*	*18*	*24*	*23*	*89*	*11.7*	*-65.84*
03-04	*32*	*129*	*18*	*21*	*19*	*71*	*14.0*	*-29.56*

BY MONTH

NH Flat	W-R	Per cent	£1 Level Stake
May	0-1	0.0	-1.00
June	0-0	0.0	0.00
July	0-0	0.0	0.00
August	0-0	0.0	0.00
September	0-0	0.0	0.00
October	0-0	0.0	0.00
November	1-2	50.0	+7.00
December	0-0	0.0	0.00
January	0-3	0.0	-3.00
February	0-1	0.0	-1.00
March	0-3	0.0	-3.00
April	1-2	50.0	+7.00

Hurdles	W-R	Per cent	£1 Level Stake
May	0-4	0.0	-4.00
June	0-1	0.0	-1.00
July	0-0	0.0	0.00
August	0-2	0.0	-2.00
September	0-0	0.0	0.00
October	0-8	0.0	-8.00
November	0-4	0.0	-4.00
December	1-10	10.0	+3.00
January	0-7	0.0	-7.00
February	0-3	0.0	-3.00
March	0-4	0.0	-4.00
April	1-7	14.3	+1.50

Chases	W-R	Per cent	£1 Level Stake
May	1-5	20.0	-0.50
June	0-1	0.0	-1.00
July	0-0	0.0	0.00
August	0-0	0.0	0.00
September	0-0	0.0	0.00
October	0-7	0.0	-7.00
November	1-11	9.1	-4.50
December	2-10	20.0	+0.50
January	0-4	0.0	-4.00
February	1-6	16.7	+3.00
March	0-4	0.0	-4.00
April	2-9	22.2	+4.25

Totals	W-R	Per cent	£1 Level Stake
May	1-10	10.0	-5.50
June	0-2	0.0	-2.00
July	0-0	0.0	0.00
August	0-2	0.0	-2.00
September	0-0	0.0	0.00
October	0-15	0.0	-15.00
November	2-17	11.8	-1.50
December	3-20	15.0	+3.50
January	0-14	0.0	-14.00
February	1-10	10.0	-1.00
March	0-11	0.0	-11.00
April	4-18	22.2	+12.75

DISTANCE

Hurdles	W-R	Per cent	£1 Level Stake
2m-2m3f	1-41	2.4	-28.00
2m4f-2m7f	1-9	11.1	-0.50
3m+	0-0	0.0	0.00

Chases	W-R	Per cent	£1 Level Stake
2m-2m3f	2-16	12.5	-9.25
2m4f-2m7f	3-28	10.7	-1.50
3m+	2-13	15.4	-2.50

TYPE OF RACE

Non-Handicaps

	W-R	Per cent	£1 Level Stake
Nov Hrdls	0-14	0.0	-14.00
Hrdls	1-3	33.3	+5.50
Nov Chs	3-5	60.0	+12.75
Chases	0-1	0.0	-1.00
Sell/Claim	0-0	0.0	0.00

Handicaps

	W-R	Per cent	£1 Level Stake
Nov Hrdls	1-2	50.0	+11.00
Hrdls	0-31	0.0	-31.00
Nov Chs	0-7	0.0	-7.00
Chases	4-44	9.1	-18.00
Sell/Claim	0-0	0.0	0.00

RACE CLASS

	W-R	Per cent	£1 Level Stake
Class 1	0-3	0.0	-3.00
Class 2	0-13	0.0	-13.00
Class 3	5-65	7.7	-41.25
Class 4	4-27	14.8	+14.50
Class 5	1-2	50.0	+7.00
Class 6	1-9	11.1	0.00

FIRST TIME OUT

	W-R	Per cent	£1 Level Stake
Bumpers	2-7	28.6	+11.00
Hurdles	1-14	7.1	-5.50
Chases	2-11	18.2	-2.25
Totals	5-32	15.6	+3.25

JOCKEYS

	W-R	Per cent	£1 Level Stake
Russ Garritty	8-81	9.9	-17.75
David O'Meara	2-23	8.7	-12.00
Stephen Craine	1-5	20.0	+4.00

COURSE RECORD

	Total W-R	Non-Hndcps Hurdles	Chases	Hndcps Hurdles	Chases	NH Flat	Per cent	£1 Level Stake
Wetherby	3-29	1-5	0-0	0-10	2-12	0-2	10.3	-10.00
Sedgefield	2-6	0-1	0-1	1-2	0-1	1-1	33.3	+16.00
Kelso	2-8	0-2	2-2	0-2	0-2	0-0	25.0	-1.25
Towcester	1-1	0-0	1-1	0-0	0-0	0-0	100.0	+10.00
Doncaster	1-4	0-1	0-0	0-1	0-1	1-1	25.0	+5.00
Carlisle	1-5	0-0	0-0	0-2	1-3	0-0	20.0	+1.50
Mrket Rsn	1-15	0-3	0-1	0-4	1-7	0-0	6.7	-6.00

WINNING HORSES

Horse	Races Run	1st	2nd	3rd	£
Silver Knight	7	2	0	2	16769
Tribal Dispute	8	2	2	0	12207
Edmo Yewkay	7	1	2	1	5673
Jonny's Kick	10	1	0	3	4437
King's Bounty	6	1	1	0	3773
Eborarry	10	1	2	1	3461
Ryhall	3	1	0	1	2933
Anchors Away	1	1	0	0	2277
Wolds Way	3	1	0	0	1850
Total winning prize-money					**£53380**
Favourites	1-780		0.1%		-777.75

DAVID M EASTERBY

SHERIFF HUTTON, N YORKS

	No. of Hrs	Races Run	1st	2nd	3rd	Unpl	Per cent	£1 Level Stake
NH Flat	0	0	0	0	0	0	0.0	0.00
Hurdles	0	0	0	0	0	0	0.0	0.00
Chases	5	12	2	2	1	7	16.7	-2.75
Totals	**5**	**12**	**2**	**2**	**1**	**7**	**16.7**	**-2.75**
04-05	5	11	2	2	1	6	18.2	-3.75
03-04	5	10	1	4	0	5	10.0	-6.25

JOCKEYS

	W-R	Per cent	£1 Level Stake
Mr T Greenall	2-9	22.2	+0.25

COURSE RECORD

	Total W-R	Non-Hndcps Hurdles	Chases	Hndcps Hurdles	Chases	NH Flat	Per cent	£1 Level Stake
Fakenham	1-1	0-0	1-1	0-0	0-0	0-0	100.0	+2.75
Stratford	1-2	0-0	1-2	0-0	0-0	0-0	50.0	+3.50

WINNING HORSES

Horse	Races Run	1st	2nd	3rd	£
*Spring Margot	2	1	0	0	3123
Sikander A Azam	4	1	0	0	2226
Total winning prize-money					**£5349**
Favourites	**1-3**		**33.3%**		**0.75**

B J ECKLEY

LLANSPYDDID, POWYS

	No. of Hrs	Races Run	1st	2nd	3rd	Unpl	Per cent	£1 Level Stake
NH Flat	3	3	0	0	0	3	0.0	-3.00
Hurdles	3	11	2	1	1	7	18.2	+38.00
Chases	1	2	0	0	0	2	0.0	-2.00
Totals	**6**	**16**	**2**	**1**	**1**	**12**	**12.5**	**+33.00**
04-05	5	22	0	5	1	16	0.0	-22.00
03-04	5	10	0	1	0	9	0.0	10.00

JOCKEYS

	W-R	Per cent	£1 Level Stake
Tom Messenger	1-3	33.3	+12.00
Mark Nicolls	1-12	8.3	+22.00

COURSE RECORD

	Total W-R	Non-Hndcps Hurdles	Chases	Hndcps Hurdles	Chases	NH Flat	Per cent	£1 Level Stake
Hereford	2-4	0-0	0-1	2-3	0-0	0-0	50.0	+45.00

WINNING HORSES

Horse	Races Run	1st	2nd	3rd	£
Abraham Smith	6	1	1	1	3904
Witness Time	6	1	0	0	3253
Total winning prize-money					**£7157**
Favourites	**0-0**		**0.0%**		**0.00**

G F EDWARDS

LUCKWELL BRIDGE, SOMERSET

	No. of Hrs	Races Run	1st	2nd	3rd	Unpl	Per cent	£1 Level Stake
NH Flat	1	2	0	0	0	2	0.0	-2.00
Hurdles	4	18	2	0	2	14	11.1	+26.00
Chases	0	0	0	0	0	0	0.0	0.00
Totals	**5**	**20**	**2**	**0**	**2**	**16**	**10.0**	**+24.00**
04-05	5	12	1	2	1	8	8.3	-4.00
03-04	4	17	0	0	3	14	0.0	-17.00

JOCKEYS

	W-R	Per cent	£1 Level Stake
Mr D Edwards	2-17	11.8	+27.00

COURSE RECORD

	Total W-R	Non-Hndcps Hurdles	Chases	Hndcps Hurdles	Chases	NH Flat	Per cent	£1 Level Stake
Taunton	2-7	0-0	0-0	2-7	0-0	0-0	28.6	+37.00

WINNING HORSES

Horse	Races Run	1st	2nd	3rd	£
Devito	10	2	0	1	8238
Total winning prize-money					**£8238**
Favourites	**0-0**		**0.0%**		**0.00**

C R EGERTON

CHADDLEWORTH, BERKS

	No. of Hrs	Races Run	1st	2nd	3rd	Unpl	Per cent	£1 Level Stake
NH Flat	7	12	2	1	0	9	16.7	-0.50
Hurdles	13	34	8	4	5	17	23.5	+60.41
Chases	10	38	11	8	6	13	28.9	+13.53
Totals	**26**	**84**	**21**	**13**	**11**	**39**	**25.0**	**+73.44**
04-05	35	84	23	14	9	38	27.4	-3.65
03-04	32	98	17	10	13	58	17.3	-19.62

BY MONTH

NH Flat	W-R	Per cent	£1 Level Stake	Hurdles	W-R	Per cent	£1 Level Stake
May	0-0	0.0	0.00	May	1-3	33.3	+10.00
June	0-0	0.0	0.00	June	0-0	0.0	0.00
July	0-0	0.0	0.00	July	0-0	0.0	0.00
August	0-0	0.0	0.00	August	0-1	0.0	-1.00
September	0-0	0.0	0.00	September	0-0	0.0	0.00
October	0-2	0.0	-2.00	October	0-1	0.0	-1.00
November	0-1	0.0	-1.00	November	2-7	28.6	+1.88
December	0-3	0.0	-3.00	December	1-5	20.0	+2.00
January	1-2	50.0	+4.50	January	0-5	0.0	-5.00
February	0-1	0.0	-1.00	February	2-5	40.0	+18.00
March	0-1	0.0	-1.00	March	1-3	33.3	+38.00
April	1-2	50.0	+3.00	April	1-4	25.0	-2.47

Chases	W-R	Per cent	£1 Level Stake	Totals	W-R	Per cent	£1 Level Stake
May	0-2	0.0	-2.00	May	1-5	20.0	+8.00
June	0-1	0.0	-1.00	June	0-1	0.0	-1.00
July	0-1	0.0	-1.00	July	0-1	0.0	-1.00
August	0-1	0.0	-1.00	August	0-2	0.0	-2.00
September	0-1	0.0	-1.00	September	0-1	0.0	-1.00
October	2-3	66.7	+2.75	October	2-6	33.3	-0.25
November	1-5	20.0	+10.00	November	3-13	23.1	+10.88
December	3-5	60.0	+4.75	December	4-13	30.8	+3.75

January	2-6	33.3	+6.33	January	3-13	23.1	+5.83	Towcester	1-3	0-0	0-1	0-0	0-0	1-2	33.3	+2.00
February	1-6	16.7	-4.50	February	3-12	25.0	+12.50	Plumpton	1-4	1-1	0-1	0-0	0-0	0-2	25.0	-2.47
March	1-5	20.0	-2.80	March	2-9	22.2	+34.20	Uttoxeter	1-4	0-0	1-2	0-0	0-1	0-1	25.0	-0.75
April	1-2	50.0	+3.00	April	3-8	37.5	+3.53	Wincanton	1-4	0-2	0-0	1-2	0-0	0-0	25.0	+3.00

DISTANCE

Hurdles	W-R	Per cent	£1 Level Stake	Chases	W-R	Per cent	£1 Level Stake
2m-2m3f	6-21	28.6	+58.41	2m-2m3f	4-11	36.4	+2.03
2m4f-2m7f	1-6	16.7	-4.00	2m4f-2m7f	2-10	20.0	-4.25
3m+	1-7	14.3	+6.00	3m+	5-17	29.4	+15.75

TYPE OF RACE

Non-Handicaps	W-R	Per cent	£1 Level Stake	Handicaps	W-R	Per cent	£1 Level Stake
Nov Hrdls	5-14	35.7	+19.41	Nov Hrdls	1-3	33.3	+38.00
Hrdls	0-6	0.0	-6.00	Hrdls	2-10	20.0	+10.00
Nov Chs	7-16	43.8	+16.50	Nov Chs	2-3	66.7	+3.70
Chases	0-1	0.0	-1.00	Chases	2-18	11.1	-5.67
Sell/Claim	0-1	0.0	-1.00	Sell/Claim	0-0	0.0	0.00

RACE CLASS / FIRST TIME OUT

	W-R	Per cent	£1 Level Stake		W-R	Per cent	£1 Level Stake
Class 1	3-15	20.0	+43.63	Bumpers	1-7	14.3	-0.50
Class 2	2-6	33.3	+4.63	Hurdles	3-12	25.0	+9.88
Class 3	6-24	25.0	+12.03	Chases	3-7	42.9	+3.08
Class 4	8-28	28.6	+12.66				
Class 5	1-2	50.0	+3.00	Totals	7-26	26.9	+12.46
Class 6	1-9	11.1	-2.50				

JOCKEYS

	W-R	Per cent	£1 Level Stake
A P McCoy	10-36	27.8	+2.53
Andrew Tinkler	5-22	22.7	+0.38
P J Brennan	3-8	37.5	+39.53
Sam Thomas	1-1	100.0	+20.00
Barry Fenton	1-3	33.3	+12.00
Robert Thornton	1-6	16.7	+7.00

COURSE RECORD

	Total W-R	Non-Hndcps Hurdles	Chases	Hndcps Hurdles	Chases	NH Flat	Per cent	£1 Level Stake
Newbury	4-13	0-3	1-1	0-2	3-7	0-0	30.8	+13.03
Sandown	2-5	0-1	1-2	0-0	1-2	0-0	40.0	+5.63
Cheltenham	2-10	0-2	1-2	1-4	0-1	0-1	20.0	+33.63
Fontwell	1-1	0-0	1-1	0-0	0-0	0-0	100.0	+4.00
Ludlow	1-1	0-0	1-1	0-0	0-0	0-0	100.0	+1.50
Mrket Rsn	1-1	1-1	0-0	0-0	0-0	0-0	100.0	+1.38
Exeter	1-2	0-0	0-0	1-1	0-1	0-0	50.0	+11.00
Huntingdon	1-2	1-1	0-0	0-1	0-0	0-0	50.0	+4.50
Leicester	1-2	0-0	1-1	0-0	0-1	0-0	50.0	-0.50
Southwell	1-2	1-1	0-1	0-0	0-0	0-0	50.0	+19.00
Taunton	1-2	0-1	0-0	0-0	0-0	1-1	50.0	+4.50
Fakenham	1-3	1-2	0-0	0-1	0-0	0-0	33.3	-1.00

WINNING HORSES

Horse	Races Run	1st	2nd	3rd	£
Shamayoun	7	3	0	1	49922
Darkness	7	4	1	1	72144
Graphic Approach	4	1	1	1	25052
The Local	7	3	0	2	18996
Rubberdubber	3	2	0	0	14313
Gallant Approach	3	2	1	0	10867
Mr Pointment	4	2	0	0	8610
Admiral Peary	7	1	2	2	4875
Valance	1	1	0	0	3953
The Entomologist	2	1	0	0	2602
Willie Pep	1	1	0	0	1713
Total winning prize-money					**£213047**
Favourites	88-102		86.3%		314.69

J P ELLIOT

KELSO, BORDERS

	No. of Hrs	Races Run	1st	2nd	3rd	Unpl	Per cent	£1 Level Stake
NH Flat	0	0	0	0	0	0	0.0	0.00
Hurdles	0	0	0	0	0	0	0.0	0.00
Chases	2	4	1	2	1	0	25.0	-2.00
Totals	**2**	**4**	**1**	**2**	**1**	**0**	**25.0**	**-2.00**

JOCKEYS

	W-R	Per cent	£1 Level Stake
Miss R Davidson	1-4	25.0	-2.00

COURSE RECORD

	Total W-R	Non-Hndcps Hurdles	Chases	Hndcps Hurdles	Chases	NH Flat	Per cent	£1 Level Stake
Sedgefield	1-1	0-0	1-1	0-0	0-0	0-0	100.0	+1.00

WINNING HORSES

Horse	Races Run	1st	2nd	3rd	£
*Lord O'All Seasons	2	1	0	1	1249
Total winning prize-money					**£1249**
Favourites	1-2		50.0%		0.00

MRS R L ELLIOT

HOWNAM, BORDERS

	No. of Hrs	Races Run	1st	2nd	3rd	Unpl	Per cent	£1 Level Stake
NH Flat	3	7	1	0	1	5	14.3	+8.00

							Per	£1 Level
Hurdles	4	11	0	1	0	10	0.0	-11.00
Chases	1	1	0	1	0	0	0.0	-1.00
Totals	**7**	**19**	**1**	**2**	**1**	**15**	**5.3**	**-4.00**
04-05	7	27	3	2	1	21	11.1	+37.00
03-04	8	22	1	0	1	20	4.5	+29.00

JOCKEYS

	W-R	Per cent	£1 Level Stake
Miss R Davidson	1-17	5.9	-2.00

COURSE RECORD

	Total W-R	Non-Hndcps Hurdles Chases	Hndcps Hurdles Chases	NH Flat	Per cent	£1 Level Stake
Newcastle	1-2	0-1 0-0	0-0 0-0	1-1	50.0	+13.00

WINNING HORSES

Horse	Races Run	1st	2nd	3rd	£
Scarvagh Diamond	3	1	0	0	1627
Total winning prize-money					**£1627**
Favourites	0-2		0.0%		-2.00

E A ELLIOTT

RUSHYFORD, CO DURHAM

	No. of Hrs	Races Run	1st	2nd	3rd	Unpl	Per cent	£1 Level Stake
NH Flat	2	2	0	0	0	2	0.0	2.00
Hurdles	3	6	1	1	0	4	16.7	+5.00
Chases	2	6	0	1	0	5	0.0	-6.00
Totals	**5**	**14**	**1**	**2**	**0**	**11**	**7.1**	**-3.00**
04-05	5	25	3	4	1	17	12.0	-5.88
03-04	5	22	1	5	1	15	4.5	-9.00

JOCKEYS

	W-R	Per cent	£1 Level Stake
T J O'Brien	1-2	50.0	+9.00

COURSE RECORD

	Total W-R	Non-Hndcps Hurdles Chases	Hndcps Hurdles Chases	NH Flat	Per cent	£1 Level Stake
Sedgefield	1-6	0-0 0-0	1-3 0-3	0-0	16.7	+5.00

WINNING HORSES

Horse	Races Run	1st	2nd	3rd	£
Two Steps To Go	2	1	0	0	2317
Total winning prize-money					**£2317**
Favourites	0-0		0.0%		0.00

B ELLISON

NORTON, N YORKS

	No. of Hrs	Races Run	1st	2nd	3rd	Unpl	Per cent	£1 Level Stake
NH Flat	0	0	0	0	0	0	0.0	0.00
Hurdles	14	41	1	2	5	33	2.4	-32.00
Chases	4	8	2	2	1	3	25.0	-0.63
Totals	**15**	**49**	**3**	**4**	**6**	**36**	**6.1**	**-32.63**
04-05	30	117	11	11	16	79	9.4	-69.96
03-04	25	110	17	17	17	59	15.5	-16.39

JOCKEYS

	W-R	Per cent	£1 Level Stake
Tony Dobbin	2-9	22.2	+4.50
Wilson Renwick	1-12	8.3	-9.13

COURSE RECORD

	Total W-R	Non-Hndcps Hurdles Chases	Hndcps Hurdles Chases	NH Flat	Per cent	£1 Level Stake
Carlisle	1-4	0-0 1-2	0-2 0-0	0-0	25.0	-1.13
Sedgefield	1-6	0-3 1-1	0-2 0-0	0-0	16.7	-1.50
Wetherby	1-10	0-5 0-0	1-4 0-1	0-0	10.0	-1.00

WINNING HORSES

Horse	Races Run	1st	2nd	3rd	£
Mister Arjay	7	1	1	1	5233
Great As Gold	7	1	2	1	4554
King Eider	2	1	0	0	4076
Total winning prize-money					**£13863**
Favourites	1-2		50.0%		0.88

D R C ELSWORTH

NEWMARKET, SUFFOLK

	No. of Hrs	Races Run	1st	2nd	3rd	Unpl	Per cent	£1 Level Stake
NH Flat	0	0	0	0	0	0	0.0	0.00
Hurdles	6	8	1	1	0	6	12.5	-1.00
Chases	1	7	1	3	1	2	14.3	-2.50
Totals	**6**	**15**	**2**	**4**	**1**	**8**	**13.3**	**-3.50**
04-05	9	27	10	4	2	11	37.0	+84.17
03-04	9	19	2	2	5	10	10.5	-7.50

JOCKEYS

	W-R	Per cent	£1 Level Stake
Andrew Thornton	1-4	25.0	+0.50
Robert Walford	1-9	11.1	-2.00

COURSE RECORD

	Total W-R	Non-Hndcps Hurdles	Chases	Hndcps Hurdles	Chases	NH Flat	Per cent	£1 Level Stake
Stratford	1-3	0-1	0-0	1-1	0-1	0-0	33.3	+4.00
Wincanton	1-4	0-0	0-0	0-0	1-4	0-0	25.0	+0.50

WINNING HORSES

Horse	Races Run	1st	2nd	3rd	£
Black De Bessy	8	2	3	1	13230
Total winning prize-money					**£13230**
Favourites	**1-5**		**20.0%**		**-0.50**

MISS E M ENGLAND

PRIORS HARDWICK, WARWICKS

	No. of Hrs	Races Run	1st	2nd	3rd	Unpl	Per cent	£1 Level Stake
NH Flat	0	0	0	0	0	0	0.0	0.00
Hurdles	1	6	1	0	0	5	16.7	+3.00
Chases	0	0	0	0	0	0	0.0	0.00
Totals	**1**	**6**	**1**	**0**	**0**	**5**	**16.7**	**+3.00**
04-05	1	4	0	0	2	2	0.0	-4.00

JOCKEYS

	W-R	Per cent	£1 Level Stake
Charlie Poste	1-2	50.0	+7.00

COURSE RECORD

	Total W-R	Non-Hndcps Hurdles	Chases	Hndcps Hurdles	Chases	NH Flat	Per cent	£1 Level Stake
Towcester	1-3	0-0	0-0	1-3	0-0	0-0	33.3	+6.00

WINNING HORSES

Horse	Races Run	1st	2nd	3rd	£
Andy Gin	6	1	0	0	4478
Total winning prize-money					**£4478**
Favourites	**0-0**		**0.0%**		**0.00**

A ENNIS

BEARE GREEN, SURREY

	No. of Hrs	Races Run	1st	2nd	3rd	Unpl	Per cent	£1 Level Stake
NH Flat	2	2	0	0	0	2	0.0	-2.00
Hurdles	7	27	1	2	2	22	3.7	-25.09
Chases	7	42	8	4	6	24	19.0	+9.50
Totals	**15**	**71**	**9**	**6**	**8**	**48**	**12.7**	**-17.59**
04-05	16	53	4	4	5	40	7.5	-18.50
03-04	11	39	1	1	9	28	2.6	-28.00

JOCKEYS

	W-R	Per cent	£1 Level Stake
William Kennedy	2-3	66.7	+17.50
P J Brennan	2-9	22.2	+1.50
Jim Crowley	2-11	18.2	-2.50
Colin Bolger	2-20	10.0	-11.09
Robert Stephens	1-3	33.3	+2.00

COURSE RECORD

	Total W-R	Non-Hndcps Hurdles	Chases	Hndcps Hurdles	Chases	NH Flat	Per cent	£1 Level Stake
Fontwell	4-17	0-3	0-2	0-1	4-10	0-1	23.5	+15.50
Taunton	1-2	1-1	0-0	0-0	0-1	0-0	50.0	-0.09
Wincanton	1-3	0-0	0-0	0-0	1-3	0-0	33.3	-0.50
Huntingdon	1-5	0-1	0-0	0-0	1-4	0-0	20.0	+0.50
Mrket Rsn	1-5	0-1	0-0	0-1	1-3	0-0	20.0	0.00
Plumpton	1-6	0-2	0-0	0-2	1-2	0-0	16.7	0.00

WINNING HORSES

Horse	Races Run	1st	2nd	3rd	£
Walcot Lad	16	4	3	1	20774
Roddy The Vet	7	2	0	2	8348
Cappanrush	5	1	0	0	5096
Ultimate Limit	10	2	1	2	7904
Total winning prize-money					**£42122**
Favourites	**4-7**		**57.1%**		**2.41**

J M P EUSTACE

NEWMARKET, SUFFOLK

	No. of Hrs	Races Run	1st	2nd	3rd	Unpl	Per cent	£1 Level Stake
NH Flat	0	0	0	0	0	0	0.0	0.00
Hurdles	4	8	1	0	0	7	12.5	-5.00
Chases	0	0	0	0	0	0	0.0	0.00
Totals	**4**	**8**	**1**	**0**	**0**	**7**	**12.5**	**-5.00**
04-05	2	5	1	0	1	3	20.0	+16.00
03-04	2	7	0	1	1	5	0.0	-7.00

JOCKEYS

	W-R	Per cent	£1 Level Stake
Mark Bradburne	1-5	20.0	-2.00

COURSE RECORD

	Total W-R	Non-Hndcps Hurdles	Chases	Hndcps Hurdles	Chases	NH Flat	Per cent	£1 Level Stake
Mrket Rsn	1-1	1-1	0-0	0-0	0-0	0-0	100.0	+2.00

WINNING HORSES

Horse	Races Run	1st	2nd	3rd	£
Orcadian	2	1	0	0	3578
Total winning prize-money					**£3578**
Favourites	1-1		100.0%		2.00

P D EVANS

PANDY, ABERGAVENNY

	No. of Hrs	Races Run	1st	2nd	3rd	Unpl	Per cent	£1 Level Stake
NH Flat	3	9	2	1	1	5	22.2	+30.50
Hurdles	9	30	1	11	6	12	3.3	-25.00
Chases	0	0	0	0	0	0	0.0	0.00
Totals	11	39	3	12	1	17	7.7	+5.50
04-05	16	40	5	5	0	30	12.5	-2.75
03-04	15	37	3	4	8	22	8.1	+22.08

JOCKEYS

	W-R	Per cent	£1 Level Stake
Antony Evans	2-12	16.7	+27.50
Robert Thornton	1-9	11.1	-4.00

COURSE RECORD

	Total W-R	Non-Hndcps Hurdles	Chases	Hndcps Hurdles	Chases	NH Flat	Per cent	£1 Level Stake
Nton Abbot	1-3	1-2	0-0	0-0	0-0	0-1	33.3	+2.00
Uttoxeter	1-3	0-1	0-0	0-1	0-0	1-1	33.3	+2.50
Worcester	1-8	0-3	0-0	0-1	0-0	1-4	12.5	+26.00

WINNING HORSES

Horse	Races Run	1st	2nd	3rd	£
*Gold Guest	4	1	1	0	4796
Don And Gerry	12	1	6	2	2002
She's Humble	4	1	0	0	1713
Total winning prize-money					**£8511**
Favourites	0-3		0.0%		-3.00

H J EVANS

HONEYBOURNE, WORCS

	No. of Hrs	Races Run	1st	2nd	3rd	Unpl	Per cent	£1 Level Stake
NH Flat	1	1	0	0	0	1	0.0	-1.00
Hurdles	3	11	1	1	0	9	9.1	+30.00
Chases	1	1	0	0	0	1	0.0	-1.00
Totals	3	13	1	1	0	11	7.7	+28.00
04-05	3	4	0	0	0	4	0.0	-4.00
03-04	1	5	0	1	0	4	0.0	-5.00

JOCKEYS

	W-R	Per cent	£1 Level Stake
Vince Slattery	1-8	12.5	+33.00

COURSE RECORD

	Total W-R	Non-Hndcps Hurdles	Chases	Hndcps Hurdles	Chases	NH Flat	Per cent	£1 Level Stake
Mrket Rsn	1-2	0-0	0-0	1-2	0-0	0-0	50.0	+39.00

WINNING HORSES

Horse	Races Run	1st	2nd	3rd	£
General Smith	7	1	1	0	3444
Total winning prize-money					**£3444**
Favourites	0-0		0.0%		0.00

M J M EVANS

KIDDERMINSTER, WORCS

	No. of Hrs	Races Run	1st	2nd	3rd	Unpl	Per cent	£1 Level Stake
NH Flat	0	0	0	0	0	0	0.0	0.00
Hurdles	4	4	0	0	0	4	0.0	-4.00
Chases	7	24	2	2	2	18	8.3	-7.00
Totals	9	28	2	2	2	22	7.1	-11.00
04-05	8	27	1	3	5	18	3.7	-10.00
03-04	6	20	0	1	0	19	0.0	-20.00

JOCKEYS

	W-R	Per cent	£1 Level Stake
Richard Johnson	1-1	100.0	+10.00
Ollie McPhail	1-4	25.0	+2.00

COURSE RECORD

	Total W-R	Non-Hndcps Hurdles	Chases	Hndcps Hurdles	Chases	NH Flat	Per cent	£1 Level Stake
Chepstow	2-7	0-0	0-1	0-0	2-6	0-0	28.6	+10.00

WINNING HORSES

Horse	Races Run	1st	2nd	3rd	£
*Fantasmic	3	1	0	1	4400
Advance East	4	1	0	1	3253
Total winning prize-money					**£7653**
Favourites	0-0		0.0%		0.00

MRS N S EVANS

PANDY, GWENT

	No. of Hrs	Races Run	1st	2nd	3rd	Unpl	Per cent	£1 Level Stake
NH Flat	6	15	0	1	2	12	0.0	-15.00

							Per	£1 Level
Hurdles	11	25	1	2	0	22	4.0	-18.00
Chases	4	10	0	1	1	8	0.0	-10.00
Totals	16	50	1	4	3	42	2.0	-43.00
04-05	11	23	0	0	1	22	0.0	-23.00
03-04	14	28	2	1	0	25	7.1	+46.00

JOCKEYS

	W-R	Per cent	£1 Level Stake
Jodie Mogford	1-43	2.3	-36.00

COURSE RECORD

	Total W-R	Non-Hndcps Hurdles	Chases	Hndcps Hurdles	Chases	NH Flat	Per cent	£1 Level Stake
Wetherby	1-1	0-0	0-0	1-1	0-0	0-0	100.0	+6.00

WINNING HORSES

Horse	Races Run	1st	2nd	3rd	£
The Pecker Dunn	7	1	0	0	2302
Total winning prize-money					**£2302**
Favourites	0-0		0.0%		0.00

J P L EWART

CRAIGCLEUCH, DUMFRIES & G'WAY

	No. of Hrs	Races Run	1st	2nd	3rd	Unpl	Per cent	£1 Level Stake
NH Flat	3	4	0	0	0	4	0.0	-4.00
Hurdles	6	14	1	3	2	8	7.1	+27.00
Chases	1	5	0	0	1	4	0.0	-5.00
Totals	8	23	1	3	3	16	4.3	+18.00
04-05	4	14	1	1	1	11	7.1	+12.00

JOCKEYS

	W-R	Per cent	£1 Level Stake
Gary Berridge	1-17	5.9	+24.00

COURSE RECORD

	Total W-R	Non-Hndcps Hurdles	Chases	Hndcps Hurdles	Chases	NH Flat	Per cent	£1 Level Stake
Carlisle	1-3	1-3	0-0	0-0	0-0	0-0	33.3	+38.00

WINNING HORSES

Horse	Races Run	1st	2nd	3rd	£
Numero Un De Solzen	3	1	1	1	3832
Total winning prize-money					**£3832**
Favourites	0-2		0.0%		-2.00

R A FAHEY

MUSLEY BANK, N YORKS

	No. of Hrs	Races Run	1st	2nd	3rd	Unpl	Per cent	£1 Level Stake
NH Flat	4	10	0	1	2	7	0.0	-10.00
Hurdles	16	40	4	7	8	21	10.0	-24.50
Chases	3	13	1	2	2	8	7.7	-9.25
Totals	20	63	5	10	12	36	7.9	-43.75
04-05	39	124	10	14	16	84	8.1	-68.59
03-04	30	102	15	16	10	61	14.7	-8.70

JOCKEYS

	W-R	Per cent	£1 Level Stake
G Lee	2-2	100.0	+4.50
Padge Whelan	2-26	7.7	-17.00
A P McCoy	1-3	33.3	+0.75

COURSE RECORD

	Total W-R	Non-Hndcps Hurdles	Chases	Hndcps Hurdles	Chases	NH Flat	Per cent	£1 Level Stake
Musselbgh	2-6	0-1	0-0	2-4	0-0	0-1	33.3	+1.50
Uttoxeter	1-1	0-0	0-0	0-0	1-1	0-0	100.0	+2.75
Worcester	1-3	1-1	0-0	0-1	0-1	0-0	33.3	+0.50
Mrket Rsn	1-5	0-2	0-0	1-3	0-0	0-0	20.0	-0.50

WINNING HORSES

Horse	Races Run	1st	2nd	3rd	£
Ball O Malt	7	1	1	3	8044
*Saif Sareea	7	2	4	0	14196
Beseiged	3	1	0	2	4836
Classical Ben	1	1	0	0	3400
Total winning prize-money					**£30476**
Favourites	3-10		30.0%		0.25

C W FAIRHURST

MIDDLEHAM MOOR, N YORKS

	No. of Hrs	Races Run	1st	2nd	3rd	Unpl	Per cent	£1 Level Stake
NH Flat	3	7	2	0	1	4	28.6	+8.00
Hurdles	7	14	0	0	1	13	0.0	-14.00
Chases	0	0	0	0	0	0	0.0	0.00
Totals	8	21	2	0	2	17	9.5	-6.00
04-05	7	25	0	2	0	23	0.0	-25.00
03-04	9	29	3	0	1	25	10.3	-10.50

JOCKEYS

	W-R	Per cent	£1 Level Stake
Mick Fitzgerald	1-1	100.0	+4.00
Barry Keniry	1-7	14.3	+3.00

COURSE RECORD

	Total W-R	Non-Hndcps Hurdles	Chases	Hndcps Hurdles	Chases	NH Flat	Per cent	£1 Level Stake
Doncaster	1-1	0-0	0-0	0-0	0-0	1-1	100.0	+9.00
Cheltenham	1-2	0-0	0-0	0-0	0-0	1-2	50.0	+3.00

WINNING HORSES

Horse	Races Run	1st	2nd	3rd	£
Burnt Oak	4	2	0	1	11669
Total winning prize-money					**£11669**
Favourites	1-1		100.0%		4.00

J R FANSHAWE

NEWMARKET, SUFFOLK

	No. of Hrs	Races Run	1st	2nd	3rd	Unpl	Per cent	£1 Level Stake
NH Flat	0	0	0	0	0	0	0.0	0.00
Hurdles	7	15	4	1	1	9	26.7	+12.82
Chases	2	6	2	2	0	2	33.3	+0.80
Totals	8	21	6	3	1	11	28.6	+13.62
04-05	6	23	7	5	2	9	30.4	-1.06
03-04	3	5	1	1	0	3	20.0	+2.00

JOKEYS

	W-R	Per cent	£1 Level Stake
A P McCoy	5-12	41.7	-0.38
P J Brennan	1-3	33.3	+20.00

COURSE RECORD

	Total W-R	Non-Hndcps Hurdles	Chases	Hndcps Hurdles	Chases	NH Flat	Per cent	£1 Level Stake
Fakenham	3-3	3-3	0-0	0-0	0-0	0-0	100.0	+23.02
Folkestone	1-1	0-0	1-1	0-0	0-0	0-0	100.0	+0.30
Huntingdon	1-2	1-2	0-0	0-0	0-0	0-0	50.0	-0.20
Cheltenham	1-6	0-2	0-0	0-3	1-1	0-0	16.7	-0.50

WINNING HORSES

Horse	Races Run	1st	2nd	3rd	£
Reveillez	4	2	2	0	50170
Bayard	4	2	1	0	11359
Cruzspiel	2	2	0	0	9698
Total winning prize-money					**£71227**
Favourites	5-8		62.5%		3.62

R A FARRANT

BAMPTON, DEVON

	No. of Hrs	Races Run	1st	2nd	3rd	Unpl	Per cent	£1 Level Stake
NH Flat	2	5	0	0	0	5	0.0	-5.00

Hurdles	6	21	2	1	3	15	9.5	-7.00
Chases	0	0	0	0	0	0	0.0	0.00
Totals	7	26	2	1	3	20	7.7	-12.00

JOCKEYS

	W-R	Per cent	£1 Level Stake
Richard Johnson	1-3	33.3	+2.00
Tom Doyle	1-5	20.0	+4.00

COURSE RECORD

	Total W-R	Non-Hndcps Hurdles	Chases	Hndcps Hurdles	Chases	NH Flat	Per cent	£1 Level Stake
Worcester	1-2	0-1	0-0	1-1	0-0	0-0	50.0	+7.00
Taunton	1-5	1-4	0-0	0-1	0-0	0-0	20.0	0.00

WINNING HORSES

Horse	Races Run	1st	2nd	3rd	£
All Square	3	1	0	1	2928
Urban Dream	9	1	1	1	2309
Total winning prize-money					**£5237**
Favourites	0-0		0.0%		0.00

LUCINDA FEATHERSTONE

NEWMARKET, SUFFOLK

	No. of Hrs	Races Run	1st	2nd	3rd	Unpl	Per cent	£1 Level Stake
NH Flat	4	4	0	0	0	4	0.0	-4.00
Hurdles	13	29	2	2	0	25	6.9	-16.00
Chases	4	9	0	0	3	6	0.0	-9.00
Totals	14	42	2	2	3	35	4.8	-29.00
04-05	9	39	2	2	5	30	5.1	-19.50
03-04	5	22	1	1	1	19	4.5	-9.00

JOCKEYS

	W-R	Per cent	£1 Level Stake
Paddy Merrigan	1-1	100.0	+4.00
John McNamara	1-12	8.3	-4.00

COURSE RECORD

	Total W-R	Non-Hndcps Hurdles	Chases	Hndcps Hurdles	Chases	NH Flat	Per cent	£1 Level Stake
Fontwell	2-5	0-1	0-0	2-3	0-1	0-0	40.0	+8.00

WINNING HORSES

Horse	Races Run	1st	2nd	3rd	£
Roman Candle	6	2	1	0	6018
Total winning prize-money					**£6018**
Favourites	0-0		0.0%		0.00

D B FEEK

BRIGHTLING, E SUSSEX

	No. of Hrs	Races Run	1st	2nd	3rd	Unpl	Per cent	£1 Level Stake
NH Flat	4	4	0	0	0	4	0.0	-4.00
Hurdles	14	37	0	5	1	31	0.0	-37.00
Chases	6	20	1	1	4	14	5.0	-10.00
Totals	18	61	1	6	5	49	1.6	-51.00
04-05	17	62	8	8	11	35	12.9	-26.84
03-04	10	42	1	3	9	29	2.4	-35.50

JOCKEYS

	W-R	Per cent	£1 Level Stake
Robert Lucey-Butler	1-11	9.1	-1.00

COURSE RECORD

	Total W-R	Non-Hndcps Hurdles	Chases	Hndcps Hurdles	Chases	NH Flat	Per cent	£1 Level Stake
Taunton	1-2	0-0	0-0	0-0	1-2	0-0	50.0	+8.00

WINNING HORSES

Horse	Races Run	1st	2nd	3rd	£
*Twentytwosilver	1	1	0	0	3769
Total winning prize-money					£3769
Favourites	0-2		0.0%		-2.00

MISS J FEILDEN

EXNING, SUFFOLK

	No. of Hrs	Races Run	1st	2nd	3rd	Unpl	Per cent	£1 Level Stake
NH Flat	0	0	0	0	0	0	0.0	0.00
Hurdles	7	22	3	2	2	15	13.6	+6.50
Chases	0	0	0	0	0	0	0.0	0.00
Totals	7	22	3	2	2	15	13.6	+6.50
04-05	3	5	0	0	1	4	0.0	-5.00
03-04	10	30	0	0	3	27	0.0	-30.00

JOCKEYS

	W-R	Per cent	£1 Level Stake
Mr Matthew Smith	3-14	21.4	+14.50

COURSE RECORD

	Total W-R	Non-Hndcps Hurdles	Chases	Hndcps Hurdles	Chases	NH Flat	Per cent	£1 Level Stake
Mrket Rsn	1-2	1-1	0-0	0-1	0-0	0-0	50.0	+9.00
Huntingdon	1-4	1-2	0-0	0-2	0-0	0-0	25.0	+8.00
Fakenham	1-5	1-4	0-0	0-1	0-0	0-0	20.0	+0.50

WINNING HORSES

Horse	Races Run	1st	2nd	3rd	£
Three Ships	3	2	1	0	6657
Dance World	5	1	1	0	2928
Total winning prize-money					£9585
Favourites	0-0		0.0%		0.00

R F FISHER

ULVERSTON, CUMBRIA

	No. of Hrs	Races Run	1st	2nd	3rd	Unpl	Per cent	£1 Level Stake
NH Flat	2	4	0	0	0	4	0.0	-4.00
Hurdles	12	49	4	7	4	34	8.2	-14.17
Chases	2	24	4	2	4	14	16.7	+4.13
Totals	14	77	8	9	8	52	10.4	-14.04
04-05	8	30	2	1	6	21	6.7	+2.00
03-04	10	36	2	1	2	31	5.6	-22.00

JOCKEYS

	W-R	Per cent	£1 Level Stake
Keith Mercer	4-39	10.3	-1.17
Richard McGrath	2-7	28.6	+10.00
G Lee	1-3	33.3	-0.38
Paddy Aspell	1-7	14.3	-1.50

COURSE RECORD

	Total W-R	Non-Hndcps Hurdles	Chases	Hndcps Hurdles	Chases	NH Flat	Per cent	£1 Level Stake
Mrket Rsn	2-7	1-2	0-0	1-2	0-3	0-0	28.6	+10.33
Newcastle	2-12	0-5	0-0	0-2	2-5	0-0	16.7	-4.38
Catterick	1-3	1-2	0-0	0-1	0-0	0-0	33.3	+9.00
Carlisle	1-4	0-0	0-0	0-0	1-4	0-0	25.0	+9.00
Uttoxeter	1-7	1-6	0-0	0-0	0-1	0-0	14.3	-1.50
Cartmel	1-9	0-6	0-0	0-1	1-2	0-0	11.1	-1.50

WINNING HORSES

Horse	Races Run	1st	2nd	3rd	£
Mikasa	16	3	1	2	7497
Lazy But Lively	14	1	1	2	3850
Rare Coincidence	7	3	2	0	8851
No Commission	5	1	0	0	2741
Total winning prize-money					£22939
Favourites	2-5		40.0%		1.96

MISS J FISHER

KIRKNEWTON, LOTHIAN

	No. of Hrs	Races Run	1st	2nd	3rd	Unpl	Per cent	£1 Level Stake
NH Flat	0	0	0	0	0	0	0.0	0.00

	No. of Hrs	Races Run	1st	2nd	3rd	Unpl	Per cent	£1 Level Stake
Hurdles	0	0	0	0	0	0	0.0	0.00
Chases	2	5	1	0	1	3	20.0	0.00
Totals	2	5	1	0	1	3	20.0	0.00
04-05	2	8	1	2	1	4	12.5	+7.00
03-04	2	5	0	0	0	5	0.0	-5.00

JOCKEYS

	W-R	Per cent	£1 Level Stake
Mr W L Morgan	1-3	33.3	+2.00

COURSE RECORD

	Total W-R	Non-Hndcps Hurdles	Chases	Hndcps Hurdles	Chases	NH Flat	Per cent	£1 Level Stake
Sedgefield	1-1	0-0	1-1	0-0	0-0	0-0	100.0	+4.00

WINNING HORSES

Horse	Races Run	1st	2nd	3rd	£
Swiftway	2	1	0	0	1526
Total winning prize-money					**£1526**
Favourites	0-2		0.0%		-2.00

T J FITZGERALD

MALTON, N YORKS

	No. of Hrs	Races Run	1st	2nd	3rd	Unpl	Per cent	£1 Level Stake
NH Flat	7	12	0	1	1	10	0.0	-12.00
Hurdles	6	16	1	2	1	12	6.3	-13.25
Chases	2	5	0	1	1	3	0.0	-5.00
Totals	13	33	1	4	3	25	3.0	-30.25
04-05	11	31	3	2	3	23	9.7	-1.50
03-04	15	44	0	5	2	37	0.0	-44.00

JOCKEYS

	W-R	Per cent	£1 Level Stake
G Lee	1-4	25.0	-1.25

COURSE RECORD

	Total W-R	Non-Hndcps Hurdles	Chases	Hndcps Hurdles	Chases	NH Flat	Per cent	£1 Level Stake
Warwick	1-1	0-0	0-0	1-1	0-0	0-0	100.0	+1.75

WINNING HORSES

Horse	Races Run	1st	2nd	3rd	£
Vicentio	5	1	1	0	3581
Total winning prize-money					**£3581**
Favourites	1-4		25.0%		-1.25

J L FLINT

KENFIG HILL, BRIDGEND

	No. of Hrs	Races Run	1st	2nd	3rd	Unpl	Per cent	£1 Level Stake
NH Flat	0	0	0	0	0	0	0.0	0.00
Hurdles	4	17	4	1	1	11	23.5	+39.00
Chases	0	0	0	0	0	0	0.0	0.00
Totals	4	17	4	1	1	11	23.5	+39.00
04-05	3	25	3	4	6	12	12.0	-9.09
03-04	3	12	0	1	1	10	0.0	-12.00

JOCKEYS

	W-R	Per cent	£1 Level Stake
Christian Williams	2-4	50.0	+32.63
Tom Scudamore	1-1	100.0	+1.38
Robert Stephens	1-5	20.0	+12.00

COURSE RECORD

	Total W-R	Non-Hndcps Hurdles	Chases	Hndcps Hurdles	Chases	NH Flat	Per cent	£1 Level Stake
Bangor	2-2	2-2	0-0	0-0	0-0	0-0	100.0	+34.63
Hereford	2-2	2-2	0-0	0-0	0-0	0-0	100.0	+17.38

WINNING HORSES

Horse	Races Run	1st	2nd	3rd	£
Fair Along	3	2	0	0	6440
Dancinginthestreet	8	2	1	0	4399
Total winning prize-money					**£10847**
Favourites	2-4		50.0%		1.00

S FLOOK

LEOMINSTER, HEREFORDSHIRE

	No. of Hrs	Races Run	1st	2nd	3rd	Unpl	Per cent	£1 Level Stake
NH Flat	0	0	0	0	0	0	0.0	0.00
Hurdles	0	0	0	0	0	0	0.0	0.00
Chases	10	37	4	2	5	26	10.8	+8.33
Totals	10	37	4	2	5	26	10.8	+8.33
04-05	7	28	3	4	4	17	10.7	-17.25
03-04	9	29	4	4	2	19	13.8	-8.93

JOCKEYS

	W-R	Per cent	£1 Level Stake
Mr D Mansell	3-4	75.0	+37.00
Mr A Wintle	1-15	6.7	-10.67

COURSE RECORD

	Total W-R	Non-Hndcps Hurdles	Chases	Hndcps Hurdles	Chases	NH Flat	Per cent	£1 Level Stake
Exeter	2-2	0-0	2-2	0-0	0-0	0-0	100.0	+24.00

Hereford	1-3	0-0	1-3	0-0	0-0	0-0	33.3	+1.33
Ludlow	1-7	0-0	1-7	0-0	0-0	0-0	14.3	+8.00

WINNING HORSES

Horse	Races Run	1st	2nd	3rd	£
Enitsag	6	2	1	1	5038
Beauchamp Oracle	7	1	1	2	2498
*Abbey Days	2	1	0	0	1249
Total winning prize-money					£8785
Favourites	0-1		0.0%		-1.00

R FORD

COTEBROOK, CHESHIRE

	No. of Hrs	Races Run	1st	2nd	3rd	Unpl	Per cent	£1 Level Stake
NH Flat	5	8	0	0	0	8	0.0	-8.00
Hurdles	14	39	7	5	9	18	17.9	-0.82
Chases	15	68	9	13	5	41	13.2	-23.00
Totals	30	115	16	18	14	67	13.9	-31.82
04-05	23	77	9	11	8	49	11.7	-8.25
03-04	32	96	10	4	13	69	10.4	-28.52

BY MONTH

NH Flat	W-R	Per cent	£1 Level Stake	Hurdles	W-R	Per cent	£1 Level Stake
May	0-0	0.0	0.00	May	0-3	0.0	-3.00
June	0-0	0.0	0.00	June	3-8	37.5	+4.85
July	0-0	0.0	0.00	July	0-4	0.0	-4.00
August	0-0	0.0	0.00	August	0-4	0.0	-4.00
September	0-1	0.0	-1.00	September	0-0	0.0	0.00
October	0-2	0.0	-2.00	October	0-2	0.0	-2.00
November	0-1	0.0	-1.00	November	1-4	25.0	-2.17
December	0-0	0.0	0.00	December	0-3	0.0	-3.00
January	0-0	0.0	0.00	January	0-1	0.0	-1.00
February	0-1	0.0	-1.00	February	0-2	0.0	-2.00
March	0-1	0.0	-1.00	March	2-5	40.0	+7.50
April	0-2	0.0	-2.00	April	1-3	33.3	+8.00

Chases	W-R	Per cent	£1 Level Stake	Totals	W-R	Per cent	£1 Level Stake
May	0-5	0.0	-5.00	May	0-8	0.0	-8.00
June	0-4	0.0	-4.00	June	3-12	25.0	+0.85
July	2-7	28.6	+12.50	July	2-11	18.2	+8.50
August	2-9	22.2	+1.00	August	2-13	15.4	-3.00
September	0-3	0.0	-3.00	September	0-4	0.0	-4.00
October	3-6	50.0	+4.50	October	3-10	30.0	+0.50
November	1-9	11.1	-7.00	November	2-14	14.3	-10.17
December	0-8	0.0	-8.00	December	0-11	0.0	-11.00
January	0-5	0.0	-5.00	January	0-6	0.0	-6.00
February	1-5	20.0	-2.00	February	1-8	12.5	-5.00
March	0-4	0.0	-4.00	March	2-10	20.0	+2.50
April	0-3	0.0	-3.00	April	1-8	12.5	+3.00

DISTANCE

Hurdles	W-R	Per cent	£1 Level Stake	Chases	W-R	Per cent	£1 Level Stake
2m-2m3f	3-19	15.8	+0.83	2m-2m3f	3-28	10.7	-18.00
2m4f-2m7f	1-8	12.5	-1.00	2m4f-2m7f	3-20	15.0	+5.50
3m+	3-12	25.0	-0.65	3m+	3-20	15.0	-10.50

TYPE OF RACE

Non-Handicaps	W-R	Per cent	£1 Level Stake	Handicaps	W-R	Per cent	£1 Level Stake
Nov Hrdls	0-7	0.0	-7.00	Nov Hrdls	1-4	25.0	-0.25
Hrdls	0-8	0.0	-8.00	Hrdls	5-12	41.7	+15.43
Nov Chs	2-8	25.0	-3.00	Nov Chs	3-21	14.3	-1.00
Chases	0-0	0.0	0.00	Chases	4-39	10.3	-19.00
Sell/Claim	0-3	0.0	-3.00	Sell/Claim	1-6	16.7	+1.00

RACE CLASS

	W-R	Per cent	£1 Level Stake
Class 1	0-4	0.0	-4.00
Class 2	0-2	0.0	-2.00
Class 3	1-15	6.7	-11.00
Class 4	14-73	19.2	-0.82
Class 5	1-12	8.3	-5.00
Class 6	0-9	0.0	-9.00

FIRST TIME OUT

	W-R	Per cent	£1 Level Stake
Bumpers	0-5	0.0	-5.00
Hurdles	1-13	7.7	-9.25
Chases	0-12	0.0	-12.00
Totals	1-30	3.3	-26.25

JOCKEYS

	W-R	Per cent	£1 Level Stake
G Lee	5-20	25.0	+4.00
Larry McGrath	2-2	100.0	+3.85
Tony Dobbin	2-8	25.0	-2.00
Miss Caroline Hurley	2-8	25.0	+0.83
Richard McGrath	2-13	15.4	-0.50
P J Brennan	2-17	11.8	-2.00
Tom Greenway	1-1	100.0	+10.00

COURSE RECORD

	Total W-R	Non-Hndcps Hurdles	Chases	Hndcps Hurdles	Chases	NH Flat	Per cent	£1 Level Stake
Kelso	2-4	0-1	1-1	0-0	1-2	0-0	50.0	+2.00
Southwell	2-4	0-0	0-0	0-0	2-4	0-0	50.0	+9.50
Huntingdon	2-6	0-1	0-0	2-2	0-3	0-0	33.3	+6.50
Uttoxeter	2-16	0-2	0-1	1-4	1-8	0-1	12.5	-1.90
Warwick	1-1	0-0	1-1	0-0	0-0	0-0	100.0	+2.00
Carlisle	1-2	0-0	0-0	0-0	1-2	0-0	50.0	+2.00
Mrket Rsn	1-4	0-0	0-1	1-1	0-2	0-0	25.0	-2.17
Cartmel	1-6	0-0	0-0	0-2	1-4	0-0	16.7	-2.00
Hexham	1-6	0-0	0-1	1-2	0-2	0-1	16.7	+5.00
Aintree	1-8	0-2	0-1	0-0	1-4	0-1	12.5	-5.50
Perth	1-10	0-2	0-1	1-3	0-4	0-0	10.0	-3.00
Worcester	1-10	0-2	0-0	1-3	0-4	0-1	10.0	-6.25

WINNING HORSES

Horse	Races Run	1st	2nd	3rd	£
Chabrimal Minster	10	2	3	1	10197
Croc An Oir	7	3	2	1	11279
Parisienne Gale	13	6	1	3	23516
Optimistic Harry	3	1	0	0	4508
Good Heart	6	2	1	0	8444
Ocean Tide	5	1	2	1	3253
*Oulton Broad	3	1	0	1	2741
Total winning prize-money					£63938
Favourites	8-24		33.3%		0.68

D M FORSTER

REDWORTH, CO DURHAM

	No. of Hrs	Races Run	1st	2nd	3rd	Unpl	Per cent	£1 Level Stake
NH Flat	1	1	0	0	1	0	0.0	-1.00
Hurdles	1	1	0	0	0	1	0.0	-1.00
Chases	3	12	2	2	1	7	16.7	+9.50
Totals	5	14	2	2	2	8	14.3	+7.50
04-05	4	17	3	3	3	8	17.6	+13.75
03-04	3	17	1	2	1	13	5.9	-7.00

JOCKEYS

	W-R	Per cent	£1 Level Stake
Richard McGrath	2-8	25.0	+13.50

COURSE RECORD

	Total W-R	Non-Hndcps Hurdles	Chases	Hndcps Hurdles	Chases	NH Flat	Per cent	£1 Level Stake
Kelso	1-1	0-0	0-0	0-0	1-1	0-0	100.0	+5.50
Haydock	1-2	0-0	0-0	0-0	1-1	0-1	50.0	+13.00

WINNING HORSES

Horse	Races Run	1st	2nd	3rd	£
Ossmoses	5	2	1	1	82496
Total winning prize-money					£82496
Favourites	0-2		0.0%		-2.00

MISS S E FORSTER

KIRK YETHOLM, BORDERS

	No. of Hrs	Races Run	1st	2nd	3rd	Unpl	Per cent	£1 Level Stake
NH Flat	4	7	0	0	0	7	0.0	-7.00
Hurdles	18	77	2	4	9	62	2.6	-61.00
Chases	10	44	6	10	4	24	13.6	-7.00
Totals	25	128	8	14	13	93	6.3	-75.00
04-05	29	118	6	8	14	90	5.1	-8.50
03-04	21	104	6	12	16	70	5.8	-33.50

JOCKEYS

	W-R	Per cent	£1 Level Stake
Mr C Storey	3-67	4.5	-49.50
Neil Mulholland	2-9	22.2	+4.50
Brian Harding	1-3	33.3	+3.00
Dougie Costello	1-10	10.0	-1.00
Tom Messenger	1-14	7.1	-7.00

COURSE RECORD

	Total W-R	Non-Hndcps Hurdles	Chases	Hndcps Hurdles	Chases	NH Flat	Per cent	£1 Level Stake
Ayr	3-13	0-1	0-2	1-5	2-4	0-1	23.1	+9.50
Sedgefield	2-16	0-1	0-3	1-9	1-1	0-2	12.5	-3.50
Cartmel	1-7	0-3	0-0	0-3	1-1	0-0	14.3	-1.50
Catterick	1-7	0-0	1-1	0-4	0-2	0-0	14.3	-0.50
Kelso	1-28	0-8	0-6	0-7	1-6	0-1	3.6	-22.00

WINNING HORSES

Horse	Races Run	1st	2nd	3rd	£
Skenfrith	8	2	0	0	11711
Persian Point	9	1	1	2	6506
*Primitive Way	4	1	2	2	4875
Carnacrack	3	1	2	0	4485
Uneven Line	12	1	2	2	3578
*Prince Adjal	7	1	2	1	2398
Star Trooper	16	1	1	2	2193
Total winning prize-money					£35746
Favourites	1-3		33.3%		2.50

C ST V FOX

GILLINGHAM, DORSET

	No. of Hrs	Races Run	1st	2nd	3rd	Unpl	Per cent	£1 Level Stake
NH Flat	0	0	0	0	0	0	0.0	0.00
Hurdles	0	0	0	0	0	0	0.0	0.00
Chases	1	6	4	0	0	2	66.7	+6.78
Totals	1	6	4	0	0	2	66.7	+6.78
04-05	1	5	2	0	1	2	40.0	+4.25
03-04	1	6	3	0	0	3	50.0	+4.94

JOCKEYS

	W-R	Per cent	£1 Level Stake
Miss C Tizzard	4-6	66.7	+6.78

COURSE RECORD

	Total W-R	Non-Hndcps Hurdles	Chases	Hndcps Hurdles	Chases	NH Flat	Per cent	£1 Level Stake
Ludlow	2-3	0-0	2-3	0-0	0-0	0-0	66.7	+1.78
Hereford	1-1	0-0	1-1	0-0	0-0	0-0	100.0	+2.00
Wincanton	1-1	0-0	1-1	0-0	0-0	0-0	100.0	+4.00

WINNING HORSES

Horse	Races Run	1st	2nd	3rd	£
Red Brook Lad	6	4	0	0	9945
Total winning prize-money					**£9945**
Favourites	1-3		33.3%		-1.09

M E D FRANCIS

LAMBOURN, BERKS

	No. of Hrs	Races Run	1st	2nd	3rd	Unpl	Per cent	£1 Level Stake
NH Flat	1	2	0	1	0	1	0.0	-2.00
Hurdles	2	7	1	0	1	5	14.3	+14.00
Chases	0	0	0	0	0	0	0.0	0.00
Totals	2	9	1	1	1	6	11.1	+12.00
04-05	2	6	1	0	0	5	16.7	+20.00
03-04	3	10	0	0	0	10	0.0	-10.00

JOCKEYS

	W-R	Per cent	£1 Level Stake
Brian Crowley	1-6	16.7	+15.00

COURSE RECORD

	Total W-R	Non-Hndcps Hurdles	Chases	Hndcps Hurdles	Chases	NH Flat	Per cent	£1 Level Stake
Doncaster	1-2	0-0	0-0	1-2	0-0	0-0	50.0	+19.00

WINNING HORSES

Horse	Races Run	1st	2nd	3rd	£
Fard Du Moulin Mas	6	1	0	1	5693
Total winning prize-money					**£5693**
Favourites	0-0		0.0%		0.00

J D FROST

SCORRITON, DEVON

	No. of Hrs	Races Run	1st	2nd	3rd	Unpl	Per cent	£1 Level Stake
NH Flat	7	9	0	1	1	7	0.0	-9.00
Hurdles	35	123	16	12	7	88	13.0	+0.61
Chases	13	41	5	3	3	30	12.2	+13.88
Totals	45	173	21	16	11	125	12.1	+5.49
04-05	55	228	14	32	18	164	6.1	-104.27
03-04	50	183	13	19	23	128	7.1	-99.46

BY MONTH

NH Flat	W-R	Per cent	£1 Level Stake	Hurdles	W-R	Per cent	£1 Level Stake
May	0-0	0.0	0.00	May	6-16	37.5	+20.45
June	0-0	0.0	0.00	June	1-9	11.1	-4.00
July	0-1	0.0	-1.00	July	0-7	0.0	-7.00
August	0-0	0.0	0.00	August	1-14	7.1	-8.50
September	0-0	0.0	0.00	September	0-0	0.0	0.00
October	0-1	0.0	-1.00	October	2-20	10.0	+27.00
November	0-2	0.0	-2.00	November	3-15	20.0	+3.25
December	0-0	0.0	0.00	December	0-14	0.0	-14.00
January	0-0	0.0	0.00	January	0-7	0.0	-7.00
February	0-0	0.0	0.00	February	0-8	0.0	-8.00
March	0-2	0.0	-2.00	March	1-8	12.5	-2.00
April	0-3	0.0	-3.00	April	2-5	40.0	+0.41

Chases	W-R	Per cent	£1 Level Stake	Totals	W-R	Per cent	£1 Level Stake
May	0-5	0.0	-5.00	May	6-21	28.6	+15.45
June	0-2	0.0	-2.00	June	1-11	9.1	-6.00
July	0-2	0.0	-2.00	July	0-10	0.0	-10.00
August	1-2	50.0	+0.38	August	2-16	12.5	-8.12
September	0-0	0.0	0.00	September	0-0	0.0	0.00
October	1-5	20.0	-2.00	October	3-26	11.5	+24.00
November	1-7	14.3	+1.50	November	4-24	16.7	+2.75
December	0-8	0.0	-8.00	December	0-22	0.0	-22.00
January	0-1	0.0	-1.00	January	0-8	0.0	-8.00
February	0-3	0.0	-3.00	February	0-11	0.0	-11.00
March	0-1	0.0	-1.00	March	1-11	9.1	-5.00
April	2-5	40.0	+36.00	April	4-13	30.8	+33.41

DISTANCE

Hurdles	W-R	Per cent	£1 Level Stake	Chases	W-R	Per cent	£1 Level Stake
2m-2m3f	13-91	14.3	-14.90	2m-2m3f	1-20	5.0	-13.00
2m4f-2m7f	1-22	4.5	+12.00	2m4f-2m7f	3-14	21.4	+30.88
3m+	2-10	20.0	+3.50	3m+	1-7	14.3	-4.00

TYPE OF RACE

Non-Handicaps	W-R	Per cent	£1 Level Stake	Handicaps	W-R	Per cent	£1 Level Stake
Nov Hrdls	6-27	22.2	+28.07	Nov Hrdls	0-13	0.0	-13.00
Hrdls	0-5	0.0	-5.00	Hrdls	4-44	9.1	-7.13
Nov Chs	1-10	10.0	-3.00	Nov Chs	1-9	11.1	-6.63
Chases	0-1	0.0	-1.00	Chases	3-21	14.3	+24.50
Sell/Claim	9-29	31.0	+16.66	Sell/Claim	0-9	0.0	-9.00

RACE CLASS

	W-R	Per cent	£1 Level Stake
Class 1	0-2	0.0	-2.00
Class 2	0-2	0.0	-2.00
Class 3	4-46	8.7	+4.38
Class 4	10-75	13.3	+14.70
Class 5	7-39	17.9	-0.59
Class 6	0-9	0.0	-9.00

FIRST TIME OUT

	W-R	Per cent	£1 Level Stake
Bumpers	0-7	0.0	-7.00
Hurdles	6-28	21.4	+43.07
Chases	0-10	0.0	-10.00
Totals	6-45	13.3	+26.07

JOCKEYS

	W-R	Per cent	£1 Level Stake
Chris Honour	8-87	9.2	-55.39
Miss S Gaisford	6-18	33.3	+65.88
Richard Johnson	4-11	36.4	+5.50

Christian Williams	2-4			50.0			+38.50	
Shane Walsh	1-19			5.3			-15.00	

COURSE RECORD

	Total W-R	Non-Hndcps Hurdles	Chases	Hndcps Hurdles	Chases	NH Flat	Per cent	£1 Level Stake
Nton Abbot 9-45	5-16	0-2	3-20	1-6	0-1	20.0	+1.73	
Exeter	5-42	2-13	1-5	0-16	2-5	0-3	11.9	+16.50
Stratford	2-8	2-5	0-0	0-1	0-7	0-0	25.0	+10.00
Towcester	1-3	1-1	0-1	0-1	0-0	0-0	33.3	0.00
Fontwell	1-5	1-3	0-0	0-1	0-1	0-0	20.0	-1.75
Ludlow	1-7	0-3	0-0	0-3	1-1	0-0	14.3	+27.00
Hereford	1-9	0-2	0-2	1-3	0-1	0-1	11.1	0.00
Chepstow	1-15	1-3	0-1	0-4	0-6	0-1	6.7	-9.00

WINNING HORSES

Horse	Races Run	1st	2nd	3rd	£
Saffron Sun	6	3	0	0	21855
Baloo	8	1	0	2	6817
Miss Lehman	6	3	0	0	10898
Fire Ranger	5	2	3	0	8147
Latin Queen	10	2	2	1	7232
Frosty Jak	4	1	0	0	3510
Temper Lad	5	2	1	0	6880
Sarena Special	2	1	1	0	3003
Longstone Lady	4	1	0	0	2741
Brochrua	11	3	0	2	6947
Critical Stage	7	1	2	0	2535
Beyondtherealm	2	1	0	0	2145
Total winning prize-money					**£82710**
Favourites	18-24		75.0%		14.98

J GALLAGHER

CHASTLETON, OXON

	No. of Hrs	Races Run	1st	2nd	3rd	Unpl	Per cent	£1 Level Stake
NH Flat	3	6	0	0	0	6	0.0	-6.00
Hurdles	8	31	3	4	0	24	9.7	-4.50
Chases	1	2	0	0	0	2	0.0	-2.00
Totals	11	39	3	4	0	32	7.7	-12.50
04-05	*10*	*34*	*2*	*3*	*2*	*27*	*5.9*	*-17.75*
03-04	*16*	*40*	*3*	*2*	*4*	*31*	*7.5*	*-22.50*

JOCKEYS

	W-R	Per cent	£1 Level Stake
Barry Fenton	2-2	100.0	+17.00
Richard Johnson	1-3	33.3	+4.50

COURSE RECORD

	Total W-R	Non-Hndcps Hurdles	Chases	Hndcps Hurdles	Chases	NH Flat	Per cent	£1 Level Stake
Leicester	1-2	0-0	0-0	1-2	0-0	0-0	50.0	+7.00
Huntingdon	1-5	0-2	0-0	1-1	0-1	0-1	20.0	+2.50

Uttoxeter	1-8	0-1	0-1	1-4	0-0	0-2	12.5	+2.00

WINNING HORSES

Horse	Races Run	1st	2nd	3rd	£
Killing Me Softly	9	2	1	0	11255
Make My Hay	5	1	2	0	3083
Total winning prize-money					**£14338**
Favourites	0-0		0.0%		0.00

D R GANDOLFO

WANTAGE, OXON

	No. of Hrs	Races Run	1st	2nd	3rd	Unpl	Per cent	£1 Level Stake
NH Flat	4	5	0	0	1	4	0.0	-5.00
Hurdles	18	50	3	5	1	41	6.0	-4.00
Chases	10	36	4	6	7	19	11.1	-7.50
Totals	26	91	7	11	9	64	7.7	-16.50
04-05	*23*	*78*	*4*	*8*	*8*	*58*	*5.1*	*-21.00*
03-04	*26*	*90*	*6*	*10*	*8*	*66*	*6.7*	*-64.31*

JOCKEYS

	W-R	Per cent	£1 Level Stake
Tom Doyle	6-45	13.3	-4.50
Sam Curling	1-13	7.7	+21.00

COURSE RECORD

	Total W-R	Non-Hndcps Hurdles	Chases	Hndcps Hurdles	Chases	NH Flat	Per cent	£1 Level Stake
Huntingdon 2-10	0-1	0-1	1-4	1-3	0-1	20.0	+37.00	
Lingfield	1-1	1-1	0-0	0-0	0-0	0-0	100.0	+3.50
Stratford	1-2	0-0	0-0	0-0	1-2	0-0	50.0	+2.00
Fakenham	1-3	0-1	0-0	0-1	1-1	0-0	33.3	+2.50
Ludlow	1-3	0-0	1-1	0-0	0-2	0-0	33.3	+3.00
Worcester	1-7	1-1	0-0	0-1	0-4	0-1	14.3	+0.50

WINNING HORSES

Horse	Races Run	1st	2nd	3rd	£
Glengarra	5	2	1	0	14188
Fleurette	6	1	2	0	5127
Rooster's Reunion	6	1	0	2	3892
Take The Oath	8	1	1	2	3290
Candarli	4	1	1	0	3253
Percipient	6	1	1	2	3080
Total winning prize-money					**£32830**
Favourites	0-3		0.0%		-3.00

MRS S GARDNER

LONGDOWN, DEVON

	No. of Hrs	Races Run	1st	2nd	3rd	Unpl	Per cent	£1 Level Stake
NH Flat	4	7	0	0	0	7	0.0	-7.00

Hurdles	5	18	1	2	0	15	5.6	-5.00
Chases	1	1	0	0	0	1	0.0	-1.00
Totals	8	26	1	2	0	23	3.8	-13.00
04-05	4	27	4	5	5	13	14.8	-11.67
03-04	10	42	0	5	2	35	0.0	-42.00

JOCKEYS

	W-R	Per cent	£1 Level Stake
Miss L Gardner	1-21	4.8	-8.00

COURSE RECORD

	Total W-R	Non-Hndcps Hurdles Chases	Hndcps Hurdles Chases	NH Flat	Per cent	£1 Level Stake
Exeter	1-10	0-3 0-0	1-5 0-1	0-1	10.0	+3.00

WINNING HORSES

Horse	Races Run	1st	2nd	3rd	£
Bak To Bill	9	1	1	0	4554
Total winning prize-money					**£4554**
Favourites	0-0		0.0%		0.00

MRS ROSEMARY GASSON

BANBURY, OXON

	No. of Hrs	Races Run	1st	2nd	3rd	Unpl	Per cent	£1 Level Stake
NH Flat	0	0	0	0	0	0	0.0	0.00
Hurdles	0	0	0	0	0	0	0.0	0.00
Chases	3	8	1	1	2	4	12.5	+1.00
Totals	3	8	1	1	2	4	12.5	+1.00
04-05	2	11	1	0	3	7	9.1	-8.50
03-04	3	8	0	2	1	5	0.0	-8.00

JOCKEYS

	W-R	Per cent	£1 Level Stake
Mr Andrew Martin	1-4	25.0	+5.00

COURSE RECORD

	Total W-R	Non-Hndcps Hurdles Chases	Hndcps Hurdles Chases	NH Flat	Per cent	£1 Level Stake
Huntingdon	1-1	0-0 1-1	0-0 0-0	0-0	100.0	+8.00

WINNING HORSES

Horse	Races Run	1st	2nd	3rd	£
Viscount Bankes	6	1	1	1	1437
Total winning prize-money					**£1437**
Favourites	0-0		0.0%		0.00

J A GEAKE

KIMPTON, HANTS

	No. of Hrs	Races Run	1st	2nd	3rd	Unpl	Per cent	£1 Level Stake
NH Flat	6	8	0	0	0	8	0.0	-8.00
Hurdles	24	59	6	6	8	39	10.2	-32.41
Chases	11	41	3	3	5	30	7.3	-28.29
Totals	34	108	9	9	13	77	8.3	-68.70
04-05	22	70	6	6	8	50	8.6	-25.75

JOCKEYS

	W-R	Per cent	£1 Level Stake
Mark Bradburne	4-26	15.4	-10.02
A P McCoy	1-1	100.0	+0.61
Paul O'Neill	1-3	33.3	+1.33
Marcus Foley	1-4	25.0	-1.13
Simon Elliott	1-21	4.8	-15.50
Jimmy McCarthy	1-29	3.4	-20.00

COURSE RECORD

	Total W-R	Non-Hndcps Hurdles Chases	Hndcps Hurdles Chases	NH Flat	Per cent	£1 Level Stake
Worcester	2-4	1-1 0-0	1-2 0-1	0-0	50.0	+1.73
Taunton	1-2	0-1 0-0	0-0 1-1	0-0	50.0	+3.50
Uttoxeter	1-2	1-2 0-0	0-0 0-0	0-0	50.0	-0.39
Towcester	1-4	0-1 0-0	1-2 0-1	0-0	25.0	+2.50
Plumpton	1-6	0-2 1-1	0-1 0-1	0-1	16.7	-3.13
Sandown	1-8	0-1 0-0	0-1 1-6	0-1	12.5	-3.67
Exeter	1-10	1-3 0-2	0-2 0-2	0-1	10.0	-1.00
Wincanton	1-15	0-4 0-0	1-2 0-8	0-1	6.7	-11.25

WINNING HORSES

Horse	Races Run	1st	2nd	3rd	£
Penneyrose Bay	6	2	1	0	12764
Latimer's Place	7	1	0	2	6799
Black Hills	4	1	0	1	5927
Supreme Tadgh	8	1	1	1	4928
*Saddlers Cloth	6	1	0	0	3457
Absolut Power	8	2	4	2	6481
Breezer	9	1	0	3	2602
Total winning prize-money					**£42958**
Favourites	5-12		41.7%		4.72

T R GEORGE

SLAD, GLOUCS

	No. of Hrs	Races Run	1st	2nd	3rd	Unpl	Per cent	£1 Level Stake
NH Flat	10	15	2	3	2	8	13.3	-5.00
Hurdles	36	101	10	5	18	68	9.9	-22.84

Chases	42	145	22	23	13	87	15.2	-32.65
Totals	**67**	**261**	**34**	**31**	**33**	**163**	**13.0**	**-60.49**
04-05	67	275	47	44	30	154	17.1	+8.09
03-04	65	311	50	50	40	171	16.1	-72.85

	W-R	Per cent	£1 Level Stake
Class 3	10-81	12.3	-23.25
Class 4	19-123	15.4	-5.24
Class 5	3-20	15.0	-7.00
Class 6	1-12	8.3	-4.00

	W-R	Per cent	£1 Level Stake
Chases	7-34	20.6	-2.75
Totals	11-67	16.4	-18.34

BY MONTH

NH Flat	W-R	Per cent	£1 Level Stake	Hurdles	W-R	Per cent	£1 Level Stake
May	0-1	0.0	-1.00	May	2-13	15.4	+1.50
June	0-1	0.0	-1.00	June	1-6	16.7	+1.00
July	0-0	0.0	0.00	July	0-6	0.0	-6.00
August	0-0	0.0	0.00	August	1-5	20.0	+21.00
September	0-0	0.0	0.00	September	0-3	0.0	-3.00
October	0-2	0.0	-2.00	October	0-5	0.0	-5.00
November	1-4	25.0	+4.00	November	2-12	16.7	-7.34
December	0-3	0.0	-3.00	December	1-10	10.0	-4.00
January	1-1	100.0	+1.00	January	1-15	6.7	-7.00
February	0-0	0.0	0.00	February	1-10	10.0	-1.00
March	0-2	0.0	-2.00	March	0-8	0.0	-8.00
April	0-1	0.0	-1.00	April	1-8	12.5	-5.00

Chases	W-R	Per cent	£1 Level Stake	Totals	W-R	Per cent	£1 Level Stake
May	2-11	18.2	-2.25	May	4-25	16.0	-1.75
June	1-12	8.3	-9.25	June	2-19	10.5	-9.25
July	1-5	20.0	-2.38	July	1-11	9.1	-8.38
August	0-2	0.0	-2.00	August	1-7	14.3	+19.00
September	0-1	0.0	1.00	September	0-4	0.0	-4.00
October	0-9	0.0	-9.00	October	0-16	0.0	-16.00
November	4-24	16.7	-7.65	November	7-40	17.5	-10.99
December	3-17	17.6	+3.75	December	4-30	13.3	-3.25
January	4-21	19.0	-4.13	January	6-37	16.2	-10.13
February	1-9	11.1	-3.00	February	2-19	10.5	-4.00
March	0-14	0.0	-14.00	March	0-24	0.0	-24.00
April	6-20	30.0	+18.25	April	7-29	24.1	+12.25

DISTANCE

Hurdles	W-R	Per cent	£1 Level Stake	Chases	W-R	Per cent	£1 Level Stake
2m-2m3f	5-48	10.4	+4.50	2m-2m3f	5-43	11.6	-24.90
2m4f-2m7f	1-39	2.6	-36.00	2m4f-2m7f	7-41	17.1	-3.50
3m+	4-14	28.6	+8.66	3m+	10-61	16.4	-4.25

TYPE OF RACE

Non-Handicaps	W-R	Per cent	£1 Level Stake	Handicaps	W-R	Per cent	£1 Level Stake
Nov Hrdls	1-35	2.9	-26.00	Nov Hrdls	2-16	12.5	0.00
Hrdls	2-10	20.0	+19.00	Hrdls	4-33	12.1	-16.84
Nov Chs	6-20	30.0	+9.63	Nov Chs	4-30	13.3	-7.75
Chases	0-5	0.0	-5.00	Chases	12-88	13.6	-27.52
Sell/Claim	0-4	0.0	-4.00	Sell/Claim	0-2	0.0	-2.00

RACE CLASS   FIRST TIME OUT

	W-R	Per cent	£1 Level Stake		W-R	Per cent	£1 Level Stake
Class 1	0-11	0.0	-11.00	Bumpers	1-10	10.0	-2.00
Class 2	1-14	7.1	-9.00	Hurdles	3-23	13.0	-13.59

JOCKEYS

	W-R	Per cent	£1 Level Stake
Jason Maguire	16-145	11.0	-37.63
Willie McCarthy	5-42	11.9	-26.52
Wayne Hutchinson	3-7	42.9	+19.50
Robert Thornton	2-7	28.6	+1.25
P J Brennan	2-9	22.2	+1.00
David Dennis	1-1	100.0	+4.00
Richard Johnson	1-3	33.3	+7.00
A P McCoy	1-5	20.0	-3.09
Paul Moloney	1-5	20.0	+1.00
Noel Fehily	1-6	16.7	+2.00
Mr R McCarthy	1-9	11.1	-7.00

COURSE RECORD

	Total W-R	Non-Hndcps Hurdles	Chases	Hndcps Hurdles	Chases	NH Flat	Per cent	£1 Level Stake
Perth	5-14	0-1	1-4	2-5	2-4	0-0	35.7	+11.25
Exeter	4-15	0-2	1-2	1-4	2-7	0-0	26.7	+6.91
Hereford	3-12	1-1	0-1	0-4	1-4	1-2	25.0	+10.00
Worcester	3-15	1-4	2-2	0-3	0-5	0-1	20.0	-3.50
Bangor	2-5	1-1	0-0	0-1	1-3	0-0	40.0	+10.00
Towcester	2-8	0-2	1-2	1-1	0-3	0-0	25.0	+3.25
Uttoxeter	2-16	0-3	0-1	0-1	2-10	0-1	12.5	-10.00
Wincanton	2-16	0-3	0-1	1-2	1-9	0-1	12.5	-7.75
Huntingdon	2-17	1-3	0-2	1-4	0-6	0-2	11.8	+19.00
Ayr	1-2	0-0	0-0	0-0	1-2	0-0	50.0	+13.00
Wetherby	1-2	0-0	0-0	0-0	0-0	1-2	50.0	0.00
Windsor	1-2	0-1	0-0	0-0	1-1	0-0	50.0	+0.10
Leicester	1-3	0-0	0-0	0-1	1-2	0-0	33.3	-0.63
Fontwell	1-8	0-2	0-1	0-2	1-3	0-0	12.5	-2.00
Lingfield	1-8	0-1	0-1	0-2	1-4	0-0	12.5	-2.50
Mrket Rsn	1-9	0-1	0-0	0-3	1-5	0-0	11.1	-5.25
Nton Abbot	1-10	0-2	1-2	0-3	0-3	0-0	10.0	-7.38
Ludlow	1-13	0-6	0-1	0-1	1-4	0-1	7.7	-9.00

WINNING HORSES

Horse	Races Run	1st	2nd	3rd	£
*Ryders Storm	4	2	0	1	16476
Curtins Hill	2	1	1	0	8606
Idle Talk	5	2	1	1	13415
Travel	5	2	0	0	12296
Stack The Pack	4	2	0	0	11950
Calvic	6	2	0	2	13337
Nowator	5	1	1	1	6825
Garryvoe	1	1	0	0	5725
Rosetown	8	2	1	2	10177
Trenance	6	2	1	0	8978
Dante Citizen	7	1	1	2	4880
Toulouse-Lautrec	3	1	2	0	4840

Mandica	9	1	0	1	4804
Mighty Matters	5	1	0	0	4128
Dawton	4	1	2	0	4046
Lord Ryeford	7	1	0	0	3904
Julies Boy	9	3	1	1	10348
Swifts Hill	3	1	0	0	3297
Ishka Baha	5	1	0	1	2967
Bar Gayne	8	1	2	2	2928
Broken Reed	1	1	0	0	2741
Dyneburg	5	1	0	1	2681
Wind Instrument	3	2	0	0	4447
Eggmount	3	1	0	0	0
Total winning prize-money					**£163796**
Favourites	17-45		37.8%		10.13

KAREN GEORGE

HIGHER EASINGTON, DEVON

	No. of Hrs	Races Run	1st	2nd	3rd	Unpl	Per cent	£1 Level Stake
NH Flat	1	1	0	0	0	1	0.0	1.00
Hurdles	14	36	1	1	6	28	2.8	-24.00
Chases	4	7	0	1	0	6	0.0	-7.00
Totals	15	44	1	2	6	35	2.3	-32.00
04-05	15	53	6	3	5	39	11.3	+53.10
03-04	21	80	2	4	4	70	2.5	-57.50

JOCKEYS

	W-R	Per cent	£1 Level Stake
Richard Johnson	1-1	100.0	+11.00

COURSE RECORD

	Total W-R	Non-Hndcps Hurdles	Chases	Hndcps Hurdles	Chases	NH Flat	Per cent	£1 Level Stake
Worcester	1-6	0-0	0-0	1-5	0-1	0-0	16.7	+6.00

WINNING HORSES

Horse	Races Run	1st	2nd	3rd	£
Achilles Wings	3	1	1	1	4823
Total winning prize-money					**£4823**
Favourites	0-0		0.0%		0.00

MISS J R GIBNEY

SHENLEY, HERTS

	No. of Hrs	Races Run	1st	2nd	3rd	Unpl	Per cent	£1 Level Stake
NH Flat	1	2	0	0	0	2	0.0	-2.00
Hurdles	4	11	0	0	1	10	0.0	-11.00
Chases	2	4	1	0	0	3	25.0	+22.00
Totals	6	17	1	0	1	15	5.9	+9.00

JOCKEYS

	W-R	Per cent	£1 Level Stake
Owyn Nelmes	1-14	7.1	+12.00

COURSE RECORD

	Total W-R	Non-Hndcps Hurdles	Chases	Hndcps Hurdles	Chases	NH Flat	Per cent	£1 Level Stake
Huntingdon	1-5	0-3	0-0	0-1	1-1	0-0	20.0	+21.00

WINNING HORSES

Horse	Races Run	1st	2nd	3rd	£
Sweet Bird	3	1	0	0	3896
Total winning prize-money					**£3896**
Favourites	0-0		0.0%		0.00

N J GIFFORD

FINDON, W SUSSEX

	No. of Hrs	Races Run	1st	2nd	3rd	Unpl	Per cent	£1 Level Stake
NH Flat	4	4	0	0	2	2	0.0	-4.00
Hurdles	17	58	13	5	6	34	22.4	+44.47
Chases	10	26	1	0	2	23	3.8	-13.00
Totals	28	88	14	5	10	59	15.9	+27.47
04-05	29	83	5	1	13	64	6.0	-44.00
03-04	26	82	9	9	8	56	11.0	-2.50

BY MONTH

NH Flat	W-R	Per cent	£1 Level Stake	Hurdles	W-R	Per cent	£1 Level Stake
May	0-0	0.0	0.00	May	0-0	0.0	0.00
June	0-0	0.0	0.00	June	0-0	0.0	0.00
July	0-0	0.0	0.00	July	0-0	0.0	0.00
August	0-0	0.0	0.00	August	0-0	0.0	0.00
September	0-0	0.0	0.00	September	0-2	0.0	-2.00
October	0-1	0.0	-1.00	October	2-6	33.3	+11.50
November	0-1	0.0	-1.00	November	3-10	30.0	+3.00
December	0-0	0.0	0.00	December	2-10	20.0	+29.00
January	0-0	0.0	0.00	January	2-7	28.6	-0.28
February	0-0	0.0	0.00	February	1-12	8.3	-8.25
March	0-2	0.0	-2.00	March	2-6	33.3	+13.50
April	0-0	0.0	0.00	April	1-5	20.0	-2.00

Chases	W-R	Per cent	£1 Level Stake	Totals	W-R	Per cent	£1 Level Stake
May	0-3	0.0	-3.00	May	0-3	0.0	-3.00
June	0-0	0.0	0.00	June	0-0	0.0	0.00
July	0-0	0.0	0.00	July	0-0	0.0	0.00
August	0-1	0.0	-1.00	August	0-1	0.0	-1.00
September	0-1	0.0	-1.00	September	0-3	0.0	-3.00
October	1-2	50.0	+11.00	October	3-9	33.3	+21.50
November	0-4	0.0	-4.00	November	3-15	20.0	-2.00
December	0-4	0.0	-4.00	December	2-14	14.3	+25.00

January	0-6	0.0	-6.00	January	2-13	15.4	-6.28
February	0-1	0.0	-1.00	February	1-13	7.7	-9.25
March	0-2	0.0	-2.00	March	2-10	20.0	+9.50
April	0-2	0.0	-2.00	April	1-7	14.3	-4.00

DISTANCE

Hurdles	W-R	Per cent	£1 Level Stake	Chases	W-R	Per cent	£1 Level Stake
2m-2m3f	10-34	29.4	+51.47	2m-2m3f	0-0	0.0	0.00
2m4f-2m7f	3-23	13.0	-6.00	2m4f-2m7f	0-8	0.0	-8.00
3m+	0-1	0.0	-1.00	3m+	1-18	5.6	-5.00

TYPE OF RACE

Non-Handicaps	W-R	Per cent	£1 Level Stake	Handicaps	W-R	Per cent	£1 Level Stake
Nov Hrdls	11-37	29.7	+52.47	Nov Hrdls	1-4	25.0	+4.50
Hrdls	1-11	9.1	-6.50	Hrdls	0-6	0.0	-6.00
Nov Chs	0-6	0.0	-6.00	Nov Chs	0-1	0.0	-1.00
Chases	0-1	0.0	-1.00	Chases	1-18	5.6	-5.00
Sell/Claim	0-0	0.0	0.00	Sell/Claim	0-0	0.0	0.00

RACE CLASS

FIRST TIME OUT

	W-R	Per cent	£1 Level Stake		W-R	Per cent	£1 Level Stake
Class 1	2-7	28.6	+4.50	Bumpers	0-4	0.0	-4.00
Class 2	0-0	0.0	0.00	Hurdles	3-16	18.8	+7.00
Class 3	5-28	17.9	+42.50	Chases	1-8	12.5	+5.00
Class 4	7-45	15.6	-11.53				
Class 5	0-5	0.0	-5.00	Totals	4-28	14.3	+8.00
Class 6	0-3	0.0	-3.00				

JOCKEYS

	W-R	Per cent	£1 Level Stake
Leighton Aspell	8-33	24.2	+38.25
A P McCoy	3-5	60.0	+4.72
Mr D H Dunsdon	1-5	20.0	-0.50
Andrew Tinkler	1-5	20.0	-1.00
James Davies	1-17	5.9	+9.00

COURSE RECORD

	Total W-R	Non-Hndcps Hurdles	Chases	Hndcps Hurdles	Chases	NH Flat	Per cent	£1 Level Stake
Fontwell	3-13	2-8	0-0	0-0	1-4	0-1	23.1	+8.25
Folkestone	2-8	2-5	0-1	0-0	0-2	0-0	25.0	-2.28
Towcester	2-9	2-7	0-1	0-1	0-0	0-0	22.2	+28.00
Plumpton	2-14	2-8	0-1	0-3	0-1	0-1	14.3	-5.50
Aintree	1-1	1-1	0-0	0-0	0-0	0-0	100.0	+2.00
Leicester	1-2	1-2	0-0	0-0	0-0	0-0	50.0	+3.50
Sandown	1-3	0-0	0-1	1-2	0-0	0-0	33.3	+5.50
Newbury	1-4	1-1	0-1	0-1	0-0	0-1	25.0	+9.00
Wincanton	1-6	1-1	0-2	0-0	0-3	0-0	16.7	+7.00

WINNING HORSES

Horse	Races Run	1st	2nd	3rd	£
Killaghy Castle	4	2	0	1	37719
Straw Bear	4	3	1	0	39359
Snowy Ford	6	1	0	0	6148
Wee Robbie	3	1	2	0	5693
Shaka's Pearl	6	1	0	1	5605
Russian Around	1	1	0	0	4778
Witness Run	5	1	0	0	3803
Just A Splash	5	1	0	2	3533
Dusky Lord	3	2	1	0	5976
Soleil Fix	3	1	0	1	3248
Total winning prize-money					**£115862**
Favourites	2 8		25.0%		-3.78

S J GILMORE

SULGRAVE, NORTHANTS

	No. of Hrs	Races Run	1st	2nd	3rd	Unpl	Per cent	£1 Level Stake
NH Flat	1	1	0	0	0	1	0.0	-1.00
Hurdles	4	8	0	1	0	7	0.0	-8.00
Chases	4	10	1	0	1	8	10.0	-3.50
Totals	7	19	1	1	1	16	5.3	-12.50
04-05	9	40	2	2	3	33	5.0	-18.00
03-04	11	56	2	9	7	38	3.6	-24.50

JOCKEYS

	W-R	Per cent	£1 Level Stake
Marcus Foley	1-4	25.0	+2.50

COURSE RECORD

	Total W-R	Non-Hndcps Hurdles	Chases	Hndcps Hurdles	Chases	NH Flat	Per cent	£1 Level Stake
Worcester	1-2	0-0	0-0	0-0	1-2	0-0	50.0	+4.50

WINNING HORSES

Horse	Races Run	1st	2nd	3rd	£
Major Euro	4	1	0	1	6848
Total winning prize-money					**£6848**
Favourites	0-0		0.0%		0.00

M J GINGELL

NORTH RUNCTON, NORFOLK

	No. of Hrs	Races Run	1st	2nd	3rd	Unpl	Per cent	£1 Level Stake
NH Flat	5	6	0	0	0	6	0.0	-6.00
Hurdles	28	95	2	2	3	88	2.1	-88.50
Chases	7	19	3	2	1	13	15.8	+9.75
Totals	31	120	5	4	4	107	4.2	-84.75

04-05	41	149	1	7	14	127	0.7	-141.50
03-04	35	142	4	3	16	118	2.8	-89.50

JOCKEYS

	W-R	Per cent	£1 Level Stake
Chris Honour	5-22	22.7	+13.25

COURSE RECORD

	Total W-R	Non-Hndcps Hurdles	Chases	Hndcps Hurdles	Chases	NH Flat	Per cent	£1 Level Stake
Fakenham	5-32	0-9	0-0	2-16	3-7	0-0	15.6	+3.25

WINNING HORSES

Horse	Races Run	1st	2nd	3rd	£
New Perk	9	5	2	1	24874
Total winning prize-money					**£24874**
Favourites	2-36		5.6%		-29.50

J S GOLDIE

UPLAWMOOR, E RENFREWS

	No. of Hrs	Races Run	1st	2nd	3rd	Unpl	Per cent	£1 Level Stake
NH Flat	0	0	0	0	0	0	0.0	0.00
Hurdles	10	30	0	3	2	24	0.0	-30.00
Chases	4	18	3	2	2	11	16.7	-7.00
Totals	**13**	**48**	**3**	**5**	**4**	**35**	**6.3**	**-37.00**
04-05	11	61	10	1	5	45	16.4	+0.38
03-04	9	59	6	10	4	39	10.2	-10.63

JOCKEYS

	W-R	Per cent	£1 Level Stake
Richard McGrath	3-12	25.0	-1.00

COURSE RECORD

	Total W-R	Non-Hndcps Hurdles	Chases	Hndcps Hurdles	Chases	NH Flat	Per cent	£1 Level Stake
Perth	3-15	0-2	3-5	0-5	0-3	0-0	20.0	-4.00

WINNING HORSES

Horse	Races Run	1st	2nd	3rd	£
Kid'Z'Play	6	3	0	2	20417
Total winning prize-money					**£20417**
Favourites	0-1		0.0%		-1.00

W K GOLDSWORTHY

YERBESTON, PEMBROKES

	No. of Hrs	Races Run	1st	2nd	3rd	Unpl	Per cent	£1 Level Stake
NH Flat	7	9	0	0	0	9	0.0	-9.00
Hurdles	17	75	5	4	6	60	6.7	-16.00
Chases	4	17	2	1	3	11	11.8	-5.75
Totals	**22**	**101**	**7**	**5**	**9**	**80**	**6.9**	**-30.75**
04-05	14	55	3	10	4	38	5.5	-36.17
03-04	6	29	7	4	3	15	24.1	+3.17

JOCKEYS

	W-R	Per cent	£1 Level Stake
James Davies	2-7	28.6	+26.50
Carl Llewellyn	2-16	12.5	+1.50
Timmy Murphy	1-11	9.1	-7.75
Richard Johnson	1-11	9.1	-3.00
Lee Stephens	1 20	5.0	-12.00

COURSE RECORD

	Total W-R	Non-Hndcps Hurdles	Chases	Hndcps Hurdles	Chases	NH Flat	Per cent	£1 Level Stake
Stratford	2-9	0-0	1-1	1-6	0-1	0-1	22.2	+5.25
Hereford	2-12	1-6	0-0	0-4	1-2	0-0	16.7	+2.50
Worcester	1-10	1-6	0-0	0-4	0-0	0-0	10.0	-2.00
Nton Abbot	1-13	0-4	0-0	1-6	0-2	0-1	7.7	-5.50
Fontwell	1-15	0-2	0-1	1-8	0-2	0-2	6.7	+11.00

WINNING HORSES

Horse	Races Run	1st	2nd	3rd	£
Imperial Rocket	15	1	2	4	7378
Charango Star	15	3	1	1	15221
Spirit Of Tenby	6	2	0	0	6259
Blue Leader	11	1	1	0	2219
Total winning prize-money					**£31077**
Favourites	1-4		25.0%		3.50

S GOLLINGS

SCAMBLESBY, LINCS

	No. of Hrs	Races Run	1st	2nd	3rd	Unpl	Per cent	£1 Level Stake
NH Flat	7	12	0	1	0	11	0.0	-12.00
Hurdles	23	69	6	10	5	48	8.7	-39.90
Chases	7	42	7	5	8	22	16.7	+24.00
Totals	**31**	**123**	**13**	**16**	**13**	**81**	**10.6**	**-27.90**
04-05	27	135	11	17	17	90	8.1	-72.05
03-04	29	118	9	9	21	79	7.6	-42.80

BY MONTH

NH Flat	W-R	Per cent	£1 Level Stake	Hurdles	W-R	Per cent	£1 Level Stake
May	0-2	0.0	-2.00	May	1-10	10.0	+2.00
June	0-0	0.0	0.00	June	0-5	0.0	-5.00
July	0-1	0.0	-1.00	July	1-5	20.0	-2.90
August	0-1	0.0	-1.00	August	1-5	20.0	-2.00
September	0-1	0.0	-1.00	September	0-2	0.0	-2.00
October	0-1	0.0	-1.00	October	0-5	0.0	-5.00
November	0-0	0.0	0.00	November	1-8	12.5	-2.00
December	0-0	0.0	0.00	December	0-6	0.0	-6.00
January	0-3	0.0	-3.00	January	0-4	0.0	-4.00
February	0-0	0.0	0.00	February	1-4	25.0	-0.75
March	0-1	0.0	-1.00	March	0-6	0.0	-6.00
April	0-2	0.0	-2.00	April	1-9	11.1	-6.25

Chases	W-R	Per cent	£1 Level Stake	Totals	W-R	Per cent	£1 Level Stake
May	2-4	50.0	+9.50	May	3-16	18.8	+9.50
June	1-4	25.0	+3.00	June	1-9	11.1	-2.00
July	0-1	0.0	-1.00	July	1-7	14.3	-4.90
August	0-3	0.0	-3.00	August	1-9	11.1	-6.00
September	0-1	0.0	-1.00	September	0-4	0.0	-4.00
October	1-3	33.3	+0.50	October	1-9	11.1	-5.50
November	2-5	40.0	+16.00	November	3-13	23.1	+14.00
December	0-3	0.0	3.00	December	0-9	0.0	-9.00
January	1-6	16.7	+15.00	January	1-13	7.7	+8.00
February	0-2	0.0	-2.00	February	1-6	16.7	-2.75
March	0-4	0.0	-4.00	March	0-11	0.0	-11.00
April	0-6	0.0	-6.00	April	1-17	5.9	-14.25

DISTANCE

Hurdles	W-R	Per cent	£1 Level Stake	Chases	W-R	Per cent	£1 Level Stake
2m-2m3f	3-48	6.3	-36.00	2m-2m3f	1-11	9.1	+10.00
2m4f-2m7f	3-16	18.8	+1.10	2m4f-2m7f	5-20	25.0	+16.00
3m+	0-5	0.0	-5.00	3m+	1-11	9.1	-2.00

TYPE OF RACE

Non-Handicaps	W-R	Per cent	£1 Level Stake	Handicaps	W-R	Per cent	£1 Level Stake
Nov Hrdls	3-20	15.0	-12.15	Nov Hrdls	0-3	0.0	-3.00
Hrdls	1-15	6.7	-11.75	Hrdls	2-27	7.4	-9.00
Nov Chs	2-13	15.4	+3.50	Nov Chs	1-11	9.1	+10.00
Chases	0-0	0.0	0.00	Chases	4-18	22.2	+10.50
Sell/Claim	0-1	0.0	-1.00	Sell/Claim	0-3	0.0	-3.00

RACE CLASS

	W-R	Per cent	£1 Level Stake
Class 1	2-16	12.5	-6.75
Class 2	0-2	0.0	-2.00
Class 3	5-39	12.8	+7.25
Class 4	6-51	11.8	-11.40
Class 5	0-4	0.0	-4.00
Class 6	0-11	0.0	-11.00

FIRST TIME OUT

	W-R	Per cent	£1 Level Stake
Bumpers	0-7	0.0	-7.00
Hurdles	1-20	5.0	-17.25
Chases	0-4	0.0	-4.00
Totals	1-31	3.2	-28.25

JOCKEYS

	W-R	Per cent	£1 Level Stake
Tom Scudamore	4-28	14.3	-16.90
William Kennedy	4-52	7.7	-22.50
Robert Thornton	2-13	15.4	+2.50
G Lee	1-1	100.0	+5.00
Mr T F Woodside	1-1	100.0	+11.00
Keith Mercer	1-2	50.0	+19.00

COURSE RECORD

	Total W-R	Non-Hndcps Hurdles	Chases	Hndcps Hurdles	Chases	NH Flat	Per cent	£1 Level Stake
Mrket Rsn	5-41	0-10	1-5	1-11	3-10	0-5	12.2	-5.00
Cartmel	1-1	1-1	0-0	0-0	0-0	0-0	100.0	+1.10
Folkestone	1-1	0-0	1-1	0-0	0-0	0-0	100.0	+8.00
Lingfield	1-2	0-0	0-0	0-0	1-2	0-0	50.0	+10.00
Wincanton	1-2	0-1	0-0	1-1	0-0	0-0	50.0	+4.00
Kelso	1-3	1-1	0-1	0-0	0-1	0-0	33.3	-0.25
Stratford	1-4	1-2	0-0	0-1	0-1	0-0	25.0	-1.00
Wetherby	1-4	0-1	0-2	0-0	1-1	0-0	25.0	+17.00
Sandown	1-5	1-3	0-0	0-1	0-1	0-0	20.0	-1.75

WINNING HORSES

Horse	Races Run	1st	2nd	3rd	£
Royal Shakespeare	12	2	2	2	45616
Vigoureux	11	1	1	1	8458
Romany Prince	8	3	4	0	16918
Seaniethesmuggler	9	2	3	2	9357
Almnadia	3	1	0	0	4901
Sunny South East	10	1	0	2	4749
Lanmire Tower	9	3	1	2	11273
Total winning prize-money					**£101272**
Favourites	4-10		40.0%		1.60

MISS A GOSCHEN

HENSTRIDGE, SOMERSET

	No. of Hss	Races Run	1st	2nd	3rd	Unpl	Per cent	£1 Level Stake
NH Flat	0	0	0	0	0	0	0.0	0.00
Hurdles	0	0	0	0	0	0	0.0	0.00
Chases	1	4	1	1	0	2	25.0	+0.50
Totals	1	4	1	1	0	2	25.0	+0.50
04-05	1	3	1	0	0	2	33.3	+1.50
03-04	1	3	2	0	0	1	66.7	+4.00

JOCKEYS

	W-R	Per cent	£1 Level Stake
Miss A Goschen	1-4	25.0	+0.50

COURSE RECORD

	Total W-R	Non-Hndcps Hurdles	Chases	Hndcps Hurdles	Chases	NH Flat	Per cent	£1 Level Stake
Ludlow	1-1	0-0	1-1	0-0	0-0	0-0	100.0	+3.50

WINNING HORSES

Horse	Races Run	1st	2nd	3rd	£
Chasing The Bride	4	1	1	0	2926
Total winning prize-money					£2926
Favourites	0-0		0.0%		0.00

MRS H O GRAHAM

PHILIP LAW, BORDERS

	No. of Hrs	Races Run	1st	2nd	3rd	Unpl	Per cent	£1 Level Stake
NH Flat	7	13	0	1	0	12	0.0	-13.00
Hurdles	15	46	2	5	8	31	4.3	-22.00
Chases	3	7	0	1	1	5	0.0	-7.00
Totals	18	66	2	7	9	48	3.0	-42.00
04-05	13	68	8	7	6	47	11.8	-14.38
03-04	8	35	1	1	0	33	2.9	-22.00

JOCKEYS

	W-R	Per cent	£1 Level Stake
Andrew Glassonbury	1-4	25.0	+7.00
Miss R Davidson	1-6	16.7	+7.00

COURSE RECORD

	Total W-R	Non-Hndcps Hurdles	Chases	Hndcps Hurdles	Chases	NH Flat	Per cent	£1 Level Stake
Wetherby	1-3	0-0	0-0	1-1	0-0	0-2	33.3	+10.00
Carlisle	1-6	0-0	0-1	1-2	0-1	0-2	16.7	+5.00

WINNING HORSES

Horse	Races Run	1st	2nd	3rd	£
Russian Sky	9	1	4	2	6987
Lofty Leader	9	1	0	3	3325
Total winning prize-money					£10312
Favourites	0-2		0.0%		-2.00

C GRANT

NEWTON BEWLEY, CO DURHAM

	No. of Hrs	Races Run	1st	2nd	3rd	Unpl	Per cent	£1 Level Stake
NH Flat	7	12	0	1	0	11	0.0	-12.00
Hurdles	17	70	2	11	9	48	2.9	-49.00
Chases	9	39	4	4	4	27	10.3	-5.50

Totals	28	121	6	16	13	86	5.0	-66.50
04-05	27	103	9	11	14	69	8.7	-51.42
03-04	41	146	6	10	14	116	4.1	-77.50

JOCKEYS

	W-R	Per cent	£1 Level Stake
Mr T Greenall	3-29	10.3	-1.00
Dougie Costello	1-3	33.3	+8.00
P J Brennan	1-4	25.0	+2.50
Richard McGrath	1-43	2.3	-34.00

COURSE RECORD

	Total W-R	Non-Hndcps Hurdles	Chases	Hndcps Hurdles	Chases	NH Flat	Per cent	£1 Level Stake
Newcastle	2-10	1-4	0-0	0-3	1-3	0-0	20.0	+9.00
Bangor	1-5	0-0	1-1	0-1	0-2	0-1	20.0	+1.50
Mrket Rsn	1-5	0-0	0-1	0-2	1-2	0-0	20.0	+5.00
Musselbgh	1-6	0-1	0-0	0-3	1-1	0-1	16.7	+2.00
Kelso	1-12	0-7	0-0	1-5	0-0	0-0	8.3	-1.00

WINNING HORSES

Horse	Races Run	1st	2nd	3rd	£
Kalou	8	1	2	0	6501
*Fiery Peace	5	1	0	1	5426
Sachsenwalzer	5	1	0	0	4705
Briar's Mist	8	1	0	0	3904
Penteli	10	1	1	2	3513
Laertes	7	1	2	2	2602
Total winning prize-money					£26651
Favourites	0-3		0.0%		-3.00

C J GRAY

MOORLAND, SOMERSET

	No. of Hrs	Races Run	1st	2nd	3rd	Unpl	Per cent	£1 Level Stake
NH Flat	1	1	0	0	0	1	0.0	-1.00
Hurdles	7	25	3	3	1	18	12.0	+21.00
Chases	3	8	0	0	0	8	0.0	-8.00
Totals	9	34	3	3	1	27	8.8	+12.00
04-05	13	53	1	1	5	46	1.9	-45.50
03-04	16	54	1	3	1	49	1.9	-31.00

JOCKEYS

	W-R	Per cent	£1 Level Stake
Bernie Wharfe	2-12	16.7	+13.00
Richard Hobson	1-9	11.1	+12.00

COURSE RECORD

	Total W-R	Non-Hndcps Hurdles	Chases	Hndcps Hurdles	Chases	NH Flat	Per cent	£1 Level Stake
Taunton	2-6	0-0	0-0	2-4	0-1	0-1	33.3	+23.00
Worcester	1-2	0-0	0-1	1-1	0-0	0-0	50.0	+15.00

WINNING HORSES

Horse	Races Run	1st	2nd	3rd	£
Charm Offensive	5	1	0	0	3083
Le Forezien	5	2	0	0	4591
Total winning prize-money					**£7674**
Favourites	1-1		100.0%		7.00

ROBERT GRAY

MALTON, N YORKS

	No. of Hrs	Races Run	1st	2nd	3rd	Unpl	Per cent	£1 Level Stake
NH Flat	1	2	0	0	0	2	0.0	-2.00
Hurdles	14	46	4	1	2	39	8.7	-12.50
Chases	7	24	3	1	3	17	12.5	+17.00
Totals	**20**	**72**	**7**	**2**	**5**	**58**	**9.7**	**+2.50**

JOCKEYS

	W-R	Per cent	£1 Level Stake
Tony Dobbin	2-9	22.2	+7.50
Andrew Thornton	2-11	18.2	+4.00
G Lee	1-4	25.0	+7.00
Tom Greenway	1-7	14.3	+19.00
Ollie McPhail	1-16	6.3	-10.00

COURSE RECORD

	Total W-R	Non-Hndcps Hurdles	Chases	Hndcps Hurdles	Chases	NH Flat	Per cent	£1 Level Stake
Mrket Rsn	3-13	0-1	0-0	2-11	1-1	0-0	23.1	+9.50
Sedgefield	2-14	1-3	0-2	1-7	0-1	0-1	14.3	+3.00
Hexham	1-1	0-0	0-0	0-0	1-1	0-0	100.0	+25.00
Haydock	1-5	0-1	0-0	0-0	1-4	0-0	20.0	+4.00

WINNING HORSES

Horse	Races Run	1st	2nd	3rd	£
*Nowator	6	1	1	0	5390
*Overstrand	10	1	0	0	5205
*Nick The Silver	5	1	0	0	4397
*El Andaluz	2	1	0	1	3900
*Rifleman	8	1	0	0	3083
*Sheer Guts	6	2	0	1	4455
Total winning prize-money					**£26430**
Favourites	0-4		0.0%		-4.00

V G GREENWAY

FITZHEAD, SOMERSET

	No. of Hrs	Races Run	1st	2nd	3rd	Unpl	Per cent	£1 Level Stake
NH Flat	0	0	0	0	0	0	0.0	0.00
Hurdles	3	6	0	1	1	4	0.0	-6.00

Chases	3	6	1	0	0	5	16.7	+61.00
Totals	**3**	**12**	**1**	**1**	**1**	**9**	**8.3**	**+55.00**
04-05	2	7	0	1	0	6	0.0	-7.00

JOCKEYS

	W-R	Per cent	£1 Level Stake
James White	1-3	33.3	+64.00

COURSE RECORD

	Total W-R	Non-Hndcps Hurdles	Chases	Hndcps Hurdles	Chases	NH Flat	Per cent	£1 Level Stake
Taunton	1-1	0-0	1-1	0-0	0-0	0-0	100.0	+66.00

WINNING HORSES

Horse	Races Run	1st	2nd	3rd	£
Joizel	4	1	0	0	3083
Total winning prize-money					**£3083**
Favourites	0-0		0.0%		0.00

S G GRIFFITHS

NANTGAREDIG, CARMARTHENS

	No. of Hrs	Races Run	1st	2nd	3rd	Unpl	Per cent	£1 Level Stake
NH Flat	0	0	0	0	0	0	0.0	0.00
Hurdles	2	10	1	1	2	6	10.0	-7.50
Chases	2	5	0	1	0	4	0.0	-5.00
Totals	**3**	**15**	**1**	**2**	**2**	**10**	**6.7**	**-12.50**
04-05	3	20	2	1	1	16	10.0	-2.00
03-04	3	12	0	3	1	8	0.0	-12.00

JOCKEYS

	W-R	Per cent	£1 Level Stake
Robert Stephens	1-9	11.1	-6.50

COURSE RECORD

	Total W-R	Non-Hndcps Hurdles	Chases	Hndcps Hurdles	Chases	NH Flat	Per cent	£1 Level Stake
Hereford	1-5	1-3	0-0	0-1	0-1	0-0	20.0	-2.50

WINNING HORSES

Horse	Races Run	1st	2nd	3rd	£
Tirikumba	7	1	1	2	3341
Total winning prize-money					**£3341**
Favourites	1-1		100.0%		1.50

MRS D M GRISSELL

BRIGHTLING, E SUSSEX

	No. of Hrs	Races Run	1st	2nd	3rd	Unpl	Per cent	£1 Level Stake
NH Flat	0	0	0	0	0	0	0.0	0.00
Hurdles	0	0	0	0	0	0	0.0	0.00
Chases	9	11	1	2	1	7	9.1	-9.38
Totals	**9**	**11**	**1**	**2**	**1**	**7**	**9.1**	**-9.38**
04-05	4	7	0	1	2	4	0.0	-7.00
03-04	10	17	2	0	2	13	11.8	-7.13

JOCKEYS

	W-R	Per cent	£1 Level Stake
Mr P G Hall	1-7	14.3	-5.38

COURSE RECORD

	Total W-R	Non-Hndcps Hurdles	Chases	Hndcps Hurdles	Chases	NH Flat	Per cent	£1 Level Stake
Folkestone	1-5	0-0	1-5	0-0	0-0	0-0	20.0	-3.38

WINNING HORSES

Horse	Races Run	1st	2nd	3rd	£
Satchmo	2	1	0	0	1876
Total winning prize-money					**£1876**
Favourites	1-2	50.0%			-0.39

J GROUCOTT

MUCH WENLOCK, SHROPSHIRE

	No. of Hrs	Races Run	1st	2nd	3rd	Unpl	Per cent	£1 Level Stake
NH Flat	0	0	0	0	0	0	0.0	0.00
Hurdles	0	0	0	0	0	0	0.0	0.00
Chases	6	19	4	2	3	10	21.1	+6.16
Totals	**6**	**19**	**4**	**2**	**3**	**10**	**21.1**	**+6.16**
04-05	3	7	1	0	2	4	14.3	+9.00
03-04	2	4	1	1	0	2	25.0	+2.50

JOCKEYS

	W-R	Per cent	£1 Level Stake
Mr W Hill	3-8	37.5	+13.41
Mr J M Pritchard	1-4	25.0	-0.25

COURSE RECORD

	Total W-R	Non-Hndcps Hurdles	Chases	Hndcps Hurdles	Chases	NH Flat	Per cent	£1 Level Stake
Fontwell	1-1	0-0	1-1	0-0	0-0	0-0	100.0	+2.75
Huntingdon	1-1	0-0	1-1	0-0	0-0	0-0	100.0	+0.91
Bangor	1-2	0-0	1-2	0-0	0-0	0-0	50.0	+1.50
Cheltenham	1-4	0-0	1-4	0-0	0-0	0-0	25.0	+12.00

WINNING HORSES

Horse	Races Run	1st	2nd	3rd	£
No Retreat	6	3	1	1	4048
Gatsby	5	1	0	1	3835
Total winning prize-money					**£7883**
Favourites	1-1		100.0%		0.91

R C GUEST

BRANCEPETH, CO DURHAM

	No. of Hrs	Races Run	1st	2nd	3rd	Unpl	Per cent	£1 Level Stake
NH Flat	8	20	2	2	2	14	10.0	+73.00
Hurdles	69	254	21	19	16	198	8.3	-135.96
Chases	53	241	32	27	31	151	13.3	-36.43
Totals	**92**	**515**	**55**	**48**	**49**	**363**	**10.7**	**-99.39**
04-05	84	532	62	75	63	332	11.7	-91.31
03-04	73	417	48	48	49	272	11.5	-31.11

BY MONTH

NH Flat	W-R	Per cent	£1 Level Stake		Hurdles	W-R	Per cent	£1 Level Stake
May	0-1	0.0	-1.00		May	10-45	22.2	-8.79
June	0-0	0.0	0.00		June	0-14	0.0	-14.00
July	0-0	0.0	0.00		July	3-18	16.7	+0.50
August	0-0	0.0	0.00		August	0-26	0.0	-26.00
September	0-1	0.0	-1.00		September	0-10	0.0	-10.00
October	0-2	0.0	-2.00		October	2-27	7.4	-5.00
November	0-5	0.0	-5.00		November	1-28	3.6	-23.67
December	1-3	33.3	+64.00		December	1-25	4.0	-15.00
January	1-3	33.3	+23.00		January	0-22	0.0	-22.00
February	0-2	0.0	-2.00		February	0-7	0.0	-7.00
March	0-0	0.0	0.00		March	0-5	0.0	-5.00
April	0-3	0.0	-3.00		April	4-27	14.8	0.00

Chases	W-R	Per cent	£1 Level Stake		Totals	W-R	Per cent	£1 Level Stake
May	4-32	12.5	-10.27		May	14-78	17.9	-20.06
June	1-13	7.7	-10.25		June	1-27	3.7	-24.25
July	3-15	20.0	+8.00		July	6-33	18.2	+8.50
August	1-14	7.1	-10.25		August	1-40	2.5	-36.25
September	0-5	0.0	-5.00		September	0-16	0.0	-16.00
October	5-32	15.6	-2.25		October	7-61	11.5	-9.25
November	1-22	4.5	-15.50		November	2-55	3.6	-44.17
December	1-18	5.6	-11.50		December	3-46	6.5	+37.50
January	3-25	12.0	-9.00		January	4-50	8.0	-8.00
February	3-14	21.4	+9.50		February	3-23	13.0	+0.50
March	1-5	20.0	+10.00		March	1-10	10.0	+5.00
April	9-46	19.6	+10.10		April	13-76	17.1	+7.10

DISTANCE

Hurdles	W-R	Per cent	£1 Level Stake		Chases	W-R	Per cent	£1 Level Stake
2m-2m3f	15-172	8.7	-81.86		2m-2m3f	15-99	15.2	-14.30

	W-R	Per cent	£1 Level Stake		W-R	Per cent	£1 Level Stake
2m4f-2m7f	5-68	7.4	-48.60	2m4f-2m7f	10-84	11.9	-11.13
3m+	1-14	7.1	-5.50	3m+	7-58	12.1	-11.00

TYPE OF RACE

Non-Handicaps				Handicaps			
	W-R	Per cent	£1 Level Stake		W-R	Per cent	£1 Level Stake
Nov Hrdls	3-52	5.8	-42.35	Nov Hrdls	4-28	14.3	+1.00
Hrdls	2-18	11.1	-9.75	Hrdls	10-121	8.3	-53.79
Nov Chs	6-20	30.0	+3.98	Nov Chs	7-50	14.0	-3.15
Chases	1-2	50.0	+2.00	Chases	17-168	10.1	-43.75
Sell/Claim	1-13	7.7	-11.17	Sell/Claim	1-25	4.0	-22.90

RACE CLASS / FIRST TIME OUT

	W-R	Per cent	£1 Level Stake		W-R	Per cent	£1 Level Stake
Class 1	0-9	0.0	-9.00	Bumpers	0-8	0.0	-8.00
Class 2	4-15	26.7	+22.83	Hurdles	7-52	13.5	+2.50
Class 3	13-135	9.6	-53.63	Chases	6-32	18.8	+26.50
Class 4	33-282	11.7	91.03				
Class 5	3-56	5.4	-43.57	Totals	13-92	14.1	+21.00
Class 6	2-18	11.1	+75.00				

JOCKEYS

	W-R	Per cent	£1 Level Stake
Larry McGrath	14-170	8.2	-78.55
Henry Oliver	13-112	11.6	-49.75
Paul O'Neill	7-63	11.1	-13.42
John Flavin	6-60	10.0	+4.50
William Kennedy	3-8	37.5	+3.00
Paddy Merrigan	2-8	25.0	+6.00
Timmy Murphy	1-1	100.0	+3.33
Mr J E Clare	1-1	100.0	+4.00
Brian Harding	1-1	100.0	+3.50
Wayne Kavanagh	1-1	100.0	+6.00
Barry Keniry	1-2	50.0	+2.50
Robert Stephens	1-2	50.0	+3.00
Mr C Mulhall	1-4	25.0	+6.00
Ciaran Eddery	1-5	20.0	+62.00
Dominic Elsworth	1-6	16.7	+1.00
Kenny Johnson	1-27	3.7	-18.50

COURSE RECORD

	Total W-R	Non-Hndcps Hurdles	Non-Hndcps Chases	Hndcps Hurdles	Hndcps Chases	NH Flat	Per cent	£1 Level Stake
Cartmel	6-24	4-10	0-2	1-8	1-4	0-0	25.0	+7.90
Catterick	5-25	0-4	0-1	1-9	3-8	1-3	20.0	+80.50
Towcester	4-18	2-4	1-1	0-3	1-9	0-1	22.2	-4.82
Carlisle	4-23	0-1	2-2	0-6	2-13	0-1	17.4	+1.50
Wetherby	4-26	0-5	0-1	4-12	0-7	0-1	15.4	-8.13
Hexham	4-40	0-6	3-6	1-11	0-15	0-2	10.0	-28.52
Mrket Rsn	4-40	0-6	0-1	1-19	3-12	0-2	10.0	-16.25
Sedgefield	4-47	0-6	0-2	3-20	1-17	0-2	8.5	-23.00
Worcester	3-23	0-1	1-1	1-10	1-11	0-0	13.0	-4.50
Kelso	3-32	0-5	1-2	1-10	1-15	0-0	9.4	-11.50
Bangor	2-26	0-6	0-1	0-8	2-11	0-0	7.7	-10.90

							Per cent	£1 Level Stake
Fakenham	2-26	0-5	0-0	0-10	2-11	0-0	7.7	-15.00
Uttoxeter	2-33	0-1	0-2	0-11	2-18	0-1	6.1	-16.50
Chepstow	1-2	0-0	0-1	1-1	0-0	0-0	50.0	+15.00
Huntingdon	1-7	0-0	0-0	0-2	1-5	0-0	14.3	-2.50
Stratford	1-7	0-1	0-0	0-2	1-4	0-0	14.3	+2.00
Leicester	1-10	0-3	0-0	0-3	1-4	0-0	10.0	-3.50
Haydock	1-13	0-1	0-0	1-5	0-5	0-2	7.7	-8.67
Newcastle	1-14	0-3	0-0	0-4	1-7	0-0	7.1	-7.00
Southwell	1-14	0-2	0-0	0-1	1-10	0-1	7.1	-6.50
Musselbgh	1-15	0-3	0-0	0-4	0-7	1-1	6.7	+11.00

WINNING HORSES

Horse	Races Run	1st	2nd	3rd	£
Our Armageddon	4	1	0	0	34106
Admiral	6	2	0	0	37196
Gatorade	3	1	0	0	10351
Bill's Echo	10	1	4	1	10023
Ghadames	3	1	0	0	9235
Donovan	11	2	0	1	11174
Wet Lips	8	2	2	2	12334
Time To Reflect	2	1	0	1	6715
*Pass Me By	9	3	2	1	17214
Good Outlook	6	1	2	1	6506
Drumossie	10	1	0	1	6263
Pequenita	12	2	1	1	10266
Stan	5	2	0	1	10615
*Jodante	4	2	1	0	9108
Sconced	13	1	0	2	4880
College City	16	3	3	2	12453
Beaugency	10	3	0	1	11257
Magico	8	1	1	3	4845
Mr Bigglesworth	4	3	1	0	11602
Isellido	11	2	0	1	8266
Flintoff	4	3	0	0	11681
Bergerac	6	2	1	0	7914
Move Over	6	1	0	0	3904
*Prince Adjal	4	1	0	0	3780
Apadi	10	1	0	1	3770
Red Perk	12	3	2	0	9869
Diamond Cutter	5	1	0	1	3671
North Landing	9	1	0	3	3451
He's Hot Right Now	12	2	1	0	6450
Ballyboe Boy	9	1	0	1	3073
Polished	3	2	0	1	5355
Topwell	6	1	0	1	2241
Insurgent	7	1	0	0	2056
Total winning prize-money					**£311624**
Favourites	13-45		28.9%		-11.72

B DE HAAN

LAMBOURN, BERKS

	No. of Hrs	Races Run	1st	2nd	3rd	Unpl	Per cent	£1 Level Stake
NH Flat	2	2	0	0	0	2	0.0	-2.00

Hurdles	11	26	0	2	4	20	0.0	-26.00
Chases	7	24	2	5	5	12	8.3	-17.50
Totals	**17**	**52**	**2**	**7**	**9**	**34**	**3.8**	**-45.50**
04-05	14	43	4	5	8	26	9.3	-11.00
03-04	18	47	5	5	6	31	10.6	-1.35

JOCKEYS

	W-R	Per cent	£1 Level Stake
A P McCoy	1-4	25.0	-2.00
Noel Fehily	1-21	4.8	-16.50

COURSE RECORD

	Total W-R	Non-Hndcps Hurdles	Chases	Hndcps Hurdles	Chases	NH Flat	Per cent	£1 Level Stake
Warwick	1-1	0-0	0-0	0-0	1-1	0-0	100.0	+1.00
Wincanton	1-4	0-0	0-1	0-0	1-3	0-0	25.0	+0.50

WINNING HORSES

Horse	Races Run	1st	2nd	3rd	£
Crimson Pirate	1	1	0	0	6338
Lord Dundaniel	9	1	1	3	3904
Total winning prize-money					**£10242**
Favourites	1-3		33.3%		**-1.00**

A M HALES

QUAINTON, BUCKS

	No. of Hrs	Races Run	1st	2nd	3rd	Unpl	Per cent	£1 Level Stake
NH Flat	2	2	0	0	0	2	0.0	-2.00
Hurdles	17	40	3	4	6	27	7.5	-31.68
Chases	6	21	2	4	0	15	9.5	-8.00
Totals	**18**	**63**	**5**	**8**	**6**	**44**	**7.9**	**-41.68**
04-05	16	50	3	6	3	38	6.0	-19.00
03-04	15	44	3	6	4	31	6.8	-30.67

JOCKEYS

	W-R	Per cent	£1 Level Stake
William Kennedy	3-22	13.6	-13.68
Tom Malone	1-6	16.7	+2.00
Jimmy McCarthy	1-13	7.7	-8.00

COURSE RECORD

	Total W-R	Non-Hndcps Hurdles	Chases	Hndcps Hurdles	Chases	NH Flat	Per cent	£1 Level Stake
Nton Abbot	1-1	0-0	0-0	0-0	1-1	0-0	100.0	+7.00
Fontwell	1-5	1-3	0-1	0-0	0-1	0-0	20.0	-3.43
Huntingdon	1-5	0-0	1-1	0-2	0-2	0-0	20.0	0.00
Wincanton	1-5	0-0	0-0	1-4	0-1	0-0	20.0	-0.50
Worcester	1-7	1-5	0-0	0-0	0-1	0-1	14.3	-4.75

WINNING HORSES

Horse	Races Run	1st	2nd	3rd	£
Saltango	10	3	3	2	14908
Sharp Rigging	6	1	1	0	6506
Corkan	4	1	0	0	3326
Total winning prize-money					**£24740**
Favourites	2-3		66.7%		**0.82**

G A HAM

ROOKS BRIDGE, SOMERSET

	No. of Hrs	Races Run	1st	2nd	3rd	Unpl	Per cent	£1 Level Stake
NH Flat	1	2	0	0	0	2	0.0	-2.00
Hurdles	12	55	3	3	4	45	5.5	-35.50
Chases	3	9	0	0	1	8	0.0	-9.00
Totals	**12**	**66**	**3**	**3**	**5**	**55**	**4.5**	**-46.50**
04-05	13	71	3	4	7	57	4.2	-25.50
03-04	17	68	0	3	3	62	0.0	-68.00

JOCKEYS

	W-R	Per cent	£1 Level Stake
Eamon Dehdashti	3-36	8.3	-16.50

COURSE RECORD

	Total W-R	Non-Hndcps Hurdles	Chases	Hndcps Hurdles	Chases	NH Flat	Per cent	£1 Level Stake
Nton Abbot	1-5	0-2	0-1	1-2	0-0	0-0	20.0	+4.00
Uttoxeter	1-5	1-1	0-0	0-4	0-0	0-0	20.0	-1.50
Taunton	1-7	0-1	0-0	1-5	0-1	0-0	14.3	0.00

WINNING HORSES

Horse	Races Run	1st	2nd	3rd	£
Jack Durrance	12	1	1	2	3089
Penny's Crown	16	2	0	1	4562
Total winning prize-money					**£7651**
Favourites	1-2		50.0%		**1.50**

MRS MARY HAMBRO

BOURTON-ON-THE-HILL, GLOUCS

	No. of Hrs	Races Run	1st	2nd	3rd	Unpl	Per cent	£1 Level Stake
NH Flat	3	4	0	0	0	4	0.0	-4.00
Hurdles	1	3	1	0	0	2	33.3	+0.75
Chases	2	6	0	0	0	6	0.0	-6.00
Totals	**6**	**13**	**1**	**0**	**0**	**12**	**7.7**	**-9.25**
04-05	4	6	1	0	0	5	16.7	-0.50
03-04	5	12	0	1	1	10	0.0	-12.00

JOCKEYS

	W-R	Per cent	£1 Level Stake
Carl Llewellyn	1-4	25.0	-0.25

COURSE RECORD

	Total W-R	Non-Hndcps Hurdles	Chases	Hndcps Hurdles	Chases	NH Flat	Per cent	£1 Level Stake
Taunton	1-1	1-1	0-0	0-0	0-0	0-0	100.0	+2.75

WINNING HORSES

Horse	Races Run	1st	2nd	3rd	£
Kingham	3	1	0	0	3083
Total winning prize-money					£3083
Favourites	0-0		0.0%		0.00

MRS D A HAMER

NANTYCAWS, CARMARTHENS

	No. of Hrs	Races Run	1st	2nd	3rd	Unpl	Per cent	£1 Level Stake
NH Flat	3	4	0	0	0	4	0.0	-4.00
Hurdles	20	69	7	5	8	49	10.1	+13.88
Chases	4	15	1	3	3	8	6.7	-8.50
Totals	23	88	8	8	11	61	9.1	+1.38
04-05	18	72	8	7	10	47	11.1	-6.75
03-04	22	55	6	4	5	40	10.9	+9.33

JOCKEYS

	W-R	Per cent	£1 Level Stake
Benjamin Hitchcott	3-33	9.1	-9.50
Liam Heard	2-6	33.3	+7.88
Christian Williams	1-3	33.3	+38.00
Richard Johnson	1-6	16.7	+1.00
Robert Stephens	1-13	7.7	-9.00

COURSE RECORD

	Total W-R	Non-Hndcps Hurdles	Chases	Hndcps Hurdles	Chases	NH Flat	Per cent	£1 Level Stake
Bangor	2-6	0-2	0-0	1-3	1-1	0-0	33.3	+11.50
Chepstow	2-9	0-3	0-1	2-5	0-0	0-0	22.2	+34.88
Uttoxeter	2-9	1-1	0-1	1-6	0-1	0-0	22.2	+5.00
Towcester	1-4	0-0	0-0	1-3	0-0	0-1	25.0	+6.00
Exeter	1-9	0-2	0-1	1-6	0-0	0-0	11.1	-5.00

WINNING HORSES

Horse	Races Run	1st	2nd	3rd	£
Power Unit	7	1	1	0	4716
Arm And A Leg	13	2	0	2	7542
Red Moor	9	1	2	1	3413
Carew Lad	4	1	0	1	3253

Alessandro Severo		4	1	0	0	3234
Lady Maranzi		6	2	0	1	4684
Total winning prize-money						£26842
Favourites	2-5		40.0%			1.88

MRS A HAMILTON

GREAT BAVINGTON, NORTHUMBLAND

	No. of Hrs	Races Run	1st	2nd	3rd	Unpl	Per cent	£1 Level Stake
NH Flat	1	1	0	0	0	1	0.0	-1.00
Hurdles	4	22	3	2	1	16	13.6	+5.50
Chases	4	8	2	1	0	5	25.0	+3.50
Totals	7	31	5	3	1	22	16.1	+8.00
04-05	7	37	7	5	5	19	18.9	+14.00
03-04	6	29	5	6	6	12	17.2	+4.60

JOCKEYS

	W-R	Per cent	£1 Level Stake
Paddy Aspell	2-3	66.7	+10.50
Peter Buchanan	2-12	16.7	+5.00
T J Dreaper	1-7	14.3	+1.50

COURSE RECORD

	Total W-R	Non-Hndcps Hurdles	Chases	Hndcps Hurdles	Chases	NH Flat	Per cent	£1 Level Stake
Cartmel	1-1	0-0	0-0	1-1	0-0	0-0	100.0	11.00
Newcastle	1-3	0-0	0-0	1-3	0-0	0-0	33.3	+4.00
Carlisle	1-4	0-0	1-1	0-3	0-0	0-0	25.0	+2.50
Kelso	1-5	0-0	0-0	1-3	0-2	0-0	20.0	+3.50
Sedgefield	1-5	0-1	1-2	0-2	0-0	0-0	20.0	0.00

WINNING HORSES

Horse	Races Run	1st	2nd	3rd	£
Tynedale	5	1	0	1	4840
Silver Sedge	10	2	2	0	7482
Lucky Duck	2	1	0	0	3578
Primitive Poppy	9	1	1	0	3304
Total winning prize-money					£19204
Favourites	0-0		0.0%		0.00

M D HAMMOND

MIDDLEHAM MOOR, N YORKS

	No. of Hrs	Races Run	1st	2nd	3rd	Unpl	Per cent	£1 Level Stake
NH Flat	9	14	0	2	3	9	0.0	-14.00
Hurdles	33	104	12	5	12	75	11.5	+62.58
Chases	13	56	6	9	6	35	10.7	-29.63
Totals	46	174	18	16	21	119	10.3	+18.95
04-05	34	106	16	9	11	70	15.1	-28.92
03-04	27	117	10	12	7	88	8.5	-26.58

BY MONTH

NH Flat	W-R	Per cent	£1 Level Stake	Hurdles	W-R	Per cent	£1 Level Stake
May	0-2	0.0	-2.00	May	1-7	14.3	-2.67
June	0-0	0.0	0.00	June	0-2	0.0	-2.00
July	0-1	0.0	-1.00	July	0-1	0.0	-1.00
August	0-0	0.0	0.00	August	2-3	66.7	+4.75
September	0-0	0.0	0.00	September	1-6	16.7	-1.50
October	0-1	0.0	-1.00	October	0-7	0.0	-7.00
November	0-4	0.0	-4.00	November	2-14	14.3	-0.50
December	0-0	0.0	0.00	December	2-13	15.4	+1.50
January	0-2	0.0	-2.00	January	2-11	18.2	+102.00
February	0-2	0.0	-2.00	February	0-9	0.0	-9.00
March	0-1	0.0	-1.00	March	2-17	11.8	-8.00
April	0-1	0.0	-1.00	April	0-14	0.0	-14.00

Chases	W-R	Per cent	£1 Level Stake	Totals	W-R	Per cent	£1 Level Stake
May	0-5	0.0	-5.00	May	1-14	7.1	-9.67
June	0-3	0.0	-3.00	June	0-5	0.0	-5.00
July	0-2	0.0	-2.00	July	0-4	0.0	-4.00
August	1-2	50.0	+1.50	August	3-5	60.0	+6.25
September	1-2	50.0	+2.50	September	2-8	25.0	+1.00
October	1-3	33.3	-0.38	October	1-11	9.1	-8.38
November	0-11	0.0	-11.00	November	2-29	6.9	-15.50
December	2-8	25.0	+2.25	December	4-21	19.0	+3.75
January	0-4	0.0	-4.00	January	2-17	11.8	+96.00
February	1-4	25.0	+1.50	February	1-15	6.7	-9.50
March	0-5	0.0	-5.00	March	2-23	8.7	-14.00
April	0-7	0.0	-7.00	April	0-22	0.0	-22.00

DISTANCE

Hurdles	W-R	Per cent	£1 Level Stake	Chases	W-R	Per cent	£1 Level Stake
2m-2m3f	7-67	10.4	+72.33	2m-2m3f	1-14	7.1	-7.50
2m4f-2m7f	5-32	15.6	-4.75	2m4f-2m7f	3-21	14.3	-8.25
3m+	0-5	0.0	-5.00	3m+	2-21	9.5	-13.88

TYPE OF RACE

Non-Handicaps	W-R	Per cent	£1 Level Stake	Handicaps	W-R	Per cent	£1 Level Stake
Nov Hrdls	4-50	8.0	+71.83	Nov Hrdls	3-10	30.0	+10.50
Hrdls	3-16	18.8	-0.25	Hrdls	1-23	4.3	-19.00
Nov Chs	0-4	0.0	-4.00	Nov Chs	1-6	16.7	-2.25
Chases	0-6	0.0	-6.00	Chases	4-39	10.3	-19.00
Sell/Claim	0-2	0.0	-2.00	Sell/Claim	1-3	33.3	+1.50

RACE CLASS

	W-R	Per cent	£1 Level Stake
Class 1	0-1	0.0	-1.00
Class 2	0-2	0.0	-2.00
Class 3	3-36	8.3	-21.75
Class 4	14-111	12.6	+63.21
Class 5	1-12	8.3	-7.50
Class 6	0-12	0.0	-12.00

FIRST TIME OUT

	W-R	Per cent	£1 Level Stake
Bumpers	0-9	0.0	-9.00
Hurdles	4-29	13.8	-1.25
Chases	0-8	0.0	-8.00
Totals	4-46	8.7	-18.25

JOCKEYS

	W-R	Per cent	£1 Level Stake
G Lee	6-46	13.0	-19.42
Neil Mulholland	5-55	9.1	-22.75
Barry Keniry	4-28	14.3	+88.63
Tony Dobbin	2-13	15.4	-0.50
Wilson Renwick	1-16	6.3	-11.00

COURSE RECORD

	Total W-R	Non-Hndcps Hurdles	Chases	Hndcps Hurdles	Chases	NH Flat	Per cent	£1 Level Stake
Ayr	4-21	1-6	0-1	2-8	1-4	0-2	19.0	+99.50
Sedgefield	4-22	4-7	0-4	0-4	0-7	0-0	18.2	-5.42
Wetherby	3-35	0-13	0-0	2-10	1-6	0-6	8.6	-20.75
Cartmel	2-6	0-2	0-0	1-3	1-1	0-0	33.3	+2.00
Catterick	2-8	1-3	0-1	0-1	1-2	0-1	25.0	+10.50
Hexham	2-14	0-3	1-2	0-1	1-8	0-0	14.3	-6.88
Kelso	1-11	1-7	0-0	0-1	0-3	0-0	9.1	-3.00

WINNING HORSES

Horse	Races Run	1st	2nd	3rd	£
Aston Lad	8	3	2	0	16428
Jimmy Bond	4	2	1	0	5712
Boris The Spider	7	1	0	1	4554
Mexican	7	1	0	0	4114
Karo De Vindecy	9	1	3	1	3829
Tee-Jay	10	2	1	4	6944
Snow's Ride	7	2	0	1	3388
*Serbelloni	3	1	0	0	3316
Industrial Star	2	1	0	1	3253
Green 'N' Gold	8	1	0	1	3084
High Country	3	1	0	1	2961
Calfraz	8	1	1	3	2928
Charlotte Vale	2	1	1	0	2720
Total winning prize-money					**£63231**
Favourites	5-13		38.5%		4.13

G A HARKER

THIRKLEBY, N YORKS

	No. of Hrs	Races Run	1st	2nd	3rd	Unpl	Per cent	£1 Level Stake
NH Flat	11	20	4	2	4	10	20.0	+12.50
Hurdles	16	54	8	4	3	39	14.8	-25.93
Chases	5	21	1	1	5	14	4.8	-6.00
Totals	27	95	13	7	12	63	13.7	-19.43
04-05	20	75	10	10	11	44	13.3	-5.08
03-04	21	73	11	9	4	49	15.1	-9.00

	W-R	Per cent	£1 Level Stake
Class 5	0-7	0.0	-7.00
Class 6	4-20	20.0	+12.50

	W-R	Per cent	£1 Level Stake
Totals	8-27	29.6	+33.25

BY MONTH

NH Flat	W-R	Per cent	£1 Level Stake	Hurdles	W-R	Per cent	£1 Level Stake
May	0-3	0.0	-3.00	May	0-5	0.0	-5.00
June	0-2	0.0	-2.00	June	2-4	50.0	+6.83
July	0-0	0.0	0.00	July	1-1	100.0	+0.67
August	0-0	0.0	0.00	August	1-1	100.0	+2.25
September	1-1	100.0	+5.50	September	1-2	50.0	+2.00
October	0-1	0.0	-1.00	October	0-3	0.0	-3.00
November	3-6	50.0	+20.00	November	1-8	12.5	-3.50
December	0-2	0.0	-2.00	December	0-5	0.0	-5.00
January	0-0	0.0	0.00	January	0-6	0.0	-6.00
February	0-1	0.0	-1.00	February	0-6	0.0	-6.00
March	0-2	0.0	-2.00	March	1-4	25.0	-2.43
April	0-2	0.0	-2.00	April	1-9	11.1	-6.75

Chases	W-R	Per cent	£1 Level Stake	Totals	W-R	Per cent	£1 Level Stake
May	0-1	0.0	-1.00	May	0-9	0.0	-9.00
June	0-0	0.0	0.00	June	2-6	33.3	+4.83
July	0-0	0.0	0.00	July	1-1	100.0	+0.67
August	0-0	0.0	0.00	August	1-1	100.0	+2.25
September	1-1	100.0	+14.00	September	3-4	75.0	+21.50
October	0-2	0.0	-2.00	October	0-6	0.0	-6.00
November	0-0	0.0	0.00	November	4-14	28.6	+16.50
December	0-4	0.0	-4.00	December	0-11	0.0	-11.00
January	0-4	0.0	-4.00	January	0-10	0.0	-10.00
February	0-4	0.0	-4.00	February	0-11	0.0	-11.00
March	0-3	0.0	-3.00	March	1-9	11.1	-7.43
April	0-2	0.0	-2.00	April	1-13	7.7	-10.75

DISTANCE

Hurdles	W-R	Per cent	£1 Level Stake	Chases	W-R	Per cent	£1 Level Stake
2m-2m3f	6-30	20.0	-8.68	2m-2m3f	1-11	9.1	+4.00
2m4f-2m7f	1-16	6.3	-13.75	2m4f-2m7f	0-7	0.0	-7.00
3m+	1-8	12.5	-3.50	3m+	0-3	0.0	-3.00

TYPE OF RACE

Non-Handicaps	W-R	Per cent	£1 Level Stake	Handicaps	W-R	Per cent	£1 Level Stake
Nov Hrdls	4-19	21.1	-7.01	Nov Hrdls	0-3	0.0	0.00
Hrdls	0-3	0.0	-3.00	Hrdls	4-24	16.7	-7.92
Nov Chs	1-9	11.1	+6.00	Nov Chs	0-4	0.0	-4.00
Chases	0-1	0.0	-1.00	Chases	0-7	0.0	-7.00
Sell/Claim	0-4	0.0	-4.00	Sell/Claim	0-1	0.0	-1.00

RACE CLASS / FIRST TIME OUT

	W-R	Per cent	£1 Level Stake		W-R	Per cent	£1 Level Stake
Class 1	0-0	0.0	0.00	Bumpers	4-11	36.4	+21.50
Class 2	0-2	0.0	-2.00	Hurdles	3-12	25.0	+0.75
Class 3	6-29	20.7	+3.75	Chases	1-4	25.0	+11.00
Class 4	3-37	8.1	-26.68				

JOCKEYS

	W-R	Per cent	£1 Level Stake
William Kennedy	9-28	32.1	+19.32
Richard McGrath	2-17	11.8	-4.00
Brian Harding	1-5	20.0	+8.00
N Hannity	1-8	12.5	-5.75

COURSE RECORD

	Total W-R	Non-Hndcps Hurdles	Chases	Hndcps Hurdles	Chases	NH Flat	Per cent	£1 Level Stake
Perth	6-15	1-4	1-1	3-7	0-1	1-2	40.0	+24.58
Hexham	2-5	0-2	0-0	0-0	0-0	2-3	40.0	+8.00
Mrket Rsn	2-7	2-2	0-1	0-3	0-0	0-1	28.6	-3.76
Sedgefield	2-14	0-2	0-3	1-6	0-1	1-2	14.3	+3.50
Wetherby	1-6	1-3	0-0	0-2	0-0	0-1	16.7	-3.75

WINNING HORSES

Horse	Races Run	1st	2nd	3rd	£
Farne Isle	6	1	1	0	7621
Cyborg De Sou	8	1	0	3	6809
*Top Style	7	1	1	0	5616
Rajam	4	3	0	0	4860
Jethro Tull	6	1	0	1	4759
Notaproblem	8	1	2	2	3892
Custom Design	4	2	0	1	4598
Zaffie Parson	6	1	0	0	2487
Balamory Dan	3	1	0	1	2275
Red Poker	3	1	0	0	1987
Total winning prize-money					£44904
Favourites	7-13		53.8%		8.57

M F HARRIS

EDGCOTE, NORTHANTS

	No. of Hrs	Races Run	1st	2nd	3rd	Unpl	Per cent	£1 Level Stake
NH Flat	1	1	0	0	0	1	0.0	-1.00
Hurdles	38	152	13	16	19	104	8.6	-40.13
Chases	14	65	5	4	11	45	7.7	-32.25
Totals	44	218	18	20	30	150	8.3	-81.38
04-05	38	175	9	17	16	133	5.1	-58.75
03-04	40	150	9	11	11	119	6.0	-111.07

BY MONTH

NH Flat	W-R	Per cent	£1 Level Stake	Hurdles	W-R	Per cent	£1 Level Stake
May	0-0	0.0	0.00	May	0-10	0.0	-10.00
June	0-1	0.0	-1.00	June	0-11	0.0	-11.00
July	0-0	0.0	0.00	July	2-6	33.3	+13.88
August	0-0	0.0	0.00	August	0-9	0.0	-9.00
September	0-0	0.0	0.00	September	2-11	18.2	+6.50

October	0-0	0.0	0.00
November	0-0	0.0	0.00
December	0-0	0.0	0.00
January	0-0	0.0	0.00
February	0-0	0.0	0.00
March	0-0	0.0	0.00
April	0-0	0.0	0.00

October	0-16	0.0	-16.00
November	1-10	10.0	-2.50
December	3-11	27.3	+3.00
January	1-20	5.0	-7.00
February	2-16	12.5	-6.50
March	1-16	6.3	+5.00
April	1-16	6.3	-14.50

Chases	W-R	Per cent	£1 Level Stake
May	1-5	20.0	-2.75
June	0-2	0.0	-2.00
July	1-3	33.3	+1.50
August	0-1	0.0	-1.00
September	0-6	0.0	-6.00
October	0-6	0.0	-6.00
November	0-6	0.0	-6.00
December	0-8	0.0	-8.00
January	1-5	20.0	+6.00
February	1-5	20.0	+5.00
March	1-6	16.7	-1.00
April	0-12	0.0	-12.00

Totals	W-R	Per cent	£1 Level Stake
May	1-15	6.7	-12.75
June	0-14	0.0	-14.00
July	3-9	33.3	+15.38
August	0-10	0.0	-10.00
September	2-17	11.8	+0.50
October	0-22	0.0	-22.00
November	1-16	6.3	-8.50
December	3-19	15.8	-5.00
January	2-25	8.0	-1.00
February	3-21	14.3	-1.50
March	2-22	9.1	+4.00
April	1-28	3.6	-26.50

DISTANCE

Hurdles	W-R	Per cent	£1 Level Stake
2m-2m3f	12-111	10.8	-20.13
2m4f-2m7f	1-34	2.9	-21.00
3m+	0-7	0.0	-7.00

Chases	W-R	Per cent	£1 Level Stake
2m-2m3f	2-23	8.7	-8.50
2m4f-2m7f	2-26	7.7	-10.00
3m+	1-16	6.3	-13.75

TYPE OF RACE

Non-Handicaps

	W-R	Per cent	£1 Level Stake
Nov Hrdls	2-44	4.5	-31.13
Hrdls	1-20	5.0	-18.50
Nov Chs	1-13	7.7	-8.50
Chases	0-1	0.0	-1.00
Sell/Claim	2-6	33.3	+3.50

Handicaps

	W-R	Per cent	£1 Level Stake
Nov Hrdls	1-14	7.1	+7.00
Hrdls	2-56	3.6	-31.50
Nov Chs	0-9	0.0	-9.00
Chases	4-40	10.0	-11.75
Sell/Claim	4-12	33.3	+9.50

RACE CLASS

	W-R	Per cent	£1 Level Stake
Class 1	0-1	0.0	-1.00
Class 2	0-5	0.0	-5.00
Class 3	4-50	8.0	-13.88
Class 4	4-126	3.2	-87.00
Class 5	10-35	28.6	+27.50
Class 6	0-1	0.0	-1.00

FIRST TIME OUT

	W-R	Per cent	£1 Level Stake
Bumpers	0-1	0.0	-1.00
Hurdles	1-36	2.8	-33.13
Chases	0-7	0.0	-7.00
Totals	1-44	2.3	-41.13

JOCKEYS

	W-R	Per cent	£1 Level Stake
Charlie Poste	9-96	9.4	-34.00
P J Brennan	3-44	6.8	-15.63
Mr H Engblom	1-1	100.0	+16.00
A P McCoy	1-3	33.3	-0.75
Richard Johnson	1-3	33.3	+7.00
Sam Thomas	1-4	25.0	+3.50
John Kington	1-4	25.0	+0.50
John McNamara	1-8	12.5	-3.00

COURSE RECORD

	Total W-R	Non-Hndcps Hurdles	Non-Hndcps Chases	Hndcps Hurdles	Hndcps Chases	NH Flat	Per cent	£1 Level Stake
Stratford	3-17	2-6	0-3	1-6	0-1	0-1	17.6	+12.88
Hereford	2-5	1-2	0-0	0-1	1-2	0-0	40.0	+10.00
Mrket Rsn	2-18	0-7	0-0	2-7	0-4	0-0	11.1	-8.00
Fakenham	1-3	0-1	0-0	0-1	1-1	0-0	33.3	-0.75
Newbury	1-4	0-2	0-0	1-1	0-1	0-0	25.0	+17.00
Worcester	1-4	0-0	0-2	0-0	1-2	0-0	25.0	+1.00
Cartmel	1-5	0-4	1-1	0-0	0-0	0-0	20.0	-0.50
Chepstow	1-5	1-4	0-0	0-0	0-1	0-0	20.0	-3.50
Sedgefield	1-5	0-1	0-1	0-1	1-2	0-0	20.0	+6.00
Taunton	1-7	1-4	0-1	0-2	0-0	0-0	14.3	-2.50
Warwick	1-9	1-1	0-0	0-5	0-3	0-0	11.1	+4.00
Folkestone	1-10	0-3	0-0	1-5	0-2	0-0	10.0	-6.00
Uttoxeter	1-10	0-1	0-1	1-6	0-2	0-0	10.0	-2.50
Fontwell	1-15	0-5	0-2	1-5	0-3	0-0	6.7	-7.50

WINNING HORSES

Horse	Races Run	1st	2nd	3rd	£
Paxford Jack	4	1	1	2	6776
Moonfleet	4	1	2	0	6235
Federstar	2	1	1	0	6044
*Pseudonym	11	1	1	4	5205
*Mr Fernet	2	1	0	0	5025
Salinas	2	1	0	0	4430
Before The Mast	17	3	0	5	8253
Cyborsun	3	1	0	0	3513
Leopold	13	1	1	3	3354
Pardini	13	1	1	1	3253
Herecomestanley	13	1	3	2	2741
Zeloso	12	2	2	0	4680
*Sunley Future	11	2	0	2	4275
*Lysander	8	1	2	1	0

Total winning prize-money **£63784**

Favourites **2-119** **1.7%** **-111.25**

JOHN A HARRIS

EASTWELL, LEICS

	No. of Hrs	Races Run	1st	2nd	3rd	Unpl	Per cent	£1 Level Stake
NH Flat	*1*	*2*	*0*	*0*	*0*	*2*	*0.0*	*-2.00*
Hurdles	*6*	*15*	*1*	*0*	*0*	*14*	*6.7*	*+8.00*
Chases	*1*	*1*	*0*	*0*	*0*	*1*	*0.0*	*-1.00*
Totals	**7**	**18**	**1**	**0**	**0**	**17**	**5.6**	**+5.00**
04-05	*9*	*28*	*0*	*0*	*2*	*26*	*0.0*	*-28.00*
03-04	*10*	*36*	*2*	*1*	*0*	*33*	*5.6*	*+8.00*

JOCKEYS

	W-R	Per cent	£1 Level Stake
Andrew Tinkler	1-5	20.0	+18.00

COURSE RECORD

	Total W-R	Non-Hndcps Hurdles	Chases	Hndcps Hurdles	Chases	NH Flat	Per cent	£1 Level Stake
Fakenham	1-1	1-1	0-0	0-0	0-0	0-0	100.0	+22.00

WINNING HORSES

Horse	Races Run	1st	2nd	3rd	£
*Muntami	6	1	0	0	2928
Total winning prize-money					**£2928**
Favourites	**0-0**		**0.0%**		**0.00**

P C HASLAM

MIDDLEHAM MOOR, N YORKS

	No. of Hrs	Races Run	1st	2nd	3rd	Unpl	Per cent	£1 Level Stake
NH Flat	1	5	2	1	0	2	40.0	+4.50
Hurdles	33	124	24	14	12	74	19.4	-5.53
Chases	8	28	2	4	5	17	7.1	-9.50
Totals	**40**	**157**	**28**	**19**	**17**	**93**	**17.8**	**-10.53**
04-05	19	67	11	2	10	43	16.4	7.04
03-04	16	52	18	10	4	20	34.6	+10.28

BY MONTH

NH Flat	W-R	Per cent	£1 Level Stake	Hurdles	W-R	Per cent	£1 Level Stake
May	0-0	0.0	0.00	May	1-4	25.0	+0.50
June	0-0	0.0	0.00	June	0-2	0.0	-2.00
July	0-0	0.0	0.00	July	1-7	14.3	-3.75
August	0-0	0.0	0.00	August	1-13	7.7	-10.75
September	0-0	0.0	0.00	September	3-14	21.4	-2.47
October	0-0	0.0	0.00	October	3-14	21.4	+17.00
November	2-2	100.0	+7.50	November	6-20	30.0	+8.58
December	0-0	0.0	0.00	December	1-3	33.3	0.00
January	0-0	0.0	0.00	January	3-10	30.0	-0.65
February	0-1	0.0	-1.00	February	1-10	10.0	-2.00
March	0-1	0.0	-1.00	March	2-14	14.3	-3.13
April	0-1	0.0	-1.00	April	2-13	15.4	-6.88

Chases	W-R	Per cent	£1 Level Stake	Totals	W-R	Per cent	£1 Level Stake
May	0-1	0.0	-1.00	May	1-5	20.0	-0.50
June	0-0	0.0	0.00	June	0-2	0.0	-2.00
July	0-0	0.0	0.00	July	1-7	14.3	-3.75
August	1-2	50.0	+11.00	August	2-15	13.3	+0.25
September	0-0	0.0	0.00	September	3-14	21.4	-2.47
October	0-3	0.0	-3.00	October	3-17	17.6	+14.00
November	0-3	0.0	-3.00	November	8-25	32.0	+13.08
December	1-1	100.0	+4.50	December	2-4	50.0	+4.50

January	0-3	0.0	-3.00	January	3-13	23.1	-3.65
February	0-5	0.0	-5.00	February	1-16	6.3	-8.00
March	0-4	0.0	-4.00	March	2-19	10.5	-8.13
April	0-6	0.0	-6.00	April	2-20	10.0	-13.88

DISTANCE

Hurdles	W-R	Per cent	£1 Level Stake	Chases	W-R	Per cent	£1 Level Stake
2m-2m3f	20-100	20.0	+2.92	2m-2m3f	0-4	0.0	-4.00
2m4f-2m7f	4-20	20.0	-4.45	2m4f-2m7f	1-13	7.7	0.00
3m+	0-4	0.0	-4.00	3m+	1-11	9.1	-5.50

TYPE OF RACE

Non-Handicaps	W-R	Per cent	£1 Level Stake	Handicaps	W-R	Per cent	£1 Level Stake
Nov Hrdls	13-70	18.6	-0.61	Nov Hrdls	3-14	21.4	+1.88
Hrdls	0-5	0.0	-5.00	Hrdls	2-18	11.1	-7.80
Nov Chs	1-7	14.3	-1.50	Nov Chs	1-6	16.7	+7.00
Chases	0-0	0.0	0.00	Chases	0-15	0.0	-15.00
Sell/Claim	5-12	41.7	+7.75	Sell/Claim	1-7	14.3	-3.75

RACE CLASS

	W-R	Per cent	£1 Level Stake
Class 1	0-7	0.0	-7.00
Class 2	1-5	20.0	1.50
Class 3	4-38	10.5	-4.92
Class 4	15-83	18.1	-8.62
Class 5	6-20	30.0	+6.00
Class 6	7-4	50.0	+5.50

FIRST TIME OUT

	W-R	Per cent	£1 Level Stake
Bumpers	1-1	100.0	+4.00
Hurdles	6-32	18.8	-0.96
Chases	1-7	14.3	+6.00
Totals	8-40	20.0	+9.04

JOCKEYS

	W-R	Per cent	£1 Level Stake
Paddy Merrigan	11-52	21.2	+7.73
A P McCoy	8-28	28.6	+0.91
Barry Keniry	6-44	13.6	-2.17
Robert Stephens	1-2	50.0	+1.00
T J O'Brien	1-5	20.0	0.00
Gary Bartley	1-14	7.1	-6.00

COURSE RECORD

	Total W-R	Non-Hndcps Hurdles	Chases	Hndcps Hurdles	Chases	NH Flat	Per cent	£1 Level Stake
Mrket Rsn	3-8	3-7	0-0	0-1	0-0	0-0	37.5	+1.00
Kelso	3-10	2-6	0-0	1-2	0-2	0-0	30.0	+13.50
Newcastle	3-12	1-7	1-1	1-3	0-1	0-0	25.0	+4.50
Sedgefield	3-19	0-6	0-2	2-9	1-2	0-0	15.8	+4.20
Towcester	2-7	1-3	0-0	0-1	0-2	1-1	28.6	+0.13
Wetherby	2-10	2-9	0-0	0-1	0-0	0-0	20.0	+5.50
Haydock	2-13	1-5	0-0	0-3	0-3	1-2	15.4	+5.00
Doncaster	1-1	1-1	0-0	0-0	0-0	0-0	100.0	+2.00
Fakenham	1-1	1-1	0-0	0-0	0-0	0-0	100.0	+1.10
Leicester	1-1	1-1	0-0	0-0	0-0	0-0	100.0	+3.50
Sandown	1-1	1-1	0-0	0-0	0-0	0-0	100.0	+0.83

Chepstow	1-2	1-2	0-0	0-0	0-0	0-0	50.0	+1.75
Musselbgh	1-3	1-1	0-0	0-1	0-1	0-0	33.3	0.00
Perth	1-5	1-3	0-0	0-1	0-1	0-0	20.0	0.00
Ayr	1-6	0-0	0-0	1-4	0-2	0-0	16.7	-3.13
Hexham	1-7	0-2	0-0	1-5	0-0	0-0	14.3	-3.75
Bangor	1-12	1-11	0-1	0-0	0-0	0-0	8.3	-7.67

WINNING HORSES

Horse	Races Run	1st	2nd	3rd	£
Alfred The Great	4	2	0	1	17800
Kerry's Blade	6	1	0	0	4914
Vocative	6	1	1	0	4814
Dan's Heir	7	2	1	0	4784
Mr Mischief	7	3	3	1	11787
Dalida	3	1	1	0	4212
Nocatee	9	1	0	4	4179
Red Flyer	2	1	0	0	4173
Heraldry	5	2	1	0	5544
The Pen	2	1	0	0	3612
Etoile Russe	6	2	0	0	6036
Patxaran	6	2	2	1	6415
Royal Master	4	1	1	0	3469
Comical Errors	7	1	2	1	3364
Good Investment	7	1	1	0	3147
Dennick	6	2	1	1	4973
Zando	2	1	0	0	2857
Maunby Rocker	8	1	1	1	2350
Fox Point	2	1	0	0	2277
*City Of Manchester	3	1	0	1	2193
Total winning prize-money					**£103500**
Favourites	235-253		**92.9%**		**562.01**

N J HAWKE

HEWISH, SOMERSET

	No. of Hrs	Races Run	1st	2nd	3rd	Unpl	Per cent	£1 Level Stake
NH Flat	4	8	0	0	2	6	0.0	-8.00
Hurdles	24	54	2	2	0	50	3.7	-40.00
Chases	12	54	4	5	7	38	7.4	+38.25
Totals	**33**	**116**	**6**	**7**	**9**	**94**	**5.2**	**-9.75**
04-05	*24*	*104*	*4*	*5*	*11*	*84*	*3.8*	*-69.00*
03-04	*27*	*74*	*4*	*0*	*6*	*64*	*5.4*	*-53.63*

JOCKEYS

	W-R	Per cent	£1 Level Stake
Andrew Thornton	2-11	18.2	+11.00
Keiran Burke	2-51	3.9	-37.00
David Dennis	1-6	16.7	-2.75
P J Brennan	1-19	5.3	+48.00

COURSE RECORD

	Total W-R	Non-Hndcps Hurdles	Chases	Hndcps Hurdles	Chases	NH Flat	Per cent	£1 Level Stake
Mrket Rsn	2-4	0-1	0-0	2-2	0-1	0-0	50.0	+10.00
Newbury	1-2	0-0	0-0	0-0	1-2	0-0	50.0	+5.00
Plumpton	1-6	0-1	0-0	0-1	1-4	0-0	16.7	+9.00
Worcester	1-7	0-1	0-0	0-1	1-4	0-1	14.3	+60.00
Uttoxeter	1-12	0-2	0-0	0-3	1-7	0-0	8.3	-8.75

WINNING HORSES

Horse	Races Run	1st	2nd	3rd	£
Soeur Fontenail	10	2	1	1	12320
Papua	6	1	1	0	5746
Honneur Fontenail	9	1	0	2	3817
Friendly Request	3	1	0	0	3259
Rude Health	5	1	1	0	3253
Total winning prize-money					**£28395**
Favourites	0-0		**0.0%**		**0.00**

N J HENDERSON

UPPER LAMBOURN, BERKS

	No. of Hrs	Races Run	1st	2nd	3rd	Unpl	Per cent	£1 Level Stake
NH Flat	30	52	20	9	4	19	38.5	+41.30
Hurdles	67	208	44	23	25	116	21.2	-15.25
Chases	37	129	21	12	14	82	16.3	+18.37
Totals	**118**	**389**	**85**	**44**	**43**	**217**	**21.9**	**+44.42**
04-05	*122*	*373*	*53*	*52*	*45*	*223*	*14.2*	*-61.09*
03-04	*115*	*375*	*80*	*36*	*50*	*209*	*21.3*	*+15.21*

BY MONTH

NH Flat	W-R	Per cent	£1 Level Stake	Hurdles	W-R	Per cent	£1 Level Stake
May	2-2	100.0	+7.00	May	2-13	15.4	-2.50
June	1-2	50.0	-0.09	June	0-1	0.0	-1.00
July	0-0	0.0	0.00	July	0-0	0.0	0.00
August	0-1	0.0	-1.00	August	0-0	0.0	0.00
September	0-0	0.0	0.00	September	0-1	0.0	-1.00
October	1-3	33.3	0.00	October	3-9	33.3	+6.50
November	3-9	33.3	+0.33	November	5-20	25.0	-4.13
December	1-4	25.0	+6.00	December	9-36	25.0	+5.35
January	2-4	50.0	+0.50	January	8-28	28.6	+11.46
February	3-4	75.0	+11.23	February	9-34	26.5	+0.44
March	5-11	45.5	+20.83	March	5-36	13.9	-12.00
April	2-12	16.7	-3.50	April	3-30	10.0	-18.38

Chases	W-R	Per cent	£1 Level Stake	Totals	W-R	Per cent	£1 Level Stake
May	0-0	0.0	0.00	May	4-15	26.7	+4.50
June	0-0	0.0	0.00	June	1-3	33.3	-1.09
July	0-1	0.0	-1.00	July	0-1	0.0	-1.00
August	0-0	0.0	0.00	August	0-1	0.0	-1.00
September	0-0	0.0	0.00	September	0-1	0.0	-1.00

	W-R	Per cent	£1 Level Stake		W-R	Per cent	£1 Level Stake
October	1-2	50.0	+2.33	October	5-14	35.7	+8.83
November	3-22	13.6	-3.50	November	11-51	21.6	-7.30
December	5-20	25.0	+4.00	December	15-60	25.0	+15.35
January	4-18	22.2	+3.83	January	14-50	28.0	+15.79
February	2-14	14.3	+1.00	February	14-52	26.9	+12.67
March	5-21	23.8	+25.71	March	15-68	22.1	+34.54
April	1-31	3.2	-14.00	April	6-73	8.2	-35.88

Course	W-R						Per cent	£1 Level Stake
Huntingdon	6-19	3-7	0-4	2-4	0-3	1-1	31.6	-1.68
Ludlow	6-21	1-4	0-2	3-10	0-1	2-4	28.6	+16.50
Plumpton	5-8	3-4	0-2	1-1	0-0	1-1	62.5	+7.50
Folkestone	4-6	2-3	0-1	1-1	0-0	1-1	66.7	+9.33
Wincanton	4-12	0-3	0-0	0-3	2-4	2-2	33.3	+1.73
Chepstow	3-6	1-2	1-1	0-2	0-0	1-1	50.0	+10.50
Worcester	3-6	0-1	0-0	1-2	0-0	2-3	50.0	+3.60
Warwick	3-11	0-5	1-1	0-2	1-1	1-2	27.3	+8.50
Lingfield	3-13	0-3	2-4	1-3	0-3	0-0	23.1	-0.67
Towcester	2-7	1-3	0-2	0-0	0-0	1-2	28.6	+2.50
Exeter	2-8	1-4	0-2	0-1	1-1	0-0	25.0	-1.88
Bangor	2-9	0-3	0-1	0-1	0-1	2-3	22.2	+4.00
Southwell	2-9	0-0	1-1	0-5	0-2	1-1	22.2	-3.27
Taunton	2-9	2-4	0-1	0-2	0-1	0-1	22.2	+0.13
Fontwell	2-12	0-7	0-2	1-1	0-0	1-2	16.7	+0.50
Mrket Rsn	1-1	1-1	0-0	0-0	0-0	0-0	100.0	+4.00
Nton Abbot	1-2	1-2	0-0	0-0	0-0	0-0	50.0	+4.00
Wetherby	1-2	1-1	0-0	0-0	0-1	0-0	50.0	+2.50
Windsor	1-3	0-1	0-0	0-1	1-1	0-0	33.3	-1.00
Fakenham	1-5	1-2	0-0	0-0	0-0	0-3	20.0	-2.75
Hereford	1-7	0-2	0-0	1-3	0-0	0-2	14.3	-4.38
Uttoxeter	1-7	1-1	0-0	0-4	0-2	0-0	14.3	-3.50
Ayr	1-8	1-1	0-0	0-3	0-3	0-1	12.5	-3.50
Stratford	1-9	0-1	0-1	0-3	0-1	1-3	11.1	-7.09
Aintree	1-23	0-3	0-3	0-4	1-9	0-4	4.3	-6.00

DISTANCE

Hurdles	W-R	Per cent	£1 Level Stake	Chases	W-R	Per cent	£1 Level Stake
2m-2m3f	31-133	23.3	+0.12	2m-2m3f	5-36	13.9	+17.00
2m4f-2m7f	12-64	18.8	-7.25	2m4f-2m7f	12-52	23.1	+20.00
3m+	1-11	9.1	-8.13	3m+	4-41	9.8	-18.63

TYPE OF RACE

Non-Handicaps	W-R	Per cent	£1 Level Stake	Handicaps	W-R	Per cent	£1 Level Stake
Nov Hrdls	22-76	28.9	-2.21	Nov Hrdls	5-25	20.0	+3.75
Hrdls	3-24	12.5	-7.63	Hrdls	14-82	17.1	-8.17
Nov Chs	6-31	19.4	-0.67	Nov Chs	0-12	0.0	-12.00
Chases	3-10	30.0	+1.21	Chases	12-76	15.8	+29.83
Sell/Claim	0-1	0.0	-1.00	Sell/Claim	0-0	0.0	0.00

RACE CLASS / FIRST TIME OUT

	W-R	Per cent	£1 Level Stake		W-R	Per cent	£1 Level Stake
Class 1	8-80	10.0	-2.83	Bumpers	14-30	46.7	+35.74
Class 2	8-53	15.1	-5.39	Hurdles	11-56	19.6	-13.50
Class 3	23-120	19.2	+5.21	Chases	5-32	15.6	-0.67
Class 4	27-91	29.7	+6.13				
Class 5	3-9	33.3	+15.50	Totals	30-118	25.4	+21.57
Class 6	16-36	44.4	+25.80				

JOCKEYS

	W-R	Per cent	£1 Level Stake
Mick Fitzgerald	44-181	24.3	+25.01
Marcus Foley	14-71	19.7	+14.83
Andrew Tinkler	7-65	10.8	-19.50
A P McCoy	4-11	36.4	-2.98
Mr J Snowden	3-6	50.0	+4.38
Mr T Greenall	3-6	50.0	+12.75
Sam Curling	3-18	16.7	-8.07
Charlie Studd	2-7	28.6	+4.00
Mr S Waley-Cohen	2-14	14.3	+5.00
Sam Thomas	1-1	100.0	+3.50
B J Geraghty	1-1	100.0	+6.00
Mr C R Nelson	1-1	100.0	+6.50

COURSE RECORD

	Total W-R	Non-Hndcps Hurdles	Chases	Hndcps Hurdles	Chases	NH Flat	Per cent	£1 Level Stake
Sandown	9-38	1-6	2-5	4-15	1-9	1-3	23.7	+11.08
Cheltenham	9-53	1-9	2-3	1-15	4-24	1-2	17.0	+18.54
Newbury	8-48	3-14	0-2	3-14	1-12	1-6	16.7	+2.23

WINNING HORSES

Horse	Races Run	1st	2nd	3rd	£
Fondmort	6	2	0	1	10833R
Trabolgan	1	1	0	0	71275
Liberthine	6	1	0	0	62630
Greenhope	3	1	0	0	42765
Non So	4	1	0	2	42765
Blue Shark	1	1	0	0	28510
Tysou	6	2	0	1	36211
Afsoun	5	2	1	1	30044
Karello Bay	3	2	1	0	16311
The Market Man	3	2	1	0	23832
All Star	5	1	1	0	13812
Crozan	4	1	0	0	10428
Caracciola	6	1	0	0	10192
Scots Grey	7	1	0	1	9739
Tarlac	5	2	0	1	12322
Royals Darling	4	1	2	0	9395
First Love	4	3	0	0	15136
Herakles	7	2	0	1	12021
Copsale Lad	5	2	2	1	12608
Go For Bust	7	1	0	1	7829
Tessanoora	5	2	2	0	11060
Green Iceni	4	1	1	2	6896
Saintsaire	5	1	1	0	6857
Afrad	6	1	0	1	6717
Astyanax	7	2	1	0	9899
Tanikos	8	1	1	2	6506
Lustral Du Seuil	3	1	1	0	6129
Its A Dream	4	2	0	0	8588

In Media Res	5	2	0	2	9051
Shining Strand	10	2	3	1	10350
Nas Na Riogh	3	1	0	0	5205
Temoin	4	3	0	0	14639
Au Courant	2	2	0	0	7075
Lady Of Fortune	2	1	0	0	5062
Brankley Boy	5	2	1	2	9434
*Reaching Out	4	1	0	0	4840
Capitana	5	2	1	1	8887
Unjust Law	6	3	1	0	8967
Menchikov	5	1	2	1	4372
Craven	5	2	1	0	6206
*Jack The Giant	2	1	1	0	4229
Royal Corrouge	1	1	0	0	3982
Trompette	4	2	0	1	6987
Restless D'Artaix	2	1	0	1	3721
*Princelet	2	1	0	0	3578
Classic Fiddle	2	2	0	0	5291
*Queen's Dancer	3	1	0	0	3253
Wogan	4	1	2	0	3253
Doomshakalaka	1	1	0	0	3114
Sir Jimmy Shand	3	2	0	0	4315
Amaretto Rose	2	1	0	0	2602
Jean Le Poisson	2	1	0	0	2056
Slick	5	1	0	0	2030
Bonchester Bridge	8	1	2	1	1873
Major Miller	3	1	1	0	1871
Mam Ratagan	2	1	0	0	1713
Barbers Shop	1	1	0	0	1713
Star Award	1	1	0	0	1627
Paix Eternelle	2	1	0	0	1627
Total winning prize-money					**£791738**
Favourites	38-99		**38.4%**		**0.87**

LADY HERRIES

PATCHING, W SUSSEX

	No. of Hrs	Races Run	1st	2nd	3rd	Unpl	Per cent	£1 Level Stake
NH Flat	0	0	0	0	0	0	0.0	0.00
Hurdles	5	10	3	1	1	5	30.0	+37.00
Chases	1	3	0	0	0	3	0.0	-3.00
Totals	6	13	3	1	1	8	23.1	+34.00
04-05	5	15	4	2	6	3	26.7	+21.13
03-04	5	8	0	1	1	6	0.0	-8.00

JOCKEYS

	W-R	Per cent	£1 Level Stake
Leighton Aspell	2-6	33.3	+15.00
Andrew Thornton	1-1	100.0	+25.00

COURSE RECORD

	Total W-R	Non-Hndcps Hurdles	Chases	Hndcps Hurdles	Chases	NH Flat	Per cent	£1 Level Stake
Fontwell	1-1	1-1	0-0	0-0	0-0	0-0	100.0	+25.00

Sandown	1-1	0-0	0-0	1-1	0-0	0-0	100.0	+5.00
Folkestone	1-2	1-1	0-1	0-0	0-0	0-0	50.0	+13.00

WINNING HORSES

Horse	Races Run	1st	2nd	3rd	£
Kipsigis	2	2	0	0	8751
Warningcamp	3	1	0	0	3526
Total winning prize-money					**£12277**
Favourites	0-68		**0.0%**		**-68.00**

J HETHERTON

NORTON, N YORKS

	No. of Hrs	Races Run	1st	2nd	3rd	Unpl	Per cent	£1 Level Stake
NH Flat	2	2	0	1	0	1	0.0	-2.00
Hurdles	9	44	2	5	3	33	4.5	-22.50
Chases	1	1	0	0	0	1	0.0	-1.00
Totals	11	47	2	6	3	35	4.3	-25.50
04-05	19	54	3	6	2	43	5.6	-29.00
03-04	13	71	6	8	9	48	8.5	+4.25

JOCKEYS

	W-R	Per cent	£1 Level Stake
Keith Mercer	2-6	33.3	+15.50

COURSE RECORD

	Total W-R	Non-Hndcps Hurdles	Chases	Hndcps Hurdles	Chases	NH Flat	Per cent	£1 Level Stake
Doncaster	1-2	0-1	0-0	1-1	0-0	0-0	50.0	+7.50
Mrket Rsn	1-6	0-0	0-0	1-5	0-0	0-1	16.7	+6.00

WINNING HORSES

Horse	Races Run	1st	2nd	3rd	£
Qualitair Pleasure	11	2	3	1	4320
Total winning prize-money					**£4320**
Favourites	0-0		**0.0%**		**0.00**

P W HIATT

HOOK NORTON, OXON

	No. of Hrs	Races Run	1st	2nd	3rd	Unpl	Per cent	£1 Level Stake
NH Flat	5	8	0	0	0	8	0.0	-8.00
Hurdles	14	45	2	2	4	37	4.4	+13.00
Chases	6	19	3	1	1	14	15.8	-1.65
Totals	21	72	5	3	5	59	6.9	+3.35
04-05	17	36	0	1	2	33	0.0	-36.00
03-04	7	18	2	3	2	11	11.1	-10.20

JOCKEYS

	W-R	Per cent	£1 Level Stake
Robert Thornton	2-6	33.3	-1.65
Sean Fox	1-1	100.0	+50.00
Vince Slattery	1-3	33.3	+10.00
Sean Curran	1-12	8.3	-5.00

COURSE RECORD

	Total W-R	Non-Hndcps Hurdles	Chases	Hndcps Hurdles	Chases	NH Flat	Per cent	£1 Level Stake
Stratford	2-7	0-2	0-0	0-0	2-5	0-0	28.6	-2.65
Mrket Rsn	1-3	0-0	0-2	0-0	1-1	0-0	33.3	+10.00
Uttoxeter	1-9	0-3	0-0	1-3	0-0	0-3	11.1	+42.00
Worcester	1-12	0-4	0-0	1-6	0-1	0-1	8.3	-5.00

WINNING HORSES

Horse	Races Run	1st	2nd	3rd	£
*Keltic Lord	11	3	1	2	17164
Tinstre	8	2	2	0	6202
Total winning prize-money					**£23360**
Favourites	2-4		50.0%		0.35

MRS S J HICKMAN

RYE, E SUSSEX

	No. of Hrs	Races Run	1st	2nd	3rd	Unpl	Per cent	£1 Level Stake
NH Flat	0	0	0	0	0	0	0.0	0.00
Hurdles	0	0	0	0	0	0	0.0	0.00
Chases	1	2	1	0	0	1	50.0	+11.00
Totals	1	2	1	0	0	1	50.0	+11.00
04-05	4	5	0	1	0	4	0.0	-5.00
03-04	4	5	0	0	0	5	0.0	-5.00

JOCKEYS

	W-R	Per cent	£1 Level Stake
Mr A Hickman	1-2	50.0	+11.00

COURSE RECORD

	Total W-R	Non-Hndcps Hurdles	Chases	Hndcps Hurdles	Chases	NH Flat	Per cent	£1 Level Stake
Folkestone	1-1	0-0	1-1	0-0	0-0	0-0	100.0	+12.00

WINNING HORSES

Horse	Races Run	1st	2nd	3rd	£
Swincombe	2	1	0	0	1648
Total winning prize-money					**£1648**
Favourites	0-0		0.0%		0.00

MRS T J HILL

CHINNOR, OXON

	No. of Hrs	Races Run	1st	2nd	3rd	Unpl	Per cent	£1 Level Stake
NH Flat	0	0	0	0	0	0	0.0	0.00
Hurdles	2	8	0	3	0	5	0.0	-8.00
Chases	6	27	5	0	4	18	18.5	0.00
Totals	7	35	5	3	4	23	14.3	-8.00
04-05	4	6	3	1	0	2	50.0	+4.75
03-04	2	3	0	0	0	3	0.0	-3.00

JOCKEYS

	W-R	Per cent	£1 Level Stake
Mr J E Tudor	3-9	33.3	+8.00
Andrew Thornton	1-7	14.3	-2.50
Robert Thornton	1-13	7.7	-7.50

COURSE RECORD

	Total W-R	Non-Hndcps Hurdles	Chases	Hndcps Hurdles	Chases	NH Flat	Per cent	£1 Level Stake
Uttoxeter	1-1	0-0	0-0	0-0	1-1	0-0	100.0	+4.50
Plumpton	1-3	0-0	0-1	0-0	1-2	0-0	33.3	+1.50
Cheltenham	1-4	0-0	1-3	0-0	0-1	0-0	25.0	+0.50
Folkestone	1-4	0-0	1-3	0-0	0-1	0-0	25.0	+4.00
Fontwell	1-5	0-0	1-2	0-2	0-1	0-0	20.0	-0.50

WINNING HORSES

Horse	Races Run	1st	2nd	3rd	£
*Balladeer	6	1	0	1	4044
Bell Rock	4	2	0	0	5233
Mr Splodge	3	2	0	0	5624
Total winning prize-money					**£14901**
Favourites	1-1		100.0%		4.50

M R HOAD

LEWES, E SUSSEX

	No. of Hrs	Races Run	1st	2nd	3rd	Unpl	Per cent	£1 Level Stake
NH Flat	0	0	0	0	0	0	0.0	0.00
Hurdles	7	17	0	0	0	17	0.0	-17.00
Chases	1	2	1	0	0	1	50.0	+4.50
Totals	8	19	1	0	0	18	5.3	-12.50
04-05	4	22	1	5	0	16	4.5	-18.25
03-04	5	8	2	1	0	5	25.0	+4.00

JOCKEYS

	W-R	Per cent	£1 Level Stake
Tom Scudamore	1-5	20.0	+1.50

COURSE RECORD

	Total W-R	Non-Hndcps Hurdles	Chases	Hndcps Hurdles	Chases	NH Flat	Per cent	£1 Level Stake
Towcester	1-2	0-0	0-0	0-1	1-1	0-0	50.0	+4.50

WINNING HORSES

Horse	Races Run	1st	2nd	3rd	£
The Staggery Boy	2	1	0	0	3513
Total winning prize-money					**£3513**
Favourites	0-0		0.0%		0.00

P J HOBBS

WITHYCOMBE, SOMERSET

	No. of Hrs	Races Run	1st	2nd	3rd	Unpl	Per cent	£1 Level Stake
NH Flat	20	32	3	4	4	21	9.4	-20.88
Hurdles	102	347	67	39	39	202	19.3	-10.39
Chases	72	280	42	39	36	163	15.0	-76.68
Totals	155	659	112	82	79	386	17.0	-107.95
04-05	141	627	122	99	78	328	19.5	-58.81
03-04	160	720	122	121	84	393	16.9	-153.04

BY MONTH

NH Flat	W-R	Per cent	£1 Level Stake	Hurdles	W-R	Per cent	£1 Level Stake
May	0-1	0.0	-1.00	May	3-20	15.0	-7.25
June	0-0	0.0	0.00	June	3-15	20.0	+5.00
July	0-0	0.0	0.00	July	4-15	26.7	-0.50
August	0-0	0.0	0.00	August	4-18	22.2	+3.50
September	0-0	0.0	0.00	September	3-12	25.0	+1.75
October	1-4	25.0	+1.50	October	13-42	31.0	+10.79
November	1-5	20.0	-2.13	November	5-36	13.9	-6.93
December	0-4	0.0	-4.00	December	4-33	12.1	-16.56
January	0-4	0.0	-4.00	January	3-34	8.8	-6.09
February	0-1	0.0	-1.00	February	5-36	13.9	-6.17
March	1-9	11.1	-6.25	March	8-33	24.2	-0.08
April	0-4	0.0	-4.00	April	12-53	22.6	+12.14

Chases	W-R	Per cent	£1 Level Stake	Totals	W-R	Per cent	£1 Level Stake
May	3-18	16.7	-7.00	May	6-39	15.4	-15.25
June	2-13	15.4	-8.18	June	5-28	17.9	-3.18
July	3-11	27.3	+7.50	July	7-26	26.9	+7.00
August	5-13	38.5	+19.63	August	9-31	29.0	+23.13
September	1-7	14.3	-5.64	September	4-19	21.1	-3.89
October	6-30	20.0	-8.37	October	20-76	26.3	+3.92
November	3-45	6.7	-25.50	November	9-86	10.5	-34.56
December	6-30	20.0	-3.52	December	10-67	14.9	-24.08
January	0-24	0.0	-24.00	January	3-62	4.8	-34.09
February	2-17	11.8	-4.50	February	7-54	13.0	-11.67
March	4-32	12.5	-17.04	March	13-74	17.6	-23.37
April	7-40	17.5	-0.07	April	19-97	19.6	+8.07

DISTANCE

Hurdles	W-R	Per cent	£1 Level Stake	Chases	W-R	Per cent	£1 Level Stake
2m-2m3f	43-233	18.5	-11.30	2m-2m3f	15-66	22.7	-0.31
2m4f-2m7f	18-88	20.5	+6.99	2m4f-2m7f	15-105	14.3	-37.07
3m+	6-26	23.1	-6.08	3m+	12-109	11.0	-39.30

TYPE OF RACE

Non-Handicaps	W-R	Per cent	£1 Level Stake	Handicaps	W-R	Per cent	£1 Level Stake
Nov Hrdls	23-119	19.3	-38.85	Nov Hrdls	7-30	23.3	+22.50
Hrdls	10-51	19.6	+2.82	Hrdls	27-146	18.5	+4.14
Nov Chs	20-61	32.8	+2.73	Nov Chs	0-19	0.0	-19.00
Chases	2-15	13.3	-7.75	Chases	20-185	10.8	-52.67
Sell/Claim	0-0	0.0	0.00	Sell/Claim	0-1	0.0	-1.00

RACE CLASS

	W-R	Per cent	£1 Level Stake
Class 1	11-78	14.1	-6.63
Class 2	9-75	12.0	-22.45
Class 3	47-237	19.8	-18.88
Class 4	42-232	18.1	-52.24
Class 5	1-13	7.7	+8.00
Class 6	2-24	8.3	-15.75

FIRST TIME OUT

	W-R	Per cent	£1 Level Stake
Bumpers	2-20	10.0	-11.75
Hurdles	13-83	15.7	-7.73
Chases	6-52	11.5	-24.33
Totals	21-155	13.5	-43.81

JOCKEYS

	W-R	Per cent	£1 Level Stake
Richard Johnson	83-426	19.5	-35.19
P J Brennan	17-123	13.8	-23.17
T J O'Brien	6-33	18.2	-3.33
Robert Stephens	4-43	9.3	-19.00
Noel Fehily	1-1	100.0	+2.25
A P McCoy	1-4	25.0	-0.50

COURSE RECORD

	Total W-R	Non-Hndcps Hurdles	Chases	Hndcps Hurdles	Chases	NH Flat	Per cent	£1 Level Stake
Exeter	14-56	2-14	7-12	2-16	3-13	0-1	25.0	+4.44
Nton Abbot	12-46	2-5	2-7	4-22	4-12	0-0	26.1	+40.09
Chepstow	7-30	3-12	0-1	3-10	0-4	1-3	23.3	-1.84
Cheltenham	7-65	5-12	0-10	1-14	0-24	1-5	10.8	-31.90
Stratford	6-24	2-5	1-2	2-8	1-8	0-1	25.0	+19.25
Worcester	6-33	2-7	1-3	3-14	0-8	0-1	18.2	-9.92
Bangor	5-17	1-6	2-3	1-3	0-3	1-2	29.4	+3.11
Haydock	5-20	1-8	0-1	1-3	3-5	0-3	25.0	+4.83
Mrket Rsn	5-23	1-5	1-1	3-9	0-7	0-0	21.7	+5.50
Sandown	5-30	2-4	1-5	0-7	2-14	0-0	16.7	-4.50
Taunton	5-34	3-11	1-1	1-12	0-8	0-2	14.7	-9.51
Newbury	5-41	2-10	0-1	3-9	0-18	0-3	12.2	-16.00
Hereford	4-20	1-9	3-5	0-3	0-2	0-1	20.0	-7.19
Perth	3-6	0-2	1-2	2-2	0-0	0-0	50.0	+2.28
Uttoxeter	3-17	0-4	0-0	3-6	0-7	0-0	17.6	+1.00
Aintree	3-26	2-6	0-3	1-5	0-11	0-1	11.5	-12.43

Ludlow	3-28	1-10	0-3	1-7	1-6	0-2	10.7	-18.25
Wincanton	3-55	0-10	0-4	2-13	1-25	0-3	5.5	-32.50
Doncaster	2-3	1-1	1-2	0-0	0-0	0-0	66.7	+4.75
Ayr	2-7	0-0	0-0	1-2	1-5	0-0	28.6	+2.00
Towcester	2-7	0-1	0-0	0-2	2-3	0-1	28.6	+2.83
Huntingdon	2-15	1-4	1-4	0-2	0-5	0-0	13.3	-7.75
Leicester	1-3	1-2	0-1	0-0	0-0	0-0	33.3	+0.50
Plumpton	1-10	0-5	0-0	0-2	1-2	0-1	10.0	-7.75
Fontwell	1-12	0-5	0-1	0-2	1-3	0-1	8.3	-8.00

WINNING HORSES

Horse	Races Run	1st	2nd	3rd	£
Lacdoudal	9	3	2	1	133742
*Detroit City	5	4	0	0	133577
Monkerhostin	8	1	3	1	37063
Noble Request	7	3	2	0	71625
Wellbeing	5	3	0	2	38920
Tamango	12	4	1	1	50645
Willie John Daly	7	1	0	1	23877
Captain Corelli	3	1	0	1	19478
Supreme Prince	6	1	0	1	18859
*Fair Along	6	2	1	1	27252
Boychuk	7	3	0	3	25660
Kalca Mome	9	1	1	1	16265
Motorway	8	4	0	1	34580
Double Honour	8	1	1	0	13506
Mcbain	7	2	0	0	21269
Croix De Guerre	10	3	2	2	23210
Leading Contender	3	2	0	0	11753
Gunther McBride	5	1	0	0	9759
Rooster Booster	3	1	0	0	8801
Chiaro	3	2	0	0	11696
Cool Spice	3	1	0	0	7378
Chilling Place	6	2	1	0	12552
Serpentine Rock	5	1	0	2	6893
Xellance	8	2	0	0	13371
Cousin Nicky	6	2	0	0	10735
Monticelli	6	2	0	1	11756
Yaboya	4	1	1	1	6263
Chivite	2	2	0	0	11754
Good Lord Louis	3	1	0	0	6164
Amicelli	9	4	3	1	19653
Drumbeater	8	4	2	0	20553
Rift Valley	9	2	1	0	10578
Napoleon	6	1	0	0	5543
Amarula Ridge	4	1	0	1	5517
Moscow Whisper	7	1	0	1	3486
Forever Dream	6	1	1	0	5411
Mr Fluffy	4	1	0	0	5408
Mister Flint	5	3	1	0	15158
Fool On The Hill	4	1	0	1	5258
Tom Sayers	9	1	2	1	5205
*Traprain	4	2	1	0	8133
College Ace	6	2	0	1	7968
Maharaat	3	1	0	0	4878
Supreme Serenade	6	1	3	0	4782
Castlemore	5	1	0	0	4761
Harry's Dream	5	2	2	1	8215
Zabenz	8	1	2	1	4561
O'Toole	7	2	0	1	9000
Dream Alliance	6	2	1	1	7970
Would You Believe	3	2	0	0	8239
Virtus	6	1	1	1	4271
Sunnyland	5	3	1	0	10751
Unleash	8	1	3	3	4105
Silver City	5	1	0	0	4073
From Dawn To Dusk	6	1	0	1	3904
*Bureaucrat	6	2	2	0	7157
Private Be	5	1	4	0	3891
Master D'Or	4	1	1	0	3788
Separated	5	1	0	1	3786
Savannah Bay	3	1	0	2	3741
Allumee	4	1	1	0	3708
Penny Park	5	1	0	0	3426
Wild Chimes	2	1	0	0	3220
Sandmartin	6	1	0	0	3083
*Cirrious	3	1	0	0	2928
Closed Shop	1	1	0	0	1884
Total winning prize-money					**£1058396**
Favourites	48-140		34.3%		-17.28

R J HODGES

CHARLTON ADAM, SOMERSET

	No. of His	Races Run	1st	2nd	3rd	Unpl	Per cent	£1 Level Stake
NH Flat	6	11	0	2	2	7	0.0	-11.00
Hurdles	24	114	4	8	12	90	3.5	-95.28
Chases	14	76	7	18	12	39	9.2	-34.17
Totals	37	201	11	28	26	136	5.5	-140.45
04-05	38	176	15	26	18	117	8.5	-47.79
03-04	30	135	18	13	14	90	13.3	+5.08

BY MONTH

NH Flat	W-R	Per cent	£1 Level Stake	Hurdles	W-R	Per cent	£1 Level Stake
May	0-1	0.0	-1.00	May	1-4	25.0	-2.00
June	0-0	0.0	0.00	June	0-2	0.0	-2.00
July	0-0	0.0	0.00	July	0-1	0.0	1.00
August	0-0	0.0	0.00	August	0-2	0.0	-2.00
September	0-0	0.0	0.00	September	0-1	0.0	-1.00
October	0-1	0.0	-1.00	October	0-10	0.0	-10.00
November	0-1	0.0	-1.00	November	1-15	6.7	-3.00
December	0-3	0.0	-3.00	December	0-25	0.0	-25.00
January	0-3	0.0	-3.00	January	1-21	4.8	-18.90
February	0-1	0.0	-1.00	February	0-11	0.0	-11.00
March	0-0	0.0	0.00	March	0-8	0.0	-8.00
April	0-1	0.0	-1.00	April	1-14	7.1	-11.38

Chases	W-R	Per cent	£1 Level Stake	Totals	W-R	Per cent	£1 Level Stake
May	0-7	0.0	-7.00	May	1-12	8.3	-10.00
June	0-7	0.0	-7.00	June	0-9	0.0	-9.00

July	0-8	0.0	-8.00	July	0-9	0.0	-9.00
August	1-5	20.0	+2.00	August	1-7	14.3	0.00
September	0-4	0.0	-4.00	September	0-5	0.0	-5.00
October	0-3	0.0	-3.00	October	0-14	0.0	-14.00
November	0-8	0.0	-8.00	November	1-24	4.2	-12.00
December	3-6	50.0	+17.50	December	3-34	8.8	-10.50
January	1-6	16.7	-1.67	January	2-30	6.7	-23.57
February	0-7	0.0	-7.00	February	0-19	0.0	-19.00
March	1-8	12.5	-4.25	March	1-16	6.3	-12.25
April	1-7	14.3	-3.75	April	2-22	9.1	-16.13

DISTANCE

Hurdles	W-R	Per cent	£1 Level Stake	Chases	W-R	Per cent	£1 Level Stake
2m-2m3f	1-82	1.2	-80.00	2m-2m3f	4-43	9.3	-26.17
2m4f-2m7f	3-27	11.1	-10.28	2m4f-2m7f	3-28	10.7	-3.00
3m+	0-5	0.0	-5.00	3m+	0-5	0.0	-5.00

TYPE OF RACE

Non-Handicaps	W-R	Per cent	£1 Level Stake	Handicaps	W-R	Per cent	£1 Level Stake
Nov Hrdls	0-24	0.0	-24.00	Nov Hrdls	0-14	0.0	-14.00
Hrdls	0-4	0.0	-4.00	Hrdls	1 51	2.0	-39.00
Nov Chs	2-15	13.3	+0.25	Nov Chs	2-11	18.2	-2.92
Chases	0-0	0.0	0.00	Chases	3-48	6.3	-29.50
Sell/Claim	3-16	18.8	-9.28	Sell/Claim	0-5	0.0	-5.00

RACE CLASS

	W-R	Per cent	£1 Level Stake	FIRST TIME OUT	W-R	Per cent	£1 Level Stake
Class 1	0-4	0.0	-4.00	Bumpers	0-6	0.0	-6.00
Class 2	0-7	0.0	-7.00	Hurdles	2-20	10.0	-5.38
Class 3	4-59	6.8	-22.00	Chases	1-11	9.1	+1.00
Class 4	4-91	4.4	-74.17				
Class 5	3-30	10.0	-23.27	Totals	3-37	8.1	-10.38
Class 6	0-10	0.0	-10.00				

JOCKEYS

	W-R	Per cent	£1 Level Stake
Christian Williams	3-10	30.0	+4.08
James White	3-71	4.2	-49.90
Andrew Thornton	2-4	50.0	+0.63
Jodie Mogford	1-1	100.0	+4.50
Jim Crowley	1-12	8.3	0.00
Tom Scudamore	1-27	3.7	-23.75

COURSE RECORD

	Total W-R	Non-Hndcps Hurdles	Non-Hndcps Chases	Hndcps Hurdles	Chases	NH Flat	Per cent	£1 Level Stake
Wincanton	3-32	0-7	1-1	0-13	2-10	0-1	9.4	-10.25
Taunton	2-28	0-10	1-3	0-7	1-6	0-2	7.1	-20.42
Southwell	1-1	1-1	0-0	0-0	0-0	0-0	100.0	+1.63
Huntingdon	1-3	0-0	0-0	0-0	1-3	0-0	33.3	+2.50
Worcester	1-5	0-0	0-0	0-1	1-4	0-0	20.0	+2.00
Chepstow	1-10	0-1	0-1	1-5	0-3	0-0	10.0	+2.00

Fontwell	1-12	1-5	0-0	0-3	0-4	0-0	8.3	-9.90
Nton Abbot	1-22	1-5	0-3	0-4	0-10	0-0	4.5	-20.00

WINNING HORSES

Horse	Races Run	1st	2nd	3rd	£
Wizard Of Edge	9	2	2	1	11711
Goldbrook	7	1	1	1	6338
Preacher Boy	5	2	1	1	11317
Noble Justice	5	1	0	2	5517
By Degree	2	1	0	0	4788
Jupon Vert	20	1	7	4	3793
Kings Castle	8	3	0	1	7499
Total winning prize-money					£50963
Favourites	4-13		30.8%		-1.94

M J HOGAN

NORTH END, W SUSSEX

	No. of Hrs	Races Run	1st	2nd	3rd	Unpl	Per cent	£1 Level Stake
NH Flat	0	0	0	0	0	0	0.0	0.00
Hurdles	3	14	2	3	2	7	14.3	-6.25
Chases	1	6	1	4	0	1	16.7	0.00
Totals	4	20	3	7	2	8	15.0	-6.25
04-05	3	25	0	2	4	19	0.0	-25.00
03-04	2	19	0	4	0	15	0.0	-19.00

JOCKEYS

	W-R	Per cent	£1 Level Stake
Leighton Aspell	2-10	20.0	-1.25
Robert Stephens	1-4	25.0	+1.00

COURSE RECORD

	Total W-R	Non-Hndcps Hurdles	Non-Hndcps Chases	Hndcps Hurdles	Chases	NH Flat	Per cent	£1 Level Stake
Plumpton	2-10	1-5	0-0	0-1	1-4	0-0	20.0	-1.25
Folkestone	1-2	0-0	0-0	1-2	0-0	0-0	50.0	+3.00

WINNING HORSES

Horse	Races Run	1st	2nd	3rd	£
Isam Top	9	1	1	2	4229
Mystical Star	6	1	4	0	3724
Beare Necessities	2	1	1	0	3083
Total winning prize-money					£11036
Favourites	1-5		20.0%		-2.25

H P HOGARTH

STILLINGTON, N YORKS

	No. of Hrs	Races Run	1st	2nd	3rd	Unpl	Per cent	£1 Level Stake
NH Flat	4	5	0	0	0	5	0.0	-5.00

	No. of Hrs	Races Run	1st	2nd	3rd	Unpl	Per cent	£1 Level Stake
Hurdles	4	10	0	1	1	8	0.0	-10.00
Chases	10	44	9	4	3	28	20.5	+26.25
Totals	15	59	9	5	4	41	15.3	+11.25
04-05	11	37	5	6	4	22	13.5	-6.89
03-04	7	28	4	6	4	14	14.3	+0.13

JOCKEYS

	W-R	Per cent	£1 Level Stake
David O'Meara	8-50	16.0	+17.00
Phil Kinsella	1-4	25.0	-0.75

COURSE RECORD

	Total W-R	Non-Hndcps Hurdles	Chases	Hndcps Hurdles	Chases	NH Flat	Per cent	£1 Level Stake
Hexham	3-6	0-0	2-2	0-0	1-4	0-0	50.0	+17.50
Newcastle	2-6	0-2	2-3	0-0	0-1	0-0	33.3	+7.50
Perth	1-3	0-1	0-0	0-1	1-1	0-0	33.3	+4.00
Catterick	1-4	0-0	0-0	0-0	1-2	0-2	25.0	+6.00
Mrket Rsn	1-4	0-1	0-1	0-0	1-2	0-0	25.0	+9.00
Ayr	1-5	0-1	0-1	0-0	1-3	0-0	20.0	-1.75

WINNING HORSES

Horse	Races Run	1st	2nd	3rd	£
King Killone	6	2	0	1	27195
*Master Papa	2	1	1	0	6506
Encore Cadoudal	7	1	1	0	5408
Over The Storm	6	1	0	0	4111
Cedar Rapids	8	1	0	1	3904
Tina's Scallywag	3	1	0	0	3868
Capybara	9	1	1	2	3575
Red Rampage	2	1	0	0	1249
Total winning prize-money					£55816
Favourites	1-3		33.3%		0.25

K W HOGG

ISLE OF MAN

	No. of Hrs	Races Run	1st	2nd	3rd	Unpl	Per cent	£1 Level Stake
NH Flat	0	0	0	0	0	0	0.0	0.00
Hurdles	8	38	2	1	1	34	5.3	-24.00
Chases	0	0	0	0	0	0	0.0	0.00
Totals	8	38	2	1	1	34	5.3	-24.00
04-05	8	27	2	1	4	20	7.4	+53.00
03-04	4	6	0	0	0	6	0.0	-6.00

JOCKEYS

	W-R	Per cent	£1 Level Stake
P Robson	2-7	28.6	+7.00

COURSE RECORD

	Total W-R	Non-Hndcps Hurdles	Chases	Hndcps Hurdles	Chases	NH Flat	Per cent	£1 Level Stake
Sedgefield	2-7	0-3	0-0	2-4	0-0	0-0	28.6	+7.00

WINNING HORSES

Horse	Races Run	1st	2nd	3rd	£
Ton-Chee	9	1	1	0	3354
Nifty Roy	11	1	0	1	3031
Total winning prize-money					£6385
Favourites	0-0		0.0%		0.00

A HOLLINGSWORTH

FECKENHAM, WORCS

	No. of Hrs	Races Run	1st	2nd	3rd	Unpl	Per cent	£1 Level Stake
NH Flat	1	3	0	0	0	3	0.0	-3.00
Hurdles	0	0	0	0	0	0	0.0	0.00
Chases	1	7	2	1	0	4	28.6	+8.00
Totals	2	10	2	1	0	7	20.0	+5.00
04-05	3	16	1	3	1	11	6.3	-12.50
03-04	6	19	0	1	1	17	0.0	-19.00

JOCKEYS

	W-R	Per cent	£1 Level Stake
R Walsh	1-1	100.0	+2.00
Mick Fitzgerald	1-3	33.3	+9.00

COURSE RECORD

	Total W-R	Non-Hndcps Hurdles	Chases	Hndcps Hurdles	Chases	NH Flat	Per cent	£1 Level Stake
Uttoxeter	1-2	0-0	0-0	0-0	1-2	0-0	50.0	+10.00
Stratford	1-3	0-0	0-0	0-0	1-2	0-1	33.3	0.00

WINNING HORSES

Horse	Races Run	1st	2nd	3rd	£
Gallik Dawn	7	2	1	0	13579
Total winning prize-money					£13579
Favourites	1-2		50.0%		1.00

R HOLLINSHEAD

UPPER LONGDON, STAFFS

	No. of Hrs	Races Run	1st	2nd	3rd	Unpl	Per cent	£1 Level Stake
NH Flat	2	2	0	0	0	2	0.0	-2.00
Hurdles	14	47	2	3	4	38	4.3	-8.00
Chases	4	11	2	1	2	6	18.2	+3.33
Totals	18	60	4	4	6	46	6.7	-6.67

04-05	6	28	5	3	3	17	17.9	+22.25
03-04	4	14	1	2	1	10	7.1	-3.00

JOCKEYS

	W-R	Per cent	£1 Level Stake
Tom Doyle	1-2	50.0	+2.33
David Dennis	1-7	14.3	+27.00
Miss S Sharratt	1-8	12.5	+2.00
Adam Hawkins	1-36	2.8	-31.00

COURSE RECORD

	Total W-R	Non-Hndcps Hurdles	Chases	Hndcps Hurdles	Chases	NH Flat	Per cent	£1 Level Stake
Aintree	1-1	0-0	0-0	0-0	1-1	0-0	100.0	+9.00
Mrket Rsn	1-5	0-2	0-0	1-2	0-1	0-0	20.0	0.00
Stratford	1-10	1-6	0-1	0-3	0-0	0-0	10.0	+24.00
Ludlow	1-11	0-7	1-1	0-3	0-0	0-0	9.1	-6.67

WINNING HORSES

Horse	Races Run	1st	2nd	3rd	£
*Mullensgrove	3	1	1	0	5759
Polar Passion	4	1	0	0	5434
Norma Hill	3	1	0	1	4400
Theatre Tinka	5	1	0	1	2602
Total winning prize-money					£18195
Favourites	0-0		0.0%		0.00

V J HUGHES

BRIDGEND, BRIDGEND

	No. of Hrs	Races Run	1st	2nd	3rd	Unpl	Per cent	£1 Level Stake
NH Flat	2	4	0	0	0	4	0.0	-4.00
Hurdles	4	11	1	0	1	9	9.1	+10.00
Chases	2	3	0	0	0	3	0.0	-3.00
Totals	6	18	1	0	1	16	5.6	+3.00
03-04	1	4	1	0	0	3	25.0	-1.80

JOCKEYS

	W-R	Per cent	£1 Level Stake
James Davies	1-7	14.3	+14.00

COURSE RECORD

	Total W-R	Non-Hndcps Hurdles	Chases	Hndcps Hurdles	Chases	NH Flat	Per cent	£1 Level Stake
Uttoxeter	1-2	0-0	0-0	1-2	0-0	0-0	50.0	+19.00

WINNING HORSES

Horse	Races Run	1st	2nd	3rd	£
Mick Murphy	5	1	0	0	3595
Total winning prize-money					£3595
Favourites	0-0		0.0%		0.00

MS N M HUGO

MALPAS, CHESHIRE

	No. of Hrs	Races Run	1st	2nd	3rd	Unpl	Per cent	£1 Level Stake
NH Flat	2	3	0	0	0	3	0.0	-3.00
Hurdles	0	0	0	0	0	0	0.0	0.00
Chases	1	3	1	0	0	2	33.3	+10.00
Totals	3	6	1	0	0	5	16.7	+7.00
04-05	1	2	0	0	0	2	0.0	-2.00

JOCKEYS

	W-R	Per cent	£1 Level Stake
Miss S Sharratt	1-4	25.0	+9.00

COURSE RECORD

	Total W-R	Non-Hndcps Hurdles	Chases	Hndcps Hurdles	Chases	NH Flat	Per cent	£1 Level Stake
Huntingdon	1-2	0-0	1-1	0-0	0-0	0-1	50.0	+11.00

WINNING HORSES

Horse	Races Run	1st	2nd	3rd	£
Gaiac	3	1	0	0	1498
Total winning prize-money					£1498
Favourites	0-0		0.0%		0.00

MRS E INSLEY

WATLINGTON, OXFORDSHIRE

	No. of Hrs	Races Run	1st	2nd	3rd	Unpl	Per cent	£1 Level Stake
NH Flat	0	0	0	0	0	0	0.0	0.00
Hurdles	0	0	0	0	0	0	0.0	0.00
Chases	1	3	1	0	1	1	33.3	+5.50
Totals	1	3	1	0	1	1	33.3	+5.50

JOCKEYS

	W-R	Per cent	£1 Level Stake
Mr J M Pritchard	1-2	50.0	+6.50

COURSE RECORD

	Total W-R	Non-Hndcps Hurdles	Chases	Hndcps Hurdles	Chases	NH Flat	Per cent	£1 Level Stake
Stratford	1-1	0-0	1-1	0-0	0-0	0-0	100.0	+7.50

WINNING HORSES

Horse	Races Run	1st	2nd	3rd	£
Brer Bear	3	1	0	1	3039
Total winning prize-money					£3039
Favourites	0-1		0.0%		-1.00

MISS T JACKSON

LOFTUS, CLEVELAND

	No. of Hrs	Races Run	1st	2nd	3rd	Unpl	Per cent	£1 Level Stake
NH Flat	3	3	0	0	0	3	0.0	-3.00
Hurdles	0	0	0	0	0	0	0.0	0.00
Chases	4	10	1	0	3	6	10.0	-8.56
Totals	**7**	**13**	**1**	**0**	**3**	**9**	**7.7**	**-11.56**
04-05	*6*	*26*	*0*	*1*	*1*	*24*	*0.0*	*-26.00*
03-04	*5*	*12*	*0*	*3*	*0*	*9*	*0.0*	*-12.00*

JOCKEYS

	W-R	Per cent	£1 Level Stake
Miss T Jackson	1-13	7.7	-11.56

COURSE RECORD

	Total W-R	Non-Hndcps Hurdles	Chases	Hndcps Hurdles	Chases	NH Flat	Per cent	£1 Level Stake
Ayr	1-2	0-0	1-1	0-0	0-1	0-0	50.0	-0.56

WINNING HORSES

Horse	Races Run	1st	2nd	3rd	£
Red Striker	3	1	0	1	1648
Total winning prize-money					**£1648**
Favourites	**1-1**		**100.0%**		**0.44**

J JAY

NEWMARKET, SUFFOLK

	No. of Hrs	Races Run	1st	2nd	3rd	Unpl	Per cent	£1 Level Stake
NH Flat	0	0	0	0	0	0	0.0	0.00
Hurdles	7	18	2	1	2	13	11.1	-5.50
Chases	0	0	0	0	0	0	0.0	0.00
Totals	**7**	**18**	**2**	**1**	**2**	**13**	**11.1**	**-5.50**
04-05	*2*	*3*	*0*	*0*	*0*	*3*	*0.0*	*-3.00*

JOCKEYS

	W-R	Per cent	£1 Level Stake
Timothy Bailey	1-3	33.3	+6.00
Leighton Aspell	1-5	20.0	-1.50

COURSE RECORD

	Total W-R	Non-Hndcps Hurdles	Chases	Hndcps Hurdles	Chases	NH Flat	Per cent	£1 Level Stake
Hereford	1-1	1-1	0-0	0-0	0-0	0-0	100.0	+2.50
Mrket Rsn	1-4	1-2	0-0	0-2	0-0	0-0	25.0	+5.00

WINNING HORSES

Horse	Races Run	1st	2nd	3rd	£
Gaelic Roulette	6	1	1	1	3392
Blue Mariner	4	1	0	0	2206
Total winning prize-money					**£5598**
Favourites	**0-0**		**0.0%**		**0.00**

J M JEFFERSON

NORTON, N YORKS

	No. of Hrs	Races Run	1st	2nd	3rd	Unpl	Per cent	£1 Level Stake
NH Flat	12	25	4	1	1	19	16.0	+20.33
Hurdles	29	102	14	10	4	73	13.7	-23.92
Chases	17	64	10	6	10	38	15.6	-7.86
Totals	**40**	**191**	**28**	**17**	**15**	**130**	**14.7**	**-11.45**
04-05	*42*	*189*	*21*	*12*	*23*	*133*	*11.1*	*-10.13*
03-04	*48*	*183*	*12*	*16*	*16*	*139*	*6.6*	*-76.58*

BY MONTH

NH Flat	W-R	Per cent	£1 Level Stake	Hurdles	W-R	Per cent	£1 Level Stake
May	0-0	0.0	0.00	May	3-19	15.8	-10.71
June	0-3	0.0	-3.00	June	1-6	16.7	+5.00
July	1-4	25.0	+3.50	July	2-7	28.6	-3.86
August	0-0	0.0	0.00	August	0-3	0.0	-3.00
September	0-2	0.0	-2.00	September	0-0	0.0	0.00
October	1-2	50.0	+2.33	October	0-8	0.0	-8.00
November	1-3	33.3	+4.50	November	1-12	8.3	+14.00
December	0-3	0.0	-3.00	December	1-14	7.1	-7.00
January	0-1	0.0	-1.00	January	1-8	12.5	-5.38
February	0-3	0.0	-3.00	February	3-11	27.3	-1.20
March	0-0	0.0	0.00	March	1-5	20.0	-3.27
April	1-4	25.0	+22.00	April	1-9	11.1	-0.50

Chases	W-R	Per cent	£1 Level Stake	Totals	W-R	Per cent	£1 Level Stake
May	1-5	20.0	-1.00	May	4-24	16.7	-11.71
June	0-1	0.0	-1.00	June	1-10	10.0	+1.00
July	1-5	20.0	+1.50	July	4-16	25.0	+1.14
August	0-1	0.0	-1.00	August	0-4	0.0	-4.00
September	0-4	0.0	-4.00	September	0-6	0.0	-6.00
October	0-3	0.0	-3.00	October	1-13	7.7	-8.67
November	1-6	16.7	+2.00	November	3-21	14.3	+20.50
December	3-8	37.5	+7.91	December	4-25	16.0	-2.09
January	2-9	22.2	-0.27	January	3-18	16.7	-6.65
February	0-6	0.0	-6.00	February	3-20	15.0	-10.20
March	0-6	0.0	-6.00	March	1-11	9.1	-9.27
April	2-10	20.0	+3.00	April	4-23	17.4	+24.50

DISTANCE

Hurdles	W-R	Per cent	£1 Level Stake	Chases	W-R	Per cent	£1 Level Stake
2m-2m3f	9-56	16.1	-4.49	2m-2m3f	8-40	20.0	+5.91

2m4f-2m7f	5-36	13.9	-9.43	2m4f-2m7f	2-18	11.1	-7.77
3m+	0-10	0.0	-10.00	3m+	0-6	0.0	-6.00

TYPE OF RACE

Non-Handicaps

	W-R	Per cent	£1 Level Stake
Nov Hrdls	6-42	14.3	-21.77
Hrdls	0-7	0.0	-7.00
Nov Chs	5-23	21.7	+0.64
Chases	0-2	0.0	-2.00
Sell/Claim	0-0	0.0	0.00

Handicaps

	W-R	Per cent	£1 Level Stake
Nov Hrdls	1-15	6.7	-11.00
Hrdls	7-37	18.9	+16.85
Nov Chs	0-4	0.0	-4.00
Chases	5-35	14.3	-2.50
Sell/Claim	0-1	0.0	-1.00

RACE CLASS

	W-R	Per cent	£1 Level Stake
Class 1	0-4	0.0	-4.00
Class 2	0-8	0.0	-8.00
Class 3	10-54	18.5	+17.55
Class 4	13-95	13.7	-37.84
Class 5	1-6	16.7	-0.50
Class 6	4-24	16.7	+21.33

FIRST TIME OUT

	W-R	Per cent	£1 Level Stake
Bumpers	3-12	25.0	+25.83
Hurdles	1-19	5.3	-17.71
Chases	1-9	11.1	-2.50
Totals	5-40	12.5	+5.62

JOCKEYS

	W-R	Per cent	£1 Level Stake
G Lee	11-60	18.3	-15.42
T J Dreaper	8-40	20.0	+22.23
Mr O Williams	3-7	42.9	+27.13
Paddy Merrigan	2-8	25.0	+3.83
Tony Dobbin	1-3	33.3	+5.00
Phil Kinsella	1-3	33.3	+5.50
Andrew Thornton	1-8	12.5	-6.71
Fergus King	1-12	8.3	-3.00

COURSE RECORD

	Total W-R	Non-Hndcps Hurdles	Non-Hndcps Chases	Hndcps Hurdles	Hndcps Chases	NH Flat	Per cent	£1 Level Stake
Wetherby	3-13	0-5	0-0	2-7	1-1	0-0	23.1	-0.65
Mrket Rsn	3-16	1-6	0-1	0-1	1-6	1-2	18.8	+18.07
Sedgefield	3-16	1-6	0-3	1-3	0-1	1-3	18.8	-7.37
Leicester	2-3	0-0	1-1	1-1	0-1	0-0	66.7	+30.00
Newcastle	2-4	0-2	1-1	0-0	1-1	0-0	50.0	+2.91
Ayr	2-8	0-1	1-1	1-3	0-3	0-0	25.0	-0.77
Perth	2-10	1-1	0-2	1-3	0-3	0-1	20.0	+0.07
Uttoxeter	2-12	2-5	0-1	0-3	0-1	0-2	16.7	+2.00
Hexham	2-16	1-7	0-1	0-5	0-1	0-2	12.5	-10.71
Fakenham	1-2	0-0	0-1	1-1	0-0	0-0	50.0	+5.00
Bangor	1-3	0-0	0-0	1-1	0-1	0-1	33.3	+1.00
Doncaster	1-6	0-3	1-1	0-2	0-0	0-0	16.7	+3.00
Stratford	1-8	0-4	0-1	0-1	1-2	0-0	12.5	+0.50
Worcester	1-10	0-0	0-1	0-3	0-1	1-5	10.0	-2.50
Haydock	1-11	0-1	0-1	0-3	1-5	0-1	9.1	-6.50
Catterick	1-12	0-2	0-3	0-3	0-2	1-2	8.3	-4.50

WINNING HORSES

Horse	Races Run	1st	2nd	3rd	£
Calatagan	6	2	1	0	15091
Portavadie	8	2	1	2	10831
Polar Gunner	6	5	0	0	25959
Honest Endeavour	8	1	0	1	6601
Brooklyn Brownie	10	4	2	1	21743
Classic Capers	6	1	1	2	5218
Roman Ark	8	1	2	1	5070
Dewasentah	7	3	2	1	11104
Kids Inheritance	9	1	0	0	4040
Ceannaireceach	6	1	1	0	3770
Cumbrian Knight	6	1	0	1	3731
According To Pete	5	3	1	0	7083
Oscar The Boxer	5	1	1	0	2928
Acushnet	4	1	0	0	1856
Casewick Mist	1	1	0	0	1713
Total winning prize-money					**£126738**
Favourites	**11-20**		**55.0%**		**4.22**

J R JENKINS

ROYSTON, HERTS

	No. of Hrs	Races Run	1st	2nd	3rd	Unpl	Per cent	£1 Level Stake
NH Flat	2	4	0	0	0	4	0.0	-4.00
Hurdles	14	40	1	2	1	35	2.5	-23.00
Chases	2	3	0	0	0	3	0.0	-3.00
Totals	**15**	**47**	**1**	**2**	**1**	**42**	**2.1**	**-30.00**
04-05	*30*	*101*	*2*	*4*	*6*	*89*	*2.0*	*-64.50*
03-04	*29*	*130*	*11*	*17*	*17*	*85*	*8.5*	*-61.33*

JOCKEYS

	W-R	Per cent	£1 Level Stake
Jodie Mogford	1-9	11.1	+8.00

COURSE RECORD

	Total W-R	Non-Hurdles	Non-Hurdles Chases	Hndcps Hurdles	Chases	NH Flat	Per cent	£1 Level Stake
Huntingdon	1-13	0-5	0-0	1-7	0-0	0-1	7.7	+4.00

WINNING HORSES

Horse	Races Run	1st	2nd	3rd	£
In The Hat	4	1	0	0	4798
Total winning prize-money					**£4798**
Favourites	**0-0**		**0.0%**		**0.00**

W JENKS

DEUXHILL, SHROPSHIRE

	No. of Hrs	Races Run	1st	2nd	3rd	Unpl	Per cent	£1 Level Stake
NH Flat	4	5	0	0	1	4	0.0	-5.00
Hurdles	5	23	1	1	4	17	4.3	-19.00
Chases	2	8	1	1	1	5	12.5	+26.00
Totals	9	36	2	2	6	26	5.6	+2.00
04-05	10	46	2	1	6	37	4.3	-9.00
03-04	11	43	5	6	3	29	11.6	-10.25

JOCKEYS

	W-R	Per cent	£1 Level Stake
Mark Bradburne	1-6	16.7	+28.00
Carl Llewellyn	1-19	5.3	-15.00

COURSE RECORD

	Total W-R	Non-Hndcps Hurdles	Chases	Hndcps Hurdles	Chases	NH Flat	Per cent	£1 Level Stake
Bangor	1-4	0-0	0-0	0-1	1-1	0-2	25.0	+30.00
Uttoxeter	1-6	0-1	0-0	1-4	0-1	0-0	16.7	-2.00

WINNING HORSES

Horse	Races Run	1st	2nd	3rd	£
Haile Selassie	3	1	1	0	3773
Fenney Spring	8	1	0	1	2646
Total winning prize-money					**£6419**
Favourites	1-1		100.0%		3.00

MRS L C JEWELL

SUTTON VALENCE, KENT

	No. of Hrs	Races Run	1st	2nd	3rd	Unpl	Per cent	£1 Level Stake
NH Flat	1	1	0	0	0	1	0.0	-1.00
Hurdles	14	56	1	4	7	44	1.8	-43.00
Chases	6	24	0	4	4	16	0.0	-24.00
Totals	16	81	1	8	11	61	1.2	68.00
04-05	17	67	2	7	10	48	3.0	-52.50
03-04	16	52	1	2	0	49	1.9	-44.00

JOCKEYS

	W-R	Per cent	£1 Level Stake
Benjamin Hitchcott	1-27	3.7	-14.00

COURSE RECORD

	Total W-R	Non-Hndcps Hurdles	Chases	Hndcps Hurdles	Chases	NH Flat	Per cent	£1 Level Stake
Plumpton	1-18	0-7	0-2	1-5	0-3	0-1	5.6	-5.00

WINNING HORSES

Horse	Races Run	1st	2nd	3rd	£
Silistra	9	1	1	0	3193
Total winning prize-money					**£3193**
Favourites	0-0		0.0%		0.00

R JOHNSON

NEWBURN, TYNE & WEAR

	No. of Hrs	Races Run	1st	2nd	3rd	Unpl	Per cent	£1 Level Stake
NH Flat	5	9	0	0	0	9	0.0	-9.00
Hurdles	24	65	4	7	4	50	6.2	-20.50
Chases	9	36	1	2	7	26	2.8	-30.00
Totals	29	110	5	9	11	85	4.5	-59.50
04-05	24	127	10	7	14	96	7.9	+20.50
03-04	27	139	14	7	14	104	10.1	+67.00

JOCKEYS

	W-R	Per cent	£1 Level Stake
Kenny Johnson	5-94	5.3	-43.50

COURSE RECORD

	Total W-R	Non-Hndcps Hurdles	Chases	Hndcps Hurdles	Chases	NH Flat	Per cent	£1 Level Stake
Newcastle	2-21	0-6	0-3	1-5	1-6	0-1	9.5	-2.00
Mrket Rsn	1-9	0-1	0-1	1-4	0-1	0-2	11.1	+12.00
Kelso	1-13	0-4	0-2	1-5	0-1	0-1	7.7	-8.50
Sedgefield	1-16	0-4	0-0	1-8	0-3	0-1	6.3	-10.00

WINNING HORSES

Horse	Races Run	1st	2nd	3rd	£
Piraeus	3	2	0	0	6499
Bob's Buster	8	1	1	2	2741
Seafire Lad	4	1	1	0	2282
Moyne Pleasure	8	1	1	1	2193
Total winning prize-money					**£13715**
Favourites	1-3		33.3%		1.50

B R JOHNSON

ASHTEAD, SURREY

	No. of Hrs	Races Run	1st	2nd	3rd	Unpl	Per cent	£1 Level Stake
NH Flat	3	4	0	0	0	4	0.0	-4.00
Hurdles	4	12	3	1	1	7	25.0	+2.00
Chases	1	1	0	0	0	1	0.0	-1.00
Totals	8	17	3	1	1	12	17.6	-3.00
04-05	11	25	0	2	3	20	0.0	-25.00
03-04	8	14	1	0	3	10	7.1	-8.50

JOCKEYS

	W-R	Per cent	£1 Level Stake
Matthew Batchelor	2-9	22.2	+1.25
Mick Fitzgerald	1-3	33.3	+0.75

COURSE RECORD

	Total W-R	Non-Hndcps Hurdles Chases	Hndcps Hurdles Chases	NH Flat	Per cent	£1 Level Stake
Fakenham	2-2	1-1 0-0	1-1 0-0	0-0	100.0	+8.25
Plumpton	1-1	0-0 0-0	1-1 0-0	0-0	100.0	+2.75

WINNING HORSES

Horse	Races Run	1st	2nd	3rd	£
Alph	7	2	1	1	6740
Lawaaheb	2	1	0	0	2660
Total winning prize-money					**£9400**
Favourites	2-3	66.7%			4.50

MRS S M JOHNSON

LULHAM, H'FORDS

	No. of Hrs	Races Run	1st	2nd	3rd	Unpl	Per cent	£1 Level Stake
NH Flat	5	9	0	0	1	8	0.0	-9.00
Hurdles	11	31	2	0	1	28	6.5	+3.00
Chases	0	0	0	0	0	0	0.0	0.00
Totals	15	40	2	0	2	36	5.0	-6.00
04-05	12	32	2	0	3	27	6.3	+20.00
03-04	18	59	1	4	7	47	1.7	-38.00

JOCKEYS

	W-R	Per cent	£1 Level Stake
Derek Laverty	1-5	20.0	+3.00
James Davies	1-7	14.3	+19.00

COURSE RECORD

	Total W-R	Non-Hndcps Hurdles Chases	Hndcps Hurdles Chases	NH Flat	Per cent	£1 Level Stake
Uttoxeter	1-3	0-0 0-0	1-3 0-0	0-0	33.3	+23.00
Chepstow	1-4	0-1 0-0	1-3 0-0	0-0	25.0	+4.00

WINNING HORSES

Horse	Races Run	1st	2nd	3rd	£
*Spike Jones	7	1	0	1	3904
Over Bridge	5	1	0	0	3136
Total winning prize-money					**£7040**
Favourites	0-0	0.0%			0.00

J HOWARD JOHNSON

BILLY ROW, CO DURHAM

	No. of Hrs	Races Run	1st	2nd	3rd	Unpl	Per cent	£1 Level Stake
NH Flat	13	18	5	3	2	8	27.8	+12.99
Hurdles	87	232	38	22	12	160	16.4	-52.01
Chases	29	81	15	10	8	48	18.5	-7.69
Totals	117	331	58	35	22	216	17.5	-46.71
04-05	99	317	68	36	36	176	21.5	+29.47
03-04	64	207	43	30	17	117	20.8	+11.42

BY MONTH

NH Flat	W-R	Per cent	£1 Level Stake	Hurdles	W-R	Per cent	£1 Level Stake
May	0-0	0.0	0.00	May	1-7	14.3	0.00
June	0-0	0.0	0.00	June	0-0	0.0	0.00
July	0-0	0.0	0.00	July	0-1	0.0	-1.00
August	0-0	0.0	0.00	August	1-2	50.0	+7.00
September	0-0	0.0	0.00	September	1-5	20.0	-2.00
October	0-2	0.0	-2.00	October	2-12	16.7	-7.00
November	0-2	0.0	-2.00	November	8-40	20.0	-4.60
December	0-1	0.0	-1.00	December	10-44	22.7	-14.54
January	1-3	33.3	-1.39	January	10-38	26.3	-7.38
February	0-3	0.0	-3.00	February	1-32	3.1	-6.00
March	3-3	100.0	+20.88	March	1-21	4.8	-17.00
April	1-4	25.0	+1.50	April	3-30	10.0	+0.50

Chases	W-R	Per cent	£1 Level Stake	Totals	W-R	Per cent	£1 Level Stake
May	0-1	0.0	-1.00	May	1-8	12.5	-1.00
June	0-0	0.0	0.00	June	0-0	0.0	0.00
July	0-0	0.0	0.00	July	0-1	0.0	-1.00
August	0-2	0.0	-2.00	August	1-4	25.0	+5.00
September	0-4	0.0	-4.00	September	1-9	11.1	-6.00
October	0-6	0.0	-6.00	October	2-20	10.0	-15.00
November	4-14	28.6	+8.57	November	12-56	21.4	+1.97
December	5-18	27.8	+4.08	December	15-63	23.8	-11.46
January	4-12	33.3	+7.90	January	15-53	28.3	-0.87
February	0-7	0.0	-7.00	February	1-42	2.4	-16.00
March	1-5	20.0	0.00	March	5-29	17.2	+3.88
April	1-12	8.3	-8.25	April	5-46	10.9	-6.25

DISTANCE

Hurdles	W-R	Per cent	£1 Level Stake	Chases	W-R	Per cent	£1 Level Stake
2m-2m3f	24-126	19.0	-28.97	2m-2m3f	4-21	19.0	-5.85
2m4f-2m7f	10-76	13.2	-3.94	2m4f-2m7f	6-23	26.1	+13.50
3m+	4-30	13.3	-19.10	3m+	5-37	13.5	-15.35

TYPE OF RACE

Non-Handicaps	W-R	Per cent	£1 Level Stake	Handicaps	W-R	Per cent	£1 Level Stake
Nov Hrdls	19-123	15.4	-70.07	Nov Hrdls	1-8	12.5	+7.00

Hrdls	7-30	23.3	-6.94		
Nov Chs	8-34	23.5	-6.94		
Chases	2-8	25.0	+7.00		
Sell/Claim	1-3	33.3	0.00		

Hrdls	10-68	14.7	+18.00
Nov Chs	3-9	33.3	+8.75
Chases	2-30	6.7	-16.50
Sell/Claim	0-0	0.0	0.00

RACE CLASS

	W-R	Per cent	£1 Level Stake
Class 1	5-59	8.5	-41.38
Class 2	3-29	10.3	-17.00
Class 3	20-89	22.5	+37.54
Class 4	25-134	18.7	-36.86
Class 5	0-4	0.0	-4.00
Class 6	5-16	31.3	+14.99

FIRST TIME OUT

	W-R	Per cent	£1 Level Stake
Bumpers	2-13	15.4	+8.50
Hurdles	13-77	16.9	-20.38
Chases	6-27	22.2	+7.57
Totals	21-117	17.9	-4.31

JOCKEYS

	W-R	Per cent	£1 Level Stake
G Lee	39-209	18.7	-59.97
Brian Hughes	9-53	17.0	+47.11
Tony Dobbin	5-13	38.5	+3.14
Alan Dempsey	2-27	7.4	-19.00
Joe Tizzard	1-1	100.0	+1.25
Richard Johnson	1-4	25.0	-0.25
Peter Buchanan	1-8	12.5	-3.00

COURSE RECORD

	Total W-R	Non-Hndcps Hurdles	Chases	Hndcps Hurdles	Chases	NH Flat	Per cent	£1 level Stake
Wetherby	9-33	4-14	2-6	3-10	0-2	0-1	27.3	+27.65
Sedgefield	8-51	3-27	3-5	2-12	0-3	0-4	15.7	-13.14
Carlisle	7-22	3-7	1-4	1-2	1-7	1-2	31.8	1.00
Musselbgh	6-23	4-11	1-1	0-7	1-2	0-2	26.1	-1.70
Catterick	5-14	3-10	0-1	1-2	0-0	1-1	35.7	-4.40
Mrket Rsn	5-18	2-9	1-4	0-1	1-2	1-2	27.8	-1.93
Ayr	4-20	1-5	1-4	0-4	1-6	1-1	20.0	+8.25
Haydock	3-15	1-5	0-0	1-5	1-5	0-0	20.0	+2.03
Perth	3-15	0-7	0-3	2-4	0-0	1-1	20.0	+15.50
Newcastle	2-13	2-11	0-1	0-0	0-1	0-0	15.4	-4.75
Windsor	1-1	1-1	0-0	0-0	0-0	0-0	100.0	+1.75
Cartmel	1-2	1-2	0-0	0-0	0-0	0-0	50.0	+7.00
Newbury	1-3	1-2	0-0	0-1	0-0	0-0	33.3	-1.39
Doncaster	1-9	0-6	1-1	0-1	0-0	0-1	11.1	-5.75
Hexham	1-12	1-7	0-0	0-3	0-2	0-0	8.3	0.00
Aintree	1-13	0-5	0-1	1-4	0-1	0-2	7.7	-7.00

WINNING HORSES

Horse	Races Run	1st	2nd	3rd	£
Arcalis	5	1	0	0	45072
Coat Of Honour	5	2	1	0	46215
Inglis Drever	3	2	0	0	46008
No Refuge	4	1	0	1	22915
Covent Garden	2	1	0	0	16928
Island Faith	3	1	0	0	13363
Kinburn	3	3	0	0	22862
Ortolan Bleu	3	1	1	0	9356

Kasthari	5	1	1	1	8001
Lennon	5	2	1	0	12648
Bob Justice	2	1	0	0	6571
Albany	3	1	0	0	6506
*Masafi	5	2	1	1	10026
Supreme Leisure	6	1	1	1	6506
Iron Man	4	1	1	0	6506
Hard Act To Follow	3	2	0	0	11470
Scotmail Too	5	1	0	0	6506
*Circassian	5	1	1	0	5465
*Magnificent Seven	4	2	0	0	9330
Motive	3	1	1	0	5205
Galero	4	1	0	0	5205
Renada	2	1	0	0	4893
Diamond Sal	3	1	1	1	4808
Scotmail	5	2	0	2	8175
Blairgowrie	3	1	0	0	4554
Weapons Inspector	3	1	1	0	4395
Theatre Knight	6	1	0	3	4178
San Peire	6	1	2	1	3904
*Majorca	5	1	0	0	3904
Julius Caesar	4	1	1	0	3879
Bewleys Berry	5	1	1	1	3855
Percussionist	4	2	0	1	6722
Melmount Star	2	1	0	0	3770
Sabreflight	5	2	2	0	7004
*Turnstile	5	2	0	0	6503
Nicolas Mon Ami	1	1	0	0	3444
*Estepona	2	1	0	0	3253
Some Touch	5	2	0	0	6126
*Zeitgeist	3	1	0	1	2928
Ieme Valley	3	1	0	0	2625
Astarador	3	1	1	0	2056
Wee Bertie	2	1	0	0	2056
Ovide	2	1	1	0	1850
Jack The Blaster	1	1	0	0	1713
Gold Thread	1	1	0	0	1713
Total winning prize-money					**£420922**

Favourites	29-58	50.0%	8.08

P JONES

BURNHILL GREEN, STAFFS

	No. of Hrs	Races Run	1st	2nd	3rd	Unpl	Per cent	£1 Level Stake
NH Flat	0	0	0	0	0	0	0.0	0.00
Hurdles	0	0	0	0	0	0	0.0	0.00
Chases	1	3	1	2	0	0	33.3	+4.00
Totals	1	3	1	2	0	0	33.3	+4.00
04-05	3	6	0	1	1	4	0.0	-6.00
03-04	5	12	2	1	0	9	16.7	-3.20

JOCKEYS

	W-R	Per cent	£1 Level Stake
Mr G Hanmer	1-2	50.0	+5.00

COURSE RECORD

	Total W-R	Non-Hndcps Hurdles	Chases	Hndcps Hurdles	Chases	NH Flat	Per cent	£1 Level Stake
Newbury	1-1	0-0	1-1	0-0	0-0	0-0	100.0	+6.00

WINNING HORSES

Horse	Races Run	1st	2nd	3rd	£
Christy Beamish	3	1	2	0	1648
Total winning prize-money					£1648
Favourites	0-1		0.0%		-1.00

G E JONES

BETTWS BLEDRWS, CEREDIGION

	No. of Hrs	Races Run	1st	2nd	3rd	Unpl	Per cent	£1 Level Stake
NH Flat	0	0	0	0	0	0	0.0	0.00
Hurdles	2	11	2	0	1	8	18.2	+1.00
Chases	0	0	0	0	0	0	0.0	0.00
Totals	2	11	2	0	1	8	18.2	+1.00
04-05	2	14	1	0	1	12	7.1	+12.00
03-04	4	9	0	0	0	9	0.0	-9.00

JOCKEYS

	W-R	Per cent	£1 Level Stake
T J O'Brien	2-4	50.0	+8.00

COURSE RECORD

	Total W-R	Non-Hndcps Hurdles	Chases	Hndcps Hurdles	Chases	NH Flat	Per cent	£1 Level Stake
Worcester	1-2	0-1	0-0	1-1	0-0	0-0	50.0	+3.50
Hereford	1-5	0-2	0-0	1-3	0-0	0-0	20.0	+1.50

WINNING HORSES

Horse	Races Run	1st	2nd	3rd	£
Desert Spa	9	2	0	1	5523
Total winning prize-money					£5523
Favourites	0-0		0.0%		0.00

P J JONES

EAST KENNETT, WILTS

	No. of Hrs	Races Run	1st	2nd	3rd	Unpl	Per cent	£1 Level Stake
NH Flat	2	4	1	1	0	2	25.0	+6.00
Hurdles	1	4	0	0	0	4	0.0	-4.00
Chases	3	3	0	0	0	3	0.0	-3.00
Totals	5	11	1	1	0	9	9.1	-1.00
04-05	3	12	2	1	0	9	16.7	+2.50
03-04	2	10	1	0	0	9	10.0	+5.00

JOCKEYS

	W-R	Per cent	£1 Level Stake
Gino Carenza	1-8	12.5	+2.00

COURSE RECORD

	Total W-R	Non-Hndcps Hurdles	Chases	Hndcps Hurdles	Chases	NH Flat	Per cent	£1 Level Stake
Ludlow	1-1	0-0	0-0	0-0	0-0	1-1	100.0	+9.00

WINNING HORSES

Horse	Races Run	1st	2nd	3rd	£
Lady Bling Bling	3	1	0	0	4060
Total winning prize-money					£4060
Favourites	0-0		0.0%		0.00

A P JONES

LAMBOURN, BERKS

	No. of Hrs	Races Run	1st	2nd	3rd	Unpl	Per cent	£1 Level Stake
NH Flat	1	1	0	0	0	1	0.0	-1.00
Hurdles	7	12	0	0	0	12	0.0	-12.00
Chases	2	9	1	1	2	5	11.1	-0.50
Totals	9	22	1	1	2	18	4.5	-13.50
04-05	9	26	1	2	4	19	3.8	-18.00
03-04	16	60	3	2	3	52	5.0	-40.00

JOCKEYS

	W-R	Per cent	£1 Level Stake
Mr E Imelov	1-4	25.0	+4.50

COURSE RECORD

	Total W-R	Non-Hndcps Hurdles	Chases	Hndcps Hurdles	Chases	NH Flat	Per cent	£1 Level Stake
Ludlow	1-2	0-1	0-0	0-0	1-1	0-0	50.0	+6.50

WINNING HORSES

Horse	Races Run	1st	2nd	3rd	£
Fin Bec	7	1	1	2	5402
Total winning prize-money					£5402
Favourites	0-0		0.0%		0.00

A E JONES

NEWCHAPEL, SURREY

	No. of Hrs	Races Run	1st	2nd	3rd	Unpl	Per cent	£1 Level Stake
NH Flat	4	6	0	0	0	6	0.0	-6.00
Hurdles	19	47	4	2	3	38	8.5	+26.50

Chases	8	26	6	2	2	16	23.1 +7.75
Totals	27	79	10	4	5	60	12.7 +28.25
04-05	22	74	5	3	6	60	6.8 -40.63
03-04	11	41	4	5	1	31	9.8 -2.00

BY MONTH

NH Flat	W-R	Per cent	£1 Level Stake	Hurdles	W-R	Per cent	£1 Level Stake
May	0-0	0.0	0.00	May	1-5	20.0	+4.00
June	0-3	0.0	-3.00	June	1-4	25.0	+22.00
July	0-1	0.0	-1.00	July	0-3	0.0	-3.00
August	0-0	0.0	0.00	August	1-6	16.7	-1.50
September	0-0	0.0	0.00	September	0-1	0.0	-1.00
October	0-1	0.0	-1.00	October	0-4	0.0	-4.00
November	0-1	0.0	-1.00	November	1-5	20.0	+29.00
December	0-0	0.0	0.00	December	0-1	0.0	-1.00
January	0-0	0.0	0.00	January	0-7	0.0	-7.00
February	0-0	0.0	0.00	February	0-3	0.0	3.00
March	0-0	0.0	0.00	March	0-5	0.0	-5.00
April	0-0	0.0	0.00	April	0-3	0.0	3.00

Chases	W-R	Per cent	£1 Level Stake	Totals	W-R	Per cent	£1 Level Stake
May	1-3	33.3	+2.50	May	2-8	25.0	+6.50
June	1-3	33.3	+9.00	June	2-10	20.0	+28.00
July	2-4	50.0	+7.00	July	2-8	25.0	+3.00
August	0-1	0.0	-1.00	August	1-7	14.3	-2.50
September	0-0	0.0	0.00	September	0-1	0.0	-1.00
October	0-5	0.0	-5.00	October	0-10	0.0	10.00
November	2-2	100.0	+3.25	November	3-8	37.5	+31.25
December	0-2	0.0	-2.00	December	0-3	0.0	-3.00
January	0-2	0.0	-2.00	January	0-9	0.0	-9.00
February	0-0	0.0	0.00	February	0-3	0.0	-3.00
March	0-0	0.0	0.00	March	0-5	0.0	-5.00
April	0-4	0.0	-4.00	April	0-7	0.0	-7.00

DISTANCE

Hurdles	W-R	Per cent	£1 Level Stake	Chases	W-R	Per cent	£1 Level Stake
2m-2m3f	4-40	10.0	+33.50	2m-2m3f	4-18	22.2	-2.75
2m4f-2m7f	0-4	0.0	-4.00	2m4f-2m7f	0-3	0.0	-3.00
3m+	0-3	0.0	-3.00	3m+	2-5	40.0	+13.50

TYPE OF RACE

Non-Handicaps	W-R	Per cent	£1 Level Stake	Handicaps	W-R	Per cent	£1 Level Stake
Nov Hrdls	0-15	0.0	-15.00	Nov Hrdls	0-3	0.0	-3.00
Hrdls	0-0	0.0	0.00	Hrdls	0-11	0.0	-11.00
Nov Chs	0-3	0.0	-3.00	Nov Chs	0-2	0.0	-2.00
Chases	0-0	0.0	0.00	Chases	6-21	28.6	+12.75
Sell/Claim	1-7	14.3	-2.50	Sell/Claim	3-15	20.0	+54.00

RACE CLASS | FIRST TIME OUT

	W-R	Per cent	£1 Level Stake		W-R	Per cent	£1 Level Stake
Class 1	0-1	0.0	-1.00	Bumpers	0-4	0.0	-4.00
Class 2	0-1	0.0	-1.00	Hurdles	1-17	5.9	-8.00
Class 3	3-18	16.7	-0.75	Chases	2-6	33.3	+6.00
Class 4	4-35	11.4	-14.00				
Class 5	3-19	15.8	+50.00	Totals	3-27	11.1	-6.00
Class 6	0-5	0.0	-5.00				

JOCKEYS

	W-R	Per cent	£1 Level Stake
Marcus Foley	5-19	26.3	+12.75
Derek Laverty	2-30	6.7	+13.00
Angharad Frieze	1-1	100.0	+25.00
Liam Heard	1-2	50.0	0.00
A P McCoy	1-3	33.3	+1.50

COURSE RECORD

	Total W-R	Non-Hndcps Hurdles	Non-Hndcps Chases	Hndcps Hurdles	Hndcps Chases	NH Flat	Per cent	£1 Level Stake
Nton Abbot	4-21	1-6	0-1	1-6	2-7	0-1	19.0	+20.50
Uttoxeter	2-7	0-1	0-0	0-1	2-4	0-1	28.6	+7.00
Cartmel	1-1	0-0	0-0	1-1	0-0	0-0	100.0	+8.00
Taunton	1-3	0-0	0-0	1-2	0-1	0-0	33.3	+31.00
Chepstow	1-5	0-1	0-0	0-1	1-3	0-0	20.0	-1.75
Exeter	1-7	0-2	0-0	0-3	1-2	0-0	14.3	-1.50

WINNING HORSES

Horse	Races Run	1st	2nd	3rd	£
Dangerousdanmayru	9	3	0	0	16206
Totheroadyouvgone	4	1	1	1	5538
Rolfes Delight	2	1	0	1	3730
The Mighty Sparrow	6	1	1	1	3377
Aleemdar	7	1	2	0	2975
Lucky Do	4	2	0	1	5292
Past Heritage	5	1	0	0	2365
Total winning prize-money					£39492
Favourites	2-6		33.3%		0.50

F JORDAN

ADSTONE, NORTHANTS

	No. of Hrs	Races Run	1st	2nd	3rd	Unpl	Per cent	£1 Level Stake
NH Flat	6	9	0	0	0	9	0.0	-9.00
Hurdles	22	71	2	4	6	59	2.8	-58.50
Chases	5	23	3	4	4	12	13.0	+5.13
Totals	26	103	5	8	10	80	4.9	-62.37
04-05	25	105	9	12	9	75	8.6	+7.13
03-04	27	91	5	11	7	68	5.5	-64.00

JOCKEYS

	W-R	Per cent	£1 Level Stake
Tom Doyle	3-16	18.8	+1.00
Andrew Thornton	1-2	50.0	+19.00
James Diment	1-13	7.7	-10.38

COURSE RECORD

	Total W-R	Non-Hndcps Hurdles	Chases	Hndcps Hurdles	Chases	NH Flat	Per cent	£1 Level Stake
Wetherby	1-2	0-0	0-1	1-1	0-0	0-0	50.0	+3.50
Hereford	1-4	0-1	0-0	0-2	1-1	0-0	25.0	+0.50
Leicester	1-5	0-0	0-0	1-2	0-3	0-0	20.0	+2.00
Huntingdon	1-7	0-0	0-1	0-2	1-4	0-0	14.3	+14.00
Towcester	1-12	0-5	1-2	0-2	0-1	0-2	8.3	-9.38

WINNING HORSES

Horse	Races Run	1st	2nd	3rd	£
Lubinas	11	2	2	3	8133
Oulton Broad	11	1	1	1	4056
Irish Blessing	9	2	0	1	5024
Total winning prize-money					**£17213**
Favourites	2-6		33.3%		4.00

J JOSEPH

COLESHILL, BUCKS

	No. of Hrs	Races Run	1st	2nd	3rd	Unpl	Per cent	£1 Level Stake
NH Flat	0	0	0	0	0	0	0.0	0.00
Hurdles	7	36	2	5	0	29	5.6	+6.00
Chases	0	0	0	0	0	0	0.0	0.00
Totals	7	36	2	5	0	29	5.6	+6.00
04-05	9	25	0	1	3	21	0.0	-25.00
03-04	12	37	1	1	0	35	2.7	-20.00

JOCKEYS

	W-R	Per cent	£1 Level Stake
Shane Walsh	2-31	6.5	+11.00

COURSE RECORD

	Total W-R	Non-Hndcps Hurdles	Chases	Hndcps Hurdles	Chases	NH Flat	Per cent	£1 Level Stake
Huntingdon	1-3	1-2	0-0	0-1	0-0	0-0	33.3	+5.00
Fontwell	1-5	0-1	0-0	1-4	0-0	0-0	20.0	+29.00

WINNING HORSES

Horse	Races Run	1st	2nd	3rd	£
Park City	6	1	1	0	2602
Shamsan	8	1	1	0	2240
Total winning prize-money					**£4842**
Favourites	0-0		0.0%		0.00

A G JUCKES

ABBERLEY, WORCS

	No. of Hrs	Races Run	1st	2nd	3rd	Unpl	Per cent	£1 Level Stake
NH Flat	0	0	0	0	0	0	0.0	0.00
Hurdles	8	25	1	3	2	19	4.0	-21.25
Chases	5	20	0	1	2	17	0.0	-20.00
Totals	12	45	1	4	4	36	2.2	-41.25
04-05	16	40	4	5	2	29	10.0	-12.80
03-04	14	40	2	0	2	35	5.0	-16.00

JOCKEYS

	W-R	Per cent	£1 Level Stake
Andrew Tinkler	1-11	9.1	-7.25

COURSE RECORD

	Total W-R	Non-Hndcps Hurdles	Chases	Hndcps Hurdles	Chases	NH Flat	Per cent	£1 Level Stake
Huntingdon	1-4	1-1	0-2	0-1	0-0	0-0	25.0	-0.25

WINNING HORSES

Horse	Races Run	1st	2nd	3rd	£
Mantles Prince	4	1	1	1	2261
Total winning prize-money					**£2261**
Favourites	0-1		0.0%		-1.00

D P KEANE

NORTH END, DORSET

	No. of Hrs	Races Run	1st	2nd	3rd	Unpl	Per cent	£1 Level Stake
NH Flat	7	8	0	0	1	7	0.0	-8.00
Hurdles	23	60	3	4	3	50	5.0	+67.50
Chases	17	47	7	5	2	33	14.9	+17.00
Totals	37	115	10	9	6	90	8.7	+76.50
04-05	37	151	20	22	23	86	13.2	-14.36
03-04	28	104	13	7	7	77	12.5	+40.78

BY MONTH

NH Flat	W-R	Per cent	£1 Level Stake	Hurdles	W-R	Per cent	£1 Level Stake
May	0-0	0.0	0.00	May	0-4	0.0	-4.00
June	0-0	0.0	0.00	June	0-3	0.0	-3.00
July	0-0	0.0	0.00	July	0-0	0.0	0.00
August	0-0	0.0	0.00	August	0-0	0.0	0.00
September	0-0	0.0	0.00	September	0-0	0.0	0.00
October	0-1	0.0	-1.00	October	0-5	0.0	-5.00
November	0-2	0.0	-2.00	November	1-7	14.3	+94.00
December	0-1	0.0	-1.00	December	1-11	9.1	-4.50
January	0-1	0.0	-1.00	January	0-11	0.0	-11.00
February	0-0	0.0	0.00	February	0-5	0.0	-5.00
March	0-2	0.0	-2.00	March	0-5	0.0	-5.00

April	0-1	0.0	-1.00	April	1-9	11.1	+11.00		

Chases	W-R	Per cent	£1 Level Stake	Totals	W-R	Per cent	£1 Level Stake
May	0-1	0.0	-1.00	May	0-5	0.0	-5.00
June	0-2	0.0	-2.00	June	0-5	0.0	-5.00
July	0-2	0.0	-2.00	July	0-2	0.0	-2.00
August	0-1	0.0	-1.00	August	0-1	0.0	-1.00
September	0-0	0.0	0.00	September	0-0	0.0	0.00
October	0-2	0.0	-2.00	October	0-8	0.0	-8.00
November	2-11	18.2	+6.50	November	3-20	15.0	+98.50
December	0-5	0.0	-5.00	December	1-17	5.9	-10.50
January	3-8	37.5	+20.00	January	3-20	15.0	+8.00
February	1-7	14.3	+2.00	February	1-12	8.3	-3.00
March	1-4	25.0	+5.50	March	1-11	9.1	-1.50
April	0-4	0.0	-4.00	April	1-14	7.1	+6.00

DISTANCE

Hurdles	W-R	Per cent	£1 Level Stake	Chases	W-R	Per cent	£1 Level Stake
2m-2m3f	3-35	8.6	+92.50	2m-2m3f	2-16	12.5	+0.50
2m4f-2m7f	0-23	0.0	-23.00	2m4f-2m7f	1-17	5.9	-6.00
3m+	0-2	0.0	-2.00	3m+	4-14	28.6	+22.50

TYPE OF RACE

Non-Handicaps				Handicaps			
	W-R	Per cent	£1 Level Stake		W-R	Per cent	£1 Level Stake
Nov Hrdls	1-27	3.7	+74.00	Nov Hrdls	0-4	0.0	-4.00
Hrdls	1-8	12.5	+12.00	Hrdls	0-17	0.0	-17.00
Nov Chs	0-4	0.0	-4.00	Nov Chs	0-5	0.0	-5.00
Chases	0-0	0.0	0.00	Chases	7-38	18.4	+26.00
Sell/Claim	1-1	100.0	+5.50	Sell/Claim	0-2	0.0	-2.00

RACE CLASS / FIRST TIME OUT

Race Class	W-R	Per cent	£1 Level Stake	First Time Out	W-R	Per cent	£1 Level Stake
Class 1	1-6	16.7	+3.00	Bumpers	0-7	0.0	-7.00
Class 2	0-1	0.0	-1.00	Hurdles	1-20	5.0	0.00
Class 3	4-29	13.8	+97.50	Chases	0-10	0.0	-10.00
Class 4	2-64	3.1	-43.50				
Class 5	3-7	42.9	+29.50	Totals	1-37	2.7	-17.00
Class 6	0-8	0.0	-8.00				

JOCKEYS

	W-R	Per cent	£1 Level Stake
Daryl Jacob	8-72	11.1	+10.50
Peter Buchanan	1-2	50.0	+6.00
Noel Fehily	1-29	3.4	+72.00

COURSE RECORD

	Total W-R	Non-Hndcps Hurdles	Chases	Hndcps Hurdles	Chases	NH Flat	Per cent	£1 Level Stake
Wincanton	3-29	1-10	0-1	0-5	2-12	0-1	10.3	+89.50
Chepstow	2-10	1-4	0-0	0-0	1-3	0-3	20.0	+19.50
Folkestone	1-4	0-0	0-0	0-1	1-2	0-1	25.0	+5.00
Haydock	1-5	0-1	0-0	0-1	1-3	0-0	20.0	+3.00

Plumpton	1-6	0-3	0-0	0-1	1-2	0-0	16.7	+5.00
Fontwell	1-7	0-2	0-0	0-3	1-2	0-0	14.3	+2.00
Uttoxeter	1-13	1-8	0-0	0-1	0-2	0-2	7.7	-6.50

WINNING HORSES

Horse	Races Run	1st	2nd	3rd	£
All In The Stars	6	2	1	0	38650
Barton Nic	5	2	1	0	11904
Roofing Spirit	7	1	0	0	5449
Barton Park	7	1	1	0	5075
River Of Light	4	1	0	0	3904
Joseph Beuys	8	1	1	1	3578
Barton Gate	5	1	0	0	2227
*Smokey Mountain	1	1	0	0	0
Total winning prize-money					£70787
Favourites	0-3		0.0%		-3.00

T KEDDY

NEWMARKET, SUFFOLK

	No. of Hrs	Races Run	1st	2nd	3rd	Unpl	Per cent	£1 Level Stake
NH Flat	0	0	0	0	0	0	0.0	0.00
Hurdles	0	0	0	0	0	0	0.0	0.00
Chases	1	6	1	3	1	1	16.7	+2.00
Totals	1	6	1	3	1	1	16.7	+2.00
03-04	2	2	0	0	2		0.0	-2.00

JOCKEYS

	W-R	Per cent	£1 Level Stake
Wayne Hutchinson	1-6	16.7	+2.00

COURSE RECORD

	Total W-R	Non-Hndcps Hurdles	Chases	Hndcps Hurdles	Chases	NH Flat	Per cent	£1 Level Stake
Stratford	1-2	0-0	0-0	0-0	1-2	0-0	50.0	+6.00

WINNING HORSES

Horse	Races Run	1st	2nd	3rd	£
Joey Tribbiani	6	1	3	1	6253
Total winning prize-money					£6253
Favourites	0-0		0.0%		0.00

MRS CAROLINE KEEVIL

BLAGDON, SOMERSET

	No. of Hrs	Races Run	1st	2nd	3rd	Unpl	Per cent	£1 Level Stake
NH Flat	0	0	0	0	0	0	0.0	0.00
Hurdles	0	0	0	0	0	0	0.0	0.00
Chases	4	8	2	0	2	4	25.0	+17.00
Totals	4	8	2	0	2	4	25.0	+17.00

04-05	3	5	2	1	0	2	40.0	+19.00
03-04	2	2	0	2	0	0	0.0	-2.00

JOCKEYS

	W-R	Per cent	£1 Level Stake
Mr J Snowden	2-5	40.0	+20.00

COURSE RECORD

	Total W-R	Non-Hndcps Hurdles	Chases	Hndcps Hurdles	Chases	NH Flat	Per cent	£1 Level Stake
Exeter	1-1	0-0	1-1	0-0	0-0	0-0	100.0	+3.00
Hereford	1-1	0-0	1-1	0-0	0-0	0-0	100.0	+20.00

WINNING HORSES

Horse	Races Run	1st	2nd	3rd	£
*Deep Pockets	2	1	0	1	2498
Willy Willy	3	1	0	0	1736
Total winning prize-money					**£4234**
Favourites	1-2		50.0%		2.00

C N KELLETT

WOODLANE, STAFFS

	No. of Hrs	Races Run	1st	2nd	3rd	Unpl	Per cent	£1 Level Stake
NH Flat	4	7	0	0	0	7	0.0	-7.00
Hurdles	12	26	0	1	1	24	0.0	-26.00
Chases	3	19	1	4	2	12	5.3	-13.00
Totals	16	52	1	5	3	43	1.9	-46.00
04-05	25	83	2	3	3	75	2.4	-73.50
03-04	19	56	3	4	2	47	5.4	-17.50

JOCKEYS

	W-R	Per cent	£1 Level Stake
Dave Crosse	1-13	7.7	-7.00

COURSE RECORD

	Total W-R	Non-Hndcps Hurdles	Chases	Hndcps Hurdles	Chases	NH Flat	Per cent	£1 Level Stake
Chepstow	1-1	0-0	0-0	0-0	1-1	0-0	100.0	+5.00

WINNING HORSES

Horse	Races Run	1st	2nd	3rd	£
Rookery Lad	13	1	4	1	4001
Total winning prize-money					**£4001**
Favourites	0-1		0.0%		-1.00

NICK KENT

BRIGG, LINCS

	No. of Hrs	Races Run	1st	2nd	3rd	Unpl	Per cent	£1 Level Stake
NH Flat	0	0	0	0	0	0	0.0	0.00
Hurdles	0	0	0	0	0	0	0.0	0.00
Chases	3	9	1	2	1	5	11.1	-1.00
Totals	3	9	1	2	1	5	11.1	-1.00
04-05	2	8	1	0	2	5	12.5	-1.00
03-04	1	4	0	1	0	3	0.0	-4.00

JOCKEYS

	W-R	Per cent	£1 Level Stake
Mr Nick Kent	1-9	11.1	-1.00

COURSE RECORD

	Total W-R	Non-Hndcps Hurdles	Chases	Hndcps Hurdles	Chases	NH Flat	Per cent	£1 Level Stake
Newbury	1-1	0-0	1-1	0-0	0-0	0-0	100.0	+7.00

WINNING HORSES

Horse	Races Run	1st	2nd	3rd	£
Ramirez	3	1	2	0	1648
Total winning prize-money					**£1648**
Favourites	0-0		0.0%		0.00

MISS KARIANA KEY

KNARESBOROUGH, N YORKS

	No. of Hrs	Races Run	1st	2nd	3rd	Unpl	Per cent	£1 Level Stake
NH Flat	0	0	0	0	0	0	0.0	0.00
Hurdles	3	34	4	0	5	25	11.8	-7.25
Chases	0	0	0	0	0	0	0.0	0.00
Totals	3	34	4	0	5	25	11.8	-7.25
04-05	5	55	2	3	3	47	3.6	-42.75
03-04	4	32	2	4	1	25	6.3	-12.00

JOCKEYS

	W-R	Per cent	£1 Level Stake
G Lee	2-4	50.0	+6.75
Robert Thornton	1-2	50.0	+3.00
Brian Hughes	1-7	14.3	+4.00

COURSE RECORD

	Total W-R	Non-Hndcps Hurdles	Chases	Hndcps Hurdles	Chases	NH Flat	Per cent	£1 Level Stake
Stratford	1-1	0-0	0-0	1-1	0-0	0-0	100.0	+4.00
Ayr	1-2	0-0	0-0	1-2	0-0	0-0	50.0	+1.25
Catterick	1-2	0-0	0-0	1-2	0-0	0-0	50.0	+9.00
Worcester	1-2	0-0	0-0	1-2	0-0	0-0	50.0	+5.50

2m4f-2m7f	5-78	6.4	-53.64
3m+	7-33	21.2	+32.72

2m4f-2m7f	4-37	10.8	+3.13
3m+	6-45	13.3	+0.21

WINNING HORSES

Horse	Races Run	1st	2nd	3rd	£
Mister Moussac	12	2	0	1	8356
Merryvale Man	21	2	0	4	6319
Total winning prize-money					**£14675**
Favourites	0-0		0.0%		0.00

A KING

BARBURY CASTLE, WILTS

	No. of Hrs	Races Run	1st	2nd	3rd	Unpl	Per cent	£1 Level Stake
NH Flat	20	49	10	8	6	25	20.4	+22.68
Hurdles	74	251	35	38	24	153	13.9	-18.35
Chases	29	111	18	14	12	67	16.2	1.03
Totals	108	411	63	60	42	245	15.3	+3.30
04-05	99	368	68	63	35	202	18.5	-56.17
03-04	73	264	48	32	32	152	18.2	-7.08

BY MONTH

NH Flat	W-R	Per cent	£1 Level Stake	Hurdles	W-R	Per cent	£1 Level Stake
May	1-2	50.0	+5.00	May	1-11	9.1	-6.50
June	0-0	0.0	0.00	June	0-5	0.0	-5.00
July	0-0	0.0	0.00	July	0-3	0.0	-3.00
August	0-0	0.0	0.00	August	0-3	0.0	-3.00
September	0-0	0.0	0.00	September	0-4	0.0	-4.00
October	1-1	100.0	+5.00	October	5-14	35.7	+8.91
November	2-11	18.2	-5.55	November	6-31	19.4	-13.09
December	1-5	20.0	+5.00	December	5-28	17.9	+9.75
January	1-6	16.7	-2.75	January	7-40	17.5	+55.35
February	3-8	37.5	+2.98	February	6-40	15.0	-7.44
March	0-7	0.0	-7.00	March	2-38	5.3	-26.80
April	1-9	11.1	+20.00	April	3-34	8.8	-23.53

Chases	W-R	Per cent	£1 Level Stake	Totals	W-R	Per cent	£1 Level Stake
May	0-5	0.0	-5.00	May	2-18	11.1	-6.50
June	0-4	0.0	-4.00	June	0-9	0.0	-9.00
July	0-1	0.0	-1.00	July	0-4	0.0	-4.00
August	1-3	33.3	+5.00	August	1-6	16.7	+2.00
September	0-1	0.0	-1.00	September	0-5	0.0	-5.00
October	0-1	0.0	-1.00	October	6-16	37.5	+12.91
November	2-23	8.7	-18.55	November	10-65	15.4	-37.19
December	3-16	18.8	+9.33	December	9-49	18.4	+24.08
January	2-16	12.5	-3.50	January	10-62	16.1	+49.10
February	4-14	28.6	-2.88	February	13-62	21.0	-7.34
March	3-9	33.3	+11.13	March	5-54	9.3	-22.67
April	3-18	16.7	+10.44	April	7-61	11.5	+6.91

DISTANCE

Hurdles	W-R	Per cent	£1 Level Stake	Chases	W-R	Per cent	£1 Level Stake
2m-2m3f	23-140	16.4	+2.57	2m-2m3f	8-29	27.6	-4.36

TYPE OF RACE

Non-Handicaps	W-R	Per cent	£1 Level Stake	Handicaps	W-R	Per cent	£1 Level Stake
Nov Hrdls	18-109	16.5	+34.32	Nov Hrdls	1-16	6.3	-12.00
Hrdls	5-35	14.3	-5.37	Hrdls	11-89	12.4	-33.30
Nov Chs	10-31	32.3	-6.03	Nov Chs	1-10	10.0	+13.00
Chases	1-2	50.0	+6.50	Chases	6-68	8.8	-14.50
Sell/Claim	1-3	33.3	+0.75	Sell/Claim	0-0	0.0	0.00

RACE CLASS

	W-R	Per cent	£1 Level Stake
Class 1	8-67	11.9	+4.65
Class 2	4-37	10.8	-10.50
Class 3	14-102	13.7	-31.24
Class 4	27-157	17.2	+41.96
Class 5	1-10	10.0	-6.25
Class 6	9-38	23.7	+4.68

FIRST TIME OUT

	W-R	Per cent	£1 Level Stake
Bumpers	3-20	15.0	+3.00
Hurdles	9-64	14.1	+30.35
Chases	3-24	12.5	+2.64
Totals	15-108	13.9	+35.99

JOCKEYS

	W-R	Per cent	£1 Level Stake
Robert Thornton	46-285	16.1	+29.64
Wayne Hutchinson	8-81	9.9	-27.54
Mr G Tumelty	6-24	25.0	+3.00
A P McCoy	1-1	100.0	+1.20
P J Brennan	1-2	50.0	+7.00
Warren Marston	1-3	33.3	+5.00

COURSE RECORD

	Total W-R	Non-Hndcps Hurdles	Chases	Hndcps Hurdles	Chases	NH Flat	Per cent	£1 Level Stake
Warwick	9-23	4-8	3-5	2-4	0-3	0-3	39.1	+4.32
Fontwell	5-17	4-9	0-0	0-4	0-1	1-3	29.4	+5.61
Hereford	5-24	4-13	0-1	1-6	0-1	0-3	20.8	+37.37
Huntingdon	5-24	0-4	0-2	1-5	1-8	3-5	20.8	+12.50
Wincanton	5-38	0-11	2-3	1-12	2-7	0-5	13.2	+4.66
Leicester	3-9	0-2	1-1	2-4	0-2	0-0	33.3	-1.38
Folkestone	3-12	1-6	0-0	0-0	0-2	2-4	25.0	-1.46
Exeter	3-20	1-6	2-3	0-7	0-3	0-1	15.0	-12.93
Ayr	2-5	0-0	0-0	1-1	1-4	0-0	40.0	+4.50
Southwell	2-7	0-0	0-0	1-4	1-2	0-1	28.6	+20.00
Taunton	2-8	2-3	0-0	0-3	0-2	0-0	25.0	-1.40
Towcester	2-8	1-4	0-0	1-2	0-0	0-2	25.0	+15.75
Haydock	2-10	0-2	0-0	1-4	0-2	1-2	20.0	+1.00
Chepstow	2-13	1-5	0-1	1-4	0-2	0-1	15.4	+2.20
Cheltenham	2-40	1-9	1-3	0-17	0-10	0-1	5.0	-22.50
Lingfield	1-4	1-2	0-0	0-0	0-2	0-0	25.0	+6.00
Nton Abbot	1-5	0-2	0-0	0-0	1-2	0-0	20.0	+3.00
Doncaster	1-7	1-4	0-0	0-1	0-1	0-1	14.3	+1.00
Fakenham	1-8	0-2	0-2	0-0	0-0	1-4	12.5	-6.27
Wetherby	1-9	0-4	1-3	0-1	0-0	0-1	11.1	-7.17

Plumpton	1-11	0-5	1-2	0-2	0-0	0-2	9.1	-8.50
Bangor	1-12	1-6	0-0	0-3	0-3	0-0	8.3	-7.50
Newbury	1-15	0-7	0-0	0-1	1-5	0-2	6.7	-6.00
Aintree	1-16	0-6	0-3	0-2	0-2	1-3	6.3	+13.00
Sandown	1-17	1-3	0-2	0-7	0-3	0-2	5.9	-10.50
Uttoxeter	1-20	0-6	0-2	0-4	0-5	1-3	5.0	-13.00

Hurdles	18	52	5	6	5	36	9.6	-6.50
Chases	5	23	1	1	4	17	4.3	-11.00
Totals	22	80	6	7	9	58	7.5	-22.50
04-05	16	54	3	4	3	44	5.6	+13.50
03-04	12	39	1	5	3	30	2.6	-5.00

WINNING HORSES

Horse	Races Run	1st	2nd	3rd	£
My Way De Solzen	5	3	2	0	185009
Voy Por Ustedes	6	5	1	0	118926
Pangbourne	6	3	1	0	19957
Nyrche	10	3	3	0	31336
Halcon Genelardais	6	3	0	0	41312
Senorita Rumbalita	6	3	0	1	25230
Mughas	6	1	1	2	13012
Yardbird	5	2	0	1	19422
Pretty Star	4	1	0	0	12404
Daryal	2	1	0	0	7873
First De La Brunie	6	2	1	0	10775
Kandjar D'Allier	6	1	0	1	5530
Shaadiva	2	1	0	0	5421
Shiny Thing	4	1	1	1	5348
Sea The Light	5	1	0	1	5156
Ben's Turn	5	4	1	0	10083
Mystery Lot	4	1	1	0	4554
*Blazing Bailey	5	2	2	1	7807
Alfasonic	5	2	0	0	8991
Five Colours	4	1	2	0	4229
Lantaur Lad	1	1	0	0	4202
Nykel	6	1	0	2	3904
Jackson	8	2	1	1	7202
Proprioception	6	1	1	1	3773
Incursion	2	1	1	0	3679
The Hairy Lemon	6	3	0	1	10474
Mikado Melody	3	1	0	0	3601
Siberian Highness	4	2	1	0	7124
Adjami	4	1	2	0	3570
Le Corvee	5	1	0	0	3413
Knighton Lad	5	1	1	0	3253
North Lodge	5	1	1	0	3039
Petwick	4	1	1	0	2707
Wyldello	4	1	3	0	2193
Glimmer Of Light	5	1	1	0	2082
Apollo Lady	4	2	0	1	4097
The Big Canadian	3	1	0	0	2037
Total winning prize-money					**£612725**
Favourites	28-223		12.6%		-155.20

N B KING

NEWMARKET, SUFFOLK

	No. of Hrs	Races Run	1st	2nd	3rd	Unpl	Per cent	£1 Level Stake
NH Flat	3	5	0	0	0	5	0.0	-5.00

JOCKEYS

	W-R	Per cent	£1 Level Stake
Owyn Nelmes	5-49	10.2	+5.25
Shane Walsh	1-14	7.1	-10.75

COURSE RECORD

	Total W-R	Non-Hndcps Hurdles	Chases	Hndcps Hurdles	Chases	NH Flat	Per cent	£1 Level Stake
Uttoxeter	2-8	2-6	0-0	0-2	0-0	0-0	25.0	-2.00
Fontwell	2-11	0-4	0-2	1-1	1-4	0-0	18.2	+7.00
Stratford	1-3	1-3	0-0	0-0	0-0	0-0	33.3	+23.00
Fakenham	1-16	0-4	0-1	1-7	0-4	0-0	6.3	-8.50

WINNING HORSES

Horse	Races Run	1st	2nd	3rd	£
Pangeran	9	1	0	3	4687
Festive Chimes	17	3	5	5	6444
Love Triangle	6	1	0	0	2947
Ethan Snowflake	4	1	0	0	2193
Total winning prize-money					**£16271**
Favourites		1-2		50.0%	0.75

F KIRBY

STREETLAM, N YORKS

	No. of Hrs	Races Run	1st	2nd	3rd	Unpl	Per cent	£1 Level Stake
NH Flat	0	0	0	0	0	0	0.0	0.00
Hurdles	4	6	0	0	0	6	0.0	-6.00
Chases	4	18	2	0	2	14	11.1	-7.50
Totals	5	24	2	0	2	20	8.3	-13.50
04-05	8	27	2	3	2	20	7.4	+6.50
03-04	4	19	5	2	1	11	26.3	+85.50

JOCKEYS

	W-R	Per cent	£1 Level Stake
Kenny Johnson	2-22	9.1	-11.50

COURSE RECORD

	Total W-R	Non-Hndcps Hurdles	Chases	Hndcps Hurdles	Chases	NH Flat	Per cent	£1 Level Stake
Wetherby	1-1	0-0	0-0	0-0	1-1	0-0	100.0	+6.00
Catterick	1-8	0-2	0-2	0-1	1-3	0-0	12.5	-4.50

WINNING HORSES

Horse	Races Run	1st	2nd	3rd	£
Sound Of Cheers	8	1	0	2	4554
Forest Dante	4	1	0	0	4167
Total winning prize-money					**£8721**
Favourites	**0-0**		**0.0%**		**0.00**

MISS H C KNIGHT

WEST LOCKINGE, OXON

	No. of Hrs	Races Run	1st	2nd	3rd	Unpl	Per cent	£1 Level Stake
NH Flat	21	30	1	1	1	27	3.3	-25.67
Hurdles	47	117	12	7	8	90	10.3	-64.95
Chases	34	97	14	10	14	59	14.4	-6.81
Totals	75	244	27	18	23	176	11.1	-97.43
04-05	89	291	29	23	30	208	10.0	-62.12
03-04	76	259	43	39	30	147	16.6	-29.02

BY MONTH

NH Flat	W-R	Per cent	£1 Level Stake		Hurdles	W-R	Per cent	£1 Level Stake
May	0-3	0.0	-3.00		May	1-8	12.5	-3.67
June	0-0	0.0	0.00		June	1-2	50.0	+1.50
July	0-0	0.0	0.00		July	1-2	50.0	+0.38
August	0-0	0.0	0.00		August	0-2	0.0	-2.00
September	0-0	0.0	0.00		September	0-2	0.0	-2.00
October	0-1	0.0	-1.00		October	0-11	0.0	-11.00
November	0-7	0.0	-7.00		November	0-16	0.0	-16.00
December	1-5	20.0	-0.67		December	2-13	15.4	-9.54
January	0-4	0.0	-4.00		January	2-14	14.3	-8.13
February	0-1	0.0	-1.00		February	0-16	0.0	-16.00
March	0-4	0.0	-4.00		March	4-14	28.6	+16.25
April	0-5	0.0	-5.00		April	1-17	5.9	-14.75

Chases	W-R	Per cent	£1 Level Stake		Totals	W-R	Per cent	£1 Level Stake
May	0-4	0.0	-4.00		May	1-15	6.7	-10.67
June	0-0	0.0	0.00		June	1-2	50.0	+1.50
July	0-1	0.0	-1.00		July	1-3	33.3	-0.62
August	0-1	0.0	-1.00		August	0-3	0.0	-3.00
September	0-2	0.0	-2.00		September	0-4	0.0	-4.00
October	1-10	10.0	-5.00		October	1-22	4.5	-17.00
November	4-19	21.1	+3.75		November	4-42	9.5	-19.25
December	4-19	21.1	-3.84		December	7-37	18.9	-14.05
January	0-9	0.0	-9.00		January	2-27	7.4	-21.13
February	3-11	27.3	+21.79		February	3-28	10.7	+4.79
March	0-9	0.0	-9.00		March	4-27	14.8	+3.25
April	2-12	16.7	+2.50		April	3-34	8.8	-17.25

DISTANCE

Hurdles	W-R	Per cent	£1 Level Stake		Chases	W-R	Per cent	£1 Level Stake
2m-2m3f	4-59	6.8	-32.79		2m-2m3f	5-24	20.8	-3.46
2m4f-2m7f	7-52	13.5	-29.41		2m4f-2m7f	8-44	18.2	-0.34
3m+	1-6	16.7	-2.75		3m+	1-29	3.4	-3.00

TYPE OF RACE

Non-Handicaps	W-R	Per cent	£1 Level Stake		Handicaps	W-R	Per cent	£1 Level Stake
Nov Hrdls	9-75	12.0	-38.29		Nov Hrdls	1-8	12.5	-0.50
Hrdls	2-19	10.5	-11.17		Hrdls	0-15	0.0	-15.00
Nov Chs	6-36	16.7	-9.55		Nov Chs	4-20	20.0	+1.25
Chases	1-6	16.7	0.00		Chases	3-35	8.6	+1.50
Sell/Claim	0-0	0.0	0.00		Sell/Claim	0-0	0.0	0.00

RACE CLASS

	W-R	Per cent	£1 Level Stake
Class 1	4-18	22.2	+3.00
Class 2	0-10	0.0	-10.00
Class 3	9-83	10.8	-31.95
Class 4	13-100	13.0	-29.80
Class 5	0-9	0.0	-9.00
Class 6	1-24	4.2	-19.67

FIRST TIME OUT

	W-R	Per cent	£1 Level Stake
Bumpers	1-21	4.8	-16.67
Hurdles	1-78	3.6	-23.67
Chases	2-26	7.7	-17.25
Totals	4-75	5.3	-57.59

JOCKEYS

	W-R	Per cent	£1 Level Stake
Timmy Murphy	17-73	23.3	-0.45
Sam Thomas	4-64	6.3	-44.17
A P McCoy	2-6	33.3	+1.36
Paul Moloney	2-45	4.4	-6.00
Paul O'Neill	1-2	50.0	+2.33
J Culloty	1-7	14.3	-3.50

COURSE RECORD

	Total W-R	Non-Hndcps Hurdles	Non-Hndcps Chases	Hndcps Hurdles	Hndcps Chases	NH Flat	Per cent	£1 Level Stake
Fontwell	5-16	3-8	2-4	0-1	0-3	0-0	31.3	+18.11
Sandown	4-12	1-2	1-3	0-2	2-4	0-1	33.3	+4.75
Ludlow	3-32	1-12	0-4	0-2	1-6	1-8	9.4	-17.57
Worcester	2-4	2-3	0-1	0-0	0-0	0-0	50.0	+1.88
Exeter	2-11	0-2	2-5	0-0	0-4	0-0	18.2	-6.46
Towcester	2-11	1-7	0-1	0-0	1-1	0-2	18.2	-1.17
Newbury	2-13	1-4	0-0	1-4	0-2	0-3	15.4	7.25
Taunton	2-13	1-3	1-3	0-0	0-4	0-3	15.4	-8.72
Huntingdon	2-19	0-6	1-5	0-0	1-6	0-2	10.5	+13.00
Haydock	1-1	1-1	0-0	0-0	0-0	0-0	100.0	+2.50
Leicester	1-3	0-1	0-0	0-0	1-2	0-0	33.3	+2.50
Aintree	1-7	0-2	0-1	0-1	1-1	0-2	14.3	-2.00

WINNING HORSES

Horse	Races Run	1st	2nd	3rd	£
Impek	7	2	2	2	71195
Harringay	5	3	1	0	37581
Racing Demon	4	3	0	0	35664
Harris Bay	6	4	0	1	31674

Cruising River	7	2	1	0	12572
Smart Mover	7	7	3	0	9108
General Grey	4	1	0	0	5205
Aztec Warrior	6	1	1	1	5205
Wenceslas	4	1	0	0	4801
Glasker Mill	6	2	0	2	7973
My Pal Val	1	1	0	0	4251
Tuesday's Child	5	1	0	0	3902
Chase The Sunset	8	2	0	1	6468
Maljimar	3	1	0	0	3253
Ringaroses	2	1	0	0	2453
Total winning prize-money					**£241305**
Favourites	11-22		50.0%		6.37

04-05	43	162	21	16	21	104	13.0	-12.04
03-04	37	118	13	20	7	78	11.0	-36.92

BY MONTH

NH Flat	W-R	Per cent	£1 Level Stake		Hurdles	W-R	Per cent	£1 Level Stake
May	1-1	100.0	+5.00		May	2-6	33.3	+2.50
June	0-0	0.0	0.00		June	0-6	0.0	-6.00
July	0-0	0.0	0.00		July	0-2	0.0	-2.00
August	0-0	0.0	0.00		August	1-5	20.0	-2.25
September	0-0	0.0	0.00		September	0-3	0.0	-3.00
October	0-2	0.0	-2.00		October	5-14	35.7	+13.75
November	0-1	0.0	-1.00		November	3-16	18.8	+2.83
December	0-0	0.0	0.00		December	0-18	0.0	-18.00
January	0-3	0.0	-3.00		January	0-6	0.0	-6.00
February	0-1	0.0	-1.00		February	0-7	0.0	-7.00
March	0-2	0.0	-2.00		March	1-12	8.3	-6.50
April	0-1	0.0	-1.00		April	4-14	28.6	+13.75

Chases	W-R	Per cent	£1 Level Stake		Totals	W-R	Per cent	£1 Level Stake
May	2-8	25.0	+12.00		May	5-15	33.3	+19.50
June	0-3	0.0	-3.00		June	0-9	0.0	-9.00
July	0-1	0.0	-1.00		July	0-3	0.0	-3.00
August	0-0	0.0	0.00		August	1-5	20.0	-2.25
September	0-1	0.0	-1.00		September	0-4	0.0	-4.00
October	0-6	0.0	-6.00		October	5-22	22.7	+5.75
November	2-8	25.0	+4.50		November	5-25	20.0	+6.33
December	1-4	25.0	-0.25		December	1-22	4.5	-18.25
January	4-16	25.0	+6.25		January	4-25	16.0	-2.75
February	0-3	0.0	-3.00		February	0-11	0.0	-11.00
March	2-12	16.7	+0.50		March	3-26	11.5	-8.00
April	2-13	15.4	+0.50		April	6-28	21.4	+13.25

DISTANCE

Hurdles	W-R	Per cent	£1 Level Stake		Chases	W-R	Per cent	£1 Level Stake
2m-2m3f	9-57	15.8	+2.33		2m-2m3f	1-31	3.2	-23.00
2m4f-2m7f	4-41	9.8	-25.00		2m4f-2m7f	6-20	30.0	+20.75
3m+	3-11	27.3	+4.75		3m+	6-24	25.0	+11.75

TYPE OF RACE

Non-Handicaps	W-R	Per cent	£1 Level Stake		Handicaps	W-R	Per cent	£1 Level Stake
Nov Hrdls	4-37	10.8	-21.17		Nov Hrdls	4-7	57.1	+19.50
Hrdls	1-20	5.0	-16.00		Hrdls	7-44	15.9	+0.75
Nov Chs	0-8	0.0	-8.00		Nov Chs	1-11	9.1	-7.50
Chases	0-2	0.0	-2.00		Chases	12-54	22.2	+27.00
Sell/Claim	0-0	0.0	0.00		Sell/Claim	0-0	0.0	0.00

RACE CLASS

	W-R	Per cent	£1 Level Stake
Class 1	0-13	0.0	-13.00
Class 2	0-11	0.0	-11.00
Class 3	12-66	18.2	+13.00
Class 4	17-91	18.7	+5.58

FIRST TIME OUT

	W-R	Per cent	£1 Level Stake
Bumpers	1-9	11.1	-3.00
Hurdles	8-31	25.8	+23.08
Chases	1-12	8.3	-7.00

G L LANDAU

FROME, SOMERSET

	No. of Hrs	Races Run	1st	2nd	3rd	Unpl	Per cent	£1 Level Stake
NH Flat	0	0	0	0	0	0	0.0	0.00
Hurdles	0	0	0	0	0	0	0.0	0.00
Chases	3	6	3	1	2	0	50.0	+2.45
Totals	3	6	3	1	2	0	50.0	+2.45
04-05	3	10	3	3	2	2	30.0	+10.00
03-04	1	1	0	0	0	1	0.0	-1.00

JOCKEYS

	W-R	Per cent	£1 Level Stake
Mr R Burton	3-5	60.0	+3.45

COURSE RECORD

	Total W-R	Non-Hndcps Hurdles	Chases	Hndcps Hurdles	Chases	NH Flat	Per cent	£1 Level Stake
Towcester	1-1	0-0	1-1	0-0	0-0	0-0	100.0	+1.25
Cheltenham	1-2	0-0	1-2	0-0	0-0	0-0	50.0	+2.00
Folkestone	1-2	0-0	1-2	0-0	0-0	0-0	50.0	+0.20

WINNING HORSES

Horse	Races Run	1st	2nd	3rd	£
Hot Toddy	1	1	0	0	2019
Paddy For Paddy	3	2	0	1	1874
Total winning prize-money					**£3893**
Favourites	2-4		50.0%		0.45

MISS E C LAVELLE

WILDHERN, HANTS

	No. of Hrs	Races Run	1st	2nd	3rd	Unpl	Per cent	£1 Level Stake
NH Flat	9	11	1	1	3	6	9.1	-5.00
Hurdles	39	109	16	12	9	72	14.7	-17.92
Chases	20	75	13	9	11	42	17.3	+9.50
Totals	52	195	30	22	23	120	15.4	-13.42

| Class 5 | 0-4 | 0.0 | -4.00 | Totals | 10-52 | 19.2 | +13.08 |
| Class 6 | 1-10 | 10.0 | -4.00 | | | | |

JOCKEYS

	W-R	Per cent	£1 Level Stake
Barry Fenton	16-94	17.0	+0.58
Marcus Foley	6-39	15.4	+2.75
Brian Crowley	4-24	16.7	-6.25
Noel Fehily	2-7	28.6	+4.00
Andrew Thornton	1-2	50.0	+6.50
Timmy Murphy	1-4	25.0	+4.00

COURSE RECORD

	Total W-R	Non-Hndcps Hurdles	Chases	Hndcps Hurdles	Chases	NH Flat	Per cent	£1 Level Stake
Taunton	5-12	0-3	0-0	1-3	4-5	0-1	41.7	+15.75
Exeter	4-8	0-2	0-0	2-3	2-2	0-1	50.0	+19.50
Plumpton	4-11	3-6	0-1	1-3	0-0	0-1	36.4	+12.75
Ludlow	3-9	0-3	0-1	2-3	1-2	0-0	33.3	+7.00
Southwell	2-4	0-0	0-0	1-1	1-3	0-0	50.0	+11.00
Folkestone	2-6	0-0	0-0	0-2	2-4	0-0	33.3	+0.25
Hereford	2-11	0-3	0-1	1-2	0-3	1-2	18.2	+1.50
Huntingdon	2-21	0-5	0-0	1-5	1-10	0-1	9.5	-2.50
Uttoxeter	1-3	0-1	0-0	1-1	0-1	0-0	33.3	+0.75
Windsor	1-3	0-1	0-0	1-2	0-0	0-0	33.3	+8.00
Stratford	1-9	0-1	0-0	0-2	1-6	0-0	11.1	-2.00
Wincanton	1-9	1-6	0-0	0-2	0-0	0-1	11.1	-4.67
Worcester	1-9	1-3	0-0	0-3	0-3	0-0	11.1	-6.25
Newbury	1-17	0-5	0-1	0-1	1-9	0-1	5.9	-11.50

WINNING HORSES

Horse	Races Run	1st	2nd	3rd	£
Presenting Express	7	4	1	0	31415
Umbrella Man	6	2	2	0	17406
Palua	8	1	0	1	10960
Glacial Delight	9	4	0	1	23823
Priors Dale	5	1	0	1	6935
The Bandit	6	1	0	0	6506
Tomina	2	2	0	0	10512
Presence Of Mind	4	1	1	1	5688
No Way Back	6	1	0	1	5205
Phar Out Phavorite	7	3	1	1	13965
Marjina	2	1	0	0	4076
*Blaeberry	7	1	2	1	3904
Buster Culllis	3	1	1	1	3904
Celebration Town	3	1	0	0	3715
Tritonville Lodge	3	1	1	0	3487
Kilindini	8	2	1	2	6594
Stern	1	1	0	0	3360
Madison De Vonnas	5	1	0	2	3346
None-So-Pretty	2	1	0	0	1953
Total winning prize-money					**£166754**
Favourites	8-17		47.1%		11.50

B D LEAVY

FORSBROOK, STAFFS

	No. of Hrs	Races Run	1st	2nd	3rd	Unpl	Per cent	£1 Level Stake
NH Flat	2	2	0	0	0	2	0.0	-2.00
Hurdles	9	26	2	2	2	20	7.7	+2.00
Chases	3	3	0	0	0	3	0.0	-3.00
Totals	12	31	2	2	2	25	6.5	-3.00
04-05	20	67	6	4	6	51	9.0	-16.50
03-04	21	51	3	3	4	41	5.9	-27.50

JOCKEYS

	W-R	Per cent	£1 Level Stake
Richard Hobson	1-3	33.3	+18.00
Liam Heard	1-4	25.0	+3.00

COURSE RECORD

	Total W-R	Non-Hndcps Hurdles	Chases	Hndcps Hurdles	Chases	NH Flat	Per cent	£1 Level Stake
Leicester	1-3	1-2	0-0	0-0	0-1	0-0	33.3	+4.00
Stratford	1-3	0-1	0-0	1-2	0-0	0-0	33.3	+18.00

WINNING HORSES

Horse	Races Run	1st	2nd	3rd	£
*Rojabaa	8	2	1	1	13274
Total winning prize-money					**£13274**
Favourites	0-0		0.0%		0.00

R LEE

BYTON, H'FORDS

	No. of Hrs	Races Run	1st	2nd	3rd	Unpl	Per cent	£1 Level Stake
NH Flat	2	2	0	0	0	2	0.0	-2.00
Hurdles	12	53	2	5	4	42	3.8	-40.50
Chases	20	96	7	16	17	56	7.3	-18.00
Totals	29	151	9	21	21	100	6.0	-60.50
04-05	31	190	26	24	29	111	13.7	-17.67
03-04	31	169	21	15	18	117	12.4	-4.25

JOCKEYS

	W-R	Per cent	£1 Level Stake
Robert Thornton	5-28	17.9	+34.00
Richard Johnson	2-17	11.8	+3.00
William Kennedy	1-18	5.6	-14.50
Tom Doyle	1-42	2.4	-37.00

COURSE RECORD

	Total W-R	Non-Hndcps Hurdles	Chases	Hndcps Hurdles	Chases	NH Flat	Per cent	£1 Level Stake
Hereford	2-13	0-0	0-3	1-4	1-6	0-0	15.4	+0.50

Worcester	2-14	0-2	0-3	1-2	1-6	0-1	14.3	+5.50
Nton Abbot	1-3	0-0	0-0	0-0	1-3	0-0	33.3	+0.50
Southwell	1-6	0-0	0-1	0-0	1-5	0-0	16.7	+2.00
Huntingdon	1-7	0-1	0-0	0-1	1-5	0-0	14.3	+27.00
Ludlow	1-7	0-1	0-2	0-0	1-4	0-0	14.3	0.00
Warwick	1-9	0-1	0-2	0-2	1-4	0-0	11.1	-4.00

WINNING HORSES

Horse	Races Run	1st	2nd	3rd	£
Almaydan	8	1	1	0	13012
Cosmocrat	4	1	1	0	6747
Marked Man	7	1	2	0	5579
Jolejoker	5	1	1	1	5205
Runner Bean	13	2	2	1	8386
*Walsingham	8	1	1	0	3904
Southerndown	10	1	2	3	3675
Potts Of Magic	10	1	2	1	3458
Total winning prize-money					**£49966**
Favourites	0-8		**0.0%**		**-8.00**

S T LEWIS

LONGDON, WORCS

	No. of Hrs	Races Run	1st	2nd	3rd	Unpl	Per cent	£1 Level Stake
NH Flat	3	10	0	0	1	9	0.0	-10.00
Hurdles	11	59	3	0	2	54	5.1	+23.00
Chases	7	34	0	3	2	29	0.0	-34.00
Totals	16	103	3	3	5	92	2.9	-21.00
04-05	22	99	2	3	8	86	2.0	-74.25
03-04	28	104	1	0	6	97	1.0	-101.75

JOCKEYS

	W-R	Per cent	£1 Level Stake
Patrick C Stringer	2-8	25.0	+53.00
Liam Treadwell	1-9	11.1	+12.00

COURSE RECORD

	Total W-R	Non-Hndcps Hurdles	Chases	Hndcps Hurdles	Chases	NH Flat	Per cent	£1 Level Stake
Ludlow	2-17	1-7	0-2	1-3	0-3	0-2	11.8	+44.00
Towcester	1-27	0-8	0-2	1-5	0-10	0-2	3.7	-6.00

WINNING HORSES

Horse	Races Run	1st	2nd	3rd	£
Little Rort	9	1	0	0	3718
Jug Of Punch	10	2	0	0	6135
Total winning prize-money					**£9853**
Favourites	0-1		**0.0%**		**-1.00**

B J LLEWELLYN

FOCHRIW, CAERPHILLY

	No. of Hrs	Races Run	1st	2nd	3rd	Unpl	Per cent	£1 Level Stake
NH Flat	3	3	0	0	0	3	0.0	-3.00
Hurdles	27	91	7	7	10	66	7.7	-21.67
Chases	8	20	3	3	2	12	15.0	+12.50
Totals	33	114	10	10	12	81	8.8	-12.17
04-05	21	90	15	16	7	52	16.7	+6.83
03-04	27	89	11	6	11	61	12.4	-17.42

BY MONTH

NH Flat	W-R	Per cent	£1 Level Stake	Hurdles	W-R	Per cent	£1 Level Stake
May	0-1	0.0	-1.00	May	2-9	22.2	+9.00
June	0-0	0.0	0.00	June	0-5	0.0	-5.00
July	0-0	0.0	0.00	July	0-6	0.0	-6.00
August	0-0	0.0	0.00	August	0-3	0.0	-3.00
September	0-1	0.0	-1.00	September	0-1	0.0	-1.00
October	0-0	0.0	0.00	October	1-9	11.1	+25.00
November	0-0	0.0	0.00	November	1-9	11.1	-4.67
December	0-1	0.0	-1.00	December	1-13	7.7	-9.00
January	0-0	0.0	0.00	January	1-11	9.1	-1.50
February	0-0	0.0	0.00	February	0-9	0.0	-9.00
March	0-0	0.0	0.00	March	0-7	0.0	-7.00
April	0-0	0.0	0.00	April	1-9	11.1	-3.50

Chases	W-R	Per cent	£1 Level Stake	Totals	W-R	Per cent	£1 Level Stake
May	0-0	0.0	0.00	May	2-10	20.0	+8.00
June	1-1	100.0	+9.00	June	1-6	16.7	+4.00
July	0-2	0.0	-2.00	July	0-8	0.0	-8.00
August	0-0	0.0	0.00	August	0-3	0.0	-3.00
September	0-0	0.0	0.00	September	0-2	0.0	-2.00
October	1-5	20.0	+12.00	October	2-14	14.3	+37.00
November	0-4	0.0	-4.00	November	1-13	7.7	-8.67
December	0-2	0.0	-2.00	December	1-16	6.3	-12.00
January	1-3	33.3	+2.50	January	2-14	14.3	-5.00
February	0-0	0.0	0.00	February	0-9	0.0	-9.00
March	0-2	0.0	-2.00	March	0-9	0.0	-9.00
April	0-1	0.0	-1.00	April	1-10	10.0	-4.50

DISTANCE

Hurdles	W-R	Per cent	£1 Level Stake	Chases	W-R	Per cent	£1 Level Stake
2m-2m3f	4-54	7.4	-6.67	2m-2m3f	1-6	16.7	-0.50
2m4f-2m7f	2-28	7.1	-19.00	2m4f-2m7f	1-5	20.0	+5.00
3m+	1-9	11.1	+4.00	3m+	1-9	11.1	+8.00

TYPE OF RACE

Non-Handicaps	W-R	Per cent	£1 Level Stake	Handicaps	W-R	Per cent	£1 Level Stake
Nov Hrdls	2-26	7.7	+12.33	Nov Hrdls	1-15	6.7	-2.00
Hrdls	1-10	10.0	-6.00	Hrdls	1-21	4.8	-16.00
Nov Chs	0-1	0.0	-1.00	Nov Chs	1-5	20.0	+0.50

	W-R	Per cent	£1 Level Stake		W-R	Per cent	£1 Level Stake
Chases	0-0	0.0	0.00	Chases	2-14	14.3	+13.00
Sell/Claim	1-20	5.0	-16.50	Sell/Claim	1-5	20.0	+0.50

RACE CLASS / FIRST TIME OUT

	W-R	Per cent	£1 Level Stake		W-R	Per cent	£1 Level Stake
Class 1	0-6	0.0	-6.00	Bumpers	0-3	0.0	-3.00
Class 2	0-0	0.0	0.00	Hurdles	2-25	8.0	-6.50
Class 3	1-19	5.3	+15.00	Chases	2-5	40.0	+10.50
Class 4	8-62	12.9	+0.33				
Class 5	1-24	4.2	-18.50	Totals	4-33	12.1	+1.00
Class 6	0-3	0.0	-3.00				

JOCKEYS

	W-R	Per cent	£1 Level Stake
Ollie McPhail	4-30	13.3	+17.83
Tony Dobbin	1-1	100.0	+4.50
Shane Walsh	1-2	50.0	+8.00
Tom Doyle	1-4	25.0	+13.00
Mr R McCarthy	1-6	16.7	+7.00
P J Brennan	1-9	11.1	-4.00
Christian Williams	1-20	5.0	-16.50

COURSE RECORD

	Total W-R	Non-Hndcps Hurdles	Chases	Hndcps Hurdles	Chases	NH Flat	Per cent	£1 Level Stake
Chepstow	3-15	7-11	0-0	0-2	1-2	0-0	20.0	+10.33
Bangor	1-1	0-0	0-0	1-1	0-0	0-0	100.0	+4.50
Catterick	1-2	0-0	0-0	0-0	1-2	0-0	50.0	+3.50
Cheltenham	1-3	1-2	0-0	0-1	0-0	0-0	33.3	+31.00
Leicester	1-3	1-2	0-0	0-1	0-0	0-0	33.3	+0.50
Stratford	1-6	0-2	0-0	0-1	1-2	0-1	16.7	+4.00
Plumpton	1-7	0-1	0-0	1-4	0-2	0-0	14.3	+6.00
Hereford	1-14	0-6	0-0	1-4	0-3	0-1	7.1	-9.00

WINNING HORSES

Horse	Races Run	1st	2nd	3rd	£
Alva Glen	7	1	0	1	5042
Barnbrook Empire	4	1	0	0	5058
Calon Lan	4	1	0	0	4784
Whaleef	6	1	0	1	3904
Biscar Two	5	2	0	0	7053
Anflora	6	1	1	2	3835
Random Quest	8	1	1	0	3396
Brisbane Road	3	1	0	0	2744
Ask The Umpire	2	1	0	0	2464
Total winning prize-money					**£38880**
Favourites	0-2		0.0%		-2.00

CARL LLEWELLYN

UPPER LAMBOURN, BERKS

	No. of Hrs	Races Run	1st	2nd	3rd	Unpl	Per cent	£1 Level Stake
NH Flat	3	3	0	1	0	2	0.0	-3.00
Hurdles	3	3	0	1	1	1	0.0	-3.00
Chases	6	7	1	2	0	4	14.3	+27.00
Totals	12	13	1	4	1	7	7.7	+21.00

JOCKEYS

	W-R	Per cent	£1 Level Stake
Carl Llewellyn	1-6	16.7	+28.00

COURSE RECORD

	Total W-R	Non-Hndcps Hurdles	Chases	Hndcps Hurdles	Chases	NH Flat	Per cent	£1 Level Stake
Ayr	1-1	0-0	0-0	0-0	1-1	0-0	100.0	+33.00

WINNING HORSES

Horse	Races Run	1st	2nd	3rd	£
*Run For Paddy	1	1	0	0	91232
Total winning prize-money					**£91232**
Favourites	0-3		0.0%		-3.00

L LUNGO

CARRUTHERSTOWN, D'FRIES & G'WAY

	No. of Hrs	Races Run	1st	2nd	3rd	Unpl	Per cent	£1 Level Stake
NH Flat	9	10	2	1	0	7	20.0	-0.75
Hurdles	55	164	15	9	17	123	9.1	-94.60
Chases	25	53	10	8	3	32	18.9	-17.41
Totals	69	227	27	18	20	162	11.9	-112.76
04-05	82	281	57	29	33	162	20.3	-9.00
03-04	85	313	55	33	23	202	17.6	-91.87

BY MONTH

NH Flat	W-R	Per cent	£1 Level Stake	Hurdles	W-R	Per cent	£1 Level Stake
May	1-2	50.0	+1.25	May	4-22	18.2	-5.30
June	0-0	0.0	0.00	June	1-2	50.0	-0.20
July	0-0	0.0	0.00	July	0-3	0.0	-3.00
August	0-0	0.0	0.00	August	0-1	0.0	-1.00
September	0-0	0.0	0.00	September	0-0	0.0	0.00
October	0-0	0.0	0.00	October	2-11	18.2	-2.25
November	0-3	0.0	-3.00	November	3-26	11.5	-18.39
December	0-1	0.0	-1.00	December	1-19	5.3	-14.00
January	0-1	0.0	-1.00	January	0-25	0.0	-25.00
February	1-1	100.0	+5.00	February	0-12	0.0	-12.00
March	0-1	0.0	-1.00	March	1-13	7.7	-3.00
April	0-1	0.0	-1.00	April	3-30	10.0	-10.46

Chases	W-R	Per cent	£1 Level Stake		Totals	W-R	Per cent	£1 Level Stake
May	1-3	33.3	-1.27		May	6-27	22.2	-5.32
June	0-0	0.0	0.00		June	1-2	50.0	-0.20
July	0-1	0.0	-1.00		July	0-4	0.0	-4.00
August	0-0	0.0	0.00		August	0-1	0.0	-1.00
September	0-0	0.0	0.00		September	0-0	0.0	0.00
October	0-1	0.0	-1.00		October	2-12	16.7	-3.25
November	2-11	18.2	-6.33		November	5-40	12.5	-27.72
December	1-8	12.5	-3.50		December	2-28	7.1	-18.50
January	3-10	30.0	-1.92		January	3-36	8.3	-27.92
February	2-6	33.3	+5.62		February	3-19	15.8	-1.38
March	1-3	33.3	+2.00		March	2-17	11.8	-2.00
April	0-10	0.0	-10.00		April	3-41	7.3	-21.46

DISTANCE

Hurdles	W-R	Per cent	£1 Level Stake		Chases	W-R	Per cent	£1 Level Stake
2m-2m3f	9-75	12.0	-45.80		2m-2m3f	5-13	38.5	+1.31
2m4f-2m7f	5-64	7.8	-27.80		2m4f-2m7f	3-19	15.8	-10.72
3m+	1-25	4.0	-21.00		3m+	2-21	9.5	-8.00

TYPE OF RACE

Non-Handicaps	W-R	Per cent	£1 Level Stake		Handicaps	W-R	Per cent	£1 Level Stake
Nov Hrdls	5-35	14.3	-27.17		Nov Hrdls	2-18	11.1	-11.30
Hrdls	1-9	11.1	-3.00		Hrdls	7-100	7.0	-51.13
Nov Chs	4-7	57.1	+4.03		Nov Chs	3-11	27.3	-3.17
Chases	0-2	0.0	-2.00		Chases	3-33	9.1	-16.27
Sell/Claim	0-0	0.0	0.00		Sell/Claim	0-2	0.0	-2.00

RACE CLASS / FIRST TIME OUT

	W-R	Per cent	£1 Level Stake			W-R	Per cent	£1 Level Stake
Class 1	0-11	0.0	-11.00		Bumpers	2-9	22.2	+0.25
Class 2	1-24	4.2	-14.00		Hurdles	4-47	8.5	-29.38
Class 3	9-63	14.3	-19.89		Chases	2-13	15.4	-6.83
Class 4	14-108	13.0	-57.95					
Class 5	1-13	7.7	-11.17		Totals	8-69	11.6	-35.96
Class 6	2-8	25.0	+1.25					

JOCKEYS

	W-R	Per cent	£1 Level Stake
Tony Dobbin	13-76	17.1	-28.36
Gary Berridge	5-60	8.3	-25.25
Bruce Gibson	4-40	10.0	-31.15
G Lee	1-1	100.0	+0.67
Michael McAlister	1-2	50.0	+8.00
Mr G Tumelty	1-4	25.0	+1.00
Brian Harding	1-9	11.1	-7.17
John Ennis	1-11	9.1	-6.50

COURSE RECORD

	Total W-R	Non-Hndcps Hurdles	Chases	Hndcps Hurdles	Chases	NH Flat	Per cent	£1 Level Stake
Ayr	7-43	1-9	1-2	1-19	3-9	1-4	16.3	-1.19
Kelso	4-27	2-8	0-0	1-14	0-4	1-1	14.8	-11.50
Perth	3-15	2-6	0-1	1-7	0-0	0-1	20.0	-7.53
Sedgefield	3-16	1-5	0-0	2-8	0-3	0-0	18.8	-7.39
Hexham	2-14	0-2	0-1	0-5	2-5	0-1	14.3	-9.27
Newcastle	2-17	0-3	2-4	0-7	0-3	0-0	11.8	-12.08
Aintree	1-5	0-0	0-0	1-5	0-0	0-0	20.0	+2.50
Uttoxeter	1-5	0-0	1-1	0-3	0-1	0-0	20.0	-0.50
Bangor	1-9	0-1	0-0	1-6	0-2	0-0	11.1	-6.13
Musselbgh	1-11	0-0	0-0	0-4	1-6	0-1	9.1	-9.17
Wetherby	1-11	0-1	0-0	1-10	0-0	0-0	9.1	-6.50
Carlisle	1-13	0-4	0-0	1-6	0-3	0-0	7.7	-3.00

WINNING HORSES

Horse	Races Run	1st	2nd	3rd	£
The Rajan Bandit	6	1	0	0	12526
Brooklyn Breeze	3	1	0	0	8288
Armaguedon	3	1	0	0	7807
Reap The Reward	6	1	0	0	7807
Chef De Cour	7	3	1	0	14370
Wild Cane Ridge	5	2	1	0	10494
Rasharrow	5	3	0	0	14990
Bogus Dreams	4	2	0	0	9188
Thoutmosis	7	1	0	1	5577
Villon	1	1	0	0	4196
Lovely Native	3	1	0	0	3904
Malt De Vergy	4	1	0	0	3705
Corrib Lad	4	1	0	2	3614
Brandy Wine	7	2	2	0	6305
Lutin Du Moulin	12	2	0	2	6082
Word Gets Around	6	1	1	0	3253
Silken Pearls	3	1	0	0	3083
You Do The Math	8	1	3	1	2993
The Pious Prince	1	1	0	0	1713
Total winning prize-money					**£129895**
Favourites	15-45		33.3%		-10.76

S LYCETT

NAUNTON, GLOUCS

	No. of Hrs	Races Run	1st	2nd	3rd	Unpl	Per cent	£1 Level Stake
NH Flat	1	4	0	1	1	2	0.0	-4.00
Hurdles	9	36	2	2	3	29	5.6	+3.00
Chases	4	11	2	0	0	9	18.2	-1.67
Totals	12	51	4	3	4	40	7.8	-2.67
04-05	3	9	1	1	0	7	11.1	-7.09
03-04	1	5	1	1	0	3	20.0	+2.50

JOCKEYS

	W-R	Per cent	£1 Level Stake
A P McCoy	2-4	50.0	+5.33
Keith Mercer	2-8	25.0	+31.00

COURSE RECORD

	Total W-R	Non-Hndcps Hurdles	Chases	Hndcps Hurdles	Chases	NH Flat	Per cent	£1 Level Stake
Worcester	2-5	0-1	0-0	1-1	1-3	0-0	40.0	+29.00
Folkestone	1-1	0-0	0-0	1-1	0-0	0-0	100.0	+9.00
Huntingdon	1-2	0-0	0-0	0-1	1-1	0-0	50.0	+2.33

WINNING HORSES

Horse	Races Run	1st	2nd	3rd	£
*Pardon What	13	2	1	0	7684
Jazz Night	5	2	0	0	6665
Total winning prize-money					£14349
Favourites	1-2		50.0%		2.33

J MACKIE

CHURCH BROUGHTON , DERBYS

	No. of Hrs	Races Run	1st	2nd	3rd	Unpl	Per cent	£1 Level Stake
NH Flat	3	7	0	0	0	7	0.0	-7.00
Hurdles	17	64	5	5	9	45	7.8	-29.00
Chases	6	20	2	1	6	11	10.0	+1.50
Totals	23	91	7	6	15	63	7.7	-34.50
04-05	25	102	7	13	15	67	6.9	-61.34
03-04	28	125	18	17	6	84	14.4	-7.80

JOCKEYS

	W-R	Per cent	£1 Level Stake
Paul Moloney	2-30	6.7	-8.50
William Kennedy	1-4	25.0	+3.00
Tom Siddall	1-5	20.0	+3.00
Phil Kinsella	1-5	20.0	+2.00
Warren Marston	1-6	16.7	1.00
Patrick McDonald	1-7	14.3	+1.00

COURSE RECORD

	Total W-R	Non-Hndcps Hurdles	Chases	Hndcps Hurdles	Chases	NH Flat	Per cent	£1 Level Stake
Bangor	2-4	0-0	0-0	1-3	1-1	0-0	50.0	+18.00
Doncaster	1-5	1-1	0-0	0-2	0-2	0-0	20.0	+3.00
Haydock	1-6	0-2	0-0	1-3	0-0	0-1	16.7	+1.00
Southwell	1-6	0-0	0-1	0-2	1-2	0-1	16.7	+0.50
Warwick	1-6	0-0	0-1	1-5	0-0	0-0	16.7	-1.00
Uttoxeter	1-25	0-7	0-1	1-11	0-3	0-3	4.0	-17.00

WINNING HORSES

Horse	Races Run	1st	2nd	3rd	£
*Gidam Gidam	6	1	2	0	4333
Pure Brief	12	2	1	3	8268
Speed Venture	7	2	0	2	7677
Sunisa	6	1	0	2	3477
Tiger Frog	7	1	0	0	3444
Total winning prize-money					£27199
Favourites	0-0		0.0%		0.00

P MADDISON

SKEWSBY, N YORKS

	No. of Hrs	Races Run	1st	2nd	3rd	Unpl	Per cent	£1 Level Stake
NH Flat	0	0	0	0	0	0	0.0	0.00
Hurdles	2	6	0	1	0	5	0.0	-6.00
Chases	1	4	1	1	0	2	25.0	+9.00
Totals	2	10	1	2	0	7	10.0	+3.00
04-05	3	16	1	1	0	14	6.3	-12.75

JOCKEYS

	W-R	Per cent	£1 Level Stake
Mark Bradburne	1-1	100.0	+12.00

COURSE RECORD

	Total W-R	Non-Hndcps Hurdles	Chases	Hndcps Hurdles	Chases	NH Flat	Per cent	£1 Level Stake
Doncaster	1-1	0-0	0-0	0-0	1-1	0-0	100.0	+12.00

WINNING HORSES

Horse	Races Run	1st	2nd	3rd	£
Lothian Falcon	7	1	2	0	10432
Total winning prize-money					£10432
Favourites	0-1		0.0%		-1.00

M MADGWICK

DENMEAD, HANTS

	No. of Hrs	Races Run	1st	2nd	3rd	Unpl	Per cent	£1 Level Stake
NH Flat	0	0	0	0	0	0	0.0	0.00
Hurdles	11	37	1	3	2	31	2.7	-29.00
Chases	4	10	0	1	2	7	0.0	-10.00
Totals	13	47	1	4	4	38	2.1	-39.00
04-05	16	64	3	2	5	54	4.7	-39.50
03-04	10	34	1	1	5	27	2.9	-27.00

JOCKEYS

	W-R	Per cent	£1 Level Stake
Robert Lucey-Butler	1-18	5.6	-10.00

COURSE RECORD

	Total W-R	Non-Hndcps Hurdles	Chases	Hndcps Hurdles	Chases	NH Flat	Per cent	£1 Level Stake
Wincanton	1-7	0-1	0-0	1-6	0-0	0-0	14.3	+1.00

WINNING HORSES

Horse		Races Run	1st	2nd	3rd	£
The Kirk		3	1	0	0	3115
Total winning prize-money						£3115
Favourites	0-1		0.0%			-1.00

C J MANN

UPPER LAMBOURN, BERKS

	No. of Hrs	Races Run	1st	2nd	3rd	Unpl	Per cent	£1 Level Stake
NH Flat	5	7	0	2	0	5	0.0	-7.00
Hurdles	40	119	12	14	19	74	10.1	-59.29
Chases	22	55	11	7	9	28	20.0	+49.38
Totals	61	181	23	23	28	107	12.7	-16.91
04-05	63	244	27	23	38	156	11.1	-112.19
03-04	66	235	37	35	29	134	15.7	+16.90

BY MONTH

NH Flat	W-R	Per cent	£1 Level Stake	Hurdles	W-R	Per cent	£1 Level Stake
May	0-0	0.0	0.00	May	3-14	21.4	-3.13
June	0-0	0.0	0.00	June	0-1	0.0	-1.00
July	0-0	0.0	0.00	July	0-4	0.0	-4.00
August	0-0	0.0	0.00	August	0-3	0.0	-3.00
September	0-0	0.0	0.00	September	0-1	0.0	-1.00
October	0-2	0.0	-2.00	October	1-12	8.3	-8.00
November	0-1	0.0	-1.00	November	3-23	13.0	+0.75
December	0-1	0.0	-1.00	December	2-16	12.5	-7.17
January	0-1	0.0	-1.00	January	2-15	13.3	-6.00
February	0-0	0.0	0.00	February	0-8	0.0	-8.00
March	0-1	0.0	-1.00	March	0-10	0.0	-10.00
April	0-1	0.0	-1.00	April	1-12	8.3	-8.75

Chases	W-R	Per cent	£1 Level Stake	Totals	W-R	Per cent	£1 Level Stake
May	0-6	0.0	-6.00	May	3-20	15.0	-9.13
June	1-3	33.3	+23.00	June	1-4	25.0	+22.00
July	0-2	0.0	-2.00	July	0-6	0.0	-6.00
August	0-1	0.0	-1.00	August	0-4	0.0	-4.00
September	0-0	0.0	0.00	September	0-1	0.0	-1.00
October	1-3	33.3	+14.00	October	2-17	11.8	+4.00
November	0-11	0.0	-11.00	November	3-35	8.6	-11.25

December	4-12	33.3	+22.38	December	6-29	20.7	+14.21
January	3-6	50.0	+10.00	January	5-22	22.7	+3.00
February	0-5	0.0	-5.00	February	0-13	0.0	-13.00
March	2-4	50.0	+7.00	March	2-15	13.3	-4.00
April	0-2	0.0	-2.00	April	1-15	6.7	-11.75

DISTANCE

Hurdles	W-R	Per cent	£1 Level Stake	Chases	W-R	Per cent	£1 Level Stake
2m-2m3f	6-54	11.1	-25.13	2m-2m3f	1-10	10.0	-5.50
2m4f-2m7f	5-51	9.8	-24.17	2m4f-2m7f	6-26	23.1	+30.38
3m+	1-14	7.1	-10.00	3m+	4-19	21.1	+24.50

TYPE OF RACE

Non-Handicaps	W-R	Per cent	£1 Level Stake	Handicaps	W-R	Per cent	£1 Level Stake
Nov Hrdls	4-53	7.5	-32.79	Nov Hrdls	0-6	0.0	-6.00
Hrdls	2-20	10.0	-12.50	Hrdls	4-37	10.8	-13.25
Nov Chs	3-9	33.3	+3.50	Nov Chs	2-10	20.0	+17.50
Chases	0-2	0.0	-2.00	Chases	6-33	18.2	+31.38
Sell/Claim	2-3	66.7	+5.25	Sell/Claim	0-0	0.0	0.00

RACE CLASS

	W-R	Per cent	£1 Level Stake
Class 1	0-9	0.0	-9.00
Class 2	2-15	13.3	+22.00
Class 3	9-61	14.8	-4.88
Class 4	12-86	14.0	-15.04
Class 5	0-4	0.0	-4.00
Class 6	0-6	0.0	-6.00

FIRST TIME OUT

	W-R	Per cent	£1 Level Stake
Bumpers	0-5	0.0	-5.00
Hurdles	4-38	10.5	-19.38
Chases	1-18	5.6	-1.00
Totals	5-61	8.2	-25.38

JOCKEYS

	W-R	Per cent	£1 Level Stake
Noel Fehily	19-114	16.7	+30.08
Dave Crosse	4-31	12.9	-11.00

COURSE RECORD

	Total W-R	Non-Hndcps Hurdles	Chases	Hndcps Hurdles	Chases	NH Flat	Per cent	£1 Level Stake
Mrket Rsn	4-12	1-5	0-2	2-3	1-2	0-0	33.3	+15.75
Uttoxeter	3-9	1-4	0-0	0-2	2-3	0-0	33.3	+21.21
Wetherby	2-3	0-1	2-2	0-0	0-0	0-0	66.7	+3.00
Ludlow	2-6	1-3	0-0	1-3	0-0	0-0	33.3	+2.75
Haydock	2-9	0-1	0-1	0-1	2-5	0-1	22.2	+29.00
Fontwell	2-15	1-11	0-0	0-2	1-1	0-1	13.3	0.00
Warwick	1-3	0-1	0-0	0-0	1-2	0-0	33.3	+3.50
Chepstow	1-5	1-2	0-0	0-1	0-1	0-0	20.0	-1.00
Fakenham	1-5	0-3	0-0	0-0	1-2	0-0	20.0	+2.00
Southwell	1-6	0-1	0-1	1-2	0-1	0-1	16.7	-2.50
Bangor	1-7	0-2	1-1	0-1	0-2	0-1	14.3	-0.50
Worcester	1-7	1-3	0-1	0-2	0-1	0-0	14.3	-3.50
Wincanton	1-8	1-5	0-0	0-1	0-2	0-0	12.5	-5.63
Plumpton	1-9	1-5	0-0	0-2	0-1	0-1	11.1	-4.00

WINNING HORSES

Horse	Races Run	1st	2nd	3rd	£
Rheindross	3	1	0	1	43500
Nathos	10	2	3	1	17181
Another Native	8	3	0	1	21885
Nadover	4	2	1	0	13246
*Melford	3	2	0	0	11818
Hoh Viss	6	3	1	0	13215
Prairie Moonlight	3	1	1	0	5855
Alphabetical	7	1	1	2	5530
Villair	3	1	0	1	5426
Joe McHugh	7	1	1	0	4554
Shady Grey	6	1	2	1	3507
Fandani	5	1	1	2	3476
Dearson	6	1	2	0	3310
Ziggy Zen	3	1	0	0	3045
Dunbell Boy	3	1	0	0	3031
Mr Fernet	2	1	0	0	2723
Total winning prize-money					**£161302**
Favourites	6-21		28.6%		**-6.17**

S J MARSHALL

ALNWICK, NORTHUMBERLAND

	No. of Hrs	Races Run	1st	2nd	3rd	Unpl	Per cent	£1 Level Stake
NH Flat	0	0	0	0	0	0	0.0	0.00
Hurdles	2	6	0	1	1	4	0.0	-6.00
Chases	4	28	3	3	2	20	10.7	+15.00
Totals	5	34	3	4	3	24	8.8	+9.00
04-05	4	15	2	6	1	6	13.3	+11.50
03-04	3	19	3	2	0	14	15.8	+23.00

JOCKEYS

	W-R	Per cent	£1 Level Stake
Michael McAlister	3-30	10.0	+13.00

COURSE RECORD

	Total W-R	Non-Hndcps Hurdles	Chases	Hndcps Hurdles	Chases	NH Flat	Per cent	£1 Level Stake
Kelso	3-10	0-0	0-2	0-1	3-7	0-0	30.0	+33.00

WINNING HORSES

Horse	Races Run	1st	2nd	3rd	£
Little Flora	11	2	0	1	13455
Miss Mattie Ross	8	1	2	1	5563
Total winning prize-money					**£19018**
Favourites	0-0		0.0%		**0.00**

R MATHEW

LITTLE BARRINGTON, GLOUCS

	No. of Hrs	Races Run	1st	2nd	3rd	Unpl	Per cent	£1 Level Stake
NH Flat	2	2	0	0	0	2	0.0	-2.00
Hurdles	2	2	0	0	0	2	0.0	-2.00
Chases	2	11	2	0	1	8	18.2	+0.83
Totals	4	15	2	0	1	12	13.3	-3.17
04-05	3	15	1	0	1	12	6.7	-10.67
03-04	3	8	0	1	0	7	0.0	-8.00

JOCKEYS

	W-R	Per cent	£1 Level Stake
Wayne Hutchinson	2-6	33.3	+5.83

COURSE RECORD

	Total W-R	Non-Hndcps Hurdles	Chases	Hndcps Hurdles	Chases	NH Flat	Per cent	£1 Level Stake
Exeter	1-4	0-0	0-0	0-0	1-3	0-1	25.0	+0.33
Towcester	1-4	0-0	0-2	0-0	1-2	0-0	25.0	+3.50

WINNING HORSES

Horse	Races Run	1st	2nd	3rd	£
Heartache	8	2	0	1	8063
Total winning prize-money					**£8063**
Favourites	0-0		0.0%		**0.00**

G C MAUNDRELL

MARLBROUGH, WILTS.

	No. of Hrs	Races Run	1st	2nd	3rd	Unpl	Per cent	£1 Level Stake
NH Flat	0	0	0	0	0	0	0.0	0.00
Hurdles	0	0	0	0	0	0	0.0	0.00
Chases	2	4	2	0	0	2	50.0	+0.63
Totals	2	4	2	0	0	2	50.0	+0.63

JOCKEYS

	W-R	Per cent	£1 Level Stake
Mr G Maundrell	2-4	50.0	+0.63

COURSE RECORD

	Total W-R	Non-Hndcps Hurdles	Chases	Hndcps Hurdles	Chases	NH Flat	Per cent	£1 Level Stake
Fakenham	2-2	0-0	2-2	0-0	0-0	0-0	100.0	+2.63

WINNING HORSES

Horse	Races Run	1st	2nd	3rd	£
*Rhythm King	3	2	0	0	3965

Total winning prize-money			£3965
Favourites	2-3	66.7%	1.63

D MCCAIN

CHOLMONDELEY, CHESHIRE

	No. of Hrs	Races Run	1st	2nd	3rd	Unpl	Per cent	£1 Level Stake
NH Flat	14	28	3	2	5	18	10.7	-12.25
Hurdles	43	193	23	19	26	125	11.9	+82.95
Chases	19	79	9	4	7	58	11.4	+21.33
Totals	54	300	35	25	38	201	11.7	+92.03
04-05	41	166	15	22	21	108	9.0	-54.92
03-04	32	136	8	8	7	113	5.9	-76.17

BY MONTH

NH Flat	W-R	Per cent	£1 Level Stake	Hurdles	W-R	Per cent	£1 Level Stake
May	1-5	20.0	-1.75	May	3-16	18.8	+21.20
June	0-0	0.0	0.00	June	0-4	0.0	-4.00
July	0-2	0.0	-2.00	July	1-4	25.0	-1.50
August	0-0	0.0	0.00	August	0-11	0.0	-11.00
September	0-0	0.0	0.00	September	0-7	0.0	-7.00
October	1-1	100.0	+7.00	October	0-19	0.0	-19.00
November	1-5	20.0	-0.50	November	3-24	12.5	+20.50
December	0-1	0.0	-1.00	December	4-27	14.8	+64.00
January	0-4	0.0	-4.00	January	4-21	19.0	+14.50
February	0-3	0.0	-3.00	February	5-25	20.0	+17.25
March	0-2	0.0	-2.00	March	1-16	6.3	-7.00
April	0-5	0.0	-5.00	April	2-19	10.5	-5.00

Chases	W-R	Per cent	£1 Level Stake	Totals	W-R	Per cent	£1 Level Stake
May	0-4	0.0	-4.00	May	4-25	16.0	+15.45
June	0-0	0.0	0.00	June	0-4	0.0	-4.00
July	0-3	0.0	-3.00	July	1-9	11.1	-6.50
August	0-1	0.0	-1.00	August	0-12	0.0	-12.00
September	0-0	0.0	0.00	September	0-7	0.0	-7.00
October	1-7	14.3	+1.00	October	2-27	7.4	-11.00
November	0-6	0.0	-6.00	November	4-35	11.4	+14.00
December	1-9	11.1	+1.00	December	5-37	13.5	+64.00
January	2-11	18.2	+31.00	January	6-36	16.7	+41.50
February	3-14	21.4	+0.33	February	8-42	19.0	+14.58
March	0-8	0.0	-8.00	March	1-26	3.8	-17.00
April	2-16	12.5	+10.00	April	4-40	10.0	0.00

DISTANCE

Hurdles	W-R	Per cent	£1 Level Stake	Chases	W-R	Per cent	£1 Level Stake
2m-2m3f	11-125	8.8	+30.50	2m-2m3f	1-21	4.8	-6.00
2m4f-2m7f	10-49	20.4	+58.25	2m4f-2m7f	2-24	8.3	-14.67
3m+	2-19	10.5	-5.80	3m+	6-34	17.6	+42.00

TYPE OF RACE

Non-Handicaps	W-R	Per cent	£1 Level Stake	Handicaps	W-R	Per cent	£1 Level Stake
Nov Hrdls	11-87	12.6	+13.75	Nov Hrdls	3-20	15.0	+46.00
Hrdls	2-10	20.0	+5.20	Hrdls	5-51	9.8	+5.00
Nov Chs	1-19	5.3	-14.67	Nov Chs	3-22	13.6	+3.00
Chases	0-4	0.0	-4.00	Chases	5-34	14.7	+37.00
Sell/Claim	2-24	8.3	-9.50	Sell/Claim	1-8	12.5	+21.00

RACE CLASS

	W-R	Per cent	£1 Level Stake
Class 1	1-16	6.3	+18.00
Class 2	1-14	7.1	-5.00
Class 3	6-51	11.8	+13.00
Class 4	19-149	12.8	+62.78
Class 5	5-44	11.4	+13.50
Class 6	3-26	11.5	-10.25

FIRST TIME OUT

	W-R	Per cent	£1 Level Stake
Bumpers	1-14	7.1	-6.00
Hurdles	3-33	9.1	+14.00
Chases	2-7	28.6	+16.00
Totals	6-54	11.1	+24.00

JOCKEYS

	W-R	Per cent	£1 Level Stake
Stephen Craine	19-146	13.0	+65.58
Jason Maguire	7-58	12.1	+19.50
Paddy Aspell	3-16	18.8	+4.50
G Lee	3-32	9.4	-7.75
Tony Dobbin	1-4	25.0	-1.80
Mr G Tumelty	1-6	16.7	+45.00
Dominic Elsworth	1-12	8.3	-7.00

COURSE RECORD

	Total W-R	Non-Hndcps Hurdles	Chases	Hndcps Hurdles	Chases	NH Flat	Per cent	£1 Level Stake
Haydock	8-29	2-7	0-3	3-5	3-10	0-4	27.6	+68.75
Uttoxeter	5-24	2-11	0-0	2-5	1-3	0-5	20.8	+68.50
Sedgefield	4-23	1-9	1-2	2-6	0-5	0-1	17.4	-0.17
Bangor	4-42	1-17	0-4	1-15	2-4	0-2	9.5	-10.00
Musselbgh	3-6	1-1	0-0	0-1	2-4	0-0	50.0	+12.50
Fakenham	1-3	0-0	0-0	1-3	0-0	0-0	33.3	+26.00
Exeter	1-4	0-1	0-1	0-1	0-0	1-1	25.0	+4.00
Leicester	1-4	1-1	0-2	0-1	0-0	0-0	25.0	+8.00
Ayr	1-5	1-4	0-0	0-0	0-1	0-0	20.0	+8.00
Southwell	1-5	0-0	0-0	0-1	0-2	1-1	20.0	-1.75
Hexham	1-8	1-4	0-1	0-2	0-1	0-0	12.5	+18.00
Carlisle	1-11	1-5	0-1	0-2	0-3	0-0	9.1	+6.00
Wetherby	1-11	1-1	0-1	0-6	0-3	0-0	9.1	-8.80
Towcester	1-13	0-5	0-1	0-2	0-1	1-4	7.7	-8.50
Hereford	1-16	1-10	0-1	0-3	0-1	0-1	6.3	-11.50
Ludlow	1-19	1-8	0-1	0-5	0-3	0-2	5.3	-10.00

WINNING HORSES

Horse	Races Run	1st	2nd	3rd	£
Ebony Light	9	3	0	0	63226
Cloudy Lane	8	4	3	0	24157

Bannister Lane	11	2	1	1	9558
*Nevsky Bridge	2	1	0	1	6263
Another Club Royal	11	3	2	1	13663
Triple Mint	4	1	1	2	5530
Vicario	12	3	0	2	12592
Regal Heights	7	2	0	2	7195
Itsuptoharry	8	1	1	0	3770
First Fought	8	1	2	0	3747
*Temple Place	5	1	0	1	3578
Chickapeakray	8	3	1	2	9128
Combat Drinker	8	1	1	4	3416
Reem Two	13	2	3	3	6659
Sword Of Damascus	5	2	1	0	5466
Balmoral Queen	5	1	0	1	2611
Dickie Lewis	5	1	1	0	2569
Trickstep	4	1	0	0	2555
West Hill	8	1	0	0	2398
The Wife's Sister	10	1	3	0	2082
Total winning prize-money					**£190163**
Favourites	**4-16**		**25.0%**		**-0.05**

P S MCENTEE

NEWMARKET, SUFFOLK

	No. of Hrs	Races Run	1st	2nd	3rd	Unpl	Per cent	£1 Level Stake
NH Flat	2	2	0	0	0	2	0.0	-2.00
Hurdles	2	5	1	0	0	4	20.0	-1.75
Chases	0	0	0	0	0	0	0.0	0.00
Totals	4	7	1	0	0	6	14.3	-3.75
04-05	1	1	0	0	0	1	0.0	-1.00
03-04	5	8	0	0	1	7	0.0	-8.00

JOCKEYS

	W-R	Per cent	£1 Level Stake
Robert Thornton	1-1	100.0	+2.25

COURSE RECORD

	Total W-R	Non-Hndcps Hurdles Chases		Hndcps Hurdles Chases		NH Flat	Per cent	£1 Level Stake
Mrket Rsn	1-1	1-1	0-0	0-0	0-0	0-0	100.0	+2.25

WINNING HORSES

Horse	Races Run	1st	2nd	3rd	£
*Yenaled	4	1	0	0	2741
Total winning prize-money					**£2741**
Favourites	**0-0**		**0.0%**		**0.00**

M J MCGRATH

MAIDSTONE, KENT

	No. of Hrs	Races Run	1st	2nd	3rd	Unpl	Per cent	£1 Level Stake
NH Flat	2	4	0	0	0	4	0.0	-4.00
Hurdles	7	28	1	4	2	21	3.6	-26.09
Chases	2	3	0	0	0	3	0.0	-3.00
Totals	10	35	1	4	2	28	2.9	-33.09
04-05	6	10	1	0	1	8	10.0	+5.00

JOCKEYS

	W-R	Per cent	£1 Level Stake
Timmy Murphy	1-3	33.3	-1.09

COURSE RECORD

	Total W-R	Non Hndcps Hurdles Chases		Hndcps Hurdles Chases		NH Flat	Per cent	£1 Level Stake
Mrket Rsn	1-1	1-1	0-0	0-0	0-0	0-0	100.0	+0.91

WINNING HORSES

Horse	Races Run	1st	2nd	3rd	£
Enhancer	9	1	3	1	4940
Total winning prize-money					**£4940**
Favourites	**1-3**		**33.3%**		**-1.09**

MRS J C MCGREGOR

MILNATHORT, PERTH & KINROSS

	No. of Hrs	Races Run	1st	2nd	3rd	Unpl	Per cent	£1 Level Stake
NH Flat	2	4	0	2	0	2	0.0	-4.00
Hurdles	10	31	0	0	0	31	0.0	-31.00
Chases	3	20	1	2	1	16	5.0	-8.00
Totals	13	55	1	4	1	49	1.8	-43.00
04-05	15	54	1	1	3	49	1.9	-28.00
03-04	21	96	2	9	8	77	2.1	-80.50

JOCKEYS

	W-R	Per cent	£1 Level Stake
Keith Mercer	1-7	14.3	+5.00

COURSE RECORD

	Total W-R	Non-Hndcps Hurdles Chases		Hndcps Hurdles Chases		NH Flat	Per cent	£1 Level Stake
Perth	1-21	0-6	0-2	0-4	1-6	0-3	4.8	-9.00

WINNING HORSES

Horse	Races Run	1st	2nd	3rd	£
Goodbadindiferent	9	1	0	0	6903

Total winning prize-money				£6903				
Favourites	0-0		0.0%	0.00				

Ayr	1-4	0-0	0-0	0-1	1-2	0-1	25.0	+1.50
Carlisle	1-6	0-3	0-0	0-0	1-3	0-0	16.7	+3.00

WINNING HORSES

Horse	Races Run	1st	2nd	3rd	£
*Nifty Roy	6	2	0	2	7482
Mags Two	4	1	0	1	2674
Total winning prize-money					**£10156**
Favourites	2-5		40.0%		6.00

KAREN MCLINTOCK

INGOE, NORTHUMBERLAND

	No. of Hrs	Races Run	1st	2nd	3rd	Unpl	Per cent	£1 Level Stake
NH Flat	5	6	0	0	1	5	0.0	-6.00
Hurdles	4	8	2	2	0	4	25.0	+28.00
Chases	1	1	0	0	0	1	0.0	-1.00
Totals	**9**	**15**	**2**	**2**	**1**	**10**	**13.3**	**+21.00**
04-05	4	13	2	2	1	8	15.4	+2.25

JOCKEYS

	W-R	Per cent	£1 Level Stake
Richard McGrath	1-1	100.0	+14.00
Wilson Renwick	1-5	20.0	+16.00

COURSE RECORD

	Total W-R	Non-Hndcps Hurdles	Chases	Hndcps Hurdles	Chases	NH Flat	Per cent	£1 Level Stake
Hexham	1-2	0-0	0-0	1-1	0-0	0-1	50.0	+19.00
Catterick	1-4	0-0	0-0	1-2	0-0	0-2	25.0	+11.00

WINNING HORSES

Horse	Races Run	1st	2nd	3rd	£
River Mist	6	2	1	0	9833
Total winning prize-money					**£9833**
Favourites	0-0		0.0%		0.00

I MCMATH

CUMWHINTON, CUMBRIA

	No. of Hrs	Races Run	1st	2nd	3rd	Unpl	Per cent	£1 Level Stake
NH Flat	1	1	0	0	0	1	0.0	-1.00
Hurdles	11	25	1	3	2	19	4.0	-19.50
Chases	4	9	2	0	2	5	22.2	+5.50
Totals	**11**	**35**	**3**	**3**	**4**	**25**	**8.6**	**-15.00**
04-05	10	21	1	0	0	20	4.8	-13.00
03-04	1	1	0	1	0	0	0.0	-1.00

JOCKEYS

	W-R	Per cent	£1 Level Stake
Dougie Costello	2-8	25.0	+6.50
Paddy Merrigan	1-5	20.0	+0.50

COURSE RECORD

	Total W-R	Non-Hndcps Hurdles	Chases	Hndcps Hurdles	Chases	NH Flat	Per cent	£1 Level Stake
Huntingdon	1-2	0-0	0-0	1-2	0-0	0-0	50.0	+3.50

GRAEME P MCPHERSON

STOW-ON-THE-WOLD, GLOUCS

	No. of Hrs	Races Run	1st	2nd	3rd	Unpl	Per cent	£1 Level Stake
NH Flat	0	0	0	0	0	0	0.0	0.00
Hurdles	0	0	0	0	0	0	0.0	0.00
Chases	1	1	1	0	0	0	100.0	+5.00
Totals	**1**	**1**	**1**	**0**	**0**	**0**	**100.0**	**+5.00**

JOCKEYS

	W-R	Per cent	£1 Level Stake
Mr L R Payter	1-1	100.0	+5.00

COURSE RECORD

	Total W-R	Non-Hndcps Hurdles	Chases	Hndcps Hurdles	Chases	NH Flat	Per cent	£1 Level Stake
Leicester	1-1	0-0	1-1	0-0	0-0	0-0	100.0	+5.00

WINNING HORSES

Horse	Races Run	1st	2nd	3rd	£
*Another Raleagh	1	1	0	0	6002
Total winning prize-money					**£6002**
Favourites	0-0		0.0%		0.00

MISS KATE MILLIGAN

MIDDLEHAM MOOR, N YORKS

	No. of Hrs	Races Run	1st	2nd	3rd	Unpl	Per cent	£1 Level Stake
NH Flat	4	5	0	0	0	5	0.0	-5.00
Hurdles	12	24	0	1	2	21	0.0	-24.00
Chases	8	26	3	3	4	16	11.5	+21.50
Totals	**18**	**55**	**3**	**4**	**6**	**42**	**5.5**	**-7.50**
04-05	20	89	5	8	7	69	5.6	-42.50
03-04	21	119	8	10	14	87	6.7	-17.38

JOCKEYS

	W-R	Per cent	£1 Level Stake
Michael McAlister	2-26	7.7	+17.50
Dougie Costello	1-15	6.7	-11.00

COURSE RECORD

	Total W-R	Non-Hndcps Hurdles	Chases	Hndcps Hurdles	Chases	NH Flat	Per cent	£1 Level Stake
Kelso	1-3	0-1	1-1	0-1	0-0	0-0	33.3	+1.00
Hexham	1-11	0-1	0-0	0-1	1-8	0-1	9.1	+23.00
Sedgefield	1-22	0-3	0-4	0-8	1-5	0-2	4.5	-12.50

WINNING HORSES

Horse	Races Run	1st	2nd	3rd	£
Dark Ben	8	1	3	2	5205
Inglewood	4	1	0	0	3819
Middleway	4	1	0	0	3492
Total winning prize-money					**£12516**
Favourites	0-1		0.0%		-1.00

T G MILLS

HEADLEY, SURREY

	No. of Hrs	Races Run	1st	2nd	3rd	Unpl	Per cent	£1 Level Stake
NH Flat	0	0	0	0	0	0	0.0	0.00
Hurdles	4	11	3	6	1	1	27.3	+8.50
Chases	0	0	0	0	0	0	0.0	0.00
Totals	4	11	3	6	1	1	27.3	+8.50
04-05	2	3	1	1	0	1	33.3	0.00

JOCKEYS

	W-R	Per cent	£1 Level Stake
Richard Johnson	1-1	100.0	+3.00
Tom Doyle	1-3	33.3	+10.00
Jim Crowley	1-3	33.3	-0.50

COURSE RECORD

	Total W-R	Non-Hndcps Hurdles	Chases	Hndcps Hurdles	Chases	NH Flat	Per cent	£1 Level Stake
Fontwell	2-2	2-2	0-0	0-0	0-0	0-0	100.0	+13.50
Uttoxeter	1-2	1-2	0-0	0-0	0-0	0-0	50.0	+2.00

WINNING HORSES

Horse	Races Run	1st	2nd	3rd	£
Snow Tempest	2	1	0	0	3577
Settlement Craic	3	1	2	0	3494
Keep On Movin'	3	1	1	1	3437
Total winning prize-money					**£10508**
Favourites	1-206		0.5%		-203.50

N R MITCHELL

PIDDLETRENTHIDE, DORSET

	No. of Hrs	Races Run	1st	2nd	3rd	Unpl	Per cent	£1 Level Stake
NH Flat	8	11	0	0	0	11	0.0	-11.00
Hurdles	10	38	0	1	2	35	0.0	-38.00
Chases	10	52	2	8	7	35	3.8	-40.50
Totals	23	101	2	9	9	81	2.0	-89.50
04-05	19	76	6	6	9	55	7.9	+67.50
03-04	14	60	3	3	3	51	5.0	-40.00

JOCKEYS

	W-R	Per cent	£1 Level Stake
Dave Crosse	1-10	10.0	6.00
Richard Young	1-74	4.2	-16.50

COURSE RECORD

	Total W-R	Non-Hndcps Hurdles	Chases	Hndcps Hurdles	Chases	NH Flat	Per cent	£1 Level Stake
Nton Abbot	1-6	0-1	0-0	0-1	1-4	0-0	16.7	+1.50
Plumpton	1-10	0-1	0-0	0-2	1-6	0-1	10.0	-6.00

WINNING HORSES

Horse	Races Run	1st	2nd	3rd	£
James Victor	8	1	1	1	4737
Denarius Secundus	14	1	2	1	3132
Total winning prize-money					**£7869**
Favourites	0-0		0.0%		0.00

JAMES MOFFATT

CARTMEL, CUMBRIA

	No. of Hrs	Races Run	1st	2nd	3rd	Unpl	Per cent	£1 Level Stake
NH Flat	3	7	0	0	0	7	0.0	-7.00
Hurdles	19	82	6	6	4	66	7.3	-8.67
Chases	4	17	0	2	0	15	0.0	-17.00
Totals	20	106	6	8	4	88	5.7	-32.67
04-05	20	82	2	7	8	65	2.4	-73.50
03-04	16	61	6	7	2	46	9.8	-17.00

JOCKEYS

	W-R	Per cent	£1 Level Stake
Michael McAvoy	3-25	12.0	+14.00
Richard McGrath	2-13	15.4	+0.33
Jim Crowley	1-17	5.9	+4.00

COURSE RECORD

	Total W-R	Non-Hndcps Hurdles	Chases	Hndcps Hurdles	Chases	NH Flat	Per cent	£1 Level Stake
Newcastle	1-1	0-0	0-0	1-1	0-0	0-0	100.0	+16.00
Aintree	1-3	0-1	0-0	1-2	0-0	0-0	33.3	+18.00
Catterick	1-5	0-1	0-1	1-2	0-1	0-0	20.0	+4.00
Hexham	1-15	0-6	0-0	1-4	0-3	0-2	6.7	-6.00
Cartmel	1-22	1-7	0-1	0-10	0-4	0-0	4.5	-17.67
Sedgefield	1-23	0-6	0-2	1-11	0-3	0-1	4.3	-10.00

WINNING HORSES

Horse	Races Run	1st	2nd	3rd	£
Border Tale	11	1	0	0	7491
Ball Games	10	2	1	1	5194
Faraway Echo	8	1	0	0	2713
Lanzlo	4	1	1	1	2709
Cody	10	1	2	0	2277
Total winning prize-money					£20384
Favourites	1-3		33.3%		1.33

MRS L J MONGAN

EPSOM, SURREY

	No. of Hrs	Races Run	1st	2nd	3rd	Unpl	Per cent	£1 Level Stake
NH Flat	1	1	0	0	0	1	0.0	-1.00
Hurdles	5	14	2	1	1	9	14.3	+10.25
Chases	2	9	0	1	1	7	0.0	-9.00
Totals	6	24	2	2	2	17	8.3	+0.25
04-05	5	16	1	0	4	11	6.3	-3.00
03-04	6	15	2	2	0	11	13.3	+6.33

JOCKEYS

	W-R	Per cent	£1 Level Stake
Jamie Moore	1-4	25.0	-0.75
Leighton Aspell	1-7	14.3	+14.00

COURSE RECORD

	Total W-R	Non-Hndcps Hurdles	Chases	Hndcps Hurdles	Chases	NH Flat	Per cent	£1 Level Stake
Huntingdon	1-2	1-1	0-0	0-1	0-0	0-0	50.0	+1.25
Newbury	1-2	1-2	0-0	0-0	0-0	0-0	50.0	+19.00

WINNING HORSES

Horse	Races Run	1st	2nd	3rd	£
Orange Street	6	1	1	0	4554
Saraba	4	1	0	1	3253
Total winning prize-money					£7807
Favourites	1-2		50.0%		1.25

P MONTEITH

ROSEWELL, MIDLOTHIAN

	No. of Hrs	Races Run	1st	2nd	3rd	Unpl	Per cent	£1 Level Stake
NH Flat	2	3	0	0	0	3	0.0	-3.00
Hurdles	25	95	4	12	16	63	4.2	-82.75
Chases	17	72	7	9	16	40	9.7	-8.50
Totals	36	170	11	21	32	106	6.5	-94.25
04-05	34	173	14	26	25	108	8.1	-92.79
03-04	28	147	17	12	19	99	11.6	-12.17

BY MONTH

NH Flat	W-R	Per cent	£1 Level Stake	Hurdles	W-R	Per cent	£1 Level Stake
May	0-1	0.0	-1.00	May	0-4	0.0	-4.00
June	0-0	0.0	0.00	June	0-5	0.0	-5.00
July	0-0	0.0	0.00	July	0-5	0.0	-5.00
August	0-0	0.0	0.00	August	0-5	0.0	-5.00
September	0-0	0.0	0.00	September	0-1	0.0	-1.00
October	0-0	0.0	0.00	October	0-6	0.0	-6.00
November	0-1	0.0	-1.00	November	0-12	0.0	-12.00
December	0-0	0.0	0.00	December	1-9	11.1	-6.25
January	0-1	0.0	-1.00	January	0-14	0.0	-14.00
February	0-0	0.0	0.00	February	1-16	6.3	-12.75
March	0-0	0.0	0.00	March	2-8	25.0	-1.75
April	0-0	0.0	0.00	April	0-10	0.0	-10.00

Chases	W-R	Per cent	£1 Level Stake	Totals	W-R	Per cent	£1 Level Stake
May	2-6	33.3	+18.50	May	2-11	18.2	+13.50
June	0-4	0.0	-4.00	June	0-9	0.0	-9.00
July	0-3	0.0	-3.00	July	0-8	0.0	-8.00
August	0-4	0.0	-4.00	August	0-9	0.0	-9.00
September	1-2	50.0	+7.00	September	1-3	33.3	+6.00
October	0-5	0.0	-5.00	October	0-11	0.0	-11.00
November	0-8	0.0	-8.00	November	0-21	0.0	-21.00
December	1-6	16.7	+11.00	December	2-15	13.3	+4.75
January	0-8	0.0	-8.00	January	0-23	0.0	-23.00
February	1-6	16.7	-1.50	February	2-22	9.1	-14.25
March	2-6	33.3	+2.50	March	4-14	28.6	+0.75
April	0-14	0.0	-14.00	April	0-24	0.0	-24.00

DISTANCE

Hurdles	W-R	Per cent	£1 Level Stake	Chases	W-R	Per cent	£1 Level Stake
2m-2m3f	3-81	3.7	-72.75	2m-2m3f	7-37	18.9	+26.50
2m4f-2m7f	1-11	9.1	-7.00	2m4f-2m7f	0-24	0.0	-24.00
3m+	0-3	0.0	-3.00	3m+	0-11	0.0	-11.00

TYPE OF RACE

Non-Handicaps	W-R	Per cent	£1 Level Stake	Handicaps	W-R	Per cent	£1 Level Stake
Nov Hrdls	1-30	3.3	-26.75	Nov Hrdls	0-6	0.0	-6.00
Hrdls	2-10	20.0	-5.00	Hrdls	1-46	2.2	-42.00
Nov Chs	1-14	7.1	+3.00	Nov Chs	0-12	0.0	-12.00

Chases	1-4	25.0	+17.00	Chases	5-41	12.2	-15.50		
Sell/Claim	0-5	0.0	-5.00	Sell/Claim	0-1	0.0	-1.00		

04-05	40	154	9	17	8	120	5.8	-105.00
03-04	37	192	16	25	21	130	8.3	-75.83

RACE CLASS / FIRST TIME OUT

	W-R	Per cent	£1 Level Stake		W-R	Per cent	£1 Level Stake
Class 1	0-3	0.0	-3.00	Bumpers	0-2	0.0	-2.00
Class 2	0-7	0.0	-7.00	Hurdles	0-21	0.0	-21.00
Class 3	6-69	8.7	-10.00	Chases	0-13	0.0	-13.00
Class 4	5-78	6.4	-61.25				
Class 5	0-10	0.0	-10.00	Totals	0-36	0.0	-36.00
Class 6	0-3	0.0	-3.00				

JOCKEYS

	W-R	Per cent	£1 Level Stake
G Lee	2-9	22.2	-1.25
Neil Mulholland	2-15	13.3	+9.50
Wilson Renwick	2-37	5.4	-30.25
David Da Silva	2-44	4.5	-23.00
Richard Johnson	1-2	50.0	+7.00
Mark Bradburne	1-6	16.7	-3.75
Timmy Murphy	1-19	5.3	-14.50

COURSE RECORD

	Total W-R	Non-Hndcps Hurdles	Chases	Hndcps Hurdles	Chases	NH Flat	Per cent	£1 Level Stake
Ayr	5-33	1-9	1-4	1-8	2-10	0 2	15.2	-0.25
Kelso	3-33	2-10	0-4	0-8	1-10	0-1	9.1	-24.50
Perth	2-27	0-8	1-5	0-8	1-6	0-0	7.4	+3.00
Newcastle	1-15	0-3	0-2	0-7	1-3	0-0	6.7	-10.50

WINNING HORSES

Horse	Races Run	1st	2nd	3rd	£
Moscow Dancer	7	2	1	1	17598
Gone Too Far	13	1	2	5	8210
Brave Thought	6	1	1	1	6350
Shares	9	1	2	0	5371
Polyphon	9	2	2	1	9759
First Look	6	2	2	1	5205
Nerone	8	1	0	4	4554
Auenmoon	7	1	2	1	3083
Total winning prize-money					£60130
Favourites	3-14		21.4%		-5.00

G M MOORE

MIDDLEHAM MOOR, N YORKS

	No. of Hrs	Races Run	1st	2nd	3rd	Unpl	Per cent	£1 Level Stake
NH Flat	5	9	1	2	1	5	11.1	-4.00
Hurdles	31	104	5	6	13	80	4.8	-41.50
Chases	11	44	5	3	5	31	11.4	+0.83
Totals	40	157	11	11	19	116	7.0	-44.67

BY MONTH

NH Flat	W-R	Per cent	£1 Level Stake	Hurdles	W-R	Per cent	£1 Level Stake
May	0-0	0.0	0.00	May	0-13	0.0	-13.00
June	0-0	0.0	0.00	June	0-4	0.0	-4.00
July	0-0	0.0	0.00	July	0-3	0.0	-3.00
August	0-0	0.0	0.00	August	2-3	66.7	+9.75
September	0-0	0.0	0.00	September	1-6	16.7	-2.25
October	0-0	0.0	0.00	October	1-9	11.1	+20.00
November	0-2	0.0	-2.00	November	1-17	5.9	0.00
December	0-3	0.0	-3.00	December	0-14	0.0	-14.00
January	0-0	0.0	0.00	January	0-10	0.0	-10.00
February	1-1	100.0	+4.00	February	0-7	0.0	-7.00
March	0-0	0.0	0.00	March	0-4	0.0	-4.00
April	0-3	0.0	-3.00	April	0-14	0.0	-14.00

Chases	W-R	Per cent	£1 Level Stake	Totals	W-R	Per cent	£1 Level Stake
May	2-5	40.0	+4.83	May	2-18	11.1	-8.17
June	0-2	0.0	-2.00	June	0-6	0.0	-6.00
July	0-2	0.0	-2.00	July	0-5	0.0	-5.00
August	0-3	0.0	-3.00	August	2-6	33.3	+6.75
September	0-0	0.0	0.00	September	1-6	16.7	-2.25
October	1-6	16.7	+7.00	October	2-15	13.3	+27.00
November	0-4	0.0	-4.00	November	1-23	4.3	-6.00
December	1-9	11.1	+8.00	December	1-26	3.8	-9.00
January	1-4	25.0	+1.00	January	1-14	7.1	-9.00
February	0-3	0.0	-3.00	February	1-11	9.1	-6.00
March	0-1	0.0	-1.00	March	0-5	0.0	-5.00
April	0-5	0.0	-5.00	April	0-22	0.0	-22.00

DISTANCE

Hurdles	W-R	Per cent	£1 Level Stake	Chases	W-R	Per cent	£1 Level Stake
2m-2m3f	5-61	8.2	+1.50	2m-2m3f	0-12	0.0	-12.00
2m4f-2m7f	0-31	0.0	-31.00	2m4f-2m7f	4-15	26.7	+24.83
3m+	0-12	0.0	-12.00	3m+	1-17	5.9	-12.00

TYPE OF RACE

Non-Handicaps	W-R	Per cent	£1 Level Stake	Handicaps	W-R	Per cent	£1 Level Stake
Nov Hrdls	4-53	7.5	+0.50	Nov Hrdls	0-18	0.0	-18.00
Hrdls	1-6	16.7	+3.00	Hrdls	0-24	0.0	-24.00
Nov Chs	1-9	11.1	-4.67	Nov Chs	2-6	33.3	+12.50
Chases	0-0	0.0	0.00	Chases	2-29	6.9	-7.00
Sell/Claim	0-3	0.0	-3.00	Sell/Claim	0-1	0.0	-1.00

RACE CLASS / FIRST TIME OUT

	W-R	Per cent	£1 Level Stake		W-R	Per cent	£1 Level Stake
Class 1	1-2	50.0	+27.00	Bumpers	0-5	0.0	-5.00
Class 2	0-3	0.0	-3.00	Hurdles	3-27	11.1	+2.75
Class 3	5-44	11.4	+0.83	Chases	1-8	12.5	-2.50
Class 4	4-92	4.3	-58.50				

Class 5	1-9	11.1	-4.00	Totals	4-40	10.0	-4.75
Class 6	0-7	0.0	-7.00				

JOCKEYS

	W-R	Per cent	£1 Level Stake
Barry Keniry	7-104	6.7	-15.50
Dougie Costello	4-35	11.4	-11.17

COURSE RECORD

	Total W-R	Non-Hndcps Hurdles	Chases	Hndcps Hurdles	Chases	NH Flat	Per cent	£1 Level Stake
Wetherby	7-40	1-9	1-2	0-12	4-15	1-2	17.5	+38.83
Cartmel	2-4	2-2	0-0	0-1	0-1	0-0	50.0	+8.75
Perth	1-5	1-2	0-0	0-3	0-0	0-0	20.0	-1.25
Carlisle	1-8	1-4	0-1	0-2	0-1	0-0	12.5	+9.00

WINNING HORSES

Horse	Races Run	1st	2nd	3rd	£
*Aviation	7	3	0	1	19287
Jungle Jinks	8	1	2	0	8458
Sir Storm	9	1	0	0	5729
Spring Gamble	4	1	0	1	5616
Ashnaya	4	2	1	0	10956
*Dubonai	8	1	1	0	4271
Planters Punch	7	1	0	1	2912
Kealshore Lad	4	1	2	0	2741
Total winning prize-money					**£59970**
Favourites	1-8		12.5%		-4.25

J S MOORE

UPPER LAMBOURN, BERKS

	No. of Hrs	Races Run	1st	2nd	3rd	Unpl	Per cent	£1 Level Stake
NH Flat	2	4	0	0	0	4	0.0	-4.00
Hurdles	4	15	2	0	1	12	13.3	+13.63
Chases	0	0	0	0	0	0	0.0	0.00
Totals	6	19	2	0	1	16	10.5	+9.63
04-05	9	21	0	1	1	19	0.0	-21.00
03-04	9	32	1	4	1	26	3.1	-29.00

JOCKEYS

	W-R	Per cent	£1 Level Stake
Dave Crosse	1-6	16.7	-3.38
Shane Walsh	1-6	16.7	+20.00

COURSE RECORD

	Total W-R	Non-Hndcps Hurdles	Chases	Hndcps Hurdles	Chases	NH Flat	Per cent	£1 Level Stake
Ludlow	2-3	2-3	0-0	0-0	0-0	0-0	66.7	+25.63

WINNING HORSES

Horse	Races Run	1st	2nd	3rd	£
Twist Bookie	7	1	0	0	3422
Redspin	5	1	0	1	3419
Total winning prize-money					**£6841**
Favourites	1-1		100.0%		1.63

G L MOORE

WOODINGDEAN, E SUSSEX

	No. of Hrs	Races Run	1st	2nd	3rd	Unpl	Per cent	£1 Level Stake
NH Flat	5	10	2	1	3	4	20.0	+11.33
Hurdles	75	306	41	32	28	205	13.4	+13.07
Chases	26	133	20	18	25	70	15.0	-4.37
Totals	93	449	63	51	56	279	14.0	+20.03
04-05	83	391	47	70	56	218	12.0	-128.44
03-04	64	238	36	49	23	130	15.1	-42.27

BY MONTH

NH Flat	W-R	Per cent	£1 Level Stake	Hurdles	W-R	Per cent	£1 Level Stake
May	0-2	0.0	-2.00	May	6-25	24.0	+31.00
June	0-2	0.0	-2.00	June	0-5	0.0	-5.00
July	0-0	0.0	0.00	July	0-1	0.0	-1.00
August	0-1	0.0	-1.00	August	5-7	71.4	+18.83
September	0-0	0.0	0.00	September	1-11	9.1	-6.50
October	1-2	50.0	+15.00	October	4-28	14.3	+15.00
November	0-0	0.0	0.00	November	6-47	12.8	-2.25
December	0-1	0.0	-1.00	December	2-45	4.4	-13.00
January	0-1	0.0	-1.00	January	3-32	9.4	0.00
February	0-0	0.0	0.00	February	5-33	15.2	-9.39
March	0-0	0.0	0.00	March	3-35	8.6	-19.63
April	1-1	100.0	+3.33	April	6-37	16.2	+5.00

Chases	W-R	Per cent	£1 Level Stake	Totals	W-R	Per cent	£1 Level Stake
May	3-9	33.3	+0.67	May	9-36	25.0	+29.67
June	1-7	14.3	+0.50	June	1-14	7.1	-6.50
July	0-1	0.0	-1.00	July	0-2	0.0	-2.00
August	1-3	33.3	-1.33	August	6-11	54.5	+16.50
September	0-4	0.0	-4.00	September	1-15	6.7	-10.50
October	3-10	30.0	+33.00	October	8-40	20.0	+63.00
November	2-23	8.7	-11.50	November	8-70	11.4	-13.75
December	0-14	0.0	-14.00	December	2-60	3.3	-28.00
January	2-15	13.3	+1.00	January	5-48	10.4	0.00
February	1-11	9.1	-2.00	February	6-44	13.6	-11.39
March	2-15	13.3	-9.88	March	5-50	10.0	-29.51
April	5-21	23.8	+4.17	April	12-59	20.3	+12.50

DISTANCE

Hurdles	W-R	Per cent	£1 Level Stake	Chases	W-R	Per cent	£1 Level Stake
2m-2m3f	30-233	12.9	+28.32	2m-2m3f	9-48	18.8	+9.22

	W-R	Per cent	£1 Level Stake		W-R	Per cent	£1 Level Stake
2m4f-2m7f	9-63	14.3	-14.50	2m4f-2m7f	8-58	13.8	-13.42
3m+	2-10	20.0	-0.75	3m+	3-27	11.1	-0.17

TYPE OF RACE

Non-Handicaps

	W-R	Per cent	£1 Level Stake
Nov Hrdls	15-97	15.5	+15.49
Hrdls	6-24	25.0	+22.00
Nov Chs	11-43	25.6	+2.13
Chases	1-4	25.0	+0.33
Sell/Claim	3-16	18.8	-2.50

Handicaps

	W-R	Per cent	£1 Level Stake
Nov Hrdls	3-33	9.1	-7.75
Hrdls	13-129	10.1	-15.17
Nov Chs	2-71	9.5	-7.00
Chases	7-65	10.8	+4.50
Sell/Claim	2-8	25.0	+9.00

RACE CLASS

	W-R	Per cent	£1 Level Stake
Class 1	1-29	3.4	-16.00
Class 2	0-16	0.0	-16.00
Class 3	21-134	15.7	+41.25
Class 4	33-232	14.2	-11.54
Class 5	6-28	21.4	+11.00
Class 6	2-10	20.0	+11.33

FIRST TIME OUT

	W-R	Per cent	£1 Level Stake
Bumpers	1-5	20.0	-0.67
Hurdles	16-70	22.9	+53.63
Chases	2-18	11.1	-11.20
Totals	19-93	20.4	+41.76

JOCKEYS

	W-R	Per cent	£1 Level Stake
Philip Hide	28-146	19.2	+79.37
Jamie Moore	28-207	13.5	-17.25
A P McCoy	2-8	25.0	-1.83
Eamon Dehdashti	2-36	5.6	-25.25
P J Brennan	1-1	100.0	+3.00
Richard Johnson	1-3	33.3	+4.00
Mr W Russell	1-7	14.3	+19.00

COURSE RECORD

	Total W-R	Non-Hndcps Hurdles	Chases	Hndcps Hurdles	Chases	NH Flat	Per cent	£1 Level Stake
Fontwell	19-90	6-27	4-10	6-28	2-21	1-4	21.1	+9.42
Plumpton	14-56	9-26	1-3	2-16	1-9	1-2	25.0	+41.36
Huntingdon	5-35	1-6	4-8	0-12	0-9	0-0	14.3	-2.87
Taunton	3-19	1-6	1-1	0-9	1-3	0-0	15.8	-2.25
Lingfield	3-21	1-8	0-4	0-6	2-3	0-0	14.3	+21.50
Sandown	3-31	0-7	0-3	3-17	0-4	0-0	9.7	+4.00
Towcester	2-7	1-3	0-0	1-3	0-1	0-0	28.6	-0.25
Nton Abbot	2-12	1-2	0-2	1-4	0-3	0-1	16.7	-0.50
Stratford	2-14	0-1	0-1	2-10	0-2	0-0	14.3	+29.00
Cheltenham	2-22	0-5	1-3	1-11	0-3	0-0	9.1	-3.25
Folkestone	2-27	1-12	0-4	0-4	1-7	0-0	7.4	-4.00
Warwick	1-3	1-1	0-0	0-1	0-1	0-0	33.3	-0.63
Leicester	1-4	0-0	0-1	0-2	1-1	0-0	25.0	+3.00
Worcester	1-4	0-1	0-0	1-2	0-1	0-0	25.0	+1.50
Ludlow	1-5	1-3	0-0	0-2	0-0	0-0	20.0	+7.00
Wincanton	1-13	0-3	0-2	0-6	1-2	0-0	7.7	-8.00
Aintree	1-14	1-5	0-1	0-6	0-1	0-1	7.1	-3.00

WINNING HORSES

Horse	Races Run	1st	2nd	3rd	£
Verasi	6	2	0	1	33962
Mr Boo	5	3	0	0	24271
New Entic	8	1	1	0	12526
*Here We Go	2	2	0	0	13660
Haafel	8	2	0	0	13469
*Pace Shot	7	2	2	1	11001
Flying Spirit	8	2	3	0	12139
Sesame Rambler	6	1	0	0	7516
Stormy Skye	8	1	1	1	6929
*Lewis Island	6	1	2	3	6263
Tamreen	7	1	0	1	5704
*Equilibria	5	1	1	0	5608
*Flaming Weapon	6	1	2	1	5473
Space Cowboy	8	3	0	0	12356
Stance	7	1	1	2	5421
Pardishar	6	1	3	1	5205
Adecco	6	1	0	3	5205
Idris	8	1	3	3	5205
*Heathcote	4	3	1	0	14820
Cold Turkey	2	1	0	1	5049
Twenty Degrees	9	1	1	4	5029
Anticipating	6	2	1	1	8370
High Hope	1	1	0	0	4945
Earlsfield Raider	3	2	1	0	8541
Dolzago	1	1	0	0	4827
Election Seeker	2	1	0	0	4807
Nawamees	4	1	0	1	4362
Ressource	7	1	0	0	4222
Eau Pure	12	1	2	2	4216
Party Games	9	3	1	2	11954
Master T	9	1	1	1	3723
*Kristinor	4	1	0	0	3452
Wayward Melody	10	1	0	3	3445
Maclean	11	1	2	0	3380
*Almizan	5	1	1	1	3374
*Welcome Stranger	3	1	0	0	3253
Sole Agent	6	1	0	1	2928
*Grasp	5	1	1	0	2928
Silverio	8	1	1	0	2928
Froghole Flyer	4	1	0	0	2741
White On Black	3	1	0	1	2741
Charliemoore	6	1	0	1	2702
Lightning Star	3	1	1	0	2604
Trigger Guard	6	1	0	1	2583
Assoon	8	1	1	2	2487
Barranco	9	1	1	2	2193
Mr Ex	6	1	0	3	1925
Or Jaune	1	1	0	0	1627
Total winning prize-money					**£324069**
Favourites	14-41		34.1%		-1.29

K A MORGAN

WALTHAM ON THE WOLDS, LEICS

	No. of Hrs	Races Run	1st	2nd	3rd	Unpl	Per cent	£1 Level Stake
NH Flat	1	1	0	0	1	0	0.0	-1.00
Hurdles	11	33	4	5	3	21	12.1	+0.50
Chases	3	5	0	0	1	4	0.0	-5.00
Totals	13	39	4	5	5	25	10.3	-5.50
04-05	16	48	2	4	2	40	4.2	-39.00
03-04	17	75	4	6	7	58	5.3	-45.25

JOCKEYS

	W-R	Per cent	£1 Level Stake
Patrick McDonald	1-3	33.3	+6.00
Johnny Levins	1-4	25.0	+4.00
Shane Walsh	1-8	12.5	+3.00
P J Brennan	1-11	9.1	-5.50

COURSE RECORD

	Total W-R	Non-Hndcps Hurdles	Chases	Hndcps Hurdles	Chases	NH Flat	Per cent	£1 Level Stake
Bangor	1-1	0-0	0-0	1-1	0-0	0-0	100.0	+4.50
Huntingdon	1-3	0-0	0-0	1-3	0-0	0-0	33.3	+6.00
Towcester	1-4	0-1	0-1	1-2	0-0	0-0	25.0	+7.00
Fakenham	1-6	0-1	0-0	1-5	0-0	0-0	16.7	+2.00

WINNING HORSES

Horse	Races Run	1st	2nd	3rd	£
Kingkohler	4	1	3	0	10228
Macreater	8	1	0	1	3393
Colophony	7	2	0	1	5994
Total winning prize-money					£19615
Favourites	0-2		0.0%		-2.00

C P MORLOCK

KINGSTON LISLE, OXON

	No. of Hrs	Races Run	1st	2nd	3rd	Unpl	Per cent	£1 Level Stake
NH Flat	4	5	0	0	1	4	0.0	-5.00
Hurdles	18	45	1	6	3	35	2.2	-30.00
Chases	3	6	0	0	1	5	0.0	-6.00
Totals	20	56	1	6	5	44	1.8	-41.00
04-05	18	56	0	4	3	49	0.0	-56.00
03-04	18	69	3	2	5	59	4.3	+17.00

JOCKEYS

	W-R	Per cent	£1 Level Stake
Tom Doyle	1-10	10.0	+5.00

COURSE RECORD

	Total W-R	Non-Hndcps Hurdles	Chases	Hndcps Hurdles	Chases	NH Flat	Per cent	£1 Level Stake
Uttoxeter	1-3	1-2	0-0	0-1	0-0	0-0	33.3	+12.00

WINNING HORSES

Horse	Races Run	1st	2nd	3rd	£
*Explosive Fox	7	1	2	0	3325
Total winning prize-money					£3325
Favourites	0-0		0.0%		0.00

D MORRIS

NEWMARKET, SUFFOLK

	No. of Hrs	Races Run	1st	2nd	3rd	Unpl	Per cent	£1 Level Stake
NH Flat	1	2	1	0	0	1	50.0	+2.00
Hurdles	0	0	0	0	0	0	0.0	0.00
Chases	0	0	0	0	0	0	0.0	0.00
Totals	1	2	1	0	0	1	50.0	+2.00
04-05	1	2	0	0	1	1	0.0	-2.00

JOCKEYS

	W-R	Per cent	£1 Level Stake
Mick Fitzgerald	1-1	100.0	+3.00

COURSE RECORD

	Total W-R	Non-Hndcps Hurdles	Chases	Hndcps Hurdles	Chases	NH Flat	Per cent	£1 Level Stake
Uttoxeter	1-1	0-0	0-0	0-0	0-0	1-1	100.0	+3.00

WINNING HORSES

Horse	Races Run	1st	2nd	3rd	£
Master Marmalade	2	1	0	0	1603
Total winning prize-money					£1603
Favourites	0-0		0.0%		0.00

H MORRISON

EAST ILSLEY, BERKS

	No. of Hrs	Races Run	1st	2nd	3rd	Unpl	Per cent	£1 Level Stake
NH Flat	4	6	2	0	0	4	33.3	+3.50
Hurdles	9	29	1	3	7	18	3.4	-3.00
Chases	2	8	0	0	1	7	0.0	-8.00
Totals	10	43	3	3	8	29	7.0	-7.50
04-05	14	47	3	8	4	32	6.4	-36.79
03-04	16	57	10	8	2	37	17.5	-1.38

JOCKEYS

	W-R	Per cent	£1 Level Stake
Jim Crowley	2-22	9.1	+10.00
Tom Scudamore	1-5	20.0	-1.50

COURSE RECORD

	Total W-R	Non-Hndcps Hurdles	Chases	Hndcps Hurdles	Chases	NH Flat	Per cent	£1 Level Stake
Taunton	1-1	0-0	0-0	0-0	0-0	1-1	100.0	+5.00
Chepstow	1-3	0-1	0-0	0 1	0-0	1-1	33.3	+0.50
Wincanton	1 3	1-2	0-1	0-0	0-0	0-0	33.3	+23.00

WINNING HORSES

Horse	Races Run	1st	2nd	3rd	£
Gentleman Jimmy	4	2	0	0	5303
Zanzibar Boy	4	1	0	0	1850
Total winning prize-money					**£7153**
Favourites	**0-4**		**0.0%**		**-4.00**

MRS C M MULHALL

SCARCROFT, W YORKS

	No. of Hrs	Races Run	1st	2nd	3rd	Unpl	Per cent	£1 Level Stake
NH Flat	0	0	0	0	0	0	0.0	0.00
Hurdles	0	0	0	0	0	0	0.0	0.00
Chases	2	3	1	0	0	2	33.3	+0.50
Totals	2	3	1	0	0	2	33.3	+0.50
04-05	2	6	3	0	1	2	50.0	+6.75
03-04	2	5	1	1	1	2	20.0	-2.00

JOCKEYS

	W-R	Per cent	£1 Level Stake
Mr C Mulhall	1-3	33.3	+0.50

COURSE RECORD

	Total W-R	Non-Hndcps Hurdles	Chases	Hndcps Hurdles	Chases	NH Flat	Per cent	£1 Level Stake
Cheltenham	1-2	0-0	1-2	0-0	0-0	0-0	50.0	+1.50

WINNING HORSES

Horse	Races Run	1st	2nd	3rd	£
Mister Friday	1	1	0	0	4869
Total winning prize-money					**£4869**
Favourites		**1-1**	**100.0%**		**2.50**

M MULLINEAUX

ALPRAHAM, CHESHIRE

	No. of Hrs	Races Run	1st	2nd	3rd	Unpl	Per cent	£1 Level Stake
NH Flat	3	5	0	0	0	5	0.0	-5.00
Hurdles	10	31	0	0	0	31	0.0	-31.00
Chases	5	20	1	1	1	17	5.0	-11.00
Totals	14	56	1	1	1	53	1.8	-47.00
04-05	13	61	4	2	3	52	6.6	+34.00
03-04	10	39	2	2	1	34	5.1	+8.00

JOCKEYS

	W-R	Per cent	£1 Level Stake
Alan O'Keeffe	1-6	16.7	+3.00

COURSE RECORD

	Total W-R	Non-Hndcps Hurdles	Chases	Hndcps Hurdles	Chases	NH Flat	Per cent	£1 Level Stake
Taunton	1-3	0-2	0-0	0-0	1-1	0-0	33.3	+6.00

WINNING HORSES

Horse	Races Run	1st	2nd	3rd	£
Sailor A'Hoy	8	1	1	0	3769
Total winning prize-money					**£3769**
Favourites		**0-0**	**0.0%**		**0.00**

J W MULLINS

WILSFORD-CUM-LAKE, WILTS

	No. of Hrs	Races Run	1st	2nd	3rd	Unpl	Per cent	£1 Level Stake
NH Flat	19	37	4	1	3	29	10.8	-2.00
Hurdles	38	147	10	21	14	102	6.8	-42.13
Chases	29	114	8	19	14	73	7.0	-38.34
Totals	62	298	22	41	31	204	7.4	-82.47
04-05	62	252	25	30	26	171	9.9	-39.26
03-04	53	226	23	27	25	151	10.2	+26.66

BY MONTH

NH Flat	W-R	Per cent	£1 Level Stake	Hurdles	W-R	Per cent	£1 Level Stake
May	2-3	66.7	+18.00	May	1-20	5.0	-17.00
June	1-1	100.0	+3.00	June	0-9	0.0	-9.00
July	0-0	0.0	0.00	July	0-4	0.0	-4.00
August	0-1	0.0	-1.00	August	0-1	0.0	-1.00
September	0-0	0.0	0.00	September	0-1	0.0	-1.00
October	0-5	0.0	-5.00	October	0-6	0.0	-6.00
November	0-2	0.0	-2.00	November	1-20	5.0	+9.00
December	0-1	0.0	-1.00	December	0-18	0.0	-18.00
January	0-4	0.0	-4.00	January	0-15	0.0	-15.00
February	0-6	0.0	-6.00	February	0-13	0.0	-13.00

March	0-7	0.0	-7.00	March	2-16	12.5	+10.00
April	1-7	14.3	+3.00	April	6-24	25.0	+22.88

Chases	W-R	Per cent	£1 Level Stake	Totals	W-R	Per cent	£1 Level Stake
May	1-16	6.3	-6.00	May	4-39	10.3	-5.00
June	1-6	16.7	+23.00	June	2-16	12.5	+17.00
July	0-5	0.0	-5.00	July	0-9	0.0	-9.00
August	1-5	20.0	+2.50	August	1-7	14.3	+0.50
September	0-5	0.0	-5.00	September	0-6	0.0	-6.00
October	0-7	0.0	-7.00	October	0-18	0.0	-18.00
November	0-11	0.0	-11.00	November	1-33	3.0	-4.00
December	0-13	0.0	-13.00	December	0-32	0.0	-32.00
January	0-9	0.0	-9.00	January	0-28	0.0	-28.00
February	1-6	16.7	+13.00	February	1-25	4.0	-6.00
March	1-10	10.0	-7.00	March	3-33	9.1	-4.00
April	3-21	14.3	-13.84	April	10-52	19.2	+12.04

DISTANCE

Hurdles	W-R	Per cent	£1 Level Stake	Chases	W-R	Per cent	£1 Level Stake
2m-2m3f	6-63	9.5	-6.50	2m 2m3f	4-44	9.1	-6.75
2m4f-2m7f	2-67	3.0	-29.00	2m4f-2m7f	2-41	4.9	-73.50
3m+	2-17	11.8	-6.63	3m+	2-29	6.9	-8.09

TYPE OF RACE

Non-Handicaps	W-R	Per cent	£1 Level Stake	Handicaps	W-R	Per cent	£1 Level Stake
Nov Hrdls	5-49	10.2	+23.50	Nov Hrdls	1-24	4.2	-16.50
Hrdls	0-17	0.0	-17.00	Hrdls	4-45	8.9	-20.13
Nov Chs	1-27	3.7	-25.09	Nov Chs	4-31	12.9	+6.25
Chases	1-6	16.7	+13.00	Chases	2-49	4.1	-31.50
Sell/Claim	0-6	0.0	-6.00	Sell/Claim	0-7	0.0	-7.00

RACE CLASS / FIRST TIME OUT

Race Class	W-R	Per cent	£1 Level Stake	First Time Out	W-R	Per cent	£1 Level Stake
Class 1	1-12	8.3	+7.00	Bumpers	1-19	5.3	-7.00
Class 2	0-6	0.0	-6.00	Hurdles	1-23	4.3	-16.50
Class 3	2-53	3.8	-35.00	Chases	4-20	20.0	+23.78
Class 4	14-165	8.5	-28.97				
Class 5	1-31	3.2	-23.50	Totals	6-62	9.7	+0.28
Class 6	4-31	12.9	+4.00				

JOCKEYS

	W-R	Per cent	£1 Level Stake
Richard Young	8-120	6.7	-59.75
Andrew Thornton	5-61	8.2	+10.91
Wayne Kavanagh	5-79	6.3	-24.13
Willie McCarthy	1-2	50.0	+1.00
Sean Curran	1-3	33.3	+6.00
Jamie Moore	1-3	33.3	+6.00

Simon Elliott	1-8		12.5	-0.50

COURSE RECORD

	Total W-R	Non-Hndcps Hurdles	Non-Hndcps Chases	Hndcps Hurdles	Chases	NH Flat	Per cent	£1 Level Stake
Hereford	4-10	0-2	0-1	1-2	1-3	2-2	40.0	+12.88
Wincanton	4-37	1-14	1-2	2-10	0-7	0-4	10.8	+12.00
Exeter	3-17	2-4	0-3	0-7	0-2	1-1	17.6	+18.50
Southwell	2-8	0-0	1-3	0-1	1-4	0-0	25.0	+1.41
Nton Abbot	2-19	0-6	0-1	0-6	1-4	1-2	10.5	+1.00
Newbury	2-20	1-7	0-0	0-5	1-4	0-4	10.0	+12.00
Towcester	2-21	1-6	0-3	0-2	1-8	0-2	9.5	-15.13
Chepstow	1-6	0-1	0-0	1-2	0-2	0-1	16.7	+3.00
Worcester	1-24	0-4	0-5	0-4	1-10	0-1	4.2	+5.00
Fontwell	1-31	0-11	0-6	1-7	0-2	0-5	3.2	-28.13

WINNING HORSES

Horse	Races Run	1st	2nd	3rd	£
See You Sometime	8	1	0	0	23076
Kawagino	8	1	1	0	6506
Jockser	8	1	2	1	6263
Ballyhno	8	2	0	0	8354
Lord On The Run	7	1	4	0	4554
Miss Doublet	3	1	0	0	4554
Terrible Tenant	11	2	0	3	8190
Middleham Park	8	1	2	0	4144
Special Conquest	11	1	3	1	4095
High Peak	8	1	1	3	3926
Appach	3	1	1	0	3819
Our Jolly Swagman	7	1	0	0	3793
Fallout	7	1	0	0	3584
*Avesomeofthat	3	1	0	0	3083
Hill Forts Henry	14	1	2	0	2928
Cold Mountain	4	1	0	0	2741
Pan The Man	5	1	1	0	2499
Hill Forts Timmy	9	2	2	0	3997
Swift Half	3	1	0	0	1713
Total winning prize-money					**£101819**
Favourites	7-17		41.2%		4.03

P G MURPHY

EAST GARSTON, BERKS

	No. of Hrs	Races Run	1st	2nd	3rd	Unpl	Per cent	£1 Level Stake
NH Flat	1	1	0	0	1	0	0.0	-1.00
Hurdles	9	22	4	2	1	15	18.2	+59.00
Chases	3	14	0	0	3	11	0.0	-14.00
Totals	12	37	4	2	5	26	10.8	+44.00
04-05	12	38	2	0	1	35	5.3	-4.00
03-04	8	39	1	5	5	28	2.6	-28.00

JOCKEYS

	W-R	Per cent	£1 Level Stake
Sam Thomas	2-3	66.7	+44.00
Jamie Moore	1-4	25.0	+22.00
Leighton Aspell	1-18	5.6	-10.00

COURSE RECORD

	Total W-R	Non-Hndcps Hurdles	Chases	Hndcps Hurdles	Chases	NH Flat	Per cent	£1 Level Stake
Fontwell	2-5	1-1	0-0	1-4	0-0	0-0	40.0	+27.00
Huntingdon	1-1	0-0	0-0	1-1	0-0	0-0	100.0	+7.00
Wincanton	1-2	1-1	0-0	0-0	0-1	0-0	50.0	+39.00

WINNING HORSES

Horse	Races Run	1st	2nd	3rd	£
Treaty Flyer	6	2	1	1	8196
Esters Boy	7	2	1	1	5975
Total winning prize-money					**£14171**
Favourites	**0-88**		**0.0%**		**-88.00**

FERDY MURPHY

WEST WITTON, N YORKS

	No. of Hrs	Races Run	1st	2nd	3rd	Unpl	Per cent	£1 Level Stake
NH Flat	12	17	1	0	4	12	5.9	-12.50
Hurdles	56	164	23	20	16	105	14.0	-58.39
Chases	53	203	21	28	14	140	10.3	-13.24
Totals	94	384	45	48	34	257	11.7	-84.13
04-05	81	387	55	44	46	242	14.2	-78.92
03-04	84	327	31	38	38	220	9.5	-99.33

BY MONTH

NH Flat	W-R	Per cent	£1 Level Stake	Hurdles	W-R	Per cent	£1 Level Stake
May	0-3	0.0	-3.00	May	1-14	7.1	-11.50
June	0-0	0.0	0.00	June	0-2	0.0	-2.00
July	0-0	0.0	0.00	July	0-1	0.0	-1.00
August	0-0	0.0	0.00	August	0-0	0.0	0.00
September	0-0	0.0	0.00	September	0-3	0.0	-3.00
October	0-1	0.0	-1.00	October	2-18	11.1	-12.25
November	0-5	0.0	-5.00	November	5-33	15.2	-20.39
December	1-1	100.0	+3.50	December	4-25	16.0	-10.08
January	0-2	0.0	-2.00	January	4-16	25.0	-1.42
February	0-0	0.0	0.00	February	1-15	6.7	-8.00
March	0-3	0.0	-3.00	March	3-17	17.6	-4.50
April	0-2	0.0	-2.00	April	3-20	15.0	+15.75

Chases	W-R	Per cent	£1 Level Stake	Totals	W-R	Per cent	£1 Level Stake
May	1-14	7.1	-11.25	May	2-31	6.5	-25.75
June	0-1	0.0	-1.00	June	0-3	0.0	-3.00

July	0-4	0.0	-4.00	July	0-5	0.0	-5.00
August	1-7	14.3	-3.75	August	1-7	14.3	-3.75
September	0-3	0.0	-3.00	September	0-6	0.0	-6.00
October	0-20	0.0	-20.00	October	2-39	5.1	-33.25
November	5-40	12.5	-7.25	November	10-78	12.8	-32.64
December	5-35	14.3	+13.53	December	10-61	16.4	+6.95
January	2-23	8.7	-13.13	January	6-41	14.6	-16.55
February	2-17	11.8	-4.50	February	3-32	9.4	-12.50
March	3-20	15.0	+53.50	March	6-40	15.0	+46.00
April	2-19	10.5	-12.40	April	5-41	12.2	+1.35

DISTANCE

Hurdles	W-R	Per cent	£1 Level Stake	Chases	W-R	Per cent	£1 Level Stake
2m-2m3f	5-49	10.2	-35.39	2m-2m3f	0-14	0.0	-14.00
2m4f-2m7f	9-59	15.3	-29.17	2m4f-2m7f	9-72	12.5	-22.12
3m+	9-56	16.1	+6.17	3m+	12-117	10.3	+22.88

TYPE OF RACE

Non-Handicaps	W-R	Per cent	£1 Level Stake	Handicaps	W-R	Per cent	£1 Level Stake
Nov Hrdls	13-72	18.1	-34.89	Nov Hrdls	1-15	6.7	+11.00
Hrdls	5-25	20.0	-3.25	Hrdls	4-48	8.3	-27.25
Nov Chs	6-51	11.8	+12.88	Nov Chs	1-22	4.5	-13.50
Chases	2-10	20.0	-3.63	Chases	11-117	9.4	-12.50
Sell/Claim	0-1	0.0	-1.00	Sell/Claim	0-3	0.0	-3.00

RACE CLASS

	W-R	Per cent	£1 Level Stake
Class 1	0-36	0.0	-36.00
Class 2	7-32	21.9	+84.50
Class 3	8-84	9.5	-41.14
Class 4	28-198	14.1	-68.99
Class 5	1-17	5.9	-10.00
Class 6	1-17	5.9	-12.50

FIRST TIME OUT

	W-R	Per cent	£1 Level Stake
Bumpers	0-12	0.0	-12.00
Hurdles	6-43	14.0	-23.39
Chases	1-39	2.6	-22.00
Totals	7-94	7.4	-57.39

JOCKEYS

	W-R	Per cent	£1 Level Stake
Keith Mercer	19-184	10.3	-66.80
T J Dreaper	10-79	12.7	-40.67
Patrick McDonald	9-51	17.6	-7.25
Mr R O Harding	2-3	66.7	+65.00
Joseph Byrne	1-1	100.0	+3.50
Mr G Tumelty	1-2	50.0	+2.50
G Lee	1-3	33.3	-0.90
Tony Dobbin	1-3	33.3	+1.50
Alan O'Keeffe	1-4	25.0	+13.00

COURSE RECORD

	Total W-R	Non-Hndcps Hurdles	Chases	Hndcps Hurdles	Chases	NH Flat	Per cent	£1 Level Stake
Sedgefield	9-62	2-13	4-16	0-15	3-18	0-0	14.5	-37.99
Perth	4-12	2-2	0-0	2-5	0-4	0-1	33.3	+26.25

Wetherby	4-28	2-12	1-5	1-4	0-6	0-1	14.3	+5.50
Doncaster	3-9	1-5	0-1	0-0	2-3	0-0	33.3	+7.00
Kelso	3-12	3-6	0-1	0-0	0-5	0-0	25.0	-5.25
Ayr	3-17	1-3	0-2	0-4	2-7	0-1	17.6	-2.00
Cheltenham	3-24	0-0	1-6	0-6	2-11	0-1	12.5	+61.00
Musselbgh	2-11	0-2	1-1	0-3	1-5	0-0	18.2	+1.50
Hexham	2-20	1-5	0-2	0-3	1-8	0-2	10.0	-2.00
Newcastle	2-28	1-11	0-4	0-1	1-11	0-1	7.1	-21.25
Bangor	1-5	0-0	0-0	1-2	0-1	0-2	20.0	+2.00
Ludlow	1-5	1-3	0-0	0-0	0-2	0-0	20.0	+2.00
Warwick	1-6	0-0	0-2	1-2	0-2	0-0	16.7	-0.50
Hereford	1-7	0-1	1-2	0-3	0-1	0-0	14.3	-3.25
Leicester	1-7	0-3	1-2	0-0	0-2	0-0	14.3	-0.50
Towcester	1-8	0-0	0-3	0-1	0-3	1-1	12.5	-3.50
Catterick	1-10	1-3	0-2	0-1	0-3	0-1	10.0	-7.25
Aintree	1-11	1-2	0-1	0-1	0-7	0-0	9.1	-7.25
Haydock	1-12	1-6	0-1	0-2	0-1	0-2	8.3	-10.64
Uttoxeter	1-19	1-5	0-1	0-4	0-8	0-1	5.3	-17.00

WINNING HORSES

Horse	Races Run	1st	2nd	3rd	£
You're Special	8	2	1	1	43959
Hot Weld	6	3	0	1	37388
Ivoire De Beaulieu	2	2	0	0	15294
Nine De Sivola	8	4	0	1	24986
Haut De Gamme	7	1	1	1	11315
Leading Man	5	1	0	1	11192
Ile Maurice	7	3	1	1	17111
Green Ideal	7	2	1	0	14313
*Aces Four	4	3	0	1	14964
Noir Et Vert	5	2	0	0	13012
New Alco	6	2	4	0	10790
Dolmur	3	1	0	0	6916
Swallow Magic	12	2	2	0	9049
L'Antartique	4	2	1	0	8605
Underwriter	6	1	0	1	4720
Dark Thunder	9	1	0	1	4696
Canavan	8	1	3	0	4554
Dead Mans Dante	14	2	3	1	8818
Devondale	6	2	0	1	8445
Show Me The River	6	1	3	0	4086
High Day	6	2	0	0	7195
King Of Confusion	5	2	1	2	7130
Chancers Dante	9	1	1	2	3253
Water Taxi	8	1	3	0	3083
Senora Snoopy	4	1	0	1	2521
Total winning prize-money					£297395
Favourites	18-54		33.3%		-7.13

F P MURTAGH

LOW BRAITHWAITE, CUMBRIA

	No. of Hrs	Races Run	1st	2nd	3rd	Unpl	Per cent	£1 Level Stake
NH Flat	1	1	0	0	0	1	0.0	-1.00

Hurdles	13	29	0	0	1	28	0.0	-29.00
Chases	7	28	1	3	2	22	3.6	-22.00
Totals	18	58	1	3	3	51	1.7	-52.00
04-05	25	98	4	2	4	87	4.1	-39.00
03-04	26	111	3	6	9	92	2.7	-88.50

JOCKEYS

	W-R	Per cent	£1 Level Stake
T J Dreaper	1-3	33.3	+3.00

COURSE RECORD

	Total W-R	Non-Hndcps Hurdles	Chases	Hndcps Hurdles	Chases	NH Flat	Per cent	£1 Level Stake
Carlisle	1-9	0-2	0-3	0-1	1-3	0-0	11.1	-3.00

WINNING HORSES

Horse	Races Run	1st	2nd	3rd	£
Hollows Mill	9	1	0	1	3578
Total winning prize-money					£3578
Favourites	0-2		0.0%		-2.00

MRS A M NAUGHTON

RICHMOND, N YORKS

	No. of Hrs	Races Run	1st	2nd	3rd	Unpl	Per cent	£1 Level Stake
NH Flat	0	0	0	0	0	0	0.0	0.00
Hurdles	3	11	1	0	0	10	9.1	-4.50
Chases	0	0	0	0	0	0	0.0	0.00
Totals	3	11	1	0	0	10	9.1	-4.50
04-05	4	30	0	3	2	25	0.0	-30.00
03-04	7	27	1	0	1	25	3.7	-18.00

JOCKEYS

	W-R	Per cent	£1 Level Stake
Thomas Burrows	1-4	25.0	+2.50

COURSE RECORD

	Total W-R	Non-Hndcps Hurdles	Chases	Hndcps Hurdles	Chases	NH Flat	Per cent	£1 Level Stake
Fakenham	1-1	0-0	0-0	1-1	0-0	0-0	100.0	+5.50

WINNING HORSES

Horse	Races Run	1st	2nd	3rd	£
Needwood Spirit	7	1	0	0	2535
Total winning prize-money					£2535
Favourites	0-0		0.0%		0.00

DR J R J NAYLOR

SHREWTON, WILTS

	No. of Hrs	Races Run	1st	2nd	3rd	Unpl	Per cent	£1 Level Stake
NH Flat	5	10	0	0	2	8	0.0	-10.00
Hurdles	7	25	1	0	1	23	4.0	-8.00
Chases	1	3	0	1	0	2	0.0	-3.00
Totals	11	38	1	1	3	33	2.6	-21.00
04-05	11	34	0	1	2	31	0.0	-34.00
03-04	13	51	5	6	3	37	9.8	-18.50

JOCKEYS

	W-R	Per cent	£1 Level Stake
Andrew Thornton	1-16	6.3	+1.00

COURSE RECORD

	Total W-R	Non-Hndcps Hurdles	Chases	Hndcps Hurdles	Chases	NH Flat	Per cent	£1 Level Stake
Fontwell	1-5	0-3	0-0	1-2	0-0	0-0	20.0	+12.00

WINNING HORSES

Horse	Races Run	1st	2nd	3rd	£
Hilarious	9	1	0	1	2960
Total winning prize-money					£2960
Favourites	0-1		0.0%		-1.00

P NEEDHAM

BARNARD CASTLE, CO DURHAM

	No. of Hrs	Races Run	1st	2nd	3rd	Unpl	Per cent	£1 Level Stake
NH Flat	0	0	0	0	0	0	0.0	0.00
Hurdles	3	11	1	0	1	9	9.1	0.00
Chases	2	6	0	0	0	6	0.0	-6.00
Totals	3	17	1	0	1	15	5.9	-6.00
04-05	1	2	0	0	0	2	0.0	-2.00
03-04	3	10	0	1	2	7	0.0	-10.00

JOCKEYS

	W-R	Per cent	£1 Level Stake
Barry Keniry	1-11	9.1	0.00

COURSE RECORD

	Total W-R	Non-Hndcps Hurdles	Chases	Hndcps Hurdles	Chases	NH Flat	Per cent	£1 Level Stake
Perth	1-2	1-1	0-0	0-1	0-0	0-0	50.0	+9.00

WINNING HORSES

Horse	Races Run	1st	2nd	3rd	£
Cheery Martyr	8	1	0	0	3543
Total winning prize-money					£3543
Favourites	0-0		0.0%		0.00

MRS H R J NELMES

WARMWELL, DORSET

	No. of Hrs	Races Run	1st	2nd	3rd	Unpl	Per cent	£1 Level Stake
NH Flat	4	7	0	0	0	7	0.0	-7.00
Hurdles	1	4	0	0	0	4	0.0	-4.00
Chases	1	10	2	1	5	2	20.0	+3.50
Totals	6	21	2	1	5	13	9.5	-7.50
04-05	3	6	0	0	0	6	0.0	-6.00

JOCKEYS

	W-R	Per cent	£1 Level Stake
Owyn Nelmes	2-18	11.1	-4.50

COURSE RECORD

	Total W-R	Non-Hndcps Hurdles	Chases	Hndcps Hurdles	Chases	NH Flat	Per cent	£1 Level Stake
Hereford	1-2	0-0	0-0	0-0	1-2	0-0	50.0	+6.00
Nton Abbot	1-2	0-0	0-0	0-0	1-2	0-0	50.0	+3.50

WINNING HORSES

Horse	Races Run	1st	2nd	3rd	£
Wild Power	10	2	1	5	9902
Total winning prize-money					£9902
Favourites	0-0		0.0%		0.00

A G NEWCOMBE

YARNSCOMBE, DEVON

	No. of Hrs	Races Run	1st	2nd	3rd	Unpl	Per cent	£1 Level Stake
NH Flat	1	1	0	0	0	1	0.0	-1.00
Hurdles	6	15	1	1	0	13	6.7	0.00
Chases	0	0	0	0	0	0	0.0	0.00
Totals	7	16	1	1	0	14	6.3	-1.00
04-05	5	10	2	0	0	8	20.0	+56.00
03-04	3	5	0	0	0	5	0.0	-5.00

JOCKEYS

	W-R	Per cent	£1 Level Stake
Andrew Thornton	1-4	25.0	+11.00

COURSE RECORD

	Total W-R	Non-Hndcps Hurdles	Chases	Hndcps Hurdles	Chases	NH Flat	Per cent	£1 Level Stake
Nton Abbot	1-2	1-2	0-0	0-0	0-0	0-0	50.0	+13.00

WINNING HORSES

Horse	Races Run	1st	2nd	3rd	£
Miss Skippy	8	1	1	0	2569
Total winning prize-money					£2569
Favourites	0-0		0.0%		0.00

MISS A M NEWTON-SMITH

JEVINGTON, E SUSSEX

	No. of Hrs	Races Run	1st	2nd	3rd	Unpl	Per cent	£1 Level Stake
NH Flat	0	0	0	0	0	0	0.0	0.00
Hurdles	11	41	3	2	1	35	7.3	+26.50
Chases	4	8	0	1	0	7	0.0	-8.00
Totals	11	49	3	3	1	42	6.1	+18.50
04-05	12	56	4	5	6	41	7.1	-21.50
03-04	17	71	2	5	3	61	2.8	-24.00

JOCKEYS

	W-R	Per cent	£1 Level Stake
Matthew Batchelor	3-26	11.5	+41.50

COURSE RECORD

	Total W-R	Non-Hndcps Hurdles	Chases	Hndcps Hurdles	Chases	NH Flat	Per cent	£1 Level Stake
Fontwell	3-15	0-7	0-1	3-7	0-0	0-0	20.0	+52.50

WINNING HORSES

Horse	Races Run	1st	2nd	3rd	£
Come Bye	9	2	0	0	7300
English Jim	7	1	1	0	3429
Total winning prize-money					£10729
Favourites	0-1		0.0%		-1.00

D NICHOLLS

SESSAY, N YORKS

	No. of Hrs	Races Run	1st	2nd	3rd	Unpl	Per cent	£1 Level Stake
NH Flat	1	1	0	0	0	1	0.0	-1.00
Hurdles	1	2	1	1	0	0	50.0	+1.75
Chases	0	0	0	0	0	0	0.0	0.00
Totals	2	3	1	1	0	1	33.3	+0.75
04-05	1	3	0	1	1	1	0.0	-3.00

JOCKEYS

	W-R	Per cent	£1 Level Stake
Wilson Renwick	1-2	50.0	+1.75

COURSE RECORD

	Total W-R	Non-Hndcps Hurdles	Chases	Hndcps Hurdles	Chases	NH Flat	Per cent	£1 Level Stake
Hexham	1-1	1-1	0-0	0-0	0-0	0-0	100.0	+2.75

WINNING HORSES

Horse	Races Run	1st	2nd	3rd	£
Fourth Dimension	2	1	1	0	3392
Total winning prize-money					£3392
Favourites	0-0		0.0%		0.00

P F NICHOLLS

DITCHEAT, SOMERSET

	No. of Hrs	Races Run	1st	2nd	3rd	Unpl	Per cent	£1 Level Stake
NH Flat	22	44	9	11	5	19	20.5	-19.00
Hurdles	86	273	71	34	33	135	26.0	-37.84
Chases	85	334	68	58	33	175	20.4	-54.67
Totals	158	651	148	103	71	329	22.7	-111.51
04-05	158	714	154	105	92	363	21.6	-85.93
03-04	155	673	132	135	80	326	19.6	-97.19

BY MONTH

NH Flat	W-R	Per cent	£1 Level Stake	Hurdles	W-R	Per cent	£1 Level Stake
May	0-2	0.0	-2.00	May	7-19	36.8	+13.07
June	1-3	33.3	+1.33	June	2-6	33.3	-0.45
July	0-1	0.0	-1.00	July	1-3	33.3	-0.38
August	1-1	100.0	+2.50	August	2-5	40.0	+5.83
September	0-0	0.0	0.00	September	0-1	0.0	-1.00
October	0-0	0.0	0.00	October	7-30	23.3	-7.03
November	0-8	0.0	-8.00	November	8-34	23.5	-15.07
December	2-3	66.7	+1.42	December	11-41	26.8	-4.84
January	1-10	10.0	-6.00	January	13-34	38.2	+10.93
February	2-4	50.0	-1.41	February	8-32	25.0	-18.60
March	2-7	28.6	-0.83	March	6-30	20.0	-8.31
April	0-5	0.0	-5.00	April	6-38	15.8	-12.02

Chases	W-R	Per cent	£1 Level Stake	Totals	W-R	Per cent	£1 Level Stake
May	7-17	41.2	+6.68	May	14-38	36.8	+17.75
June	2-10	20.0	-4.50	June	5-19	26.3	-3.62
July	1-7	14.3	-3.75	July	2-11	18.2	-5.13
August	0-3	0.0	-3.00	August	3-9	33.3	+5.33
September	1-4	25.0	+9.00	September	1-5	20.0	+8.00
October	8-34	23.5	-9.66	October	15-64	23.4	-16.69
November	10-57	17.5	-14.75	November	18-99	18.2	-37.82
December	12-50	24.0	+8.17	December	25-94	26.6	+4.75
January	7-32	21.9	+1.72	January	21-76	27.6	+6.65
February	7-33	21.2	-16.92	February	17-69	24.6	-36.93
March	7-32	21.9	+1.94	March	15-69	21.7	-7.20
April	6-55	10.9	-29.59	April	12-98	12.2	-46.61

DISTANCE

Hurdles	W-R	Per cent	£1 Level Stake	Chases	W-R	Per cent	£1 Level Stake
2m-2m3f	38-143	26.6	-6.99	2m-2m3f	26-95	27.4	-15.51
2m4f-2m7f	26-90	28.9	-6.28	2m4f-2m7f	18-109	16.5	-40.74
3m+	7-40	17.5	-24.57	3m+	24-130	18.5	+1.58

TYPE OF RACE

Non-Handicaps	W-R	Per cent	£1 Level Stake	Handicaps	W-R	Per cent	£1 Level Stake
Nov Hrdls	43-113	38.1	+7.80	Nov Hrdls	1-12	8.3	-4.00
Hrdls	9-37	24.3	-7.61	Hrdls	16-107	15.0	-35.94
Nov Chs	30-110	27.3	-30.64	Nov Chs	5-20	25.0	-1.59
Chases	9-34	26.5	+1.39	Chases	24-170	14.1	-23.83
Sell/Claim	2-3	66.7	+2.90	Sell/Claim	0-1	0.0	-1.00

RACE CLASS

	W-R	Per cent	£1 Level Stake
Class 1	23-167	13.8	-58.06
Class 2	12-98	12.2	-52.53
Class 3	66-202	32.7	+39.80
Class 4	33-133	24.8	-28.48
Class 5	3-8	37.5	+0.01
Class 6	11-43	25.6	-11.25

FIRST TIME OUT

	W-R	Per cent	£1 Level Stake
Bumpers	4-22	18.2	-9.55
Hurdles	18-69	26.1	-1.23
Chases	15-67	22.4	-16.11
Totals	37-158	23.4	-26.89

JOCKEYS

	W-R	Per cent	£1 Level Stake
R Walsh	63-203	31.0	+22.21
Christian Williams	32-193	16.6	-75.22
Liam Heard	20-102	19.6	-22.41
Joe Tizzard	7-41	17.1	-22.81
B J Geraghty	5-12	41.7	+13.08
A P McCoy	4-13	30.8	-1.76
P J Brennan	4-21	19.0	-12.89
Mr J Snowden	2-6	33.3	-1.79
Sam Thomas	2-7	28.6	-3.42
Mr C J Sweeney	2-9	22.2	-1.25
Mick Fitzgerald	2-9	22.2	-4.14
Leighton Aspell	1-1	100.0	+14.00
Richard Johnson	1-1	100.0	+0.73
D Gallagher	1-2	50.0	+1.25
Miss C Tizzard	1-4	25.0	+8.00
Paddy Merrigan	1-5	20.0	-3.09

COURSE RECORD

	Total W-R	Non-Hndcps Hurdles	Non-Hndcps Chases	Hndcps Hurdles	Hndcps Chases	NH Flat	Per cent	£1 Level Stake
Wincanton	28-84	10-23	2-9	4-21	8-24	4-7	33.3	+25.67
Chepstow	13-52	6-19	3-7	1-11	2-10	1-5	25.0	-6.81
Cheltenham	13-93	5-17	2-20	3-20	3-33	0-3	14.0	-15.61
Newbury	11-32	3-6	2-5	1-5	5-15	0-1	34.4	+15.75
Sandown	10-41	3-9	7-14	0-6	0-12	0-0	24.4	-15.52
Worcester	9-27	5-8	0-5	0-2	2-4	2-8	33.3	+21.86
Taunton	8-39	2-7	1-9	3-8	1-8	1-7	20.5	-15.68
Stratford	7-21	2-4	3-6	1-4	1-7	0-0	33.3	+7.05
Warwick	5-15	2-3	2-6	0-3	1-2	0-1	33.3	+3.35
Aintree	5-50	1-8	3-9	0-8	1-22	0-3	10.0	-31.13
Hereford	4-10	2-5	2-3	0-1	0-0	0-1	40.0	-0.80
Ludlow	4-13	0-3	1-2	1-2	2-4	0-2	30.8	+0.32
Exeter	4-34	3-11	0-9	0-6	1-6	0-7	11.8	22.75
Folkestone	3-8	2-4	1-2	0-0	0-1	0-1	37.5	-2.52
Huntingdon	3-9	2-3	1-4	0-0	0-2	0-0	33.3	-3.41
Lingfield	3-12	1-2	0-4	0-3	2-3	0-0	25.0	-1.38
Nton Abbot	3-13	1-3	1-2	1-2	0-6	0-0	23.1	-2.58
Fontwell	3-14	0-4	2-4	0-1	0-3	1-2	21.4	-10.16
Wetherby	2-7	1-2	1-3	0-0	0-2	0-0	28.6	-1.85
Haydock	2-10	1-2	1-4	0-2	0-2	0-0	20.0	-7.09
Southwell	1-2	0-0	0-0	1-1	0-1	0-0	50.0	+0.25
Fakenham	1-3	0-1	1-2	0-0	0-0	0-0	33.3	0.00
Leicester	1-3	0-0	1-3	0-0	0-0	0-0	33.3	-1.60
Windsor	1-5	1-2	0-1	0-2	0-0	0-0	20.0	-2.25
Mrket Rsn	1-6	0-0	1-2	0-1	0-3	0-0	16.7	-3.63
Doncaster	1-7	0-0	0-2	1-1	0-4	0-0	14.3	-3.00
Bangor	1-9	1-3	0-2	0-2	0-2	0-0	11.1	-7.92
Plumpton	1-10	0-1	1-4	0-1	0-3	0-1	10.0	-8.09

WINNING HORSES

Horse	Races Run	1st	2nd	3rd	£
Star De Mohaison	6	4	1	1	144953
Kauto Star	3	1	1	0	71275
L'Aventure	6	1	0	1	57020
Noland	5	4	0	1	105849
Eurotrek	4	2	0	0	50052
*Desert Quest	10	5	2	1	67322
Natal	9	5	0	1	55388
Hoo La Baloo	8	3	2	0	44338
Royal Auclair	8	1	1	0	28510
Napolitain	9	4	2	0	65297
Goblet Of Fire	7	2	1	1	32246
Be Be King	5	3	0	0	31972
Denman	5	4	1	0	38084
Bold Fire	5	2	2	0	22601
Armaturk	7	2	1	1	36259
Almost Broke	6	1	0	1	10700
Albuliera	7	2	1	2	22410
Neptune Collonges	7	4	1	1	53740
Darrias	12	6	1	2	17142
Cerium	6	3	0	1	30193
Sweet Diversion	6	3	3	0	23596
Spring Margot	1	1	0	0	12378
Le Jaguar	7	1	0	1	11435
Taranis	5	4	0	0	35057
East Lawyer	7	1	0	1	11060
Ladalko	7	1	2	2	10359
Reflected Glory	6	1	3	1	10345
Pirate Flagship	8	3	2	0	25645
Fair Prospect	2	1	0	0	10273
Inca Trail	6	3	0	0	10149

Horse					
Le Volfoni	11	4	3	2	30733
Gungadu	6	2	2	1	11872
Comanche War Paint	6	2	0	0	13985
Magic Sky	6	1	0	0	8190
Hors La Loi III	5	1	1	1	7937
The Luder	7	2	2	1	11060
Nippy Des Mottes	11	4	2	0	24828
Turko	7	2	3	0	11711
Were In Touch	1	1	0	0	7114
Cornish Sett	8	2	3	0	7059
Luneray	8	2	1	2	13401
Made In Montot	2	1	0	0	6665
Stavordale Lad	7	2	3	0	10943
Nycteos	5	2	1	0	10224
Mouseski	9	1	1	2	6252
Andreas	6	2	1	1	11309
Spidam	3	1	0	2	5621
Lord Anner	6	2	1	0	10915
L'Oudon	4	1	0	0	5205
Blu Teen	5	1	0	0	5205
Perouse	5	1	0	0	4706
Leroy's Sister	1	1	0	0	4690
Give Me Love	10	1	2	2	4384
Geeveem	3	2	0	0	7157
Ho Ho Hill	2	1	1	0	4144
*Smart Cavalier	5	1	2	0	3904
*Vale De Lobo	3	1	0	0	3614
Twist Magic	5	1	0	1	3590
Silence Reigns	4	3	0	0	6617
Azzemour	5	1	0	0	3549
Nanga Parbat	7	1	2	1	3533
Bee Hawk	4	1	1	0	3445
*Caspers Case	1	1	0	0	3445
*Colorado Pearl	1	1	0	0	3426
Grande Creole	4	1	0	0	3333
Kaldouas	3	1	0	0	3289
Opera Mundi	3	1	1	0	3253
Raffaello	2	1	1	0	3083
Dear Villez	2	1	0	1	2928
Hot 'N' Holy	5	2	1	0	4742
Pepporoni Pete	3	1	0	1	2357
Teeton Babysham	2	1	1	0	2277
Morson Boy	1	1	0	0	2191
Kicks For Free	4	2	0	2	4111
Fountain Crumble	5	1	1	0	1907
Delena	3	1	0	0	1850
Silverburn	2	1	1	0	1713
Notre Cyborg	2	1	0	0	1627
Houlihans Free	6	1	0	2	1506
Total winning prize-money					**£1474337**
Favourites	85-206		41.3%		-16.13

MISS V J NICHOLLS

YELVERTON, DEVON

	No. of Hrs	Races Run	1st	2nd	3rd	Unpl	Per cent	£1 Level Stake
NH Flat	0	0	0	0	0	0	0.0	0.00
Hurdles	0	0	0	0	0	0	0.0	0.00
Chases	1	3	1	0	0	2	33.3	+10.00
Totals	1	3	1	0	0	2	33.3	+10.00

JOCKEYS

	W-R	Per cent	£1 Level Stake
Miss S Gaisford	1-2	50.0	+11.00

COURSE RECORD

	Total W-R	Non-Hndcps Hurdles	Chases	Hndcps Hurdles	Chases	NH Flat	Per cent	£1 Level Stake
Exeter	1-3	0-0	1-3	0-0	0-0	0-0	33.3	+10.00

WINNING HORSES

Horse	Races Run	1st	2nd	3rd	£
Virgos Bambino	3	1	0	0	2805
Total winning prize-money					**£2805**
Favourites	0-0		0.0%		0.00

J NICOL

NEWMARKET, SUFFOLK

	No. of Hrs	Races Run	1st	2nd	3rd	Unpl	Per cent	£1 Level Stake
NH Flat	2	5	2	1	0	2	40.0	+6.88
Hurdles	0	0	0	0	0	0	0.0	0.00
Chases	0	0	0	0	0	0	0.0	0.00
Totals	2	5	2	1	0	2	40.0	+6.88
04-05	2	3	0	0	0	3	0.0	-3.00

JOCKEYS

	W-R	Per cent	£1 Level Stake
Mick Fitzgerald	2-3	66.7	+8.88

COURSE RECORD

	Total W-R	Non-Hndcps Hurdles	Chases	Hndcps Hurdles	Chases	NH Flat	Per cent	£1 Level Stake
Ludlow	1-1	0-0	0-0	0-0	0-0	1-1	100.0	+1.88
Worcester	1-1	0-0	0-0	0-0	0-0	1-1	100.0	+8.00

WINNING HORSES

Horse	Races Run	1st	2nd	3rd	£
Tooting	3	1	1	0	2277
Shakerattleandroll	2	1	0	0	1506

Total winning prize-money		£3783
Favourites	15-15 100.0%	28.13

P D NIVEN

BARTON-LE-STREET, N YORKS

	No. of Hrs	Races Run	1st	2nd	3rd	Unpl	Per cent	£1 Level Stake
NH Flat	4	9	2	1	0	6	22.2	+16.50
Hurdles	18	44	6	3	1	34	13.6	+32.50
Chases	4	16	1	0	1	14	6.3	-10.00
Totals	**20**	**69**	**9**	**4**	**2**	**54**	**13.0**	**+39.00**
04-05	30	112	8	7	10	87	7.1	-12.50
03-04	21	94	4	6	10	74	4.3	-40.25

JOCKEYS

	W-R	Per cent	£1 Level Stake
Miss L Haagensen	2-2	100.0	+32.50
G Lee	2-7	28.6	+8.00
Jim Crowley	2-23	8.7	-11.00
Noel Fehily	1-1	100.0	+3.50
Brian Hughes	1-3	33.3	+18.00
Mr T Greenall	1-3	33.3	+18.00

COURSE RECORD

	Total W R	Non-Hndcps Hurdles	Chases	Hndcps Hurdles	Chases	NH Flat	Per cent	£1 Level Stake
Mrket Rsn	2-9	0-2	0-0	2-5	0-2	0-0	22.2	+20.00
Wetherby	2-11	1-5	0-0	1-5	0-0	0-1	18.2	+3.50
Carlisle	1-1	0-0	0-0	1-1	0-0	0-0	100.0	+25.00
Huntingdon	1-2	0-0	0-0	0-1	0-0	1-1	50.0	+2.50
Ayr	1-3	0-1	0-0	0-0	0-0	1-2	33.3	+18.00
Uttoxeter	1-6	0-2	0-0	1-2	0-2	0-0	16.7	+1.00
Hexham	1-8	0-1	0-1	0-2	1-4	0-0	12.5	-2.00

WINNING HORSES

Horse	Races Run	1st	2nd	3rd	£
Panmure	10	1	0	0	3751
Talarive	9	2	2	0	6118
Wise Tale	5	2	1	0	5666
Twotiming Gent	5	2	0	1	5893
Grecian Groom	1	1	0	0	2056
Stolen Moments	4	1	1	0	2056
Total winning prize-money					**£25540**
Favourites	1-3	33.3%			1.50

R NIXON

ETTRICKBRIDGE, BORDERS

	No. of Hrs	Races Run	1st	2nd	3rd	Unpl	Per cent	£1 Level Stake
NH Flat	3	4	0	1	1	2	0.0	-4.00
Hurdles	8	50	1	2	5	42	2.0	-39.00
Chases	4	16	0	0	2	14	0.0	-16.00
Totals	**10**	**70**	**1**	**3**	**8**	**58**	**1.4**	**-59.00**
04-05	10	83	3	4	9	67	3.6	-49.25
03-04	10	61	2	5	5	49	3.3	-34.00

JOCKEYS

	W-R	Per cent	£1 Level Stake
Gareth Thomas	1-52	1.9	-41.00

COURSE RECORD

	Total W-R	Non-Hndcps Hurdles	Chases	Hndcps Hurdles	Chases	NH Flat	Per cent	£1 Level Stake
Sedgefield	1-6	0-1	0-1	1-3	0-1	0-0	16.7	+5.00

WINNING HORSES

Horse	Races Run	1st	2nd	3rd	£
Political Cruise	11	1	0	1	2082
Total winning prize-money					**£2082**
Favourites	0-0	0.0%			0.00

MRS SUSAN NOCK

ICOMB, GLOUCS

	No. of Hrs	Races Run	1st	2nd	3rd	Unpl	Per cent	£1 Level Stake
NH Flat	1	1	0	0	0	1	0.0	-1.00
Hurdles	4	10	1	0	0	9	10.0	-4.50
Chases	3	8	0	1	3	4	0.0	-8.00
Totals	**7**	**19**	**1**	**1**	**3**	**14**	**5.3**	**-13.50**
04-05	6	25	1	0	6	18	4.0	-21.25
03-04	7	29	4	4	2	19	13.8	-4.75

JOCKEYS

	W-R	Per cent	£1 Level Stake
Tom Scudamore	1-6	16.7	-0.50

COURSE RECORD

	Total W-R	Non-Hndcps Hurdles	Chases	Hndcps Hurdles	Chases	NH Flat	Per cent	£1 Level Stake
Towcester	1-1	1-1	0-0	0-0	0-0	0-0	100.0	+4.50

WINNING HORSES

Horse	Races Run	1st	2nd	3rd	£
Molostiep	2	1	0	0	3904
Total winning prize-money					**£3904**
Favourites	0-0	0.0%			0.00

MRS L B NORMILE

DUNCRIEVIE, PERTH & KINROSS

	No. of Hrs	Races Run	1st	2nd	3rd	Unpl	Per cent	£1 Level Stake
NH Flat	8	15	0	0	2	13	0.0	-15.00
Hurdles	25	50	0	2	2	46	0.0	-50.00
Chases	12	39	3	5	2	29	7.7	+45.00
Totals	37	104	3	7	6	88	2.9	-20.00
04-05	36	115	7	8	6	94	6.1	+18.40
03-04	32	118	6	5	11	96	5.1	-65.06

JOCKEYS

	W-R	Per cent	£1 Level Stake
Dougie Costello	1-3	33.3	+64.00
Neil Mulholland	1-20	5.0	-9.00
Des Flavin	1-66	1.5	-60.00

COURSE RECORD

	Total W-R	Non-Hndcps Hurdles	Chases	Hndcps Hurdles	Chases	NH Flat	Per cent	£1 Level Stake
Newcastle	1-4	0-2	0-0	0-1	1-1	0-0	25.0	+2.00
Hexham	1-9	0-3	0-3	0-0	1-3	0-0	11.1	+58.00
Sedgefield	1-10	0-2	0-3	0-0	1-4	0-1	10.0	+1.00

WINNING HORSES

Horse	Races Run	1st	2nd	3rd	£
Flaming Heck	7	2	1	0	7336
Toad Hall	6	1	0	0	3332
Total winning prize-money					£10668
Favourites	0-1		0.0%		-1.00

JEDD O'KEEFFE

MIDDLEHAM MOOR, N YORKS

	No. of Hrs	Races Run	1st	2nd	3rd	Unpl	Per cent	£1 Level Stake
NH Flat	0	0	0	0	0	0	0.0	0.00
Hurdles	8	33	6	3	3	21	18.2	+23.25
Chases	2	10	1	1	2	5	10.0	-4.00
Totals	10	43	7	4	5	26	16.3	+19.25
04-05	11	45	3	4	5	33	6.7	-21.25
03-04	11	43	3	1	7	32	7.0	-20.67

JOCKEYS

	W-R	Per cent	£1 Level Stake
Brian Harding	7-27	25.9	+35.25

COURSE RECORD

	Total W-R	Non-Hndcps Hurdles	Chases	Hndcps Hurdles	Chases	NH Flat	Per cent	£1 Level Stake
Kelso	1-1	0-0	0-0	1-1	0-0	0-0	100.0	+12.00
Huntingdon	1-2	1-1	0-0	0-1	0-0	0-0	50.0	+13.00

Ayr	1-3	0-1	0-1	1-1	0-0	0-0	33.3	+3.50
Hexham	1-3	1-1	0-1	0-1	0-0	0-0	33.3	+0.75
Newcastle	1-4	0-1	0-0	1-3	0-0	0-0	25.0	+1.00
Wetherby	1-4	1-2	0-0	0-2	0-0	0-0	25.0	+9.00
Sedgefield	1-7	0-2	1-2	0-3	0-0	0-0	14.3	-1.00

WINNING HORSES

Horse	Races Run	1st	2nd	3rd	£
Sir Night	5	1	1	0	5499
Habitual Dancer	7	2	1	0	10410
Beat The Heat	7	1	0	2	4144
United Spirit	4	2	0	0	6781
*Lankawi	6	1	1	1	3440
Total winning prize-money					£30274
Favourites	0-3		0.0%		-3.00

O O'NEILL

CLEEVE HILL, GLOUCS

	No. of Hrs	Races Run	1st	2nd	3rd	Unpl	Per cent	£1 Level Stake
NH Flat	1	1	0	0	0	1	0.0	-1.00
Hurdles	2	12	1	0	1	10	8.3	+29.00
Chases	0	0	0	0	0	0	0.0	0.00
Totals	3	13	1	0	1	11	7.7	+28.00
04-05	7	32	1	0	2	29	3.1	-15.00
03-04	4	9	0	0	0	9	0.0	-9.00

JOCKEYS

	W-R	Per cent	£1 Level Stake
Matthew Batchelor	1-5	20.0	+36.00

COURSE RECORD

	Total W-R	Non-Hndcps Hurdles	Chases	Hndcps Hurdles	Chases	NH Flat	Per cent	£1 Level Stake
Mrket Rsn	1-2	0-1	0-0	1-1	0-0	0-0	50.0	+39.00

WINNING HORSES

Horse	Races Run	1st	2nd	3rd	£
Sylcan Express	5	1	0	0	2246
Total winning prize-money					£2246
Favourites	0-0		0.0%		0.00

JONJO O'NEILL

CHELTENHAM, GLOUCS

	No. of Hrs	Races Run	1st	2nd	3rd	Unpl	Per cent	£1 Level Stake
NH Flat	30	47	11	5	3	28	23.4	-6.27
Hurdles	134	417	59	44	37	276	14.1	-101.60
Chases	80	247	35	39	24	149	14.2	-67.72
Totals	187	711	105	88	64	453	14.8	-175.59

04-05	156	525	97	69	49	310	18.5	-145.06
03-04	174	640	102	73	52	413	15.9	-114.21

Class 3	34-240	14.2	-94.08
Class 4	37-275	13.5	-52.72
Class 5	2-17	11.8	-2.00
Class 6	14-44	31.8	+2.52

Chases	8-52	15.4	-16.38
Totals	28-187	15.0	-76.67

BY MONTH

NH Flat	W-R	Per cent	£1 Level Stake	Hurdles	W-R	Per cent	£1 Level Stake
May	0-0	0.0	0.00	May	1-11	9.1	-9.80
June	0-1	0.0	-1.00	June	2-19	10.5	-10.25
July	1-1	100.0	+2.00	July	6-32	18.8	-4.56
August	1-2	50.0	+1.50	August	2-21	9.5	-11.00
September	2-4	50.0	+3.23	September	1-11	9.1	-2.00
October	1-5	20.0	-1.75	October	12-48	25.0	+2.20
November	2-13	15.4	-4.25	November	5-49	10.2	-24.83
December	0-3	0.0	-3.00	December	7-36	19.4	-14.07
January	1-4	25.0	-2.00	January	4-48	8.3	-5.67
February	1-4	25.0	+3.50	February	9-57	15.8	+0.24
March	2-6	33.3	-0.50	March	4-49	8.2	-24.75
April	0-4	0.0	-4.00	April	6-36	16.7	+2.89

Chases	W-R	Per cent	£1 Level Stake	Totals	W-R	Per cent	£1 Level Stake
May	5-8	62.5	+8.92	May	6-19	31.6	-0.88
June	1-13	7.7	-10.90	June	3-33	9.1	-22.15
July	2-15	13.3	-2.75	July	9-48	18.8	-5.31
August	4-21	19.0	-2.75	August	7-44	15.9	-12.25
September	2-18	11.1	-9.50	September	5-33	15.2	-8.27
October	3-34	8.8	-23.77	October	16-87	18.4	-23.32
November	5-35	14.3	-2.75	November	12-97	12.4	-31.83
December	2-25	8.0	-15.50	December	9-64	14.1	-32.57
January	2-19	10.5	+1.00	January	7-71	9.9	-6.67
February	4-22	10.2	-0.04	February	14-83	16.9	+3.70
March	3-21	14.3	-15.17	March	9-76	11.8	-40.42
April	2-16	12.5	+5.50	April	8-56	14.3	+4.39

DISTANCE

Hurdles	W-R	Per cent	£1 Level Stake	Chases	W-R	Per cent	£1 Level Stake
2m-2m3f	32-219	14.6	-58.07	2m-2m3f	8-58	13.8	-18.13
2m4f-2m7f	20-131	15.3	-8.31	2m4f-2m7f	17-104	16.3	-15.29
3m+	7-67	10.4	-35.22	3m+	10-85	11.8	-34.29

TYPE OF RACE

Non-Handicaps	W-R	Per cent	£1 Level Stake	Handicaps	W-R	Per cent	£1 Level Stake
Nov Hrdls	28-159	17.6	-47.50	Nov Hrdls	3-23	13.0	+9.63
Hrdls	7-56	12.5	-6.31	Hrdls	21-175	12.0	-53.42
Nov Chs	14-64	21.9	-17.63	Nov Chs	4-23	17.4	+8.75
Chases	2-12	16.7	+4.83	Chases	15-148	10.1	-63.67
Sell/Claim	0-2	0.0	-2.00	Sell/Claim	0-2	0.0	-2.00

RACE CLASS / FIRST TIME OUT

	W-R	Per cent	£1 Level Stake		W-R	Per cent	£1 Level Stake
Class 1	6-71	8.5	-38.97	Bumpers	8-30	26.7	+3.23
Class 2	12-64	18.8	+10.67	Hurdles	12-105	11.4	-63.52

JOCKEYS

	W-R	Per cent	£1 Level Stake
A P McCoy	69-366	18.9	-43.65
Noel Fehily	9-84	10.7	-34.21
Mr A J Berry	5-37	13.5	-13.57
Jamie Moore	4-32	12.5	0.38
Mick Fitzgerald	4-36	11.1	+2.60
Mr J P Magnier	3-5	60.0	+4.50
Shane Walsh	3-13	23.1	+6.50
Mr J T McNamara	2-6	33.3	-2.04
Brian Harding	2-19	10.5	-6.25
Barry Fenton	1-7	14.3	-1.00
Richard Johnson	1-12	8.3	-3.00
Wayne Jones	1-13	7.7	-6.00
Richard McGrath	1-19	5.3	-17.09

COURSE RECORD

	Total W-R	Non-Hndcps Hurdles	Non-Hndcps Chases	Hndcps Hurdles	Chases	NH Flat	Per cent	£1 Level Stake
Cheltenham	8-52	3-10	3-11	1-16	1-12	0-3	15.4	-3.83
Stratford	7-32	2-8	2-4	1-6	2-12	0-2	21.9	+3.38
Mrket Rsn	7-49	1-12	1-4	1-13	2-18	2-2	14.3	-27.02
Worcester	6-62	0-13	0-5	2-25	2-13	2-6	9.7	-30.75
Carlisle	5-15	2-3	0-0	2-4	1-6	0-2	33.3	+18.50
Nton Abbot	5-19	0-1	0-1	3-12	1-4	1-1	26.3	+7.50
Sandown	5-25	2-5	0-1	3-13	0-6	0-0	20.0	+15.56
Wetherby	5-26	3-9	0-3	1-7	1-7	0-0	19.2	-11.29
Uttoxeter	5-35	4-13	0-2	1-12	0-7	0-1	14.3	-8.62
Leicester	4-18	0-5	1-3	0-2	3-8	0-0	22.2	+6.50
Haydock	4-22	1-8	0-1	1-7	0-2	2-4	18.2	-5.50
Bangor	4-26	2-9	2-3	0-5	0-8	0-1	15.4	-18.66
Huntingdon	4-29	1-10	1-4	2-8	0-6	0-1	13.8	-12.71
Chepstow	4-30	2-8	0-2	1-9	1-7	0-4	13.3	-20.77
Plumpton	3-22	1-14	0-0	1-2	0-5	1-1	13.6	+28.50
Newbury	3-24	0-10	0-4	0-5	1-2	2-3	12.5	-10.00
Exeter	3-26	2-9	0-3	1-9	0-4	0-1	11.5	-3.80
Doncaster	2-2	1-1	0-0	0-0	1-1	0-0	100.0	+4.38
Hereford	2-9	1-4	0-0	0-2	0-0	1-3	22.2	+8.25
Folkestone	2-11	1-5	1-1	0-0	0-4	0-1	18.2	-3.77
Towcester	2-12	1-5	0-0	1-5	0-1	0-1	16.7	-7.65
Southwell	2-18	0-1	0-3	0-5	2-8	0-1	11.1	-6.00
Warwick	2-18	0-5	2-7	0-4	0-2	0-0	11.1	-14.63
Ludlow	2-20	1-9	1-2	0-5	0-2	0-2	10.0	-14.52
Aintree	2-25	1-4	0-5	1-5	0-9	0-2	8.0	-19.63
Sedgefield	1-2	0-1	1-1	0-0	0-0	0-0	50.0	-0.67
Newcastle	1-5	1-3	0-0	0-0	0-2	0-0	20.0	+2.50
Lingfield	1-7	0-2	0-1	1-1	0-3	0-0	14.3	+2.00
Fakenham	1-8	1-6	0-1	0-0	0-1	0-0	12.5	-6.27
Taunton	1-9	0-4	0-1	0-2	1-2	0-0	11.1	-1.00
Wincanton	1-17	1-9	0-0	0-5	0-1	0-2	5.9	-15.56
Fontwell	1-19	0-8	1-3	0-4	0-3	0-1	5.3	-13.00

WINNING HORSES

Horse	Races Run	1st	2nd	3rd	£
Black Jack Ketchum	5	5	0	0	125447
Bold Bishop	6	2	2	0	48337
Lingo	1	1	0	0	28510
Refinement	7	6	0	1	65595
Fire Dragon	8	2	3	0	27612
Iris's Gift	6	3	1	0	31108
Olaso	3	1	0	1	13012
Hasty Prince	8	1	0	1	12526
Be My Better Half	8	1	1	2	12526
Ursis	4	2	0	0	19315
Nor'Nor'East	5	2	1	1	14285
Exotic Dancer	4	1	0	2	9864
Millenaire	7	3	0	0	23700
Feel The Pride	10	4	1	1	26469
Wild Is The Wind	7	1	3	0	7166
Two Miles West	4	1	1	1	7053
Schapiro	2	1	0	0	6942
East Tycoon	8	1	0	0	6929
Tigers Lair	4	3	0	0	17831
Royal Hector	6	2	1	0	11479
The Pennys Dropped	2	1	0	1	6656
Alright Now M'Lad	5	2	0	0	10735
Mikado	8	2	2	0	9028
Be The Tops	4	1	1	1	5655
Personal Assurance	2	1	0	0	5551
Music To My Ears	2	1	0	1	5486
Spirit Of New York	3	2	0	0	7378
Lake Merced	8	2	1	1	9542
The Sister	5	1	0	0	5343
Don't Push It	2	2	0	0	7197
Old Feathers	7	1	0	1	5205
Clan Royal	4	1	0	2	5205
Manners	3	2	0	0	8133
Olival	4	1	0	1	5205
Catchthebug	3	2	0	0	8251
Zarakash	5	1	1	2	4854
Wee Anthony	7	1	0	0	4554
Inaro	5	1	2	0	4489
Youlbesolucky	10	2	2	2	6220
Fier Normand	5	2	1	0	7771
High Gear	7	2	1	1	6778
Englishtown	4	2	1	1	7606
Native Chancer	9	1	2	1	4134
*Sasso	4	1	0	1	4118
Parkinson	7	3	0	0	11060
Haloo Baloo	8	1	1	0	3904
Predator	6	1	2	0	3822
Wichita Lineman	4	2	0	0	5917
Taking My Cut	4	1	1	0	3578
Briscoe Place	5	2	0	0	3578
Gironde	2	1	1	0	3562
New Time	2	1	0	1	3445

Horse	Races Run	1st	2nd	3rd	£
Knife Edge	5	2	1	0	5413
*Darasim	3	1	1	0	3423
Goss	4	1	0	1	3326
Square Mile	3	1	0	1	3311
*Prize Fighter	6	1	0	1	3203
Money Line	6	1	0	0	3010
Long Road Home	2	1	0	0	2583
Albertas Run	3	2	0	0	3645
Cockspur	2	1	0	0	1713
Dancewiththedevil	3	1	0	0	1627
Drombeag	4	2	0	0	2249
Buck Whaley	2	1	0	0	0
Total winning prize-money					**£743169**
Favourites	50-130		38.5%		-21.22

J G M O'SHEA

ELTON, GLOUCS

	No. of Hrs	Races Run	1st	2nd	3rd	Unpl	Per cent	£1 Level Stake
NH Flat	6	12	0	0	1	11	0.0	-12.00
Hurdles	27	96	3	9	10	74	3.1	-83.42
Chases	6	8	0	0	0	8	0.0	-8.00
Totals	35	116	3	9	11	93	2.6	-103.42
04-05	32	143	10	17	14	102	7.0	-82.79
03-04	32	131	12	17	15	87	9.2	-89.17

JOCKEYS

	W-R	Per cent	£1 Level Stake
Andrew Thornton	1-3	33.3	+0.25
Nick Carter	1-6	16.7	-1.00
Steven Crawford	1-9	11.1	-4.67

COURSE RECORD

	Total W-R	Non-Hndcps Hurdles	Chases	Hndcps Hurdles	Chases	NH Flat	Per cent	£1 Level Stake
Hereford	2-29	1-15	0-0	1-6	0-4	0-4	6.9	-19.67
Towcester	1-4	1-3	0-0	0-0	0-0	0-1	25.0	-0.75

WINNING HORSES

Horse	Races Run	1st	2nd	3rd	£
Tom Bell	9	1	1	1	10589
Cullian	7	1	0	1	2602
Mickey Pearce	10	1	0	1	2082
Total winning prize-money					**£15273**
Favourites	1-5		20.0%		-0.67

J A B OLD

BARBURY CASTLE, WILTS

	No. of Hrs	Races Run	1st	2nd	3rd	Unpl	Per cent	£1 Level Stake
NH Flat	11	20	3	2	1	14	15.0	-2.00

Hurdles	30	71	7	8	0	56	9.9	-21.59
Chases	13	31	5	5	1	20	16.1	+9.44
Totals	**42**	**122**	**15**	**15**	**2**	**90**	**12.3**	**-14.15**
04-05	42	144	14	12	17	101	9.7	-47.38
03-04	45	130	9	14	14	93	6.9	-42.80

Class 2	3-6	50.0	+17.00	Hurdles	2-24	8.3	-1.00
Class 3	2-24	8.3	-8.50	Chases	1-7	14.3	+5.00
Class 4	6-62	9.7	-16.15				
Class 5	1-8	12.5	-2.50	Totals	3-42	7.1	-7.00
Class 6	3-15	20.0	+3.00				

BY MONTH

NH Flat	W-R	Per cent	£1 Level Stake	Hurdles	W-R	Per cent	£1 Level Stake
May	0-1	0.0	-1.00	May	0-4	0.0	-4.00
June	0-0	0.0	0.00	June	0-0	0.0	0.00
July	0-0	0.0	0.00	July	0-0	0.0	0.00
August	0-0	0.0	0.00	August	0-0	0.0	0.00
September	0-0	0.0	0.00	September	0-0	0.0	0.00
October	0-0	0.0	0.00	October	0-5	0.0	-5.00
November	0-2	0.0	-2.00	November	1-11	9.1	+4.00
December	0-2	0.0	-2.00	December	2-16	12.5	+2.00
January	1-2	50.0	+1.50	January	1-9	11.1	-0.50
February	1-3	33.3	+10.00	February	1-7	14.3	-3.50
March	0-5	0.0	-5.00	March	2-11	18.2	-6.59
April	1-5	20.0	-3.50	April	0-8	0.0	-8.00

Chases	W-R	Per cent	£1 Level Stake	Totals	W-R	Per cent	£1 Level Stake
May	0-1	0.0	-1.00	May	0-6	0.0	-6.00
June	0-0	0.0	0.00	June	0-0	0.0	0.00
July	0-0	0.0	0.00	July	0-0	0.0	0.00
August	0-0	0.0	0.00	August	0-0	0.0	0.00
September	0-0	0.0	0.00	September	0-0	0.0	0.00
October	0-0	0.0	0.00	October	0-5	0.0	-5.00
November	0-3	0.0	-3.00	November	1-16	6.3	-1.00
December	1-4	25.0	+8.00	December	3-22	13.6	+8.00
January	3-9	33.3	+18.00	January	5-20	25.0	+19.00
February	0-5	0.0	-5.00	February	2-15	13.3	+1.50
March	1-7	14.3	-5.56	March	3-23	13.0	-17.15
April	0-2	0.0	-2.00	April	1-15	6.7	-13.50

DISTANCE

Hurdles	W-R	Per cent	£1 Level Stake	Chases	W-R	Per cent	£1 Level Stake
2m-2m3f	0-39	0.0	-39.00	2m-2m3f	1-5	20.0	-3.56
2m4f-2m7f	2-16	12.5	-6.09	2m4f-2m7f	2-9	22.2	+1.00
3m+	5-16	31.3	+23.50	3m+	2-17	11.8	+12.00

TYPE OF RACE

Non-Handicaps	W-R	Per cent	£1 Level Stake	Handicaps	W-R	Per cent	£1 Level Stake
Nov Hrdls	4-32	12.5	-9.09	Nov Hrdls	1-10	10.0	-2.00
Hrdls	0-15	0.0	-15.00	Hrdls	2-14	14.3	+4.50
Nov Chs	1-5	20.0	+7.00	Nov Chs	0-4	0.0	-4.00
Chases	1-1	100.0	+0.44	Chases	3-21	14.3	+6.00
Sell/Claim	0-0	0.0	0.00	Sell/Claim	0-0	0.0	0.00

RACE CLASS

	W-R	Per cent	£1 Level Stake		W-R	Per cent	£1 Level Stake
Class 1	0-7	0.0	-7.00	Bumpers	0-11	0.0	-11.00

JOCKEYS

	W-R	Per cent	£1 Level Stake
Jason Maguire	8-58	13.8	-7.50
Mark Bradburne	4-20	20.0	+3.91
Timmy Murphy	1-3	33.3	+14.00
P J Brennan	1-7	14.3	-5.56
Wayne Hutchinson	1-19	5.3	-4.00

COURSE RECORD

	Total W-R	Non-Hndcps Hurdles	Non-Hndcps Chases	Hndcps Hurdles	Hndcps Chases	NH Flat	Per cent	£1 Level Stake
Warwick	3-10	2-2	1-2	0-2	0-2	0-2	30.0	+8.00
Cheltenham	2-5	0-3	0-0	2-2	0-0	0-0	40.0	+13.50
Folkestone	2-6	0-2	0-0	0-0	1-2	1-2	33.3	+3.00
Wincanton	2-7	0-0	0-0	1-2	1-4	0-1	28.6	+18.00
Towcester	2-12	1-6	0-0	0-3	0-0	1-3	16.7	+2.91
Windsor	1-1	1-1	0-0	0-0	0-0	0-0	100.0	+14.00
Leicester	1-6	0-3	1-1	0-1	0-1	0-0	16.7	-4.56
Lingfield	1-6	0-2	0-0	0-2	1-2	0-0	16.7	-1.50
Taunton	1-8	0-2	0-0	0-2	0-1	1-3	12.5	-6.50

WINNING HORSES

Horse	Races Run	1st	2nd	3rd	£
Attorney General	5	2	0	0	31302
Wain Mountain	7	1	1	0	16265
Kildonnan	6	2	2	0	10410
Boundary House	5	1	0	0	5704
The Duckpond	1	1	0	0	5413
Sargasso Sea	5	1	1	0	3999
Colline De Fleurs	6	2	3	0	5712
Smeathe's Ridge	5	1	1	0	3578
Thedreamstillalive	2	1	1	0	3570
Super Lord	4	1	0	1	3526
Kelv	2	1	0	0	2056
Top Ram	5	1	0	0	1627
Total winning prize-money					£93162
Favourites	5-10		50.0%		2.85

ROSS OLIVER

NEWQUAY, CORNWALL

	No. of Hrs	Races Run	1st	2nd	3rd	Unpl	Per cent	£1 Level Stake
NH Flat	0	0	0	0	0	0	0.0	0.00
Hurdles	0	0	0	0	0	0	0.0	0.00
Chases	1	5	1	0	0	4	20.0	+6.00
Totals	**1**	**5**	**1**	**0**	**0**	**4**	**20.0**	**+6.00**
04-05	1	3	1	0	1	1	33.3	+8.00

JOCKEYS

	W-R	Per cent	£1 Level Stake
Miss P Gundry	1-3	33.3	+8.00

COURSE RECORD

	Total W-R	Non-Hndcps Hurdles	Non-Hndcps Chases	Hndcps Hurdles	Hndcps Chases	NH Flat	Per cent	£1 Level Stake
Cheltenham	1-1	0-0	1-1	0-0	0-0	0-0	100.0	+10.00

WINNING HORSES

Horse	Races Run	1st	2nd	3rd	£
Let's Fly	5	1	0	0	3290
Total winning prize-money					£3290
Favourites	0-1		0.0%		-1.00

J F PANVERT

HILDENBOROUGH, KENT

	No. of Hrs	Races Run	1st	2nd	3rd	Unpl	Per cent	£1 Level Stake
NH Flat	2	2	0	0	0	2	0.0	-2.00
Hurdles	3	11	1	0	2	8	9.1	-6.00
Chases	1	1	0	0	0	1	0.0	-1.00
Totals	6	14	1	0	2	11	7.1	-9.00
04-05	4	7	0	0	0	7	0.0	-7.00
03-04	6	23	2	2	5	14	8.7	-4.00

JOCKEYS

	W-R	Per cent	£1 Level Stake
P J Brennan	1-10	10.0	-5.00

COURSE RECORD

	Total W-R	Non-Hndcps Hurdles	Non-Hndcps Chases	Hndcps Hurdles	Hndcps Chases	NH Flat	Per cent	£1 Level Stake
Fontwell	1-3	1-1	0-1	0-0	0-0	0-1	33.3	+2.00

WINNING HORSES

Horse	Races Run	1st	2nd	3rd	£
*Miss Merenda	6	1	0	1	3335
Total winning prize-money					£3335
Favourites	0-0		0.0%		0.00

A PARKER

ECCLEFECHAN, D'FRIES & G'WAY

	No. of Hrs	Races Run	1st	2nd	3rd	Unpl	Per cent	£1 Level Stake
NH Flat	4	6	0	0	0	6	0.0	-6.00
Hurdles	15	29	1	3	2	23	3.4	-24.00
Chases	9	43	1	4	5	33	2.3	-34.50
Totals	19	78	2	7	7	62	2.6	-64.50
04-05	18	100	8	9	9	74	8.0	-48.00
03-04	22	90	10	5	15	60	11.1	-11.60

JOCKEYS

	W-R	Per cent	£1 Level Stake
Timmy Murphy	1-3	33.3	+5.50
Alan Dempsey	1-37	2.7	-32.00

COURSE RECORD

	Total W-R	Non-Hndcps Hurdles	Non-Hndcps Chases	Hndcps Hurdles	Hndcps Chases	NH Flat	Per cent	£1 Level Stake
Uttoxeter	1-3	0-0	0-0	1-2	0-1	0-0	33.3	+2.00
Ayr	1-14	0-2	0-0	0-2	1-8	0-2	7.1	-5.50

WINNING HORSES

Horse	Races Run	1st	2nd	3rd	£
D J Flippance	7	1	1	0	6792
Overserved	2	1	0	0	5790
Total winning prize-money					£12582
Favourites	0-1		0.0%		-1.00

DAVE PARKER

CAPHEATON, NORTHUMB

	No. of Hrs	Races Run	1st	2nd	3rd	Unpl	Per cent	£1 Level Stake
NH Flat	0	0	0	0	0	0	0.0	0.00
Hurdles	0	0	0	0	0	0	0.0	0.00
Chases	2	2	1	1	0	0	50.0	+1.25
Totals	2	2	1	1	0	0	50.0	+1.25
04-05	1	2	1	0	0	1	50.0	+9.00
03-04	2	3	0	0	1	2	0.0	-3.00

JOCKEYS

	W-R	Per cent	£1 Level Stake
Miss P Robson	1-2	50.0	+1.25

COURSE RECORD

	Total W-R	Non-Hndcps Hurdles	Non-Hndcps Chases	Hndcps Hurdles	Hndcps Chases	NH Flat	Per cent	£1 Level Stake
Carlisle	1-1	0-0	1-1	0-0	0-0	0-0	100.0	+2.25

WINNING HORSES

Horse	Races Run	1st	2nd	3rd	£
Mr Woodentop	1	1	0	0	1978
Total winning prize-money					£1978
Favourites	1-2		50.0%		1.25

J R PAYNE

BROMPTON REGIS, SOMERSET

	No. of Hrs	Races Run	1st	2nd	3rd	Unpl	Per cent	£1 Level Stake
NH Flat	2	4	0	0	0	4	0.0	-4.00
Hurdles	0	0	0	0	0	0	0.0	0.00
Chases	1	4	1	0	0	3	25.0	+8.00
Totals	**3**	**8**	**1**	**0**	**0**	**7**	**12.5**	**+4.00**
04-05	3	13	1	0	1	11	7.7	-5.50
03-04	3	20	1	5	1	13	5.0	-11.00

JOCKEYS

	W-R	Per cent	£1 Level Stake
Christian Williams	1-2	50.0	+10.00

COURSE RECORD

	Total W-R	Non-Hndcps Hurdles	Chases	Hndcps Hurdles	Chases	NH Flat	Per cent	£1 Level Stake
Nton Abbot	1-3	0-0	0-0	0-0	1-2	0-1	33.3	+9.00

WINNING HORSES

Horse	Races Run	1st	2nd	3rd	£
Athnowen	4	1	0	0	4761
Total winning prize-money					**£4761**
Favourites	0-0		0.0%		0.00

MRS A J PERRETT

PULBOROUGH, W SUSSEX

	No. of Hrs	Races Run	1st	2nd	3rd	Unpl	Per cent	£1 Level Stake
NH Flat	0	0	0	0	0	0	0.0	0.00
Hurdles	6	7	1	0	0	6	14.3	+3.00
Chases	1	3	1	0	1	1	33.3	-1.00
Totals	**6**	**10**	**2**	**0**	**1**	**7**	**20.0**	**+2.00**
04-05	3	9	0	3	2	4	0.0	-9.00
03-04	7	25	7	6	6	6	28.0	+1.18

JOCKEYS

	W-R	Per cent	£1 Level Stake
Jim Crowley	2-10	20.0	+2.00-

COURSE RECORD

	Total W-R	Non-Hndcps Hurdles	Chases	Hndcps Hurdles	Chases	NH Flat	Per cent	£1 Level Stake
Nton Abbot	1-2	1-2	0-0	0-0	0-0	0-0	50.0	+8.00
Plumpton	1-4	0-2	1-2	0-0	0-0	0-0	25.0	-2.00

WINNING HORSES

Horse	Races Run	1st	2nd	3rd	£
Big Moment	4	1	0	1	5429
Dream Along	2	1	0	0	5356
Total winning prize-money					**£10785**
Favourites	1-2		50.0%		0.00

R T PHILLIPS

ADLESTROP, GLOUCS

	No. of Hrs	Races Run	1st	2nd	3rd	Unpl	Per cent	£1 Level Stake
NH Flat	14	21	3	2	3	13	14.3	-7.50
Hurdles	45	123	9	8	13	93	7.3	-78.47
Chases	24	64	5	7	9	43	7.8	+25.13
Totals	**63**	**208**	**17**	**17**	**25**	**149**	**8.2**	**-60.04**
04-05	59	192	27	17	19	129	14.1	-3.96
03-04	55	152	13	12	11	116	8.6	-94.82

BY MONTH

NH Flat	W-R	Per cent	£1 Level Stake	Hurdles	W-R	Per cent	£1 Level Stake
May	1-1	100.0	+2.75	May	0-9	0.0	-9.00
June	0-1	0.0	-1.00	June	0-1	0.0	-1.00
July	0-1	0.0	-1.00	July	0-2	0.0	-2.00
August	0-0	0.0	0.00	August	0-7	0.0	-7.00
September	0-0	0.0	0.00	September	0-0	0.0	0.00
October	0-0	0.0	0.00	October	0-1	0.0	-1.00
November	1-2	50.0	+0.75	November	2-12	16.7	-5.14
December	1-5	20.0	+2.00	December	4-17	23.5	+11.00
January	0-1	0.0	-1.00	January	1-22	4.5	-20.33
February	0-2	0.0	-2.00	February	0-15	0.0	-15.00
March	0-6	0.0	-6.00	March	1-19	5.3	-16.50
April	0-2	0.0	-2.00	April	1-18	5.6	-12.50

Chases	W-R	Per cent	£1 Level Stake	Totals	W-R	Per cent	£1 Level Stake
May	1-4	25.0	+30.00	May	2-14	14.3	+23.75
June	0-2	0.0	-2.00	June	0-4	0.0	-4.00
July	0-0	0.0	0.00	July	0-3	0.0	-3.00
August	0-0	0.0	0.00	August	0-7	0.0	-7.00
September	0-1	0.0	-1.00	September	0-1	0.0	-1.00
October	0-0	0.0	0.00	October	0-1	0.0	-1.00
November	1-7	14.3	+8.00	November	4-21	19.0	+3.61
December	1-6	16.7	+28.00	December	6-28	21.4	+41.00
January	0-8	0.0	-8.00	January	1-31	3.2	-29.33
February	0-12	0.0	-12.00	February	0-29	0.0	-29.00
March	2-9	22.2	-2.88	March	3-34	8.8	-25.38
April	0-15	0.0	-15.00	April	1-35	2.9	-29.50

DISTANCE

Hurdles	W-R	Per cent	£1 Level Stake	Chases	W-R	Per cent	£1 Level Stake
2m-2m3f	4-42	9.5	-19.14	2m-2m3f	0-8	0.0	-8.00

2m4f-2m7f	2-50	4.0	-38.00	2m4f-2m7f	4-29	13.8	+26.13
3m+	3-31	9.7	-21.33	3m+	1-27	3.7	+7.00

TYPE OF RACE

Non-Handicaps	W-R	Per cent	£1 Level Stake	Handicaps	W-R	Per cent	£1 Level Stake
Nov Hrdls	3-55	5.5	-47.47	Nov Hrdls	2-10	20.0	+6.00
Hrdls	3-18	16.7	-2.50	Hrdls	1-39	2.6	-33.50
Nov Chs	2-20	10.0	-13.88	Nov Chs	1-7	14.3	+27.00
Chases	0-2	0.0	-2.00	Chases	2-35	5.7	+14.00
Sell/Claim	0-0	0.0	0.00	Sell/Claim	0-2	0.0	-2.00

RACE CLASS / FIRST TIME OUT

	W-R	Per cent	£1 Level Stake		W-R	Per cent	£1 Level Stake
Class 1	0-4	0.0	-4.00	Bumpers	3-14	21.4	-0.50
Class 2	0-4	0.0	-4.00	Hurdles	3-34	8.8	-19.64
Class 3	4-56	7.1	+0.17	Chases	2-15	13.3	+34.00
Class 4	9-112	8.0	-37.01				
Class 5	1-13	7.7	-10.50	Totals	8-63	12.7	+13.86
Class 6	3-19	15.8	-5.50				

JOCKEYS

	W-R	Per cent	£1 Level Stake
Richard Johnson	8-61	13.1	+6.41
Sean Quinlan	3-27	11.1	-4.00
Warren Marston	3-59	5.1	-47.00
Wayne Hutchinson	1-8	12.5	-4.75
Robert Thornton	1-12	8.3	-4.50
Jimmy McCarthy	1-17	5.9	+17.00

COURSE RECORD

	Total W-R	Non-Hndcps Hurdles	Chases	Hndcps Hurdles	Chases	NH Flat	Per cent	£1 Level Stake
Uttoxeter	3-13	1-6	0-1	0-1	0-1	2-4	23.1	-1.89
Towcester	2-16	1-5	1-4	0-2	0-2	0-3	12.5	-7.25
Chepstow	2-20	0-4	0-4	1-4	1-5	0-3	10.0	+19.50
Doncaster	1-1	0-0	0-0	1-1	0-0	0-0	100.0	+6.00
Carlisle	1-4	0-1	1-3	0-0	0-0	0-0	25.0	-1.13
Mrket Rsn	1-4	0-2	0-0	0-1	0-0	1-1	25.0	-0.25
Plumpton	1-4	1-3	0-0	0-1	0-0	0-0	25.0	+0.50
Stratford	1-4	0-1	0-0	0-2	1-1	0-0	25.0	+30.00
Windsor	1-4	1-2	0-0	0-1	0-1	0-0	25.0	+3.50
Newcastle	1-6	0-1	0-0	0-2	0-1	0-1	16.7	-4.33
Huntingdon	1-8	0-1	0-0	0-3	1-3	0-1	12.5	+7.00
Exeter	1-12	0-3	0-1	1-6	0-2	0-0	8.3	-3.00
Worcester	1-15	1-6	0-2	0-2	0-3	0-2	6.7	-12.50

WINNING HORSES

Horse	Races Run	1st	2nd	3rd	£
Dark'n Sharp	3	1	0	0	7222
Lonesome Man	2	1	0	0	6877
On Y Va	5	2	0	1	10221
Cash And New	5	1	1	2	5010
Datito	4	1	1	0	4157
Sharp Jack	6	1	1	0	3904
Giovanna	3	1	0	1	3803
Caesarean Hunter	8	2	1	0	6704
What A Vintage	5	2	1	0	5325
Pedros Brief	3	1	0	0	3299
The Mick Weston	3	1	0	0	2987
Return Ticket	4	1	0	0	2398
Baron Romeo	6	1	1	0	2008
Alaskan Fizz	2	1	0	0	1995
Total winning prize-money					£65910
Favourites	5-18		27.8%		-6.47

S PIKE

SIDBURY, DEVON

	No. of Hrs	Races Run	1st	2nd	3rd	Unpl	Per cent	£1 Level Stake
NH Flat	1	3	1	0	0	2	33.3	+14.00
Hurdles	0	0	0	0	0	0	0.0	0.00
Chases	0	0	0	0	0	0	0.0	0.00
Totals	1	3	1	0	0	2	33.3	+14.00
04-05	1	2	0	1	0	1	0.0	-2.00
03-04	2	7	1	0	1	5	14.3	-5.75

JOCKEYS

	W-R	Per cent	£1 Level Stake
Robert Thornton	1-2	50.0	+15.00

COURSE RECORD

	Total W-R	Non-Hndcps Hurdles	Chases	Hndcps Hurdles	Chases	NH Flat	Per cent	£1 Level Stake
Warwick	1-1	0-0	0-0	0-0	0-0	1-1	100.0	+16.00

WINNING HORSES

Horse	Races Run	1st	2nd	3rd	£
Sovietica	3	1	0	0	1939
Total winning prize-money					£1939
Favourites	0-0		0.0%		0.00

M C PIPE

NICHOLASHAYNE, DEVON

	No. of Hrs	Races Run	1st	2nd	3rd	Unpl	Per cent	£1 Level Stake
NH Flat	19	26	6	5	2	13	23.1	-6.13
Hurdles	149	568	61	69	53	385	10.7	-240.75
Chases	81	286	45	33	29	179	15.7	-30.70
Totals	195	880	112	107	84	577	12.7	-277.58
04-05	230	1185	195	135	101	753	16.5	-205.47
03-04	240	1099	180	129	111	679	16.4	-248.54

BY MONTH

NH Flat	W-R	Per cent	£1 Level Stake	Hurdles	W-R	Per cent	£1 Level Stake
May	0-3	0.0	-3.00	May	5-49	10.2	-4.46
June	0-2	0.0	-2.00	June	8-39	20.5	-6.12
July	1-2	50.0	+1.75	July	4-34	11.8	-21.82
August	1-2	50.0	+0.88	August	2-42	4.8	-37.52
September	1-3	33.3	+2.00	September	5-16	31.3	+9.38
October	0-2	0.0	-2.00	October	8-49	16.3	-8.99
November	1-4	25.0	-1.63	November	7-59	11.9	-22.38
December	1-1	100.0	+2.25	December	3-56	5.4	-43.09
January	0-0	0.0	0.00	January	6-62	9.7	-18.83
February	0-0	0.0	0.00	February	6-60	10.0	-23.00
March	0-5	0.0	-5.00	March	1-49	2.0	-46.25
April	1-2	50.0	+0.63	April	6-53	11.3	-17.66

Chases	W-R	Per cent	£1 Level Stake	Totals	W-R	Per cent	£1 Level Stake
May	2-20	10.0	-12.50	May	7-72	9.7	-19.96
June	2-19	10.5	-12.63	June	10-60	16.7	-20.75
July	7-18	38.9	+41.95	July	12-54	22.2	+21.88
August	3-17	17.6	-11.53	August	6-61	9.8	-48.17
September	1-7	14.3	-2.00	September	7-26	26.9	+9.38
October	1-8	12.5	+5.00	October	9-59	15.3	-5.99
November	6-33	18.2	-4.13	November	14-96	14.6	-28.14
December	3-29	10.3	-13.25	December	7-86	8.1	-54.09
January	6-27	22.2	-2.86	January	12-89	13.5	-21.69
February	7-33	21.2	-11.25	February	13-93	14.0	-34.25
March	3-39	7.7	-8.50	March	4-93	4.3	-50.75
April	4-36	11.1	+1.00	April	11-91	12.1	-16.03

DISTANCE

Hurdles	W-R	Per cent	£1 Level Stake	Chases	W-R	Per cent	£1 Level Stake
2m-2m3f	38-307	12.4	-116.98	2m-2m3f	14-77	18.2	-15.26
2m4f-2m7f	15-172	8.7	-80.38	2m4f-2m7f	21-98	21.4	+31.35
3m+	8-89	9.0	-43.40	3m+	10-111	9.0	-46.79

TYPE OF RACE

Non-Handicaps	W-R	Per cent	£1 Level Stake	Handicaps	W-R	Per cent	£1 Level Stake
Nov Hrdls	23-137	16.8	-76.04	Nov Hrdls	3-49	6.1	-30.13
Hrdls	5-53	9.4	-13.17	Hrdls	24-271	8.9	-92.78
Nov Chs	16-70	22.9	-25.08	Nov Chs	1-15	6.7	-11.50
Chases	3-19	15.8	-4.75	Chases	24-181	13.3	+7.13
Sell/Claim	5-36	13.9	-22.14	Sell/Claim	3-26	11.5	-3.17

RACE CLASS

	W-R	Per cent	£1 Level Stake
Class 1	13-152	8.6	-24.25
Class 2	7-103	6.8	-16.77
Class 3	40-231	17.3	-41.86
Class 4	35-305	11.5	-176.26
Class 5	11-66	16.7	-14.31
Class 6	6-23	26.1	-3.13

FIRST TIME OUT

	W-R	Per cent	£1 Level Stake
Bumpers	5-19	26.3	-2.38
Hurdles	14-124	11.3	-26.31
Chases	11-52	21.2	+24.88
Totals	30-195	15.4	-3.81

JOCKEYS

	W-R	Per cent	£1 Level Stake
Timmy Murphy	44-268	16.4	-70.75
A P McCoy	22-103	21.4	-39.69
Andrew Glassonbury	13-103	12.6	-9.98
Tom Scudamore	11-124	8.9	-65.77
Tom Malone	6-95	6.3	-47.92
Jamie Moore	5-33	15.2	+31.72
R J Greene	5-58	8.6	-11.20
Daryl Jacob	1-1	100.0	+10.00
Mr C Wallis	1-4	25.0	+0.50
Richard Johnson	1-5	20.0	-1.75
Paddy Merrigan	1-7	14.3	-0.50
Gerry Supple	1-18	5.6	-14.75
Robert Quinn	1-20	5.0	-16.50

COURSE RECORD

	Total W-R	Non-Hndcps Hurdles	Chases	Hndcps Hurdles	Chases	NH Flat	Per cent	£1 Level Stake
Nton Abbot	18-99	6-26	5-13	2-40	3-17	2-3	18.2	-35.90
Cheltenham	11-107	0-12	0-14	5-48	6-31	0-2	10.3	-28.00
Exeter	9-69	1-19	1-6	3-31	2-10	2-3	13.0	-24.13
Mrket Rsn	7-24	2-6	1-2	1-8	3-8	0-0	29.2	+32.48
Folkestone	5-14	3-10	0-0	2-4	0-0	0-0	35.7	+4.92
Stratford	5-30	3-9	0-2	1-9	0-7	1-3	16.7	-11.65
Taunton	5-45	4-21	1-2	0-18	0-4	0-0	11.1	-15.39
Haydock	4-24	1-1	2-2	1-15	0-6	0-0	16.7	+16.98
Chepstow	4-31	0-12	0-0	2-11	2-8	0-0	12.9	-6.88
Newbury	4-37	1-11	0-3	1-8	2-14	0-1	10.8	-4.75
Uttoxeter	4-46	1-8	2-3	0-22	1-10	0-3	8.7	-29.50
Lingfield	3-11	0-3	2-5	0-1	1-2	0-0	27.3	-2.50
Leicester	3-14	2-5	0-1	0-5	1-3	0-0	21.4	-5.34
Ludlow	3-28	1-10	1-6	1-9	0-3	0-0	10.7	-14.59
Wincanton	3-30	0-6	1-1	1-11	1-11	0-1	10.0	-13.75
Worcester	3-41	1-9	1-4	1-20	0-5	0-3	7.3	-20.13
Fakenham	2-6	0-1	0-2	1-2	1-1	0-0	33.3	+1.08
Bangor	2-11	2-5	0-0	0-2	0-3	0-1	18.2	-7.77
Plumpton	2-14	0-4	0-2	2-6	0-2	0-0	14.3	+2.50
Southwell	2-14	0-2	1-2	1-6	0-4	0-0	14.3	-10.10
Hereford	2-19	2-11	0-4	0-3	0-0	0-1	10.5	-14.77
Huntingdon	2-19	0-5	0-1	2-8	0-4	0-1	10.5	-10.00
Fontwell	2-20	0-5	0-2	1-8	1-5	0-0	10.0	-13.50
Aintree	2-33	1-5	1-3	0-13	0-11	0-1	6.1	-22.27
Windsor	1-2	0-1	0-0	1-1	0-0	0-0	50.0	+6.50
Wetherby	1-3	0-0	0-0	0-1	1-2	0-0	33.3	+7.00
Towcester	1-8	0-5	0-0	0-1	0-1	1-1	12.5	-5.63
Warwick	1-16	0-4	1-3	0-4	0-4	0-1	6.3	-13.50
Sandown	1-41	0-2	0-3	1-26	0-9	0-1	2.4	-15.00

WINNING HORSES

Horse	Races Run	1st	2nd	3rd	£
Celestial Gold	2	1	0	0	85530
Our Vic	5	3	0	0	148654
Desert Air	6	1	1	0	57020

Iris Bleu	6	1	0	0	39914	Earn Out	8	1	0	0	3031
Tango Royal	7	1	0	0	37700	Milan Deux Mille	5	1	1	1	2977
Therealbandit	5	1	0	0	29013	Lutea	4	1	0	0	2653
Standin Obligation	6	4	0	0	50515	Better Moment	11	2	0	2	5001
Don't Be Shy	7	2	1	0	39073	Saratogane	4	1	1	0	2487
Buena Vista	8	4	1	2	35899	*Strathtay	6	1	2	0	2330
Celtic Son	6	1	2	0	19957	Green Prospect	2	1	0	0	2247
Nous Voila	6	3	0	1	28140	Painter Man	1	1	0	0	2056
Joaaci	4	1	0	0	16910	Twelve Paces	5	1	0	1	1848
Acambo	5	2	0	1	22235	Flying Spur	6	1	0	0	1813
Mr Cool	5	1	0	0	16576	Horus	6	1	0	1	0

Total winning prize-money   **£1040243**

Favourites   64-160   40.0%   10.09

Itsmyboy	6	3	1	0	19809
Not Left Yet	6	1	2	0	11320
Bannow Strand	5	2	1	0	17310
*Getoutwhenyoucan	7	3	3	0	19841
Whispered Secret	13	4	3	1	22119
*Whirling	3	1	1	0	8346
Madison Du Berlais	7	3	0	3	20190
Windsor Boy	5	1	0	0	7807
Hever Road	7	2	1	2	14112
Korelo	7	1	0	2	7543
Bumper	4	1	1	0	7543
Nobody Tells Me	3	2	1	0	10704
*Wee Dinns	5	1	2	1	6889
Neveesou	3	1	1	0	6490
Yes My Lord	4	2	0	0	9266
Honan	17	5	2	2	20493
Tonic Du Charmil	9	3	4	0	16961
Lough Derg	6	1	1	1	5927
Sardagna	10	1	1	0	5558
Fontanesi	14	2	0	1	10903
Commercial Flyer	3	1	0	0	5530
Meneur De Jeu	4	1	0	1	5525
He's A Leader	1	1	0	0	5514
Time Bandit	2	1	0	1	5421
Figaro Du Rocher	8	1	3	0	5408
Kilty Storm	7	2	2	1	8288
Paro	4	2	0	1	5205
Cantgeton	10	3	0	2	13502
Yourman	5	2	2	0	9173
Dont Ask Me	7	1	1	1	4810
Alikat	13	1	2	1	4635
Red Echo	5	1	0	0	4554
Mioche D'Estruval	8	1	3	1	4527
Tamarinbleu	4	1	1	0	4384
Milord Lescribaa	3	1	2	0	4105
Basilea Star	3	1	1	0	3943
Magnifico	5	2	0	0	7163
Happy Shopper	8	1	0	0	3904
Bertiebanoo	4	1	0	0	3751
Fourty Acers	4	1	2	1	3533
Noble Sham	4	1	2	0	3452
Boulevardofdreams	4	1	2	0	3445
Philippa Yeates	2	1	0	0	3268
*Topkat	4	1	0	1	3253
Doc Row	4	1	0	1	3253
Wardash	10	3	1	0	7987

M PITMAN

UPPER LAMBOURN, BERKS

	No. of Hrs	Races Run	1st	2nd	3rd	Unpl	Per cent	£1 Level Stake
NH Flat	15	30	5	6	4	15	16.7	+17.38
Hurdles	24	61	8	6	8	39	13.1	-4.50
Chases	13	41	5	7	4	25	12.2	0.00
Totals	**45**	**132**	**18**	**19**	**16**	**79**	**13.6**	**+12.88**
04-05	44	167	23	19	19	106	13.8	-23.54
03-04	38	118	22	14	8	74	18.6	+16.57

BY MONTH

NH Flat	W-R	Per cent	£1 Level Stake	Hurdles	W-R	Per cent	£1 Level Stake
May	0-1	0.0	-1.00	May	1-7	14.3	+2.00
June	0-0	0.0	0.00	June	0-3	0.0	-3.00
July	0-0	0.0	0.00	July	0-1	0.0	-1.00
August	0-0	0.0	0.00	August	0-1	0.0	-1.00
September	0-0	0.0	0.00	September	1-1	100.0	+3.50
October	2-3	66.7	+3.50	October	2-5	40.0	+7.50
November	0-6	0.0	-6.00	November	1-10	10.0	-3.00
December	0-3	0.0	-3.00	December	0-12	0.0	-12.00
January	2-6	33.3	+0.88	January	1-9	11.1	-5.50
February	0-5	0.0	-5.00	February	0-6	0.0	-6.00
March	1-5	20.0	+29.00	March	2-6	33.3	+14.00
April	0-1	0.0	-1.00	April	0-0	0.0	0.00

Chases	W-R	Per cent	£1 Level Stake	Totals	W-R	Per cent	£1 Level Stake
May	0-2	0.0	-2.00	May	1-10	10.0	-1.00
June	0-2	0.0	-2.00	June	0-5	0.0	-5.00
July	0-0	0.0	0.00	July	0-1	0.0	-1.00
August	0-0	0.0	0.00	August	0-1	0.0	-1.00
September	0-0	0.0	0.00	September	1-1	100.0	+3.50
October	2-3	66.7	+10.50	October	6-11	54.5	+21.50
November	2-8	25.0	+10.00	November	3-24	12.5	+1.00
December	0-1	0.0	-1.00	December	0-16	0.0	-16.00
January	1-12	8.3	-2.50	January	4-27	14.8	-7.12
February	0-6	0.0	-6.00	February	0-17	0.0	-17.00
March	0-5	0.0	-5.00	March	3-16	18.8	+38.00
April	0-2	0.0	-2.00	April	0-3	0.0	-3.00

DISTANCE

Hurdles	W-R	Per cent	£1 Level Stake	Chases	W-R	Per cent	£1 Level Stake
2m-2m3f	1-30	3.3	-26.50	2m-2m3f	2-8	25.0	+8.50
2m4f-2m7f	6-24	25.0	+24.00	2m4f-2m7f	2-17	11.8	+0.50
3m+	1-7	14.3	-2.00	3m+	1-16	6.3	-9.00

TYPE OF RACE

Non-Handicaps	W-R	Per cent	£1 Level Stake	Handicaps	W-R	Per cent	£1 Level Stake
Nov Hrdls	4-28	14.3	-5.00	Nov Hrdls	0-6	0.0	-6.00
Hrdls	1-4	25.0	+1.00	Hrdls	3-22	13.6	+6.50
Nov Chs	1-8	12.5	-1.00	Nov Chs	0-0	0.0	0.00
Chases	0-2	0.0	-2.00	Chases	4-31	12.9	+3.00
Sell/Claim	0-1	0.0	-1.00	Sell/Claim	0-0	0.0	0.00

RACE CLASS

	W-R	Per cent	£1 Level Stake
Class 1	1-17	5.9	-14.13
Class 2	2-6	33.3	+10.50
Class 3	3-33	9.1	-7.00
Class 4	7-39	17.9	+11.00
Class 5	2-14	14.3	+25.00
Class 6	3-23	13.0	-12.50

FIRST TIME OUT

	W-R	Per cent	£1 Level Stake
Bumpers	3-15	20.0	-4.50
Hurdles	3-20	15.0	+8.50
Chases	3-10	30.0	+13.50
Totals	9-45	20.0	+17.50

JOCKEYS

	W-R	Per cent	£1 Level Stake
Timmy Murphy	4-13	30.8	+12.38
Andrew Tinkler	4-22	18.2	+9.00
Paul Moloney	3-27	11.1	-9.50
Robert Lucey-Butler	2-10	20.0	-1.00
Noel Fehily	2-12	16.7	+1.50
Carl Llewellyn	2-27	7.4	+18.00
William Kennedy	1-2	50.0	+1.50

COURSE RECORD

	Total W-R	Non-Hndcps Hurdles	Chases	Hndcps Hurdles	Chases	NH Flat	Per cent	£1 Level Stake
Warwick	3-5	1-1	0-0	1-1	0-1	1-2	60.0	+19.88
Newbury	2-5	0-0	0-1	0-0	1-2	1-2	40.0	+40.00
Fakenham	2-6	0-3	0-1	1-1	0-0	1-1	33.3	+6.00
Plumpton	2-8	1-3	0-1	1-2	0-0	0-2	25.0	+1.00
Sandown	2-9	0-1	1-1	0-2	1-4	0-1	22.2	+7.50
Southwell	1-2	0-0	0-0	0-0	0-1	1-1	50.0	+2.00
Lingfield	1-3	1-3	0-0	0-0	0-0	0-0	33.3	+0.50
Wetherby	1-3	1-2	0-0	0-0	0-0	0-1	33.3	+2.00
Bangor	1-4	1-2	0-0	0-0	0-0	0-2	25.0	+4.00
Exeter	1-5	0-0	0-0	0-0	1-3	0-2	20.0	+1.50
Huntingdon	1-5	0-1	0-1	0-1	1-1	0-1	20.0	+2.00
Uttoxeter	1-9	0-3	0-1	0-1	0-2	1-2	11.1	-5.50

WINNING HORSES

Horse	Races Run	1st	2nd	3rd	£
Run For Paddy	5	1	1	0	13437
Too Forward	5	1	1	0	12626
Dempsey	3	1	1	0	12526
Roll Along	2	2	0	0	8927
Without A Doubt	5	1	1	1	5465
Good Samaritan	3	1	1	0	4915
Bay Island	8	1	3	1	4784
*Be My Destiny	1	1	0	0	4111
Red Dahlia	8	2	1	2	7016
Ask The Gatherer	5	2	0	1	6791
Snakebite	4	1	2	0	3253
Pontiff	2	1	0	1	3083
Joyryder	2	1	0	0	2056
Nightfly	2	1	0	0	2056
Hennessy	4	1	1	0	1981
Total winning prize-money					**£93027**
Favourites	3-13	23.1%			-2.63

C T POGSON

FARNSFIELD, NOTTS

	No. of Hrs	Races Run	1st	2nd	3rd	Unpl	Per cent	£1 Level Stake
NH Flat	1	2	0	0	0	2	0.0	-2.00
Hurdles	8	42	5	7	2	28	11.9	-15.75
Chases	5	8	0	1	1	6	0.0	-8.00
Totals	10	52	5	8	3	36	9.6	-25.75
04-05	9	63	8	10	7	38	12.7	+58.50
03-04	6	40	4	6	4	26	10.0	+102.00

JOCKEYS

	W-R	Per cent	£1 Level Stake
Adam Pogson	5-52	9.6	-25.75

COURSE RECORD

	Total W-R	Non-Hndcps Hurdles	Chases	Hndcps Hurdles	Chases	NH Flat	Per cent	£1 Level Stake
Sedgefield	3-6	3-4	0-1	0-0	0-0	0-1	50.0	+3.25
Towcester	1-3	1-3	0-0	0-0	0-0	0-0	33.3	+1.00
Uttoxeter	1-11	0-6	0-0	1-5	0-0	0-0	9.1	+2.00

WINNING HORSES

Horse	Races Run	1st	2nd	3rd	£
Emmasflora	12	3	2	2	11290
Major Catch	8	1	2	0	2928
Idlewild	12	1	1	0	2401
Total winning prize-money					**£16619**
Favourites	2-6	33.3%			-0.25

B N POLLOCK

MEDBOURNE, LEICS

	No. of Hrs	Races Run	1st	2nd	3rd	Unpl	Per cent	£1 Level Stake
NH Flat	1	1	0	0	0	1	0.0	-1.00
Hurdles	18	49	3	3	2	41	6.1	-22.75
Chases	11	38	4	4	2	28	10.5	+8.50
Totals	24	88	7	7	4	70	8.0	-15.25
04-05	19	60	5	4	3	48	8.3	+8.50
03-04	18	45	1	8	6	30	2.2	-40.67

JOCKEYS

	W-R	Per cent	£1 Level Stake
Tom Messenger	5-66	7.6	-12.25
Andrew Thornton	2-17	11.8	+2.00

COURSE RECORD

	Total W-R	Non-Hndcps Hurdles	Chases	Hndcps Hurdles	Chases	NH Flat	Per cent	£1 Level Stake
Towcester	2-13	0-3	0-1	0-1	2-7	0-1	15.4	+14.50
Catterick	1-1	1-1	0-0	0-0	0-0	0-0	100.0	+2.25
Southwell	1-3	0-0	0-0	0-0	1-3	0-0	33.3	+14.00
Uttoxeter	1-5	1-4	0-0	0-1	0-0	0-0	20.0	+3.00
Fakenham	1-6	0-1	0-1	1-4	0-0	0-0	16.7	+9.00
Leicester	1-9	0-3	1-3	0-0	0-3	0-0	11.1	-7.00

WINNING HORSES

Horse	Races Run	1st	2nd	3rd	£
A Glass In Thyne	3	1	0	0	34212
Launde	6	1	2	0	4754
Never Awol	8	2	1	0	7654
Beau Torero	2	2	0	0	5994
*Prairie Law	10	1	1	0	2082
Total winning prize-money					£54696
Favourites	2-4		50.0%		1.25

MRS NORMA POOK

PENN BOTTOM, BUCKS

	No. of Hrs	Races Run	1st	2nd	3rd	Unpl	Per cent	£1 Level Stake
NH Flat	1	2	0	0	1	1	0.0	-2.00
Hurdles	3	5	1	0	0	4	20.0	+10.00
Chases	0	0	0	0	0	0	0.0	0.00
Totals	3	7	1	0	1	5	14.3	+8.00

JOCKEYS

	W-R	Per cent	£1 Level Stake
Willie McCarthy	1-1	100.0	+14.00

COURSE RECORD

	Total W-R	Non-Hndcps Hurdles	Chases	Hndcps Hurdles	Chases	NH Flat	Per cent	£1 Level Stake
Mrket Rsn	1-1	0-0	0-0	1-1	0-0	0-0	100.0	+14.00

WINNING HORSES

Horse	Races Run	1st	2nd	3rd	£
Malay	1	1	0	0	5205
Total winning prize-money					£5205
Favourites	0-0		0.0%		0.00

C L POPHAM

WEST BAGBOROUGH, SOMERSET

	No. of Hrs	Races Run	1st	2nd	3rd	Unpl	Per cent	£1 Level Stake
NH Flat	2	6	0	0	1	5	0.0	-6.00
Hurdles	10	31	1	3	2	25	3.2	-24.50
Chases	4	18	1	2	1	14	5.6	-10.00
Totals	13	55	2	5	4	44	3.6	-40.50
04-05	7	23	0	3	3	17	0.0	-23.00
03-04	11	41	0	3	6	32	0.0	-41.00

JOCKEYS

	W-R	Per cent	£1 Level Stake
Robert Walford	1-16	6.3	-9.50
Tom Messenger	1-18	5.6	-10.00

COURSE RECORD

	Total W-R	Non-Hndcps Hurdles	Chases	Hndcps Hurdles	Chases	NH Flat	Per cent	£1 Level Stake
Towcester	2-8	1-4	0-0	0-0	1-3	0-1	25.0	+6.50

WINNING HORSES

Horse	Races Run	1st	2nd	3rd	£
Purple Patch	8	1	2	1	5192
*Petolinski	6	1	2	0	4368
Total winning prize-money					£9560
Favourites	0-0		0.0%		0.00

J G PORTMAN

COMPTON, BERKS

	No. of Hrs	Races Run	1st	2nd	3rd	Unpl	Per cent	£1 Level Stake
NH Flat	3	4	0	0	0	4	0.0	-4.00
Hurdles	9	28	3	2	1	22	10.7	-17.09
Chases	5	20	3	2	3	12	15.0	-1.50
Totals	14	52	6	4	4	38	11.5	-22.59

04-05	19	73	5	5	5	58	6.8	-42.95
03-04	14	62	8	10	11	33	12.9	-22.34

JOCKEYS

	W-R	Per cent	£1 Level Stake
Joe Tizzard	3-12	25.0	+1.50
Timmy Murphy	1-6	16.7	-2.00
Andrew Tinkler	1-7	14.3	-5.09
Stephen Craine	1-10	10.0	0.00

COURSE RECORD

	Total W-R	Non-Hndcps Hurdles	Chases	Hndcps Hurdles	Chases	NH Flat	Per cent	£1 Level Stake
Chepstow	1-2	0-0	0-0	0-0	1 2	0-0	50.0	+8.00
Exeter	1-3	0-0	0-1	1-1	0-1	0-0	33.3	+2.00
Fontwell	1-3	1-1	0-0	0-1	0-1	0-0	33.3	-1.09
Stratford	1-3	0-0	0-0	0-2	1-1	0-0	33.3	+2.00
Taunton	1-3	0-0	0-0	1-3	0-0	0-0	33.3	+1.00
Wincanton	1-5	0-0	0-0	0-1	1-4	0-0	20.0	-1.50

WINNING HORSES

Horse	Races Run	1st	2nd	3rd	£
*L'Oiseau	5	2	0	1	10306
Hiers De Brouage	8	1	0	2	5322
Dash For Cover	3	1	1	0	3549
*Desert Secrets	9	1	1	1	3253
*Lizzie Bathwick	3	1	2	0	2741
Total winning prize-money					**£25171**
Favourites	**3-4**		**75.0%**		**5.41**

JAMIE POULTON

TELSCOMBE, E SUSSEX

	No. of Hrs	Races Run	1st	2nd	3rd	Unpl	Per cent	£1 Level Stake
NH Flat	1	2	1	0	0	1	50.0	+8.00
Hurdles	5	15	0	1	2	12	0.0	-15.00
Chases	3	12	1	2	3	6	8.3	-8.50
Totals	**8**	**29**	**2**	**3**	**5**	**19**	**6.9**	**15.50**
04-05	7	27	3	4	1	19	11.1	-2.50
03-04	11	33	4	3	2	24	12.1	+5.00

JOCKEYS

	W-R	Per cent	£1 Level Stake
Colin Bolger	1-12	8.3	-8.50
Matthew Batchelor	1-17	5.9	-7.00

COURSE RECORD

	Total W-R	Non-Hndcps Hurdles	Chases	Hndcps Hurdles	Chases	NH Flat	Per cent	£1 Level Stake
Fontwell	1-6	0-3	0-0	0-2	0-0	1-1	16.7	+4.00
Plumpton	1-6	0-0	0-2	0-1	1-3	0-0	16.7	-2.50

WINNING HORSES

Horse	Races Run	1st	2nd	3rd	£
Tommy Carson	9	1	2	2	4791
Pairtree	2	1	0	0	1904
Total winning prize-money					**£6695**
Favourites	**0-0**		**0.0%**		**0.00**

B G POWELL

MORESTEAD, HANTS

	No. of Hrs	Races Run	1st	2nd	3rd	Unpl	Per cent	£1 Level Stake
NH Flat	18	26	4	3	3	16	15.4	+22.00
Hurdles	64	201	19	16	19	147	9.5	-82.27
Chases	34	103	9	14	8	71	8.7	-43.00
Totals	**90**	**330**	**32**	**33**	**30**	**234**	**9.7**	**-103.27**
04-05	89	258	27	30	26	175	10.5	+56.74
03-04	72	220	21	16	21	162	9.5	-64.93

BY MONTH

NH Flat	W-R	Per cent	£1 Level Stake	Hurdles	W-R	Per cent	£1 Level Stake
May	2-4	50.0	+14.00	May	0-12	0.0	12.00
June	0-1	0.0	-1.00	June	0-14	0.0	-14.00
July	0-0	0.0	0.00	July	0-7	0.0	-7.00
August	0-0	0.0	0.00	August	1-9	11.1	-4.00
September	0-0	0.0	0.00	September	1-11	9.1	-6.50
October	1-1	100.0	+16.00	October	4-14	28.6	+0.32
November	1-4	25.0	+9.00	November	0-23	0.0	-23.00
December	0-5	0.0	-5.00	December	2-23	8.7	-17.20
January	0-3	0.0	-3.00	January	6-22	27.3	+22.94
February	0-3	0.0	-3.00	February	0-18	0.0	-18.00
March	0-0	0.0	0.00	March	1-21	4.8	-11.50
April	0-5	0.0	-5.00	April	4-27	14.8	+7.67

Chases	W-R	Per cent	£1 Level Stake	Totals	W-R	Per cent	£1 Level Stake
May	1-10	10.0	-4.50	May	3-26	11.5	-2.50
June	0-5	0.0	-5.00	June	0-20	0.0	-20.00
July	1 5	20.0	+1.50	July	1-12	8.3	-5.50
August	0-6	0.0	-6.00	August	1-15	6.7	-10.00
September	1-2	50.0	+1.50	September	2-13	15.4	-5.00
October	0-7	0.0	-7.00	October	5-22	22.7	+9.32
November	1-10	10.0	-4.00	November	2-37	5.4	-18.00
December	1-11	9.1	-5.50	December	3-39	7.7	-27.70
January	0-11	0.0	-11.00	January	6-36	16.7	+8.94
February	0-9	0.0	-9.00	February	0-30	0.0	-30.00
March	2-13	15.4	+2.00	March	3-34	8.8	-9.50
April	2-14	14.3	+4.00	April	6-46	13.0	+6.67

DISTANCE

Hurdles	W-R	Per cent	£1 Level Stake	Chases	W-R	Per cent	£1 Level Stake
2m-2m3f	15-117	12.8	-14.78	2m-2m3f	3-20	15.0	-1.50

| 2m4f-2m7f | 3-69 | 4.3 | -61.98 | 2m4f-2m7f | 4-43 | 9.3 | -13.00 |
| 3m+ | 1-15 | 6.7 | -5.50 | 3m+ | 2-40 | 5.0 | -28.50 |

TYPE OF RACE

Non-Handicaps	W-R	Per cent	£1 Level Stake	Handicaps	W-R	Per cent	£1 Level Stake
Nov Hrdls	13-89	14.6	-16.23	Nov Hrdls	1-13	7.7	-8.50
Hrdls	2-20	10.0	-16.53	Hrdls	1-62	1.6	-58.00
Nov Chs	2-23	8.7	-9.50	Nov Chs	0-17	0.0	-17.00
Chases	1-9	11.1	-5.50	Chases	5-52	9.6	-14.50
Sell/Claim	0-12	0.0	-12.00	Sell/Claim	2-7	28.6	+27.00

RACE CLASS / FIRST TIME OUT

	W-R	Per cent	£1 Level Stake		W-R	Per cent	£1 Level Stake
Class 1	0-8	0.0	-8.00	Bumpers	3-18	16.7	+13.00
Class 2	0-9	0.0	-9.00	Hurdles	2-53	3.8	-27.00
Class 3	4-74	5.4	-58.48	Chases	1-19	5.3	-13.50
Class 4	22-180	12.2	-50.78				
Class 5	2-33	6.1	+1.00	Totals	6-90	6.7	-27.50
Class 6	4-26	15.4	+22.00				

JOCKEYS

	W-R	Per cent	£1 Level Stake
Timmy Murphy	10-49	20.4	-3.18
Johnny Levins	5-49	10.2	-23.95
Charlie Studd	5-67	7.5	+13.00
A P McCoy	2-4	50.0	-0.31
G Lee	2-5	40.0	+5.00
Mr S P Jones	2-8	25.0	+14.00
Joe Tizzard	2-23	8.7	-12.50
Mr S Walker	1-1	100.0	+12.00
Tom Doyle	1-7	14.3	+2.50
Robert Thornton	1-7	14.3	-5.33
James Davies	1-41	2.4	-35.50

COURSE RECORD

	Total W-R	Non-Hndcps Hurdles	Chases	Hndcps Hurdles	Chases	NH Flat	Per cent	£1 Level Stake
Fontwell	8-43	6-20	1-4	1-10	0-6	0-3	18.6	-10.58
Worcester	4-27	0-6	1-4	0-4	2-11	1-2	14.8	+7.00
Hereford	3-10	2-5	0-1	0-0	0-1	1-3	30.0	+26.25
Taunton	3-11	0-4	0-1	2-3	1-2	0-1	27.3	+8.50
Ludlow	3-14	1-3	0-3	1-4	0-2	1-2	21.4	+20.75
Fakenham	2-4	2-2	0-0	0-0	0-0	0-2	50.0	-0.76
Towcester	2-16	0-5	2-3	0-6	0-1	0-1	12.5	-2.50
Wincanton	2-26	1-10	0-0	0-9	1-5	0-2	7.7	-12.00
Sedgefield	1-1	1-1	0-0	0-0	0-0	0-0	100.0	+4.00
Wetherby	1-6	1-4	0-1	0-0	0-1	0-0	16.7	-4.43
Cheltenham	1-10	0-4	0-0	0-2	0-2	1-2	10.0	+7.00
Folkestone	1-13	0-1	0-5	0-1	1-3	0-3	7.7	-7.00
Newbury	1-17	1-8	0-1	0-3	0-3	0-2	5.9	-7.50

WINNING HORSES

Horse	Races Run	1st	2nd	3rd	£
Flotta	5	3	1	0	18792
Waltzing Beau	6	1	0	0	6263
Muttley Maguire	5	2	1	1	9443
Sunley Shines	6	2	1	1	8458
Tokala	7	4	1	0	9434
Blueberry Ice	6	1	0	1	4241
Palace Walk	6	2	0	1	7403
Scarrabus	6	1	0	0	3994
Lahinch Lad	9	1	1	0	3907
Bubble Boy	7	1	1	1	3904
Calusa Charlie	6	1	1	2	3904
Tora Bora	6	2	2	0	7137
Lucky Sinna	11	1	3	1	3748
Sitting Duck	9	1	3	1	3578
Graceful Dancer	5	1	0	0	3516
Wembury Point	10	2	0	0	6802
*Take A Mile	6	1	1	2	3203
*Screen Test	2	1	0	1	3058
*Barella	4	1	0	0	2602
Keralam	1	1	0	0	2534
*Methodical	7	1	1	1	2193
Legal Glory	3	1	0	0	1919
Total winning prize-money					**£120033**
Favourites	5-22		**22.7%**		**-13.27**

R J PRICE

ULLINGSWICK, H'FORDS

	No. of Hrs	Races Run	1st	2nd	3rd	Unpl	Per cent	£1 Level Stake
NH Flat	1	2	0	0	0	2	0.0	-2.00
Hurdles	18	47	2	2	0	43	4.3	-11.00
Chases	5	12	1	0	1	10	8.3	-6.00
Totals	19	61	3	2	1	55	4.9	-19.00
04-05	27	119	6	6	15	92	5.0	-71.50
03-04	26	105	13	14	10	67	12.4	+33.25

JOCKEYS

	W-R	Per cent	£1 Level Stake
Wayne Hutchinson	2-8	25.0	+28.00
Alan O'Keeffe	1-22	4.5	-16.00

COURSE RECORD

	Total W-R	Non-Hndcps Hurdles	Chases	Hndcps Hurdles	Chases	NH Flat	Per cent	£1 Level Stake
Worcester	2-16	0-6	0-0	1-8	1-2	0-0	12.5	+5.00
Uttoxeter	1-7	0-2	0-0	1-5	0-0	0-0	14.3	+14.00

WINNING HORSES

Horse	Races Run	1st	2nd	3rd	£
Bobsbest	5	1	0	0	5138
Lilac	2	1	0	0	3897
Court One	2	1	1	0	3510
Total winning prize-money					£12545
Favourites	0-0		0.0%		0.00

C J PRICE

PUDLESTON, H'FORDS

	No. of Hrs	Races Run	1st	2nd	3rd	Unpl	Per cent	£1 Level Stake
NH Flat	3	5	1	0	0	4	20.0	+29.00
Hurdles	4	8	0	1	1	6	0.0	-8.00
Chases	0	0	0	0	0	0	0.0	0.00
Totals	6	13	1	1	1	10	7.7	+21.00
04-05	6	20	1	3	1	15	5.0	-16.50
03-04	8	20	1	5	0	14	5.0	-14.00

JOCKEYS

	W-R	Per cent	£1 Level Stake
Wayne Hutchinson	1-6	16.7	+28.00

COURSE RECORD

	Total W-R	Non-Hndcps Hurdles	Chases	Hndcps Hurdles	Chases	NH Flat	Per cent	£1 Level Stake
Ludlow	1-4	0-1	0-0	0-1	0-0	1-2	25.0	+30.00

WINNING HORSES

Horse	Races Run	1st	2nd	3rd	£
Risk Challenge	2	1	0	0	2602
Total winning prize-money					£2602
Favourites	0-0		0.0%		0.00

J K PRICE

EBBW VALE, BLAENAU GWENT

	No. of Hrs	Races Run	1st	2nd	3rd	Unpl	Per cent	£1 Level Stake
NH Flat	0	0	0	0	0	0	0.0	0.00
Hurdles	1	3	1	0	0	2	33.3	+12.00
Chases	0	0	0	0	0	0	0.0	0.00
Totals	1	3	1	0	0	2	33.3	+12.00
04-05	3	12	0	0	0	12	0.0	-12.00
03-04	1	2	0	0	0	2	0.0	-2.00

JOCKEYS

	W-R	Per cent	£1 Level Stake
Robert Stephens	1-2	50.0	+13.00

COURSE RECORD

	Total W-R	Non-Hndcps Hurdles	Chases	Hndcps Hurdles	Chases	NH Flat	Per cent	£1 Level Stake
Hereford	1-3	0-1	0-0	1-2	0-0	0-0	33.3	+12.00

WINNING HORSES

Horse	Races Run	1st	2nd	3rd	£
*Penric	3	1	0	0	3437
Total winning prize-money					£3437
Favourites	0-0		0.0%		0.00

A E PRICE

LEOMINSTER, H'FORDS

	No. of Hrs	Races Run	1st	2nd	3rd	Unpl	Per cent	£1 Level Stake
NH Flat	3	7	0	1	0	6	0.0	-7.00
Hurdles	5	15	1	0	1	13	6.7	-7.50
Chases	5	24	3	2	4	15	12.5	-6.00
Totals	10	46	4	3	5	34	8.7	-20.50
04-05	12	41	3	3	3	32	7.3	-19.50
03-04	10	27	0	1	2	24	0.0	-27.00

JOCKEYS

	W-R	Per cent	£1 Level Stake
Owyn Nelmes	3-20	15.0	-3.00
A P McCoy	1-2	50.0	+6.50

COURSE RECORD

	Total W-R	Non-Hndcps Hurdles	Chases	Hndcps Hurdles	Chases	NH Flat	Per cent	£1 Level Stake
Hereford	1-2	1-1	0-0	0-0	0-1	0-0	50.0	+5.50
Warwick	1-2	0-0	0-0	0-0	1-1	0-1	50.0	+6.50
Folkestone	1-4	0-2	0-1	0-0	1-1	0-0	25.0	+0.50
Ludlow	1-11	0-1	0-2	0-2	1-3	0-3	9.1	-6.00

WINNING HORSES

Horse	Races Run	1st	2nd	3rd	£
Moscow Gold	6	2	1	0	8040
Midnight Gunner	7	1	1	1	3486
Sistema	8	1	0	1	2082
Total winning prize-money					£13608
Favourites	1-1		100.0%		4.00

MISS JOANNE PRIEST

STOURPORT, WORCS

	No. of Hrs	Races Run	1st	2nd	3rd	Unpl	Per cent	£1 Level Stake
NH Flat	0	0	0	0	0	0	0.0	0.00
Hurdles	3	8	1	1	0	6	12.5	+26.00
Chases	2	4	0	0	0	4	0.0	-4.00
Totals	3	12	1	1	0	10	8.3	+22.00
03-04	1	1	0	0	0	1	0.0	-1.00

JOCKEYS

	W-R	Per cent	£1 Level Stake
Jason Maguire	1-9	11.1	+25.00

COURSE RECORD

	Total W-R	Non-Hndcps Hurdles	Chases	Hndcps Hurdles	Chases	NH Flat	Per cent	£1 Level Stake
Taunton	1-2	0 0	0-0	1-2	0-0	0-0	50.0	+32.00

WINNING HORSES

Horse	Races Run	1st	2nd	3rd	£
*Squantum	3	1	0	0	3578
Total winning prize-money					£3578
Favourites	0-0		0.0%		0.00

DR P PRITCHARD

PURTON, GLOUCS

	No. of Hrs	Races Run	1st	2nd	3rd	Unpl	Per cent	£1 Level Stake
NH Flat	1	1	0	0	0	1	0.0	-1.00
Hurdles	16	62	2	0	4	56	3.2	-7.00
Chases	14	77	3	5	10	59	3.9	-53.00
Totals	20	140	5	5	14	116	3.6	-61.00
04-05	27	151	9	3	6	133	6.0	-6.00
03-04	29	198	4	16	29	149	2.0	-176.80

JOCKEYS

	W-R	Per cent	£1 Level Stake
Charlie Poste	1-1	100.0	+9.00
James Davies	1-8	12.5	-2.00
Mr David Turner	1-12	8.3	-4.00
Dr P Pritchard	1-31	3.2	-10.00
T J Phelan	1-32	3.1	+2.00

COURSE RECORD

	Total W-R	Non-Hndcps Hurdles	Chases	Hndcps Hurdles	Chases	NH Flat	Per cent	£1 Level Stake
Chepstow	3-11	0-1	0-1	1-2	2-7	0-0	27.3	+28.00
Nton Abbot	1-17	0-5	0-0	0-4	1-8	0-0	5.9	-11.00
Worcester	1-22	0-2	0-1	1-8	0-10	0-1	4.5	+12.00

WINNING HORSES

Horse	Races Run	1st	2nd	3rd	£
Get The Point	6	1	0	1	3748
Ashgan	17	1	0	2	2702
Sunday Habits	7	1	0	1	2515
Blazing Batman	17	1	0	4	2277
Knockrigg	3	1	0	0	2082
Total winning prize-money					£13324
Favourites	0-0		0.0%		0.00

M G QUINLAN

NEWMARKET, SUFFOLK

	No. of Hrs	Races Run	1st	2nd	3rd	Unpl	Per cent	£1 Level Stake
NH Flat	0	0	0	0	0	0	0.0	0.00
Hurdles	9	25	2	6	1	16	8.0	-12.00
Chases	2	3	0	1	1	1	0.0	-3.00
Totals	9	28	2	7	2	17	7.1	-15.00
04-05	3	8	3	0	0	5	37.5	+2.25

JOCKEYS

	W-R	Per cent	£1 Level Stake
Mick Fitzgerald	1-1	100.0	+3.50
Paul Moloney	1-9	11.1	-0.50

COURSE RECORD

	Total W-R	Non-Hndcps Hurdles	Chases	Hndcps Hurdles	Chases	NH Flat	Per cent	£1 Level Stake
Ludlow	1-3	1-3	0-0	0-0	0-0	0-0	33.3	+5.50
Plumpton	1-4	0-3	0-0	1-1	0-0	0-0	25.0	+0.50

WINNING HORSES

Horse	Races Run	1st	2nd	3rd	£
Air Guitar	6	1	2	1	3455
Kyno	7	1	3	1	3083
Total winning prize-money					£6538
Favourites	1-120		0.8%		-115.50

J J QUINN

SETTRINGTON, N YORKS

	No. of Hrs	Races Run	1st	2nd	3rd	Unpl	Per cent	£1 Level Stake
NH Flat	6	10	1	4	1	4	10.0	-6.25
Hurdles	24	67	13	8	7	39	19.4	-1.90
Chases	5	17	5	0	5	7	29.4	+15.50
Totals	30	94	19	12	13	50	20.2	+7.35
04-05	25	75	11	9	9	46	14.7	-11.06
03-04	11	35	5	6	3	21	14.3	+16.63

BY MONTH

NH Flat	W-R	Per cent	£1 Level Stake	Hurdles	W-R	Per cent	£1 Level Stake
May	0-0	0.0	0.00	May	1-9	11.1	+2.00
June	0-0	0.0	0.00	June	1-4	25.0	+1.00
July	0-0	0.0	0.00	July	0-5	0.0	-5.00
August	0-0	0.0	0.00	August	4-4	100.0	+12.50
September	0-0	0.0	0.00	September	1-5	20.0	+1.50
October	1-1	100.0	+2.75	October	1-7	14.3	-4.00
November	0-3	0.0	-3.00	November	2-7	28.6	+6.00
December	0-0	0.0	0.00	December	0-7	0.0	-7.00
January	0-2	0.0	-2.00	January	0-3	0.0	-3.00
February	0-2	0.0	-2.00	February	1-6	16.7	-0.50
March	0-0	0.0	0.00	March	0-5	0.0	-5.00
April	0-2	0.0	-2.00	April	2-5	40.0	-0.40

Chases	W-R	Per cent	£1 Level Stake	Totals	W-R	Per cent	£1 Level Stake
May	1-1	100.0	+14.00	May	2-10	20.0	+16.00
June	1-1	100.0	+3.50	June	2-5	40.0	+4.50
July	0-0	0.0	0.00	July	0-5	0.0	-5.00
August	0-1	0.0	-1.00	August	4-5	80.0	+11.50
September	0-0	0.0	0.00	September	1-5	20.0	+1.50
October	0-1	0.0	-1.00	October	2-9	22.2	-2.25
November	0-2	0.0	-2.00	November	2-12	16.7	+1.00
December	0-2	0.0	-2.00	December	0-9	0.0	-9.00
January	1-4	25.0	+0.33	January	1-9	11.1	-4.67
February	0-3	0.0	-3.00	February	1-11	9.1	-5.50
March	1-1	100.0	+3.33	March	1-6	16.7	1.67
April	1-1	100.0	+3.33	April	3-8	37.5	+0.93

DISTANCE

Hurdles	W-R	Per cent	£1 Level Stake	Chases	W-R	Per cent	£1 Level Stake
2m-2m3f	10-58	17.2	-3.50	2m-2m3f	3-8	37.5	+15.83
2m4f-2m7f	2-7	28.6	+1.10	2m4f-2m7f	0-4	0.0	-4.00
3m+	1-2	50.0	+0.50	3m+	2-5	40.0	+3.67

TYPE OF RACE

Non-Handicaps	W-R	Per cent	£1 Level Stake	Handicaps	W-R	Per cent	£1 Level Stake
Nov Hrdls	6-25	24.0	-4.40	Nov Hrdls	3-9	33.3	+7.00
Hrdls	1-4	25.0	+2.00	Hrdls	3-26	11.5	-3.50
Nov Chs	3-12	25.0	+11.67	Nov Chs	1-1	100.0	+3.33
Chases	0-0	0.0	0.00	Chases	1-4	25.0	+0.50
Sell/Claim	0-4	0.0	-4.00	Sell/Claim	0-0	0.0	0.00

RACE CLASS

	W-R	Per cent	£1 Level Stake
Class 1	0-3	0.0	-3.00
Class 2	1-5	20.0	+0.50
Class 3	4-31	12.9	-9.17
Class 4	13-42	31.0	+28.27
Class 5	0-5	0.0	-5.00
Class 6	1-8	12.5	-4.25

FIRST TIME OUT

	W-R	Per cent	£1 Level Stake
Bumpers	1-6	16.7	-2.25
Hurdles	3-23	13.0	-6.50
Chases	0-1	0.0	-1.00
Totals	4-30	13.3	-9.75C

JOCKEYS

	W-R	Per cent	£1 Level Stake
Russ Garritty	9-38	23.7	+8.43
Dougie Costello	4-24	16.7	+5.00
Tony Dobbin	2-5	40.0	+1.83
Fergus King	1-1	100.0	+5.00
Mr R Tierney	1-1	100.0	+2.75
Stephen Craine	1-1	100.0	+3.33
T J O'Brien	1-3	33.3	+2.00

COURSE RECORD

	Total W-R	Non-Hndcps Hurdles	Chases	Hndcps Hurdles	Chases	NH Flat	Per cent	£1 Level Stake
Bangor	3-5	2-2	0-1	1-2	0-0	0-0	60.0	+9.50
Hexham	3-6	1-1	0-0	0-3	1-1	1-1	50.0	+4.75
Uttoxeter	2-3	1-2	0-0	1-1	0-0	0-0	66.7	+6.50
Catterick	2-6	1-2	1-2	0-0	0-1	0-1	33.3	+5.33
Sedgefield	2-9	1-4	1-2	0-0	0-0	0-3	22.2	+8.10
Carlisle	1-1	0-0	0-0	0-0	1-1	0-0	100.0	+3.33
Hereford	1-2	0-0	0-0	1-2	0-0	0-0	50.0	+3.00
Cartmel	1-3	1-2	0-0	0-1	0-0	0-0	33.3	-1.00
Wetherby	1-3	0-0	0-0	1-2	0-1	0-0	33.3	+3.00
Musselbgh	1-4	0-0	0-1	1-2	0-0	0-1	25.0	+1.50
Kelso	1-6	0-2	1-1	0-2	0-1	0-0	16.7	-1.67
Mrket Rsn	1-12	0-4	0-1	1-6	0-0	0-1	8.3	-1.00

WINNING HORSES

Horse	Races Run	1st	2nd	3rd	£
Crow Wood	5	2	0	1	22184
Jake Black	4	1	0	0	7352
Goldstar Dancer	5	3	1	0	13839
Bellaney Jewel	7	3	0	3	15113
Adjawar	4	2	1	0	5395
Aleron	5	1	0	1	5205
Hilltime	3	1	1	1	4927
Master Nimbus	8	3	1	1	10220
Kirkham Abbey	5	1	1	1	3461
Character Building	6	1	3	1	3253
One More Step	1	1	0	0	1904
Total winning prize-money					**£92853**
Favourites	2-14		14.3%		-9.90

MRS JULIE READ

NEWMARKET, SUFFOLK

	No. of Hrs	Races Run	1st	2nd	3rd	Unpl	Per cent	£1 Level Stake
NH Flat	0	0	0	0	0	0	0.0	0.00
Hurdles	0	0	0	0	0	0	0.0	0.00
Chases	3	6	1	0	0	5	16.7	0.00
Totals	3	6	1	0	0	5	16.7	0.00
04-05	2	6	1	1	0	4	16.7	-3.13
03-04	3	6	0	1	0	5	0.0	-6.00

JOCKEYS

	W-R	Per cent	£1 Level Stake
Mr M Mackley	1-4	25.0	+2.00

COURSE RECORD

	Total W-R	Non-Hndcps Hurdles	Chases	Hndcps Hurdles	Chases	NH Flat	Per cent	£1 Level Stake
Fakenham	1-3	0-0	1-3	0-0	0-0	0-0	33.3	+3.00

WINNING HORSES

Horse	Races Run	1st	2nd	3rd	£
*Galway Breeze	3	1	0	0	3297
Total winning prize-money					**£3297**
Favourites	**0-0**		**0.0%**		**0.00**

W T REED

HAYDON BRIDGE, NORTHUMBERLAND

	No. of Hrs	Races Run	1st	2nd	3rd	Unpl	Per cent	£1 Level Stake
NH Flat	2	5	0	0	0	5	0.0	-5.00
Hurdles	3	11	0	0	2	9	0.0	-11.00
Chases	5	19	1	0	1	17	5.3	-13.50
Totals	7	35	1	0	3	31	2.9	-29.50
04-05	10	38	2	3	5	28	5.3	-24.25
03-04	5	16	4	2	0	10	25.0	+3.50

JOCKEYS

	W-R	Per cent	£1 Level Stake
Andrew Thornton	1-5	20.0	+0.50

COURSE RECORD

	Total W-R	Non-Hndcps Hurdles	Chases	Hndcps Hurdles	Chases	NH Flat	Per cent	£1 Level Stake
Wetherby	1-6	0-1	0-1	0-0	1-2	0-2	16.7	-0.50

WINNING HORSES

Horse	Races Run	1st	2nd	3rd	£
Helvetius	8	1	0	0	3917
Total winning prize-money					**£3917**
Favourites	**0-1**		**0.0%**		**-1.00**

MRS E J REED

HEXHAM, NORTHUMBERLAND

	No. of Hrs	Races Run	1st	2nd	3rd	Unpl	Per cent	£1 Level Stake
NH Flat	0	0	0	0	0	0	0.0	0.00
Hurdles	0	0	0	0	0	0	0.0	0.00
Chases	2	4	2	1	0	1	50.0	+0.32
Totals	2	4	2	1	0	1	50.0	+0.32

JOCKEYS

	W-R	Per cent	£1 Level Stake
Mr R Morgan	2-3	66.7	+1.32

COURSE RECORD

	Total W-R	Non-Hndcps Hurdles	Chases	Hndcps Hurdles	Chases	NH Flat	Per cent	£1 Level Stake
Perth	1-1	0-0	1-1	0-0	0-0	0-0	100.0	+1.75
Kelso	1-2	0-0	1-2	0-0	0-0	0-0	50.0	-0.43

WINNING HORSES

Horse	Races Run	1st	2nd	3rd	£
*Coomakista	3	2	1	0	4997
Total winning prize-money					**£4997**
Favourites	**1-1**		**100.0%**		**0.57**

D A REES

CLARBESTON, PEMBROKES

	No. of Hrs	Races Run	1st	2nd	3rd	Unpl	Per cent	£1 Level Stake
NH Flat	3	3	0	0	0	3	0.0	-3.00
Hurdles	9	21	1	3	2	15	4.8	-16.00
Chases	2	4	0	0	0	4	0.0	-4.00
Totals	11	28	1	3	2	22	3.6	-23.00
04-05	8	29	1	0	1	27	3.4	-6.00
03-04	7	25	0	2	2	21	0.0	-25.00

JOCKEYS

	W-R	Per cent	£1 Level Stake
William Kennedy	1-4	25.0	+1.00

COURSE RECORD

	Total W-R	Non-Hndcps Hurdles	Chases	Hndcps Hurdles	Chases	NH Flat	Per cent	£1 Level Stake
Plumpton	1-1	0-0	0-0	1-1	0-0	0-0	100.0	+4.00

WINNING HORSES

Horse	Races Run	1st	2nd	3rd	£
Bonny Boy	5	1	1	0	2398
Total winning prize-money					**£2398**
Favourites	**1-2**		**50.0%**		**3.00**

K G REVELEY

LINGDALE, REDCAR & CLEVELAND

	No. of Hrs	Races Run	1st	2nd	3rd	Unpl	Per cent	£1 Level Stake
NH Flat	18	30	4	1	3	22	13.3	-16.07
Hurdles	46	169	21	22	15	111	12.4	-17.65
Chases	17	69	7	5	8	49	10.1	-40.80
Totals	63	268	32	28	26	182	11.9	-74.52
04-05	55	244	30	28	25	160	12.3	-96.45

BY MONTH

NH Flat	W-R	Per cent	£1 Level Stake	Hurdles	W-R	Per cent	£1 Level Stake
May	0-2	0.0	-2.00	May	1-16	6.3	-11.50
June	0-2	0.0	-2.00	June	0-4	0.0	-4.00
July	0-1	0.0	1.00	July	0-4	0.0	-4.00
August	0-0	0.0	0.00	August	0-5	0.0	-5.00
September	1-1	100.0	15.50	September	1-5	20.0	+4.00
October	1-2	50.0	-0.70	October	0-17	0.0	-17.00
November	2-6	33.3	+0.13	November	7-32	21.9	+27.25
December	0-3	0.0	-3.00	December	2-19	10.5	-9.00
January	0-3	0.0	-3.00	January	3-20	15.0	-11.40
February	0-2	0.0	-2.00	February	4-19	21.1	+30.50
March	0-5	0.0	-5.00	March	0-11	0.0	-11.00
April	0-3	0.0	-3.00	April	3-17	17.6	-6.50

Chases	W-R	Per cent	£1 Level Stake	Totals	W-R	Per cent	£1 Level Stake
May	0-2	0.0	-2.00	May	1-20	5.0	-15.50
June	0-1	0.0	-1.00	June	0-7	0.0	7.00
July	0-1	0.0	-1.00	July	0-6	0.0	-6.00
August	0-0	0.0	0.00	August	0-5	0.0	-5.00
September	0-1	0.0	-1.00	September	2-7	28.6	+8.50
October	0-2	0.0	-2.00	October	1-21	4.8	-19.70
November	0-11	0.0	-11.00	November	9-49	18.4	+16.38
December	3-18	16.7	-1.72	December	5-40	12.5	-13.72
January	2-10	20.0	-5.58	January	5-33	15.2	-19.98
February	0-10	0.0	-10.00	February	4-31	12.9	+18.50
March	1-6	16.7	-3.00	March	1-22	4.5	-19.00
April	1-7	14.3	-2.50	April	4-27	14.8	-12.00

DISTANCE

Hurdles	W-R	Per cent	£1 Level Stake	Chases	W-R	Per cent	£1 Level Stake
2m-2m3f	10-72	13.9	+13.63	2m-2m3f	1-18	5.6	-15.38
2m4f-2m7f	10-76	13.2	-15.77	2m4f-2m7f	4-23	17.4	-11.23
3m+	1-21	4.8	-15.50	3m+	2-28	7.1	-14.20

TYPE OF RACE

Non-Handicaps	W-R	Per cent	£1 Level Stake	Handicaps	W-R	Per cent	£1 Level Stake
Nov Hrdls	5-46	10.9	+0.10	Nov Hrdls	1-20	5.0	-11.00
Hrdls	2-10	20.0	-3.50	Hrdls	12-83	14.5	+1.25
Nov Chs	5-11	45.5	+0.70	Nov Chs	1-10	10.0	-5.50
Chases	0-7	0.0	-7.00	Chases	1-41	2.4	-29.00

Sell/Claim	1-3	33.3	+2.50
Sell/Claim	0-8	0.0	-8.00

RACE CLASS

	W-R	Per cent	£1 Level Stake
Class 1	1-19	5.3	-12.50
Class 2	1-16	6.3	-14.00
Class 3	11-77	14.3	+26.63
Class 4	13-111	11.7	-52.58
Class 5	2-19	10.5	-10.00
Class 6	4-26	15.4	-12.07

FIRST TIME OUT

	W-R	Per cent	£1 Level Stake
Bumpers	4-18	22.2	-4.07
Hurdles	5-34	14.7	+9.13
Chases	0-11	0.0	-11.00
Totals	9-63	14.3	-5.94

JOCKEYS

	W-R	Per cent	£1 Level Stake
Richard McGrath	13-108	12.0	-71.83
Jim Crowley	8-45	17.8	-6.57
Phil Kinsella	4-33	12.1	+16.00
James Reveley	4-54	7.4	-4.50
Fergus King	1-2	50.0	+10.00
Andrew Thornton	1-5	20.0	+0.50
G Lee	1-6	16.7	-3.13

COURSE RECORD

	Total W-R	Non-Hndcps Hurdles	Chases	Hndcps Hurdles	Chases	NH Flat	Per cent	£1 Level Stake
Huntingdon	8-24	1-2	2-3	3-9	0-7	2-3	33.3	+1.93
Catterick	4-23	0-4	2-3	1-6	1-7	0-3	17.4	+6.43
Wetherby	4-43	2-16	0-2	1-15	0-5	1-5	9.3	-24.90
Ayr	3-9	0-2	0-0	3-5	0-1	0-1	33.3	0.00
Musselbgh	3-14	1-4	1-1	1-3	0-4	0-2	21.4	+26.40
Plumpton	2-5	1-2	0-0	1-3	0-0	0-0	40.0	+8.50
Bangor	1-1	1-1	0-0	0-0	0-0	0-0	100.0	+4.50
Leicester	1-4	1-2	0-0	0-0	0-2	0-0	25.0	+1.50
Sandown	1-4	0-0	0-0	1-3	0-1	0-0	25.0	+2.50
Stratford	1-6	0-2	0-0	0-1	0-1	1-2	16.7	+0.50
Perth	1-7	0-1	0-0	0-2	1-2	0-2	14.3	-2.50
Doncaster	1-13	0-2	0-1	1-7	0-1	0-2	7.7	+10.00
Kelso	1-15	1-4	0-1	0-6	0-4	0-0	6.7	-12.00
Sedgefield	1-15	0-2	0-5	1-6	0-2	0-0	6.7	-12.38

WINNING HORSES

Horse	Races Run	1st	2nd	3rd	£
Ungaro	8	3	1	1	38406
Into The Shadows	4	2	0	1	17406
Sun King	5	1	1	0	7807
Clouding Over	8	4	0	1	20907
Robbo	10	1	0	2	6994
October Mist	5	1	0	0	6974
Hernando's Boy	5	2	1	0	9040
Top Brass	5	1	0	1	5205
*Toss The Caber	4	1	2	0	4784
Birdwatch	7	3	1	0	11551
Welcome To Unos	7	3	1	0	11447
Rambling Minster	5	1	0	0	3904
Celtic Legend	11	1	1	1	3522

Time Marches On	4	1	0	0	3504
Diklers Rose	5	1	2	0	3416
Supreme's Legacy	7	3	2	0	7888
Finns Cross	1	1	0	0	3109
Jass	2	1	0	1	1898
Brave Rebellion	7	1	1	3	1817
Total winning prize-money					**£169579**
Favourites	14-36		38.9%		1.60

N G RICHARDS

GREYSTOKE, CUMBRIA

	No. of Hrs	Races Run	1st	2nd	3rd	Unpl	Per cent	£1 Level Stake
NH Flat	19	29	8	4	4	13	27.6	+6.25
Hurdles	71	197	36	26	22	113	18.3	-16.28
Chases	20	51	15	11	5	20	29.4	+3.17
Totals	92	277	59	41	31	146	21.3	-6.86
04-05	70	239	53	33	22	131	22.2	+62.56
03-04	56	174	38	29	13	94	21.8	+2.33

BY MONTH

NH Flat	W-R	Per cent	£1 Level Stake	Hurdles	W-R	Per cent	£1 Level Stake
May	2-3	66.7	+4.25	May	3-16	18.8	+3.50
June	1-1	100.0	+2.00	June	2-11	18.2	+1.50
July	0-0	0.0	0.00	July	2-7	28.6	-0.33
August	0-1	0.0	-1.00	August	1-4	25.0	-2.33
September	0-0	0.0	0.00	September	0-7	0.0	-7.00
October	1-2	50.0	+0.50	October	2-13	15.4	-5.00
November	0-3	0.0	-3.00	November	2-23	8.7	-9.50
December	1-2	50.0	+7.00	December	4-23	17.4	-1.38
January	1-4	25.0	+2.50	January	9-29	31.0	+34.72
February	0-3	0.0	-3.00	February	3-18	16.7	-8.50
March	2-7	28.6	0.00	March	4-16	25.0	-7.31
April	0-3	0.0	-3.00	April	4-30	13.3	-14.65

Chases	W-R	Per cent	£1 Level Stake	Totals	W-R	Per cent	£1 Level Stake
May	2-5	40.0	+0.13	May	7-24	29.2	+7.88
June	0-3	0.0	-3.00	June	3-15	20.0	+0.50
July	0-2	0.0	-2.00	July	2-9	22.2	-2.33
August	2-2	100.0	+4.63	August	3-7	42.9	+1.30
September	1-3	33.3	-0.25	September	1-10	10.0	-7.25
October	0-1	0.0	-1.00	October	3-16	18.8	-5.50
November	3-5	60.0	+7.40	November	5-31	16.1	-5.10
December	1-4	25.0	-1.38	December	6-29	20.7	+4.24
January	1-2	50.0	-0.33	January	11-35	31.4	+36.89
February	2-8	25.0	-3.21	February	5-29	17.2	-14.71
March	1-8	12.5	-6.09	March	7-31	22.6	-13.40
April	2-8	25.0	+8.29	April	6-41	14.6	-9.36

DISTANCE

Hurdles	W-R	Per cent	£1 Level Stake	Chases	W-R	Per cent	£1 Level Stake
2m-2m3f	15-90	16.7	-16.66	2m-2m3f	2-5	40.0	-2.31

	W-R	Per cent	£1 Level Stake		W-R	Per cent	£1 Level Stake
2m4f-2m7f	14-76	18.4	+1.97	2m4f-2m7f	6-20	30.0	-4.92
3m+	7-31	22.6	-1.58	3m+	7-26	26.9	+10.41

TYPE OF RACE

Non-Handicaps	W-R	Per cent	£1 Level Stake	Handicaps	W-R	Per cent	£1 Level Stake
Nov Hrdls	15-55	27.3	-7.99	Nov Hrdls	5-19	26.3	+10.25
Hrdls	4-26	15.4	-4.11	Hrdls	12-88	13.6	-5.42
Nov Chs	6-15	40.0	-4.62	Nov Chs	1-4	25.0	+11.00
Chases	2-10	20.0	-3.88	Chases	6-22	27.3	+0.67
Sell/Claim	1-4	25.0	+3.00	Sell/Claim	0-7	0.0	-7.00

RACE CLASS / FIRST TIME OUT

	W-R	Per cent	£1 Level Stake		W-R	Per cent	£1 Level Stake
Class 1	2-27	7.4	-16.71	Bumpers	8-19	42.1	+16.25
Class 2	5-19	26.3	+26.25	Hurdles	12-64	18.8	+18.25
Class 3	10-68	14.7	-37.19	Chases	3-9	33.3	-3.10
Class 4	30-114	26.3	+18.09				
Class 5	2-20	10.0	-8.67	Totals	23-92	25.0	+31.40
Class 6	10-29	34.5	+12.38				

JOCKEYS

	W-R	Per cent	£1 Level Stake
Tony Dobbin	37-136	27.2	-6.72
Miss R Davidson	9-27	33.3	+26.74
Brian Harding	8-65	12.3	-11.50
A P McCoy	1-1	100.0	+2.50
Alan Dempsey	1-1	100.0	+14.00
Ewan Whillans	1-7	14.3	-3.00
Mr C J Callow	1-7	14.3	-4.38
Scott Marshall	1-9	11.1	-0.50

COURSE RECORD

	Total W-R	Non-Hndcps Hurdles	Chases	Hndcps Hurdles	Chases	NH Flat	Per cent	£1 Level Stake
Ayr	12-46	4-14	3-3	3-18	0-4	2-7	26.1	-3.82
Kelso	10-34	4-15	1-5	5-12	0-0	0-2	29.4	+9.59
Perth	8-35	2-9	1-2	1-18	3-5	1-1	22.9	-12.54
Carlisle	5-12	1-4	2-2	1-3	0-1	1-2	41.7	+18.16
Newcastle	5-16	3-8	0-1	1-6	1-1	0-0	31.3	+6.71
Musselbgh	4-14	1-5	0-0	1-4	2-2	0-3	28.6	+1.79
Hexham	4-17	0-6	0-2	2-5	1-1	1-3	23.5	+16.50
Bangor	2-6	0-2	1-1	0-1	0-0	1-2	33.3	+2.50
Sedgefield	2-13	1-2	0-2	0-7	0-1	1-1	15.4	-3.50
Ludlow	1-1	0-0	0-0	1-1	0-0	0-0	100.0	+4.00
Catterick	1-3	0-0	0-0	0-2	0-0	1-1	33.3	+1.00
Uttoxeter	1-3	1-2	0-0	0-0	0-1	0-0	33.3	+0.50
Cartmel	1-8	1-2	0-0	0-3	0-3	0-0	12.5	-2.00
Cheltenham	1-14	1-4	0-3	0-3	0-2	0-2	7.1	-1.00
Haydock	1-14	0-3	0-0	1-9	0-0	0-2	7.1	-10.75
Aintree	1-16	0-3	0-1	1-9	0-2	0-1	6.3	-9.00

WINNING HORSES

Horse	Races Run	1st	2nd	3rd	£
Direct Access	3	1	0	0	33804
Monet's Garden	4	3	1	0	37185
Jazz D'Estruval	1	1	0	0	13585
The French Furze	4	1	0	1	13152
Premier Dane	4	1	2	0	12572
According To John	4	4	0	0	20838
Possextown	5	2	3	0	8190
Turpin Green	5	1	2	1	7352
Harmony Brig	6	3	1	1	12594
Native Coral	4	2	1	0	11564
Ben Britten	3	2	0	1	9085
Bob's Gone	1	1	0	0	5603
*Bohemian Spirit	6	3	1	1	11768
Ever Present	4	2	0	2	8635
Rising Generation	13	1	1	2	4901
Topanberry	6	2	0	1	8207
Zaffaran Express	5	1	1	2	4554
Muckle Flugga	5	1	1	0	3897
Camden Bella	5	2	1	0	6443
Lahib The Fifth	3	3	0	0	8407
Marlborough Sound	3	1	1	0	3683
Echo Point	2	1	1	0	3679
Bafana Boy	4	1	0	0	3578
Money Trix	4	3	1	0	9932
Glenmoss Rosy	1	1	0	0	3393
One Sniff	2	1	1	0	3383
*The Names Bond	4	2	0	0	6489
Nubel	5	1	0	1	3253
Etched In Stone	3	2	0	0	5407
*Nuzzle	5	1	0	0	2655
Emperor Ross	5	1	0	1	2384
Telemoss	4	1	1	0	2143
Westgrove Berry	2	1	0	0	2056
Linda's Theatre	1	1	0	0	1932
Young Albert	2	1	0	0	1891
Sparron Hawk	3	1	0	0	1713
Gunner Jack	1	1	0	0	1713
Rayshan	2	1	0	0	0
Total winning prize-money					**£301620**
Favourites	30-78		38.5%		-7.94

MRS L RICHARDS

FUNTINGTON, W SUSSEX

	No. of Hrs	Races Run	1st	2nd	3rd	Unpl	Per cent	£1 Level Stake
NH Flat	0	0	0	0	0	0	0.0	0.00
Hurdles	3	8	1	0	2	5	12.5	-1.00
Chases	2	14	1	1	3	9	7.1	+7.00
Totals	**5**	**22**	**2**	**1**	**5**	**14**	**9.1**	**+6.00**

04-05	5	21	2	0	2	17	9.5	-4.50
03-04	7	27	0	0	0	27	0.0	-27.00

JOCKEYS

	W-R	Per cent	£1 Level Stake
John McNamara	1-2	50.0	+5.00
Matthew Batchelor	1-15	6.7	+6.00

COURSE RECORD

	Total W-R	Non-Hndcps Hurdles	Chases	Hndcps Hurdles	Chases	NH Flat	Per cent	£1 Level Stake
Folkestone	1-5	0-1	0-0	0-0	1-4	0-0	20.0	+16.00
Plumpton	1-8	0-1	0-0	1-3	0-4	0-0	12.5	-1.00

WINNING HORSES

Horse	Races Run	1st	2nd	3rd	£
New Leader	6	1	1	0	4060
Manque Neuf	5	1	0	2	2494
Total winning prize-money					**£6554**
Favourites	0-0		0.0%		0.00

M G RIMELL

LEAFIELD, OXON

	No. of Hrs	Races Run	1st	2nd	3rd	Unpl	Per cent	£1 Level Stake
NH Flat	10	14	2	3	1	8	14.3	-8.52
Hurdles	10	24	3	0	7	14	12.5	-10.25
Chases	4	14	1	1	4	8	7.1	-12.27
Totals	**21**	**52**	**6**	**4**	**12**	**30**	**11.5**	**-31.04**
04-05	8	28	9	2	1	16	32.1	+28.75
03-04	10	36	3	4	2	27	8.3	+4.00

JOCKEYS

	W-R	Per cent	£1 Level Stake
Jamie Moore	4-26	15.4	-11.27
A P McCoy	1-4	25.0	-2.27
G Lee	1-8	12.5	-3.50

COURSE RECORD

	Total W-R	Non-Hndcps Hurdles	Chases	Hndcps Hurdles	Chases	NH Flat	Per cent	£1 Level Stake
Taunton	2-5	1-3	1-1	0-0	0-1	0-0	40.0	+2.23
Towcester	1-2	0-0	0-1	1-1	0-0	0-0	50.0	+1.75
Worcester	1-2	0-0	0-0	0-1	0-0	1-1	50.0	-0.27
Wincanton	1-3	0-0	0-0	1-2	0-0	0-1	33.3	+1.50
Plumpton	1-5	0-1	0-1	0-1	0-0	1-2	20.0	-1.25

WINNING HORSES

Horse	Races Run	1st	2nd	3rd	£
Pearly Bay	3	1	0	1	7339

Horse	Races Run	1st	2nd	3rd	£
Crossbow Creek	6	1	0	2	5514
Ellway Prospect	4	1	0	1	3904
Nesnaas	6	1	0	3	3763
Ice Tea	2	1	1	0	1967
Sun Pageant	1	1	0	0	1946
Total winning prize-money					£24433
Favourites	4-7		57.1%		3.95

P C RITCHENS

SHIPTON BELLINGER, HANTS

	No. of Hrs	Races Run	1st	2nd	3rd	Unpl	Per cent	£1 Level Stake
NH Flat	1	2	0	0	0	2	0.0	-2.00
Hurdles	5	14	0	2	2	10	0.0	-14.00
Chases	4	13	1	0	1	11	7.7	-9.75
Totals	7	29	1	2	3	23	3.4	-25.75
04-05	7	37	4	3	5	25	10.8	0.00
03-04	8	52	2	2	3	45	3.8	-31.00

JOCKEYS

	W-R	Per cent	£1 Level Stake
Andrew Thornton	1-18	5.6	-14.75

COURSE RECORD

	Total W-R	Non-Hndcps Hurdles	Chases	Hndcps Hurdles	Chases	NH Flat	Per cent	£1 Level Stake
Fontwell	1-4	0-0	0-1	0-0	1-3	0-0	25.0	-0.75

WINNING HORSES

Horse	Races Run	1st	2nd	3rd	£
Foxmeade Dancer	9	1	0	2	3666
Total winning prize-money					£3666
Favourites	1-3		33.3%		0.25

C ROBERTS

NEWPORT, NEWPORT

	No. of Hrs	Races Run	1st	2nd	3rd	Unpl	Per cent	£1 Level Stake
NH Flat	8	16	1	0	0	15	6.3	-1.00
Hurdles	21	69	8	0	3	58	11.6	+5.50
Chases	5	20	1	1	2	16	5.0	-9.00
Totals	26	105	10	1	5	89	9.5	-4.50
04-05	24	89	8	4	7	70	9.0	+34.00
03-04	14	34	3	2	0	29	8.8	+39.00

BY MONTH

	NH Flat W-R	Per cent	£1 Level Stake	Hurdles W-R	Per cent	£1 Level Stake	Chases W-R	Per cent	£1 Level Stake	Totals W-R	Per cent	£1 Level Stake
May	0-2	0.0	-2.00	0-2	0.0	-2.00	0-0	0.0	0.00	0-4	0.0	-4.00
June	0-3	0.0	-3.00	0-3	0.0	-3.00	0-1	0.0	-1.00	0-7	0.0	-7.00
July	0-1	0.0	-1.00	1-3	33.3	+10.00	0-2	0.0	-2.00	1-6	16.7	+7.00
August	0-2	0.0	-2.00	0-3	0.0	-3.00	0-2	0.0	-2.00	0-7	0.0	-7.00
September	0-0	0.0	0.00	0-6	0.0	-6.00	0-0	0.0	0.00	0-6	0.0	-6.00
October	0-1	0.0	1.00	0-3	0.0	-3.00	0-1	0.0	-1.00	0-5	0.0	-5.00
November	0-1	0.0	-1.00	1-10	10.0	+3.00	0-2	0.0	-2.00	1-13	7.7	0.00
December	0-3	0.0	-3.00	0-6	0.0	-6.00	1-2	50.0	+9.00	1-11	9.1	0.00
January	0-2	0.0	-2.00	0-9	0.0	-9.00	0-2	0.0	-2.00	0-13	0.0	-13.00
February	0-0	0.0	0.00	0-5	0.0	-5.00	0-2	0.0	-2.00	0-7	0.0	-7.00
March	0-0	0.0	0.00	3-6	50.0	+7.50	0-3	0.0	-3.00	3-9	33.3	+4.50
April	1-1	100.0	+14.00	3-13	23.1	+22.00	0-3	0.0	-3.00	4-17	23.5	+33.00

DISTANCE

Hurdles	W-R	Per cent	£1 Level Stake	Chases	W-R	Per cent	£1 Level Stake
2m-2m3f	6-43	14.0	+17.50	2m-2m3f	0-2	0.0	-2.00
2m4f-2m7f	2-15	13.3	-1.00	2m4f-2m7f	0-6	0.0	-6.00
3m+	0-11	0.0	-11.00	3m+	1-12	8.3	-1.00

TYPE OF RACE

Non-Handicaps	W-R	Per cent	£1 Level Stake	Handicaps	W-R	Per cent	£1 Level Stake
Nov Hrdls	2-29	6.9	-4.00	Nov Hrdls	3-11	27.3	+23.50
Hrdls	0-9	0.0	-9.00	Hrdls	2-17	11.8	-12.00
Nov Chs	0-6	0.0	-6.00	Nov Chs	0-4	0.0	-4.00
Chases	0-0	0.0	0.00	Chases	1-9	11.1	+2.00
Sell/Claim	1-4	25.0	0.00	Sell/Claim	1-1	100.0	+9.00

RACE CLASS

	W-R	Per cent	£1 Level Stake
Class 1	0-3	0.0	-3.00
Class 2	0-2	0.0	-2.00
Class 3	1-19	5.3	-8.00
Class 4	6-56	10.7	+4.50
Class 5	2-10	20.0	+4.00
Class 6	1-15	6.7	0.00

FIRST TIME OUT

	W-R	Per cent	£1 Level Stake
Bumpers	1-8	12.5	+7.00
Hurdles	2-16	12.5	-2.00
Chases	0-2	0.0	-2.00
Totals	3-26	11.5	+3.00

JOCKEYS

	W-R	Per cent	£1 Level Stake
Lee Stephens	4-32	12.5	+11.00
Ollie McPhail	3-26	11.5	+6.50

Andrew Thornton	2-7	28.6	+16.00
Miss E J Jones	1-1	100.0	+1.00

COURSE RECORD

	Total W-R	Non-Hndcps Hurdles	Chases	Hndcps Hurdles	Chases	NH Flat	Per cent	£1 Level Stake
Wincanton	2-4	1-2	0-0	1-2	0-0	0-0	50.0	+20.00
Mrket Rsn	1-1	0-0	0-0	0-0	1-1	0-0	100.0	+10.00
Huntingdon	1-2	0-1	0-0	1-1	0-0	0-0	50.0	0.00
Towcester	1-4	1-2	0-1	0-1	0-0	0-0	25.0	0.00
Taunton	1-5	0 3	0-0	1-1	0-1	0-0	20.0	+3.50
Uttoxeter	1-5	0-0	0-0	1-3	0-1	0-1	20.0	+8.00
Worcester	1-11	0-1	0-0	0-5	0-2	1-3	9.1	+4.00
Hereford	1-12	0-6	0-1	1-2	0-0	0-3	8.3	+1.00
Chepstow	1-19	0-7	0-3	1-7	0-0	0-2	5.3	-9.00

WINNING HORSES

Horse	Races Run	1st	2nd	3rd	£
Victory Gunner	11	1	0	2	6002
*Picot De Say	9	3	0	0	11386
Little Brave	5	2	0	0	6814
*Dreams Jewel	5	1	0	0	2741
Queen Excalibur	10	1	0	0	2723
Sou'Wester	1	1	0	0	2277
Ballymena	3	1	0	0	2097
Total winning prize-money					£34040
Favourites	2-2		100.0%		3.00

MRS P ROBESON
TYRINGHAM, MILTON KEYNES

	No. of Hrs	Races Run	1st	2nd	3rd	Unpl	Per cent	£1 Level Stake
NH Flat	3	3	0	0	0	2	0.0	-3.00
Hurdles	9	27	2	1	2	22	7.4	-3.00
Chases	3	8	1	0	0	7	12.5	-3.00
Totals	14	38	3	1	2	31	7.9	-9.00
04-05	15	46	5	2	3	36	10.9	+1.00
03-04	10	34	5	1	3	25	14.7	+94.50

JOCKEYS

	W-R	Per cent	£1 Level Stake
Marcus Foley	1-1	100.0	+4.00
Russ Garritty	1-5	20.0	0.00
Jimmy McCarthy	1-25	4.0	-6.00

COURSE RECORD

	Total W-R	Non-Hndcps Hurdles	Chases	Hndcps Hurdles	Chases	NH Flat	Per cent	£1 Level Stake
Wetherby	2-3	1-2	1-1	0-0	0-0	0-0	66.7	+7.00
Huntingdon	1-7	0-2	0-0	1-3	0-1	0-1	14.3	+12.00

WINNING HORSES

Horse	Races Run	1st	2nd	3rd	£
Olney Lad	5	1	0	0	5205
Ponderon	2	1	0	1	4940
Coralbrook	6	1	0	1	3253
Total winning prize-money					£13398
Favourites	0-1		0.0%		-1.00

MRS C J ROBINSON
SHIFNAL, SHROPSHIRE

	No. of Hrs	Races Run	1st	2nd	3rd	Unpl	Per cent	£1 Level Stake
NH Flat	0	0	0	0	0	0	0.0	0.00
Hurdles	0	0	0	0	0	0	0.0	0.00
Chases	3	4	1	0	0	3	25.0	+4.00
Totals	3	4	1	0	0	3	25.0	+4.00
04-05	1	3	0	0	0	3	0.0	-3.00
03-04	3	4	0	0	0	4	0.0	-4.00

JOCKEYS

	W-R	Per cent	£1 Level Stake
Mr R Burton	1-3	33.3	+5.00

COURSE RECORD

	Total W-R	Non-Hndcps Hurdles	Chases	Hndcps Hurdles	Chases	NH Flat	Per cent	£1 Level Stake
Aintree	1-1	0-0	1-1	0-0	0-0	0-0	100.0	+7.00

WINNING HORSES

Horse	Races Run	1st	2nd	3rd	£
Honest Yer Honour	2	1	0	0	2470
Total winning prize-money					£2470
Favourites	0-0		0.0%		0.00

MISS SARAH ROBINSON
BRIDGWATER, SOMERSET

	No. of Hrs	Races Run	1st	2nd	3rd	Unpl	Per cent	£1 Level Stake
NH Flat	0	0	0	0	0	0	0.0	0.00
Hurdles	0	0	0	0	0	0	0.0	0.00
Chases	3	6	1	0	0	5	16.7	-3.00
Totals	3	6	1	0	0	5	16.7	-3.00
04-05	3	8	2	2	0	4	25.0	-1.50
03-04	2	3	0	1	0	2	0.0	-3.00

JOCKEYS

	W-R	Per cent	£1 Level Stake
Miss Sarah Robinson	1-3	33.3	0.00

COURSE RECORD

	Total W-R	Non-Hndcps Hurdles	Chases	Hndcps Hurdles	Chases	NH Flat	Per cent	£1 Level Stake
Bangor	1-2	0-0	1-2	0-0	0-0	0-0	50.0	+1.00

WINNING HORSES

Horse	Races Run	1st	2nd	3rd	£
Johns Legacy	1	1	0	0	1433
Total winning prize-money					**£1433**
Favourites	1-1		100.0%		2.00

MISS P ROBSON

KIRKHARLE, NORTHUMBERLAND

	No. of Hrs	Races Run	1st	2nd	3rd	Unpl	Per cent	£1 Level Stake
NH Flat	0	0	0	0	0	0	0.0	0.00
Hurdles	6	10	0	1	1	8	0.0	-10.00
Chases	5	17	2	5	3	7	11.8	-7.50
Totals	9	27	2	6	4	15	7.4	-17.50
04-05	7	29	4	3	1	21	13.8	-18.77
03-04	5	12	5	1	2	4	41.7	+13.50

JOCKEYS

	W-R	Per cent	£1 Level Stake
Richard McGrath	2-9	22.2	+0.50

COURSE RECORD

	Total W-R	Non-Hndcps Hurdles	Chases	Hndcps Hurdles	Chases	NH Flat	Per cent	£1 Level Stake
Catterick	1-2	0-0	1-1	0-1	0-0	0-0	50.0	+3.50
Ayr	1-9	0-1	0-0	0-2	1-6	0-0	11.1	-5.00

WINNING HORSES

Horse	Races Run	1st	2nd	3rd	£
King Barry	6	2	2	1	9652
Total winning prize-money					**£9652**
Favourites	1-8		12.5%		-4.00

P R RODFORD

ASH, SOMERSET

	No. of Hrs	Races Run	1st	2nd	3rd	Unpl	Per cent	£1 Level Stake
NH Flat	2	5	0	0	0	5	0.0	-5.00
Hurdles	9	35	3	4	1	27	8.6	+13.00

Chases	6	20	0	2	4	14	0.0	-20.00
Totals	13	60	3	6	5	46	5.0	-12.00
04-05	16	59	3	5	7	44	5.1	+163.50
03-04	7	27	0	0	5	22	0.0	-27.00

JOCKEYS

	W-R	Per cent	£1 Level Stake
Robert Thornton	2-2	100.0	+20.00
Keiran Burke	1-49	2.0	-23.00

COURSE RECORD

	Total W-R	Non-Hndcps Hurdles	Chases	Hndcps Hurdles	Chases	NH Flat	Per cent	£1 Level Stake
Worcester	2-10	2-4	0-2	0-1	0-1	0-2	20.0	+31.00
Fontwell	1-3	1-2	0-0	0-0	0-1	0-0	33.3	+4.00

WINNING HORSES

Horse	Races Run	1st	2nd	3rd	£
Beechwood	3	1	0	0	3458
Outside Investor	12	7	1	0	5509
Total winning prize-money					**£8967**
Favourites	0-0		0.0%		0.00

B S ROTHWELL

NAWTON, N YORKS

	No. of Hrs	Races Run	1st	2nd	3rd	Unpl	Per cent	£1 Level Stake
NH Flat	1	2	0	0	0	2	0.0	-2.00
Hurdles	8	15	0	0	1	14	0.0	-15.00
Chases	1	6	1	0	0	5	16.7	+11.00
Totals	9	23	1	0	1	21	4.3	-6.00
04-05	9	46	1	3	2	40	2.2	-37.50
03-04	17	73	3	4	4	62	4.1	-25.00

JOCKEYS

	W-R	Per cent	£1 Level Stake
Anthony Ross	1-15	6.7	+2.00

COURSE RECORD

	Total W-R	Non-Hndcps Hurdles	Chases	Hndcps Hurdles	Chases	NH Flat	Per cent	£1 Level Stake
Sedgefield	1-3	0-0	1-2	0-0	0-1	0-0	33.3	+14.00

WINNING HORSES

Horse	Races Run	1st	2nd	3rd	£
Celtic Blaze	11	1	0	1	4857
Total winning prize-money					**£4857**
Favourites	0-0		0.0%		0.00

R ROWE

SULLINGTON, W SUSSEX

	No. of Hrs	Races Run	1st	2nd	3rd	Unpl	Per cent	£1 Level Stake
NH Flat	5	6	0	0	0	6	0.0	-6.00
Hurdles	19	43	2	4	3	34	4.7	-26.67
Chases	11	39	4	3	3	29	10.3	+19.50
Totals	30	88	6	7	6	69	6.8	-13.17
04-05	34	128	7	12	7	102	5.5	-100.02
03-04	32	147	11	16	14	106	7.5	-61.50

JOCKEYS

	W-R	Per cent	£1 Level Stake
Brian Crowley	3-29	10.3	+12.50
Paul Moloney	1-4	25.0	+17.00
Matthew Batchelor	1-6	16.7	+2.00
Leighton Aspell	1-10	10.0	-5.67

COURSE RECORD

	Total W-R	Non-Hndcps Hurdles	Non-Hndcps Chases	Hndcps Hurdles	Chases	NH Flat	Per cent	£1 Level Stake
Plumpton	2-11	0-3	0-0	2-5	0-2	0-1	18.2	+5.33
Exeter	1-3	0-0	0-0	0-0	1-2	0-1	33.3	+18.00
Nton Abbot	1-6	0-2	0-0	0-2	1-2	0-0	16.7	+2.00
Folkestone	1-12	0-5	0-1	0-4	1-2	0-0	8.3	-3.50
Fontwell	1-13	0-3	0-0	0-2	1-8	0-0	7.7	+8.00

WINNING HORSES

Horse	Races Run	1st	2nd	3rd	£
Magic Of Sydney	5	1	0	1	6880
King Coal	5	1	0	1	4880
Lord 'N' Master	4	1	1	0	4737
Touch Of Fate	4	1	1	0	4677
French Direction	6	1	0	0	4066
Up At Midnight	3	1	0	0	3253
Total winning prize-money					£28493
Favourites	0-0		0.0%		0.00

MISS M E ROWLAND

LOWER BLIDWORTH, NOTTS

	No. of Hrs	Races Run	1st	2nd	3rd	Unpl	Per cent	£1 Level Stake
NH Flat	3	9	0	0	0	9	0.0	-9.00
Hurdles	8	21	2	1	0	18	9.5	+13.00
Chases	2	6	0	0	0	6	0.0	-6.00
Totals	11	36	2	1	0	33	5.6	-2.00
04-05	11	30	0	0	2	28	0.0	-30.00
03-04	7	18	1	0	0	16	5.6	+11.00

JOCKEYS

	W-R	Per cent	£1 Level Stake
Jodie Mogford	2-14	14.3	+20.00

COURSE RECORD

	Total W-R	Non-Hndcps Hurdles	Non-Hndcps Chases	Hndcps Hurdles	Chases	NH Flat	Per cent	£1 Level Stake
Fakenham	1-2	0-1	0-0	1-1	0-0	0-0	50.0	+19.00
Sedgefield	1-6	1-2	0-1	0-3	0-0	0-0	16.7	+7.00

WINNING HORSES

Horse	Races Run	1st	2nd	3rd	£
Miss Jessica	7	1	0	0	3360
Real Chief	1	1	0	0	2398
Total winning prize-money					£5758
Favourites	0-0		0.0%		0.00

MISS LUCINDA V RUSSELL

ARLARY, PERTH & KINROSS

	No. of Hrs	Races Run	1st	2nd	3rd	Unpl	Per cent	£1 Level Stake
NH Flat	5	8	0	2	1	5	0.0	-8.00
Hurdles	39	145	4	10	15	116	2.8	-70.80
Chases	34	132	8	15	13	96	6.1	-66.00
Totals	62	285	12	27	29	217	4.2	-144.80
04-05	46	241	29	37	23	151	12.0	-67.95
03-04	43	208	14	31	27	135	6.7	-42.89

BY MONTH

NH Flat	W-R	Per cent	£1 Level Stake	Hurdles	W-R	Per cent	£1 Level Stake
May	0-0	0.0	0.00	May	0-14	0.0	-14.00
June	0-0	0.0	0.00	June	0-8	0.0	-8.00
July	0-0	0.0	0.00	July	0-3	0.0	-3.00
August	0-0	0.0	0.00	August	0-5	0.0	-5.00
September	0-0	0.0	0.00	September	1-7	14.3	-4.80
October	0-0	0.0	0.00	October	0-18	0.0	-18.00
November	0-2	0.0	-2.00	November	0-20	0.0	-20.00
December	0-0	0.0	0.00	December	0-10	0.0	-10.00
January	0-1	0.0	-1.00	January	2-17	11.8	+4.00
February	0-3	0.0	-3.00	February	1-13	7.7	+38.00
March	0-1	0.0	-1.00	March	0-13	0.0	-13.00
April	0-1	0.0	-1.00	April	0-17	0.0	-17.00

Chases	W-R	Per cent	£1 Level Stake	Totals	W-R	Per cent	£1 Level Stake
May	0-10	0.0	-10.00	May	0-24	0.0	-24.00
June	0-8	0.0	-8.00	June	0-16	0.0	-16.00
July	0-4	0.0	-4.00	July	0-7	0.0	-7.00
August	0-4	0.0	-4.00	August	0-9	0.0	-9.00
September	0-5	0.0	-5.00	September	1-12	8.3	-9.80
October	2-10	20.0	+11.00	October	2-28	7.1	-7.00

November	0-13	0.0	-13.00
December	0-10	0.0	-10.00
January	4-18	22.2	+6.00
February	0-14	0.0	-14.00
March	2-19	10.5	+2.00
April	0-17	0.0	-17.00

November	0-35	0.0	-35.00
December	0-20	0.0	-20.00
January	6-36	16.7	+9.00
February	1-30	3.3	+21.00
March	2-33	6.1	-12.00
April	0-35	0.0	-35.00

DISTANCE

Hurdles	W-R	Per cent	£1 Level Stake	Chases	W-R	Per cent	£1 Level Stake
2m-2m3f	2-63	3.2	+3.00	2m-2m3f	4-46	8.7	-11.00
2m4f-2m7f	0-54	0.0	-54.00	2m4f-2m7f	1-43	2.3	-34.00
3m+	2-28	7.1	-19.80	3m+	3-43	7.0	-21.00

TYPE OF RACE

Non-Handicaps	W-R	Per cent	£1 Level Stake	Handicaps	W-R	Per cent	£1 Level Stake
Nov Hrdls	2-42	4.8	+11.20	Nov Hrdls	0-14	0.0	-14.00
Hrdls	0-12	0.0	-12.00	Hrdls	2-66	3.0	-45.00
Nov Chs	1-35	2.9	-20.00	Nov Chs	1-26	3.8	-24.00
Chases	0-2	0.0	-2.00	Chases	6-69	8.7	-20.00
Sell/Claim	0-5	0.0	-5.00	Sell/Claim	0-8	0.0	8.00

RACE CLASS

	W-R	Per cent	£1 Level Stake	FIRST TIME OUT	W-R	Per cent	£1 Level Stake
Class 1	0-8	0.0	-8.00	Bumpers	0-5	0.0	-5.00
Class 2	0-9	0.0	-9.00	Hurdles	0-33	0.0	-33.00
Class 3	6-84	7.1	-25.00	Chases	0-24	0.0	-24.00
Class 4	5-157	3.2	-81.80				
Class 5	1-21	4.8	-15.00	Totals	0-62	0.0	-62.00
Class 6	0-6	0.0	-6.00				

JOCKEYS

	W-R	Per cent	£1 Level Stake
Peter Buchanan	11-231	4.8	-105.80
Dougie Costello	1-7	14.3	+8.00

COURSE RECORD

	Total W-R	Non-Hndcps Hurdles	Chases	Hndcps Hurdles	Chases	NH Flat	Per cent	£1 Level Stake
Wetherby	3-20	0-5	0-2	0-2	3-10	0-1	15.0	-2.00
Ayr	3-64	0-10	0-8	1-22	2-21	0-3	4.7	-44.00
Hexham	2-27	1-8	1-1	0-7	0-10	0-1	7.4	-9.80
Kelso	2-27	0-10	0-6	1-6	1-5	0-0	7.4	+1.00
Musselbgh	1-4	1-3	0-0	0-1	0-0	0-0	25.0	+47.00
Haydock	1-10	0-1	0-0	0-5	1-4	0-0	10.0	-4.00

WINNING HORSES

Horse	Races Run	1st	2nd	3rd	£
Kerry Lads	6	2	1	0	22121
Culcabock	11	1	0	1	7807
Seeyaaj	6	1	0	0	6506
Master Sebastian	6	1	0	1	6506

Catch The Perk	8	2	1	2	8939
Oliverjohn	7	2	0	3	10275
Your Advantage	3	1	1	0	4290
Lerida	7	1	0	0	3253
Caesar's Palace	12	1	1	0	2398
Total winning prize-money					£72095
Favourites	3-12		25.0%		-1.80

B J M RYALL

RIMPTON, SOMERSET

	No. of Hrs	Races Run	1st	2nd	3rd	Unpl	Per cent	£1 Level Stake
NH Flat	2	3	0	0	1	2	0.0	-3.00
Hurdles	3	5	0	1	0	4	0.0	-5.00
Chases	8	42	8	2	4	28	19.0	+16.75
Totals	12	50	8	3	5	34	16.0	+8.75
04-05	10	48	5	4	7	32	10.4	-12.25
03-04	11	43	0	5	2	36	0.0	-43.00

JOCKEYS

	W-R	Per cent	£1 Level Stake
Owyn Nelmes	5-13	38.5	+26.50
Joe Tizzard	2-19	10.5	-3.00
Richard Johnson	1-2	50.0	+1.25

COURSE RECORD

	Total W-R	Non-Hndcps Hurdles	Chases	Hndcps Hurdles	Chases	NH Flat	Per cent	£1 Level Stake
Worcester	3-9	0-2	0-1	0-0	3-5	0-1	33.3	+12.00
Fontwell	2-4	0-0	0-0	0-0	2-4	0-0	50.0	+17.50
Cartmel	1-1	0-0	0-0	0-0	1-1	0-0	100.0	+2.25
Ludlow	1-2	0-0	0-0	0-0	1-2	0-0	50.0	+6.00
Exeter	1-4	0-1	0-0	0-0	1-3	0-0	25.0	+1.00

WINNING HORSES

Horse	Races Run	1st	2nd	3rd	£
Sir Frosty	5	1	0	0	8268
Bronzesmith	8	2	0	0	12405
Wild Oats	5	1	0	1	5205
Quizzling	9	2	0	2	8276
Alcatras	8	2	2	1	8344
Total winning prize-money					£42498
Favourites	1-4		25.0%		-0.75

J RYAN

NEWMARKET, SUFFOLK

	No. of Hrs	Races Run	1st	2nd	3rd	Unpl	Per cent	£1 Level Stake
NH Flat	1	2	0	0	0	2	0.0	-2.00
Hurdles	6	10	1	0	0	9	10.0	-5.00
Chases	2	4	0	0	0	4	0.0	-4.00
Totals	6	16	1	0	0	15	6.3	-11.00

JOCKEYS

	W-R	Per cent	£1 Level Stake
Barry Fenton	1-1	100.0	+4.00

COURSE RECORD

	Total W-R	Non-Hndcps Hurdles	Chases	Hndcps Hurdles	Chases	NH Flat	Per cent	£1 Level Stake
Uttoxeter	1-1	0-0	0-0	1-1	0-0	0-0	100.0	+4.00

WINNING HORSES

Horse	Races Run	1st	2nd	3rd	£
*Buster	2	1	0	0	2946
Total winning prize-money					£2946
Favourites	0-0		0.0%		0.00

M J RYAN

NEWMARKET, SUFFOLK

	No. of Hrs	Races Run	1st	2nd	3rd	Unpl	Per cent	£1 Level Stake
NH Flat	0	0	0	0	0	0	0.0	0.00
Hurdles	6	8	0	0	0	8	0.0	-8.00
Chases	1	4	1	0	1	2	25.0	+5.00
Totals	6	12	1	0	1	10	8.3	-3.00
04-05	12	37	3	2	3	29	8.1	+27.50
03-04	15	39	4	3	3	29	10.3	-6.75

JOCKEYS

	W-R	Per cent	£1 Level Stake
Robert Thornton	1-3	33.3	+6.00

COURSE RECORD

	Total W-R	Non-Hndcps Hurdles	Chases	Hndcps Hurdles	Chases	NH Flat	Per cent	£1 Level Stake
Huntingdon	1-5	0-1	0-0	0-3	1-1	0-0	20.0	+4.00

WINNING HORSES

Horse	Races Run	1st	2nd	3rd	£
Count Oski	5	1	0	1	3581
Total winning prize money					£3581
Favourites	0-0		0.0%		0.00

K A RYAN

HAMBLETON, N YORKS

	No. of Hrs	Races Run	1st	2nd	3rd	Unpl	Per cent	£1 Level Stake
NH Flat	2	2	1	0	0	1	50.0	+4.50
Hurdles	6	10	0	0	1	9	0.0	-10.00

Chases	1	1	0	0	0	1	0.0	-1.00
Totals	9	13	1	0	1	11	7.7	-6.50
04-05	9	39	5	5	2	27	12.8	-2.33
03-04	9	32	7	7	2	16	21.9	+25.80

JOCKEYS

	W R	Per cent	£1 Level Stake
Tony Dobbin	1-1	100.0	+5.50

COURSE RECORD

	Total W-R	Non-Hndcps Hurdles	Chases	Hndcps Hurdles	Chases	NH Flat	Per cent	£1 Level Stake
Musselbgh	1-1	0-0	0-0	0-0	0-0	1-1	100.0	+5.50

WINNING HORSES

Horse	Races Run	1st	2nd	3rd	£
New Dancer	1	1	0	0	2056
Total winning prize-money					£2056
Favourites	0-1		0.0%		-1.00

MRS K M SANDERSON

TIVERTON, DEVON

	No. of Hrs	Races Run	1st	2nd	3rd	Unpl	Per cent	£1 Level Stake
NH Flat	1	2	0	1	1	0	0.0	-2.00
Hurdles	2	11	1	0	0	10	9.1	-6.00
Chases	1	4	0	0	0	4	0.0	-4.00
Totals	4	17	1	1	1	14	5.9	-12.00
04-05	1	7	2	1	0	4	28.6	-0.63
03-04	1	7	1	2	2	2	14.3	-3.75

JOCKEYS

	W-R	Per cent	£1 Level Stake
T J O'Brien	1-12	8.3	-7.00

COURSE RECORD

	Total W-R	Non-Hndcps Hurdles	Chases	Hndcps Hurdles	Chases	NH Flat	Per cent	£1 Level Stake
Worcester	1-6	1-3	0-0	0-1	0-0	0-2	16.7	-1.00

WINNING HORSES

Horse	Races Run	1st	2nd	3rd	£
*Giust In Temp	7	1	0	0	3406
Total winning prize-money					£3406
Favourites	0-0		0.0%		0.00

MRS DIANNE SAYER

HACKTHORPE, CUMBRIA

	No. of Hrs	Races Run	1st	2nd	3rd	Unpl	Per cent	£1 Level Stake
NH Flat	1	1	0	0	0	1	0.0	-1.00
Hurdles	4	17	2	0	0	15	11.8	-1.00
Chases	3	11	0	1	1	9	0.0	-11.00
Totals	5	29	2	1	1	25	6.9	-13.00
04-05	5	22	1	4	3	14	4.5	-5.00
03-04	10	28	1	1	1	25	3.6	-15.00

JOCKEYS

	W-R	Per cent	£1 Level Stake
Miss J Sayer	1-1	100.0	+7.50
Richard McGrath	1-3	33.3	+4.50

COURSE RECORD

	Total W-R	Non-Hndcps Hurdles	Chases	Hndcps Hurdles	Chases	NH Flat	Per cent	£1 Level Stake
Wetherby	1-1	0-0	0-0	1-1	0-0	0-0	100.0	+7.50
Carlisle	1-3	0-0	0-0	1-1	0-1	0-1	33.3	+4.50

WINNING HORSES

Horse	Races Run	1st	2nd	3rd	£
*Front Rank	4	1	0	0	2928
Getinbybutonlyjust	3	1	1	0	2860
Total winning prize-money					£5788
Favourites	0-0		0.0%		0.00

MISS V SCOTT

ELSDON, NORTHUMBERLAND

	No. of Hrs	Races Run	1st	2nd	3rd	Unpl	Per cent	£1 Level Stake
NH Flat	0	0	0	0	0	0	0.0	0.00
Hurdles	6	8	0	2	2	4	0.0	-8.00
Chases	2	5	1	0	0	4	20.0	+21.00
Totals	7	13	1	2	2	8	7.7	+13.00
04-05	14	42	2	4	4	32	4.8	-30.25
03-04	14	33	3	1	2	27	9.1	+7.00

JOCKEYS

	W-R	Per cent	£1 Level Stake
Sam Stronge	1-4	25.0	+22.00

COURSE RECORD

	Total W-R	Non-Hndcps Hurdles	Chases	Hndcps Hurdles	Chases	NH Flat	Per cent	£1 Level Stake
Hexham	1-2	0-1	0-0	0-0	1-1	0-0	50.0	+24.00

WINNING HORSES

Horse	Races Run	1st	2nd	3rd	£
Loy's Lad	4	1	0	0	3304
Total winning prize-money					£3304
Favourites	0-0		0.0%		0.00

M SCUDAMORE

BROMSASH, HEREFORDSHIRE

	No. of Hrs	Races Run	1st	2nd	3rd	Unpl	Per cent	£1 Level Stake
NH Flat	16	22	0	0	1	21	0.0	-22.00
Hurdles	45	139	9	11	15	104	6.5	-31.40
Chases	22	77	6	11	13	47	7.8	-33.00
Totals	63	238	15	22	29	172	6.3	-86.40
04-05	60	263	24	36	24	179	9.1	-69.00
03-04	35	135	7	10	18	100	5.2	-93.75

BY MONTH

NH Flat	W-R	Per cent	£1 Level Stake	Hurdles	W-R	Per cent	£1 Level Stake
May	0-1	0.0	-1.00	May	1-12	8.3	-2.00
June	0-0	0.0	0.00	June	1-8	12.5	+43.00
July	0-0	0.0	0.00	July	0-3	0.0	-3.00
August	0-0	0.0	0.00	August	0-4	0.0	-4.00
September	0-2	0.0	-2.00	September	0-3	0.0	-3.00
October	0-1	0.0	-1.00	October	1-12	8.3	-1.00
November	0-3	0.0	-3.00	November	2-20	10.0	-11.06
December	0-2	0.0	-2.00	December	1-15	6.7	+2.00
January	0-5	0.0	-5.00	January	3-23	13.0	-13.34
February	0-0	0.0	0.00	February	0-12	0.0	-12.00
March	0-4	0.0	-4.00	March	0-14	0.0	-14.00
April	0-4	0.0	-4.00	April	0-13	0.0	-13.00

Chases	W-R	Per cent	£1 Level Stake	Totals	W-R	Per cent	£1 Level Stake
May	0-2	0.0	-2.00	May	1-15	6.7	-5.00
June	0-3	0.0	-3.00	June	1-11	9.1	+40.00
July	0-2	0.0	-2.00	July	0-5	0.0	-5.00
August	0-3	0.0	-3.00	August	0-7	0.0	-7.00
September	0-2	0.0	-2.00	September	0-7	0.0	-7.00
October	3-13	23.1	+7.00	October	4-26	15.4	+5.00
November	1-9	11.1	-3.50	November	3-32	9.4	-17.56
December	0-13	0.0	-13.00	December	1-30	3.3	-13.00
January	1-6	16.7	-0.50	January	4-34	11.8	-18.84
February	0-6	0.0	-6.00	February	0-18	0.0	-18.00
March	1-7	14.3	+6.00	March	1-25	4.0	-12.00
April	0-11	0.0	-11.00	April	0-28	0.0	-28.00

DISTANCE

Hurdles	W-R	Per cent	£1 Level Stake	Chases	W-R	Per cent	£1 Level Stake
2m-2m3f	5-80	6.3	+8.41	2m-2m3f	1-29	3.4	-23.50

2m4f-2m7f	4-37	10.8	-17.81		2m4f-2m7f	1-13	7.7	-11.00
3m+	0-22	0.0	-22.00		3m+	4-35	11.4	+1.50

TYPE OF RACE

Non-Handicaps	W-R	Per cent	£1 Level Stake	Handicaps	W-R	Per cent	£1 Level Stake
Nov Hrdls	4-48	8.3	+12.19	Nov Hrdls	1-27	3.7	-25.09
Hrdls	0-12	0.0	-12.00	Hrdls	2-40	5.0	-12.00
Nov Chs	1-11	9.1	+2.00	Nov Chs	2-16	12.5	-6.00
Chases	0-1	0.0	-1.00	Chases	3-49	6.1	-28.00
Sell/Claim	0-5	0.0	-5.00	Sell/Claim	1-7	14.3	+3.00

RACE CLASS / FIRST TIME OUT

	W-R	Per cent	£1 Level Stake		W-R	Per cent	£1 Level Stake
Class 1	0-6	0.0	-6.00	Bumpers	0-16	0.0	-16.00
Class 2	0-5	0.0	-5.00	Hurdles	4-37	10.8	+36.00
Class 3	1-45	2.2	-28.00	Chases	0-10	0.0	-10.00
Class 4	13-143	9.1	-18.40				
Class 5	1-22	4.5	-12.00	Totals	4-63	6.3	+10.00
Class 6	0-17	0.0	-17.00				

JOCKEYS

	W-R	Per cent	£1 Level Stake
Tom Scudamore	6-112	5.4	-72.56
John Kington	3-81	3.7	-11.50
Tom Malone	2-6	33.3	+14.00
Tony Dobbin	1-1	100.0	+2.25
R J Greene	1-3	33.3	+10.00
Richard Spate	1-3	33.3	-1.09
Brian Crowley	1-12	8.3	-7.50

COURSE RECORD

	Total W-R	Non-Hndcps Hurdles	Chases	Hndcps Hurdles	Chases	NH Flat	Per cent	£1 Level Stake
Uttoxeter	3-25	0-7	0-0	1-8	2-8	0-2	12.0	+3.00
Lingfield	1-1	1-1	0-0	0-0	0-0	0-0	100.0	+0.44
Folkestone	1-2	0-0	0-0	1-1	0-0	0-1	50.0	-0.09
Sandown	1-3	0-1	0-0	1-2	0-0	0-0	33.3	+14.00
Wetherby	1-3	1-1	0-0	0-1	0-0	0-1	33.3	+1.50
Fakenham	1-4	0-1	0-1	0-0	1-1	0-1	25.0	+1.50
Haydock	1-5	1-1	0-1	0-1	0-0	0-2	20.0	-1.75
Taunton	1-8	0-3	0-0	1-3	0-1	0-1	12.5	+3.00
Wincanton	1-11	1-3	0-1	0-4	0-3	0-0	9.1	-3.50
Warwick	1-12	0-1	0-0	0-5	1-4	0-2	8.3	-6.50
Chepstow	1-13	0-1	1-4	0-1	0-6	0-1	7.7	0.00
Worcester	1-14	0-4	0-0	0-5	1-3	0-2	7.1	-12.00
Hereford	1-23	1-7	0-1	0-7	0-7	0-1	4.3	+28.00

WINNING HORSES

Horse	Races Run	1st	2nd	3rd	£
Albarino	6	2	0	2	9976
Heltornic	10	2	0	0	7934
Grey Tune	2	1	0	0	4241
Waynesworld	11	2	0	2	7485
Amadeus	12	1	3	4	4125
Hi Laurie	9	2	4	0	7270
Beauchamp Prince	6	1	1	0	3810
Finzi	7	1	4	2	3578
Ballyjohnboy Lord	5	1	0	2	3253
Idle Journey	5	1	0	1	3094
Angie's Double	1	1	0	0	2457
Total winning prize-money					£57223
Favourites	4-22		18.2%		-13.40

MRS MARILYN SCUDAMORE

NAUNTON, GLOUCS

	No. of Hrs	Races Run	1st	2nd	3rd	Unpl	Per cent	£1 Level Stake
NH Flat	0	0	0	0	0	0	0.0	0.00
Hurdles	0	0	0	0	0	0	0.0	0.00
Chases	5	8	1	0	1	6	12.5	-4.00
Totals	5	8	1	0	1	6	12.5	-4.00
04-05	4	6	2	1	0	3	33.3	+6.00

JOCKEYS

	W-R	Per cent	£1 Level Stake
Miss C Stucley	1-6	16.7	-2.00

COURSE RECORD

	Total W-R	Non-Hndcps Hurdles	Chases	Hndcps Hurdles	Chases	NH Flat	Per cent	£1 Level Stake
Cheltenham	1-1	0-0	1-1	0-0	0-0	0-0	100.0	+3.00

WINNING HORSES

Horse	Races Run	1st	2nd	3rd	£
Galway	3	1	0	1	3024
Total winning prize-money					£3024
Favourites	0-1		0.0%		-1.00

I SEMPLE

CARLUKE, S LANARKS

	No. of Hrs	Races Run	1st	2nd	3rd	Unpl	Per cent	£1 Level Stake
NH Flat	0	0	0	0	0	0	0.0	0.00
Hurdles	2	6	1	0	1	4	16.7	-3.00
Chases	0	0	0	0	0	0	0.0	0.00
Totals	2	6	1	0	1	4	16.7	-3.00
04-05	4	6	1	2	0	3	16.7	-3.38

JOCKEYS

	W-R	Per cent	£1 Level Stake
Jim Crowley	1-4	25.0	-1.00

COURSE RECORD

	Total W-R	Non-Hndcps Hurdles	Chases	Hndcps Hurdles	Chases	NH Flat	Per cent	£1 Level Stake
Perth	1-2	1-1	0-0	0-1	0-0	0-0	50.0	+1.00

WINNING HORSES

Horse	Races Run	1st	2nd	3rd	£
Millagros	5	1	0	1	3445
Total winning prize-money					£3445
Favourites	0-0		0.0%		0.00

R SHAIL

HOLLYBUSH, H'FORDS

	No. of Hrs	Races Run	1st	2nd	3rd	Unpl	Per cent	£1 Level Stake
NH Flat	0	0	0	0	0	0	0.0	0.00
Hurdles	0	0	0	0	0	0	0.0	0.00
Chases	1	4	1	0	1	2	25.0	-0.50
Totals	1	4	1	0	1	2	25.0	-0.50
04-05	2	6	0	0	2	4	0.0	-6.00
03-04	1	7	1	1	1	4	14.3	-2.50

JOCKEYS

	W-R	Per cent	£1 Level Stake
Mr D Barlow	1-3	33.3	+0.50

COURSE RECORD

	Total W-R	Non-Hndcps Hurdles	Chases	Hndcps Hurdles	Chases	NH Flat	Per cent	£1 Level Stake
Folkestone	1-1	0-0	1-1	0-0	0-0	0-0	100.0	+2.50

WINNING HORSES

Horse	Races Run	1st	2nd	3rd	£
Maggies Brother	4	1	0	1	3458
Total winning prize-money					£3458
Favourites	0-0		0.0%		0.00

M SHEPPARD

EASTNOR, H'FORDS

	No. of Hrs	Races Run	1st	2nd	3rd	Unpl	Per cent	£1 Level Stake
NH Flat	0	0	0	0	0	0	0.0	0.00
Hurdles	18	64	5	5	9	45	7.8	-25.13
Chases	17	57	6	7	6	38	10.5	-27.25
Totals	25	121	11	12	15	83	9.1	-52.38
04-05	22	93	10	6	11	66	10.8	-6.50
03-04	13	59	5	10	5	39	8.5	-14.60

BY MONTH

NH Flat	W-R	Per cent	£1 Level Stake		Hurdles	W-R	Per cent	£1 Level Stake
May	0-0	0.0	0.00		May	2-6	33.3	+2.50
June	0-0	0.0	0.00		June	1-5	20.0	-2.63
July	0-0	0.0	0.00		July	0-7	0.0	-7.00
August	0-0	0.0	0.00		August	0-7	0.0	-7.00
September	0-0	0.0	0.00		September	0-1	0.0	-1.00
October	0-0	0.0	0.00		October	1-8	12.5	+3.00
November	0-0	0.0	0.00		November	0-6	0.0	-6.00
December	0-0	0.0	0.00		December	0-6	0.0	-6.00
January	0-0	0.0	0.00		January	0-8	0.0	-8.00
February	0-0	0.0	0.00		February	0-1	0.0	-1.00
March	0-0	0.0	0.00		March	0-3	0.0	-3.00
April	0-0	0.0	0.00		April	1-6	16.7	+11.00

Chases	W-R	Per cent	£1 Level Stake		Totals	W-R	Per cent	£1 Level Stake
May	0-3	0.0	-3.00		May	2-9	22.2	-0.50
June	1-4	25.0	+2.50		June	2-9	22.2	-0.13
July	0-0	0.0	0.00		July	0-7	0.0	-7.00
August	0-2	0.0	-2.00		August	0-9	0.0	-9.00
September	0-2	0.0	-2.00		September	0-3	0.0	-3.00
October	0-4	0.0	-4.00		October	1-12	8.3	-1.00
November	2-8	25.0	-0.50		November	2-14	14.3	-6.50
December	1-11	9.1	-5.50		December	1-17	5.9	-11.50
January	1-9	11.1	-2.00		January	1-17	5.9	-10.00
February	1-7	14.3	-3.75		February	1-8	12.5	-4.75
March	0-4	0.0	-4.00		March	0-7	0.0	-7.00
April	0-3	0.0	-3.00		April	1-9	11.1	+8.00

DISTANCE

Hurdles	W-R	Per cent	£1 Level Stake		Chases	W-R	Per cent	£1 Level Stake
2m-2m3f	5-40	12.5	-1.13		2m-2m3f	1-18	5.6	-11.50
2m4f-2m7f	0-17	0.0	-17.00		2m4f-2m7f	0-17	0.0	-17.00
3m+	0-7	0.0	-7.00		3m+	5-22	22.7	+1.25

TYPE OF RACE

Non-Handicaps	W-R	Per cent	£1 Level Stake		Handicaps	W-R	Per cent	£1 Level Stake
Nov Hrdls	0-9	0.0	-9.00		Nov Hrdls	1-12	8.3	+5.00
Hrdls	0-5	0.0	-5.00		Hrdls	2-28	7.1	-12.50
Nov Chs	0-9	0.0	-9.00		Nov Chs	2-10	20.0	-2.50
Chases	0-0	0.0	0.00		Chases	3-37	8.1	-21.25
Sell/Claim	2-8	25.0	-1.63		Sell/Claim	0-2	0.0	-2.00

RACE CLASS

	W-R	Per cent	£1 Level Stake
Class 1	0-0	0.0	0.00
Class 2	0-4	0.0	-4.00
Class 3	3-30	10.0	-16.75
Class 4	6-80	7.5	-31.00

FIRST TIME OUT

	W-R	Per cent	£1 Level Stake
Bumpers	0-0	0.0	0.00
Hurdles	1-15	6.7	-4.00
Chases	1-10	10.0	-4.50

Class 5	2-7	28.6	-0.63	Totals	2-25	8.0	-8.50
Class 6	0-0	0.0	0.00				

JOCKEYS

	W-R	Per cent	£1 Level Stake
Andrew Thornton	3-6	50.0	+8.50
David Dennis	3-19	15.8	-6.13
Mark Bradburne	2-24	8.3	-15.25
Christian Williams	1-2	50.0	+15.00
P J Brennan	1-8	12.5	+3.00
Lee Stephens	1-13	7.7	-8.50

COURSE RECORD

	Total W-R	Non-Hndcps Hurdles	Chases	Hndcps Hurdles	Chases	NH Flat	Per cent	£1 Level Stake
Warwick	2-5	0-0	0-0	0-3	2-2	0-0	40.0	+3.75
Hereford	2-20	1-3	1-2	0-6	0-9	0-0	10.0	-9.50
Exeter	1-1	0-0	0-0	1-1	0-0	0-0	100.0	+16.00
Hexham	1-1	0-0	0-0	0-0	1-1	0-0	100.0	+1.00
Lingfield	1-1	0-0	0-0	0-0	1-1	0-0	100.0	+4.50
Towcester	1-2	0-0	0-0	1-2	0-0	0-0	50.0	+9.00
Bangor	1-4	0-0	0-0	1-2	0-2	0-0	25.0	+0.50
Chepstow	1-10	0-2	0-1	0-3	1-4	0-0	10.0	-3.00
Worcester	1-22	1-8	0-1	0-6	0-7	0-0	4.5	-19.63

WINNING HORSES

Horse	Races Run	1st	2nd	3rd	£
Moorlands Again	9	2	2	0	12004
Forzacurity	11	1	1	0	6479
Precious Bane	8	3	2	?	12656
Rudetski	6	1	0	1	3712
*Young Tot	6	2	0	0	7027
Burning Truth	7	2	0	1	5418
Total winning prize-money					**£47296**
Favourites	3-8		37.5%		**-0.38**

O SHERWOOD

UPPER LAMBOURN, BERKS

	No. of Hrs	Races Run	1st	2nd	3rd	Unpl	Per cent	£1 Level Stake
NH Flat	11	17	2	1	1	13	11.8	-10.25
Hurdles	30	101	10	11	12	68	9.9	-31.04
Chases	17	65	8	10	8	39	12.3	-9.13
Totals	49	183	20	22	21	120	10.9	-50.42
04-05	45	153	16	25	21	91	10.5	-72.47
03-04	43	155	22	27	17	89	14.2	-83.44

BY MONTH

NH Flat	W-R	Per cent	£1 Level Stake	Hurdles	W-R	Per cent	£1 Level Stake
May	0-1	0.0	-1.00	May	0-8	0.0	-8.00
June	0-0	0.0	0.00	June	0-1	0.0	-1.00
July	0-0	0.0	0.00	July	0-2	0.0	-2.00
August	0-0	0.0	0.00	August	0-0	0.0	0.00
September	0-0	0.0	0.00	September	0-0	0.0	0.00
October	0-1	0.0	-1.00	October	0-7	0.0	-7.00
November	1-5	20.0	-1.00	November	2-13	15.4	-2.38
December	0-1	0.0	-1.00	December	3-18	16.7	+18.00
January	0-0	0.0	0.00	January	1-14	7.1	-9.67
February	0-2	0.0	-2.00	February	0-11	0.0	-11.00
March	0-3	0.0	-3.00	March	1-12	8.3	-5.50
April	1-4	25.0	-1.25	April	3-15	20.0	-2.50

Chases	W-R	Per cent	£1 Level Stake	Totals	W-R	Per cent	£1 Level Stake
May	0-1	0.0	-1.00	May	0-10	0.0	-10.00
June	0-0	0.0	0.00	June	0-1	0.0	-1.00
July	1-1	100.0	+10.00	July	1-3	33.3	+8.00
August	0-1	0.0	-1.00	August	0-1	0.0	-1.00
September	0-1	0.0	-1.00	September	0-1	0.0	-1.00
October	1-2	50.0	+0.75	October	1-10	10.0	-7.25
November	3-10	30.0	+4.13	November	6-28	21.4	+0.75
December	0-14	0.0	-14.00	December	3-33	9.1	+3.00
January	0-7	0.0	-7.00	January	1-21	4.8	-16.67
February	1-7	14.3	-1.00	February	1-20	5.0	-14.00
March	2-10	20.0	+12.00	March	3-25	12.0	+3.50
April	0-11	0.0	-11.00	April	4-30	13.3	-14.75

DISTANCE

Hurdles	W-R	Per cent	£1 Level Stake	Chases	W-R	Per cent	£1 Level Stake
2m-2m3f	6-52	11.5	-12.88	2m-2m3f	2-18	11.1	-6.25
2m4f-2m7f	3-33	9.1	-8.67	2m4f-2m7f	1-14	7.1	-8.00
3m+	1-16	6.3	-9.50	3m+	5-33	15.2	+5.13

TYPE OF RACE

Non-Handicaps	W-R	Per cent	£1 Level Stake	Handicaps	W-R	Per cent	£1 Level Stake
Nov Hrdls	6-47	12.8	-12.04	Nov Hrdls	0-10	0.0	-10.00
Hrdls	2-18	11.1	+2.00	Hrdls	1-25	4.0	-17.00
Nov Chs	1-7	14.3	-4.25	Nov Chs	1-8	12.5	+3.00
Chases	0-4	0.0	-4.00	Chases	6-46	13.0	-3.88
Sell/Claim	0-0	0.0	0.00	Sell/Claim	1-1	100.0	+6.00

RACE CLASS

	W-R	Per cent	£1 Level Stake
Class 1	1-9	11.1	-1.00
Class 2	2-10	20.0	+7.00
Class 3	6-52	11.5	-12.42
Class 4	8-93	8.6	-38.75
Class 5	1-6	16.7	+1.00
Class 6	2-13	15.4	-6.25

FIRST TIME OUT

	W-R	Per cent	£1 Level Stake
Bumpers	1-11	9.1	-7.00
Hurdles	3-24	12.5	+12.00
Chases	1-14	7.1	-11.38
Totals	5-49	10.2	-6.38

JOCKEYS

	W-R	Per cent	£1 Level Stake
Leighton Aspell	16-134	11.9	-24.92
Owyn Nelmes	2-27	7.4	-14.00

P J Brennan	1-3	33.3	-0.50
G Lee	1-4	25.0	+4.00

COURSE RECORD

	Total W-R	Non-Hndcps Hurdles	Chases	Hndcps Hurdles	Chases	NH Flat	Per cent	£1 Level Stake
Leicester	2-3	2-2	0-1	0-0	0-0	0-0	66.7	+9.33
Mrket Rsn	2-7	2-3	0-0	0-2	0-1	0-1	28.6	-1.88
Huntingdon	2-15	0-6	0-1	1-3	1-4	0-1	13.3	0.00
Fontwell	2-17	1-8	0-1	0-3	1-4	0-1	11.8	-11.38
Warwick	1-2	1-2	0-0	0-0	0-0	0-0	50.0	+9.00
Stratford	1-4	0-1	0-0	0-0	1-3	0-0	25.0	+7.00
Wetherby	1-5	0-1	0-0	0-1	1-2	0-1	20.0	+1.00
Worcester	1-5	0-1	0-0	0-2	0-1	1-1	20.0	-2.25
Bangor	1-6	0-2	0-0	0-2	1-2	0-0	16.7	+3.00
Windsor	1-6	0-3	0-0	0-2	1-1	0-0	16.7	-2.50
Hereford	1-7	0-0	0-1	0-2	0-2	1-2	14.3	-3.00
Folkestone	1-9	1-4	0-1	0-0	0-2	0-2	11.1	+8.00
Sandown	1-10	0-1	0-1	0-4	1-3	0-1	10.0	+3.00
Towcester	1-10	0-4	1-3	0-1	0-1	0-1	10.0	-7.25
Ludlow	1-11	1-4	0-0	0-1	0-4	0-2	9.1	-4.50
Newbury	1-12	0-1	0-0	1-3	0-6	0-7	8.3	-4.00

WINNING HORSES

Horse	Races Run	1st	2nd	3rd	£
Manorson	4	1	0	0	17106
Claymore	5	1	0	1	12526
*Prime Contender	4	1	0	0	9300
Eric's Charm	3	1	1	0	7807
Kausse De Thaix	8	2	0	1	11927
Brumous	3	2	1	0	9906
Caribou	3	2	0	0	10227
Winsley	7	1	3	2	5460
Mini Dare	7	1	0	1	5452
Super Road Train	7	1	1	2	5322
Lyes Green	7	2	1	1	7697
Bel Ombre	6	1	0	0	4229
Love Of Classics	7	1	3	1	3333
Quotable	5	1	0	0	2741
Rosita Bay	4	1	0	1	1932
Mount Sandel	3	1	1	0	1713
Total winning prize-money					**£116678**
Favourites	6-16		37.5%		1.25

S E H SHERWOOD

BREDENBURY, H'FORDS

	No. of Hrs	Races Run	1st	2nd	3rd	Unpl	Per cent	£1 Level Stake
NH Flat	1	1	0	0	0	1	0.0	-1.00
Hurdles	7	14	0	1	1	12	0.0	-14.00
Chases	6	16	4	1	1	10	25.0	+34.25
Totals	11	31	4	2	2	23	12.9	+19.25
04-05	14	50	4	5	8	33	8.0	-13.00
03-04	21	54	6	3	2	43	11.1	+7.17

JOCKEYS

	W-R	Per cent	£1 Level Stake
Joe Tizzard	4-18	22.2	+32.25

COURSE RECORD

	Total W-R	Non-Hndcps Hurdles	Chases	Hndcps Hurdles	Chases	NH Flat	Per cent	£1 Level Stake
Stratford	1-1	0-0	0-0	0-0	1-1	0-0	100.0	+20.00
Huntingdon	1-2	0-0	1-1	0-0	0-1	0-0	50.0	+1.25
Haydock	1-3	0-0	0-0	0-1	1-2	0-0	33.3	+6.00
Worcester	1-5	0-2	1-2	0-1	0-0	0-0	20.0	+12.00

WINNING HORSES

Horse	Races Run	1st	2nd	3rd	£
On The Outside	5	3	0	0	18574
Il'Athou	4	1	1	0	5400
Total winning prize-money					**£23974**
Favourites	0-1		0.0%		-1.00

MISS L C SIDDALL

COLTON, N YORKS

	No. of Hrs	Races Run	1st	2nd	3rd	Unpl	Per cent	£1 Level Stake
NH Flat	1	1	0	0	0	1	0.0	-1.00
Hurdles	7	33	2	1	2	28	6.1	-18.00
Chases	3	17	0	0	1	16	0.0	-17.00
Totals	10	51	2	1	3	45	3.9	-36.00
04-05	11	65	5	6	5	49	7.7	-34.50
03-04	9	51	3	4	6	38	5.9	-41.63

JOCKEYS

	W-R	Per cent	£1 Level Stake
Andrew Thornton	1-8	12.5	+1.00
Tom Siddall	1-24	4.2	-18.00

COURSE RECORD

	Total W-R	Non-Hndcps Hurdles	Chases	Hndcps Hurdles	Chases	NH Flat	Per cent	£1 Level Stake
Southwell	1-3	1-3	0-0	0-0	0-0	0-0	33.3	+6.00
Mrket Rsn	1-7	0-0	0-0	1-5	0-2	0-0	14.3	-1.00

WINNING HORSES

Horse	Races Run	1st	2nd	3rd	£
Super Boston	6	1	0	0	2961
Lazy Lena	10	1	1	1	2172
Total winning prize-money					**£5133**
Favourites	0-1		0.0%		-1.00

MISS VICKY SIMPSON

NORTH BERWICK, EAST LOTHIAN

	No. of Hrs	Races Run	1st	2nd	3rd	Unpl	Per cent	£1 Level Stake
NH Flat	0	0	0	0	0	0	0.0	0.00
Hurdles	0	0	0	0	0	0	0.0	0.00
Chases	1	3	1	1	1	0	33.3	+3.50
Totals	1	3	1	1	1	0	33.3	+3.50

JOCKEYS

	W-R	Per cent	£1 Level Stake
Miss Vicky Simpson	1-3	33.3	+3.50

COURSE RECORD

	Total W-R	Non-Hndcps Hurdles	Chases	Hndcps Hurdles	Chases	NH Flat	Per cent	£1 Level Stake
Kelso	1-1	0-0	1-1	0-0	0-0	0-0	100.0	+5.50

WINNING HORSES

Horse	Races Run	1st	2nd	3rd	£
Jacksonville	3	1	1	1	2637
Total winning prize-money					**£2637**
Favourites	0-0	0.0%			0.00

MRS E SLACK

HILTON, CUMBRIA

	No. of Hrs	Races Run	1st	2nd	3rd	Unpl	Per cent	£1 Level Stake
NH Flat	5	6	1	0	0	5	16.7	+5.00
Hurdles	16	64	2	4	7	51	3.1	-42.50
Chases	6	15	1	3	1	10	6.7	-12.38
Totals	20	85	4	7	8	66	4.7	-49.88
04-05	17	96	9	6	14	67	9.4	-44.88
03-04	14	74	6	9	10	49	8.1	-30.90

JOCKEYS

	W-R	Per cent	£1 Level Stake
Steven Gagan	2-42	4.8	-34.88
Michael McAlister	1-4	25.0	+7.00
Brian Harding	1-17	5.9	0.00

COURSE RECORD

	Total W-R	Non-Hndcps Hurdles	Chases	Hndcps Hurdles	Chases	NH Flat	Per cent	£1 Level Stake
Kelso	1-5	0-2	0-1	1-2	0-0	0-0	20.0	-0.50
Wetherby	1-6	0-2	0-0	1-3	0-0	0-1	16.7	+11.00
Hexham	1-8	0-2	0-0	0-5	0-0	1-1	12.5	+3.00
Sedgefield	1-23	0-7	1-1	0-6	0-6	0-3	4.3	-20.38

WINNING HORSES

Horse	Races Run	1st	2nd	3rd	£
Red Man	15	2	3	3	7897
Stoneravinmad	2	1	0	1	2713
King Daniel	2	1	0	0	1028
Total winning prize-money					**£11638**
Favourites	1-2	50.0%			0.63

MRS P SLY

THORNEY, CAMBS

	No. of Hrs	Races Run	1st	2nd	3rd	Unpl	Per cent	£1 Level Stake
NH Flat	4	7	0	0	1	6	0.0	-7.00
Hurdles	19	61	8	7	6	40	13.1	+14.25
Chases	4	13	1	2	1	9	7.7	10.13
Totals	22	81	9	9	8	55	11.1	-2.88
04-05	21	86	5	15	5	61	5.8	-13.75
03-04	19	88	7	5	10	66	8.0	+58.00

JOCKEYS

	W-R	Per cent	£1 Level Stake
Warren Marston	5-42	11.9	+15.13
Paul Moloney	2-16	12.5	-3.00
Gino Carenza	1-3	33.3	+1.00
Miss L Allan	1-6	16.7	-2.00

COURSE RECORD

	Total W-R	Non-Hndcps Hurdles	Chases	Hndcps Hurdles	Chases	NH Flat	Per cent	£1 Level Stake
Huntingdon	3-20	3-7	0-2	0-6	0-4	0-1	15.0	-3.75
Fakenham	2-10	0-3	1-1	1-2	0-4	0-0	20.0	-0.13
Sandown	1-1	0-0	0-0	1-1	0-0	0-0	100.0	+3.00
Stratford	1-3	0-1	0-0	1-2	0-0	0-0	33.3	+7.00
Uttoxeter	1-4	0-0	0-0	1-3	0-0	0-1	25.0	+30.00
Warwick	1-5	0-3	0-0	1-2	0-0	0-0	20.0	-1.00

WINNING HORSES

Horse	Races Run	1st	2nd	3rd	£
Dhehdaah	5	1	2	0	6766
Hawthorn Prince	3	2	0	0	11366
Vertical Bloom	5	1	1	3	4857
Fullards	4	1	0	0	4799
Harrycone Lewis	9	2	2	0	7213
Upright Ima	11	1	3	1	3904
Harley	1	1	0	0	3536
Total winning prize-money					**£42441**
Favourites	2-5	40.0%			1.88

C SMITH

TEMPLE BRUER, LINCS

	No. of Hrs	Races Run	1st	2nd	3rd	Unpl	Per cent	£1 Level Stake
NH Flat	1	1	0	0	0	1	0.0	-1.00
Hurdles	2	20	3	2	1	14	15.0	-8.50
Chases	0	0	0	0	0	0	0.0	0.00
Totals	3	21	3	2	1	15	14.3	-9.50
04-05	2	9	0	0	3	6	0.0	-9.00
03-04	1	1	0	0	0	1	0.0	-1.00

JOCKEYS

	W-R	Per cent	£1 Level Stake
A P McCoy	1-2	50.0	+2.50
Wayne Hutchinson	1-2	50.0	+1.75
David Dennis	1-5	20.0	-1.75

COURSE RECORD

	Total W-R	Non-Hndcps Hurdles	Chases	Hndcps Hurdles	Chases	NH Flat	Per cent	£1 Level Stake
Mrket Rsn	2-7	1-4	0-0	1-2	0-0	0-1	28.6	+0.75
Towcester	1-1	1-1	0-0	0-0	0-0	0-0	100.0	+2.75

WINNING HORSES

Horse	Races Run	1st	2nd	3rd	£
Smart Boy Prince	14	3	2	1	14860
Total winning prize-money					£14860
Favourites	0-0		0.0%		0.00

M SMITH

KIRKHEATON, NORTHUMBERLAND

	No. of Hrs	Races Run	1st	2nd	3rd	Unpl	Per cent	£1 Level Stake
NH Flat	0	0	0	0	0	0	0.0	0.00
Hurdles	2	8	2	0	2	4	25.0	+8.50
Chases	1	3	0	0	0	3	0.0	-3.00
Totals	3	11	2	0	2	7	18.2	+5.50
04-05	2	4	1	0	0	3	25.0	+7.00
03-04	3	7	0	0	1	6	0.0	-7.00

JOCKEYS

	W-R	Per cent	£1 Level Stake
Michael McAlister	2-8	25.0	+8.50

COURSE RECORD

	Total W-R	Non-Hndcps Hurdles	Chases	Hndcps Hurdles	Chases	NH Flat	Per cent	£1 Level Stake
Hexham	1-1	0-0	0-0	1-1	0-0	0-0	100.0	+9.00
Catterick	1-3	0-0	0-0	1-1	0-2	0-0	33.3	+3.50

WINNING HORSES

Horse	Races Run	1st	2nd	3rd	£
Texas Holdem	7	2	0	2	12023
Total winning prize-money					£12023
Favourites	0-0		0.0%		0.00

V SMITH

EXNING, SUFFOLK

	No. of Hrs	Races Run	1st	2nd	3rd	Unpl	Per cent	£1 Level Stake
NH Flat	1	1	0	0	0	1	0.0	-1.00
Hurdles	4	14	1	1	0	12	7.1	-6.00
Chases	0	0	0	0	0	0	0.0	0.00
Totals	5	15	1	1	0	13	6.7	-7.00
04-05	8	13	0	1	1	11	0.0	-13.00
03-04	1	2	0	0	1	1	0.0	-2.00

JOCKEYS

	W-R	Per cent	£1 Level Stake
Philip Hide	1-5	20.0	+3.00

COURSE RECORD

	Total W-R	Non-Hndcps Hurdles	Chases	Hndcps Hurdles	Chases	NH Flat	Per cent	£1 Level Stake
Stratford	1-1	1-1	0-0	0-0	0-0	0-0	100.0	+7.00

WINNING HORSES

Horse	Races Run	1st	2nd	3rd	£
Harrycat	4	1	1	0	6322
Total winning prize-money					£6322
Favourites	0-1		0.0%		-1.00

J S SMITH

TIRLEY, GLOUCS

	No. of Hrs	Races Run	1st	2nd	3rd	Unpl	Per cent	£1 Level Stake
NH Flat	1	3	0	0	0	3	0.0	-3.00
Hurdles	4	12	2	1	0	9	16.7	-6.25
Chases	3	13	1	3	0	9	7.7	-6.00
Totals	6	28	3	4	0	21	10.7	-15.25
04-05	6	25	3	1	3	18	12.0	-12.10
03-04	7	31	5	5	7	14	16.1	+22.50

JOCKEYS

	W-R	Per cent	£1 Level Stake
Paul Moloney	2-10	20.0	-4.25
Mr G Tumelty	1-1	100.0	+6.00

COURSE RECORD

	Total W-R	Non-Hndcps Hurdles	Chases	Hndcps Hurdles	Chases	NH Flat	Per cent	£1 Level Stake
Wincanton	1-1	0-0	0-0	1-1	0-0	0-0	100.0	+1.88
Warwick	1-3	0-1	0-0	1-1	0-1	0-0	33.3	-0.13
Hereford	1-4	0-2	0-0	0-1	1-1	0-0	25.0	+3.00

WINNING HORSES

Horse	Races Run	1st	2nd	3rd	£
Return Home	4	2	1	0	7353
Valley Warrior	7	1	1	0	3253
Total winning prize-money					**£10606**
Favourites	1-3		33.3%		-0.13

G J SMITH

SIX HILLS, LEICS

	No. of Hrs	Races Run	1st	2nd	3rd	Unpl	Per cent	£1 Level Stake
NH Flat	2	4	0	0	0	4	0.0	-4.00
Hurdles	11	21	3	1	2	15	14.3	+68.50
Chases	6	12	1	1	1	9	8.3	-3.50
Totals	14	37	4	2	3	28	10.8	+61.00
04-05	8	25	0	0	1	24	0.0	-25.00
03-04	6	11	1	0	1	9	9.1	+4.00

JOCKEYS

	W-R	Per cent	£1 Level Stake
Jodie Mogford	4-21	19.0	+77.00

COURSE RECORD

	Total W-R	Non-Hndcps Hurdles	Chases	Hndcps Hurdles	Chases	NH Flat	Per cent	£1 Level Stake
Uttoxeter	2-7	2-5	0-1	0-1	0-0	0-0	28.6	+69.50
Stratford	1-1	1-1	0-0	0-0	0-0	0-0	100.0	+12.00
Bangor	1-2	0-0	1-1	0-1	0-0	0-0	50.0	+6.50

WINNING HORSES

Horse	Races Run	1st	2nd	3rd	£
Fisherman Jack	6	1	1	1	4132
Red Nose Lady	8	2	1	1	5928
Euro Route	3	1	0	1	2275
Total winning prize-money					**£12335**
Favourites	0-0		0.0%		0.00

MRS S J SMITH

HIGH ELDWICK, W YORKS

	No. of Hrs	Races Run	1st	2nd	3rd	Unpl	Per cent	£1 Level Stake
NH Flat	23	38	3	0	3	32	7.9	-11.00
Hurdles	69	183	26	19	16	122	14.2	-13.55
Chases	46	191	31	26	23	111	16.2	+3.91
Totals	105	412	60	45	42	265	14.6	-20.64
04-05	99	478	62	65	52	299	13.0	-172.32
03-04	97	436	69	55	76	236	15.8	+1.58

BY MONTH

NH Flat	W-R	Per cent	£1 Level Stake	Hurdles	W-R	Per cent	£1 Level Stake
May	0-1	0.0	-1.00	May	1-15	6.7	-10.50
June	0-1	0.0	-1.00	June	2-10	20.0	-2.42
July	0-1	0.0	-1.00	July	0-8	0.0	-8.00
August	0-3	0.0	-3.00	August	1-6	16.7	+2.50
September	1-2	50.0	+2.50	September	0-5	0.0	-5.00
October	0-3	0.0	-3.00	October	0-14	0.0	-14.00
November	0-10	0.0	-10.00	November	2-15	13.3	+15.00
December	0-5	0.0	-5.00	December	1-24	4.2	-21.13
January	0-2	0.0	-2.00	January	3-18	16.7	-3.50
February	1-3	33.3	+14.00	February	7-21	33.3	+32.38
March	0-3	0.0	-3.00	March	3-16	18.8	-7.25
April	1-4	25.0	+1.50	April	6-31	19.4	+8.37

Chases	W-R	Per cent	£1 Level Stake	Totals	W-R	Per cent	£1 Level Stake
May	3-15	20.0	-0.63	May	4-31	12.9	-12.13
June	3-7	42.9	+6.88	June	5-18	27.8	+3.46
July	0-8	0.0	-8.00	July	0-17	0.0	-17.00
August	3-16	18.8	-2.92	August	4-25	16.0	-3.42
September	2-3	66.7	+23.50	September	3-10	30.0	+21.00
October	5-18	27.8	+16.25	October	5-35	14.3	-0.75
November	7-30	23.3	+22.75	November	9-55	16.4	+27.75
December	2-24	8.3	-15.70	December	3-53	5.7	-41.83
January	1-18	5.6	-12.00	January	4-38	10.5	-17.50
February	0-17	0.0	-17.00	February	8-41	19.5	+29.38
March	2-9	22.2	-1.13	March	5-28	17.9	-11.38
April	3-26	11.5	-8.10	April	10-61	16.4	+1.77

DISTANCE

Hurdles	W-R	Per cent	£1 Level Stake	Chases	W-R	Per cent	£1 Level Stake
2m-2m3f	8-68	11.8	-28.89	2m-2m3f	3-21	14.3	+5.00
2m4f-2m7f	12-84	14.3	+15.25	2m4f-2m7f	15-76	19.7	+9.61
3m+	6-31	19.4	+0.08	3m+	13-94	13.8	-10.70

TYPE OF RACE

Non-Handicaps	W-R	Per cent	£1 Level Stake	Handicaps	W-R	Per cent	£1 Level Stake
Nov Hrdls	10-60	16.7	-4.43	Nov Hrdls	2-19	10.5	-11.00

Hrdls	2-19	10.5	-4.75	Hrdls	11-81	13.6	-6.38
Nov Chs	7-36	19.4	-2.68	Nov Chs	2-12	16.7	-2.00
Chases	2-12	16.7	-1.00	Chases	20-130	15.4	+10.58
Sell/Claim	0-3	0.0	-3.00	Sell/Claim	1-2	50.0	+15.00

RACE CLASS

	W-R	Per cent	£1 Level Stake
Class 1	3-38	7.9	-15.00
Class 2	5-35	14.3	+38.50
Class 3	25-128	19.5	+13.61
Class 4	23-167	13.8	-57.75
Class 5	1-9	11.1	+8.00
Class 6	3-35	8.6	-8.00

FIRST TIME OUT

	W-R	Per cent	£1 Level Stake
Bumpers	0-23	0.0	-23.00
Hurdles	2-48	4.2	-36.50
Chases	4-34	11.8	-14.13
Totals	6-105	5.7	-73.63

JOCKEYS

	W-R	Per cent	£1 Level Stake
Dominic Elsworth	43-243	17.7	+26.98
David O'Meara	6-27	22.2	+1.88
Padge Whelan	6-42	14.3	+15.00
Michael O'Connell	3-24	12.5	+2.50
Andrew Adams	1-9	11.1	-4.50
T Halliday	1-16	6.3	-11.50

COURSE RECORD

	Total W-R	Non-Hndcps Hurdles	Chases	Hndcps Hurdles	Chases	NH Flat	Per cent	£1 Level Stake
Mrket Rsn	9-42	2-10	1-2	1-13	4-14	1-3	21.4	+28.65
Wetherby	8-51	0-8	2-6	3-15	3-18	0-4	15.7	-13.07
Carlisle	6-18	0-3	0-1	3-6	3-8	0-0	33.3	+16.50
Worcester	5-25	2-6	1-6	0-5	2-4	0-4	20.0	+2.04
Sedgefield	5-38	2-9	1-8	1-8	0-8	1-5	13.2	+8.75
Kelso	4-13	1-3	1-3	1-3	1-4	0-0	30.8	+3.62
Newcastle	4-17	1-5	0-0	0-2	3-9	0-1	23.5	-2.50
Hexham	3-10	0-2	0-1	1-2	1-3	1-2	30.0	+14.00
Southwell	3-23	0-1	1-5	2-6	0-10	0-1	13.0	-4.25
Haydock	3-26	1-8	1-1	1-5	0-8	0-4	11.5	+23.00
Cartmel	2-9	0-2	1-2	0-2	1-3	0-0	22.2	-1.63
Uttoxeter	2-19	1-2	0-2	1-9	0-4	0-2	10.5	-10.75
Catterick	2-30	2-9	0-2	0-6	0-6	0-7	6.7	-23.75
Stratford	1-2	0-0	0-0	0-0	1-2	0-0	50.0	+2.50
Newbury	1-5	0-1	0-0	0-0	1-4	0-0	20.0	+12.00
Huntingdon	1-7	0-0	0-3	0-1	1-3	0-0	14.3	-3.75
Bangor	1-22	0-4	0-1	0-6	1-7	0-4	4.5	-17.00

WINNING HORSES

Horse	Races Run	1st	2nd	3rd	£
St Matthew	5	2	0	0	58341
Mister McGoldrick	10	1	1	3	28845
Ross Comm	10	5	1	1	54116
Little Big Horse	9	3	0	2	47181
Royal Emperor	6	1	1	1	22915
Town Crier	8	2	1	0	29843
Smiths Landing	1	1	0	0	14883
Presumptuous	4	2	0	0	18983
Supreme Breeze	6	1	0	1	13127
Undeniable	6	2	1	3	18581
Corlande	6	2	0	0	19032
Bushido	8	3	0	1	18434
Darina's Boy	6	2	1	1	11999
Rebel Rhythm	7	2	2	1	10785
Sharp Belline	8	2	1	0	9655
Oso Magic	8	3	0	0	14551
Cool Cossack	1	1	0	0	5434
Bougoure	5	2	0	1	8760
*Willies Way	4	1	1	0	5205
*Atlantic Jane	2	1	0	0	5205
Infini	6	1	0	0	4680
Pebble Bay	7	1	2	2	4589
After Me Boys	4	1	0	1	4173
Stagecoach Diamond	7	2	2	1	6951
*Farington Lodge	5	1	2	0	3937
*Imtihan	6	2	3	0	6987
Ding Dong Belle	1	1	0	0	3497
Like A Lord	3	1	0	0	3484
Tomenoso	7	1	0	3	3445
Flake	7	1	1	0	3253
Cash King	5	1	0	0	3253
Boulders Beach	6	1	1	1	3253
Blackergreen	6	2	2	1	6167
Tous Chez	6	1	1	2	2928
Losing Grip	4	1	0	0	2193
Rising Tempest	5	1	0	0	1911
Autograph	2	1	0	0	1713
Stagecoach Opal	4	1	0	1	1713
Total winning prize-money					**£484002**
Favourites	20-42		47.6%		15.56

MISS SUZY SMITH

LEWES, E SUSSEX

	No. of Hrs	Races Run	1st	2nd	3rd	Unpl	Per cent	£1 Level Stake
NH Flat	7	11	0	0	1	10	0.0	-11.00
Hurdles	6	14	3	2	2	7	21.4	+26.00
Chases	6	23	3	4	0	16	13.0	+3.13
Totals	16	48	6	6	3	33	12.5	+18.13
04-05	8	21	2	7	0	12	9.5	-6.00
03-04	7	27	5	5	3	14	18.5	+26.38

JOCKEYS

	W-R	Per cent	£1 Level Stake
Daryl Jacob	3-10	30.0	+34.00
Colin Bolger	2-19	10.5	0.00
T J O'Brien	1-1	100.0	+2.13

COURSE RECORD

	Total W-R	Non-Hndcps Hurdles	Chases	Hndcps Hurdles	Chases	NH Flat	Per cent	£1 Level Stake
Cheltenham	1-1	0-0	0-0	1-1	0-0	0-0	100.0	+20.00

Wincanton	1-2	0-1	0-0	1-1	0-0	0-0	50.0	+11.00
Fontwell	1-4	0-1	0-0	1-1	0-2	0-0	25.0	+2.00
Huntingdon	1-4	0-0	0-0	0-0	1-3	0-1	25.0	-0.88
Warwick	1-4	0-0	0-0	0-0	1-2	0-1	25.0	+2.00
Ludlow	1-8	0-1	0-2	0-0	1-3	0-2	12.5	+9.00

WINNING HORSES

Horse	Races Run	1st	2nd	3rd	£
Material World	3	1	1	1	18789
Golden Bay	3	2	0	0	20308
*Boardroom Dancer	4	2	0	0	6568
Cool Song	7	1	3	0	3381
Total winning prize-money					**£49046**
Favourites	1-5		20.0%		-1.88

M E SOWERSBY

GOODMANHAM, E YORKS

	No. of Hrs	Races Run	1st	2nd	3rd	Unpl	Per cent	£1 Level Stake
NH Flat	2	3	0	1	0	2	0.0	-3.00
Hurdles	25	108	2	4	4	98	1.9	-94.50
Chases	4	15	0	0	3	12	0.0	-15.00
Totals	30	126	2	5	7	112	1.6	-112.50
04-05	21	96	2	2	5	87	2.1	-76.00
03-04	18	86	1	5	6	74	1.2	-75.00

JOCKEYS

	W-R	Per cent	£1 Level Stake
Phil Kinsella	1-6	16.7	+0.50
Keith Mercer	1-10	10.0	-3.00

COURSE RECORD

	Total W-R	Non-Hndcps Hurdles	Chases	Hndcps Hurdles	Chases	NH Flat	Per cent	£1 Level Stake
Catterick	1-16	0-5	0-0	1-9	0-1	0-1	6.3	-9.50
Mrket Rsn	1-50	0-26	0-1	1-13	0-9	0-1	2.0	-43.00

WINNING HORSES

Horse	Races Run	1st	2nd	3rd	£
Karathatha	10	1	0	2	4849
*Uncle John	5	1	0	0	2741
Total winning prize-money					**£7590**
Favourites	0-2		0.0%		-2.00

J L SPEARING

KINNERSLEY, WORCS

	No. of Hrs	Races Run	1st	2nd	3rd	Unpl	Per cent	£1 Level Stake
NH Flat	8	14	0	1	1	12	0.0	-14.00
Hurdles	20	47	1	4	6	36	2.1	-44.25

Chases	12	52	13	14	3	22	25.0	+63.75
Totals	34	113	14	19	10	70	12.4	+5.50
04-05	22	94	10	11	12	61	10.6	-7.55
03-04	22	69	11	9	9	40	15.9	+19.88

BY MONTH

NH Flat	W-R	Per cent	£1 Level Stake	Hurdles	W-R	Per cent	£1 Level Stake
May	0-2	0.0	-2.00	May	1-7	14.3	-4.25
June	0-3	0.0	-3.00	June	0-5	0.0	-5.00
July	0-1	0.0	-1.00	July	0-2	0.0	-2.00
August	0-0	0.0	0.00	August	0-1	0.0	-1.00
September	0-0	0.0	0.00	September	0-1	0.0	-1.00
October	0-0	0.0	0.00	October	0-7	0.0	-7.00
November	0-0	0.0	0.00	November	0-3	0.0	-3.00
December	0-2	0.0	-2.00	December	0-4	0.0	-4.00
January	0-0	0.0	0.00	January	0-4	0.0	-4.00
February	0-2	0.0	-2.00	February	0-4	0.0	-4.00
March	0-3	0.0	-3.00	March	0-7	0.0	-2.00
April	0-1	0.0	-1.00	April	0-7	0.0	-7.00

Chases	W-R	Per cent	£1 Level Stake	Totals	W-R	Per cent	£1 Level Stake
May	0-5	0.0	-5.00	May	1-14	7.1	-11.25
June	0-1	0.0	-1.00	June	0-9	0.0	-9.00
July	1-6	16.7	+1.50	July	1-9	11.1	-1.50
August	2-4	50.0	+18.00	August	2-5	40.0	+17.00
September	0-1	0.0	-1.00	September	0-2	0.0	-2.00
October	1-5	20.0	-1.50	October	1-12	8.3	-8.50
November	1-4	25.0	+15.00	November	1-7	14.3	+12.00
December	0-5	0.0	-5.00	December	0-11	0.0	-11.00
January	1-6	16.7	+4.00	January	1-10	10.0	0.00
February	1-3	33.3	-0.25	February	1-9	11.1	-6.25
March	2-5	40.0	+15.00	March	2-10	20.0	+10.00
April	4-7	57.1	+24.00	April	4-15	26.7	+16.00

DISTANCE

Hurdles	W-R	Per cent	£1 Level Stake	Chases	W-R	Per cent	£1 Level Stake
2m-2m3f	1-28	3.6	-25.25	2m-2m3f	7-26	26.9	+25.75
2m4f-2m7f	0-18	0.0	-18.00	2m4f-2m7f	3-17	17.6	+14.00
3m+	0-1	0.0	-1.00	3m+	3-9	33.3	+24.00

TYPE OF RACE

Non-Handicaps	W-R	Per cent	£1 Level Stake	Handicaps	W-R	Per cent	£1 Level Stake
Nov Hrdls	0-17	0.0	-17.00	Nov Hrdls	0-7	0.0	-7.00
Hrdls	0-3	0.0	-3.00	Hrdls	0-16	0.0	-16.00
Nov Chs	2-12	16.7	+12.00	Nov Chs	1-5	20.0	+10.00
Chases	0-1	0.0	-1.00	Chases	10-34	29.4	+54.75
Sell/Claim	1-3	33.3	-0.25	Sell/Claim	0-3	0.0	-3.00

RACE CLASS   FIRST TIME OUT

	W-R	Per cent	£1 Level Stake		W-R	Per cent	£1 Level Stake
Class 1	1-1	100.0	+10.00	Bumpers	0-8	0.0	-8.00
Class 2	1-3	33.3	+12.00	Hurdles	0-16	0.0	-16.00

Class 3	8-37	21.6	+24.25	Chases	1-10	10.0	+2.00
Class 4	3-50	6.0	-21.50				
Class 5	1-10	10.0	-7.25	Totals	1-34	2.9	-22.00
Class 6	0-12	0.0	-12.00				

JOCKEYS

	W-R	Per cent	£1 Level Stake
P J Brennan	5-18	27.8	+31.50
Antony Evans	2-17	11.8	-1.00
Leighton Aspell	1-1	100.0	+14.00
Andrew Thornton	1-1	100.0	+5.00
T J Dreaper	1-2	50.0	+10.00
A P McCoy	1-4	25.0	-0.50
G Lee	1-6	16.7	-3.25
Robert Thornton	1-8	12.5	+3.00
William Kennedy	1-16	6.3	-13.25

COURSE RECORD

	Total W-R	Non-Hndcps Hurdles	Chases	Hndcps Hurdles	Chases	NH Flat	Per cent	£1 Level Stake
Stratford	3-12	0-1	1-1	0-2	2-6	0-2	25.0	+1.00
Aintree	2-4	0-0	0-0	0-1	2-3	0-0	50.0	+26.00
Bangor	2-9	0-1	0-1	0-2	2-5	0-0	22.2	+8.00
Wetherby	1-1	0-0	0-0	0-0	1-1	0-0	100.0	+11.00
Sandown	1-2	0-0	0-0	0-0	1-2	0-0	50.0	+0.75
Fontwell	1-4	1-1	0-0	0-2	0-1	0-0	25.0	-1.25
Newbury	1-4	0-1	0-0	0-0	1-3	0-0	25.0	+1.00
Wincanton	1-4	0-1	1-1	0-1	0-1	0-0	25.0	+6.00
Nton Abbot	1-5	0-1	0-0	0-1	1-2	0-1	20.0	+6.00
Uttoxeter	1-6	0-1	0-1	0-1	1-3	0-0	16.7	+9.00

WINNING HORSES

Horse	Races Run	1st	2nd	3rd	£
Jacks Craic	10	3	4	0	55815
Hakim	8	4	3	0	56032
Simon	7	3	1	1	30242
Tom's Prize	3	1	0	0	7673
Dickensbury Lad	5	1	3	0	6889
Knight's Emperor	11	1	1	1	5473
Borehill Joker	5	1	3	0	2359
Total winning prize-money					£164483
Favourites	4-9		44.4%		4.50

IAN D STARK

ASHKIRK, SCOTTISH BORDERS

	No. of Hrs	Races Run	1st	2nd	3rd	Unpl	Per cent	£1 Level Stake
NH Flat	0	0	0	0	0	0	0.0	0.00
Hurdles	0	0	0	0	0	0	0.0	0.00
Chases	1	1	1	0	0	0	100.0	+6.00
Totals	1	1	1	0	0	0	100.0	+6.00
04-05	2	3	0	0	0	3	0.0	-3.00

JOCKEYS

	W-R	Per cent	£1 Level Stake
Mr R S Brown	1-1	100.0	+6.00

COURSE RECORD

	Total W-R	Non-Hndcps Hurdles	Chases	Hndcps Hurdles	Chases	NH Flat	Per cent	£1 Level Stake
Kelso	1-1	0-0	1-1	0-0	0-0	0-0	100.0	+6.00

WINNING HORSES

Horse	Races Run	1st	2nd	3rd	£
*Birkwood	1	1	0	0	2498
Total winning prize-money					£2498
Favourites	0-0		0.0%		0.00

D R STODDART

ADSTONE, NORTHANTS

	No. of Hrs	Races Run	1st	2nd	3rd	Unpl	Per cent	£1 Level Stake
NH Flat	0	0	0	0	0	0	0.0	0.00
Hurdles	3	9	1	1	4	3	11.1	-1.50
Chases	2	4	0	0	0	4	0.0	-4.00
Totals	4	13	1	1	4	7	7.7	-5.50
04-05	3	17	0	1	0	16	0.0	-17.00
03-04	2	9	2	2	1	4	22.2	+3.50

JOCKEYS

	W-R	Per cent	£1 Level Stake
Tom Doyle	1-5	20.0	+2.50

COURSE RECORD

	Total W-R	Non-Hndcps Hurdles	Chases	Hndcps Hurdles	Chases	NH Flat	Per cent	£1 Level Stake
Uttoxeter	1-3	1-2	0-0	0-1	0-0	0-0	33.3	+4.50

WINNING HORSES

Horse	Races Run	1st	2nd	3rd	£
Killonemoonlight	6	1	1	3	2625
Total winning prize-money					£2625
Favourites	0-0		0.0%		0.00

W STOREY

MUGGLESWICK, CO DURHAM

	No. of Hrs	Races Run	1st	2nd	3rd	Unpl	Per cent	£1 Level Stake
NH Flat	3	5	1	0	0	4	20.0	+96.00
Hurdles	14	55	2	7	2	44	3.6	+21.00
Chases	0	0	0	0	0	0	0.0	0.00
Totals	16	60	3	7	2	48	5.0	+117.00

04-05	16	68	2	5	3	58	2.9	-46.00
03-04	18	82	6	12	8	56	7.3	-44.20

JOCKEYS

	W-R	Per cent	£1 Level Stake
Alan Dempsey	1-2	50.0	+65.00
G Lee	1-6	16.7	+3.00
Neil Mulholland	1-27	3.7	+74.00

COURSE RECORD

	Total W-R	Non-Hndcps Hurdles	Chases	Hndcps Hurdles	Chases	NH Flat	Per cent	£1 Level Stake
Musselbgh	1-7	0-5	0-0	0-0	0-0	1-2	14.3	+94.00
Catterick	1-12	0-5	0-0	1-6	0-0	0-1	8.3	-3.00
Kelso	1-13	1-7	0-0	0-6	0-0	0-0	7.7	+54.00

WINNING HORSES

Horse	Races Run	1st	2nd	3rd	£
Singhalongtasveer	4	1	0	0	3904
Colway Ritz	5	1	0	0	2741
Eden Linty	2	1	0	0	2056
Total winning prize-money					**£8701**
Favourites	0-1		**0.0%**		**-1.00**

B STOREY

KIRKLINTON, CUMBRIA

	No. of Hrs	Races Run	1st	2nd	3rd	Unpl	Per cent	£1 Level Stake
NH Flat	8	12	0	0	0	12	0.0	-12.00
Hurdles	18	53	4	2	1	46	7.5	-4.00
Chases	6	23	1	1	1	20	4.3	-16.00
Totals	26	88	5	3	2	78	5.7	-32.00
04-05	6	12	0	0	1	11	0.0	-12.00

JOCKEYS

	W-R	Per cent	£1 Level Stake
Mr M Seston	1-2	50.0	+9.00
Tony Dobbin	1-4	25.0	+5.00
Brian Harding	1-15	6.7	+2.00
Richard McGrath	1-16	6.3	-9.00
Michael McAlister	1-34	2.9	-22.00

COURSE RECORD

	Total W-R	Non-Hndcps Hurdles	Chases	Hndcps Hurdles	Chases	NH Flat	Per cent	£1 Level Stake
Sedgefield	2-13	0-3	0-2	2-5	0-0	0-3	15.4	+13.00
Carlisle	1-6	0-3	0-0	1-2	0-1	0-0	16.7	+5.00
Hexham	1-9	0-5	0-1	1-1	0-2	0-0	11.1	+3.00
Ayr	1-21	0-6	0-2	0-7	1-6	0-0	4.8	-14.00

WINNING HORSES

Horse	Races Run	1st	2nd	3rd	£
Do L'Enfant D'Eau	5	1	0	0	7620
*General Duroc	8	3	0	1	10829
Plenty Courage	3	1	0	0	3066
Total winning prize-money					**£21515**
Favourites	0-3		**0.0%**		**-3.00**

R M STRONGE

BEEDON COMMON, BERKS

	No. of Hrs	Races Run	1st	2nd	3rd	Unpl	Per cent	£1 Level Stake
NH Flat	2	3	0	0	0	3	0.0	-3.00
Hurdles	12	40	3	4	3	30	7.5	+34.00
Chases	3	3	0	0	0	3	0.0	-3.00
Totals	15	46	3	4	3	36	6.5	+28.00
04-05	14	49	1	7	5	36	2.0	-43.00
03-04	15	59	4	3	3	49	6.8	-20.25

JOCKEYS

	W-R	Per cent	£1 Level Stake
A P McCoy	1-2	50.0	+4.00
Barry Fenton	1-7	14.3	+10.00
Shane Walsh	1-13	7.7	+38.00

COURSE RECORD

	Total W-R	Non-Hndcps Hurdles	Chases	Hndcps Hurdles	Chases	NH Flat	Per cent	£1 Level Stake
Bangor	1-1	0-0	0-0	1-1	0-0	0-0	100.0	+16.00
Cheltenham	1-1	0-0	0-0	1-1	0-0	0-0	100.0	+50.00
Ludlow	1-2	0-0	0-0	1-2	0-0	0-0	50.0	+4.00

WINNING HORSES

Horse	Races Run	1st	2nd	3rd	£
Water King	7	2	0	0	15001
*Always Waining	3	1	0	0	6181
Total winning prize-money					**£21182**
Favourites	0-2		**0.0%**		**-2.00**

MISS TOR STURGIS

KINGSTON LISLE, OXON

	No. of Hrs	Races Run	1st	2nd	3rd	Unpl	Per cent	£1 Level Stake
NH Flat	0	0	0	0	0	0	0.0	0.00
Hurdles	4	10	0	1	1	8	0.0	-10.00
Chases	3	10	3	0	1	6	30.0	+6.25
Totals	6	20	3	1	2	14	15.0	-3.75

JOCKEYS

	W-R	Per cent	£1 Level Stake
Robert Thornton	1-1	100.0	+2.75
A P McCoy	1-3	33.3	+0.50
Marcus Foley	1-6	16.7	+3.00

COURSE RECORD

	Total W-R	Non-Hndcps Hurdles	Chases	Hndcps Hurdles	Chases	NH Flat	Per cent	£1 Level Stake
Hereford	1-1	0-0	0-0	0-0	1-1	0-0	100.0	+2.75
Fontwell	1-3	0-1	1-2	0-0	0-0	0-0	33.3	+6.00
Ludlow	1-4	0-1	0-0	0-0	1-3	0-0	25.0	-0.50

WINNING HORSES

Horse	Races Run	1st	2nd	3rd	£
*Welsh Main	4	2	0	1	8189
Dedrunknmunky	2	1	0	0	4662
Total winning prize-money					**£12851**
Favourites	**1-2**		**50.0%**		1.75

G A SWINBANK

MELSONBY, N YORKS

	No. of Hrs	Races Run	1st	2nd	3rd	Unpl	Per cent	£1 Level Stake
NH Flat	18	35	10	1	5	19	28.6	-1.28
Hurdles	20	32	2	1	4	25	6.3	-12.63
Chases	4	12	3	0	2	7	25.0	+19.00
Totals	37	79	15	2	11	51	19.0	+5.09
04-05	26	71	8	8	8	47	11.3	-28.13
03-04	31	78	14	8	8	48	17.9	+20.64

BY MONTH

NH Flat	W-R	Per cent	£1 Level Stake	Hurdles	W-R	Per cent	£1 Level Stake
May	1-3	33.3	+0.75	May	0-0	0.0	0.00
June	1-4	25.0	-0.75	June	0-0	0.0	0.00
July	0-1	0.0	-1.00	July	0-0	0.0	0.00
August	0-0	0.0	0.00	August	1-3	33.3	+14.00
September	0-0	0.0	0.00	September	0-1	0.0	-1.00
October	0-1	0.0	-1.00	October	1-3	33.3	-0.63
November	1-4	25.0	0.00	November	0-10	0.0	-10.00
December	2-3	66.7	+7.00	December	0-7	0.0	-7.00
January	2-7	28.6	-1.59	January	0-2	0.0	-2.00
February	1-2	50.0	-0.27	February	0-2	0.0	-2.00
March	0-3	0.0	-3.00	March	0-2	0.0	-2.00
April	2-7	28.6	-1.42	April	0-2	0.0	-2.00

Chases	W-R	Per cent	£1 Level Stake	Totals	W-R	Per cent	£1 Level Stake
May	1-2	50.0	+15.00	May	2-5	40.0	+15.75
June	0-0	0.0	0.00	June	1-4	25.0	-0.75
July	0-0	0.0	0.00	July	0-1	0.0	-1.00

August	0-0	0.0	0.00	August	1-3	33.3	+14.00
September	0-1	0.0	-1.00	September	0-2	0.0	-2.00
October	0-0	0.0	0.00	October	1-4	25.0	-1.63
November	0-0	0.0	0.00	November	1-14	7.1	-10.00
December	0-2	0.0	-2.00	December	2-12	16.7	-2.00
January	2-4	50.0	+10.00	January	4-13	30.8	+6.41
February	0-2	0.0	-2.00	February	1-6	16.7	-4.27
March	0-1	0.0	-1.00	March	0-6	0.0	-6.00
April	0-0	0.0	0.00	April	2-9	22.2	-3.42

DISTANCE

Hurdles	W-R	Per cent	£1 Level Stake	Chases	W-R	Per cent	£1 Level Stake
2m-2m3f	0-20	0.0	-20.00	2m-2m3f	0-1	0.0	-1.00
2m4f-2m7f	0-8	0.0	-8.00	2m4f-2m7f	0-2	0.0	-2.00
3m+	2-4	50.0	+15.38	3m+	3-9	33.3	+22.00

TYPE OF RACE

Non-Handicaps	W-R	Per cent	£1 Level Stake	Handicaps	W-R	Per cent	£1 Level Stake
Nov Hrdls	0-15	0.0	-15.00	Nov Hrdls	0-1	0.0	-1.00
Hrdls	0-4	0.0	-4.00	Hrdls	1-10	10.0	+7.00
Nov Chs	0-0	0.0	0.00	Nov Chs	0-2	0.0	-2.00
Chases	0-0	0.0	0.00	Chases	3-10	30.0	+21.00
Sell/Claim	1-1	100.0	+1.38	Sell/Claim	0-0	0.0	0.00

RACE CLASS

	W-R	Per cent	£1 Level Stake
Class 1	0-3	0.0	-3.00
Class 2	0-2	0.0	-2.00
Class 3	4-17	23.5	+31.00
Class 4	0-23	0.0	-23.00
Class 5	2-7	28.6	-1.13
Class 6	9-27	33.3	+3.22

FIRST TIME OUT

	W-R	Per cent	£1 Level Stake
Bumpers	5-18	27.8	+3.25
Hurdles	1-17	5.9	+4.00
Chases	1-2	50.0	+15.00
Totals	7-37	18.9	+18.25

JOCKEYS

	W-R	Per cent	£1 Level Stake
Dougie Costello	5-35	14.3	+0.98
Tony Dobbin	4-10	40.0	+7.75
Jim Crowley	3-17	17.6	+6.13
Tom Doyle	2-3	66.7	+2.41
Mr T Greenall	1-2	50.0	-0.17

COURSE RECORD

	Total W-R	Non-Hndcps Hurdles	Chases	Hndcps Hurdles	Chases	NH Flat	Per cent	£1 Level Stake
Catterick	2-8	0-0	0-0	0-2	2-6	0-0	25.0	+6.00
Mrket Rsn	2-8	0-2	0-0	1-2	0-1	1-3	25.0	+12.25
Wetherby	2-8	0-2	0-0	0-1	0-0	2-5	25.0	-1.00
Sedgefield	2-11	0-3	0-0	0-1	1-1	1-6	18.2	+9.75
Fakenham	1-1	0-0	0-0	0-0	0-0	1-1	100.0	+2.75
Uttoxeter	1-1	1-1	0-0	0-0	0-0	0-0	100.0	+1.38
Doncaster	1-2	0-0	0-0	0-0	0-0	1-2	50.0	+4.50
Southwell	1-3	0-0	0-0	0-0	0-1	1-2	33.3	-1.09

Carlisle	1-5	0-2	0-0	0-1	0-1	1-1	20.0	-3.27
Ayr	1-6	0-2	0-0	0-1	0-0	1-3	16.7	-2.00
Hexham	1-6	0-3	0-0	0-0	0-0	1-3	16.7	-4.17

WINNING HORSES

Horse	Races Run	1st	2nd	3rd	£
Prince Of Slane	6	3	0	1	24949
Midnight Creek	2	2	0	0	6963
Dand Nee	2	1	0	0	2768
Barton Belle	2	1	0	1	2741
Alfie Flits	4	3	0	0	6283
Lindbergh Law	3	2	1	0	3724
Programme Girl	1	1	0	0	1829
The Music Queen	3	1	0	1	1713
Sir Boreas Hawk	2	1	0	1	1028
Total winning prize-money					**£51998**
Favourites	**7-14**		**50.0%**		**4.09**

T P TATE

TADCASTER, N YORKS

	No. of Hrs	Races Run	1st	2nd	3rd	Unpl	Per cent	£1 Level Stake
NH Flat	7	10	1	1	2	6	10.0	-4.50
Hurdles	6	20	6	3	2	9	30.0	-6.33
Chases	2	6	2	1	0	3	33.3	+0.25
Totals	**14**	**36**	**9**	**5**	**4**	**18**	**25.0**	**-10.58**
04-05	13	20	2	2	2	14	10.0	-9.50
03-04	12	30	7	1	6	16	23.3	+10.33

JOCKEYS

	W-R	Per cent	£1 Level Stake
Jason Maguire	5-19	26.3	-6.33
Mr R T A Tate	2-5	40.0	+1.25
Dominic Elsworth	1-2	50.0	0.00
Brian Harding	1-4	25.0	+0.50

COURSE RECORD

	Total W-R	Non-Hndcps Hurdles Chases		Hndcps Hurdles	Chases	NH Flat	Per cent	£1 Level Stake
Newcastle	2-2	1 1	1 1	0-0	0-0	0-0	100.0	+2.07
Wetherby	2-9	1-5	1-2	0-0	0-0	0-2	22.2	-3.15
Catterick	1-1	1-1	0-0	0-0	0-0	0-0	100.0	+1.00
Hexham	1-1	1-1	0-0	0-0	0-0	0-0	100.0	+1.00
Ayr	1-2	1-1	0-0	0-0	0-0	0-1	50.0	-0.50
Haydock	1-3	0-0	0-1	0-0	0-0	1-2	33.3	+2.50
Kelso	1-3	1-2	0-1	0-0	0-0	0-0	33.3	+1.50

WINNING HORSES

Horse	Races Run	1st	2nd	3rd	£
The Duke's Speech	5	2	0	2	6739
Gardasee	7	3	2	0	9956
Ally Shrimp	2	1	1	0	3383

Bleak House		2	1	1	0	1713
The Butterwick Kid		5	2	1	0	2782
Total winning prize-money						**£24573**
Favourites	**76-78**		**97.4%**			**316.92**

MRS L C TAYLOR

UPPER LAMBOURN, BERKS

	No. of Hrs	Races Run	1st	2nd	3rd	Unpl	Per cent	£1 Level Stake
NH Flat	0	0	0	0	0	0	0.0	0.00
Hurdles	6	22	0	1	7	14	0.0	-22.00
Chases	8	18	2	3	3	10	11.1	-4.00
Totals	**11**	**40**	**2**	**4**	**10**	**24**	**5.0**	**-26.00**
04-05	16	75	11	10	8	46	14.7	+5.54
03-04	14	68	9	7	10	42	13.2	+6.50

JOCKEYS

	W-R	Per cent	£1 Level Stake
Mark Bradburne	2-12	16.7	+2.00

COURSE RECORD

	Total W-R	Non-Hndcps Hurdles Chases		Hndcps Hurdles	Chases	NH Flat	Per cent	£1 Level Stake
Exeter	1-3	0-0	1-1	0-1	0-1	0 0	33.3	+1.50
Lingfield	1-4	0-0	1-1	0-3	0-0	0-0	25.0	+5.50

WINNING HORSES

Horse	Races Run	1st	2nd	3rd	£
Montgermont	6	2	2	1	24796
Total winning prize-money					**£24796**
Favourites	**0-1**		**0.0%**		**-1.00**

MRS C L TAYLOR

ASHFORD, KENT

	No. of Hrs	Races Run	1st	2nd	3rd	Unpl	Per cent	£1 Level Stake
NH Flat	0	0	0	0	0	0	0.0	0.00
Hurdles	0	0	0	0	0	0	0.0	0.00
Chases	1	4	1	0	1	2	25.0	+0.50
Totals	**1**	**4**	**1**	**0**	**1**	**2**	**25.0**	**+0.50**

JOCKEYS

	W-R	Per cent	£1 Level Stake
Mr P G Hall	1-1	100.0	+3.50

COURSE RECORD

	Total W-R	Non-Hndcps Hurdles Chases		Hndcps Hurdles	Chases	NH Flat	Per cent	£1 Level Stake
Folkestone	1-2	0-0	1-2	0-0	0-0	0-0	50.0	+2.50

WINNING HORSES

Horse	Races Run	1st	2nd	3rd	£
*Millenium Way	4	1	0	1	1736
Total winning prize-money					**£1736**
Favourites	**0-0**		**0.0%**		**0.00**

D W THOMPSON

BOLAM, CO DURHAM

	No. of Hrs	Races Run	1st	2nd	3rd	Unpl	Per cent	£1 Level Stake
NH Flat	2	2	0	0	0	2	0.0	-2.00
Hurdles	16	72	2	7	7	56	2.8	-61.00
Chases	3	8	0	0	1	7	0.0	-8.00
Totals	**17**	**82**	**2**	**7**	**8**	**65**	**2.4**	**-71.00**
04-05	18	70	4	4	4	58	5.7	-31.50
03-04	12	54	5	2	4	43	9.3	-2.63

JOCKEYS

	W-R	Per cent	£1 Level Stake
G Lee	1-2	50.0	+2.50
Paddy Merrigan	1-4	25.0	+2.50

COURSE RECORD

	Total W-R	Non-Hndcps Hurdles	Chases	Hndcps Hurdles	Chases	NH Flat	Per cent	£1 Level Stake
Southwell	1-6	0-1	0-0	1-3	0-1	0-1	16.7	+0.50
Sedgefield	1-13	1-2	0-2	0-9	0-0	0-0	7.7	-8.50

WINNING HORSES

Horse	Races Run	1st	2nd	3rd	£
*Charlie Tango	4	1	0	0	3064
*Perfect Balance	7	1	1	2	2741
Total winning prize-money					**£5805**
Favourites	**0-0**		**0.0%**		**0.00**

MISS E THOMPSON

SOUTH MOLTON, DEVON

	No. of Hrs	Races Run	1st	2nd	3rd	Unpl	Per cent	£1 Level Stake
NH Flat	0	0	0	0	0	0	0.0	0.00
Hurdles	0	0	0	0	0	0	0.0	0.00
Chases	2	2	1	1	0	0	50.0	+2.00
Totals	**2**	**2**	**1**	**1**	**0**	**0**	**50.0**	**+2.00**

JOCKEYS

	W-R	Per cent	£1 Level Stake
Mr R Woollacott	1-2	50.0	+2.00

COURSE RECORD

	Total W-R	Non-Hndcps Hurdles	Chases	Hndcps Hurdles	Chases	NH Flat	Per cent	£1 Level Stake
Exeter	1-1	0-0	1-1	0-0	0-0	0-0	100.0	+3.00

WINNING HORSES

Horse	Races Run	1st	2nd	3rd	£
Teddy Boy	1	1	0	0	3416
Total winning prize-money					**£3416**
Favourites	**0-0**		**0.0%**		**0.00**

PATRICK THOMPSON

NANTWICH, CHESHIRE

	No. of Hrs	Races Run	1st	2nd	3rd	Unpl	Per cent	£1 Level Stake
NH Flat	0	0	0	0	0	0	0.0	0.00
Hurdles	0	0	0	0	0	0	0.0	0.00
Chases	1	6	1	0	1	4	16.7	0.00
Totals	**1**	**6**	**1**	**0**	**1**	**4**	**16.7**	**0.00**
04-05	2	4	0	1	0	3	0.0	-4.00

JOCKEYS

	W-R	Per cent	£1 Level Stake
Miss Tessa Clark	1-4	25.0	+2.00

COURSE RECORD

	Total W-R	Non-Hndcps Hurdles	Chases	Hndcps Hurdles	Chases	NH Flat	Per cent	£1 Level Stake
Uttoxeter	1-1	0-0	1-1	0-0	0-0	0-0	100.0	+5.00

WINNING HORSES

Horse	Races Run	1st	2nd	3rd	£
Raiseapearl	6	1	0	1	2324
Total winning prize-money					**£2324**
Favourites	**0-0**		**0.0%**		**0.00**

MRS B K THOMSON

LAMBDEN, BORDERS

	No. of Hrs	Races Run	1st	2nd	3rd	Unpl	Per cent	£1 Level Stake
NH Flat	1	1	0	1	0	0	0.0	-1.00
Hurdles	2	4	0	0	0	4	0.0	-4.00
Chases	3	14	1	1	1	11	7.1	-6.00
Totals	**5**	**19**	**1**	**2**	**1**	**15**	**5.3**	**-11.00**
04-05	7	38	2	3	3	30	5.3	-22.00
03-04	5	40	4	1	6	29	10.0	-12.90

JOCKEYS

	W-R	Per cent	£1 Level Stake
Wilson Renwick	1-8	12.5	0.00

COURSE RECORD

	Total W-R	Non-Hndcps Hurdles	Chases	Hndcps Hurdles	Chases	NH Flat	Per cent	£1 Level Stake
Kelso	1-7	0-0	0-1	0-2	1-4	0-0	14.3	+1.00

WINNING HORSES

Horse	Races Run	1st	2nd	3rd	£
Interdit	8	1	1	1	4554
Total winning prize-money					**£4554**
Favourites	0-1	0.0%			-1.00

January	0-1	0.0	-1.00	January	1-5	20.0	+4.00
February	0-0	0.0	0.00	February	2-7	28.6	+4.25
March	0-0	0.0	0.00	March	0-6	0.0	-6.00
April	0-0	0.0	0.00	April	1-15	6.7	-9.00

DISTANCE

Hurdles	W-R	Per cent	£1 Level Stake	Chases	W-R	Per cent	£1 Level Stake
2m-2m3f	3-44	6.8	-26.75	2m-2m3f	0-9	0.0	-9.00
2m4f-2m7f	3-33	9.1	-10.50	2m4f-2m7f	2-10	20.0	-2.25
3m+	3-18	16.7	+6.00	3m+	0-3	0.0	-3.00

TYPE OF RACE

Non-Handicaps	W-R	Per cent	£1 Level Stake	Handicaps	W-R	Per cent	£1 Level Stake
Nov Hrdls	0-19	0.0	-19.00	Nov Hrdls	2-15	13.3	-1.50
Hrdls	0-6	0.0	-6.00	Hrdls	6-44	13.6	+0.25
Nov Chs	0-3	0.0	-3.00	Nov Chs	0-3	0.0	-3.00
Chases	0-0	0.0	0.00	Chases	2-15	13.3	-7.25
Sell/Claim	1-8	12.5	-2.00	Sell/Claim	0-5	0.0	-5.00

MRS A M THORPE

BRONWYDD ARMS, CARMARTHENS

	No. of Hrs	Races Run	1st	2nd	3rd	Unpl	Per cent	£1 Level Stake
NH Flat	7	10	0	2	4	4	0.0	-10.00
Hurdles	22	95	9	12	14	60	9.5	-31.25
Chases	5	22	2	1	4	15	9.1	-14.25
Totals	29	127	11	15	22	79	8.7	-55.50
04-05	28	115	8	6	13	88	7.0	-52.00
03-04	25	91	9	4	5	73	9.9	-7.75

BY MONTH

NH Flat	W-R	Per cent	£1 Level Stake	Hurdles	W-R	Per cent	£1 Level Stake
May	0-2	0.0	-2.00	May	3-9	33.3	+8.50
June	0-1	0.0	-1.00	June	2-8	25.0	+12.00
July	0-0	0.0	0.00	July	0-11	0.0	-11.00
August	0-1	0.0	-1.00	August	0-6	0.0	-6.00
September	0-0	0.0	0.00	September	0-5	0.0	-5.00
October	0-4	0.0	-4.00	October	0-8	0.0	-8.00
November	0-0	0.0	0.00	November	0-10	0.0	-10.00
December	0-1	0.0	-1.00	December	0-7	0.0	-7.00
January	0-0	0.0	0.00	January	1-4	25.0	+5.00
February	0-0	0.0	0.00	February	2-7	28.6	+4.25
March	0-0	0.0	0.00	March	0-6	0.0	-6.00
April	0-1	0.0	-1.00	April	1-14	7.1	-8.00

Chases	W-R	Per cent	£1 Level Stake	Totals	W-R	Per cent	£1 Level Stake
May	1-3	33.3	+0.25	May	4-14	28.6	+6.75
June	1-1	100.0	+3.50	June	3-10	30.0	+14.50
July	0-2	0.0	-2.00	July	0-13	0.0	-13.00
August	0-2	0.0	-2.00	August	0-9	0.0	-9.00
September	0-2	0.0	-2.00	September	0-7	0.0	-7.00
October	0-3	0.0	-3.00	October	0-15	0.0	-15.00
November	0-3	0.0	-3.00	November	0-13	0.0	-13.00
December	0-5	0.0	-5.00	December	0-13	0.0	-13.00

RACE CLASS

	W-R	Per cent	£1 Level Stake
Class 1	0-0	0.0	0.00
Class 2	0-1	0.0	-1.00
Class 3	2-23	8.7	-13.25
Class 4	9-77	11.7	-15.25
Class 5	0-16	0.0	-16.00
Class 6	0-10	0.0	-10.00

FIRST TIME OUT

	W-R	Per cent	£1 Level Stake
Bumpers	0-7	0.0	-7.00
Hurdles	3-18	16.7	+6.50
Chases	0-4	0.0	-4.00
Totals	3-29	10.3	-4.50

JOCKEYS

	W-R	Per cent	£1 Level Stake
Christian Williams	3-8	37.5	+12.25
Richard Johnson	3-22	13.6	-0.50
Shane Walsh	2-5	40.0	+8.00
G Lee	1-3	33.3	+6.00
A P McCoy	1-5	20.0	-1.75
Derek Laverty	1-43	2.3	-38.50

COURSE RECORD

	Total W-R	Non-Hndcps Hurdles	Chases	Hndcps Hurdles	Chases	NH Flat	Per cent	£1 Level Stake
Fontwell	4-14	0-5	0-0	3-7	1-1	0-1	28.6	+9.50
Perth	2-3	0-1	0-0	2-2	0-0	0-0	66.7	+17.00
Nton Abbot	2-11	0-3	0-0	1-5	1-3	0-0	18.2	-2.00
Stratford	1-7	0-0	0-0	1-6	0-0	0-1	14.3	-0.50
Exeter	1-8	0-3	0-0	1-5	0-0	0-0	12.5	-1.50
Ludlow	1-9	1-4	0-0	0-4	0-0	0-1	11.1	-3.00

WINNING HORSES

Horse	Races Run	1st	2nd	3rd	£
*Amanpuri	11	3	2	1	16600

Altitude Dancer	6	3	0	2	12938
September Moon	8	1	3	0	5626
Maidstone Monument	6	2	1	2	8871
Red Chief	4	1	1	2	4290
*Simonovski	3	1	0	0	3253
Total winning prize-money					**£51578**
Favourites	**2-10**		**20.0%**		**-3.50**

C TINKLER

COMPTON, BERKS

	No. of Hrs	Races Run	1st	2nd	3rd	Unpl	Per cent	£1 Level Stake
NH Flat	10	14	1	4	1	8	7.1	-4.00
Hurdles	17	60	9	7	8	36	15.0	-20.24
Chases	4	19	4	1	1	13	21.1	+7.13
Totals	**28**	**93**	**14**	**12**	**10**	**57**	**15.1**	**-17.11**
04-05	27	82	22	14	9	37	26.8	+30.38
03-04	14	45	11	4	5	25	24.4	+48.25

BY MONTH

NH Flat	W-R	Per cent	£1 Level Stake	Hurdles	W-R	Per cent	£1 Level Stake
May	0-1	0.0	-1.00	May	0-4	0.0	-4.00
June	0-0	0.0	0.00	June	0-3	0.0	-3.00
July	0-1	0.0	-1.00	July	1-3	33.3	+6.00
August	0-1	0.0	-1.00	August	0-1	0.0	-1.00
September	0-0	0.0	0.00	September	1-2	50.0	+3.00
October	0-1	0.0	-1.00	October	1-8	12.5	-5.38
November	0-0	0.0	0.00	November	2-5	40.0	-1.99
December	0-2	0.0	-2.00	December	2-9	22.2	+5.75
January	0-2	0.0	-2.00	January	0-8	0.0	-8.00
February	0-1	0.0	-1.00	February	1-5	20.0	-1.88
March	1-2	50.0	+8.00	March	0-5	0.0	-5.00
April	0-3	0.0	-3.00	April	1-7	14.3	-4.75

Chases	W-R	Per cent	£1 Level Stake	Totals	W-R	Per cent	£1 Level Stake
May	0-0	0.0	0.00	May	0-5	0.0	-5.00
June	0-0	0.0	0.00	June	0-3	0.0	-3.00
July	0-0	0.0	0.00	July	1-4	25.0	+5.00
August	0-0	0.0	0.00	August	0-2	0.0	-2.00
September	0-0	0.0	0.00	September	1-2	50.0	+3.00
October	1-2	50.0	+3.50	October	2-11	18.2	-2.88
November	1-1	100.0	+3.50	November	3-6	50.0	+1.51
December	0-5	0.0	-5.00	December	2-16	12.5	-1.25
January	0-2	0.0	-2.00	January	0-12	0.0	-12.00
February	0-3	0.0	-3.00	February	1-9	11.1	-5.88
March	1-3	33.3	+10.00	March	2-10	20.0	+13.00
April	1-3	33.3	+0.13	April	2-13	15.4	-7.62

DISTANCE

Hurdles	W-R	Per cent	£1 Level Stake	Chases	W-R	Per cent	£1 Level Stake
2m-2m3f	5-26	19.2	-2.88	2m-2m3f	0-0	0.0	0.00
2m4f-2m7f	2-20	10.0	-16.09	2m4f-2m7f	2-5	40.0	+11.13
3m+	2-14	14.3	-1.27	3m+	2-14	14.3	-4.00

TYPE OF RACE

Non-Handicaps	W-R	Per cent	£1 Level Stake	Handicaps	W-R	Per cent	£1 Level Stake
Nov Hrdls	5-18	27.8	-4.24	Nov Hrdls	1-5	20.0	-1.25
Hrdls	1-11	9.1	-8.75	Hrdls	2-26	7.7	-6.00
Nov Chs	2-7	28.6	+9.13	Nov Chs	0-2	0.0	-2.00
Chases	0-1	0.0	-1.00	Chases	2-10	20.0	0.00
Sell/Claim	0-0	0.0	0.00	Sell/Claim	0-0	0.0	0.00

RACE CLASS

	W-R	Per cent	£1 Level Stake
Class 1	0-5	0.0	-5.00
Class 2	0-8	0.0	-8.00
Class 3	6-32	18.8	+12.73
Class 4	7-34	20.6	-12.84
Class 5	0-1	0.0	-1.00
Class 6	1-13	7.7	-3.00

FIRST TIME OUT

	W-R	Per cent	£1 Level Stake
Bumpers	1-10	10.0	0.00
Hurdles	3-15	20.0	-3.63
Chases	2-3	66.7	+4.63
Totals	**6-28**	**21.4**	**+1.00**

JOCKEYS

	W-R	Per cent	£1 Level Stake
Tom Doyle	9-58	15.5	-3.96
Tom Scudamore	2-5	40.0	+9.13
Andrew Thornton	1-1	100.0	+0.73
Mick Fitzgerald	1-5	20.0	-1.25
Andrew Tinkler	1-13	7.7	-10.75

COURSE RECORD

	Total W-R	Non-Hndcps Hurdles	Non-Hndcps Chases	Hndcps Hurdles	Hndcps Chases	NH Flat	Per cent	£1 Level Stake
Stratford	3-10	0-2	1-1	1-5	1-2	0-0	30.0	+17.50
Chepstow	2-3	1-1	0-0	0-1	0-0	1-1	66.7	+9.25
Bangor	2-6	1-1	0-0	1-2	0-2	0-1	33.3	+8.13
Lingfield	1-2	0-1	0-0	1-1	0-0	0-0	50.0	+1.75
Sandown	1-2	0-0	0-0	0-1	1-1	0-0	50.0	+2.50
Windsor	1-2	1-2	0-0	0-0	0-0	0-0	50.0	-0.71
Taunton	1-4	1-2	0-1	0-1	0-0	0-0	25.0	-2.27
Wetherby	1-4	0-2	1-1	0-0	0-1	0-0	25.0	-0.88
Huntingdon	1-7	1-3	0-1	0-1	0-0	0-2	14.3	-2.00
Uttoxeter	1-7	1-2	0-1	0-2	0-0	0-2	14.3	-4.38

WINNING HORSES

Horse	Races Run	1st	2nd	3rd	£
Valley Ride	6	1	0	0	8334
Native Ivy	4	1	0	1	8139
Smart Savannah	3	1	0	0	7543
Bob Ar Aghaidh	6	2	1	0	10188
Dominican Monk	4	1	0	0	6131
Present Glory	4	1	1	0	5465
Call Oscar	4	1	1	1	3904
Oscar Park	6	2	3	0	7460
Play The Melody	2	1	0	0	3468
Dr Cerullo	6	1	0	2	3073

Northaw Lad	3	1	1	1	2602
Sound Accord	1	1	0	0	1627
Total winning prize-money					**£67934**
Favourites	7-22		31.8%		-2.36

N TINKLER

LANGTON, N YORKS

	No. of Hrs	Races Run	1st	2nd	3rd	Unpl	Per cent	£1 Level Stake
NH Flat	2	5	1	1	0	3	20.0	+3.00
Hurdles	2	4	0	0	0	4	0.0	-4.00
Chases	0	0	0	0	0	0	0.0	0.00
Totals	3	9	1	1	0	7	11.1	-1.00
04-05	4	7	0	0	1	6	0.0	-7.00
03-04	1	1	0	0	1	1	0.0	-1.00

JOCKEYS

	W-R	Per cent	£1 Level Stake
Russ Garritty	1-4	25.0	+4.00

COURSE RECORD

	Total W-R	Non-Hndcps Hurdles	Chases	Hndcps Hurdles	Chases	NH Flat	Per cent	£1 Level Stake
Uttoxeter	1-1	0-0	0-0	0-0	0-0	1-1	100.0	+7.00

WINNING HORSES

Horse	Races Run	1st	2nd	3rd	£
Scotts Court	3	1	1	0	2065
Total winning prize-money					**£2065**
Favourites	0-0	0.0%			0.00

C L TIZZARD

MILBORNE PORT, DORSET

	No. of Hrs	Races Run	1st	2nd	3rd	Unpl	Per cent	£1 Level Stake
NH Flat	8	23	1	3	5	14	4.3	-17.50
Hurdles	21	67	7	8	8	44	10.4	-5.13
Chases	24	108	16	15	13	64	14.8	-2.25
Totals	40	198	24	26	26	122	12.1	-24.88
04-05	38	176	20	20	20	116	11.4	-93.18
03-04	34	190	22	29	21	117	11.6	+18.53

BY MONTH

NH Flat	W-R	Per cent	£1 Level Stake	Hurdles	W-R	Per cent	£1 Level Stake
May	0-1	0.0	-1.00	May	0-8	0.0	-8.00
June	0-2	0.0	-2.00	June	1-6	16.7	+28.00
July	0-0	0.0	0.00	July	1-4	25.0	+1.00
August	0-0	0.0	0.00	August	0-4	0.0	-4.00
September	0-0	0.0	0.00	September	0-3	0.0	-3.00
October	0-0	0.0	0.00	October	0-3	0.0	-3.00
November	0-6	0.0	-6.00	November	2-8	25.0	-1.50
December	0-2	0.0	-2.00	December	0-8	0.0	-8.00
January	1-3	33.3	+2.50	January	1-7	14.3	0.00
February	0-5	0.0	-5.00	February	1-7	14.3	0.00
March	0-4	0.0	-4.00	March	0-5	0.0	-5.00
April	0-0	0.0	0.00	April	1-4	25.0	-1.63

Chases	W-R	Per cent	£1 Level Stake	Totals	W-R	Per cent	£1 Level Stake
May	4-9	44.4	+30.50	May	4-18	22.2	+21.50
June	1-4	25.0	-0.50	June	2-12	16.7	+25.50
July	1-5	20.0	+1.00	July	2-9	22.2	+2.00
August	1-5	20.0	+1.00	August	1-9	11.1	-3.00
September	0-4	0.0	-4.00	September	0-7	0.0	-7.00
October	0-6	0.0	-6.00	October	0-9	0.0	-9.00
November	3-15	20.0	+3.50	November	5-29	17.2	-4.00
December	1-14	7.1	-10.25	December	1-24	4.2	-20.25
January	2-13	15.4	-9.50	January	4-23	17.4	-7.00
February	1-11	9.1	-4.50	February	2-23	8.7	-9.50
March	1-13	7.7	-3.00	March	1-22	4.5	-12.00
April	1-9	11.1	-0.50	April	2-13	15.4	-2.13

DISTANCE

Hurdles	W-R	Per cent	£1 Level Stake	Chases	W-R	Per cent	£1 Level Stake
2m-2m3f	4-36	11.1	+14.00	2m-2m3f	2-17	11.8	-5.00
2m4f-2m7f	3-24	12.5	-12.13	2m4f-2m7f	6-40	15.0	+7.25
3m+	0-7	0.0	-7.00	3m+	8-51	15.7	-4.50

TYPE OF RACE

Non-Handicaps	W-R	Per cent	£1 Level Stake	Handicaps	W-R	Per cent	£1 Level Stake
Nov Hrdls	4-30	13.3	-11.13	Nov Hrdls	1-8	12.5	+26.00
Hrdls	0-5	0.0	-5.00	Hrdls	0-20	0.0	-20.00
Nov Chs	4-21	19.0	-4.00	Nov Chs	1-10	10.0	+5.00
Chases	0-3	0.0	-3.00	Chases	11-72	15.3	+1.75
Sell/Claim	0-4	0.0	-4.00	Sell/Claim	0-1	0.0	-1.00

RACE CLASS / FIRST TIME OUT

	W-R	Per cent	£1 Level Stake		W-R	Per cent	£1 Level Stake
Class 1	0-10	0.0	-10.00	Bumpers	0-8	0.0	-8.00
Class 2	0-6	0.0	-6.00	Hurdles	2-13	15.4	-6.63
Class 3	5-43	11.6	-13.85	Chases	3-19	15.8	+13.50
Class 4	18-104	17.3	+34.47				
Class 5	0-11	0.0	-11.00	Totals	5-40	12.5	-1.13
Class 6	1-24	4.2	-18.50				

JOCKEYS

	W-R	Per cent	£1 Level Stake
Joe Tizzard	18-146	12.3	-19.25
Richard Young	2-8	25.0	+7.50
Dave Crosse	1-1	100.0	+7.50
Mr N Williams	1-2	50.0	+0.38
Miss C Tizzard	1-3	33.3	+2.00
Christian Williams	1-4	25.0	+11.00

COURSE RECORD

	Total W-R	Non-Hndcps Hurdles	Chases	Hndcps Hurdles	Chases	NH Flat	Per cent	£1 Level Stake
Exeter	6-25	2-8	1-6	0-3	2-6	1-2	24.0	+22.88
Plumpton	4-18	1-4	1-1	0-1	2-10	0-2	22.2	+8.50
Chepstow	4-31	1-6	2-2	0-5	1-13	0-5	12.9	-16.50
Nton Abbot	3-23	1-5	0-2	1-7	1-9	0-0	13.0	+22.00
Fontwell	2-15	1-1	0-4	0-0	1-8	0-2	13.3	-4.50
Cartmel	1-3	0-1	0-0	0-0	1-2	0-0	33.3	+4.00
Hereford	1-3	0-1	0-0	0-0	1-2	0-0	33.3	+0.50
Stratford	1-4	0-0	0-0	0-1	1-3	0-0	25.0	+2.00
Warwick	1-4	0-1	0-0	0-0	1-2	0-1	25.0	-0.25
Towcester	1-5	0-0	0-1	0-1	1-3	0-0	20.0	+3.50

WINNING HORSES

Horse	Races Run	1st	2nd	3rd	£
Earl's Kitchen	7	1	1	1	12526
Blakeney Coast	5	3	0	0	18512
Bob Bob Bobbin	8	2	1	1	11828
Lord Killeshanra	6	1	2	1	7469
*Ebony Jack	11	2	3	1	9378
Pass Me A Dime	4	2	0	2	10058
Bring Me Sunshine	6	1	0	1	4554
Eljay's Boy	3	1	0	0	4437
Uncle Mick	11	2	1	1	7549
Billy Ballbreaker	9	2	2	0	7146
Gemini Dancer	9	1	1	2	3436
Mister Quasimodo	7	2	3	0	6038
Malaga Boy	10	1	2	2	3094
Red Canyon	11	1	0	3	2618
Brave Spirit	8	1	3	0	2542
Leading Authority	3	1	1	1	2056
Total winning prize-money					**£113241**
Favourites	7-19		36.8%		2.63

M TODHUNTER

ORTON, CUMBRIA

	No. of Hrs	Races Run	1st	2nd	3rd	Unpl	Per cent	£1 Level Stake
NH Flat	2	3	0	0	0	3	0.0	-3.00
Hurdles	30	84	10	6	3	65	11.9	-26.46
Chases	16	63	7	5	9	42	11.1	+15.75
Totals	40	150	17	11	12	110	11.3	-13.71
04-05	39	142	16	21	20	85	11.3	-59.79
03-04	43	133	23	12	9	89	17.3	+39.11

BY MONTH

NH Flat	W-R	Per cent	£1 Level Stake
May	0-0	0.0	0.00
June	0-0	0.0	0.00
July	0-0	0.0	0.00
August	0-0	0.0	0.00
September	0-0	0.0	0.00
October	0-0	0.0	0.00
November	0-0	0.0	0.00
December	0-1	0.0	-1.00
January	0-0	0.0	0.00
February	0-0	0.0	0.00
March	0-2	0.0	-2.00
April	0-0	0.0	0.00

Hurdles	W-R	Per cent	£1 Level Stake
May	1-5	20.0	+16.00
June	0-2	0.0	-2.00
July	1-6	16.7	-1.00
August	4-9	44.4	+5.88
September	2-6	33.3	-1.83
October	2-7	28.6	+5.50
November	0-8	0.0	-8.00
December	0-13	0.0	-13.00
January	0-12	0.0	-12.00
February	0-8	0.0	-8.00
March	0-4	0.0	-4.00
April	0-4	0.0	-4.00

Chases	W-R	Per cent	£1 Level Stake
May	0-1	0.0	-1.00
June	0-2	0.0	-2.00
July	0-2	0.0	-2.00
August	0-2	0.0	-2.00
September	1-3	33.3	+7.00
October	2-7	28.6	+5.75
November	2-12	16.7	-3.00
December	1-10	10.0	+24.00
January	0-6	0.0	-6.00
February	1-4	25.0	+9.00
March	0-4	0.0	-4.00
April	0-10	0.0	-10.00

Totals	W-R	Per cent	£1 Level Stake
May	1-6	16.7	+15.00
June	0-4	0.0	-4.00
July	1-8	12.5	-3.00
August	4-11	36.4	+3.88
September	3-9	33.3	+5.17
October	4-14	28.6	+11.25
November	2-20	10.0	-11.00
December	1-24	4.2	+10.00
January	0-18	0.0	-18.00
February	1-12	8.3	+1.00
March	0-10	0.0	-10.00
April	0-14	0.0	-14.00

DISTANCE

Hurdles	W-R	Per cent	£1 Level Stake
2m-2m3f	6-51	11.8	-4.63
2m4f-2m7f	3-28	10.7	-22.83
3m+	1-5	20.0	+1.00

Chases	W-R	Per cent	£1 Level Stake
2m-2m3f	5-25	20.0	+47.00
2m4f-2m7f	2-20	10.0	-13.25
3m+	0-18	0.0	-18.00

TYPE OF RACE

Non-Handicaps	W-R	Per cent	£1 Level Stake
Nov Hrdls	4-34	11.8	-22.00
Hrdls	3-12	25.0	+15.67
Nov Chs	0-9	0.0	-9.00
Chases	0-1	0.0	-1.00
Sell/Claim	1-6	16.7	-3.63

Handicaps	W-R	Per cent	£1 Level Stake
Nov Hrdls	1-8	12.5	+1.00
Hrdls	1-25	4.0	-18.50
Nov Chs	1-11	9.1	-8.00
Chases	6-42	14.3	+33.75
Sell/Claim	0-1	0.0	-1.00

RACE CLASS

	W-R	Per cent	£1 Level Stake
Class 1	0-3	0.0	-3.00
Class 2	1-12	8.3	-5.50
Class 3	2-33	6.1	-18.00
Class 4	14-90	15.6	+24.79
Class 5	0-9	0.0	-9.00
Class 6	0-3	0.0	-3.00

FIRST TIME OUT

	W-R	Per cent	£1 Level Stake
Bumpers	0-2	0.0	-2.00
Hurdles	3-26	11.5	-10.33
Chases	2-12	16.7	+0.75
Totals	5-40	12.5	-11.58

JOCKEYS

	W-R	Per cent	£1 Level Stake
Tony Dobbin	7-30	23.3	+6.13
G Lee	6-47	12.8	-17.83
Alan Dempsey	4-35	11.4	+36.00

COURSE RECORD

	Total W-R	Non-Hndcps Hurdles	Chases	Hndcps Hurdles	Chases	NH Flat	Per cent	£1 Level Stake
Hexham	4-13	3-7	0-1	0-1	1-4	0-0	30.8	+15.92
Cartmel	3-12	2-4	0-2	1-4	0-2	0-0	25.0	+3.83
Wetherby	2-8	0-2	0-0	1-3	1-3	0-0	25.0	+7.50
Perth	2-10	2-4	0-1	0-2	0-3	0-0	20.0	-5.96
Sedgefield	2-10	0-1	0-2	0-3	2-4	0-0	20.0	+30.00
Uttoxeter	1-3	0-1	0-0	0-1	1-1	0-0	33.3	+7.00
Cheltenham	1-5	1-1	0-0	0-1	0-3	0-0	20.0	+1.00
Carlisle	1-6	0-0	0-1	0-0	1-5	0-0	16.7	+7.00
Ayr	1-19	0-5	0-0	0-4	1-7	0-3	5.3	-16.00

WINNING HORSES

Horse	Races Run	1st	2nd	3rd	£
Crathorne	7	3	0	0	15912
Provocative	4	1	0	0	7110
Ostfanni	6	4	0	0	8560
*Loulou Nivernais	8	2	1	0	8310
Longdale	10	2	0	1	7960
Alfy Rich	8	2	0	2	7907
Silver Jack	6	1	1	3	4212
Baawrah	4	1	1	0	4173
Overstrand	3	1	0	0	3596
Total winning prize-money					**£68040**
Favourites	6-18		33.3%		-4.96

M H TOMPKINS

NEWMARKET, SUFFOLK

	No. of Hrs	Races Run	1st	2nd	3rd	Unpl	Per cent	£1 Level Stake
NH Flat	0	0	0	0	0	0	0.0	0.00
Hurdles	5	14	4	2	2	6	28.6	+8.25
Chases	0	0	0	0	0	0	0.0	0.00
Totals	5	14	4	2	2	6	28.6	+8.25
04-05	4	6	0	1	2	3	0.0	-6.00
03-04	1	6	2	2	2	0	33.3	-1.84

JOCKEYS

	W-R	Per cent	£1 Level Stake
Leighton Aspell	3-11	27.3	+6.25
Colin Bolger	1-2	50.0	+3.00

COURSE RECORD

	Total W-R	Non-Hndcps Hurdles	Chases	Hndcps Hurdles	Chases	NH Flat	Per cent	£1 Level Stake
Worcester	2-3	2-2	0-0	0-1	0-0	0-0	66.7	+10.25
Southwell	1-1	0-0	0-0	1-1	0-0	0-0	100.0	+3.00
Fakenham	1-2	1-2	0-0	0-0	0-0	0-0	50.0	+3.00

WINNING HORSES

Horse	Races Run	1st	2nd	3rd	£
Rajayoga	5	3	1	1	11934
Toparudi	2	1	1	0	3448
Total winning prize-money					**£15382**
Favourites	2-2		100.0%		4.25

A R TROTTER

DUNS, BORDERS

	No. of Hrs	Races Run	1st	2nd	3rd	Unpl	Per cent	£1 Level Stake
NH Flat	0	0	0	0	0	0	0.0	0.00
Hurdles	0	0	0	0	0	0	0.0	0.00
Chases	2	4	1	0	0	3	25.0	+5.00
Totals	2	4	1	0	0	3	25.0	+5.00

JOCKEYS

	W-R	Per cent	£1 Level Stake
Mr R Trotter	1-4	25.0	+5.00

COURSE RECORD

	Total W-R	Non-Hndcps Hurdles	Chases	Hndcps Hurdles	Chases	NH Flat	Per cent	£1 Level Stake
Musselbgh	1-1	0-0	1-1	0-0	0-0	0-0	100.0	+8.00

WINNING HORSES

Horse	Races Run	1st	2nd	3rd	£
Albatros	2	1	0	0	1978
Total winning prize-money					**£1978**
Favourites	0-0		0.0%		0.00

J C TUCK

OLDBURY ON THE HILL, GLOUCS

	No. of Hrs	Races Run	1st	2nd	3rd	Unpl	Per cent	£1 Level Stake
NH Flat	2	4	0	0	0	4	0.0	-4.00
Hurdles	14	43	5	3	4	31	11.6	+4.25
Chases	3	7	0	0	0	7	0.0	-7.00
Totals	17	54	5	3	4	42	9.3	-6.75
04-05	19	70	4	5	7	54	5.7	-45.00
03-04	23	73	3	3	3	64	4.1	-54.00

JOCKEYS

	W-R	Per cent	£1 Level Stake
Jodie Mogford	5-39	12.8	+8.25

COURSE RECORD

	Total W-R	Non-Hndcps Hurdles	Chases	Hndcps Hurdles	Chases	NH Flat	Per cent	£1 Level Stake
Towcester	2-5	1-1	0-0	1-2	0-1	0-1	40.0	+8.00
Chepstow	1-5	1-1	0-0	0-4	0-0	0-0	20.0	+21.00
Exeter	1-5	0-0	0-0	1-4	0-1	0-0	20.0	-0.50
Fontwell	1-8	1-5	0-0	0-2	0-1	0-0	12.5	-4.25

WINNING HORSES

Horse	Races Run	1st	2nd	3rd	£
Sunnyarjun	6	2	1	0	7472
Indian Star	3	2	1	0	5208
Can Can Flyer	4	1	0	0	2082
Total winning prize-money					£14762
Favourites	1-2		50.0%		2.50

E W TUER

GREAT SMEATON, N YORKS

	No. of Hrs	Races Run	1st	2nd	3rd	Unpl	Per cent	£1 Level Stake
NH Flat	2	4	0	0	0	4	0.0	-4.00
Hurdles	14	60	4	8	3	45	6.7	-28.00
Chases	2	3	0	0	1	2	0.0	-3.00
Totals	15	67	4	8	4	51	6.0	-35.00
04-05	11	43	5	6	3	29	11.6	+23.25
03-04	10	49	2	3	5	39	4.1	-24.00

JOCKEYS

	W-R	Per cent	£1 Level Stake
Alan Dempsey	4-18	22.2	+14.00

COURSE RECORD

	Total W-R	Non-Hndcps Hurdles	Chases	Hndcps Hurdles	Chases	NH Flat	Per cent	£1 Level Stake
Newcastle	2-14	0-4	0-0	2-9	0-1	0-0	14.3	-1.50
Wetherby	1-5	0-2	0-0	1-3	0-0	0-0	20.0	+3.50
Sedgefield	1-12	0-3	0-0	1-8	0-0	0-1	8.3	-1.00

WINNING HORSES

Horse	Races Run	1st	2nd	3rd	£
Euro American	8	3	2	0	18080
*Villago	6	1	1	1	3142
Total winning prize-money					£21222
Favourites	0-35		0.0%		-35.00

MRS A F TULLIE

WHITEMIRE, BORDERS

	No. of Hrs	Races Run	1st	2nd	3rd	Unpl	Per cent	£1 Level Stake
NH Flat	2	4	0	0	0	4	0.0	-4.00
Hurdles	4	9	1	0	1	7	11.1	-3.50
Chases	0	0	0	0	0	0	0.0	0.00
Totals	5	13	1	0	1	11	7.7	-7.50
04-05	2	5	0	0	0	5	0.0	-5.00

JOCKEYS

	W-R	Per cent	£1 Level Stake
Dougie Costello	1-9	11.1	-3.50

COURSE RECORD

	Total W-R	Non-Hndcps Hurdles	Chases	Hndcps Hurdles	Chases	NH Flat	Per cent	£1 Level Stake
Ayr	1-1	1-1	0-0	0-0	0-0	0-0	100.0	+4.50

WINNING HORSES

Horse	Races Run	1st	2nd	3rd	£
More Likely	7	1	0	1	2741
Total winning prize-money					£2741
Favourites	0-0		0.0%		0.00

ANDREW TURNELL

BROAD HINTON, WILTS

	No. of Hrs	Races Run	1st	2nd	3rd	Unpl	Per cent	£1 Level Stake
NH Flat	3	3	0	0	0	3	0.0	-3.00
Hurdles	18	42	4	3	3	32	9.5	-25.93
Chases	15	50	6	4	4	36	12.0	-16.92
Totals	29	95	10	7	7	71	10.5	-45.85
04-05	12	54	5	8	6	35	9.3	-15.63
03-04	11	35	1	4	5	25	2.9	-27.00

BY MONTH

NH Flat	W-R	Per cent	£1 Level Stake	Hurdles	W-R	Per cent	£1 Level Stake
May	0-0	0.0	0.00	May	2-5	40.0	+0.07
June	0-0	0.0	0.00	June	0-1	0.0	-1.00
July	0-0	0.0	0.00	July	0-0	0.0	0.00
August	0-0	0.0	0.00	August	0-0	0.0	0.00
September	0-0	0.0	0.00	September	0-1	0.0	-1.00
October	0-0	0.0	0.00	October	0-0	0.0	0.00
November	0-2	0.0	-2.00	November	1-5	20.0	-1.50
December	0-0	0.0	0.00	December	0-10	0.0	-10.00
January	0-0	0.0	0.00	January	0-6	0.0	-6.00
February	0-0	0.0	0.00	February	0-8	0.0	-8.00
March	0-1	0.0	-1.00	March	0-2	0.0	-2.00

	W-R	Per cent	£1 Level Stake		W-R	Per cent	£1 Level Stake
April	0-0	0.0	0.00	April	1-4	25.0	+3.50

Chases	W-R	Per cent	£1 Level Stake	Totals	W-R	Per cent	£1 Level Stake
May	0-5	0.0	-5.00	May	2-10	20.0	-4.93
June	0-0	0.0	0.00	June	0-1	0.0	-1.00
July	0-2	0.0	-2.00	July	0-2	0.0	-2.00
August	0-1	0.0	-1.00	August	0-1	0.0	-1.00
September	1-1	100.0	+9.00	September	1-2	50.0	+8.00
October	3-6	50.0	+9.58	October	3-6	50.0	+9.58
November	0-6	0.0	-6.00	November	1-13	7.7	-9.50
December	1-6	16.7	-2.00	December	1-16	6.3	-12.00
January	0-6	0.0	-6.00	January	0-12	0.0	-12.00
February	1-6	16.7	-2.50	February	1-14	7.1	-10.50
March	0-2	0.0	-2.00	March	0-5	0.0	-5.00
April	0-9	0.0	-9.00	April	1-13	7.7	-5.50

DISTANCE

Hurdles	W-R	Per cent	£1 Level Stake	Chases	W-R	Per cent	£1 Level Stake
2m-2m3f	2-37	5.4	-26.00	2m-2m3f	2-19	10.5	-6.00
2m4f-2m7f	2-4	50.0	+1.07	2m4f-2m7f	2-19	10.5	-4.67
3m+	0-1	0.0	-1.00	3m+	2-12	16.7	-6.25

TYPE OF RACE

Non-Handicaps	W-R	Per cent	£1 Level Stake	Handicaps	W-R	Per cent	£1 Level Stake
Nov Hrdls	2-22	9.1	-12.93	Nov Hrdls	0-4	0.0	-4.00
Hrdls	1-8	12.5	-4.50	Hrdls	1-8	12.5	-4.50
Nov Chs	2-11	18.2	-3.50	Nov Chs	0-7	0.0	-7.00
Chases	0-0	0.0	0.00	Chases	4-31	12.9	-5.42
Sell/Claim	0-0	0.0	0.00	Sell/Claim	0-1	0.0	-1.00

RACE CLASS / FIRST TIME OUT

	W-R	Per cent	£1 Level Stake		W-R	Per cent	£1 Level Stake
Class 1	0-1	0.0	-1.00	Bumpers	0-3	0.0	-3.00
Class 2	0-3	0.0	-3.00	Hurdles	0-15	0.0	-15.00
Class 3	1-25	4.0	-21.00	Chases	2-11	18.2	+3.33
Class 4	9-57	15.8	-11.85				
Class 5	0-6	0.0	-6.00	Totals	2-29	6.9	-14.67
Class 6	0-3	0.0	-3.00				

JOCKEYS

	W-R	Per cent	£1 Level Stake
Gino Carenza	3-17	17.6	-0.50
Richard Johnson	2-3	66.7	+4.00
G Lee	2-13	15.4	-1.43
P J Brennan	2-20	10.0	-8.17
James Diment	1-4	25.0	-1.75

COURSE RECORD

	Total W-R	Non-Hndcps Hurdles	Chases	Hndcps Hurdles	Chases	NH Flat	Per cent	£1 Level Stake
Wincanton	3-17	0-5	0-0	1-3	2-8	0-1	17.6	-6.92
Worcester	2-4	0-1	0-1	0-0	2-2	0-0	50.0	+15.00

	W-R						Per cent	£1 Level Stake
Mrket Rsn	2-6	1-2	1-1	0-1	0-2	0-0	33.3	+1.50
Hexham	1-1	1-1	0-0	0-0	0-0	0-0	100.0	+0.57
Southwell	1-2	0-0	1-1	0-0	0-1	0-0	50.0	+1.50
Towcester	1-6	1-3	0-2	0-0	0-1	0-0	16.7	+1.50

WINNING HORSES

Horse	Races Run	1st	2nd	3rd	£
Bishop's Bridge	9	3	1	0	12350
Squires Lane	5	1	1	0	5205
*Nick The Jewel	4	1	1	0	5161
*Breaking Breeze	1	1	0	0	4778
*Charmatic	4	1	0	1	4437
*Tudor King	5	2	0	1	8340
*Lord Nellsson	3	1	1	0	3525
Total winning prize-money					£43796
Favourites	3-7		42.9%		0.32

J R TURNER

NORTON-LE-CLAY, N YORKS

	No. of Hrs	Races Run	1st	2nd	3rd	Unpl	Per cent	£1 Level Stake
NH Flat	8	10	0	0	2	8	0.0	-10.00
Hurdles	3	15	1	1	1	12	6.7	0.00
Chases	2	5	1	0	1	3	20.0	+3.00
Totals	9	30	2	1	4	23	6.7	-7.00
04-05	10	33	2	1	3	27	6.1	-24.50
03-04	11	41	5	2	3	31	12.2	+0.33

JOCKEYS

	W-R	Per cent	£1 Level Stake
Tony Dobbin	1-4	25.0	+4.00
G Lee	1-8	12.5	+7.00

COURSE RECORD

	Total W-R	Non-Hndcps Hurdles	Chases	Hndcps Hurdles	Chases	NH Flat	Per cent	£1 Level Stake
Kelso	1-5	0-2	0-0	0-1	1-2	0-0	20.0	+3.00
Sedgefield	1-5	1-2	0-0	0-2	0-0	0-1	20.0	+10.00

WINNING HORSES

Horse	Races Run	1st	2nd	3rd	£
Rosie Redman	4	1	0	1	7807
Air Of Affection	6	1	0	1	2720
Total winning prize-money					£10527
Favourites	0-3		0.0%		-3.00

W G M TURNER

SIGWELLS, SOMERSET

	No. of Hrs	Races Run	1st	2nd	3rd	Unpl	Per cent	£1 Level Stake
NH Flat	2	4	1	1	1	1	25.0	+9.00
Hurdles	17	62	3	6	10	43	4.8	-40.00
Chases	4	13	1	1	3	8	7.7	-2.00
Totals	18	79	5	8	14	52	6.3	-33.00
04-05	16	55	5	5	7	38	9.1	+44.00
03-04	11	56	3	8	6	39	5.4	-35.00

JOCKEYS

	W-R	Per cent	£1 Level Stake
Robert Lucey-Butler	2-29	6.9	-11.00
Stuart Haddon	1-4	25.0	+9.00
T J O'Brien	1-6	16.7	-2.00
Richard Gordon	1-20	5.0	-9.00

COURSE RECORD

	Total W-R	Non-Hndcps Hurdles	Chases	Hndcps Hurdles	Chases	NH Flat	Per cent	£1 Level Stake
Leicester	1-3	0-2	0-0	1-1	0-0	0-0	33.3	+4.00
Plumpton	1-4	0-3	0-0	0-0	1-1	0-0	25.0	+9.00
Fontwell	1-6	1-5	0-0	0-0	0-1	0-0	16.7	+5.00
Wincanton	1-10	0-4	0-0	1-4	0-2	0-0	10.0	-6.00
Ludlow	1-13	0-5	0-0	0-3	1-3	0-2	7.7	-2.00

WINNING HORSES

Horse	Races Run	1st	2nd	3rd	£
Ede'Iff	10	1	1	3	9545
Looks The Business	5	1	1	1	3110
Rojabaa	6	1	0	2	2967
Mizinky	4	1	0	0	2082
It's My Party	14	1	2	2	1890
Total winning prize-money					**£19594**
Favourites	0-1		0.0%		**-1.00**

\

N A TWISTON-DAVIES

NAUNTON, GLOUCS

	No. of Hrs	Races Run	1st	2nd	3rd	Unpl	Per cent	£1 Level Stake
NH Flat	29	46	9	6	3	28	19.6	+37.88
Hurdles	65	220	24	24	22	150	10.9	-98.98
Chases	56	206	26	6	11	163	12.6	-22.17
Totals	116	472	59	36	36	341	12.5	-83.27
04-05	97	389	69	51	35	234	17.7	-14.08
03-04	89	394	83	48	42	220	21.1	+77.13

BY MONTH

NH Flat	W-R	Per cent	£1 Level Stake		Hurdles	W-R	Per cent	£1 Level Stake
May	0-3	0.0	-3.00		May	0-6	0.0	-6.00
June	0-0	0.0	0.00		June	1-6	16.7	-2.50
July	0-1	0.0	-1.00		July	0-3	0.0	-3.00
August	1-1	100.0	+3.50		August	0-5	0.0	-5.00
September	0-0	0.0	0.00		September	2-4	50.0	+2.41
October	0-10	0.0	-10.00		October	9-24	37.5	+15.90
November	2-6	33.3	+13.50		November	1-26	3.8	-18.50
December	1-6	16.7	+4.00		December	4-31	12.9	-13.90
January	2-7	28.6	-0.13		January	2-23	8.7	-14.50
February	1-2	50.0	+24.00		February	4-36	11.1	-12.89
March	1-6	16.7	+3.00		March	0-29	0.0	-29.00
April	1-4	25.0	+4.00		April	1-27	3.7	-12.00

Chases	W-R	Per cent	£1 Level Stake		Totals	W-R	Per cent	£1 Level Stake
May	2-7	28.6	+8.00		May	2-16	12.5	-1.00
June	1-5	20.0	+8.00		June	2-11	18.2	+5.50
July	2-4	50.0	+13.00		July	2-8	25.0	+9.00
August	0-1	0.0	-1.00		August	1-7	14.3	-2.50
September	0-1	0.0	-1.00		September	2-5	40.0	+1.41
October	6-32	18.8	-8.25		October	15-66	22.7	-2.35
November	2-33	6.1	-27.92		November	5-65	7.7	-32.92
December	5-26	19.2	+14.50		December	10-63	15.9	+4.60
January	2-23	8.7	-1.00		January	6-53	11.3	-15.63
February	5-26	19.2	+17.00		February	10-64	15.6	+28.11
March	0-29	0.0	-29.00		March	1-64	1.6	-55.00
April	1-19	5.3	-14.50		April	3-50	6.0	-22.50

DISTANCE

Hurdles	W-R	Per cent	£1 Level Stake		Chases	W-R	Per cent	£1 Level Stake
2m-2m3f	9-73	12.3	-34.98		2m-2m3f	6-33	18.2	-4.67
2m4f-2m7f	12-85	14.1	-23.50		2m4f-2m7f	11-75	14.7	-14.50
3m+	3-62	4.8	-40.50		3m+	9-98	9.2	-3.00

TYPE OF RACE

Non-Handicaps	W-R	Per cent	£1 Level Stake		Handicaps	W-R	Per cent	£1 Level Stake
Nov Hrdls	14-95	14.7	-35.38		Nov Hrdls	2-26	7.7	-14.50
Hrdls	4-29	13.8	-14.59		Hrdls	3-64	4.7	-32.00
Nov Chs	6-28	21.4	-5.92		Nov Chs	3-32	9.4	-2.75
Chases	2-14	14.3	-3.75		Chases	15-132	11.4	-9.75
Sell/Claim	1-3	33.3	+0.50		Sell/Claim	0-3	0.0	-3.00

RACE CLASS

	W-R	Per cent	£1 Level Stake
Class 1	3-67	4.5	-55.75
Class 2	0-29	0.0	-29.00
Class 3	17-120	14.2	-5.93
Class 4	29-194	14.9	-17.96

FIRST TIME OUT

	W-R	Per cent	£1 Level Stake
Bumpers	5-29	17.2	+13.50
Hurdles	10-44	22.7	+5.18
Chases	9-43	20.9	+22.50

Class 5	3-27	11.1	-6.50	Totals	24-116	20.7	+41.18
Class 6	7-35	20.0	+31.88				

JOCKEYS

	W-R	Per cent	£1 Level Stake
Carl Llewellyn	31-235	13.2	-54.38
Antony Evans	11-101	10.9	-19.09
Marc Goldstein	6-28	21.4	+30.83
Steven Crawford	5-30	16.7	-6.63
Mr D England	3-14	21.4	+0.75
Bernie Wharfe	2-20	10.0	+6.00
Tom Scudamore	1-16	6.3	-12.75

COURSE RECORD

	Total W-R	Non-Hndcps Hurdles	Chases	Hndcps Hurdles	Chases	NH Flat	Per cent	£1 Level Stake
Chepstow	9-36	3-11	1-2	1-7	2-10	2-6	25.0	+6.13
Haydock	6-21	1-4	0-1	2-5	1-8	2-3	28.6	+49.57
Towcester	5-24	2-7	1-2	0-5	1-6	1-4	20.8	+9.25
Ludlow	5-34	0-8	1-2	0-7	3-12	1-5	14.7	+7.50
Mrket Rsn	4-10	0-3	0-0	1-3	3-4	0-0	40.0	+26.50
Uttoxeter	4-25	2-6	1-2	0-2	1-12	0-3	16.0	-12.68
Leicester	3-13	0-3	2-5	0-1	1-4	0-0	23.1	-2.42
Perth	3-14	2-5	0-0	1-6	0-3	0-0	21.4	-4.09
Newcastle	2-5	2-2	0-0	0-0	0-3	0-0	40.0	+4.12
Bangor	2-13	1-2	0-2	0-3	0-2	1-4	15.4	-5.63
Hereford	2-16	0-4	0-0	0-4	2-8	0-0	12.5	+0.25
Wetherby	2-18	0-5	1-3	0-3	0-5	1-2	11.1	-5.25
Aintree	2-19	1-4	1-3	0-4	0-7	0-1	10.5	-11.25
Huntingdon	2-27	0-7	0-1	0-7	1-11	1-1	7.4	-8.00
Stratford	1-3	1-1	0-1	0-0	0-1	0-0	33.3	+2.50
Carlisle	1-8	1-5	0-0	0-0	0-3	0-0	12.5	-5.80
Taunton	1-10	1-4	0-0	0-1	0-5	0-0	10.0	-2.00
Wincanton	1-13	0-2	0-2	0-6	1-3	0-0	7.7	+8.00
Exeter	1-14	1-5	0-2	0-2	0-3	0-2	7.1	-10.50
Warwick	1-19	1-8	0-1	0-2	0-4	0-4	5.3	-17.47
Worcester	1-20	0-6	0-1	0-5	1-6	0-2	5.0	-11.00
Cheltenham	1-51	0-12	0-9	0-5	1-20	0-5	2.0	-42.00

WINNING HORSES

Horse	Races Run	1st	2nd	3rd	£
Ollie Magern	6	1	0	0	45750
Rimsky	10	2	2	0	21001
Baby Run	1	1	0	0	15004
Lord Maizey	5	1	0	0	9683
Va Vavoom	12	2	2	0	14193
Bob The Builder	9	3	0	2	18684
Jeremy Cuddle Duck	6	3	0	0	11295
Maxie McDonald	1	1	0	0	6663
Naunton Brook	8	2	0	1	12018
Lord Brock	3	1	0	0	6506
Day Of Claies	7	2	0	1	12122
Red Georgie	4	1	0	1	5785
You Owe Me	7	1	0	0	5700
Florida Dream	8	2	0	0	10214

Montecorvino	4	1	0	0	5387
Miss Shakira	9	3	1	1	14579
Scotch Corner	10	1	0	0	5298
Billyandi	10	1	3	1	5205
The Cool Guy	3	2	1	0	8660
The Gangerman	9	1	2	3	4960
Randolph O'Brien	6	1	1	2	4909
No Guarantees	6	1	1	3	4880
Excellent Vibes	8	2	0	0	8327
Ardaghey	8	1	1	1	4120
Icy Prospect	3	1	0	0	4115
*Phildari	5	2	0	1	7456
Prestbury Knight	4	1	0	0	3881
Champagne Harry	5	1	1	0	3653
Harry Blade	2	1	1	0	3653
Ballyfitz	2	2	0	0	6940
Patman Du Charmil	7	2	0	2	6814
Nikola	4	1	1	0	3253
Best Profile	6	1	3	0	3017
Mahogany Blaze	9	1	1	2	2741
Bermuda Pointe	1	1	0	0	2602
Scribano Eile	9	1	0	0	2398
The Hollow Bottom	3	1	0	2	2388
Ballyshan	6	1	3	1	2277
Asudo	3	1	1	0	1891
Night Safe	3	2	0	0	3556
Larkbarrow	3	1	0	0	1713
Dark Corner	3	1	0	0	1627
Total winning prize-money					**£324918**
Favourites	20-41		48.8%		15.23

JOHN R UPSON

MAIDFORD, NORTHANTS

	No. of Hrs	Races Run	1st	2nd	3rd	Unpl	Per cent	£1 Level Stake
NH Flat	3	4	0	0	0	4	0.0	-4.00
Hurdles	11	33	2	2	2	27	6.1	-21.00
Chases	9	37	4	2	5	26	10.8	-11.00
Totals	**17**	**74**	**6**	**4**	**7**	**57**	**8.1**	**-36.00**
04-05	23	102	3	5	8	86	2.9	-77.00
03-04	19	93	7	8	4	74	7.5	-32.17

JOCKEYS

	W-R	Per cent	£1 Level Stake
Mark Nicolls	4-32	12.5	-4.00
P Flynn	1-6	16.7	-1.00
Jamie Goldstein	1-7	14.3	-2.00

COURSE RECORD

	Total W-R	Non-Hndcps Hurdles	Chases	Hndcps Hurdles	Chases	NH Flat	Per cent	£1 Level Stake
Towcester	2-20	0-5	0-1	0-3	2-8	0-3	10.0	-7.50
Haydock	1-2	0-1	0-0	0-0	1-1	0-0	50.0	+4.50
Warwick	1-3	1-1	0-0	0-0	0-1	0-1	33.3	+4.00

Plumpton	1-4	0-1	0-0	1-1	0-2	0-0	25.0	+1.00
Uttoxeter	1-6	0-1	0-0	0-2	1-3	0-0	16.7	+1.00

WINNING HORSES

Horse	Races Run	1st	2nd	3rd	£
Blunham Hill	7	3	0	1	20333
Over Zealous	3	1	0	1	4115
Gritti Palace	6	1	2	1	3546
Strolling Vagabond	6	1	0	1	3253
Total winning prize-money					**£31247**
Favourites	**0-1**		**0.0%**		**-1.00**

TIM VAUGHAN

BRIDGEND

	No. of Hrs	Races Run	1st	2nd	3rd	Unpl	Per cent	£1 Level Stake
NH Flat	0	0	0	0	0	0	0.0	0.00
Hurdles	5	8	0	0	0	8	0.0	-8.00
Chases	1	2	1	0	0	1	50.0	+5.50
Totals	**5**	**10**	**1**	**0**	**0**	**9**	**10.0**	**-2.50**

JOCKEYS

	W-R	Per cent	£1 Level Stake
Richard Johnson	1-3	33.3	+4.50

COURSE RECORD

	Total W-R	Non-Hndcps Hurdles	Chases	Hndcps Hurdles	Chases	NH Flat	Per cent	£1 Level Stake
Aintree	1-1	0-0	0-0	0-0	1-1	0-0	100.0	+6.50

WINNING HORSES

Horse	Races Run	1st	2nd	3rd	£
*Lonesome Man	3	1	0	0	6187
Total winning prize-money					**£6187**
Favourites	**0-0**		**0.0%**		**0.00**

J WADE

MORDON, CO DURHAM

	No. of Hrs	Races Run	1st	2nd	3rd	Unpl	Per cent	£1 Level Stake
NH Flat	8	12	0	0	2	10	0.0	-12.00
Hurdles	16	46	2	4	4	36	4.3	-35.50
Chases	9	24	2	1	3	18	8.3	-12.00
Totals	**28**	**82**	**4**	**5**	**9**	**64**	**4.9**	**-59.50**
04-05	26	91	12	9	9	61	13.2	+32.21
03-04	14	40	1	6	2	31	2.5	-28.00

JOCKEYS

	W-R	Per cent	£1 Level Stake
Paddy Aspell	4-62	6.5	-39.50

COURSE RECORD

	Total W-R	Non-Hndcps Hurdles	Chases	Hndcps Hurdles	Chases	NH Flat	Per cent	£1 Level Stake
Carlisle	2-7	0-2	0-2	0-1	2-2	0-0	28.6	+5.00
Ayr	1-4	1-2	0-0	0-0	0-1	0-1	25.0	+4.00
Hexham	1-4	1-1	0-0	0-1	0-1	0-1	25.0	-1.50

WINNING HORSES

Horse	Races Run	1st	2nd	3rd	£
Recent Edition	6	2	0	1	7482
Love That Benny	3	1	1	1	3253
Silent Bay	5	1	0	2	3083
Total winning prize-money					**£13810**
Favourites	**0-1**		**0.0%**		**-1.00**

MRS L WADHAM

NEWMARKET, SUFFOLK

	No. of Hrs	Races Run	1st	2nd	3rd	Unpl	Per cent	£1 Level Stake
NH Flat	2	3	1	0	0	2	33.3	+23.00
Hurdles	22	73	7	11	13	42	9.6	-36.40
Chases	8	28	6	6	3	13	21.4	+5.88
Totals	**28**	**104**	**14**	**17**	**16**	**57**	**13.5**	**-7.52**
04-05	29	121	18	16	19	68	14.9	+18.27
03-04	20	89	9	10	18	52	10.1	-42.50

BY MONTH

NH Flat	W-R	Per cent	£1 Level Stake	Hurdles	W-R	Per cent	£1 Level Stake
May	0-0	0.0	0.00	May	2-4	50.0	+5.25
June	0-0	0.0	0.00	June	0-5	0.0	-5.00
July	0-0	0.0	0.00	July	0-3	0.0	-3.00
August	0-0	0.0	0.00	August	0-1	0.0	-1.00
September	0-0	0.0	0.00	September	0-2	0.0	-2.00
October	0-0	0.0	0.00	October	0-4	0.0	-4.00
November	0-0	0.0	0.00	November	1-13	7.7	-11.00
December	0-1	0.0	-1.00	December	0-8	0.0	-8.00
January	0-0	0.0	0.00	January	0-7	0.0	-7.00
February	0-0	0.0	0.00	February	1-11	9.1	-5.00
March	1-1	100.0	+25.00	March	2-8	25.0	+9.25
April	0-1	0.0	-1.00	April	1-7	14.3	-4.90

Chases	W-R	Per cent	£1 Level Stake	Totals	W-R	Per cent	£1 Level Stake
May	0-0	0.0	0.00	May	2-4	50.0	+5.25
June	0-0	0.0	0.00	June	0-5	0.0	-5.00
July	0-0	0.0	0.00	July	0-3	0.0	-3.00
August	0-1	0.0	-1.00	August	0-2	0.0	-2.00

	W-R	Per cent	£1 Level Stake		W-R	Per cent	£1 Level Stake
September	0-0	0.0	0.00	September	0-2	0.0	-2.00
October	1-2	50.0	-0.17	October	1-6	16.7	-4.17
November	0-4	0.0	-4.00	November	1-17	5.9	-15.00
December	1-2	50.0	+5.00	December	1-11	9.1	-4.00
January	1-4	25.0	-0.75	January	1-11	9.1	-7.75
February	2-6	33.3	+10.80	February	3-17	17.6	+5.80
March	0-5	0.0	-5.00	March	3-14	21.4	+29.25
April	1-4	25.0	+1.00	April	2-12	16.7	-4.90

DISTANCE

Hurdles	W-R	Per cent	£1 Level Stake	Chases	W-R	Per cent	£1 Level Stake
2m-2m3f	6-56	10.7	-34.40	2m-2m3f	1-7	14.3	+8.00
2m4f-2m7f	1-15	6.7	0.00	2m4f-2m7f	4-11	36.4	+2.88
3m+	0-2	0.0	-2.00	3m+	1-10	10.0	-5.00

TYPE OF RACE

Non-Handicaps	W-R	Per cent	£1 Level Stake	Handicaps	W-R	Per cent	£1 Level Stake
Nov Hrdls	4-29	13.8	-15.50	Nov Hrdls	0-1	0.0	-1.00
Hrdls	1-7	14.3	-4.90	Hrdls	2-34	5.9	-13.00
Nov Chs	4-13	30.8	+2.63	Nov Chs	0-2	0.0	-2.00
Chases	0-1	0.0	-1.00	Chases	2-11	18.2	+7.25
Sell/Claim	0-3	0.0	-3.00	Sell/Claim	0-0	0.0	0.00

RACE CLASS

	W-R	Per cent	£1 Level Stake	FIRST TIME OUT	W-R	Per cent	£1 Level Stake
Class 1	0-11	0.0	-11.00	Bumpers	1-2	50.0	+24.00
Class 2	1-5	20.0	+10.00	Hurdles	3-21	14.3	-9.75
Class 3	3-32	9.4	-18.17	Chases	1-5	20.0	-3.17
Class 4	8-47	17.0	-8.60				
Class 5	1-4	25.0	-0.75	Totals	5-28	17.9	+11.08
Class 6	1-5	20.0	+21.00				

JOCKEYS

	W-R	Per cent	£1 Level Stake
Leighton Aspell	13-64	20.3	+25.48
Jimmy McCarthy	1-9	11.1	-2.00

COURSE RECORD

	Total W-R	Non-Hndcps Hurdles	Chases	Hndcps Hurdles	Chases	NH Flat	Per cent	£1 Level Stake
Towcester	2-5	1-2	0-1	1-2	0-0	0-0	40.0	+3.00
Mrket Rsn	2-7	1-4	1-1	0-2	0-0	0-0	28.6	-2.95
Uttoxeter	2-9	0-4	0-0	1-3	0-1	1-1	22.2	+32.00
Huntingdon	2-13	1-4	1-4	0-2	0-2	0-1	15.4	-2.75
Ludlow	1-1	0-0	1-1	0-0	0-0	0-0	100.0	+4.00
Plumpton	1-2	1-2	0-0	0-0	0-0	0-0	50.0	+0.10
Fontwell	1-4	0-1	0-0	0-2	1-1	0-0	25.0	-0.75
Lingfield	1-4	1-3	0-0	0-1	0-0	0-0	25.0	+2.00
Leicester	1-6	0-3	0-1	0-1	1-1	0-0	16.7	+9.00
Fakenham	1-8	0-2	1-3	0-1	0-2	0-0	12.5	-6.17

WINNING HORSES

Horse	Races Run	1st	2nd	3rd	£
Heir To Be	6	1	1	0	11464
The Dark Lord	7	2	0	2	16270
Viciana	5	2	1	1	10624
Migwell	6	1	0	0	5478
Executive Decision	4	1	1	0	4754
Naked Oat	4	1	1	0	4193
Brigadier Du Bois	7	1	2	2	3578
Resplendent Star	7	1	2	1	3325
Victorias Groom	5	1	1	3	3253
Sonnengold	5	1	1	0	3253
Ken's Dream	3	1	1	0	2928
Chaim	2	1	0	0	1627
Total winning prize-money					**£70747**
Favourites	7-11	63.6%			5.48

MISS TRACY WAGGOTT

SPENNYMOOR, CO DURHAM

	No. of Hrs	Races Run	1st	2nd	3rd	Unpl	Per cent	£1 Level Stake
NH Flat	0	0	0	0	0	0	0.0	0.00
Hurdles	8	25	2	1	1	21	8.0	+14.00
Chases	2	5	0	0	0	5	0.0	-5.00
Totals	8	30	2	1	1	26	6.7	+9.00

JOCKEYS

	W-R	Per cent	£1 Level Stake
Miss C Metcalfe	2-6	33.3	+33.00

COURSE RECORD

	Total W-R	Non-Hndcps Hurdles	Chases	Hndcps Hurdles	Chases	NH Flat	Per cent	£1 Level Stake
Ayr	1-1	0-0	0-0	1-1	0-0	0-0	100.0	+12.00
Sedgefield	1-6	0-0	0-0	1-4	0-2	0-0	16.7	+20.00

WINNING HORSES

Horse	Races Run	1st	2nd	3rd	£
*Longstone Lass	6	2	0	0	6289
Total winning prize-money					**£6289**
Favourites	0-0	0.0%			0.00

J S WAINWRIGHT

KENNYTHORPE, N YORKS

	No. of Hrs	Races Run	1st	2nd	3rd	Unpl	Per cent	£1 Level Stake
NH Flat	1	2	0	0	0	2	0.0	-2.00
Hurdles	12	48	3	4	2	39	6.3	-14.00

Chases	1	1	0	0	0	1	0.0	-1.00
Totals	12	51	3	4	2	42	5.9	-17.00
04-05	15	52	0	4	8	40	0.0	-52.00
03-04	14	45	3	1	6	35	6.7	-6.00

JOCKEYS

	W-R	Per cent	£1 Level Stake
Paddy Aspell	2-12	16.7	+9.00
Anthony Ross	1-15	6.7	-2.00

COURSE RECORD

	Total W-R	Non-Hndcps Hurdles	Chases	Hndcps Hurdles	Chases	NH Flat	Per cent	£1 Level Stake
Bangor	1-3	0-2	0-0	1-1	0-0	0-0	33.3	+10.00
Stratford	1-5	0-2	0-0	1-1	0-0	0-2	20.0	+3.00
Mrket Rsn	1-16	1-5	0-0	0-11	0-0	0-0	6.3	-3.00

WINNING HORSES

Horse	Races Run	1st	2nd	3rd	£
Little Task	13	2	3	2	8450
*Ivana Illyich	3	1	0	0	3575
Total winning prize-money					£12025
Favourites	0-3		0.0%		-3.00

MRS K WALDRON

STOKE BLISS, WORCS

	No. of Hrs	Races Run	1st	2nd	3rd	Unpl	Per cent	£1 Level Stake
NH Flat	3	6	0	2	0	4	0.0	-6.00
Hurdles	21	54	4	8	9	33	7.4	-30.00
Chases	15	56	8	4	9	35	14.3	-2.63
Totals	28	116	12	14	18	72	10.3	-38.63
04-05	17	50	2	5	3	40	4.0	-36.00
03-04	20	61	7	5	5	44	11.5	+12.00

BY MONTH

NH Flat	W-R	Per cent	£1 Level Stake	Hurdles	W-R	Per cent	£1 Level Stake
May	0-2	0.0	-2.00	May	1-9	11.1	+1.00
June	0-0	0.0	0.00	June	0-3	0.0	-3.00
July	0-0	0.0	0.00	July	2-10	20.0	0.00
August	0-0	0.0	0.00	August	0-6	0.0	-6.00
September	0-0	0.0	0.00	September	0-3	0.0	-3.00
October	0-1	0.0	-1.00	October	0-4	0.0	-4.00
November	0-2	0.0	-2.00	November	1-5	20.0	-1.00
December	0-0	0.0	0.00	December	0-2	0.0	-2.00
January	0-0	0.0	0.00	January	0-0	0.0	0.00
February	0-0	0.0	0.00	February	0-2	0.0	-2.00
March	0-0	0.0	0.00	March	0-6	0.0	-6.00
April	0-1	0.0	-1.00	April	0-4	0.0	-4.00

Chases	W-R	Per cent	£1 Level Stake	Totals	W-R	Per cent	£1 Level Stake
May	0-3	0.0	-3.00	May	1-14	7.1	-4.00
June	0-2	0.0	-2.00	June	0-5	0.0	-5.00
July	0-6	0.0	-6.00	July	2-16	12.5	-6.00
August	0-4	0.0	-4.00	August	0-10	0.0	-10.00
September	0-1	0.0	-1.00	September	0-4	0.0	-4.00
October	0-0	0.0	0.00	October	0-5	0.0	-5.00
November	1-4	25.0	+1.00	November	2-11	18.2	-2.00
December	1-7	14.3	+14.00	December	1-9	11.1	+12.00
January	2-5	40.0	+2.00	January	2-5	40.0	+2.00
February	1-10	10.0	-8.47	February	1-12	8.3	-10.47
March	3-10	30.0	+8.83	March	3-16	18.8	+2.83
April	0-4	0.0	-4.00	April	0-9	0.0	-9.00

DISTANCE

Hurdles	W-R	Per cent	£1 Level Stake	Chases	W-R	Per cent	£1 Level Stake
2m-2m3f	0-17	0.0	-17.00	2m-2m3f	0-11	0.0	-11.00
2m4f-2m7f	4-25	16.0	-1.00	2m4f-2m7f	4-26	15.4	-3.67
3m+	0-12	0.0	-12.00	3m+	4-19	21.1	+12.03

TYPE OF RACE

Non-Handicaps	W-R	Per cent	£1 Level Stake	Handicaps	W-R	Per cent	£1 Level Stake
Nov Hrdls	1-11	9.1	-6.50	Nov Hrdls	0-2	0.0	-2.00
Hrdls	0-7	0.0	-7.00	Hrdls	1-17	5.9	-13.00
Nov Chs	0-12	0.0	-12.00	Nov Chs	1-3	33.3	+1.33
Chases	1-13	7.7	-11.47	Chases	6-28	21.4	+19.50
Sell/Claim	2-14	14.3	-4.00	Sell/Claim	1-8	12.5	+2.00

RACE CLASS

	W-R	Per cent	£1 Level Stake
Class 1	0-2	0.0	-2.00
Class 2	0-3	0.0	-3.00
Class 3	0-18	0.0	-18.00
Class 4	6-53	11.3	-4.17
Class 5	5-28	17.9	-1.00
Class 6	1-12	8.3	-10.47

FIRST TIME OUT

	W-R	Per cent	£1 Level Stake
Bumpers	0-3	0.0	-3.00
Hurdles	1-17	5.9	-13.00
Chases	0-8	0.0	-8.00
Totals	1-28	3.6	-24.00

JOCKEYS

	W-R	Per cent	£1 Level Stake
Richard Spate	10-97	10.3	-24.67
Mr J Snowden	1-1	100.0	+2.50
Mr R Burton	1-3	33.3	-1.47

COURSE RECORD

	Total W-R	Non-Hndcps Hurdles	Chases	Hndcps Hurdles	Chases	NH Flat	Per cent	£1 Level Stake
Uttoxeter	4-35	0-7	0-1	1-16	3-8	0-3	11.4	-0.50
Folkestone	1-1	0-0	0-0	0-0	1-1	0-0	100.0	+2.50
Taunton	1-4	0-2	0-0	0-1	1-1	0-0	25.0	+0.33
Warwick	1-4	0-0	1-2	0-1	0-1	0-0	25.0	-2.47
Mrket Rsn	1-5	1-1	0-2	0-0	0-2	0-0	20.0	+0.50

	Total W-R	Non-Hndcps Hurdles	Chases	Hndcps Hurdles	Chases	NH Flat	Per cent	£1 Level Stake
Southwell	1-5	1-2	0-1	0-1	0-1	0-0	20.0	-0.50
Ludlow	1-8	0-2	0-2	1-1	0-1	0-2	12.5	+2.00
Hereford	1-9	0-3	0-1	0-2	1-2	0-1	11.1	-5.50
Leicester	1-9	0-0	0-5	0-0	1-4	0-0	11.1	+1.00

WINNING HORSES

Horse	Races Run	1st	2nd	3rd	£
Merry Storm	10	3	1	1	13276
Young Lorcan	8	4	2	1	15879
Major Benefit	7	1	1	0	4974
*Angie's Double	8	2	0	0	4991
Somewin	6	1	0	1	2541
Foly Pleasant	3	1	0	1	1319
Total winning prize-money					£42980
Favourites	3-10		30.0%		0.03

R WALEY-COHEN

RATLEY, WARWICK

	No. of Hrs	Races Run	1st	2nd	3rd	Unpl	Per cent	£1 Level Stake
NH Flat	0	0	0	0	0	0	0.0	0.00
Hurdles	2	8	0	1	1	6	0.0	-8.00
Chases	5	8	2	1	2	3	25.0	+4.50
Totals	6	16	2	2	3	9	12.5	-3.50
04-05	4	11	3	1	0	7	27.3	+0.46
03-04	4	6	0	0	1	5	0.0	-6.00

JOCKEYS

	W-R	Per cent	£1 Level Stake
Mr S Waley-Cohen	2-16	12.5	-3.50

COURSE RECORD

	Total W-R	Non-Hndcps Hurdles	Chases	Hndcps Hurdles	Chases	NH Flat	Per cent	£1 Level Stake
Kelso	1-1	0-0	1-1	0-0	0-0	0-0	100.0	+5.00
Aintree	1-1	0-0	1-1	0-0	0-0	0-0	100.0	+5.50

WINNING HORSES

Horse	Races Run	1st	2nd	3rd	£
Katarino	1	1	0	0	21007
Mel In Blue	3	1	0	1	7508
Total winning prize-money					£28515
Favourites	0-0		0.0%		0.00

T D WALFORD

SHERIFF HUTTON, N YORKS

	No. of Hrs	Races Run	1st	2nd	3rd	Unpl	Per cent	£1 Level Stake
NH Flat	7	13	0	1	3	9	0.0	-13.00
Hurdles	8	21	2	0	5	14	9.5	+0.33

Chases	4	17	1	2	1	13	5.9	-9.00
Totals	15	51	3	3	9	36	5.9	-21.67
04-05	11	41	2	4	2	33	4.9	-27.50
03-04	11	44	6	5	4	29	13.6	+69.63

JOCKEYS

	W-R	Per cent	£1 Level Stake
Robert Walford	3-27	11.1	+2.33

COURSE RECORD

	Total W-R	Non-Hndcps Hurdles	Chases	Hndcps Hurdles	Chases	NH Flat	Per cent	£1 Level Stake
Sedgefield	1-3	0-0	0-1	0-1	1-1	0-0	33.3	+5.00
Uttoxeter	1-6	0-0	0-0	1-3	0-0	0-3	16.7	+11.00
Mrket Rsn	1-8	1-2	0-0	0-1	0-3	0-2	12.5	-3.67

WINNING HORSES

Horse	Races Run	1st	2nd	3rd	£
Miss Pross	10	1	1	3	4880
Weston Rock	5	2	0	1	9253
Total winning prize-money					£14133
Favourites	0-3		0.0%		-3.00

T WALL

HARTON, SHROPSHIRE

	No. of Hrs	Races Run	1st	2nd	3rd	Unpl	Per cent	£1 Level Stake
NH Flat	1	1	0	0	0	1	0.0	-1.00
Hurdles	12	43	1	1	0	41	2.3	-28.00
Chases	2	2	0	0	0	2	0.0	-2.00
Totals	14	46	1	1	0	44	2.2	-31.00
04-05	12	51	1	3	4	43	2.0	-38.00
03-04	11	27	1	0	1	25	3.7	-1.00

JOCKEYS

	W-R	Per cent	£1 Level Stake
Owyn Nelmes	1-9	11.1	+6.00

COURSE RECORD

	Total W-R	Non-Hndcps Hurdles	Chases	Hndcps Hurdles	Chases	NH Flat	Per cent	£1 Level Stake
Uttoxeter	1-7	0-1	0-0	1-5	0-0	0-1	14.3	+8.00

WINNING HORSES

Horse	Races Run	1st	2nd	3rd	£
Margarets Wish	9	1	0	0	2317
Total winning prize-money					£2317
Favourites	0-0		0.0%		0.00

MRS S WALL

DALLINGTON, E SUSSEX

	No. of Hrs	Races Run	1st	2nd	3rd	Unpl	Per cent	£1 Level Stake
NH Flat	1	1	0	0	0	1	0.0	-1.00
Hurdles	0	0	0	0	0	0	0.0	0.00
Chases	2	9	3	0	0	6	33.3	+16.00
Totals	3	10	3	0	0	7	30.0	+15.00
04-05	2	8	0	1	1	6	0.0	-8.00
03-04	6	13	0	0	0	13	0.0	-13.00

JOCKEYS

	W-R	Per cent	£1 Level Stake
Mr G Tumelty	3-8	37.5	+17.00

COURSE RECORD

	Total W-R	Non-Hndcps Hurdles	Chases	Hndcps Hurdles	Chases	NH Flat	Per cent	£1 Level Stake
Plumpton	2-4	0-0	0-0	0-0	2-3	0-1	50.0	+12.00
Folkestone	1-3	0-0	0-1	0-0	1-2	0-0	33.3	+6.00

WINNING HORSES

Horse	Races Run	1st	2nd	3rd	£
Tallow Bay	7	3	0	0	10325
Total winning prize-money					**£10325**
Favourites	0-0		0.0%		0.00

M J WALLACE

NEWMARKET, SUFFOLK

	No. of Hrs	Races Run	1st	2nd	3rd	Unpl	Per cent	£1 Level Stake
NH Flat	0	0	0	0	0	0	0.0	0.00
Hurdles	1	4	1	1	0	2	25.0	+1.00
Chases	0	0	0	0	0	0	0.0	0.00
Totals	1	4	1	1	0	2	25.0	+1.00
03-04	1	2	0	0	0	2	0.0	-2.00

JOCKEYS

	W-R	Per cent	£1 Level Stake
Barry Fenton	1-2	50.0	+3.00

COURSE RECORD

	Total W-R	Non-Hndcps Hurdles	Chases	Hndcps Hurdles	Chases	NH Flat	Per cent	£1 Level Stake
Fakenham	1-1	1-1	0-0	0-0	0-0	0-0	100.0	+4.00

WINNING HORSES

Horse	Races Run	1st	2nd	3rd	£
Arry Dash	4	1	1	0	3405
Total winning prize-money					**£3405**
Favourites	0-0		0.0%		0.00

MRS K WALTON

MIDDLEHAM MOOR, N YORKS

	No. of Hrs	Races Run	1st	2nd	3rd	Unpl	Per cent	£1 Level Stake
NH Flat	6	13	0	3	1	9	0.0	-13.00
Hurdles	14	39	4	3	6	26	10.3	-4.13
Chases	6	30	1	7	6	16	3.3	-27.50
Totals	22	82	5	13	13	51	6.1	-44.63
04-05	18	87	13	3	8	63	14.9	+20.83
03-04	16	75	10	7	7	51	13.3	-9.13

JOCKEYS

	W-R	Per cent	£1 Level Stake
Richard McGrath	3-37	8.1	-5.88
Tony Dobbin	1-2	50.0	-0.75
Colm Sharkey	1-23	4.3	-18.00

COURSE RECORD

	Total W-R	Non-Hndcps Hurdles	Chases	Hndcps Hurdles	Chases	NH Flat	Per cent	£1 Level Stake
Ayr	2-8	1-4	0-0	1-1	0-1	0-2	25.0	-4.13
Carlisle	1-1	0-0	0-0	0-0	1-1	0-0	100.0	+1.50
Perth	1-6	0-1	0-0	1-3	0-2	0-0	16.7	-1.00
Haydock	1-7	0-2	0-0	1-1	0-0	0-4	14.3	+19.00

WINNING HORSES

Horse	Races Run	1st	2nd	3rd	£
*Huka Lodge	4	1	0	0	7807
Fantastico	4	1	0	0	4269
*Jimmy Bond	2	1	1	0	3666
*Morgan Be	6	2	1	1	7157
Total winning prize-money					**£22899**
Favourites	3-6		50.0%		0.38

G WAREHAM

FINDON, SUSSEX

	No. of Hrs	Races Run	1st	2nd	3rd	Unpl	Per cent	£1 Level Stake
NH Flat	0	0	0	0	0	0	0.0	0.00
Hurdles	0	0	0	0	0	0	0.0	0.00
Chases	1	6	1	0	0	5	16.7	+11.00
Totals	1	6	1	0	0	5	16.7	+11.00

04-05	1	7	0	0	0	7	0.0	-7.00
03-04	1	8	4	1	0	3	50.0	+6.10

JOCKEYS

	W-R	Per cent	£1 Level Stake
Mick Fitzgerald	1-1	100.0	+16.00

COURSE RECORD

	Total W-R	Non-Hndcps Hurdles	Chases	Hndcps Hurdles	Chases	NH Flat	Per cent	£1 Level Stake
Plumpton	1-2	0-0	0-0	0-0	1-2	0-0	50.0	+15.00

WINNING HORSES

Horse	Races Run	1st	2nd	3rd	£
The Newsman	6	1	0	0	4384
Total winning prize-money					£4384
Favourites	0-0		0.0%		0.00

MRS BARBARA WARING

ETTINGTON, WARWICKS

	No. of Hrs	Races Run	1st	2nd	3rd	Unpl	Per cent	£1 Level Stake
NH Flat	0	0	0	0	0	0	0.0	0.00
Hurdles	8	21	1	1	1	18	4.8	+5.00
Chases	1	3	0	0	0	3	0.0	-3.00
Totals	8	24	1	1	1	21	4.2	+2.00
04-05	11	44	0	1	2	41	0.0	-44.00
03-04	8	36	3	1	4	28	8.3	-7.50

JOCKEYS

	W-R	Per cent	£1 Level Stake
Marcus Foley	1-3	33.3	+23.00

COURSE RECORD

	Total W-R	Non-Hndcps Hurdles	Chases	Hndcps Hurdles	Chases	NH Flat	Per cent	£1 Level Stake
Worcester	1-5	0-2	0-0	1-3	0-0	0-0	20.0	+21.00

WINNING HORSES

Horse	Races Run	1st	2nd	3rd	£
Southerncrosspatch	4	1	0	0	2996
Total winning prize-money					£2996
Favourites	0-0		0.0%		0.00

W J WARNER

NORTHAMPTON, NORTHANTS

	No. of Hrs	Races Run	1st	2nd	3rd	Unpl	Per cent	£1 Level Stake
NH Flat	0	0	0	0	0	0	0.0	0.00
Hurdles	0	0	0	0	0	0	0.0	0.00
Chases	2	7	1	3	0	3	14.3	-3.50
Totals	2	7	1	3	0	3	14.3	-3.50
04-05	2	4	1	1	0	2	25.0	+0.50

JOCKEYS

	W-R	Per cent	£1 Level Stake
Mr S Morris	1-7	14.3	-3.50

COURSE RECORD

	Total W-R	Non-Hndcps Hurdles	Chases	Hndcps Hurdles	Chases	NH Flat	Per cent	£1 Level Stake
Huntingdon	1-2	0-0	1-2	0-0	0-0	0-0	50.0	+1.50

WINNING HORSES

Horse	Races Run	1st	2nd	3rd	£
Coolefind	3	1	0	0	1617
Total winning prize-money					£1617
Favourites	0-1		0.0%		-1.00

MRS S A WATT

BROMPTON-ON-SWALE, N YORKS

	No. of Hrs	Races Run	1st	2nd	3rd	Unpl	Per cent	£1 Level Stake
NH Flat	1	1	0	0	0	1	0.0	-1.00
Hurdles	5	22	0	2	0	20	0.0	-22.00
Chases	3	13	2	1	1	9	15.4	-2.25
Totals	7	36	2	3	1	30	5.6	-25.25
04-05	4	28	4	3	2	19	14.3	-0.50
03-04	3	22	3	3	2	14	13.6	-6.50

JOCKEYS

	W-R	Per cent	£1 Level Stake
Peter Buchanan	1-7	14.3	0.00
Keith Mercer	1-17	5.9	-13.25

COURSE RECORD

	Total W-R	Non-Hndcps Hurdles	Chases	Hndcps Hurdles	Chases	NH Flat	Per cent	£1 Level Stake
Sedgefield	2-6	0-1	0-0	0-0	2-5	0-0	33.3	+4.75

WINNING HORSES

Horse	Races Run	1st	2nd	3rd	£
Now Then Sid	8	2	1	1	8869
Total winning prize-money					**£8869**
Favourites	**0-3**		**0.0%**		**-3.00**

P R WEBBER

MOLLINGTON, OXON

	No. of Hrs	Races Run	1st	2nd	3rd	Unpl	Per cent	£1 Level Stake
NH Flat	23	33	6	2	1	23	18.2	+44.75
Hurdles	33	66	7	1	7	51	10.6	-36.18
Chases	19	55	9	7	12	27	16.4	-4.75
Totals	63	154	22	10	20	101	14.3	+3.82
04-05	*64*	*212*	*29*	*25*	*20*	*138*	*13.7*	*-31.76*
03-04	*73*	*231*	*36*	*28*	*26*	*141*	*15.6*	*-1.39*

BY MONTH

NH Flat	W-R	Per cent	£1 Level Stake	Hurdles	W-R	Per cent	£1 Level Stake
May	0-1	0.0	-1.00	May	2-6	33.3	+2.25
June	1-1	100.0	+2.00	June	3-4	75.0	+3.57
July	0-0	0.0	0.00	July	1-3	33.3	+6.00
August	0-1	0.0	-1.00	August	0-5	0.0	-5.00
September	0-0	0.0	0.00	September	0-0	0.0	0.00
October	0-2	0.0	-2.00	October	0-2	0.0	-2.00
November	0-5	0.0	-5.00	November	0-11	0.0	-11.00
December	0-1	0.0	-1.00	December	0-3	0.0	-3.00
January	1-8	12.5	-2.50	January	0-19	0.0	-19.00
February	0-1	0.0	-1.00	February	0-2	0.0	-2.00
March	1-4	25.0	+47.00	March	0-4	0.0	-4.00
April	3-9	33.3	+9.25	April	1-7	14.3	-2.00

Chases	W-R	Per cent	£1 Level Stake	Totals	W-R	Per cent	£1 Level Stake
May	0-1	0.0	-1.00	May	2-8	25.0	+0.25
June	0-2	0.0	-2.00	June	4-7	57.1	+3.57
July	0-2	0.0	-2.00	July	1-5	20.0	+4.00
August	0-1	0.0	-1.00	August	0-7	0.0	-7.00
September	3-4	75.0	+7.00	September	3-4	75.0	+7.00
October	1-8	12.5	-3.50	October	1-12	8.3	-7.50
November	0-9	0.0	-9.00	November	0-25	0.0	-25.00
December	0-5	0.0	-5.00	December	0-9	0.0	-9.00
January	0-5	0.0	-5.00	January	1-32	3.1	-26.50
February	1-6	16.7	+7.00	February	1-9	11.1	+4.00
March	0-4		-4.00	March	1-12	8.3	+39.00
April	4-8	50.0	+13.75	April	8-24	33.3	+21.00

DISTANCE

Hurdles	W-R	Per cent	£1 Level Stake	Chases	W-R	Per cent	£1 Level Stake
2m-2m3f	7-48	14.6	-18.18	2m-2m3f	4-26	15.4	-4.00
2m4f-2m7f	0-16	0.0	-16.00	2m4f-2m7f	5-21	23.8	+7.25
3m+	0-2	0.0	-2.00	3m+	0-8	0.0	-8.00

TYPE OF RACE

Non-Handicaps	W-R	Per cent	£1 Level Stake	Handicaps	W-R	Per cent	£1 Level Stake
Nov Hrdls	4-41	9.8	-29.68	Nov Hrdls	0-3	0.0	-3.00
Hrdls	2-9	22.2	+5.00	Hrdls	1-12	8.3	-7.50
Nov Chs	2-19	10.5	-9.50	Nov Chs	2-6	33.3	+12.00
Chases	0-0	0.0	0.00	Chases	5-29	17.2	-6.25
Sell/Claim	0-0	0.0	0.00	Sell/Claim	0-1	0.0	-1.00

RACE CLASS

	W-R	Per cent	£1 Level Stake
Class 1	0-11	0.0	-11.00
Class 2	3-13	23.1	+8.25
Class 3	3-40	7.5	-27.18
Class 4	11-59	18.6	+38.00
Class 5	1-9	11.1	-3.50
Class 6	4-22	18.2	-0.75

FIRST TIME OUT

	W-R	Per cent	£1 Level Stake
Bumpers	5-23	21.7	+3.75
Hurdles	3-24	12.5	-6.75
Chases	3-16	18.8	-3.25
Totals	11-63	17.5	-6.25

JOCKEYS

	W-R	Per cent	£1 Level Stake
Tom Doyle	20-118	16.9	+27.82
James Davies	2-15	13.3	-3.00

COURSE RECORD

	Total W-R	Non-Hndcps Hurdles	Chases	Hndcps Hurdles	Chases	NH Flat	Per cent	£1 Level Stake
Uttoxeter	3-8	1-2	0-0	0-3	0-1	2-2	37.5	+4.25
Hexham	2-2	2-2	0-0	0-0	0-0	0-0	100.0	+2.57
Fontwell	2-4	0-1	1-1	0-0	1-1	0-1	50.0	+4.75
Worcester	2-6	1-2	1-2	0-2	0-0	0-0	33.3	+7.00
Huntingdon	2-9	0-2	0-0	0-1	2-3	0-3	22.2	-0.25
Ludlow	2-14	0-7	0-1	1-1	0-0	1-5	14.3	-0.50
Chepstow	1-4	1-2	0-1	0-0	0-1	0-0	25.0	+1.00
Haydock	1-4	0-0	0-0	0-1	1-1	0-2	25.0	+9.00
Hereford	1-5	1-3	0-0	0-1	0-1	0-0	20.0	-2.00
Sandown	1-5	0-0	0-0	0-0	1-4	0-1	20.0	-1.25
Towcester	1-5	0-1	0-1	0-0	0-0	1-3	20.0	-1.25
Stratford	1-6	0-2	0-1	0-0	0-1	1-1	16.7	+45.00
Wetherby	1-7	0-1	0-2	0-0	1-4	0-0	14.3	-2.50
Wincanton	1-7	0-4	0-2	0-0	1-1	0-0	14.3	+0.50
Newbury	1-11	0-4	0-0	0-2	0-2	1-3	9.1	-5.50

WINNING HORSES

Horse	Races Run	1st	2nd	3rd	£
No Full	6	1	1	1	13012
Full House	6	2	0	0	21807
Duke Of Buckingham	7	1	1	2	6988
Uncle Wallace	3	1	0	0	6506
Miami Explorer	3	3	0	0	12468
Thalys	3	1	1	0	4794
Kentmere	5	1	1	1	4739
Space Star	3	1	1	1	4705

Tighe Caster	4	1	1	0	4085
Spinaround	5	1	1	1	3904
State Of Play	2	1	0	0	3751
Decisive	1	1	0	0	3444
Don Castille	3	1	0	0	3253
Kate's Gift	1	1	0	0	2702
Star Shot	4	2	0	0	4576
Pressgang	2	1	1	0	2398
Granny Shona	5	1	0	0	2303
Off Spin	2	1	0	0	2058
Total winning prize-money					**£107493**
Favourites	71-84		**84.5%**		183.82

L WELLS

BURDOCKS, W SUSSEX

	No. of Hrs	Races Run	1st	2nd	3rd	Unpl	Per cent	£1 Level Stake
NH Flat	6	8	0	0	0	8	0.0	-8.00
Hurdles	15	40	2	3	3	32	5.0	-9.00
Chases	11	36	1	3	4	28	2.8	-24.00
Totals	23	84	3	6	7	68	3.6	-41.00
04-05	22	71	8	5	8	50	11.3	+35.68
03-04	24	92	5	9	10	68	5.4	-33.00

JOCKEYS

	W-R	Per cent	£1 Level Stake
Jamie Moore	1-6	16.7	-4.00
Leighton Aspell	1-20	5.0	-8.00
Justin Morgan	1-46	2.2	-17.00

COURSE RECORD

	Total W-R	Non-Hndcps Hurdles	Chases	Hndcps Hurdles	Chases	NH Flat	Per cent	£1 Level Stake
Nton Abbot	3-4	1-1	1-1	1-2	0-0	0-0	75.0	+39.00

WINNING HORSES

Horse	Races Run	1st	2nd	3rd	£
One Cornetto	8	1	1	1	6119
Lease Back	3	1	0	0	3444
Big Quick	6	1	0	0	2782
Total winning prize-money					**£12345**
Favourites	0-1		0.0%		-1.00

MISS SHEENA WEST

FALMER, E SUSSEX

	No. of Hrs	Races Run	1st	2nd	3rd	Unpl	Per cent	£1 Level Stake
NH Flat	1	2	1	1	0	0	50.0	+24.00
Hurdles	16	53	8	6	4	35	15.1	+31.00
Chases	1	3	1	0	1	1	33.3	-1.27
Totals	17	58	10	7	5	36	17.2	+53.73

04-05	8	35	6	5	0	24	17.1	+73.38
03-04	9	30	2	2	1	25	6.7	-18.50

BY MONTH

NH Flat	W-R	Per cent	£1 Level Stake	Hurdles	W-R	Per cent	£1 Level Stake
May	0-0	0.0	0.00	May	0-4	0.0	-4.00
June	0-0	0.0	0.00	June	1-4	25.0	-0.25
July	0-0	0.0	0.00	July	0-5	0.0	-5.00
August	0-0	0.0	0.00	August	1-3	33.3	+2.50
September	0-0	0.0	0.00	September	3-5	60.0	+9.75
October	0-0	0.0	0.00	October	0-2	0.0	-2.00
November	1-1	100.0	+25.00	November	2-9	22.2	+46.00
December	0-0	0.0	0.00	December	0-3	0.0	-3.00
January	0-1	0.0	-1.00	January	1-3	33.3	+2.00
February	0-0	0.0	0.00	February	0-2	0.0	-2.00
March	0-0	0.0	0.00	March	0-6	0.0	-6.00
April	0-0	0.0	0.00	April	0-7	0.0	-7.00

Chases	W-R	Per cent	£1 Level Stake	Totals	W-R	Per cent	£1 Level Stake
May	0-0	0.0	0.00	May	0-4	0.0	-4.00
June	0-0	0.0	0.00	June	1-4	25.0	-0.25
July	0-0	0.0	0.00	July	0-5	0.0	-5.00
August	0-0	0.0	0.00	August	1-3	33.3	+2.50
September	0-0	0.0	0.00	September	3-5	60.0	+9.75
October	0-0	0.0	0.00	October	0-7	0.0	-2.00
November	0-0	0.0	0.00	November	3-10	30.0	+71.00
December	0-0	0.0	0.00	December	0-3	0.0	-3.00
January	0-0	0.0	0.00	January	1-4	25.0	+1.00
February	0-1	0.0	1.00	February	0-3	0.0	-3.00
March	1-1	100.0	+0.73	March	1-7	14.3	-5.27
April	0-1	0.0	-1.00	April	0-8	0.0	-8.00

DISTANCE

Hurdles	W-R	Per cent	£1 Level Stake	Chases	W-R	Per cent	£1 Level Stake
2m-2m3f	4-28	14.3	+16.75	2m-2m3f	0-0	0.0	0.00
2m4f-2m7f	4-23	17.4	+16.25	2m4f-2m7f	0-1	0.0	-1.00
3m+	0-2	0.0	-2.00	3m+	1-2	50.0	-0.27

TYPE OF RACE

Non-Handicaps	W-R	Per cent	£1 Level Stake	Handicaps	W-R	Per cent	£1 Level Stake
Nov Hrdls	3-23	13.0	+13.75	Nov Hrdls	1-4	25.0	+22.00
Hrdls	2-9	22.2	+0.25	Hrdls	2-14	14.3	-2.00
Nov Chs	1-2	50.0	-0.27	Nov Chs	0-0	0.0	0.00
Chases	0-0	0.0	0.00	Chases	0-1	0.0	-1.00
Sell/Claim	0-1	0.0	-1.00	Sell/Claim	0-1	0.0	-1.00

RACE CLASS

	W-R	Per cent	£1 Level Stake
Class 1	0-3	0.0	-3.00
Class 2	2-4	50.0	+30.00
Class 3	3-17	17.6	+18.73
Class 4	4-30	13.3	-14.00

FIRST TIME OUT

	W-R	Per cent	£1 Level Stake
Bumpers	1-1	100.0	+25.00
Hurdles	1-16	6.3	+13.00
Chases	0-0	0.0	0.00

| Class 5 | 0-3 | 0.0 | -3.00 | Totals | 2-17 | 11.8 | +38.00 |
| Class 6 | 1-1 | 100.0 | +25.00 | | | | |

JOCKEYS

	W-R	Per cent	£1 Level Stake
Jamie Goldstein	9-48	18.8	+37.73
Paddy Merrigan	1-1	100.0	+25.00

COURSE RECORD

	Total W-R	Non-Hndcps Hurdles	Chases	Hndcps Hurdles	Chases	NH Flat	Per cent	£1 Level Stake
Fontwell	3-12	2-7	0-0	1-5	0-0	0-0	25.0	+0.25
Warwick	2-5	0-3	1-1	0-0	0-0	1-1	40.0	+22.73
Huntingdon	2-7	2-6	0-0	0-1	0-0	0-0	28.6	+25.75
Taunton	1-1	1-1	0-0	0-0	0-0	0-0	100.0	+4.00
Newbury	1-2	0-0	0-0	1-2	0-0	0-0	50.0	+24.00
Plumpton	1-6	0-5	0-0	1-1	0-0	0-0	16.7	+2.00

WINNING HORSES

Horse	Races Run	1st	2nd	3rd	£
*Kalmini	5	2	1	0	13480
Screenplay	12	3	3	1	21087
Its Wallace Jnr	4	1	0	1	6506
*Captain Cloudy	4	2	0	0	7278
Dubai Ace	5	1	1	0	3332
Belita	2	1	1	0	2275
Total winning prize-money					**£53958**
Favourites	**1-5**		**20.0%**		**-3.27**

M H WESTON

HINDLIP, WORCS

	No. of Hrs	Races Run	1st	2nd	3rd	Unpl	Per cent	£1 Level Stake
NH Flat	1	2	0	0	0	2	0.0	-2.00
Hurdles	0	0	0	0	0	0	0.0	0.00
Chases	1	6	1	1	0	4	16.7	-4.09
Totals	**2**	**8**	**1**	**1**	**0**	**6**	**12.5**	**-6.09**
04-05	1	4	2	2	0	0	50.0	+3.91
03-04	1	1	1	0	0	0	100.0	+5.00

JOCKEYS

	W-R	Per cent	£1 Level Stake
Mr T Weston	1-7	14.3	-5.09

COURSE RECORD

	Total W-R	Non-Hndcps Hurdles	Chases	Hndcps Hurdles	Chases	NH Flat	Per cent	£1 Level Stake
Cheltenham	1-2	0-0	1-2	0-0	0-0	0-0	50.0	-0.09

WINNING HORSES

Horse	Races Run	1st	2nd	3rd	£
Caught At Dawn	6	1	1	0	3526
Total winning prize-money					**£3526**
Favourites	**1-2**		**50.0%**		**-0.09**

A C WHILLANS

NEWMILL-ON-SLITRIG, BORDERS

	No. of Hrs	Races Run	1st	2nd	3rd	Unpl	Per cent	£1 Level Stake
NH Flat	8	13	0	2	0	11	0.0	-13.00
Hurdles	19	70	2	3	5	60	2.9	-41.00
Chases	6	10	0	0	2	8	0.0	-10.00
Totals	**26**	**93**	**2**	**5**	**7**	**79**	**2.2**	**-64.00**
04-05	25	88	9	5	6	68	10.2	+49.25
03-04	28	107	6	14	14	73	5.6	-58.25

JOCKEYS

	W-R	Per cent	£1 Level Stake
Paul O'Neill	1-1	100.0	+11.00
Ewan Whillans	1-55	1.8	-38.00

COURSE RECORD

	Total W-R	Non-Hndcps Hurdles	Chases	Hndcps Hurdles	Chases	NH Flat	Per cent	£1 Level Stake
Cartmel	1-1	0-0	0-0	1-1	0-0	0-0	100.0	+11.00
Ayr	1-20	0-5	0-0	1-9	0-2	0-4	5.0	-3.00

WINNING HORSES

Horse	Races Run	1st	2nd	3rd	£
Sotovik	8	1	1	2	6506
Crystal Gift	2	1	0	0	5753
Total winning prize-money					**£12259**
Favourites	**0-1**		**0.0%**		**-1.00**

D W WHILLANS

HAWICK, BORDERS

	No. of Hrs	Races Run	1st	2nd	3rd	Unpl	Per cent	£1 Level Stake
NH Flat	6	7	0	0	0	7	0.0	-7.00
Hurdles	9	23	1	1	1	20	4.3	-15.50
Chases	0	0	0	0	0	0	0.0	0.00
Totals	**12**	**30**	**1**	**1**	**1**	**27**	**3.3**	**-22.50**
04-05	12	44	5	3	3	33	11.4	+27.00
03-04	10	46	4	7	2	33	8.7	+45.50

JOCKEYS

	W-R	Per cent	£1 Level Stake
Peter Buchanan	1-4	25.0	+3.50

COURSE RECORD

	Total W R	Non-Hndcps Hurdles	Chases	Hndcps Hurdles	Chases	NH Flat	Per cent	£1 Level Stake
Newcastle	1-4	0-1	0-0	1-2	0-0	0-1	25.0	+3.50

WINNING HORSES

Horse	Races Run	1st	2nd	3rd	£
Mr Midaz	3	1	0	1	3253
Total winning prize-money					**£3253**
Favourites	0-0		0.0%		0.00

BEN WHITE

HARDINGTON MOOR, SOMERSET

	No. of Hrs	Races Run	1st	2nd	3rd	Unpl	Per cent	£1 Level Stake
NH Flat	0	0	0	0	0	0	0.0	0.00
Hurdles	0	0	0	0	0	0	0.0	0.00
Chases	1	2	1	0	1	0	50.0	16.00
Totals	1	2	1	0	1	0	50.0	+6.00

JOCKEYS

	W-R	Per cent	£1 Level Stake
Mr M G Miller	1-2	50.0	+6.00

COURSE RECORD

	Total W-R	Non-Hndcps Hurdles	Chases	Hndcps Hurdles	Chases	NH Flat	Per cent	£1 Level Stake
Taunton	1-1	0-0	1-1	0-0	0-0	0-0	100.0	+7.00

WINNING HORSES

Horse	Races Run	1st	2nd	3rd	£
*Highway Oak	2	1	0	1	1978
Total winning prize-money					**£1978**
Favourites	0-1		0.0%		-1.00

A J WHITING

NORTH NIBLEY, GLOUCS

	No. of Hrs	Races Run	1st	2nd	3rd	Unpl	Per cent	£1 Level Stake
NH Flat	3	4	0	0	0	4	0.0	-4.00
Hurdles	3	4	0	0	0	4	0.0	-4.00
Chases	2	12	2	1	1	8	16.7	+3.00
Totals	7	20	2	1	1	16	10.0	-5.00

04-05	7	39	3	4	6	26	7.7	-19.17
03-04	6	32	1	2	4	25	3.1	-27.00

JOCKEYS

	W-R	Per cent	£1 Level Stake
Willie McCarthy	2-5	40.0	+10.00

COURSE RECORD

	Total W-R	Non-Hndcps Hurdles	Chases	Hndcps Hurdles	Chases	NH Flat	Per cent	£1 Level Stake
Plumpton	1-3	0-0	0-0	0-0	1-2	0-1	33.3	+5.00
Fontwell	1-6	0-3	0-0	0-0	1-3	0-0	16.7	+1.00

WINNING HORSES

Horse	Races Run	1st	2nd	3rd	£
Hazeljack	7	2	1	1	19893
Total winning prize-money					**£19893**
Favourites	0-0		0.0%		0.00

MISS J WICKENS

LINGFIELD, SURREY

	No. of Hrs	Races Run	1st	2nd	3rd	Unpl	Per cent	£1 Level Stake
NH Flat	0	0	0	0	0	0	0.0	0.00
Hurdles	0	0	0	0	0	0	0.0	0.00
Chases	1	2	1	0	0	1	50.0	+3.50
Totals	1	2	1	0	0	1	50.0	+3.50
04-05	1	3	0	0	0	3	0.0	-3.00
03-04	1	1	0	0	0	1	0.0	-1.00

JOCKEYS

	W-R	Per cent	£1 Level Stake
Miss J Wickens	1-2	50.0	+3.50

COURSE RECORD

	Total W-R	Non-Hndcps Hurdles	Chases	Hndcps Hurdles	Chases	NH Flat	Per cent	£1 Level Stake
Southwell	1-1	0-0	1-1	0-0	0-0	0-0	100.0	+4.50

WINNING HORSES

Horse	Races Run	1st	2nd	3rd	£
Abalvino	2	1	0	0	1648
Total winning prize-money					**£1648**
Favourites	0-0		0.0%		0.00

M WIGHAM

NEWMARKET, SUFFOLK

	No. of Hrs	Races Run	1st	2nd	3rd	Unpl	Per cent	£1 Level Stake
NH Flat	1	2	1	0	0	1	50.0	+19.00
Hurdles	7	25	2	2	0	21	8.0	-11.50
Chases	0	0	0	0	0	0	0.0	0.00
Totals	8	27	3	2	0	22	11.1	+7.50
04-05	8	32	1	0	2	29	3.1	-15.00
03-04	4	5	0	0	0	5	0.0	-5.00

JOCKEYS

	W-R	Per cent	£1 Level Stake
Noel Fehily	1-1	100.0	+4.50
Stephen Craine	1-1	100.0	+20.00
Wayne Hutchinson	1-2	50.0	+6.00

COURSE RECORD

	Total W-R	Non-Hndcps Hurdles	Chases	Hndcps Hurdles	Chases	NH Flat	Per cent	£1 Level Stake
Ludlow	1-1	1-1	0-0	0-0	0-0	0-0	100.0	+7.00
Sedgefield	1-1	1-1	0-0	0-0	0-0	0-0	100.0	+4.50
Musselbgh	1-2	0-0	0-0	0-1	0-0	1-1	50.0	+19.00

WINNING HORSES

Horse	Races Run	1st	2nd	3rd	£
Parsley's Return	4	2	1	0	8452
Rocca's Boy	2	1	0	0	2056
Total winning prize-money					£10508
Favourites	0-0		0.0%		0.00

MRS W WILD

ROSS-ON-WYE, H'FORDS

	No. of Hrs	Races Run	1st	2nd	3rd	Unpl	Per cent	£1 Level Stake
NH Flat	0	0	0	0	0	0	0.0	0.00
Hurdles	0	0	0	0	0	0	0.0	0.00
Chases	1	2	1	0	0	1	50.0	+3.00
Totals	1	2	1	0	0	1	50.0	+3.00
04-05	1	3	0	1	1	1	0.0	-3.00
03-04	1	1	0	1	0	0	0.0	-1.00

JOCKEYS

	W-R	Per cent	£1 Level Stake
Mr G Brewer	1-1	100.0	+4.00

COURSE RECORD

	Total W-R	Non-Hndcps Hurdles	Chases	Hndcps Hurdles	Chases	NH Flat	Per cent	£1 Level Stake
Cartmel	1-1	0-0	1-1	0-0	0-0	0-0	100.0	+4.00

WINNING HORSES

Horse	Races Run	1st	2nd	3rd	£
Victoria's Boy	2	1	0	0	1568
Total winning prize-money					£1568
Favourites	0-0		0.0%		0.00

MRS C WILESMITH

UPTON-ON-SEVERN, GLOUCS

	No. of Hrs	Races Run	1st	2nd	3rd	Unpl	Per cent	£1 Level Stake
NH Flat	0	0	0	0	0	0	0.0	0.00
Hurdles	0	0	0	0	0	0	0.0	0.00
Chases	1	3	1	0	0	2	33.3	+1.00
Totals	1	3	1	0	0	2	33.3	+1.00
04-05	1	1	0	0	1	0	0.0	-1.00

JOCKEYS

	W-R	Per cent	£1 Level Stake
Mr M Wilesmith	1-3	33.3	+1.00

COURSE RECORD

	Total W-R	Non-Hndcps Hurdles	Chases	Hndcps Hurdles	Chases	NH Flat	Per cent	£1 Level Stake
Wincanton	1-1	0-0	1-1	0-0	0-0	0-0	100.0	+3.00

WINNING HORSES

Horse	Races Run	1st	2nd	3rd	£
Be My Dream	3	1	0	0	3445
Total winning prize-money					£3445
Favourites	1-1		100.0%		3.00

D L WILLIAMS

GREAT SHEFFORD, BERKS

	No. of Hrs	Races Run	1st	2nd	3rd	Unpl	Per cent	£1 Level Stake
NH Flat	0	0	0	0	0	0	0.0	0.00
Hurdles	9	22	1	0	1	20	4.5	-7.00
Chases	12	38	2	0	1	35	5.3	-24.50
Totals	14	60	3	0	2	55	5.0	-31.50
04-05	13	49	2	3	2	42	4.1	-40.38
03-04	15	57	4	5	8	40	7.0	-25.50

JOCKEYS

	W-R	Per cent	£1 Level Stake
Miss L Horner	2-30	6.7	-16.50
Charlie Studd	1-8	12.5	+7.00

COURSE RECORD

	Total W-R	Non-Hndcps Hurdles	Chases	Hndcps Hurdles	Chases	NH Flat	Per cent	£1 Level Stake
Fontwell	1-4	0-1	0-0	0-0	1-3	0-0	25.0	+4.00
Fakenham	1-5	0-1	0-2	0-0	1-2	0-0	20.0	+0.50
Mrket Rsn	1-6	0-1	0-0	1-2	0-3	0-0	16.7	+9.00

WINNING HORSES

Horse	Races Run	1st	2nd	3rd	£
Make It Easy	9	1	0	1	5213
Thornton Bridge	5	1	0	0	4875
Joint Authority	3	1	0	0	4401
Total winning prize-money					**£14489**
Favourites	**1-2**		**50.0%**		**3.50**

IAN WILLIAMS

PORTWAY, WORCS

	No. of Hrs	Races Run	1st	2nd	3rd	Unpl	Per cent	£1 Level Stake
NH Flat	12	13	0	3	3	7	0.0	-13.00
Hurdles	72	214	22	26	17	149	10.3	+25.44
Chases	41	109	6	11	16	76	5.5	-68.88
Totals	93	336	28	40	36	232	8.3	-56.44
04-05	92	360	41	45	37	237	11.4	-82.91
03-04	102	368	53	42	37	235	14.4	-44.81

BY MONTH

NH Flat	W-R	Per cent	£1 Level Stake	Hurdles	W-R	Per cent	£1 Level Stake
May	0-1	0.0	-1.00	May	3-17	17.6	+13.07
June	0-1	0.0	-1.00	June	2-14	14.3	-3.00
July	0-0	0.0	0.00	July	0-8	0.0	-8.00
August	0-0	0.0	0.00	August	0-10	0.0	-10.00
September	0-0	0.0	0.00	September	2-7	28.6	+5.00
October	0-3	0.0	-3.00	October	0-18	0.0	-18.00
November	0-1	0.0	-1.00	November	0-20	0.0	-20.00
December	0-4	0.0	-4.00	December	4-24	16.7	+3.66
January	0-0	0.0	0.00	January	2-19	10.5	+88.00
February	0-0	0.0	0.00	February	5-33	15.2	+3.88
March	0-3	0.0	-3.00	March	2-20	10.0	-16.42
April	0-0	0.0	0.00	April	2-24	8.3	-12.75

Chases	W-R	Per cent	£1 Level Stake	Totals	W-R	Per cent	£1 Level Stake
May	3-13	23.1	+8.13	May	6-31	19.4	+20.20
June	0-8	0.0	-8.00	June	2-23	8.7	-12.00
July	0-13	0.0	-13.00	July	0-21	0.0	-21.00
August	0-4	0.0	-4.00	August	0-14	0.0	-14.00
September	0-2	0.0	-2.00	September	2-9	22.2	+3.00
October	2-11	18.2	-1.50	October	2-32	6.3	-22.50
November	0-12	0.0	-12.00	November	0-33	0.0	-33.00
December	0-10	0.0	-10.00	December	4-38	10.5	-10.34
January	0-3	0.0	-3.00	January	2-22	9.1	+85.00
February	1-11	9.1	-1.50	February	6-44	13.6	+2.38
March	0-5	0.0	-5.00	March	2-28	7.1	-24.42
April	0-17	0.0	-17.00	April	2-41	4.9	-29.75

DISTANCE

Hurdles	W-R	Per cent	£1 Level Stake	Chases	W-R	Per cent	£1 Level Stake
2m-2m3f	15-130	11.5	-48.56	2m-2m3f	2-44	4.5	-37.88
2m4f-2m7f	7-60	11.7	+98.00	2m4f-2m7f	3-47	6.4	-17.00
3m+	0-24	0.0	-24.00	3m+	1-18	5.6	-14.00

TYPE OF RACE

Non-Handicaps	W-R	Per cent	£1 Level Stake	Handicaps	W-R	Per cent	£1 Level Stake
Nov Hrdls	8-76	10.5	+54.46	Nov Hrdls	1-17	5.9	-8.00
Hrdls	7-32	21.9	+14.23	Hrdls	5-73	6.8	-45.25
Nov Chs	2-14	14.3	-4.50	Nov Chs	0-20	0.0	-20.00
Chases	1-2	50.0	+1.13	Chases	3-73	4.1	-45.50
Sell/Claim	0-10	0.0	-10.00	Sell/Claim	1-6	16.7	+20.00

RACE CLASS

	W-R	Per cent	£1 Level Stake
Class 1	0-10	0.0	-10.00
Class 2	2-15	13.3	-3.88
Class 3	10-92	10.9	-27.00
Class 4	15-193	7.8	-15.56
Class 5	1-13	7.7	+13.00
Class 6	0-13	0.0	-13.00

FIRST TIME OUT

	W-R	Per cent	£1 Level Stake
Bumpers	0-12	0.0	-12.00
Hurdles	4-56	7.1	-22.18
Chases	4-25	16.0	-9.38
Totals	8-93	8.6	-43.56

JOCKEYS

	W-R	Per cent	£1 Level Stake
David Dennis	9-68	13.2	+2.25
Wayne Hutchinson	5-61	8.2	-30.25
A P McCoy	3-13	23.1	-5.30
Jim Crowley	2-9	22.2	+1.50
David Boland	2-25	8.0	-14.67
John McNamara	1-1	100.0	+8.50
Jimmy McCarthy	1-4	25.0	+97.00
Jason Maguire	1-6	16.7	+11.00
Richard Johnson	1-8	12.5	-5.50
Paul O'Neill	1-9	11.1	+8.00
G Lee	1-15	6.7	-12.13
Robert Thornton	1-17	5.9	-13.75

COURSE RECORD

	Total W-R	Non-Hndcps Hurdles	Chases	Hndcps Hurdles	Chases	NH Flat	Per cent	£1 Level Stake
Mrket Rsn	4-21	2-10	0-1	2-4	0-6	0-0	19.0	-3.26

Ludlow	3-15	3-8	0-2	0-0	0-4	0-1	20.0 +90.07
Uttoxeter	3-20	1-6	0-1	2-8	0-4	0-1	15.0	28.00
Fontwell	2-9	1-5	1-3	0-1	0-0	0-0	22.2 -0.25
Warwick	2-21	0-12	1-1	1-6	0-1	0-1	9.5 -14.63
Stratford	2-22	1-6	1-1	0-7	0-8	0-0	9.1 -15.00
Hereford	2-24	2-7	0-1	0-6	0-9	0-1	8.3 -4.75
Wincanton	1-6	0-4	0-0	0-0	1-2	0-0	16.7 +3.50
Leicester	1-7	0-0	0-1	1-1	0-5	0-0	14.3 +1.00
Wetherby	1-7	1-5	0-0	0-2	0-0	0-0	14.3 -1.00
Aintree	1-8	0-1	0-0	1-3	0-3	0-1	12.5 -2.00
Towcester	1-9	1-4	0-0	0-3	0-2	0-0	11.1 -6.50
Cheltenham	1-13	1-3	0-0	0-6	0-3	0-1	7.7 -5.00
Exeter	1-13	1-6	0-2	0-3	0-2	0-0	7.7 -6.50
Huntingdon	1-15	1-6	0-0	0-5	0-3	0-1	6.7 -12.13
Bangor	1-17	0-5	0-0	0-6	1-6	0-0	5.9 -2.00
Worcester	1-30	0-3	0-0	0-11	1-14	0-2	3.3 -27.00

WINNING HORSES

Horse	Races Run	1st	2nd	3rd	£
Kristoffersen	9	2	2	0	15886
Bambi De L'Orme	5	1	0	0	10114
Spectrometer	7	1	1	1	9759
Oscatello	7	4	3	0	17934
Kilgowan	4	1	0	1	7516
*Livingonaknifedge	7	2	2	1	6889
Idealko	3	1	0	0	6308
Keenan's Future	4	2	0	1	8783
Star Member	4	2	0	0	10613
Iceberge	1	1	0	0	5434
Detonateur	3	1	1	0	5317
Manoram	7	1	0	2	4193
At Your Request	2	2	0	0	7423
Reseda	3	1	1	0	3970
Secured	4	1	0	0	3904
Caliban	4	1	2	0	3790
Nagano	8	1	2	0	3669
*Mith Hill	4	1	0	1	3578
Uncle John	6	1	0	0	3427
*Linnet	5	1	1	1	3253
Total winning prize-money					**£141760**
Favourites	10-42		23.8%		-16.81

NICK WILLIAMS

GEORGE NYMPTON, DEVON

	No. of Hrs	Races Run	1st	2nd	3rd	Unpl	Per cent	£1 Level Stake
NH Flat	2	3	0	0	0	3	0.0	-3.00
Hurdles	10	28	6	2	3	17	21.4	+14.33
Chases	9	48	5	3	8	32	10.4	+1.75
Totals	20	79	11	5	11	52	13.9	+13.08
04-05	13	66	9	6	5	46	13.6	-2.25
03-04	9	48	11	2	9	26	22.9	+47.38

BY MONTH

NH Flat	W-R	Per cent	£1 Level Stake	Hurdles	W-R	Per cent	£1 Level Stake
May	0-0	0.0	0.00	May	0-2	0.0	-2.00
June	0-0	0.0	0.00	June	0-1	0.0	-1.00
July	0-0	0.0	0.00	July	1-2	50.0	+3.50
August	0-0	0.0	0.00	August	0-1	0.0	-1.00
September	0-0	0.0	0.00	September	0-0	0.0	0.00
October	0-0	0.0	0.00	October	0-4	0.0	-4.00
November	0-1	0.0	-1.00	November	1-4	25.0	-2.17
December	0-0	0.0	0.00	December	1-2	50.0	+3.00
January	0-0	0.0	0.00	January	1-2	50.0	+1.50
February	0-2	0.0	-2.00	February	1-2	50.0	+7.50
March	0-0	0.0	0.00	March	0-3	0.0	-3.00
April	0-0	0.0	0.00	April	1-5	20.0	+12.00

Chases	W-R	Per cent	£1 Level Stake	Totals	W-R	Per cent	£1 Level Stake
May	1-4	25.0	+6.00	May	1-6	16.7	+4.00
June	0-2	0.0	-2.00	June	0-3	0.0	-3.00
July	0-2	0.0	-2.00	July	1-4	25.0	+1.50
August	0-3	0.0	-3.00	August	0-4	0.0	-4.00
September	1-4	25.0	+4.00	September	1-4	25.0	+4.00
October	0-6	0.0	-6.00	October	0-10	0.0	-10.00
November	0-9	0.0	-9.00	November	1-14	7.1	-12.17
December	1-4	25.0	+13.00	December	2-6	33.3	+16.00
January	0-2	0.0	-2.00	January	1-4	25.0	-0.50
February	1-6	16.7	+5.00	February	2-10	20.0	+10.50
March	0-3	0.0	-3.00	March	0-6	0.0	-6.00
April	1-3	33.3	+0.75	April	2-8	25.0	+12.75

DISTANCE

Hurdles	W-R	Per cent	£1 Level Stake	Chases	W-R	Per cent	£1 Level Stake
2m-2m3f	4-20	20.0	-4.17	2m-2m3f	0-13	0.0	-13.00
2m4f-2m7f	2-5	40.0	+21.50	2m4f-2m7f	2-10	20.0	+1.75
3m+	0-3	0.0	-3.00	3m+	3-25	12.0	+13.00

TYPE OF RACE

Non-Handicaps	W-R	Per cent	£1 Level Stake	Handicaps	W-R	Per cent	£1 Level Stake
Nov Hrdls	1-7	14.3	-1.50	Nov Hrdls	1-3	33.3	+14.00
Hrdls	0-1	0.0	-1.00	Hrdls	4-17	23.5	+2.83
Nov Chs	0-14	0.0	-14.00	Nov Chs	1-5	20.0	-1.25
Chases	0-0	0.0	0.00	Chases	4-29	13.8	+17.00
Sell/Claim	0-0	0.0	0.00	Sell/Claim	0-0	0.0	0.00

RACE CLASS | FIRST TIME OUT

RACE CLASS	W-R	Per cent	£1 Level Stake	FIRST TIME OUT	W-R	Per cent	£1 Level Stake
Class 1	1-9	11.1	-5.50	Bumpers	0-2	0.0	-2.00
Class 2	3-5	60.0	+20.50	Hurdles	1-9	11.1	-3.50
Class 3	3-33	9.1	-6.17	Chases	2-9	22.2	+4.75

	W-R	Per cent	£1 Level Stake			W-R	Per cent	£1 Level Stake
Class 4	4-29	13.8	+7.25					
Class 5	0-0	0.0	0.00	Totals		3-20	15.0	-0.75
Class 6	0-3	0.0	-3.00					

JOCKEYS

	W-R	Per cent	£1 Level Stake
P J Brennan	3-13	23.1	+10.00
G Lee	2-2	100.0	+10.83
Wayne Hutchinson	2-4	50.0	+22.50
S Durack	1-1	100.0	+2.75
A P McCoy	1-1	100.0	+2.50
Andrew Thornton	1-5	20.0	+0.50
Christian Williams	1-8	12.5	+9.00

COURSE RECORD

	Total W-R	Non-Hndcps Hurdles	Chases	Hndcps Hurdles	Chases	NH Flat	Per cent	£1 Level Stake
Lingfield	2-3	0-0	0-0	2-2	0-1	0-0	66.7	+5.50
Uttoxeter	2-6	0-1	0-2	1-1	1-2	0-0	33.3	+11.50
Nton Abbot	2-12	1-3	0-1	1-2	0-6	0-0	16.7	+10.50
Haydock	1-1	0-0	0-0	1-1	0-0	0-0	100.0	+0.83
Newcastle	1-1	0-0	0-0	0-0	1-1	0-0	100.0	+10.00
Hereford	1-2	0-0	0-0	0-1	1-1	0-0	50.0	+8.00
Worcester	1-2	0-0	0-0	0-0	1-2	0-0	50.0	+1.75
Exeter	1-12	0-1	0-4	0-3	1-4	0-0	8.3	+5.00

WINNING HORSES

Horse	Races Run	1st	2nd	3rd	£
Philson Run	7	1	1	0	46478
Dom D'Orgeval	8	3	1	2	51244
Dead-Eyed Dick	6	3	0	0	23265
Theocritus	7	2	1	1	8087
Complete Outsider	4	1	0	0	4554
He's The Biz	8	1	0	3	4290
Total winning prize-money					**£137918**
Favourites	2-4	50.0%			1.33

EVAN WILLIAMS

COWBRIDGE, VALE OF GLAMORGAN

	No. of Hrs	Races Run	1st	2nd	3rd	Unpl	Per cent	£1 Level Stake
NH Flat	7	11	1	1	2	7	9.1	-8.80
Hurdles	63	161	26	18	12	105	16.1	+26.07
Chases	46	168	29	24	14	101	17.3	+80.62
Totals	93	340	56	43	28	213	16.5	+97.89
04-05	57	219	33	26	23	137	15.1	+40.23
03-04	26	92	12	9	8	63	13.0	+35.92

BY MONTH

NH Flat	W-R	Per cent	£1 Level Stake	Hurdles	W-R	Per cent	£1 Level Stake
May	0-0	0.0	0.00	May	2-12	16.7	-2.75
June	0-1	0.0	-1.00	June	1-8	12.5	-3.50
July	0-0	0.0	0.00	July	3-17	17.6	-5.50
August	0-0	0.0	0.00	August	2-19	10.5	+17.63
September	0-0	0.0	0.00	September	1-10	10.0	-3.00
October	1-1	100.0	+1.20	October	1-14	7.1	-12.39
November	0-4	0.0	-4.00	November	0-8	0.0	-8.00
December	0-0	0.0	0.00	December	3-11	27.3	+9.00
January	0-2	0.0	-2.00	January	5-17	29.4	+9.58
February	0-0	0.0	0.00	February	4-13	30.8	+28.63
March	0-3	0.0	-3.00	March	1-12	8.3	+5.00
April	0-0	0.0	0.00	April	3-20	15.0	-8.63

Chases	W-R	Per cent	£1 Level Stake	Totals	W-R	Per cent	£1 Level Stake
May	5-10	50.0	+22.33	May	7-22	31.8	+19.58
June	4-15	26.7	+3.25	June	5-24	20.8	-1.25
July	3-17	17.6	-6.04	July	6-34	17.6	-11.54
August	2-24	8.3	+3.00	August	4-43	9.3	+20.63
September	2-11	18.2	-2.17	September	3-21	14.3	-5.17
October	5-22	22.7	+46.00	October	7-37	18.9	+34.81
November	2-13	15.4	+16.25	November	2-25	8.0	+4.25
December	2-12	16.7	+2.00	December	5-23	21.7	+11.00
January	2-11	18.2	+1.00	January	7-30	23.3	+8.58
February	0-10	0.0	-10.00	February	4-23	17.4	+18.63
March	1-6	16.7	-1.00	March	2-21	9.5	+1.00
April	1-17	5.9	+6.00	April	4-37	10.8	-2.63

DISTANCE

Hurdles	W-R	Per cent	£1 Level Stake	Chases	W-R	Per cent	£1 Level Stake
2m-2m3f	8-67	11.9	-7.93	2m-2m3f	8-52	15.4	-11.67
2m4f 2m7f	8-50	16.0	3.13	2m4f 2m7f	12-54	22.2	+53.46
3m+	10-44	22.7	+37.13	3m+	9-62	14.5	+38.83

TYPE OF RACE

Non-Handicaps	W-R	Per cent	£1 Level Stake	Handicaps	W-R	Per cent	£1 Level Stake
Nov Hrdls	2-31	6.5	+5.38	Nov Hrdls	8-24	33.3	+29.00
Hrdls	1-22	4.5	-15.00	Hrdls	11-59	18.6	+17.21
Nov Chs	8-49	16.3	+9.71	Nov Chs	7-32	21.9	+35.00
Chases	1-3	33.3	+1.33	Chases	13-83	15.7	+35.58
Sell/Claim	3-8	37.5	-0.51	Sell/Claim	1-17	5.9	-10.00

RACE CLASS

	W-R	Per cent	£1 Level Stake
Class 1	0-5	0.0	-5.00
Class 2	3-15	20.0	+13.88
Class 3	14-71	19.7	+50.46
Class 4	31-195	15.9	+46.87
Class 5	7-45	15.6	-1.51
Class 6	1-9	11.1	-6.80

FIRST TIME OUT

	W-R	Per cent	£1 Level Stake
Bumpers	1-7	14.3	-4.80
Hurdles	7-49	14.3	+16.88
Chases	8-37	21.6	+37.92
Totals	16-93	17.2	+50.00

JOCKEYS

	W-R	Per cent	£1 Level Stake
Christian Williams	28-157	17.8	+11.81
Paul Moloney	13-69	18.8	+80.63

Mr N Williams	5-17	29.4	+24.13
A P McCoy	2-3	66.7	+2.50
Mr J E Tudor	2-6	33.3	+3.00
Tony Dobbin	1-3	33.3	+6.00
Lee Stephens	1-5	20.0	-0.67
T J O'Brien	1-6	16.7	-0.50
Mr Rhys Hughes	1-6	16.7	+11.00
Joseph Byrne	1-12	8.3	+9.00
Paul O'Neill	1-15	6.7	-8.00

COURSE RECORD

	Total W-R	Non-Hndcps Hurdles	Chases	Hndcps Hurdles	Chases	NH Flat	Per cent	£1 Level Stake
Ludlow	9-33	2-3	0-4	4-8	2-15	1-3	27.3	+11.81
Worcester	7-36	1-8	2-7	2-10	2-10	0-1	19.4	+28.50
Uttoxeter	6-35	0-3	0-3	1-14	5-14	0-1	17.1	+5.83
Southwell	4-12	1-1	1-2	2-4	0-5	0-0	33.3	+4.96
Exeter	4-17	0-1	1-3	3-10	0-3	0-0	23.5	+39.00
Bangor	3-11	0-1	0-2	1-3	2-5	0-0	27.3	+19.50
Chepstow	3-35	0-11	1-7	2-6	0-9	0-2	8.6	0.50
Warwick	2-3	1-2	0-0	1-1	0-0	0-0	66.7	+8.50
Sedgefield	2-11	0-2	1-2	0-4	1-3	0-0	18.2	+1.63
Towcester	2-11	0-1	0-0	1-6	1-3	0-1	18.2	+6.00
Fontwell	2-14	0-4	0-2	1-6	1-2	0-0	14.3	-3.00
Hereford	2-15	0-2	0-1	1-5	1-6	0-1	13.3	-5.67
Fakenham	1-2	0-0	1-2	0-0	0-0	0-0	50.0	+3.00
Perth	1-2	0-0	0-0	0-0	1-2	0-0	50.0	+1.25
Plumpton	1-2	0-0	1-1	0-1	0-0	0-0	50.0	+1.25
Folkestone	1-3	1-2	0-0	0-0	0-1	0-0	33.3	+0.25
Aintree	1-4	0-0	0-0	0-1	1-3	0-0	25.0	+19.00
Newbury	1-6	0-3	0-0	0-1	1-2	0-0	16.7	+20.00
Cheltenham	1-9	0-3	0-2	0-0	1-4	0-0	11.1	+2.00
Huntingdon	1-9	0-2	0-0	0-3	1-4	0-0	11.1	-2.00
Stratford	1-11	0-0	1-1	0-3	0-7	0-0	9.1	-6.67
Nton Abbot	1-16	0-2	0-4	1-5	0-5	0-0	6.3	-13.75

WINNING HORSES

Horse	Races Run	1st	2nd	3rd	£
*State Of Play	4	3	0	0	43520
Osiris	4	1	0	0	18079
She's Our Native	7	4	0	2	25469
Danish Decorum	6	2	1	0	13976
Koumba	9	2	1	1	12433
Parisian Storm	7	1	0	2	8073
Nazimabad	12	3	1	3	15965
Nayodabayo	6	1	1	0	6399
Demi Beau	5	1	1	1	6369
Boobee	4	1	1	1	6211
Sky Warrior	4	1	1	1	5922
Cherry Gold	3	1	0	0	5564
Dancer Life	5	1	1	0	5395
*Piran	5	3	1	0	12945
Cannon Fire	9	2	1	2	8239
Multeen Gunner	6	1	1	1	4755

Merry Path	3	1	0	0	4485
In The Frame	7	2	3	0	8583
Nick Junior	3	1	0	0	4440
Oh So Brave	2	1	1	0	4183
Miss Muscat	6	1	0	0	4173
Good Man Again	6	1	1	1	4134
Desert Tommy	6	2	2	1	7243
Mayoun	4	1	2	0	3904
*Dorneys Well	4	2	1	0	3904
Galtee View	4	1	2	0	3731
Rosses Point	8	2	2	0	6662
*Galteemountain Boy	1	1	0	0	3577
Mill Bank	6	1	1	1	3536
Graffiti Tongue	3	2	1	0	6127
*Moscow Blue	2	1	0	0	3374
Fu Fighter	6	2	2	0	6496
*Wages	6	1	2	0	3253
Harry Potter	6	2	2	0	5070
Tell Henry	2	1	0	0	2386
Ghabesh	9	1	0	0	2308
Sheer Guts	4	1	0	1	2254
Total winning prize-money					**£293137**
Favourites	14-46		30.4%		-1.94

MRS C WILLIAMS

LLANCARFAN

	No. of Hrs	Races Run	1st	2nd	3rd	Unpl	Per cent	£1 Level Stake
NH Flat	0	0	0	0	0	0	0.0	0.00
Hurdles	0	0	0	0	0	0	0.0	0.00
Chases	1	1	1	0	0	0	100.0	+1.75
Totals	1	1	1	0	0	0	100.0	+1.75
04-05	1	1	0	0	0	1	0.0	-1.00

JOCKEYS

	W-R	Per cent	£1 Level Stake
Mr D S Jones	1-1	100.0	+1.75

COURSE RECORD

	Total W-R	Non-Hndcps Hurdles	Chases	Hndcps Hurdles	Chases	NH Flat	Per cent	£1 Level Stake
Chepstow	1-1	0-0	1-1	0-0	0-0	0-0	100.0	+1.75

WINNING HORSES

Horse	Races Run	1st	2nd	3rd	£
*Cannon Bridge	1	1	0	0	2498
Total winning prize-money					**£2498**
Favourites	1-1		100.0%		1.75

MRS S D WILLIAMS

MARIANSLEIGH, DEVON

	No. of Hrs	Races Run	1st	2nd	3rd	Unpl	Per cent	£1 Level Stake
NH Flat	0	0	0	0	0	0	0.0	0.00
Hurdles	15	32	2	2	1	27	6.3	-21.00
Chases	4	13	0	1	0	12	0.0	-13.00
Totals	16	45	2	3	1	39	4.4	-34.00
04-05	16	61	6	1	2	52	9.8	+33.00
03-04	15	53	6	5	9	33	11.3	-16.27

JOCKEYS

	W-R	Per cent	£1 Level Stake
Richard Johnson	2-7	28.6	+4.00

COURSE RECORD

	Total W-R	Non Hndcps Hurdles	Chases	Hndcps Hurdles	Chases	NH Flat	Per cent	£1 Level Stake
Chepstow	1-3	0-1	0-0	1-1	0-1	0-0	33.3	+1.50
Exeter	1-14	0-2	0-7	1-5	0-0	0-0	7.1	-7.50

WINNING HORSES

Horse	Races Run	1st	2nd	3rd	£
Bally Bolshoi	7	2	2	0	10118
Total winning prize-money					**£10118**
Favourites	0-3		0.0%		-3.00

MISS C J WILLIAMS

BRIDGWATER, SOMERSET

	No. of Hrs	Races Run	1st	2nd	3rd	Unpl	Per cent	£1 Level Stake
NH Flat	3	7	0	0	1	6	0.0	-7.00
Hurdles	1	1	0	0	0	1	0.0	-1.00
Chases	1	3	1	0	0	2	33.3	+12.00
Totals	5	11	1	0	1	9	9.1	+4.00
04-05	1	1	0	1	0	0	0.0	-1.00

JOCKEYS

	W-R	Per cent	£1 Level Stake
Robert Stephens	1-2	50.0	+13.00

COURSE RECORD

	Total W-R	Non-Hndcps Hurdles	Chases	Hndcps Hurdles	Chases	NH Flat	Per cent	£1 Level Stake
Worcester	1-3	0-0	1-1	0-0	0-2	0-0	33.3	+12.00

WINNING HORSES

Horse	Races Run	1st	2nd	3rd	£
Hold On Harry	3	1	0	0	4183
Total winning prize-money					**£4183**
Favourites	0-0		0.0%		0.00

MISS VENETIA WILLIAMS

KINGS CAPLE, H'FORDS

	No. of Hrs	Races Run	1st	2nd	3rd	Unpl	Per cent	£1 Level Stake
NH Flat	11	17	2	5	1	9	11.8	+0.25
Hurdles	66	202	30	20	22	129	14.9	-7.76
Chases	52	256	45	41	19	151	17.6	-33.55
Totals	112	475	77	66	42	289	16.2	-41.06
04-05	123	537	82	59	80	316	15.3	-59.36
03-04	120	570	90	87	74	319	15.8	-44.62

BY MONTH

NH Flat	W-R	Per cent	£1 Level Stake	Hurdles	W-R	Per cent	£1 Level Stake
May	0-0	0.0	0.00	May	2-14	14.3	-6.00
June	0-0	0.0	0.00	June	1-4	25.0	+2.00
July	0-0	0.0	0.00	July	1-8	12.5	-3.67
August	0-0	0.0	0.00	August	1-2	50.0	+2.00
September	0-0	0.0	0.00	September	1-4	25.0	0.00
October	2-4	50.0	+13.25	October	0-9	0.0	-9.00
November	0-1	0.0	-1.00	November	2-15	13.3	+1.25
December	0-5	0.0	-5.00	December	8-34	23.5	+17.00
January	0-2	0.0	-2.00	January	3-30	10.0	-21.75
February	0-1	0.0	-1.00	February	5-27	18.5	+6.25
March	0-4	0.0	-4.00	March	2-27	7.4	+22.00
April	0-0	0.0	0.00	April	4-28	14.3	-17.84

Chases	W-R	Per cent	£1 Level Stake	Totals	W-R	Per cent	£1 Level Stake
May	3-15	20.0	-1.13	May	5-29	17.2	-7.13
June	2-7	28.6	+2.50	June	3-11	27.3	+4.50
July	1-2	50.0	+0.10	July	2-10	20.0	-3.57
August	0-1	0.0	-1.00	August	1-3	33.3	+1.00
September	0-0	0.0	0.00	September	1-4	25.0	0.00
October	1-16	6.3	-10.50	October	3-29	10.3	-6.25
November	6-37	16.2	-3.79	November	8-53	15.1	-3.54
December	10-35	28.6	+7.65	December	18-74	24.3	+19.65
January	8-39	20.5	-9.27	January	11-71	15.5	-33.02
February	7-37	18.9	-10.12	February	12-65	18.5	-4.87
March	4-34	11.8	-3.50	March	6-65	9.2	+14.50
April	3-33	9.1	-4.50	April	7-61	11.5	-22.34

DISTANCE

Hurdles	W-R	Per cent	£1 Level Stake	Chases	W-R	Per cent	£1 Level Stake
2m-2m3f	21-119	17.6	-12.51	2m-2m3f	17-75	22.7	+12.85
2m4f-2m7f	6-63	9.5	-19.25	2m4f-2m7f	13-86	15.1	-26.28
3m+	3-20	15.0	+24.00	3m+	15-95	15.8	-20.13

TYPE OF RACE

Non-Handicaps	W-R	Per cent	£1 Level Stake	Handicaps	W-R	Per cent	£1 Level Stake
Nov Hrdls	7-56	12.5	-13.50	Nov Hrdls	2-20	10.0	-16.59
Hrdls	4-22	18.2	-4.25	Hrdls	17-104	16.3	+26.58
Nov Chs	11-40	27.5	-2.31	Nov Chs	7-26	26.9	+16.26
Chases	1-5	20.0	-3.38	Chases	26-185	14.1	-44.12
Sell/Claim	0-0	0.0	0.00	Sell/Claim	0-0	0.0	0.00

RACE CLASS / FIRST TIME OUT

	W-R	Per cent	£1 Level Stake		W-R	Per cent	£1 Level Stake
Class 1	0-32	0.0	-32.00	Bumpers	2-11	18.2	+6.25
Class 2	2-42	4.8	-30.50	Hurdles	8-54	14.8	-3.00
Class 3	32-186	17.2	+35.83	Chases	7-47	14.9	-12.67
Class 4	39-191	20.4	-14.39				
Class 5	2-13	15.4	-6.25	Totals	17-112	15.2	-9.42
Class 6	2-11	18.2	+6.25				

JOCKEYS

	W-R	Per cent	£1 Level Stake
Sam Thomas	42-264	15.9	-64.18
Paul O'Neill	14-69	20.3	+2.08
Liam Treadwell	7-26	26.9	+24.66
Alan O'Keeffe	7-79	8.9	-38.00
Mr W Biddick	2-11	18.2	+2.50
Noel Fehily	1-1	100.0	+12.00
T J O'Brien	1-1	100.0	+3.00
Phil Kinsella	1-1	100.0	+3.00
A P McCoy	1-4	25.0	-1.13
Lee Stephens	1-9	11.1	+25.00

COURSE RECORD

	Total W-R	Non-Hndcps Hurdles	Chases	Hndcps Hurdles	Chases	NH Flat	Per cent	£1 Level Stake
Towcester	8-27	0-5	2-4	2-3	4-13	0-2	29.6	+34.38
Huntingdon	5-14	0-3	0-3	1-2	4-6	0-0	35.7	+22.50
Plumpton	5-15	0-3	2-3	0-2	2-4	1-3	33.3	+3.15
Aintree	4-11	0-0	0-1	2-4	1-5	1-1	36.4	+24.50
Haydock	4-21	1-2	1-2	1-7	1-10	0-0	19.0	+12.38
Exeter	4-22	1-3	0-3	3-11	0-5	0-0	18.2	-1.25
Ludlow	4-22	2-3	0-0	2-4	0-14	0-1	18.2	+2.50
Fontwell	4-26	0-7	2-4	0-7	2-8	0-0	15.4	-15.10
Doncaster	3-6	1-1	0-0	0-1	2-4	0-0	50.0	+18.00
Warwick	3-11	0-1	0-1	2-3	1-4	0-2	27.3	+0.50
Folkestone	3-12	0-4	2-3	0-0	1-4	0-1	25.0	-2.63
Chepstow	3-19	2-5	0-0	0-6	1-8	0-0	15.8	-1.50
Uttoxeter	3-22	1-2	2-3	0-6	0-11	0-0	13.6	-10.15
Sandown	3-23	0-1	0-1	0-7	3-13	0-1	13.0	-1.67
Taunton	2-13	0-3	0-0	0-4	2-6	0-0	15.4	-4.00
Hereford	2-16	0-3	0-3	0-3	2-7	0-0	12.5	-1.00
Leicester	2-16	1-4	0-2	0-5	1-5	0-0	12.5	-10.00
Bangor	2-18	1-5	0-0	1-6	0-6	0-1	11.1	-8.00
Wincanton	2-22	0-2	0-1	1-8	1-10	0-0	9.1	-17.72
Musselbgh	1-1	0-0	0-0	1-1	0-0	0-0	100.0	+0.50
Worcester	1-2	0-0	0-0	1-1	0-1	0-0	50.0	+2.00
Perth	1-4	0-1	0-0	0-1	1-2	0-0	25.0	+1.00
Ayr	1-5	0-0	0-0	1-1	0-4	0-0	20.0	+8.00
Windsor	1-5	0-0	0-0	0-2	1-3	0-0	20.0	-3.27
Nton Abbot	1-6	0-2	0-0	1-3	0-1	0-0	16.7	-1.67
Southwell	1-7	1-1	0-0	0-2	0-4	0-0	14.3	-5.00
Stratford	1-9	0-3	0-0	0-2	1-3	0-1	11.1	-4.50
Fakenham	1-13	0-1	1-3	0-2	0-7	0-0	7.7	-8.50
Newbury	1-20	0-4	0-0	0-4	1-11	0-1	5.0	-14.50
Cheltenham	1-28	0-1	0-2	0-8	1-15	0-2	3.6	-21.00

WINNING HORSES

Horse	Races Run	1st	2nd	3rd	£
Mon Mome	9	4	3	0	38556
Flying Enterprise	8	1	0	0	12921
Misty Dancer	5	1	1	0	12676
Gods Token	5	3	0	0	22039
Kelrev	6	1	1	0	10608
Lorient Express	9	5	1	1	30344
Bleu Superbe	10	1	4	2	10058
Lord Olympia	9	2	2	1	13959
Schuh Shine	5	2	0	0	16864
Kelly	2	2	0	0	14287
Noisetine	5	1	1	0	7861
Sonevafushi	7	2	0	1	14313
Nephite	9	2	1	0	13712
Tribal Dancer	12	1	3	0	6506
*Jericho III	4	1	0	0	6506
Nice Try	7	2	0	2	10084
*Magico	5	2	1	0	12036
The Outlier	6	2	1	1	10242
Idole First	5	1	0	0	6286
De Blanc	10	3	2	2	15347
After Eight	1	1	0	0	5569
Huckster	5	1	0	0	5504
*Border Castle	5	1	1	1	5400
Avitta	8	2	3	0	10099
Gan Eagla	5	1	0	0	5205
*Gustavo	7	2	0	0	7980
Ranelagh Gray	3	1	0	0	5070
Sir Cumference	9	1	3	1	4927
Glory Be	2	1	0	0	4906
*Caribbean Cove	4	1	0	0	4554
Jolly Boy	10	5	0	1	19452
Ma Yahab	1	1	0	0	4118
Fabulous Jet	4	1	0	0	3904
My Lady Link	4	2	1	1	7654
Fair Question	4	1	0	0	3578
Meggie's Beau	7	1	1	0	3578
Spartacus Bay	3	1	1	0	3546
Ashgreen	4	2	0	0	7061
Marathea	7	2	3	1	6149
Woody Valentine	8	1	1	2	3484
*Golden Feather	5	2	0	1	5446
Coach Lane	6	1	0	2	3155

Darkshape	6	1	0	0	3111
Mars Rock	6	2	1	0	4973
*Shingle Street	9	1	2	0	3050
Sweet Oona	8	1	2	1	2928
Flying Falcon	1	1	0	0	2741
Total winning prize-money					**£432347**
Favourites	34-87		39.1%		12.11

MRS L WILLIAMSON

SAIGHTON, CHESHIRE

	No. of Hrs	Races Run	1st	2nd	3rd	Unpl	Per cent	£1 Level Stake
NH Flat	0	0	0	0	0	0	0.0	0.00
Hurdles	7	21	0	0	1	20	0.0	-21.00
Chases	10	58	4	8	7	39	6.9	-33.00
Totals	15	79	4	8	8	59	5.1	-54.00
04-05	21	113	9	13	11	80	8.0	-37.65
03-04	27	111	4	8	10	89	3.6	-67.25

JOCKEYS

	W-R	Per cent	£1 Level Stake
Tom Scudamore	3-5	60.0	+13.50
Tom Messenger	1-6	16.7	+0.50

COURSE RECORD

	Total W-R	Non-Hndcps Hurdles	Chases	Hndcps Hurdles	Chases	NH Flat	Per cent	£1 Level Stake
Sedgefield	1-1	0-0	0-0	0-0	1-1	0-0	100.0	+3.00
Southwell	1-4	0-0	0-1	0-0	1-3	0-0	25.0	+2.50
Warwick	1-4	0-0	0-1	0-0	1-3	0-0	25.0	-0.50
Bangor	1-10	0-1	0-0	0-2	1-7	0-0	10.0	+1.00

WINNING HORSES

Horse	Races Run	1st	2nd	3rd	£
Lost In Normandy	13	1	3	2	4167
Lambrini Bianco	9	3	1	2	11450
Total winning prize-money					**£15617**
Favourites	1-3		33.3%		1.00

N WILSON

UPPER HELMSLEY, N YORKS

	No. of Hrs	Races Run	1st	2nd	3rd	Unpl	Per cent	£1 Level Stake
NH Flat	1	3	0	1	1	1	0.0	-3.00
Hurdles	12	38	3	6	4	25	7.9	-15.50
Chases	7	14	0	2	0	12	0.0	-14.00
Totals	17	55	3	9	5	38	5.5	-32.50
04-05	28	80	4	6	13	57	5.0	-42.50
03-04	20	69	4	10	11	44	5.8	-39.00

JOCKEYS

	W-R	Per cent	£1 Level Stake
Wilson Renwick	2-27	7.4	-11.50
Colm Sharkey	1-10	10.0	-3.00

COURSE RECORD

	Total W-R	Non-Hndcps Hurdles	Chases	Hndcps Hurdles	Chases	NH Flat	Per cent	£1 Level Stake
Bangor	1-1	0-0	0-0	1-1	0-0	0-0	100.0	+4.50
Cartmel	1-2	0-1	0-0	1-1	0-0	0-0	50.0	+8.00
Stratford	1-2	0-1	0-0	1-1	0-0	0-0	50.0	+5.00

WINNING HORSES

Horse	Races Run	1st	2nd	3rd	£
Michaels Dream	6	2	1	1	7963
Sterling Guarantee	8	1	2	2	3582
Total winning prize-money					**£11545**
Favourites	0-3		0.0%		-3.00

A J WILSON

HAM, GLOUCS

	No. of Hrs	Races Run	1st	2nd	3rd	Unpl	Per cent	£1 Level Stake
NH Flat	3	4	0	0	0	4	0.0	-4.00
Hurdles	7	25	1	2	1	21	4.0	-10.00
Chases	2	2	0	0	0	2	0.0	-2.00
Totals	9	31	1	2	1	27	3.2	-16.00
04-05	9	19	0	0	0	19	0.0	-19.00
03-04	7	21	0	1	1	19	0.0	-21.00

JOCKEYS

	W-R	Per cent	£1 Level Stake
Mr D England	1-2	50.0	+13.00

COURSE RECORD

	Total W-R	Non-Hndcps Hurdles	Chases	Hndcps Hurdles	Chases	NH Flat	Per cent	£1 Level Stake
Huntingdon	1-4	0-2	0-0	1-2	0-0	0-0	25.0	+11.00

WINNING HORSES

Horse	Races Run	1st	2nd	3rd	£
Vivante	6	1	2	1	3426
Total winning prize-money					**£3426**
Favourites	0-0		0.0%		0.00

C R WILSON

MANFIELD, N YORKS

	No. of Hrs	Races Run	1st	2nd	3rd	Unpl	Per cent	£1 Level Stake
NH Flat	1	1	0	0	0	1	0.0	-1.00
Hurdles	6	13	0	0	0	13	0.0	-13.00
Chases	3	11	1	1	1	8	9.1	-3.50
Totals	7	25	1	1	1	22	4.0	-17.50
04-05	8	25	0	1	1	23	0.0	-25.00
03-04	7	33	1	2	0	30	3.0	-29.25

JOCKEYS

	W-R	Per cent	£1 Level Stake
Paddy Aspell	1-16	6.3	-8.50

COURSE RECORD

	Total W-R	Non-Hndcps Hurdles	Chases	Hndcps Hurdles	Chases	NH Flat	Per cent	£1 Level Stake
Sedgefield	1-8	0-1	0-1	0-1	1-5	0-0	12.5	-0.50

WINNING HORSES

Horse	Races Run	1st	2nd	3rd	£
Celtic Flow	7	1	1	1	3255
Total winning prize-money					£3255
Favourites	0-0		0.0%		0.00

MISS S J WILTON

WETLEY ROCKS, STAFFS

	No. of Hrs	Races Run	1st	2nd	3rd	Unpl	Per cent	£1 Level Stake
NH Flat	0	0	0	0	0	0	0.0	0.00
Hurdles	11	39	2	3	2	32	5.1	-20.50
Chases	1	2	0	0	0	2	0.0	-2.00
Totals	11	41	2	3	2	34	4.9	-22.50
04-05	13	74	1	8	12	53	1.4	-70.00
03-04	15	76	6	6	11	53	7.9	+11.33

JOCKEYS

	W-R	Per cent	£1 Level Stake
Henry Oliver	1-6	16.7	+4.00
Noel Fehily	1-11	9.1	-2.50

COURSE RECORD

	Total W-R	Non-Hndcps Hurdles	Chases	Hndcps Hurdles	Chases	NH Flat	Per cent	£1 Level Stake
Mrket Rsn	1-1	1-1	0-0	0-0	0-0	0-0	100.0	+7.50
Hereford	1-7	1-3	0-0	0-4	0-0	0-0	14.3	+3.00

WINNING HORSES

Horse	Races Run	1st	2nd	3rd	£
*Baie Des Flamands	5	1	0	0	3832
*Astronomical	3	1	0	0	3337
Total winning prize-money					£7169
Favourites	0-0		0.0%		0.00

P WINKWORTH

RAMSNEST COMMON, SURREY

	No. of Hrs	Races Run	1st	2nd	3rd	Unpl	Per cent	£1 Level Stake
NH Flat	3	4	1	0	0	3	25.0	+7.00
Hurdles	15	49	3	0	9	37	6.1	-20.50
Chases	10	41	6	1	7	27	14.6	-1.25
Totals	24	94	10	1	16	67	10.6	-14.75
04-05	23	99	8	10	12	69	8.1	-49.50
03-04	23	75	3	5	8	59	4.0	-59.50

BY MONTH

NH Flat	W-R	Per cent	£1 Level Stake	Hurdles	W-R	Per cent	£1 Level Stake
May	0-0	0.0	0.00	May	0-6	0.0	-6.00
June	0-0	0.0	0.00	June	0-0	0.0	0.00
July	0-0	0.0	0.00	July	0-0	0.0	0.00
August	0-0	0.0	0.00	August	0-0	0.0	0.00
September	0-0	0.0	0.00	September	0-0	0.0	0.00
October	0-0	0.0	0.00	October	0-3	0.0	-3.00
November	0-1	0.0	-1.00	November	0-4	0.0	-4.00
December	0-0	0.0	0.00	December	1-10	10.0	+5.00
January	1-1	100.0	+10.00	January	2-10	20.0	+3.50
February	0-2	0.0	-2.00	February	0-7	0.0	-7.00
March	0-0	0.0	0.00	March	0-5	0.0	-5.00
April	0-0	0.0	0.00	April	0-4	0.0	-4.00

Chases	W-R	Per cent	£1 Level Stake	Totals	W-R	Per cent	£1 Level Stake
May	0-1	0.0	-1.00	May	0-7	0.0	-7.00
June	0-1	0.0	-1.00	June	0-1	0.0	-1.00
July	0-0	0.0	0.00	July	0-0	0.0	0.00
August	0-0	0.0	0.00	August	0-0	0.0	0.00
September	0-0	0.0	0.00	September	0-0	0.0	0.00
October	0-0	0.0	0.00	October	0-3	0.0	-3.00
November	0-0	0.0	0.00	November	0-5	0.0	-5.00
December	0-4	0.0	-4.00	December	1-14	7.1	+1.00
January	4-11	36.4	+20.75	January	7-22	31.8	+34.25
February	2-10	20.0	-2.00	February	2-19	10.5	-11.00
March	0-8	0.0	-8.00	March	0-13	0.0	-13.00
April	0-6	0.0	-6.00	April	0-10	0.0	-10.00

DISTANCE

Hurdles	W-R	Per cent	£1 Level Stake	Chases	W-R	Per cent	£1 Level Stake
2m-2m3f	2-29	6.9	-9.50	2m-2m3f	3-16	18.8	+4.75

2m4f-2m7f	1-19	5.3	-10.00	2m4f-2m7f	2-14	14.3	-6.00
3m+	0-1	0.0	-1.00	3m+	1-11	9.1	0.00

TYPE OF RACE

Non-Handicaps	W-R	Per cent	£1 Level Stake	Handicaps	W-R	Per cent	£1 Level Stake
Nov Hrdls	1-17	5.9	-8.00	Nov Hrdls	1-6	16.7	-1.50
Hrdls	0-1	0.0	-1.00	Hrdls	1-22	4.5	-7.00
Nov Chs	1-8	12.5	+3.00	Nov Chs	2-6	33.3	+1.75
Chases	0-0	0.0	0.00	Chases	3-27	11.1	-6.00
Sell/Claim	0-3	0.0	-3.00	Sell/Claim	0-0	0.0	0.00

RACE CLASS / FIRST TIME OUT

RACE CLASS	W-R	Per cent	£1 Level Stake	FIRST TIME OUT	W-R	Per cent	£1 Level Stake
Class 1	0-1	0.0	-1.00	Bumpers	1-3	33.3	+8.00
Class 2	0-1	0.0	-1.00	Hurdles	1-13	7.7	-4.00
Class 3	3-20	15.0	-3.00	Chases	2-8	25.0	+9.50
Class 4	6-58	10.3	-6.75				
Class 5	0-10	0.0	-10.00	Totals	4-24	16.7	+13.50
Class 6	1-4	25.0	+7.00				

JOCKEYS

	W-R	Per cent	£1 Level Stake
Philip Hide	7-60	11.7	-2.75
Leighton Aspell	3-17	17.6	+5.00

COURSE RECORD

	Total W-R	Non-Hndcps Hurdles	Chases	Hndcps Hurdles	Chases	NH Flat	Per cent	£1 Level Stake
Folkestone	2-13	0-3	1-2	0-2	1-5	0-1	15.4	+1.25
Plumpton	2-16	1-6	0-2	0-3	0-3	1-2	12.5	+4.00
Fontwell	2-21	0-4	0-2	2-8	0-7	0-0	9.5	-1.50
Huntingdon	1-1	0-0	0-0	0-0	1-1	0-0	100.0	+12.00
Leicester	1-3	0-0	0-0	0-1	1-2	0-0	33.3	+1.50
Sandown	1-3	0-0	0-0	0-2	1-1	0-0	33.3	+0.50
Warwick	1-6	0-0	0-0	0-4	1-2	0-0	16.7	-1.50

WINNING HORSES

Horse	Races Run	1st	2nd	3rd	£
Roznic	6	3	0	1	17241
Dunsfold Duke	5	1	0	1	5205
Nobel Bleu De Kerpaul	6	1	0	1	4880
*Jack Fuller	4	1	0	1	4554
Concert Pianist	6	1	0	1	3904
Just A Touch	4	1	0	0	3904
Wenger	8	1	0	2	3417
Safari Adventures	2	1	0	0	1713
Total winning prize-money					**£44818**
Favourites	2-4		50.0%		2.75

D J WINTLE

NAUNTON, GLOUCS

	No. of Hrs	Races Run	1st	2nd	3rd	Unpl	Per cent	£1 Level Stake
NH Flat	7	8	0	1	0	7	0.0	-8.00
Hurdles	31	111	7	6	21	77	6.3	-36.00
Chases	10	29	6	1	5	17	20.7	+80.50
Totals	38	148	13	8	26	101	8.8	+36.50
04-05	33	91	6	4	10	71	6.6	-31.88
03-04	33	124	8	9	14	93	6.5	-64.92

BY MONTH

NH Flat	W-R	Per cent	£1 Level Stake	Hurdles	W-R	Per cent	£1 Level Stake
May	0-0	0.0	0.00	May	0-7	0.0	-7.00
June	0-1	0.0	-1.00	June	0-9	0.0	-9.00
July	0-0	0.0	0.00	July	0-4	0.0	-4.00
August	0-0	0.0	0.00	August	2-3	66.7	+27.00
September	0-0	0.0	0.00	September	0-2	0.0	-2.00
October	0-1	0.0	-1.00	October	1-9	11.1	+12.00
November	0-1	0.0	-1.00	November	1-14	7.1	-7.50
December	0-1	0.0	-1.00	December	0-9	0.0	-9.00
January	0-0	0.0	0.00	January	0-10	0.0	-10.00
February	0-1	0.0	-1.00	February	1-10	10.0	-1.50
March	0-2	0.0	-2.00	March	0-18	0.0	18.00
April	0-1	0.0	-1.00	April	2-16	12.5	-7.00

Chases	W-R	Per cent	£1 Level Stake	Totals	W-R	Per cent	£1 Level Stake
May	0-0	0.0	0.00	May	0-7	0.0	-7.00
June	0-0	0.0	0.00	June	0-10	0.0	-10.00
July	0-1	0.0	-1.00	July	0-5	0.0	-5.00
August	1-4	25.0	+4.00	August	3-7	42.9	+31.00
September	0-0	0.0	0.00	September	0-2	0.0	-2.00
October	1-1	100.0	+66.00	October	2-11	18.2	+77.00
November	1-4	25.0	+4.00	November	2-19	10.5	-4.50
December	1-5	20.0	+8.00	December	1-15	6.7	-2.00
January	0-2	0.0	-2.00	January	0-12	0.0	-12.00
February	1-6	16.7	+0.50	February	2-17	11.8	-2.00
March	0-4	0.0	-4.00	March	0-24	0.0	-24.00
April	1-2	50.0	+5.00	April	3-19	15.8	-3.00

DISTANCE

Hurdles	W-R	Per cent	£1 Level Stake	Chases	W-R	Per cent	£1 Level Stake
2m-2m3f	4-63	6.3	-14.00	2m-2m3f	4-13	30.8	+22.50
2m4f-2m7f	2-33	6.1	-24.00	2m4f-2m7f	2-11	18.2	+63.00
3m+	1-15	6.7	+2.00	3m+	0-5	0.0	-5.00

TYPE OF RACE

Non-Handicaps	W-R	Per cent	£1 Level Stake	Handicaps	W-R	Per cent	£1 Level Stake
Nov Hrdls	0-30	0.0	-30.00	Nov Hrdls	1-14	7.1	-7.50
Hrdls	2-9	22.2	+6.50	Hrdls	2-34	5.9	+4.00
Nov Chs	2-7	28.6	+9.00	Nov Chs	1-8	12.5	-1.50

| Chases | 0-0 | 0.0 | 0.00 | Chases | 3-14 | 21.4 | +73.00 |
| Sell/Claim | 1-14 | 7.1 | -5.50 | Sell/Claim | 1-12 | 8.3 | -5.50 |

RACE CLASS

	W-R	Per cent	£1 Level Stake
Class 1	0-1	0.0	-1.00
Class 2	0-1	0.0	-1.00
Class 3	3-39	7.7	-16.00
Class 4	7-67	10.4	+77.00
Class 5	3-35	8.6	-17.50
Class 6	0-5	0.0	-5.00

FIRST TIME OUT

	W-R	Per cent	£1 Level Stake
Bumpers	0-7	0.0	-7.00
Hurdles	1-28	3.6	-21.50
Chases	0-3	0.0	-3.00
Totals	1-38	2.6	-31.50

JOCKEYS

	W-R	Per cent	£1 Level Stake
Warren Marston	8-67	11.9	+72.50
Ryan Cummings	2-29	6.9	-5.50
Jason Maguire	1-1	100.0	+6.00
Carl Llewellyn	1-8	12.5	0.00
Jodie Mogford	1-12	8.3	-5.50

COURSE RECORD

	Total W-R	Non-Hndcps Hurdles	Chases	Hndcps Hurdles	Chases	NH Flat	Per cent	£1 Level Stake
Leicester	2-9	0-4	1-1	1-3	0-1	0-0	22.2	+5.50
Nton Abbot	2-9	0-2	1-3	1-3	0-1	0-0	22.2	+16.00
Worcester	2-10	2-4	0-0	0-6	0-0	0-0	20.0	+5.50
Hereford	2-15	0-8	0-0	1-5	1-1	0-1	13.3	-2.00
Perth	1-1	0-0	0-0	0-0	1-1	0-0	100.0	+6.00
Southwell	1-3	1-1	0-0	0-0	0-2	0-0	33.3	+5.50
Uttoxeter	1-11	0-2	0-1	0-5	1-3	0-0	9.1	+56.00
Warwick	1-13	0-5	0-0	1-6	0-1	0-1	7.7	+8.00
Towcester	1-15	0-4	0-0	0-7	1-2	0-2	6.7	-2.00

WINNING HORSES

Horse	Races Run	1st	2nd	3rd	£
Key Phil	7	1	1	1	13012
Scalloway	6	1	0	3	7956
Lord Lington	10	2	0	2	8873
Yassar	6	2	0	0	8733
Baron Blitzkrieg	7	1	0	2	4384
Seveneightsix	5	1	0	1	4148
*Doris Souter	5	1	0	1	3556
Bustisu	8	1	1	1	3335
Ceoperk	3	1	1	1	2741
Benefit Fund	4	1	0	0	2398
Storm Clear	5	1	0	1	2331
Total winning prize-money					**£61467**
Favourites	1-7		**14.3%**		**-4.50**

R S WOOD

NAWTON, N YORKS

	No. of Hrs	Races Run	1st	2nd	3rd	Unpl	Per cent	£1 Level Stake
NH Flat	0	0	0	0	0	0	0.0	0.00
Hurdles	1	13	1	0	0	12	7.7	-7.00
Chases	1	1	0	0	0	1	0.0	-1.00
Totals	1	14	1	0	0	13	7.1	-8.00
04-05	2	19	3	1	4	11	15.8	+5.75
03-04	2	23	2	1	3	17	8.7	+7.50

JOCKEYS

	W-R	Per cent	£1 Level Stake
Tom Messenger	1-4	25.0	+2.00

COURSE RECORD

	Total W-R	Non-Hndcps Hurdles	Chases	Hndcps Hurdles	Chases	NH Flat	Per cent	£1 Level Stake
Hexham	1-2	0-0	0-0	1-2	0-0	0-0	50.0	+4.00

WINNING HORSES

Horse	Races Run	1st	2nd	3rd	£
Ramblees Holly	14	1	0	0	3434
Total winning prize-money					**£3434**
Favourites	0-0		**0.0%**		**0.00**

R D E WOODHOUSE

WELBURN, N YORKS

	No. of Hrs	Races Run	1st	2nd	3rd	Unpl	Per cent	£1 Level Stake
NH Flat	0	0	0	0	0	0	0.0	0.00
Hurdles	1	5	2	0	0	3	40.0	+11.50
Chases	3	8	1	0	0	7	12.5	-5.50
Totals	4	13	3	0	0	10	23.1	+6.00
04-05	9	41	5	3	6	27	12.2	+13.75
03-04	14	63	1	3	3	56	1.6	-52.00

JOCKEYS

	W-R	Per cent	£1 Level Stake
G Lee	1-1	100.0	+5.50
Jim Crowley	1-3	33.3	+7.00
Mr B Woodhouse	1-6	16.7	-3.50

COURSE RECORD

	Total W-R	Non-Hndcps Hurdles	Chases	Hndcps Hurdles	Chases	NH Flat	Per cent	£1 Level Stake
Ayr	1-1	0-0	1-1	0-0	0-0	0-0	100.0	+1.50
Musselbgh	1-1	0-0	0-0	1-1	0-0	0-0	100.0	+5.50
Sedgefield	1-3	0-0	0-2	1-1	0-0	0-0	33.3	+7.00

WINNING HORSES

Horse	Races Run	1st	2nd	3rd	£
Tickateal	5	2	0	0	6221
Barryscourt Lad	4	1	0	0	1648
Total winning prize-money					**£7869**
Favourites	1-2		50.0%		0.50

R H YORK

MARTYR'S GREEN, SURREY

	No. of Hrs	Races Run	1st	2nd	3rd	Unpl	Per cent	£1 Level Stake
NH Flat	3	3	0	0	1	2	0.0	-3.00
Hurdles	2	4	0	0	1	3	0.0	-4.00
Chases	4	9	2	1	0	6	22.2	+27.75
Totals	7	16	2	1	2	11	12.5	+20.75
04-05	7	16	1	2	1	12	6.3	+1.00
03-04	9	21	2	3	2	14	9.5	-11.13

JOCKEYS

	W-R	Per cent	£1 Level Stake
Mr G Tumelty	1-1	100.0	+1.75
Mr G Gallagher	1-2	50.0	+32.00

COURSE RECORD

	Total W-R	Non-Hndcps Hurdles	Chases	Hndcps Hurdles	Chases	NH Flat	Per cent	£1 Level Stake
Mrket Rsn	1-1	0-0	0-0	0-0	1-1	0-0	100.0	+1.75
Plumpton	1-3	0-1	0-0	0-0	1-1	0-1	33.3	+31.00

WINNING HORSES

Horse	Races Run	1st	2nd	3rd	£
*Kirov King	3	2	0	0	8676
Total winning prize-money					**£8676**
Favourites	1-1		100.0%		1.75

MRS L J YOUNG

BRIDGWATER, SOMERSET

	No. of Hrs	Races Run	1st	2nd	3rd	Unpl	Per cent	£1 Level Stake
NH Flat	0	0	0	0	0	0	0.0	0.00
Hurdles	3	4	0	0	0	4	0.0	-4.00
Chases	3	6	1	1	0	4	16.7	0.00
Totals	5	10	1	1	0	8	10.0	-4.00
04-05	3	6	2	1	1	2	33.3	+49.50
03-04	4	12	0	0	1	11	0.0	-12.00

JOCKEYS

	W-R	Per cent	£1 Level Stake
Mark Bradburne	1-1	100.0	+5.00

COURSE RECORD

	Total W-R	Non-Hndcps Hurdles	Chases	Hndcps Hurdles	Chases	NH Flat	Per cent	£1 Level Stake
Perth	1-1	0-0	0-0	0-0	1-1	0-0	100.0	+5.00

WINNING HORSES

Horse	Races Run	1st	2nd	3rd	£
Noble Buck	3	1	1	0	15658
Total winning prize-money					**£15658**
Favourites	0-0		0.0%		0.00

MRS JEREMY YOUNG

CHARLTON MACKRELL, SOMERSET

	No. of Hrs	Races Run	1st	2nd	3rd	Unpl	Per cent	£1 Level Stake
NH Flat	0	0	0	0	0	0	0.0	0.00
Hurdles	7	16	3	1	3	9	18.8	-0.13
Chases	7	13	1	4	3	5	7.7	-9.75
Totals	12	29	4	5	6	14	13.8	-9.88
04-05	20	73	4	11	12	46	5.5	-54.63
03-04	13	48	2	2	5	39	4.2	-35.00

JOCKEYS

	W-R	Per cent	£1 Level Stake
Jason Maguire	2-9	22.2	-2.13
Noel Fehily	1-3	33.3	+0.25
Sam Thomas	1-6	16.7	+3.00

COURSE RECORD

	Total W-R	Non-Hndcps Hurdles	Chases	Hndcps Hurdles	Chases	NH Flat	Per cent	£1 Level Stake
Worcester	2-4	2-3	0-0	0-1	0-0	0-0	50.0	+2.88
Southwell	1-4	0-1	0-2	1-1	0-0	0-0	25.0	+5.00
Wetherby	1-4	0-1	0-0	0-1	1-2	0-0	25.0	-0.75

WINNING HORSES

Horse	Races Run	1st	2nd	3rd	£
Giorgio	2	1	1	0	7480
Walsingham	2	1	0	0	4024
Cream Cracker	6	2	0	2	6795
Total winning prize-money					**£18299**
Favourites	1-3		33.3%		-0.13

WINNING TRAINERS

BY MONTH 2001–2006

LEADING JUMPS TRAINERS IN JANUARY

	Total W-R	Nov Hdle	H'cap Hdle	Other Hdle	Nov Chase	H'cap Chase	Other Chase	Hunter Chase	N.H. Flat	Per cent	£1 Level stake
M C Pipe	99-638	22-155	19-188	18-86	23-58	13-123	4-20	0-0	2-18	15.5	- 183.95
P F Nicholls	73-354	15-70	10-49	10-45	15-58	13-91	7-26	0-0	3-17	20.6	- 26.87
Miss V Williams	66-380	19-68	8-82	5-26	10-52	19-133	5-11	0-0	0-11	17.4	+ 23.04
N J Henderson	64-292	21-82	9-59	4-27	8-35	5-46	3-15	0-0	14-30	21.9	- 12.14
P J Hobbs	43-348	15-101	5-63	3-24	7-43	10-93	3-9	0-0	0-16	12.4	- 136.35
Jonjo O'Neill	42-299	9-90	15-65	5-32	4-37	5-54	0-4	0-0	4-18	14.0	- 72.07
J H Johnson	42-194	16-82	9-35	4-18	8-14	3-30	1-7	0-0	1-10	21.6	+ 41.46
A King	39-249	20-83	4-44	2-30	7-29	3-34	1-7	0-0	2-23	15.7	+ 45.21
L Lungo	34-210	15-58	4 66	1-11	5-24	2-19	4-7	0-0	3-25	16.2	- 86.03
Ferdy Murphy	33-012	8-86	5-30	0-17	5-54	10-92	3-17	0 0	2-16	10.6	- 109.42
Mrs M Reveley	30-231	6-46	8-59	2-22	6-28	0-40	0-3	0-0	2-24	13.0	- 84.54
Miss H C Knight	29-208	8-64	1-17	3-22	5-38	8-36	2-11	0-0	2-20	13.9	- 07.10
N G Richards	27-125	11-38	3-31	3-23	4-13	3-8	1-1	0-0	2-11	21.6	- 24.61
H D Daly	25-178	5-40	1-10	2-21	5-34	6-49	3-8	0-0	3-16	14.0	+ 6.41
T R George	23-186	1-42	2-21	4 23	6-25	8-61	0-7	0-0	2-7	12.4	- 46.79
M W Easterby	20-154	5-40	1-29	3-12	2-15	3-21	2-5	0-0	4 33	13.0	- 27.72
Mrs S J Smith	20-191	3-34	4-31	1-19	3-29	7-54	1-8	0-0	1-16	10.5	- 17.54
R H Alner	20-201	3-41	1 26	3-15	8-30	4-71	1-9	0-0	0-9	10.0	- 48.72
N A T'stn-Davies	19-244	3-57	4-35	1-23	3-29	4 66	1-4	0 0	3-30	7.8	- 102.38
C J Mann	19-172	6-46	5-45	1-16	1-12	4-39	2-7	0-0	0-8	11.0	- 27.18
M Pitman	19-145	7-45	0-12	0-10	4-23	4-28	2-8	0-0	2-19	13.1	- 23.70
G L Moore	18-178	8-69	2-52	2-14	3-14	2-19	1-9	0-0	0-3	10.1	- 62.28
T D Easterby	17-122	6-30	4-21	2-12	3-13	1-30	1-5	0-0	0-11	13.9	- 49.55
Miss E C Lavelle	17-94	3-26	1-13	2-11	3-14	6-21	1-5	0-0	1-6	18.1	+ 9.75
Ian Williams	16-164	7-56	2-35	1-14	3-20	2-26	0-5	0-0	1-8	9.8	+ 83.00
B G Powell	16-137	5-36	3-19	2-18	2-14	1-25	2-9	0-0	1-16	11.7	+147.88
C R Egerton	15-65	3-18	3-9	1-15	2-6	2-7	1-2	0-0	3-8	23.1	+ 1.91
P R Webber	15-141	3-37	1-10	0-13	4-25	3-27	1-6	0-0	3-23	10.6	- 28.87
K C Bailey	14-156	1-31	2-22	3-20	1-23	5-39	1-10	0-0	1-11	9.0	- 36.25
R Rowe	14-110	1-26	5-21	0-9	5-13	3-35	0-1	0-0	0-5	12.7	+ 9.38
R C Guest	13-148	0-31	3-46	0-7	2-16	7-40	0-1	0-0	1-8	8.8	- 49.75
J M Jefferson	12-135	2-32	3-29	1-10	2-20	2-16	2-7	0-0	0-21	8.9	- 71.03
J A B Old	12-111	1-29	1-20	0-13	2-5	4-29	0-2	0-0	4-13	10.8	- 36.67
P Winkworth	12-86	1-22	0-16	3-8	2-6	4-20	1-7	0-0	1-7	14.0	- 2.25
R T Phillips	12-127	4-40	1-26	1-18	2-9	2-23	0-1	0-0	2-10	9.4	- 69.02
P Bowen	11-84	1-26	0-24	1-4	2-3	3-16	0-5	0-0	1-6	13.1	- 2.75
N B Mason	11-61	1-13	2-14	0-3	3-5	5-25	0-0	0-0	0 1	18.0	+ 8.50
K G Reveley	11-68	1-17	3-23	2-5	0-3	1-9	2-3	0-0	2-8	16.2	- 15.40
R Johnson	10-87	0-20	3-17	0-6	1-16	6-20	0-4	0-0	0-4	11.5	+ 12.38
R J Hodges	10-122	0-23	5-39	3-13	2-15	0-19	0-2	0-0	0-11	8.2	- 69.32
D McCain	10-89	4-27	1-14	2-5	1-13	2-16	0-5	0-0	0-9	11.2	+ 51.50
V R A Dartnall	10-48	3-14	1-14	3-5	1-6	0-2	0-0	0-0	2-7	20.8	- 5.54
C L Tizzard	10-113	2-28	1-12	0-8	1-15	3-32	1-6	0-0	2-12	8.8	- 54.38
O Sherwood	9-105	2-31	2-18	1-15	1-19	2-17	0-3	0-0	1-4	8.6	- 52.92
Noel T Chance	9-84	2-37	2-14	3-9	0-7	0-6	1-1	0-0	1-10	10.7	- 50.92
Miss L V Russell	9-102	1-19	3-21	0-4	2-19	3-28	0-4	0-0	0-7	8.8	- 36.50
Miss A M N-Smith	9-58	0-9	3-12	2-8	0-3	4-25	0-1	0-0	0-0	15.5	+ 31.00
D P Keane	9-57	1-15	0-13	0-7	0-2	7-16	1-1	0-0	0-3	15.8	+ 6.30
G M Moore	8-114	3-45	0-16	0-4	1-15	4-22	0-2	0-0	0-10	7.0	- 39.00
R H Buckler	8-104	0-27	2-8	1-7	1-15	4-30	0-7	0-0	0-10	7.7	- 24.63
Mrs L C Taylor	8-49	0-4	2-6	0-2	3-17	2-12	1-5	0-0	0-3	16.3	+ 37.75

LEADING JUMPS TRAINERS IN FEBRUARY

	Total W-R	Nov Hdle	H'cap Hdle	Other Hdle	Nov Chase	H'cap Chase	Other Chase	Hunter Chase	N.H. Flat	Per cent	£1 Level stake
M C Pipe	107-600	25-102	22-197	21-99	11-46	13-96	10-39	0-0	5-21	17.8	- 12.42
P F Nicholls	98-422	17-72	4-53	8-39	21-71	10-84	22-57	10-23	6-23	23.2	- 66.91
N J Henderson	65-303	19-87	8-53	4-36	11-34	4-37	6-21	1-2	12-33	21.5	+ 20.47
Miss V Williams	57-343	10-56	11-72	2-33	16-44	13-104	3-25	0-0	2-9	16.6	- 21.99
Jonjo O'Neill	56-354	14-113	16-93	6-24	8-34	5-55	1-5	2-3	4-27	15.8	- 54.58
P J Hobbs	38-310	14-71	4-69	2-42	5-22	10-73	1-10	0-2	2-21	12.3	- 118.03
N A T'stn-Davies	33-269	8-64	4-48	2-27	4-28	11-62	2-14	0-0	2-26	12.3	- 51.47
A King	31-204	7-72	1-32	10-31	6-15	1-19	1-8	0-1	5-26	15.2	- 52.60
J H Johnson	27-177	12-56	5-42	3-19	4-16	1-26	1-4	0-1	1-13	15.3	- 45.19
L Lungo	27-149	8-42	7-46	1-6	6-14	2-20	0-3	0-0	3-18	18.1	- 53.56
H D Daly	26-174	5-51	1-14	1-11	6-24	6-39	5-10	1-3	1-22	14.9	- 48.43
Mrs M Reveley	24-205	3-38	9-65	2-15	3-16	4-43	1-7	0 0	2-21	11.7	- 58.97
Miss H C Knight	23-171	5-58	3 10	1-10	8-35	2-24	1-10	1-3	2-21	13.5	- 56.05
R C Guest	23-132	1-22	3-35	1-7	6-18	12-41	0-0	0-0	0-9	17.4	+ 59.75
T R George	22-160	8-44	2-26	0-15	5-24	5-42	1-4	1-1	0-4	13.8	+ 33.52
Ferdy Murphy	21-212	5-47	1-32	2-15	4-31	6-62	2-17	0-0	1-8	9.9	- 20.00
N G Richards	21-96	6-26	4-26	2-9	2-6	1-12	0-2	3-5	3-10	21.9	- 25.67
Mrs S J Smith	20-171	6-33	5-35	1-10	5-26	1-45	0-7	0-0	2-15	11.7	- 12.05
G L Moore	20-151	7-47	6-52	4-22	2-13	1-12	0-2	0-0	0-3	13.2	- 22.00
Ian Williams	19-185	6-46	5-50	2-22	0-16	3-34	2-7	0-0	1-10	10.3	- 29.38
P R Webber	16-122	1-27	2-8	0-8	6-22	5-23	0-10	0-1	2-23	13.1	+ 5.50
C L Tizzard	16-116	2-15	0-13	1-7	3-25	6-27	1-7	0-0	3-22	13.8	+ 22.90
T D Easterby	15-89	5-28	2-14	2-2	1-13	5-24	0-1	0-1	0-6	16.9	+ 12.70
R H Alner	14-184	4-39	0-29	0-17	4-19	6-57	0-10	0-0	0-13	7.6	- 90.15
R T Phillips	14-111	3-27	3-29	1-19	1-5	4-17	0-6	0-1	2-7	12.6	- 47.27
R Lee	13-84	0-8	4-21	1-8	1-6	6-27	0-7	1-5	0-2	15.5	+ 67.75
M W Easterby	13-124	4-36	2-22	1-7	2-10	3-18	0-5	0-2	1-24	10.5	- 63.13
K C Bailey	12-122	0-24	0-14	2-14	3-14	3-34	2-10	0-0	2-12	9.8	- 37.50
D McCain	11-122	4-35	0-13	1-15	4-19	0-23	2-10	0-0	0-7	9.0	- 22.42
J M Jefferson	11-108	4-31	2-29	0-8	2-7	1-18	0-3	0-0	2-12	10.2	- 33.25
Noel T Chance	11-58	6-24	0-4	1-4	0-0	0-2	0-6	0-0	4-18	19.0	- 5.03
O Sherwood	10-96	4-27	0-14	1-10	1-9	3-22	0-4	0-2	1-8	10.4	- 53.63
R Dickin	10-107	1-25	1-8	0-12	3-10	5-34	0-12	0-0	0-6	9.3	- 29.25
P Bowen	9-62	4-15	2-22	0-5	0-2	3-12	0-3	0-0	0-3	14.5	- 6.44
J W Mullins	9-130	1-25	2-19	0-9	0-19	1-17	3-8	1-8	1-25	6.9	- 46.00
C J Mann	9-138	1-36	5-41	1-14	1-9	1-27	0-7	0-0	0-4	6.5	- 0.50
M Todhunter	9-60	1-15	2-11	0-4	2-6	2-14	2-4	0-0	0-6	15.0	- 8.38
M Pitman	9-108	2-29	0-11	1-9	2-15	1-17	1-2	0-1	2-24	8.3	- 43.09
P Beaumont	8-95	2-24	1-11	0-5	1-14	2-18	0-1	1-4	1-18	8.4	+ 4.91
J A B Old	8-92	1-20	4-21	1-7	0-5	1-18	0-3	0-0	1-18	8.7	- 2.00
M D Hammond	8-93	3-28	1-17	0-2	0-10	3-24	0-1	0-0	1-11	8.6	- 54.95
C R Egerton	8-54	3-14	0-8	2-12	1-5	0-3	1-2	0-0	1-10	14.8	- 14.38
E W Tuer	8-35	1-11	3-12	0-2	1-1	0-1	0-1	2-4	1-3	22.9	+ 35.17
R Johnson	7-61	1-14	3-16	0-3	0-7	2-12	1-7	0-1	0-1	11.5	+ 13.00
T P Tate	7-27	3-11	0-1	1-1	0-1	0-0	0-0	2-7	1-6	25.9	+ 7.58
R H Buckler	7-84	0-15	2-13	1-13	1-6	2-25	1-3	0-0	0-9	8.3	- 27.75
A Parker	7-64	0-10	2-11	0-3	1-7	3-27	1-2	0-1	0-3	10.9	- 15.85
B Ellison	7-51	2-19	1-14	1-7	2-5	1-4	0-2	0-0	0-0	13.7	+ 4.50
Mrs L Wadham	7-58	1-13	1-20	2-12	0-5	2-5	1-2	0-1	0-0	12.1	+ 17.30
Evan Williams	7-40	1-5	4-12	0-5	2-6	0-7	0-3	0-2	0-0	17.5	+ 23.12
N J Gifford	7-39	4-13	1-6	0-4	1-2	1-4	0-1	0-4	0-5	17.9	+ 18.25

LEADING JUMPS TRAINERS IN MARCH

	Total W-R	Nov Hdle	H'cap Hdle	Other Hdle	Nov Chase	H'cap Chase	Other Chase	Hunter Chase	N.H. Flat	Per cent	£1 Level stake
P F Nicholls	82-418	16-65	6-60	7-45	18-52	16-108	10-56	4-15	5-24	19.6	- 82.00
M C Pipe	72-663	10-119	19-223	15-117	10-36	10-124	7-56	0-2	2-24	10.9	- 216.97
P J Hobbs	64-400	12-79	18-93	7-40	11-38	4-88	7-28	0-1	5-38	16.0	- 65.50
N J Henderson	58-392	11-80	5-84	8-62	5-34	11-61	4-23	1-2	13-55	14.8	- 66.31
Jonjo O'Neill	54-375	13-88	12-106	6-56	7-20	6-58	3-24	1-4	9-36	14.4	- 15.06
Miss V Williams	52-379	10-60	7-84	5-42	13-42	10-114	2-22	0-0	5-22	13.7	- 58.58
Mrs S J Smith	41-206	11-43	9-41	1-17	6-22	10-48	2-14	0-0	2-22	19.9	+ 23.04
H D Daly	33-221	9-52	0-22	2-19	10-27	8-56	1-10	2-5	1-30	14.9	- 20.15
G L Moore	32-212	7-70	10-68	6-33	2-8	5-23	2-6	0-0	0-7	15.1	- 49.31
A King	32-216	9-59	9-47	4-36	1-13	5-23	1-5	0-1	3-36	14.8	- 45.26
J H Johnson	31-163	12-62	6-31	3-17	0-6	5-23	2-14	0-1	3-12	19.0	+ 39.40
L Lungo	30-193	7-58	7-58	5-22	5-9	2-18	1-5	0-2	4-20	15.5	I 15.06
Ian Williams	28-233	7-54	3-59	4-19	3-19	10-54	1-5	0-2	0-23	12.0	- 89.75
Ferdy Murphy	26-234	3-35	7-35	4-25	2-26	8-76	1-22	0-0	1-21	11.1	- 33.25
R H Alner	26-225	7-44	5-42	2-25	4-29	8-56	0-13	0-0	0-18	11.6	- 32.77
N G Richards	25-115	8-29	5-22	3-19	3-10	1-7	1-4	0-3	4-22	21.7	- 36.64
Miss H C Knight	24-187	5-40	1-24	3-20	2-16	5-29	4-24	0-2	5-36	12.8	- 7.27
R T Phillips	24-161	6-42	3-40	3-26	2-6	1-16	4-11	0-0	5-23	14.9	- 63.06
T R George	21-155	3-32	3-26	1-12	4-19	5-41	2-15	0-3	3-8	13.5	- 2.54
P R Webber	20-153	5-27	3-14	2-16	3-16	2-29	1-13	0-0	4-38	13.1	+ 64.31
N A T'stn-Davies	18-271	5-74	2-51	1-19	2-18	2-65	0-12	0-0	6-35	6.6	- 146.90
R C Guest	18-154	2-21	3-35	0-9	3-14	8-54	1-7	0-1	1-13	11.7	- 56.34
R Lee	15-110	1-12	1-20	0-7	2-11	7-44	1-5	3-8	0-3	12.7	- 19.12
M W Easterby	15-161	2-36	1-22	2-16	1-16	3-25	2-11	0-2	4-34	9.3	+ 37.93
K C Bailey	14-134	1-20	1-20	5-14	5-19	1-40	1-9	0-0	0-12	10.4	- 50.40
Heather Dalton	14-95	2-17	1-12	1-18	2-9	7-20	0-4	0-2	1-14	14.7	- 21.70
B G Powell	14-136	2-33	2-32	2-20	2-11	5-25	0-3	0-3	1-10	10.3	- 50.90
Mrs M Reveley	13-186	2-25	2-53	1-23	2-14	4-44	1-5	0-1	1-24	7.0	- 89.50
J Mackie	13-66	2-11	10-39	0-4	1-1	0-3	0-3	0-0	0-5	19.7	+ 40.74
Miss E C Lavelle	13-90	6-21	2-14	0-15	1-10	4-20	0-1	0-0	0-10	14.4	+ 9.42
R J Hodges	12-108	4-19	1-30	1-13	3-14	2-16	0-5	0-0	1-11	11.1	- 29.18
N B Mason	12-55	1-7	4-15	2-8	1-5	4-19	0-0	0-2	0-0	21.8	+ 4.35
J W Mullins	12-149	2-29	2-21	4-27	1-16	0-26	1-9	2-5	0-20	8.1	+ 4.94
J M Jefferson	11-84	4-21	2-20	0-10	1-6	1-12	0-2	0-0	3-14	13.1	- 10.92
P Monteith	11-74	4-19	1-22	4-9	0-4	2-14	0-5	0-0	0-1	14.9	- 26.58
Miss L V Russell	11-114	3-26	0-23	0-9	4-13	4-31	0-11	0-0	0-1	9.6	+ 12.11
C J Mann	11-132	2-32	0-36	2-21	4-11	3-25	0-4	0-0	0-6	8.3	- 85.27
Mrs L Wadham	11-67	3-12	3-25	2-17	0-2	2-13	0-0	0-2	1-2	16.4	+ 40.13
T D Easterby	11-94	1-18	1-15	1-9	3-7	1-23	2-10	0-1	2-11	11.7	- 26.92
O Sherwood	10-119	2-23	1-25	0-13	1-10	3-27	1-5	0-2	2-16	8.4	- 68.85
R Dickin	10-120	1-20	1-20	2-10	3-18	2-40	0-3	0-1	1-8	8.3	- 54.56
C Tinkler	10-25	4-7	2-7	0-2	0-1	0-1	2-2	0-0	2-6	40.0	+ 30.50
Mrs S Bradburne	10-80	4-15	0-18	0-9	2-8	4-20	0-4	0-1	0-7	12.5	- 7.00
Noel T Chance	10-68	6-21	1-13	1-8	0-4	0-1	0-3	0-0	2-18	14.7	- 7.37
D McCain	9-112	1-27	0-16	3-17	2-17	2-20	1-7	0-0	0-8	8.0	- 8.00
G B Balding	9-60	3-15	1-16	0-6	1-7	1-9	2-2	0-0	1-5	15.0	+ 33.33
B Ellison	9-70	0-17	3-21	1-10	1-5	3-15	1-3	0-0	0-0	12.9	- 20.62
R Ford	9-78	1-14	5-16	1-10	0-8	1-23	1-2	0-0	0-5	11.5	- 14.00
M Pitman	9-106	1-24	3-21	1-12	2-13	1-12	0-5	0-1	1-19	8.5	- 6.00
J L Spearing	8-51	2-12	2-12	0-5	1-3	2-7	1-2	0-0	0-11	15.7	+ 17.50
A C Whillans	8-71	0-9	3-20	0-5	0-4	3-18	0-0	0-0	2-15	11.3	- 6.38

LEADING JUMPS TRAINERS IN APRIL

	Total W-R	Nov Hdle	H'cap Hdle	Other Hdle	Nov Chase	H'cap Chase	Other Chase	Hunter Chase	N.H. Flat	Per cent	£1 Level stake
P F Nicholls	116-585	26-97	13-79	8-51	29-103	17-153	9-42	9-33	6-37	19.8	- 75.52
M C Pipe	106-761	23-134	28-238	17-131	12-54	17-201	4-35	2-4	6-22	13.9	- 149.17
P J Hobbs	78-443	20-101	17-115	11-54	10-46	14-110	3-10	0-4	4-23	17.6	- 43.39
Jonjo O'Neill	46-266	12-51	10-71	10-56	3-17	8-47	0-8	1-3	5-26	17.3	+ 84.46
L Lungo	43-194	14-43	12-64	2-19	3-18	4-25	1-2	1-1	6-27	22.2	- 28.35
Ferdy Murphy	36-287	4-47	8-46	5-33	6-33	6-83	3-20	0-1	4-28	12.5	+ 18.08
N J Henderson	35-330	3-60	4-68	6-53	4-32	6-66	3-19	0-0	9-49	10.6	- 153.28
Miss V Williams	34-320	10-49	5-66	3-42	6-45	8-105	1-12	1-2	1-16	10.6	- 141.76
Ian Williams	28-240	5-45	5-62	2-21	2-21	13-71	1-6	0-2	0-17	11.7	- 70.46
N G Richards	27-155	10-40	5-44	5-27	4-11	0-14	1-2	0-4	2-17	17.4	- 2.05
Mrs S J Smith	25-211	8-52	7-39	0-14	6-25	3-55	0-11	0-0	1-17	11.8	- 39.23
A King	24-185	9-51	2-46	2-22	4-16	3-35	1-2	0-0	3-20	13.0	- 14.72
J H Johnson	23-195	6-51	9-46	1-26	2-19	3-34	1-4	0-0	1-21	11.8	- 52.63
J W Mullins	23-170	5-45	5-22	0-20	4-18	3-32	1-8	1-4	4-22	13.5	+ 42.30
G L Moore	23-162	5-45	7-52	2-21	3-14	3-23	1-4	0-0	2-8	14.2	- 17.28
N A T'stn-Davies	22-238	2-36	5-56	3-33	0-22	7-66	0-5	0-0	5-30	9.2	- 2.00
R H Alner	22-215	6-51	2-40	1-20	5-29	7-64	0-5	0-0	1-11	10.2	+ 3.58
H D Daly	22-169	6-41	2-13	3-22	7-26	3-36	0-4	1-5	0-25	13.0	- 71.34
R C Guest	22-161	3-14	3-45	1-8	7-21	5-62	2-4	1-2	0-6	13.7	- 37.83
T R George	19-140	2-28	2-27	2-14	3-15	7-44	2-4	0-3	1-8	13.6	+ 2.34
P R Webber	19-146	2-30	1-16	2-12	5-22	5-33	1-5	0-0	3-30	13.0	- 40.41
Mrs M Reveley	17-153	6-33	1-37	1-12	3-17	4-32	0-4	0-0	2-20	11.1	- 37.27
Miss H C Knight	16-176	6-51	0-12	1-25	5-29	2-32	2-10	0-1	0-18	9.1	- 105.83
C J Mann	14-122	5-36	2-30	2-18	3-8	1-28	0-1	0-0	1-6	11.5	- 42.93
B G Powell	14-130	5-28	1-28	3-18	0-17	4-17	0-4	0-6	1-12	10.8	- 17.79
R T Phillips	13-147	4-40	3-36	2-16	1-7	2-26	0-5	0-0	1-17	8.8	- 57.50
T D Easterby	13-85	1-14	1-13	3-8	4-13	1-26	2-3	0-0	1-10	15.3	+ 6.00
Miss E C Lavelle	12-89	2-17	3-22	0-11	3-10	4-18	0-2	0-1	0-9	13.5	- 12.25
R Lee	11-87	2-10	1-18	0-8	3-9	5-37	0-1	0-5	0-2	12.6	- 21.50
O Sherwood	11-125	3-27	2-27	1-13	1-10	0-23	1-7	0-1	3-22	8.8	- 73.69
G B Balding	11-43	1-9	5-15	0-0	3-5	1-7	0-1	0-0	1-6	25.6	+ 22.75
Evan Williams	11-68	2-11	3-14	1-9	0-8	2-14	0-3	3-8	0-1	16.2	+ 5.13
P Beaumont	10-114	1-24	1-10	1-17	1-19	2-27	3-4	0-2	1-12	8.8	+ 34.50
R J Hodges	10-94	2-20	0-18	2-11	3-8	2-24	1-4	0-0	0-9	10.6	+ 3.63
M W Easterby	10-94	3-23	4-23	0-6	1-12	1-15	0-3	1-1	0-12	10.6	- 45.65
J L Spearing	10-49	1-15	2-11	1-5	1-1	3-11	1-1	0-0	1-5	20.4	+ 47.00
P Bowen	10-75	0-11	5-25	2-12	0-1	4-23	0-2	0-0	0-5	13.3	- 4.75
Heather Dalton	10-88	1-10	2-12	1-13	2-11	2-24	2-3	0-4	0-12	11.4	+ 6.12
J D Frost	10-81	1-26	3-16	2-10	0-8	3-9	1-2	0-0	0-10	12.3	+ 1.41
D McCain	9-95	2-15	1-17	0-9	1-17	4-23	0-2	0-2	1-11	9.5	- 3.50
J M Jefferson	9-93	1-16	2-23	1-11	1-8	3-16	0-1	0-0	1-19	9.7	- 30.50
K C Bailey	9-116	2-14	2-22	0-11	2-12	2-41	0-3	0-0	1-13	7.8	- 49.13
R Dickin	8-128	2-26	1-16	0-22	2-19	3-39	0-2	0-0	0-4	6.3	- 63.13
K Bishop	8-67	1-12	5-21	1-7	1-3	1-20	0-0	0-0	0-7	11.9	- 7.00
P Monteith	8-83	2-16	3-25	0-4	1-13	1-13	0-3	0-2	1-7	9.6	- 18.75
C J Down	8-72	1-18	1-14	1-10	1-4	1-6	0-2	1-4	2-14	11.1	- 5.25
Noel T Chance	8-61	2-12	2-12	0-7	0-2	0-3	0-7	0-0	4-19	13.1	- 20.18
N B Mason	8-74	0-11	2-17	2-5	1-7	3-26	0-3	0-3	0-2	10.8	- 1.37
M Todhunter	8-68	1-14	4-14	0-4	1-6	2-22	0-0	0-0	0-8	11.8	+ 0.53
M Pitman	8-82	3-17	0-14	1-10	2-9	1-14	0-4	0-0	1-17	9.8	- 39.00
B Ellison	7-63	1-10	2-22	3-11	0-3	2-18	0-2	0-0	0-1	11.1	- 15.25

LEADING JUMPS TRAINERS IN MAY

	Total W-R	Nov Hdle	H'cap Hdle	Other Hdle	Nov Chase	H'cap Chase	Other Chase	Hunter Chase	N.H. Flat	Per cent	£1 Level stake
M C Pipe	81-365	20-76	15-120	11-49	16-34	7-49	7-19	2-7	3-11	22.2	- 34.41
P F Nicholls	60-223	14-29	4-32	4-21	6-21	11-49	8-26	7-18	6-27	26.9	+ 38.42
P J Hobbs	53-252	10-40	13-71	5-24	9-33	9-57	4-11	0-0	3-16	21.0	- 44.85
Jonjo O'Neill	37-166	7-30	10-62	3-10	9-19	6-32	2-3	0-0	0-10	22.3	- 15.12
L Lungo	31-145	6-27	7-53	11-31	0-2	4-15	1-5	0-0	2-12	21.4	- 22.39
Miss V Williams	31-187	2-36	7-40	6-22	2-11	10-61	2-9	0-0	2-8	16.6	- 18.58
G L Moore	29-109	6-18	12-42	4-17	2-8	1-12	4-6	0-1	0-5	26.6	+ 47.03
R C Guest	28-186	4-33	8-43	3-24	4-16	7-58	2-9	0-0	0-3	15.1	- 55.76
C J Mann	26-102	8-25	4-23	8-22	1-4	3-16	1-8	0-0	1-4	25.5	+ 32.08
T R George	26-120	7-18	6-24	2-12	5-16	4-34	0-9	0-1	2-6	21.7	+ 26.30
Ian Williams	26-156	5-28	7-40	3-18	3-14	6-36	2-11	0-0	0-9	16.7	- 5.06
Mrs S J Smith	25-173	2-35	5-32	2-19	3-16	11-51	2-15	0-0	0-5	14.5	- 20.80
Ferdy Murphy	24-177	3-30	6-40	3-23	2-16	6-39	3-10	0-1	1-18	13.6	- 73.38
N A T'stn-Davies	23-165	5-36	3-33	3-19	3-16	5-36	2-6	0-1	2-18	13.9	+ 6.47
Mrs M Reveley	21-125	3-22	3-42	5-16	4-13	3-17	1-5	0-0	2-10	16.8	- 8.70
N J Henderson	21-136	7-30	0-30	4-21	2-6	2-16	2-11	1-1	3-21	15.4	- 53.08
N G Richards	19-77	2-9	7-33	2-13	3-8	2-8	0-0	1-1	2-5	24.7	+ 22.52
A King	19-112	7-25	2-23	1-9	4-18	4-20	0-5	0-0	1-12	17.0	+ 3.67
P R Webber	18-84	6-23	1-8	2-8	3-10	2-14	1-2	0-0	3-19	21.4	+ 33.70
J W Mullins	15-150	4-32	2-27	0-16	3-24	4-26	0-9	0-4	2-12	10.0	- 40.25
B G Powell	15-145	2-33	1-33	1-17	2-16	3-26	3-8	0-3	3-9	10.3	- 52.38
P Monteith	13-72	1-5	2-21	3-11	1-4	5-22	1-7	0-1	0-1	18.1	+ 16.58
H D Daly	13-93	2-21	0-6	3-14	1-11	2-27	1-3	0-0	4-11	14.0	- 16.35
G M Moore	11-67	2-17	4-19	0-8	4-13	0-6	0-0	0-0	1-4	16.4	6.67
D L Williams	10-46	3-8	0-3	0-5	0-6	3-13	0-2	4-7	0-2	21.7	- 15.57
K C Bailey	10-109	4-26	2-21	0-13	1-10	2-23	0-3	0-0	1-13	9.2	- 20.25
Miss H C Knight	10-84	3-22	0-3	1-8	4-18	1-8	1-7	0-0	0-18	11.9	- 50.10
Heather Dalton	10-84	0-15	3-17	1-3	1-6	3-20	1-5	1-6	0-12	11.9	- 27.66
Evan Williams	10-39	0-10	2-8	0-1	0-1	6-12	1-2	1-4	0-1	25.6	+ 15.25
R Dickin	9-122	2-26	0-14	0-10	2-16	3-41	0-7	2-4	0-4	7.4	+ 50.93
R J Price	9-64	0-8	7-29	1-8	0-3	1-11	0-2	0-3	0-0	14.1	+ 31.00
J Mackie	9-75	1-15	6-40	2-4	0-5	0-10	0-0	0-0	0-1	12.0	- 31.26
P Bowen	9-92	0-12	1-36	4-8	2-5	2-21	0-3	0-0	0-7	9.8	- 47.75
A C Whillans	9-57	0-4	6-29	0-7	1-1	2-12	0-2	0-0	0-2	15.8	+ 15.25
B Ellison	9-54	1-9	2-18	2-9	1-3	2-12	1-2	0-0	0-1	16.7	- 10.87
A W Carroll	9-68	3-13	1-23	1-7	3-10	1-11	0-0	0-0	0-4	13.2	+ 23.58
O Brennan	8-58	3-13	4-9	0-7	0-9	1-11	0-3	0-0	0-6	13.8	- 0.02
R A Fahey	8-30	0-3	5-11	0-1	0-2	1-3	0-2	0-0	2-8	26.7	+ 2.55
Mrs L Wadham	8-33	4-8	4-16	0-2	0-1	0-3	0-1	0-0	0-2	24.2	+ 20.50
Miss E C Lavelle	8-43	3-10	1-11	1-2	0-4	2-13	0-1	0-0	1-2	18.6	+ 22.00
R Lee	7-89	0-7	2-26	0-5	0-9	3-28	1-10	1-3	0-1	7.9	- 49.75
R J Hodges	7-63	2-11	0-7	2-9	1-9	2-18	0-7	0-0	0-2	11.1	- 28.25
D McCain	7-96	2-21	1-22	3-18	0-8	0-12	0-5	0-0	1-10	7.3	- 12.22
Mrs S Bradburne	7-59	0-6	1-17	1-10	0-6	4-13	1-6	0-0	0-1	11.9	- 13.25
J G M O'Shea	7-64	0-9	2-21	5-16	0-8	0-5	0-1	0-0	0-4	10.9	- 36.00
Noel T Chance	7-49	1-9	1-8	1-5	2-4	0-5	0-1	0-2	2-15	14.3	- 29.38
R H Alner	7-97	3-20	0-10	0-4	0-10	3-38	0-3	1-5	0-7	7.2	- 64.47
Mrs K Walton	7-35	1-9	0-5	1-4	3-4	1-11	0-0	0-0	1-2	20.0	+ 11.00
R Ford	7-57	1-8	1-18	1-5	1-4	2-13	0-3	1-5	0-1	12.3	- 2.25
A Crook	7-58	2-5	0-14	0-8	1-9	3-19	0-1	0-0	1-2	12.1	- 11.67
G A Swinbank	7-34	1-6	0-8	3-8	0-0	1-3	0-0	0-0	2-9	20.6	+ 1.30

LEADING JUMPS TRAINERS IN JUNE

	Total W-R	Nov Hdle	H'cap Hdle	Other Hdle	Nov Chase	H'cap Chase	Other Chase	Hunter Chase	N.H. Flat	Per cent	£1 Level stake
M C Pipe	67-297	14-54	10-88	11-44	16-38	10-56	2-7	2-4	2-6	22.6	- 58.13
P J Hobbs	31-161	6-29	9-58	2-7	10-24	3-37	1-3	0-0	0-3	19.3	+ 18.21
Mrs S J Smith	24-112	3-25	2-19	2-10	9-18	7-32	1-2	0-0	0-6	21.4	+ 19.19
Jonjo O'Neill	22-114	2-26	9-42	2-8	3-17	3-16	0-0	0-0	3-5	19.3	- 30.58
Ian Williams	17-118	3-22	6-37	3-9	0-13	5-32	0-1	0-0	0-4	14.4	- 4.50
P Bowen	16-86	5-13	4-23	1-12	2-6	3-19	0-0	0-0	1-13	18.6	- 17.68
T R George	16-60	5-10	3-8	0-6	5-17	2-15	0-2	0-0	1-2	26.7	+ 18.40
P F Nicholls	15-80	4-11	1-12	1-3	2-9	5-36	1-3	0-1	1-5	18.8	- 20.88
Ferdy Murphy	12-62	4-15	2-11	1-4	3-10	2-18	0-1	0-0	0-3	19.4	- 8.94
P R Webber	12-51	5-12	0-4	1-9	1-8	2-14	1-1	0-0	2-3	23.5	- 10.86
N A T'stn-Davies	11-66	2-13	2-14	4-11	0-4	3-15	0-1	0-1	0-7	16.7	- 1.75
N G Richards	11-46	2-10	4-20	0-1	2-3	2-10	0-0	0-0	1-2	23.9	- 1.50
C J Mann	10-63	3-15	3-19	1-10	2-5	1-13	0-1	0-0	0-0	15.9	+ 14.48
R Ford	10-38	2-5	5-10	0-6	0-5	3-10	0-1	0-1	0-0	26.3	+ 6.33
Miss V Williams	10-63	2-13	2-9	1-7	0-2	5-25	0-3	0-0	0-4	15.9	- 22.53
N J Henderson	9-40	4-12	0-5	1-5	1-3	1-3	0-2	0-0	2-10	22.5	- 10.60
J W Mullins	9-73	2-18	1-18	0-7	2-12	2-8	0-5	0-0	2-5	12.3	+ 37.25
M Todhunter	9-41	4-10	3-17	0-3	0-4	2-7	0-0	0-0	0-0	22.0	+ 21.20
L Lungo	8-38	4-16	1-15	1-1	0-0	1-4	1-1	0-0	0-1	21.1	- 14.71
Mrs A M Thorpe	8-50	2-6	2-18	1-5	0-5	3-11	0-2	0-0	0-3	16.0	+ 72.50
B G Powell	7-88	2-19	1-19	0-11	1-13	1-17	0-1	0-0	2-8	8.0	- 14.27
Miss L V Russell	6-81	2-20	1-17	0-4	1-17	2-20	0-0	0-0	0-3	7.4	- 34.00
J S Goldie	6-16	1-2	2-6	0-1	3-3	0-4	0-0	0-0	0-0	37.5	+ 7.23
Evan Williams	6-41	1-8	1-8	0-6	2-7	2-9	0-1	0-0	0-2	14.6	- 11.75
A King	6-33	2-10	3-7	0-2	0-3	1-9	0-1	0-0	0-1	18.2	- 15.07
Mrs M Reveley	5-37	2-10	1-9	0-1	0-5	1-9	0-0	0-0	1-3	13.5	- 16.75
R J Price	5-35	1-7	2-12	0-2	0-5	2-6	0-1	0-1	0-1	14.3	+ 25.50
D Burchell	5-43	1-7	3-16	1-4	0-4	0-11	0-0	0-0	0-1	11.6	- 16.67
P Monteith	5-49	1-10	2-12	0-2	1-8	1-15	0-1	0-0	0-1	10.2	- 21.00
B J Llewellyn	5-46	2-12	1-15	0-4	0-5	2-7	0-0	0-0	0-3	10.9	- 4.00
C R Egerton	5-15	3-6	0-1	1-3	1-2	0-2	0-0	0-0	0-1	33.3	- 5.79
G L Moore	5-52	0-6	2-18	0-3	2-9	1-12	0-0	0-0	0-4	9.6	- 16.00
M J Gingell	5-49	3-16	2-15	0-8	0-2	0-4	0-1	0-0	0-3	10.2	+ 8.25
Mrs L Wadham	5-17	1-9	1-4	1-1	0-0	0-0	1-1	0-0	1-2	29.4	+ 20.87
Heather Dalton	5-51	0-10	0-5	0-2	3-13	1-15	0-0	0-0	1-6	9.8	- 24.49
C L Tizzard	5-42	1-2	0-6	0-4	0-8	4-18	0-0	0-0	0-3	11.9	+ 8.50
A E Jones	5-23	0-4	3-10	0-0	0-1	2-5	0-0	0-0	0-3	21.7	+ 42.00
J D Frost	5-40	1-7	1-20	2-4	0-3	1-4	0-0	0-0	0-2	12.5	- 18.25
B J M Ryall	4-29	0-4	0-4	0-0	1-5	3-14	0-0	0-1	0-1	13.8	+ 26.00
R Lee	4-30	0-4	0-3	1-2	0-7	3-13	0-1	0-0	0-0	13.3	- 2.25
J M Jefferson	4-29	3-8	0-5	0-0	0-6	0-5	0-0	0-0	1-5	13.8	+ 3.25
R G Frost	4-23	0-6	2-8	1-2	0-1	1-5	0-0	0-0	0-1	17.4	+ 15.00
D R Gandolfo	4-23	2-5	0-5	1-3	0-2	1-7	0-0	0-0	0-1	17.4	+ 5.50
J R Adam	4-11	0-2	0-0	0-0	1-4	3-5	0-0	0-0	0-0	36.4	+ 13.25
R T Phillips	4-22	1-4	1-9	0-1	1-1	0-3	0-1	0-0	1-3	18.2	- 9.02
Miss Kate Milligan	4-36	0-4	1-13	0-1	1-4	1-11	1-1	0-0	0-2	11.1	+ 28.50
B D Leavy	4-29	0-1	1-14	1-5	0-2	2-6	0-1	0-0	0-0	13.8	+ 26.50
Mrs L B Normile	4-31	0-11	0-4	0-5	1-4	2-6	0-0	0-0	1-1	12.9	+ 78.40
Mrs Barbara Waring	3-18	0-5	1-7	0-1	1-1	1-3	0-0	0-0	0-1	16.7	+ 18.50
O Brennan	3-14	0-4	0-0	0-1	0-2	3-5	0-0	0-0	0-2	21.4	+ 29.00
R Dickin	3-62	1-14	1-10	0-4	1-17	0-14	0-1	0-0	0-2	4.8	- 11.00

LEADING JUMPS TRAINERS IN JULY

	Total W-R	Nov Hdle	H'cap Hdle	Other Hdle	Nov Chase	H'cap Chase	Other Chase	Hunter Chase	N.H. Flat	Per cent	£1 Level stake
M C Pipe	52-237	11-51	13-72	4-25	8-23	9-51	5-11	0-0	2-4	21.9	- 39.54
P J Hobbs	36-126	12-21	5-37	3-7	5-21	8-31	2-5	0-0	1-4	28.6	+ 0.53
Jonjo O'Neill	28-127	9-34	3-39	2-7	2-9	6-28	1-4	0-0	5-6	22.0	- 2.08
Evan Williams	16-69	5-20	4-17	1-7	1-12	0-5	4-7	0-0	1-1	23.2	+ 89.33
P Bowen	14-77	1-11	3-24	0-6	1-5	4-19	4-6	0-0	1-6	18.2	- 21.03
Miss V Williams	14-59	4-16	2-15	2-8	1-1	4-16	1-3	0-0	0-0	23.7	- 1.51
R C Guest	12-103	2-22	2-26	0-4	2-12	6-38	0-1	0-0	0-0	11.7	- 7.45
Mrs S J Smith	11-103	4-25	2-21	0-4	2-6	2-36	1-8	0-0	0-3	10.7	- 20.47
Ian Williams	9-91	0-15	4-30	0-5	2-6	2-29	0-3	0-0	1-3	9.9	- 41.87
P F Nicholls	8-39	3-4	0-4	0-1	2-7	2-18	1-3	0-0	0-2	20.5	- 5.25
N G Richards	8-32	1-5	2-15	3-5	1-3	1-4	0-0	0-0	0-0	25.0	+ 18.13
N A T'sn-Davies	7-40	2-9	2-11	0-3	0-4	3-15	0-1	0-0	0-3	16.2	+ 8.67
J M Jefferson	7-36	3-7	2-10	0-1	0-6	1-6	0-0	0-0	1-6	19.4	- 1.86
P C Haslam	6-24	5-20	0-1	1-3	0-0	0-0	0-0	0-0	0-0	25.0	+ 2.58
C R Egerton	6-13	2-4	1-2	1-1	0-1	0-2	0-0	0-0	2-3	46.2	+ 7.96
C J Mann	6-49	4-19	1-13	1-6	0-6	0-3	0-1	0-0	0-1	12.2	+ 0.10
T R George	6-35	2-6	1-8	0-1	0-4	1-11	2-4	0-0	0-1	17.1	- 13.23
Heather Dalton	6-46	2-8	1-6	0-5	2-7	1-15	0-2	0-0	0-3	13.0	- 21.68
B G Powell	6-56	1-14	1-14	0-9	1-6	3-10	0-2	0-0	0-1	10.7	- 20.00
N J Henderson	5-21	0-3	0-3	0-2	3-7	0-2	0-1	0-0	2-3	23.8	- 7.10
Dr P Pritchard	5-50	0-3	3-13	0-2	0-9	1-18	1-4	0-0	0-1	10.0	+ 35.50
Karen George	5-41	0-8	4-17	0-5	0-3	0-4	1-3	0-0	0-1	12.2	+ 9.50
R Dickin	4-46	0-9	0-4	0-1	1-10	3-20	0-2	0-0	0-0	8.7	+ 2.50
D J Wintle	4-40	1-10	1-11	1-6	0-3	1-8	0-1	0-0	0-1	10.0	- 18.75
D L Williams	4-38	2-17	0-3	0-1	1-6	1-9	0-2	0-0	0-0	10.5	- 30.30
D Burchell	4-26	1-1	1-11	0-1	1-3	1-9	0-0	0-0	0-1	15.4	+ 15.33
J G M O'Shea	4-33	0-8	3-12	1-5	0-5	0-2	0-1	0-0	0-0	12.1	- 9.95
B Ellison	4-22	0-6	1-6	0-0	1-3	2-5	0-2	0-0	0-0	18.2	+ 21.75
Ferdy Murphy	4-32	1-7	1-6	1-4	1-5	0-6	0-3	0-0	0-1	12.5	- 6.22
B J Llewellyn	4-34	0-4	2-11	1-5	1-7	0-4	0-2	0-0	0-1	11.8	- 18.42
J W Mullins	4-32	1-4	0-7	1-4	1-5	0-6	1-5	0-0	0-1	12.5	- 4.75
R Ford	4-29	0-5	1-8	0-2	1-4	2-10	0-0	0-0	0-0	13.8	+ 11.50
Miss Kate Milligan	4-36	1-4	2-15	1-4	0-0	0-10	0-3	0-0	0-0	11.1	+ 0.62
P R Webber	4-32	2-4	1-5	1-6	0-4	0-12	0-1	0-0	0-0	12.5	- 0.78
M Todhunter	4-24	2-6	0-7	1-2	1-2	0-6	0-1	0-0	0-0	16.7	- 5.25
C P Morlock	4-15	1-2	2-6	0-0	0-0	1-4	0-0	0-0	0-3	26.7	+ 29.50
M Pitman	4-19	1-5	2-6	0-0	0-2	1-4	0-2	0-0	0-0	21.1	+ 6.50
Nick Williams	4-18	2-7	1-2	0-2	0-0	1-7	0-0	0-0	0-0	22.2	+ 12.00
Mrs A M Thorpe	4-45	0-5	3-23	0-4	0-3	1-9	0-0	0-0	0-1	8.9	- 12.50
J D Frost	4-35	0-6	1-8	0-6	1-1	2-8	0-2	0-0	0-4	11.4	+ 1.50
P Monteith	3-29	0-6	0-5	0-3	1-6	2-7	0-2	0-0	0-0	10.3	- 3.00
P W Hiatt	3-16	0-3	0-3	0-1	1-4	2-4	0-0	0-0	0-1	18.8	+ 1.35
C J Down	3-39	1-11	0-8	0-7	0-1	1-7	1-3	0-0	0-2	7.7	- 16.75
M F Harris	3-31	1-11	1-7	0-4	0-2	0-4	1-3	0-0	0-0	9.7	- 6.63
M D Hammond	3-12	0-3	0-0	0-2	0-2	3-4	0-0	0-0	0-1	25.0	- 2.00
R S Brookhouse	3-17	1-5	2-9	0-1	0-0	0-0	0-1	0-0	0-1	17.6	+ 10.91
W M Brisbourne	3-21	1-6	0-3	0-1	0-1	0-0	0-1	0-0	2-9	14.3	- 1.75
Mrs D A Hamer	3-32	1-6	1-11	0-7	0-1	0-1	0-2	0-0	1-4	9.4	+ 3.00
Mrs K Walton	3-12	0-1	0-3	0-0	0-0	2-7	1-1	0-0	0-0	25.0	+ 4.25
Miss L V Russell	3-39	0-9	0-10	0-1	1-2	2-10	0-7	0-0	0-0	7.7	- 22.50
R T Phillips	3-19	0-4	0-4	2-5	0-0	0-4	1-1	0-0	0-1	15.8	- 3.80

LEADING JUMPS TRAINERS IN AUGUST

	Total W-R	Nov Hdle	H'cap Hdle	Other Hdle	Nov Chase	H'cap Chase	Other Chase	Hunter Chase	N.H. Flat	Per cent	£1 Level stake
M C Pipe	51-239	17-55	9-73	13-50	5-16	3-34	3-6	0-0	1-5	21.3	- 99.50
P J Hobbs	49-157	15-29	8-47	4-16	6-20	11-35	4-8	0-0	1-2	31.2	+ 21.35
Jonjo O'Neill	32-154	8-24	6-44	4-22	3-11	8-40	1-7	0-0	2-6	20.8	- 34.53
Mrs S J Smith	23-138	1-17	5-26	1-18	7-19	9-41	0-7	0-0	0-10	16.7	- 2.37
P Bowen	21-73	3-8	6-21	0-10	4-10	6-16	2-4	0-0	0-4	28.8	+ 33.38
P F Nicholls	14-34	1-3	3-6	2-3	3-8	3-10	0-0	0-0	2-4	41.2	+ 17.59
Evan Williams	14-79	5-15	0-16	2-9	2-6	3-22	1-8	0-0	1-3	17.7	+ 39.98
Ian Williams	12-84	1-17	4-19	3-24	1-3	1-16	1-3	0-0	1-2	14.3	- 41.65
Miss V Williams	11-46	0-7	4-9	1-8	1-3	3-15	2-3	0-0	0-1	23.9	- 13.22
M D Hammond	10-22	4-7	2-3	1-2	0-1	3-9	0-0	0-0	0-0	45.5	+ 11.73
D J Wintle	8-32	0-3	1-10	3-4	2-7	2-7	0-1	0-0	0-0	25.0	+ 28.10
G L Moore	8-37	3-10	1-7	3-5	0-4	0-6	1-4	0-0	0-1	21.6	- 3.50
P R Webber	8-30	2-8	1-6	0-5	1-3	4-6	0-1	0-0	0-1	26.7	+ 10.27
M Todhunter	8-43	3-13	0-12	3-6	1-7	1-4	0-1	0-0	0-0	18.6	- 15.03
C L Tizzard	8-44	0-4	0-4	1-6	2-5	4-18	1-3	0-0	0-4	18.2	- 15.05
R C Guest	8-101	2-22	3-31	0-9	1-8	2-28	0-3	0-0	0-0	7.9	- 11.38
J S King	7-18	0-3	0-0	0-3	0-0	6-11	1-1	0-0	0-0	38.9	+ 45.26
C J Mann	7-37	5-13	1-12	1-6	0-1	0-3	0-2	0-0	0-0	18.9	- 12.62
Heather Dalton	7-37	0-3	1-9	0-3	3-5	3-12	0-2	0-0	0-3	18.9	+ 7.73
R Lee	6-29	1-3	0-6	1-5	1-4	3-10	0-1	0-0	0-0	20.7	+ 10.75
R Dickin	6-32	0-5	0-1	1-3	2-7	3-11	0-4	0-0	0-1	18.8	+ 19.58
M C Chapman	6-63	2-12	3-29	0-8	1-6	0-5	0-3	0-0	0-0	9.5	- 4.00
P C Haslam	6-37	2-24	1-4	2-5	1-2	0-1	0-1	0-0	0-0	16.2	- 3.46
Mrs D A Hamer	6-32	0-8	4-9	1-11	0-0	0-0	0-0	0-0	1-4	18.8	+ 45.75
Miss L V Russell	6-47	2-11	1-11	0-3	1-7	2-14	0-1	0-0	0-0	12.8	- 1.50
J J Quinn	6-19	5-13	0-3	1-2	0-0	0-0	0-0	0-0	0-0	31.6	+ 21.50
N G Richards	6-24	1-7	0-6	1-1	0-1	4-7	0-0	0-0	0-2	25.0	- 5.97
J M Jefferson	5-20	1-8	4-8	0-1	0-0	0-1	0-1	0-0	0-1	25.0	+ 11.00
D Burchell	5-34	0-5	2-13	0-4	1-5	2-6	0-0	0-0	0-1	14.7	- 7.00
B Ellison	5-26	2-5	1-8	0-4	0-5	1-3	1-1	0-0	0-0	19.2	- 0.63
G A Swinbank	5-10	1-3	3-4	0-1	1-1	0-0	0-0	0-0	0-1	50.0	+ 26.94
A King	5-24	3-7	0-6	0-3	0-0	1-7	0-0	0-0	1-1	20.8	- 0.38
G M Moore	4-42	2-15	0-5	1-6	0-6	1-9	0-1	0-0	0-0	9.5	- 23.00
Mrs M Reveley	4-37	1-9	1-7	1-8	0-6	1-7	0-0	0-0	0-0	10.8	- 5.63
M Scudamore	4-16	0-2	1-4	0-1	0-0	2-7	0-1	0-0	1-1	25.0	+ 6.25
R G Frost	4-19	0-4	3-8	0-1	0-3	0-2	0-0	0-0	1-1	21.1	- 7.63
K Bishop	4-13	1-1	0-2	1-2	0-0	1-6	1-1	0-0	0-1	30.8	+132.67
S Dow	4-9	2-5	0-0	0-2	2-2	0-0	0-0	0-0	0-0	44.4	- 0.43
R H Buckler	4-21	0-4	0-2	0-1	2-4	2-9	0-0	0-0	0-1	19.0	+ 12.00
Dr P Pritchard	4-56	0-1	0-7	1-11	0-7	3-28	0-2	0-0	0-0	7.1	- 37.00
N B Mason	4-48	0-7	2-14	0-1	1-11	1-13	0-0	0-0	0-2	8.3	- 10.00
G Prodromou	4-10	2-3	0-2	2-3	0-0	0-2	0-0	0-0	0-0	40.0	+ 9.63
A Berry	4-8	1-2	3-4	0-1	0-0	0-0	0-1	0-0	0-0	50.0	+ 18.50
A Bailey	3-8	1-3	0-2	2-3	0-0	0-0	0-0	0-0	0-0	37.5	+ 18.00
N A T'stn-Davies	3-44	1-8	0-11	0-5	0-4	0-9	0-1	0-0	2-6	6.8	- 28.59
R Bastiman	3-10	0-2	2-5	0-1	0-0	0-0	1-2	0-0	0-0	30.0	+ 5.08
J L Spearing	3-22	0-3	0-7	0-5	1-2	2-4	0-0	0-0	0-1	13.6	+ 5.50
C J Down	3-25	1-9	0-4	0-3	0-0	0-7	1-1	0-0	1-1	12.0	- 0.50
M F Harris	3-28	0-5	1-8	1-10	1-1	0-3	0-0	0-0	0-1	10.7	- 16.25
P D Evans	3-19	0-2	0-3	2-9	1-2	0-0	0-0	0-0	0-3	15.8	- 5.17
L Lungo	3-8	0-3	1-2	0-0	0-1	2-2	0-0	0-0	0-0	37.5	+ 0.80

LEADING JUMPS TRAINERS IN SEPTEMBER

	Total W-R	Nov Hdle	H'cap Hdle	Other Hdle	Nov Chase	H'cap Chase	Other Chase	Hunter Chase	N.H. Flat	Per cent	£1 Level stake
M C Pipe	42-164	13-30	13-68	5-25	6-15	4-23	0-0	0-0	1-3	25.6	- 25.35
P J Hobbs	33-137	8-28	5-39	4-12	10-21	6-34	0-3	0-0	0-0	24.1	- 26.64
Jonjo O'Neill	30-141	7-25	6-40	2-7	5-18	3-29	0-6	0-0	7-16	21.3	- 24.43
N A T'ston-Davies	26-65	8-16	6-17	1-6	3-7	4-11	0-1	0-0	4-7	40.0	+ 52.04
Mrs S J Smith	17-69	1-14	4-14	1-4	4-13	5-16	0-2	0-0	2-6	24.6	+ 62.83
P Bowen	12-42	1-6	3-13	2-6	3-6	3-6	0-2	0-0	0-3	28.6	+ 16.49
G M Moore	9-37	6-20	0-4	2-3	0-5	1-3	0-0	0-0	0-2	24.3	+ 8.25
Ian Williams	9-60	1-12	1-21	3-6	1-6	3-15	0-0	0-0	0-0	15.0	- 15.85
M Pitman	8-26	0-7	2-8	3-4	3-4	0-2	0-0	0-0	0-1	30.8	+ 31.10
G L Moore	7-41	3-15	2-11	1-4	0-2	1-8	0-1	0-0	0-0	17.1	+ 0.19
G A Swinbank	7-18	0-7	3-4	0-0	1-1	0-2	0-0	0-0	3-4	38.9	- 0.01
Evan Williams	7-60	0-12	1-13	0-9	1-9	2-7	3-8	0-0	0-2	11.7	24.92
Mrs M Reveley	6-31	1-3	0-6	2-8	2-7	1-6	0-0	0-0	0-1	19.4	+ 3.75
M C Chapman	6-30	0-1	3-19	0-2	0-1	3-7	0-0	0-0	0-0	20.0	+ 26.00
P C Haslam	6-33	1-20	1-4	4-9	0-0	0-0	0-0	0-0	0-0	18.2	- 9.30
P R Webber	6-22	0-3	0-2	0-1	0-1	4-11	2-4	0-0	0-0	27.3	+ 6.50
Miss V Williams	6-47	2-9	0-5	1-7	2-11	1-12	0-3	0-0	0-0	12.8	- 31.35
G A Harker	6-9	0-0	3-4	0-0	1-2	0-0	0-0	0-0	2-3	66.7	+ 32.83
R C Guest	6-61	1-8	0-18	1-4	2-5	2-23	0-0	0-0	0-3	9.8	- 31.88
D J Wintle	5-22	0-4	2-10	0-1	0-2	3-5	0-0	0-0	0-0	22.7	+ 10.83
J M Jefferson	5-37	1-4	2-11	0-2	2-7	0-6	0-2	0-0	0-5	13.5	- 18.25
J I Spearing	5-18	0-1	1-6	2-3	1-3	0-1	1-1	0-0	0-3	27.8	+ 2.48
M F Harris	5-41	3-16	2-14	0-3	0-3	0-1	0-2	0-0	0-2	12.2	- 0.27
P F Nicholls	5-22	2-3	2-3	0-0	0-3	1-11	0-2	0-0	0-0	22.7	+ 8.60
M Todhunter	5-28	2-6	1-7	0-3	0-4	2-6	0-1	0-0	0-1	17.9	- 2.83
Nick Williams	5-17	1-5	1-2	0-1	0-2	3-6	0-1	0-0	0-0	29.4	+ 15.75
B G Powell	5-46	2-10	0-10	0-4	1-6	0-9	2-4	0-0	0-3	10.9	- 28.13
R J Price	4-30	0-8	2-11	0-2	1-3	1-4	0-0	0-0	0-2	13.3	- 10.00
M D Hammond	4-20	3-9	0-3	0-1	0-0	1-6	0-0	0-0	0-1	20.0	+ 32.25
Miss Sheena West	4-9	1-5	2-3	1-1	0-0	0-0	0-0	0-0	0-0	44.4	+ 9.75
Miss L V Russell	4-45	1-9	0-10	0-3	0-9	3-10	0-0	0-0	0-4	8.9	- 22.80
C J Mann	4-25	2-9	1-6	0-3	0-4	1-3	0-0	0-0	0-0	16.0	- 1.63
J J Quinn	4-13	4-8	0-1	0-3	0-0	0-0	0-0	0-0	0-1	30.8	+ 17.75
C L Tizzard	4-32	0-2	0-5	0-2	3-7	1-14	0-1	0-0	0-1	12.5	- 6.17
D McCain	3-24	0-10	1-7	2-4	0-0	0-2	0-0	0-0	0-1	12.5	- 5.00
D W P Arbuthnot	3-7	0-1	2-3	1-3	0-0	0-0	0-0	0-0	0-0	42.9	+ 14.13
P Monteith	3-25	0-5	0-3	1-4	0-1	2-8	0-0	0-0	0-1	12.0	- 1.00
J H Johnson	3-25	2-6	0-6	1-5	0-2	0-4	0-0	0-0	0-2	12.0	- 16.88
R H Buckler	3-19	0-2	0-3	0-3	1-2	2-7	0-1	0-0	0-1	15.8	- 9.50
N A Graham	3-4	2-2	0-0	1-2	0-0	0-0	0-0	0-0	0-0	75.0	+ 22.50
J G M O'Shea	3-21	0-2	2-9	0-6	1-1	0-2	0-1	0-0	0-0	14.3	- 6.00
B Ellison	3-27	2-12	1-8	0-4	0-0	0-3	0-0	0-0	0-0	11.1	- 16.43
Jamie Poulton	3-22	1-6	0-4	0-4	1-2	0-5	0-0	0-0	1-1	13.6	+ 15.00
R H Alner	3-27	0-4	0-2	0-2	0-3	3-14	0-0	0-0	0-2	11.1	- 15.75
B J Llewellyn	3-19	0-2	3-14	0-0	0-1	0-1	0-0	0-0	0-1	15.8	+ 3.50
D E Cantillon	3-5	0-2	0-0	1-1	0-0	0-0	0-0	0-0	2-2	60.0	+ 7.10
C R Egerton	3-16	1-5	0-3	1-3	1-4	0-1	0-0	0-0	0-0	18.8	- 6.00
Mrs D A Hamer	3-24	1-6	2-11	0-3	0-0	0-1	0-1	0-0	0-2	12.5	+ 52.33
L Wells	3-16	2-4	0-5	0-0	0-2	0-1	0-0	0-0	1-4	18.8	- 2.60
M J Gingell	3-41	0-1	1-15	2-9	0-7	0-3	0-5	0-0	0-1	7.3	+ 27.00
Heather Dalton	3-24	0-4	0-6	0-1	1-3	1-6	1-2	0-0	0-2	12.5	- 4.00

LEADING JUMPS TRAINERS IN OCTOBER

	Total W-R	Nov Hdle	H'cap Hdle	Other Hdle	Nov Chase	H'cap Chase	Other Chase	Hunter Chase	N.H. Flat	Per cent	£1 Level stake
P J Hobbs	82-290	22-54	10-77	11-27	12-41	17-66	8-18	0-0	3-8	28.3	+ 2.01
P F Nicholls	82-253	15-44	10-36	7-25	18-46	20-70	7-17	0-0	5-17	32.4	+ 11.45
Jonjo O'Neill	67-297	18-66	18-69	8-32	9-36	5-51	2-10	0-0	7-33	22.6	- 8.54
M C Pipe	62-309	20-81	18-103	10-47	7-24	4-43	1-4	0-0	2-9	20.1	- 96.38
N A T'stn-Davies	48-258	13-62	3-33	5-20	7-33	8-63	3-12	0-0	9-35	18.6	- 55.80
Mrs S J Smith	32-162	2-29	7-27	2-7	5-24	14-51	2-10	0-0	0-14	19.8	+ 20.82
Mrs M Reveley	21-101	3-20	4-33	4-9	3-10	6-20	0-2	0-0	1-7	20.8	+ 9.41
Miss V Williams	21-118	4-25	1-18	3-6	4-15	4-43	2-4	0-0	3-7	17.8	- 25.20
M W Easterby	20-100	5-15	1-12	1-13	0-7	2-18	0-3	0-0	11-32	20.0	+ 5.78
J M Jefferson	19-98	6-25	4-21	2-4	3-12	2-10	0-5	0-0	2-21	19.4	+ 29.50
Ian Williams	19-142	4-32	8-41	1-22	2-12	0-24	4-6	0-0	0-5	13.4	- 2.86
Miss H C Knight	18-95	3-28	0-2	0-8	9-21	4-16	0-10	0-0	2-10	18.9	- 11.22
M Pitman	17-69	5-18	3-14	0-3	1-6	2-11	1-2	0-0	5-15	24.6	+ 18.79
P Bowen	16-77	4-14	6-15	0-8	2-8	3-22	0-2	0-0	1-9	20.8	+ 5.41
G L Moore	16-109	5-38	2-28	5-19	1-8	2-11	0-4	0-0	1-2	14.7	+ 30.88
N G Richards	16-66	4-20	6-26	3-5	1-3	1-4	0-2	0-0	1-6	24.2	+ 25.10
R H Alner	15-135	5-32	2-20	0-8	3-19	5-45	0-10	0-0	0-1	11.1	- 46.13
N J Henderson	14-53	4-12	3-16	1-6	1-3	3-9	1-1	0-0	1-6	26.4	+ 9.34
Heather Dalton	14-63	2-10	2-7	0-3	2-6	6-25	1-3	0-0	1-9	22.2	+ 7.89
A King	14-68	6-21	3-16	2-12	1-5	1-12	0-2	0-0	1-1	20.6	- 1.06
B G Powell	14-92	6-25	0-18	1-8	3-12	2-14	0-3	0-0	2-13	15.2	+ 11.05
J H Johnson	13-85	3-30	2-17	3-5	2-9	2-17	1-2	0-0	0-5	15.3	- 17.20
R C Guest	13-142	3-21	2-37	0-12	1-18	6-50	1-1	0-0	0-3	9.2	- 64.30
R H Buckler	12-94	5-26	1-19	0-5	1-10	4-20	0-2	0-0	1-12	12.8	- 3.90
Ferdy Murphy	12-152	5-39	1-22	1-14	1-18	1-48	3-7	0-0	0-4	7.9	- 93.55
Miss E C Lavelle	12-61	3-17	6-15	0-5	1-7	2-14	0-0	0-0	0-3	19.7	+ 4.95
G M Moore	11-84	7-32	2-14	0-4	1-9	1-14	0-3	0-0	0-8	13.1	+ 20.90
Noel T Chance	10-29	3-8	1-7	0-2	2-3	0-2	0-0	0-0	4-7	34.5	- 0.26
L Lungo	10-65	3-16	3-24	1-5	0-5	1-7	0-0	0-0	2-8	15.4	- 21.12
C R Egerton	10-39	6-14	0-5	1-4	1-4	0-2	2-4	0-0	0-6	25.6	+ 6.32
R Ford	10-47	0-8	1-8	1-4	2-6	4-13	2-4	0-0	0-4	21.3	+ 16.75
P R Webber	10-55	1-12	1-6	1-6	3-9	3-11	0-4	0-0	1-7	18.2	- 12.28
R Rowe	9-45	1-13	3-8	0-1	4-8	1-12	0-0	0-0	0-3	20.0	- 4.53
C C Bealby	9-60	0-13	1-9	3-7	4-9	1-11	0-1	0-0	0-10	15.0	+ 41.50
Evan Williams	9-71	0-14	1-12	1-9	4-11	1-15	1-9	0-0	1-1	12.7	+ 9.57
D McCain	8-92	3-20	0-19	1-11	1-13	2-22	0-2	0-0	1-5	8.7	- 15.50
Miss L V Russell	8-82	1-20	1-18	0-5	1-11	4-23	1-3	0-0	0-2	9.8	- 36.00
C J Mann	8-77	2-21	1-19	2-11	0-2	3-14	0-5	0-0	0-5	10.4	- 26.40
M Todhunter	8-58	3-16	1-11	0-1	2-10	2-13	0-4	0-0	0-3	13.8	- 15.46
H D Daly	8-48	2-8	0-4	0-4	3-11	3-18	0-3	0-0	0-0	16.7	- 2.75
A W Carroll	8-64	2-22	2-12	3-14	1-4	0-6	0-4	0-0	0-2	12.5	- 9.25
J W Mullins	7-90	2-29	2-17	2-5	1-14	0-10	0-3	0-0	0-12	7.8	- 37.00
Mrs H O Graham	7-31	2-10	5-16	0-1	0-0	0-1	0-0	0-0	0-3	22.6	+ 52.25
T R George	7-94	3-14	1-22	1-7	1-15	1-24	0-2	0-0	0-10	7.4	- 54.60
G A Swinbank	7-31	2-7	0-10	1-4	0-0	1-4	0-0	0-0	3-6	22.6	+ 19.11
R Lee	6-40	2-6	0-6	0-2	0-1	3-22	1-3	0-0	0-0	15.0	- 12.50
M Scudamore	6-58	1-23	2-10	0-2	2-9	1-9	0-2	0-0	0-3	10.3	+ 7.50
G B Balding	6-32	0-10	4-9	0-1	0-2	1-6	1-2	0-0	0-2	18.8	+ 8.00
W Storey	6-61	0-23	1-15	0-6	0-1	5-10	0-1	0-0	0-5	9.8	- 28.75
K Bishop	6-32	2-7	3-10	0-0	0-1	1-8	0-1	0-0	0-5	18.8	- 6.73
K C Bailey	6-53	1-15	3-11	0-4	0-1	1-13	0-1	0-0	1-8	11.3	- 12.75

LEADING JUMPS TRAINERS IN NOVEMBER

	Total W-R	Nov Hdle	H'cap Hdle	Other Hdle	Nov Chase	H'cap Chase	Other Chase	Hunter Chase	N.H. Flat	Per cent	£1 Level stake
M C Pipe	118-532	37-127	24-139	13-68	15-40	23-129	2-11	0-0	7-30	22.2	- 48.76
P F Nicholls	104-455	19-75	9-65	6-41	31-81	33-138	3-34	0-0	4-29	22.9	- 41.01
Jonjo O'Neill	77-414	17-92	18-97	5-45	14-53	13-85	1-9	0-0	10-43	18.6	- 99.75
P J Hobbs	66-418	19-94	9-77	11-39	11-59	10-125	4-15	0-0	3-20	15.8	- 71.91
N J Henderson	60-232	13-58	12-38	5-30	8-34	10-41	6-15	0-0	6-22	25.9	+ 28.41
Ferdy Murphy	50-367	10-86	1-53	6-29	6-48	21-108	6-29	0-0	0-15	13.6	- 152.63
Miss H C Knight	49-257	7-56	0-8	5-37	17-71	7-39	7-16	0-0	6-34	19.1	- 10.53
Mrs M Reveley	48-251	7-52	14-70	7-27	5-23	8-50	1-3	0-0	6-29	19.1	- 40.74
L Lungo	48-248	11-64	14-87	2-11	8-25	3-27	3-8	0-0	7-26	19.4	- 55.67
N A T'stn-Davies	43-298	10-70	10-33	5-28	8-36	7-87	1-7	0-0	3-40	14.4	- 81.83
J H Johnson	41-176	11-61	9-36	5-18	0-10	9-27	5-11	0-0	2-13	23.3	+ 37.23
Miss V Williams	41-260	5-47	8-50	5-25	6-21	15-97	0-0	0-0	2-18	15.8	- 72.42
A King	36-224	14-62	9-52	0-26	4-24	6-31	0-5	0-0	3-30	16.1	- 51.51
R H Alner	34-246	8-43	2-23	2-15	7-42	11-92	4-12	0-0	0-19	13.8	- 44.48
N G Richards	30-124	7-30	7-35	4-22	5-12	2-9	1-5	0-0	4-13	24.2	+ 45.69
Mrs S J Smith	28-270	4-57	2-40	2-25	5-28	14-79	1-13	0-0	0-30	10.4	- 101.78
O Sherwood	27-108	4-21	4-11	4-13	2-19	5-23	3-4	0-0	6-18	25.0	+ 10.23
G L Moore	26-221	9-69	6-64	7-33	2-19	2-26	0-9	0-0	0-6	11.8	- 42.60
Ian Williams	25-231	6-71	6-55	3-18	2-25	5-50	3-5	0-0	0-9	10.8	- 58.34
H D Daly	24-175	7-45	2-16	2-19	6-34	5-37	0-9	0-0	2-15	13.7	- 46.90
C J Mann	23-167	9-46	4-26	3-16	3-23	3-45	1-4	0-0	0-7	13.8	+ 21.35
T R George	21-170	3-32	2-19	0-10	5-36	8-50	1-9	0-0	2-14	12.4	- 43.58
P C Haslam	19-70	9-30	3-14	4-12	1-4	0-5	0-2	0-0	2-3	27.1	+ 20.16
R Dickin	18-128	3-33	3-16	1-8	1-14	9-45	1-3	0-0	0-9	14.1	- 8.09
M W Easterby	17-160	2-47	6-31	2-23	1-11	5-24	0-3	0-0	1-21	10.6	- 32.50
K C Bailey	16-167	2-34	1-29	1-9	4-25	5-46	2-8	0-0	1-16	9.6	- 18.00
C R Egerton	16-55	7-18	3-16	3-9	2-4	0-4	0-1	0-0	1-5	29.1	+ 25.14
T D Easterby	16-145	7-50	0-22	1-11	1-7	5-42	1-3	0-0	1-11	11.0	- 60.39
M Pitman	16-104	4-30	0-9	4-7	2-13	3-22	2-6	0-0	1-17	15.4	+ 7.85
C L Tizzard	15-111	1-22	1-9	3-6	4-27	3-27	2-8	0-0	1-12	13.5	+ 12.33
P Bowen	14-96	2-18	3-22	1-12	2-9	6-26	0-3	0-0	0-7	14.6	+ 4.71
R Rowe	14-101	2-29	3-19	2-5	5-18	2-26	0-1	0-0	0-3	13.9	+ 35.63
Miss E C Lavelle	14-74	3-18	4-16	1-6	3-11	3-12	0-4	0-0	0-7	18.9	+ 32.16
J M Jefferson	13-108	1-31	4-29	2-8	2-7	2-11	0-4	0-0	2-18	12.0	- 7.03
Noel T Chance	13-66	1-6	3-14	1-6	2-6	1-3	1-1	0-0	4-20	19.7	+ 15.74
R T Phillips	13-87	3-20	4-25	1-14	1-7	1-9	1-5	0-0	2-8	14.9	- 25.73
D McCain	12-111	0-33	2-15	0-9	3-18	3-22	0-2	0-0	1-12	10.8	+ 4.33
K G Reveley	12-84	3-12	5-30	1-11	0-5	1-9	0-5	0-0	2-13	14.3	- 5.62
Heather Dalton	12-78	2-18	1-6	2-14	2-9	4-15	1-2	0-0	0-14	15.4	+ 7.78
G M Moore	11-135	4-45	1-18	0-11	4-19	2-28	0-5	0-0	0-9	8.1	- 39.38
R Lee	11-92	2-11	4-24	1-6	0-11	4-39	0-0	0-0	0-1	12.0	- 19.50
M Scudamore	11-82	4-24	1-16	2-11	2-8	2-11	0-2	0-0	0-10	13.4	- 0.44
P Monteith	11-87	2-28	2-22	3-8	1-7	3-16	0-3	0-0	0-3	12.6	+ 10.19
A Parker	11-70	2-14	1-9	0-2	1-9	7-33	0-0	0-0	0-3	15.7	- 8.00
J W Mullins	11-123	1-29	1-17	3-17	2-20	1-18	3-6	0-0	0-16	8.9	- 34.42
M Todhunter	11-94	3-29	0-18	0-3	2-15	5-25	1-3	0-0	0-1	11.7	+ 12.56
C Tinkler	10-23	2-6	2-5	1-2	0-1	2-3	0-2	0-0	3-4	43.5	+ 29.02
J A B Old	10-73	3-29	2-8	0-8	1-6	3-15	0-0	0-0	1-7	13.7	+ 31.21
John R Upson	10-74	0-18	1-8	0-4	1-4	8-35	0-1	0-0	0-4	13.5	+ 19.46
G A Harker	10-47	4-12	1-11	0-4	0-1	0-1	0-1	0-0	5-17	21.3	+ 31.00
B G Powell	10-138	1-38	1-18	0-20	2-17	5-29	0-1	0-0	1-15	7.2	- 82.98

LEADING JUMPS TRAINERS IN DECEMBER

	Total W-R	Nov Hdle	H'cap Hdle	Other Hdle	Nov Chase	H'cap Chase	Other Chase	Hunter Chase	N.H. Flat	Per cent	£1 Level stake
P F Nicholls	101-426	22-86	10-47	10-49	22-63	22-124	12-43	0-0	4-17	23.7	- 25.50
M C Pipe	93-598	28-144	18-186	8-81	15-47	12-109	6-35	0-0	6-17	15.6	- 182.73
N J Henderson	81-317	18-79	15-60	13-45	13-41	10-48	9-31	0-0	4-24	25.6	+ 75.85
Miss V Williams	68-343	15-63	12-72	3-18	7-32	25-123	3-12	0-0	4-25	19.8	- 4.76
Jonjo O'Neill	63-364	21-89	12-70	8-36	7-39	4-76	5-23	0-0	6-35	17.3	- 71.51
P J Hobbs	54-350	15-97	7-57	5-45	6-44	13-84	8-22	0-0	0-9	15.4	- 104.07
A King	41-215	9-60	9-31	6-28	6-26	9-38	0-8	0-0	2-27	19.1	+ 45.62
J H Johnson	38-166	17-54	5-40	5-23	2-8	5-25	4-13	0-0	0-5	22.9	- 30.82
Ferdy Murphy	37-312	7-60	2-37	2-22	8-44	14-104	2-33	0-0	2-12	11.9	- 111.79
R H Alner	36-236	7-51	6-33	2-10	7-38	11-80	3-16	0-0	0-8	15.3	+ 17.58
L Lungo	36-169	11-52	6-57	0-8	3-12	7-20	3-8	0-0	6-13	21.3	- 20.16
N A T'stn-Davies	34-266	7-53	4-39	4-29	6-35	10-73	1-11	0-0	2-28	12.8	- 72.72
Miss H C Knight	32-234	6-57	0-7	1-24	9-48	2-36	8-31	0-0	6-31	13.7	- 51.26
Mrs S J Smith	30-222	4-53	9-47	0-10	3-22	5-59	7-14	0-0	2-17	13.5	- 65.23
T R George	29-178	4-25	7-26	3-18	4-34	8-53	3-8	0-0	0-15	16.3	+ 34.13
H D Daly	24-165	3-40	4-15	3-15	3-26	9-45	1-11	0-0	1-14	14.5	- 32.73
Mrs M Reveley	21-177	3-31	5-63	3-18	4-12	4-34	2-7	0-0	1-17	11.9	- 19.70
N G Richards	21-110	7-27	5-34	0-14	4-14	3-11	0-4	0-0	2-7	19.1	- 24.79
R C Guest	21-120	5-21	5-37	2-16	4-14	2-25	2-3	0-0	1-4	17.5	+190.75
C J Mann	19-168	3-35	2-34	2-20	3-16	7-48	1-9	0-0	1-10	11.3	- 31.96
C R Egerton	17-62	5-15	3-9	1-11	3-7	1-2	0-1	0-0	4-17	27.4	+ 3.41
R T Phillips	17-94	6-24	2-26	2-9	2-7	1-12	0-2	0-0	4-14	18.1	+ 14.75
Ian Williams	17-187	3-42	2-40	4-21	3-23	4-42	1-7	0-0	0-12	9.1	- 104.69
T D Easterby	16-99	3-29	1-16	1-4	3-10	6-32	0-3	0-0	2-5	16.2	+ 14.40
M W Easterby	15-142	3-45	4-31	0-11	3-12	3-23	0-6	0-0	2-14	10.6	- 45.47
P R Webber	15-136	1-37	1-9	2-11	3-23	4-32	3-10	0-0	1-15	11.0	- 25.25
G L Moore	13-192	4-69	6-61	4-25	0-17	0-19	0-3	0-0	1-5	6.8	- 79.97
J Mackie	12-88	2-18	6-44	0-8	2-4	2-8	0-2	0-0	0-4	13.6	- 16.25
P Bowen	12-88	1-22	5-20	0-7	1-14	5-15	0-8	0-0	0-2	13.6	- 34.97
Noel T Chance	12-69	3-16	3-11	1-9	0-6	0-4	2-4	0-0	3-19	17.4	- 15.60
V R A Dartnall	12-45	6-13	4-10	0-4	0-6	0-4	1-3	0-0	1-7	26.7	+ 11.78
R J Hodges	11-121	3-27	2-28	1-11	0-14	4-26	1-5	0-0	0-10	9.1	- 7.00
O Sherwood	11-119	5-35	0-15	2-17	1-17	2-23	1-9	0-0	0-5	9.2	- 50.01
K C Bailey	11-134	1-32	0-17	0-13	0-26	9-30	0-6	0-0	1-11	8.2	- 34.50
K G Reveley	11-87	3-20	3-27	0-6	2-9	2-10	1-9	0-0	0-7	12.6	- 28.96
J M Jefferson	10-106	3-36	3-24	0-9	1-10	2-10	1-4	0-0	0-14	9.4	- 56.22
G A Swinbank	10-51	3-13	2-13	3-7	0-0	0-5	0-0	0-0	2-13	19.6	- 17.70
D P Keane	10-72	1-23	4-16	1-9	2-8	1-10	0-2	0-0	1-6	13.9	+ 35.38
R Johnson	9-56	0-12	3-12	0-3	0-9	6-19	0-1	0-0	0-0	16.1	- 7.12
P Monteith	9-83	0-15	4-21	1-16	0-9	2-11	2-8	0-0	0-4	10.8	- 23.42
P C Haslam	9-24	4-10	1-3	2-5	1-2	1-3	0-1	0-0	0-0	37.5	+ 14.09
John R Upson	9-65	2-16	0-3	0-3	1-6	5-29	1-5	0-0	0-3	13.8	+ 24.33
J W Mullins	9-145	1-35	0-17	1-19	3-22	4-24	0-12	0-0	0-16	6.2	- 84.67
Heather Dalton	9-80	1-17	0-12	0-7	2-10	3-15	1-3	0-0	2-16	11.3	+ 9.00
M Pitman	9-109	3-30	2-15	1-13	1-13	2-13	0-6	0-0	0-19	8.3	- 50.32
Miss E C Lavelle	9-80	2-26	1-18	0-13	2-7	3-12	0-0	0-0	1-6	11.3	- 4.02
B G Powell	9-129	2-47	1-11	1-16	1-16	2-18	2-9	0-0	0-12	7.0	- 85.70
P Beaumont	8-81	1-26	0-2	0-6	3-18	3-13	1-10	0-0	0-6	9.9	- 40.67
R Dickin	8-94	1-18	0-13	0-10	1-12	5-29	1-4	0-0	0-8	8.5	- 50.75
Mrs L Wadham	8-59	2-17	4-25	1-7	1-4	0-3	0-2	0-0	0-2	13.6	- 18.50
C L Tizzard	8-101	1-17	0-10	0-4	4-16	3-43	0-5	0-0	0-6	7.9	- 54.14

WINNING TRAINERS

BY COURSE 2001–2006

LEADING JUMPS TRAINERS AT AINTREE

	Total W-R	Nov Hdle	H'cap Hdle	Other Hdle	Nov Chase	H'cap Chase	Other Chase	Hunter Chase	N.H. Flat	Per cent	£1 Level stake
Jonjo O'Neill	21-112	5-18	3-25	6-26	2-9	6-35	0-1	0-1	2-9	18.8	+ 47.06
P F Nicholls	14-151	3-20	0-12	0-11	6-30	3-58	1-13	1-8	0-6	9.3	- 59.76
M C Pipe	12-237	3-37	4-68	3-67	1-14	1-82	2-15	0-1	0-4	5.1	- 142.52
Miss Venetia Williams	11-92	3-14	3-20	1-14	2-16	2-34	0-1	0-0	1-5	12.0	- 5.17
P J Hobbs	10-100	4-20	1-26	1-25	2-11	3-30	0-2	0-1	0-3	10.0	- 10.93
N J Henderson	8-105	1-20	1-21	0-22	2-14	3-29	0-6	0-0	1-8	7.6	- 51.88
N A Twiston-Davies	7-77	0-10	1-12	1-13	2-9	2-31	0-2	0-0	1-9	9.1	+ 32.38
J Howard Johnson	7-62	2-17	2-11	0-10	1-6	1-18	1-3	0-0	0-3	11.3	- 25.43
P Bowen	6-25	2-4	2-7	1-6	1-1	0-8	0-1	0-0	1-2	24.0	+ 9.75
Mrs S J Smith	5-79	0-12	0-9	0-3	1-13	4-35	0-3	0-0	0-6	6.3	- 37.00
L Lungo	5-25	1-4	2-13	0-6	0-0	0-3	0-0	0-0	2-4	20.0	+ 15.63
R Ford	5-25	1-9	0-0	1-3	0-1	2-9	0-0	1-2	0-1	20.0	+ 29.00
T D Easterby	5-33	2-6	1-7	1-3	1-3	0-14	0-1	0-0	0-1	15.2	+ 16.00
N G Richards	5-33	4-13	0-8	1-5	0-1	0-4	0-0	0-0	0-4	15.2	+ 7.25
A King	5-52	2-17	1-14	0-10	0-4	0-9	0-1	0-0	2-4	9.6	+ 12.25
Ferdy Murphy	4-53	0-6	0-3	1-4	2-8	1-32	0-0	0-0	0-1	7.5	- 32.25
Heather Dalton	4-17	1-3	1-2	0-1	0-1	2-8	0-0	0-0	0-3	23.5	+ 1.75
F Doumen	3-21	1-2	0-3	0-6	0-1	0-7	2-5	0-0	0-0	14.3	- 0.50
W P Mullins	3-18	0-2	0-0	0-2	0-1	2-8	1-1	0-1	0-3	16.7	+ 4.50
Miss H C Knight	3-45	0-12	0-2	0-5	2-8	1-9	0-5	0-0	0-6	6.7	- 22.50
Ian Williams	3-51	1-12	1-13	0-9	0-3	1-13	0-0	0-1	0-3	5.9	- 41.28
H D Daly	3-39	2-10	0-4	1-4	0-5	0-12	0-2	0-0	0-4	7.7	- 25.25
Mrs M Reveley	2-28	0-4	0-11	0-3	0-4	1-5	0-1	0-0	1-2	7.1	+ 19.00
D McCain	2-45	0-11	0-2	0-3	0-3	2-20	0-0	0-1	0-5	4.4	+ 6.00
K Bishop	2-5	0-0	1-3	0-1	1-1	0-0	0-0	0-0	0-1	40.0	+ 8.00
J L Spearing	2-6	0-1	0-1	0-0	0-0	2-4	0-0	0-0	0-0	33.3	+ 24.00
R Waley-Cohen	2-3	0-0	0-0	0-0	0-0	0-0	0-0	2-3	0-0	66.7	+ 7.83
A L T Moore	2-24	0-0	0-3	0-3	0-2	0-13	2-5	0-1	0-0	8.3	- 17.42
Mrs John Harrington	2-6	0-1	0-0	0-1	0-1	0-1	2-2	0-0	0-0	33.3	- 2.56
E J O'Grady	2-12	0-3	0-0	1-2	0-0	0-3	0-0	0-2	1-2	16.7	+ 2.00
John Queally	2-5	1-1	0-0	1-2	0-0	0-1	0-0	0-0	0-1	40.0	+ 33.00

LEADING JUMPS TRAINERS AT ASCOT

	Total W-R	Nov Hdle	H'cap Hdle	Other Hdle	Nov Chase	H'cap Chase	Other Chase	Hunter Chase	N.H. Flat	Per cent	£1 Level stake
M C Pipe	38-141	6-25	9-43	5-18	5-10	10-40	2-5	0-0	1-5	27.0	+ 64.84
N J Henderson	15-83	3-15	3-21	2-11	2-12	3-20	1-3	0-0	2-6	18.1	+ 24.99
M Pitman	8-35	2-10	1-4	0-3	2-9	2-6	1-1	0-0	0-2	22.9	+ 30.75
P J Hobbs	7-78	1-13	2-28	0-10	4-8	0-20	0-0	0-0	0-3	9.0	- 52.13
F Doumen	7-12	2-5	0-0	4-5	0-0	1-2	0-0	0-0	0-0	58.3	+ 5.54
Jonjo O'Neill	6-46	1-8	0-12	0-6	1-3	1-11	0-0	0-0	3-7	13.0	- 24.90
P F Nicholls	6-44	1-9	0-3	0-3	4-9	1-15	0-5	0-0	0-1	13.6	- 27.81
Miss Venetia Williams	6-52	1-4	1-17	1-2	1-3	3-22	0-3	0-0	0-2	11.5	+ 29.88
Noel T Chance	5-14	3-5	0-1	0-0	0-0	0-0	0-0	0-0	2-8	35.7	+ 19.25
R H Alner	5-28	1-7	1-3	0-1	0-2	3-13	0-0	0-0	0-2	17.9	+ 22.33
Ian Williams	5-30	0-7	1-10	0-1	0-3	3-6	0-0	0-0	1-3	16.7	+ 12.75
H D Daly	5-22	1-5	1-1	0-2	0-4	2-6	1-1	0-0	0-3	22.7	+ 19.75
Miss H C Knight	4-37	1-6	0-3	0-3	1-8	1-9	0-2	0-0	1-6	10.8	- 19.00

G L Moore	4-31	2-11	1-16	1-2	0-0	0-0	0-0	0-0	0-3	12.9	- 6.88
Miss E C Lavelle	4-23	2-7	1-9	0-1	0-0	1-3	0-1	0-0	0-2	17.4	+ 2.33
N A Twiston-Davies	3-39	1-12	0-5	0-2	2-7	0-7	0-0	0-0	0-6	7.7	- 29.82
L Wells	3-8	2-3	0-0	0-0	0-0	1-3	0-0	0-0	0-2	37.5	+ 33.00
H Morrison	3-8	1-3	1-4	0-1	1-1	0-0	0-0	0-0	0-0	37.5	+ 9.13
Mrs M Reveley	2-15	0-1	0-5	0-3	0-1	2-5	0-0	0-0	0-2	13.3	- 4.00
G B Balding	2-14	0-1	1-3	0-0	0-3	0-3	0-0	0-0	1-4	14.3	+ 4.50
K C Bailey	2-19	0-4	0-5	0-2	1-4	0-2	1-1	0-0	0-2	10.5	- 0.00
J A B Old	2-28	1-11	0-4	0-4	1-2	0-4	0-0	0-0	0-3	7.1	- 7.00
M Bradstock	2-4	0-1	1-2	0-0	0-0	0-0	0-0	0-0	1-1	50.0	+ 10.50
Ferdy Murphy	2-4	2-3	0-0	0-0	0-0	0-1	0-0	0-0	0-0	50.0	+ 13.50
P R Webber	2-22	0-4	1-6	0-3	0-0	1-5	0-0	0-0	0-5	9.1	- 12.75
S E H Sherwood	2-4	0-2	0-0	0-0	1-1	1-1	0-0	0-0	0-0	50.0	+ 5.20
A King	2-38	1-14	0-8	1-3	0-2	0-7	0-0	0-0	0-4	5.3	- 29.00
N A Gaselee	1-3	0-0	0-0	0-0	1-1	0-0	0-0	0-0	0-2	33.3	- 1.17
R Lee	1-8	0-0	1-6	0-0	0-0	0-2	0-0	0-0	0-0	12.5	+ 26.00
M J Ryan	1-6	0-2	0-1	0-0	1-2	0-0	0-0	0-0	0-1	16.7	- 0.50
C Weedon	1-5	0-2	1-2	0-0	0-0	0-0	0-0	0-0	0-1	20.0	+ 6.00

LEADING JUMPS TRAINERS AT AYR

	Total W-R	Nov Hdle	H'cap Hdle	Other Hdle	Nov Chase	H'cap Chase	Other Chase	Hunter Chase	N.H. Flat	Per£1 Level centstake	
L Lungo	55-231	18-62	7-55	3-16	10-25	6-29	2-6	0-0	9-38	23.8	- 37.71
N G Richards	42-155	14-40	7-45	3-11	7-14	3-16	2-6	1-2	5-21	27.1	+ 5.14
P Monteith	16-137	4-37	5-31	2-10	1-15	2-24	2-8	0-1	0-11	11.7	- 35.08
J Howard Johnson	16-59	8-21	0-9	0-0	1-6	1-14	2-4	0-0	1-5	27.1	+ 26.06
Ferdy Murphy	16-105	2-23	1-9	0-6	4-17	8-33	1-8	0-0	0-9	15.2	+ 0.30
Miss Lucinda V Russell	16-211	1-45	1-40	2-12	4-35	7-50	1-14	0-1	0-14	7.6	- 72.72
Mrs M Reveley	11-86	2-16	2-19	0-3	1-10	4-19	1-3	0-0	1-16	12.8	- 47.67
A C Whillans	10-95	1-24	7-24	0-4	0-5	2-20	0-3	0-0	0-15	10.5	- 6.88
P F Nicholls	10-70	3-11	1-13	0-0	2-18	2-26	0-0	1-1	1-1	14.3	- 30.80
M C Pipe	8-65	1-10	3-16	0-0	2-9	2-29	0-0	0-1	0-0	12.3	- 15.34
Mrs S C Bradburne	8-103	3-30	1-15	0-11	1-13	3-20	0-6	0-2	0-6	7.8	- 52.00
A Parker	8-97	1-23	1-12	0-5	3-12	3-29	0-5	0-3	0-8	8.2	- 37.75
P J Hobbs	7-28	0-1	3-6	0-0	1-6	2-14	0-0	0-0	1-1	25.0	+ 8.50
M Todhunter	7-67	2-16	1-14	0-6	2-5	1-16	1-2	0-0	0-8	10.4	- 32.50
Jonjo O'Neill	6-26	0-2	4-8	0-1	1-6	1-6	0-0	0-0	0-3	23.1	+ 9.50
J S Goldie	6-94	0-27	1-18	0-4	0-8	5-30	0-2	0-0	0-5	6.4	- 35.00
J M Jefferson	5-29	1-8	1-6	0-1	0-2	1-5	1-1	0-0	1-6	17.2	+ 14.73
F P Murtagh	5-39	0-13	0-5	0-2	3-4	2-9	0-2	0-0	0-4	12.8	- 13.42
Miss S E Forster	5-28	0-5	2-8	0-1	0-0	2-6	0-4	0-1	1-3	17.0	+ 36.50
R C Guest	5-39	1-6	1-7	0-4	1-4	1-15	1-1	0-0	0-2	12.8	- 17.13
N J Henderson	4-31	3-7	0-8	0-0	1-4	0-7	0-0	0-0	0-5	12.9	- 19.88
T P Tate	4-12	2-6	0-0	1-1	0-1	0-0	0-0	0-0	1-4	33.3	+ 6.50
M D Hammond	4-29	3-8	0-6	0-2	0-1	1-7	0-1	0-0	0-4	13.8	+ 91.50
R T Phillips	4-14	2-4	0-2	0-1	2-3	0-3	0-0	0-0	0-1	28.6	- 6.47
A Crook	4-17	0-3	0-0	1-3	1-1	2-7	0-1	0-0	0-2	23.5	+ 4.00
J R Bewley	4-18	2-6	0-4	0-0	1-4	1-2	0-1	0-0	0-1	22.2	+ 28.33
J N R Billinge	4-48	0-13	3-13	0-4	0-4	0-2	0-4	0-0	1-8	8.3	- 10.50
Miss Venetia Williams	4-22	2-3	2-5	0-0	0-4	0-10	0-0	0-0	0-0	18.2	+ 2.50
C Grant	4-43	1-15	0-2	0-2	0-3	1-10	0-2	0-3	2-6	9.3	- 25.20
Miss P Robson	4-17	0-1	0-2	0-0	0-0	1-9	0-1	3-4	0-0	23.5	- 1.23
G A Swinbank	4-21	1-6	0-4	1-1	0-0	0-0	0-0	0-0	2-10	19.0	+ 6.88

LEADING JUMPS TRAINERS AT BANGOR-ON-DEE

	Total W-R	Nov Hdle	H'cap Hdle	Other Hdle	Nov Chase	H'cap Chase	Other Chase	Hunter Chase	N.H. Flat	Per£1 Level centstake	
Jonjo O'Neill	35-154	10-43	10-36	1-6	8-20	4-35	1-4	0-0	1-10	22.7	- 16.33
M C Pipe	32-123	13-34	6-38	3-7	1-12	4-20	5-7	0-1	0-4	26.0	- 29.79
Miss Venetia Williams	21-121	4-25	4-29	1-4	4-14	5-41	2-2	0-0	1-6	17.4	- 31.66
P F Nicholls	16-46	4-12	1-5	0-1	4-8	4-15	1-1	1-2	1-2	34.8	+ 28.65
N A Twiston-Davies	14-85	4-19	1-17	0-3	1-8	3-18	0-2	0-0	5-18	16.5	- 14.34
P R Webber	12-52	3-14	1-5	1-1	3-9	2-9	0-3	0-0	2-11	23.1	+ 49.67
A King	12-48	6-18	3-11	0-2	0-4	2-11	0-0	0-0	1-2	25.0	+ 32.13
P J Hobbs	11-58	5-22	2-11	1-2	2-9	0-9	0-1	0-0	1-4	19.0	- 17.66
D McCain	11-145	2-49	2-27	1-12	2-26	3-16	1-4	0-1	0-10	7.6	- 46.50
Mrs S J Smith	9-99	2-23	1-19	0-11	2-13	3-25	0-0	0-0	1-8	9.1	- 20.17
Heather Dalton	9-52	1-12	1-9	0-2	1-7	6-11	0-3	0-1	0-7	17.3	+ 3.00
R C Guest	9-72	1-20	2-18	0-1	3-12	3-21	0-0	0-0	0-0	12.5	- 8.40
T R George	8-39	3-8	0-5	0-1	1-9	3-13	1-1	0-0	0-2	20.5	+ 12.83
H D Daly	8-59	3-17	0-4	0-5	2-9	3-20	0-1	0-0	0-3	13.6	- 16.39
Miss H C Knight	7-39	4-11	0-4	0-1	3-7	0-7	0-1	0-0	0-8	17.9	- 15.25
R J Price	6-35	0-6	3-14	1-2	1-6	1-6	0-0	0-0	0-1	17.1	+ 12.00
J M Jefferson	6-35	2-11	2-9	0-0	2-4	0-4	0-1	0-0	0-6	17.1	- 18.46
Ian Williams	6-63	1-19	3-19	0-3	0-6	2-12	0-0	0-0	0-4	9.5	- 19.90
N G Richards	6-22	2-5	1-5	0-1	0-2	1-2	0-0	1-1	1-6	27.3	+ 16.00
J Mackie	5-54	0-13	4-25	0-3	1-4	0-6	0-0	0-0	0-3	9.3	+ 8.00
N J Henderson	5-36	1-15	0-5	1-3	1-5	0-2	0-0	0-0	2-6	13.9	- 15.13
P Beaumont	4-44	0-11	0-3	0-1	2-11	1-5	1-3	0-3	0-7	9.1	- 19.67
Mrs Edward Crow	4-13	0-0	0-0	0-0	0-0	0-0	0-0	4-13	0-0	30.8	+ 0.87
Mrs L Williamson	4-84	1-33	0-2	0-6	1-18	1-14	0-5	0-2	1-4	4.8	- 30.00
M Sheppard	4-16	0-3	3-5	0-1	0-0	1-7	0-0	0-0	0-0	25.0	+ 7.50
Evan Williams	4-19	0-3	2-5	0-0	0-3	2-6	0-0	0-1	0-1	21.1	+ 15.25
A Bailey	3-30	1-12	0-10	2-2	0-2	0-0	0-2	0-0	0-2	10.0	- 4.00
R Lee	3-46	1-4	1-12	0-2	1-11	0-14	0-3	0-0	0-0	6.5	- 23.00
R Dickin	3-34	0-9	1-2	0-1	0-7	2-12	0-0	0-0	0-3	8.8	- 11.00
D J Wintle	3-20	0-5	2-8	0-1	0-2	1-3	0-0	0-0	0-1	15.0	- 1.50
C Tinkler	3-10	2-4	1-2	0-0	0-0	0-2	0-0	0-0	0-2	30.0	+ 7.38

LEADING JUMPS TRAINERS AT CARLISLE

	Total W-R	Nov Hdle	H'cap Hdle	Other Hdle	Nov Chase	H'cap Chase	Other Chase	Hunter Chase	N.H. Flat	Per£1 Level centstake	
L Lungo	32-149	9-52	10-35	1-6	7-18	2-17	1-3	0-0	2-18	21.5	+ 7.18
Mrs S J Smith	23-128	6-34	4-18	1-7	2-14	7-32	2-9	0-0	1-14	18.0	- 8.55
J Howard Johnson	20-81	5-25	4-12	1-6	5-11	4-18	0-0	0-0	1-9	24.7	- 4.41
N G Richards	17-66	5-22	4-15	2-7	4-6	0-6	0-3	0-0	2-7	25.8	- 15.45
R C Guest	15-72	3-10	1-12	0-2	4-11	4-27	1-2	1-1	1-7	20.8	+ 5.79
Mrs M Reveley	13-64	5-14	4-19	0-4	0-6	4-14	0-2	0-0	0-5	20.3	- 1.31
Jonjo O'Neill	13-69	3-20	3-13	0-3	1-7	1-17	0-0	0-0	5-9	18.8	- 2.12
Ferdy Murphy	13-107	4-36	0-3	1-7	1-18	3-30	1-4	0-1	3-8	12.1	- 40.42
A Parker	9-81	2-17	2-13	0-1	1-7	4-34	0-0	0-0	0-9	11.1	- 27.17
Miss Lucinda V Russell	8-98	4-27	0-16	0-5	2-17	1-21	1-7	0-0	0-5	8.2	- 21.00
J M Jefferson	7-53	2-20	2-6	0-5	1-6	1-6	0-1	0-0	1-9	13.2	- 9.14

	W-R									Per£1 Level
M W Easterby	7-44	2-6	2-8	1-3	0-4	0-5	1-5	0-0	1-13	15.9	+ 7.62
M Todhunter	6-52	2-17	0-12	0-1	1-8	2-9	1-2	0-0	0-3	11.5	- 14.27
F P Murtagh	5-66	1-22	1-15	0-5	0-2	3-14	0-4	0-0	0-4	7.6	- 16.00
R Johnson	4-40	2-13	1-9	0-3	0-6	1-5	0-2	0-1	0-1	10.0	+ 66.00
Miss Venetia Williams	4-20	1-1	0-4	0-0	1-3	2-10	0-0	0-0	0-2	20.0	- 0.84
J Wade	3-28	1-9	0-2	0-3	0-4	2-3	0-2	0-0	0-5	10.7	- 14.67
D McCain	3-36	0-9	0-2	1-6	1-4	1-10	0-1	0-0	0-4	8.3	+ 10.50
P Monteith	3-39	0-8	1-17	2-3	0-4	0-3	0-2	0-0	0-2	7.7	- 26.83
Mrs A Hamilton	3-12	0-1	0-5	1-1	0-0	0-1	1-1	0-1	1-2	25.0	+ 9.00
J B Walton	3-13	0-0	0-0	0-1	1-4	2-6	0-0	0-0	0-2	23.1	+ 6.75
A C Whillans	3-53	0-7	0-13	0-5	0-8	0-8	0-0	0-0	3-12	5.7	+ 2.50
N B Mason	3-29	0-7	0-4	0-0	1-5	2-11	0-0	0-1	0-1	10.3	+ 1.75
R A Fahey	3-19	1-10	0-4	0-1	0-0	2-2	0-0	0-0	0-2	15.8	- 0.50
Mrs A M Naughton	3-19	0-2	2-13	0-0	0-0	1-4	0-0	0-0	0-0	15.8	- 0.25
W S Coltherd	3-20	0-7	0-0	0-1	2-5	1-3	0-1	0-0	0-3	15.0	- 1.25
Miss P Robson	3-10	1-2	0-2	0-1	0-1	1-3	0-0	1-1	0-0	30.0	+ 1.83
Miss S E Forster	3-39	1-14	1-7	0-4	0-4	0-6	0-1	0-0	1-3	7.7	+ 20.00
P D Niven	3-16	1-6	0-4	0-1	1-3	0-0	1-1	0-0	0-1	18.8	+ 47.00
G M Moore	2-54	2-20	0-7	0-3	0-8	0-9	0-3	0-0	0-4	3.7	- 33.75
P Beaumont	2-32	1-9	0-0	0-2	0-10	0-4	1-1	0-0	0-6	6.3	- 8.00

LEADING JUMPS TRAINERS AT CARTMEL

	Total W-R	Nov Hdle	H'cap Hdle	Other Hdle	Nov Chase	H'cap Chase	Other Chase	Hunter Chase	N.H. Flat	Per£1 Level centstake
R C Guest	9-57	5-17	0-14	1-9	2-5	1-8	0-4	0-0	0-0	15.8	- 16.92
Mrs S J Smith	7-42	0-7	0-4	1-7	2-5	3-15	1-4	0-0	0-0	16.7	- 10.50
M C Chapman	6-56	2-13	3-19	0-8	0-5	1-7	0-4	0-0	0-0	10.7	- 6.50
D Burchell	6-21	1-4	0-6	0-1	1-3	4-7	0-0	0-0	0-0	28.6	+ 12.50
M Todhunter	6-39	4-13	1-12	1-5	0-6	0-1	0-2	0-0	0-0	15.4	- 11.42
J J Lambe	6-55	0-10	2-11	1-12	2-7	0-9	1-6	0-0	0-0	10.9	- 17.60
A Berry	5-16	1-4	4-8	0-3	0-0	0-0	0-1	0-0	0-0	31.3	+ 16.00
P Monteith	4-16	1-1	1-7	1-1	1-1	0-4	0-2	0-0	0-0	25.0	+ 1.50
M D Hammond	4-14	1-5	1-3	0-0	1-1	1-5	0-0	0-0	0-0	28.6	+ 1.25
A Sadik	4-9	0-0	0-2	0-2	1-1	2-3	1-1	0-0	0-0	44.4	+ 6.50
Miss S E Forster	4-16	0-4	0-4	1-3	1-2	2-2	0-1	0-0	0-0	25.0	+ 9.67
G M Moore	3-26	2-13	0-2	1-5	0-2	0-3	0-1	0-0	0-0	11.5	- 10.00
A C Whillans	3-4	0-0	2-3	0-0	0-0	1-1	0-0	0-0	0-0	75.0	+ 30.00
Ferdy Murphy	3-22	1-5	1-6	0-1	1-3	0-5	0-2	0-0	0-0	13.6	+ 2.17
C J Mann	3-8	2-4	0-0	1-2	0-0	0-2	0-0	0-0	0-0	37.5	- 1.55
R Ford	3-26	0-3	1-9	0-1	1-3	0-7	0-0	1-3	0-0	11.5	- 13.25
N Wilson	3-12	1-4	1-2	0-3	0-0	0-1	1-2	0-0	0-0	25.0	+ 16.00
James Moffatt	3-46	1-12	2-21	0-8	0-1	0-3	0-1	0-0	0-0	6.5	- 29.67
Mrs E Slack	2-17	0-3	2-10	0-1	0-1	0-2	0-0	0-0	0-0	11.8	- 7.25
P C Haslam	2-11	0-5	0-1	1-2	1-2	0-0	0-1	0-0	0-0	18.2	- 7.65
M F Harris	2-9	0-3	0-0	1-5	0-0	0-0	1-1	0-0	0-0	22.2	- 0.75
B Ellison	2-12	0-3	1-4	0-0	0-2	1-2	0-1	0-0	0-0	16.7	+ 2.88
N B Mason	2-20	0-2	1-8	0-0	0-4	1-6	0-0	0-0	0-0	10.0	- 1.00
C R Egerton	2-2	2-2	0-0	0-0	0-0	0-0	0-0	0-0	0-0	100.0	+ 3.60
Mrs K Walton	2-13	0-2	0-4	0-1	1-1	1-5	0-0	0-0	0-0	15.4	- 5.50
J J Quinn	2-10	2-5	0-1	0-4	0-0	0-0	0-0	0-0	0-0	20.0	- 5.00
Miss Venetia Williams	2-14	0-4	0-0	1-4	0-0	1-4	0-2	0-0	0-0	14.3	- 0.75
C Grant	2-22	0-7	0-2	1-5	1-4	0-3	0-1	0-0	0-0	9.1	- 14.17
E W Tuer	2-4	2-2	0-2	0-0	0-0	0-0	0-0	0-0	0-0	50.0	+ 4.25
D W Thompson	2-13	1-1	1-7	0-2	0-2	0-1	0-0	0-0	0-0	15.4	+ 0.50
S Mellor	1-2	0-0	0-0	0-0	0-0	1-2	0-0	0-0	0-0	50.0	+ 0.10

LEADING JUMPS TRAINERS AT CATTERICK

	Total W-R	Nov Hdle	H'cap Hdle	Other Hdle	Nov Chase	H'cap Chase	Other Chase	Hunter Chase	N.H. Flat	Per£1 Level centstake	
J Howard Johnson	19-88	10-41	4-20	0-2	2-4	2-12	0-5	0-0	1-4	21.6	- 12.13
Mrs S J Smith	14-116	5-36	3-25	1-3	1-12	0-15	2-6	0-0	2-19	12.1	- 46.63
Mrs M Reveley	10-89	2-14	3-22	0-6	1-16	1-14	2-5	0-1	1-11	11.2	- 28.30
T D Easterby	10-59	5-23	2-9	1-4	2-6	0-10	0-2	0-0	0-5	16.9	- 15.78
R C Guest	10-66	1-13	3-22	0-3	2-6	3-13	0-2	0-0	1-7	15.2	+ 70.50
L Lungo	9-40	2-12	0-10	0-1	0-3	1-5	1-2	0-0	5-7	22.5	+ 3.79
M D Hammond	8-57	3-17	0-9	0-1	1-8	2-11	1-4	0-0	1-7	14.0	- 2.70
K G Reveley	8-51	1-15	2-12	1-2	0-2	1-8	2-5	0-0	1-7	15.7	- 2.99
M W Easterby	7-93	1-26	0-14	1-3	0-7	3-16	0-4	0-0	2-23	7.5	- 44.46
R A Fahey	7-40	1-16	1-6	0-2	2-4	0-1	2-4	0-0	1-7	17.5	+ 23.50
J M Jefferson	6-60	3-22	0-11	0-1	1-8	1-7	0-4	0-0	1-7	10.0	- 27.50
Ferdy Murphy	6-72	1-18	1-11	0-2	0-11	3-22	1-5	0-0	0-3	8.3	- 46.00
F Kirby	5-34	0-7	1-5	0-4	1-2	3-11	0-4	0-0	0-1	14.7	+ 53.25
P Beaumont	4-55	1-24	0-5	0-1	0-7	3-7	0-3	0-0	0-8	7.3	- 29.00
N B Mason	4-39	1-9	0-12	1-2	1-2	1-12	0-2	0-0	0-0	10.3	- 21.75
G A Swinbank	4-39	1-11	0-6	0-2	0-2	2-8	0-0	0-0	1-10	10.3	- 17.63
W Storey	3-44	0-11	2-24	0-1	0-0	1-6	0-1	0-0	0-1	6.8	- 15.00
M E Sowersby	3-78	0-27	3-29	0-11	0-5	0-1	0-1	0-0	0-4	3.8	- 51.50
J J Quinn	3-19	2-8	0-4	0-0	0-0	0-2	1-2	0-0	0-3	15.8	- 4.92
D M Forster	3-7	1-2	0-0	0-0	0-0	1-4	0-0	0-0	1-1	42.9	+ 25.50
N G Richards	3-14	0-4	1-4	1-1	0-1	0-2	0-0	0-0	1-2	21.4	- 0.83
James Moffatt	3-21	0-4	3-12	0-1	0-0	0-1	0-1	0-0	0-2	14.3	+ 3.50
G M Moore	2-66	1-35	0-11	0-5	1-8	0-2	0-2	0-0	0-3	3.0	- 46.00
J Mackie	2-31	0-7	1-10	0-0	0-4	1-5	0-3	0-0	0-2	6.5	- 15.25
M C Chapman	2-23	0-5	0-6	1-5	1-4	0-0	0-2	0-0	0-1	8.7	+ 7.00
Mrs E Slack	2-31	0-5	1-16	0-2	0-1	1-5	0-0	0-0	0-2	6.5	- 16.00
T P Tate	2-12	1-6	0-0	0-0	1-1	0-0	0-0	0-1	0-4	16.7	- 8.47
J L Spearing	2-4	1-1	0-1	0-0	0-1	1-1	0-0	0-0	0-0	50.0	+ 1.95
P C Haslam	2-18	2-13	0-4	0-0	0-0	0-0	0-1	0-0	0-0	11.1	- 9.13
P Bowen	2-5	0-1	1-1	0-0	0-1	0-0	0-1	0-0	1-1	40.0	+ 4.00
A Parker	2-17	1-3	0-4	0-0	0-0	1-5	0-0	0-0	0-1	11.8	- 2.25

LEADING JUMPS TRAINERS AT CHELTENHAM

	Total W-R	Nov Hdle	H'cap Hdle	Other Hdle	Nov Chase	H'cap Chase	Other Chase	Hunter Chase	N.H. Flat	Per£1 Level centstake	
M C Pipe	79-641	12-95	22-218	7-102	14-38	23-167	3-53	1-3	1-13	12.3	- 21.20
P F Nicholls	57-361	8-39	11-55	6-32	11-42	11-122	6-54	5-20	1-8	15.8	- 11.59
P J Hobbs	28-277	6-46	7-84	10-39	1-19	2-79	2-14	0-2	1-9	10.1	- 127.52
Jonjo O'Neill	28-213	7-35	5-62	6-49	5-13	2-37	3-20	1-2	2-16	13.1	+ 6.25
N J Henderson	24-219	2-34	2-41	1-25	1-11	14-78	2-22	0-0	2-12	11.0	- 24.72
A King	12-122	3-28	0-31	5-29	0-5	3-25	1-4	0-0	0-6	9.8	- 42.17
N A Twiston-Davies	11-214	2-48	2-33	0-14	4-30	3-62	0-13	0-1	0-18	5.1	- 147.84
Miss Venetia Williams	11-148	3-18	1-37	1-19	1-11	5-62	0-6	0-1	0-3	7.4	- 55.42
Miss H C Knight	9-128	0-21	0-11	0-9	2-15	3-37	3-26	0-0	1-11	7.0	- 81.69
Ferdy Murphy	9-97	1-4	1-18	0-9	0-8	6-41	1-22	0-0	0-2	9.3	+ 27.50
H D Daly	9-63	1-4	0-7	1-4	1-6	5-32	1-9	0-0	0-2	14.3	+ 9.25
R H Alner	6-46	0-6	0-8	1-6	2-6	3-16	0-7	0-1	0-1	13.0	- 13.20
F Doumen	5-45	1-8	0-2	2-16	0-1	2-12	0-5	0-0	0-1	11.1	- 10.12
J Howard Johnson	5-51	3-13	0-12	1-11	0-2	0-4	1-10	0-0	0-1	9.8	+ 40.83

	Total W-R	Nov Hdle	H'cap Hdle	Other Hdle	Nov Chase	H'cap Chase	Other Chase	Hunter Chase	N.H. Flat	Per£1 centstake	Level	
E J O'Grady	5-30	1-8	1-4	1-5	0-0	0-2	0-7	0-3	2-3	16.7	+	8.83
E Bolger	5-18	0-0	0-0	0-0	0-0	3-10	2-6	0-2	0-0	27.8	+	9.63
Ian Williams	5-84	4-17	0-33	0-10	1-4	0-21	0-2	0-0	0-1	6.0	-	36.50
Mrs John Harrington	4-24	0-4	1-3	0-4	0-1	0-4	3-7	0-0	0-1	16.7	-	1.25
P Bowen	4-29	1-6	2-7	1-5	0-0	0-7	0-5	0-0	0-1	13.8	-	18.10
D T Hughes	4-23	1-5	1-3	3-9	0-0	0-2	0-7	0-0	0-0	17.4	+	33.50
J R Fanshawe	4-23	1-7	0-5	2-9	1-2	0-1	0-0	0-0	0-0	17.4	+	0.13
T R George	4-84	1-14	1-14	0-8	0-15	2-20	0-9	0-0	0-6	4.8	-	52.25
H Morrison	4-31	0-5	0-4	0-7	0-1	3-10	0-1	0-0	1-3	12.9	-	7.75
Mrs M Reveley	3-30	2-3	0-10	0-6	0-3	0-6	0-0	0-0	1-6	10.0	-	11.00
K Bishop	3-19	0-1	2-7	1-3	0-1	1-7	0-1	0-0	0-1	15.8	+	12.50
P C Haslam	3-17	1-7	1-5	0-1	0-0	1-4	0-0	0-0	0-0	17.6	-	3.42
W P Mullins	3-69	0-11	0-4	1-12	0-1	0-10	1-14	0-2	1-15	4.3	-	21.50
M F Harris	3-30	2-11	0-4	0-4	0-2	0-3	1-4	0-1	0-1	10.0	+	17.50
Noel T Chance	3-27	1-2	1-8	0-4	0-1	0-2	0-3	0-1	1-6	11.1	-	15.92
Nool Meade	3-53	1-15	0-10	1-8	0-1	1-8	0-10	0-1	0-2	5.7	-	24.59
C R Egerton	3-32	2-9	0-8	0-6	1-3	0-1	0-2	0-0	0-5	9.4	+	15.12

LEADING JUMPS TRAINERS AT CHEPSTOW

	Total W-R	Nov Hdle	H'cap Hdle	Other Hdle	Nov Chase	H'cap Chase	Other Chase	Hunter Chase	N.H. Flat	Per£1 centstake	Level	
P F Nicholls	69-248	12-39	8-46	7-39	10-20	18-62	6-15	1-2	7-27	27.8	+	3.60
M C Pipe	37-218	4-36	8-67	9-42	6-13	5-49	3-6	0-0	2-7	17.0	-	91.03
P J Hobbs	30-139	8-29	4-37	3-18	2-10	8-32	3-3	0-0	3-11	21.6	+	4.65
N A Twiston-Davies	22-118	2-17	2-20	5-23	1-8	6-33	1-1	0-0	5-16	18.6	-	1.84
Jonjo O'Neill	16-113	3-24	5-36	2-12	0-4	4-20	0-2	0-0	2-15	14.2	-	30.58
R H Alner	15-120	3-28	1-22	1-11	3-10	7-40	0-5	0-0	0-4	12.5	-	7.75
Miss Venetia Williams	11-99	1-17	2-23	4-17	0-3	4-34	0-1	0-0	0-4	11.1	-	39.18
C L Tizzard	9-74	0-8	0-7	2-10	1-7	3-26	1-2	0-0	2-14	12.2	-	17.43
Evan Williams	8-70	2-13	0-8	1-17	1-9	0-12	0-5	4-4	0-2	11.4	+	17.42
A King	8-32	2-5	3-11	1-6	1-2	1-3	0-1	0-0	0-5	25.0	+	12.95
R Lee	7-55	1-7	2-8	0-5	1-1	2-26	1-6	0-1	0-1	12.7	-	3.92
T R George	7-51	1-11	0-6	2-9	0-3	2-16	0-2	1-1	1-3	13.7	-	14.05
P Bowen	6-36	2-8	2-5	0-6	0-2	2-10	0-2	0-0	0-4	16.7	-	5.92
J G Portman	6-22	0-4	2-5	1-3	1-1	2-6	0-2	0-0	0-1	27.3	+	22.50
N J Henderson	5-33	0-11	0-5	2-2	0-5	0-2	1-2	0-0	2-6	15.2	-	7.25
J A B Old	5-71	3-21	0-12	0-13	0-1	2-19	0-1	0-0	0-5	7.0	-	33.50
Noel T Chance	5-27	0-6	2-5	0-4	0-0	0-1	0-1	0-0	3-10	18.5	+	3.88
B J Llewellyn	5-53	2-17	0-13	1-16	0-2	2-5	0-0	0-0	0-0	9.4	-	12.92
C Roberts	5-37	1-8	3-13	1-9	0-0	0-0	0-3	0-0	0-4	13.5	+	61.50
H D Daly	5-41	2-12	0-1	0-7	3-6	0-11	0-1	0-0	0-3	12.2	-	24.50
D Burchell	4-61	2-11	2-26	0-9	0-1	0-12	0-0	0-0	0-2	6.6	+	63.00
R T Phillips	4-36	0-5	1-3	0-7	1-1	1-9	0-5	0-0	1-0	11.1	+	9.87
A W Carroll	4-29	2-12	1-8	0-2	0-2	1-5	0-0	0-0	0-0	13.8	+	8.00
Mrs M Reveley	3-8	0-1	0-1	2-4	0-0	0-1	0-0	0-0	1-1	37.5	+	3.08
R J Hodges	3-31	0-4	2-11	1-5	0-1	0-7	0-1	0-0	0-2	9.7	+	6.00
R Dickin	3-37	0-2	0-4	1-11	0-0	2-17	0-2	0-0	0-1	8.1	-	9.00
C Tinkler	3-8	0-1	1-3	1-2	0-0	0-0	0-0	0-0	1-2	37.5	+	21.25
N R Mitchell	3-37	0-2	1-5	0-3	0-3	2-19	0-1	0-0	0-4	8.1	+	5.00
R H Buckler	3-54	0-6	0-10	1-5	0-2	2-21	0-2	0-0	0-8	5.6	-	19.00
M J M Evans	3-17	0-0	0-2	0-0	0-1	3-13	0-1	0-0	0-0	17.6	+	4.33
Dr P Pritchard	3-50	0-7	1-13	0-8	0-2	2-18	0-2	0-0	0-0	6.0	-	11.00

LEADING JUMPS TRAINERS AT DONCASTER

	Total W-R	Nov Hdle	H'cap Hdle	Other Hdle	Nov Chase	H'cap Chase	Other Chase	Hunter Chase	N.H. Flat	Per£1 Level centstake	
Jonjo O'Neill	14-42	4-13	7-15	1-1	2-6	0-4	0-0	0-0	0-3	33.3	+ 16.95
M C Pipe	13-43	2-7	1-8	2-3	4-4	3-17	0-2	0-0	1-2	30.2	+ 0.49
Miss Venetia Williams	10-47	2-7	0-10	1-2	1-6	6-22	0-0	0-0	0-0	21.3	+ 20.00
T D Easterby	10-43	3-9	0-7	1-3	1-4	1-12	0-1	0-0	4-7	23.3	+ 65.73
Mrs M Reveley	9-103	1-19	2-28	1-17	2-6	1-23	1-3	0-0	1-7	8.7	- 14.20
N J Henderson	8-40	2-10	2-11	0-2	3-8	0-3	0-3	0-0	1-3	20.0	- 14.56
P J Hobbs	7-18	2-5	0-2	0-0	0-3	2-5	3-3	0-0	0-0	38.9	+ 13.38
Mrs S J Smith	7-92	2-17	3-18	0-8	1-10	1-28	0-3	0-0	0-8	7.6	- 13.13
A King	7-44	3-20	1-6	0-3	2-6	1-6	0-1	0-0	0-2	15.9	+ 4.82
S Gollings	6-39	2-16	2-12	0-0	0-2	1-2	0-0	0-0	1-7	15.4	- 4.50
T P Tate	5-16	1-3	0-0	1-1	0-0	2-6	0-0	0-0	1-6	31.3	+ 9.25
J Howard Johnson	5-24	1-7	1-6	0-0	2-2	1-6	0-0	0-0	0-3	20.8	- 5.67
Ferdy Murphy	5-70	1-24	0-4	0-3	2-11	2-22	0-3	0-0	0-3	7.1	- 49.00
P F Nicholls	5-25	0-2	1-2	0-0	1-5	2-14	1 2	0-0	0-0	20.0	+ 1.83
J Mackie	4-41	1-11	1-15	0-3	1-4	1-5	0-1	0-0	0-2	9.8	- 18.50
K C Bailey	4-23	0-6	0-4	0-1	1-4	2-5	1-3	0-0	0-0	17.4	+ 3.75
N B Mason	4-22	0-6	2-5	0-2	0-2	2-6	0-0	0-0	0-1	18.2	+ 0.38
C J Mann	4-20	3-10	0-4	0-1	0-1	1-3	0-0	0-0	0-0	20.0	+ 17.25
T R George	4-20	1-6	2-3	0-0	0-6	1-4	0-1	0-0	0-0	20.0	+ 19.50
M Pitman	4-19	2-6	0-2	0-0	1-4	1-5	0-1	0-0	0-1	21.1	+ 11.50
H D Daly	4-24	0-8	1-3	1-1	0-6	2-4	0-0	0-0	0-2	16.7	- 3.25
G M Moore	3-22	2-12	0-1	0-1	0-2	0-3	0-2	0-0	1-1	13.6	+ 15.00
P Beaumont	3-31	1-10	0-0	0-2	1-8	0-4	1-4	0-0	0-3	9.7	- 11.80
O Sherwood	3-26	2-11	1-2	0-1	0-6	0-2	0-3	0-0	0-1	11.5	- 14.70
P C Haslam	3-10	0-2	1-2	2-4	0-0	0-1	0-0	0-0	0-1	30.0	+ 1.75
Noel T Chance	3-9	1-2	1-2	1-2	0-1	0-1	0-0	0-0	0-1	33.3	+ 1.33
R T Phillips	3-20	1-7	0-5	0-2	1-2	0-1	0-0	0-0	1-3	15.0	- 6.62
K G Reveley	3-37	1-11	1-12	1-5	0-1	0-0	0-3	0-0	0-5	8.1	- 8.00
P R Webber	3-32	0-10	0-1	0-1	0-8	2-8	1-1	0-0	0-3	9.4	- 9.00
R C Guest	3-38	0-8	0-10	0-1	1-5	2-11	0-1	0-0	0-2	7.9	- 22.25
O Brennan	2-42	1-13	0-3	0-4	1-6	0-8	0-2	0-0	0-6	4.8	- 33.75

LEADING JUMPS TRAINERS AT EXETER

	Total W-R	Nov Hdle	H'cap Hdle	Other Hdle	Nov Chase	H'cap Chase	Other Chase	Hunter Chase	N.H. Flat	Per£1 Level centstake	
P J Hobbs	67-315	26-101	7-66	2-13	12-52	8-55	10-16	0-0	2-12	21.3	- 43.12
M C Pipe	57-365	14-120	12-119	4-17	14-34	6-45	3-13	0-0	4-17	15.6	- 66.85
P F Nicholls	38-206	12-60	6-25	2-7	9-44	5-36	1-12	1-5	2-17	18.4	- 64.61
R H Alner	23-208	10-61	2-30	0-8	1-27	7-60	2-13	0-0	1-9	11.1	+ 31.95
Miss H C Knight	17-90	7-34	0-3	0-5	4-26	3-12	2-4	0-0	1-6	18.9	+ 23.58
J D Frost	17-181	5-77	3-41	2-11	2-15	4-14	1-6	0-0	0-17	9.4	- 33.75
K Bishop	16-102	4-24	10-37	0-4	1-8	1-18	0-3	0-0	0-8	15.7	+ 26.52
Miss Venetia Williams	13-80	4-20	7-26	1-5	1-9	0-19	0-1	0-0	0-0	16.3	- 28.81
C L Tizzard	12-92	2-22	0-8	0-3	5-22	3-26	0-4	0-0	2-7	13.0	+ 21.38
N A Twiston-Davies	11-93	2-31	3-17	1-5	0-4	4-23	0-3	0-0	1-10	11.8	- 16.75
A King	11-63	3-23	2-16	1-5	2-9	2-6	1-2	0-0	0-2	17.5	- 13.11
R J Hodges	9-105	6-33	2-33	0-2	0-11	1-10	0-2	0-0	0-14	8.6	- 14.43
Jonjo O'Neill	9-70	4-21	3-19	0-6	0-5	1-9	0-1	0-1	1-8	12.9	- 0.30
Mrs S D Williams	8-69	3-26	4-20	0-4	1-15	0-1	0-2	0-0	0-1	11.6	+ 66.70

Name	Total W-R	Nov Hdle	H'cap Hdle	Other Hdle	Nov Chase	H'cap Chase	Other Chase	Hunter Chase	N.H. Flat	Per£1 Level centstake	
N J Henderson	8-38	3-13	1-6	0-2	1-4	2-3	0-4	0-0	1-6	21.1	+ 12.72
Miss E C Lavelle	8-57	3-20	1-14	0-3	1-5	3-9	0-2	0-0	0-4	14.0	- 7.27
J W Mullins	7-107	4-41	1-23	1-6	0-10	0-8	0-8	0-0	1-11	6.5	- 15.50
T R George	7-41	1-13	1-5	0-2	2-7	2-11	1-3	0-0	0-0	17.1	+ 11.91
Ian Williams	7-50	1-19	5-16	0-2	0-2	1-6	0-3	0-1	0-1	14.0	- 22.23
H D Daly	7-40	2-9	2-3	0-2	0-10	2-10	0-2	0-1	1-3	17.5	- 4.26
J C Tuck	6-54	2-25	4-23	0-1	0-1	0-2	0-0	0-0	0-2	11.1	- 5.50
G B Balding	5-45	2-17	0-7	0-1	2-8	1-9	0-0	0-0	0-3	11.1	+ 36.75
M Bradstock	5-12	1-4	0-0	0-1	0-0	3-5	0-0	0-0	1-2	41.7	+ 22.75
Mrs L C Taylor	5-22	0-2	2-5	0-1	1-5	1-7	1-1	0-0	0-1	22.7	+ 27.00
Nick Williams	5-34	0-11	0-7	0-0	1-6	3-7	0-1	0-0	1-2	14.7	+ 14.50
Mrs A M Thorpe	5-28	1-11	4-12	0-0	0-3	0-2	0-0	0-0	0-0	17.9	+ 39.00
R Lee	4-35	2-6	0-10	0-0	0-5	1-10	0-2	1-2	0-0	11.4	- 14.25
R G Frost	4-37	1-17	2-10	0-1	1-4	0-5	0-0	0-0	0-0	10.8	- 15.27
K C Bailey	4-29	1-6	0-3	1-3	0-2	2-14	0-0	0-0	0-1	13.8	- 10.25
R H Buckler	4-64	1-23	1-13	0-3	0-6	0-7	0-4	0-0	2-8	6.3	+ 41.00
P Bowen	4-32	0-8	3-13	0-0	0-2	1-6	0-1	0-0	0-2	12.5	+ 6.75

LEADING JUMPS TRAINERS AT FAKENHAM

	Total W-R	Nov Hdle	H'cap Hdle	Other Hdle	Nov Chase	H'cap Chase	Other Chase	Hunter Chase	N.H. Flat	Per£1 Level centstake	
Ferdy Murphy	12-69	2-15	2-10	1-6	1-11	6-22	0-2	0-0	0-3	17.4	- 5.82
Mrs P Sly	10-58	2-8	1-14	1-5	3-8	1-13	1-2	1-2	0-6	17.2	+ 62.38
M J Gingell	9-160	1-33	3-56	0-26	2-13	3-24	0-1	0-0	0-7	5.6	- 97.75
Miss Venetia Williams	9-50	0-8	1-6	3-5	2-9	2-16	0-4	0-0	1-2	18.0	- 13.39
N J Henderson	8-32	1-4	1-6	2-7	0-1	1-3	0-1	0-0	3-10	25.0	- 10.72
C J Mann	8-26	2-4	1-3	0-3	2-4	3-10	0-0	0-0	0-2	30.8	+ 6.00
Mrs L Wadham	8-38	4-12	3-12	0-5	1-2	0-5	0-0	0-1	0-1	21.1	+ 5.08
O Brennan	7-47	2-3	0-3	0-4	0-3	3-19	1-5	0-0	1-10	14.9	- 4.52
P F Nicholls	7-17	0-1	0-3	1-3	3-5	1-2	0-1	2-2	0-0	41.2	+ 2.70
C C Bealby	7-58	1-8	1-8	0-6	1-6	0-13	2-3	1-3	1-11	12.1	+ 15.87
A G Blackmore	6-16	2-3	4-7	0-3	0-3	0-0	0-0	0-0	0-0	37.5	+ 17.25
N B Mason	6-23	0-2	3-8	0-2	0-1	3-7	0-0	0-2	0-1	26.1	- 1.77
R C Guest	6-46	0-4	1-16	0-6	1-3	4-17	0-0	0-0	0-0	13.0	- 19.00
Jonjo O'Neill	5-17	0-4	1-2	2-5	0-2	1-2	1-1	0-0	0-1	29.4	+ 2.31
G Prodromou	5-47	0-10	1-15	1-6	1-5	2-10	0-0	0-0	0-1	10.6	- 13.00
Heather Dalton	5-27	0-1	0-6	0-4	2-2	3-11	0-0	0-1	0-2	18.5	+ 10.04
K A Morgan	4-43	1-10	2-20	0-1	0-2	1-4	0-0	0-0	0-6	9.3	- 9.50
H Alexander	4-16	0-0	4-10	0-4	0-2	0-0	0-0	0-0	0-0	25.0	+ 38.50
Noel T Chance	4-14	1-2	0-1	1-6	1-2	0-0	0-0	0-0	1-3	28.6	- 1.75
Ian Williams	4-21	1-5	0-5	0-0	2-5	1-5	0-1	0-0	0-0	19.0	- 5.02
N A Twiston-Davies	3-13	0-0	1-1	0-1	1-2	0-3	0-1	0-0	1-2	23.1	- 7.61
M C Chapman	3-40	1-7	1-15	1-5	0-4	0-8	0-1	0-0	0-0	7.5	22.25
J M Jefferson	3-13	1-2	1-3	0-1	1-3	0-2	0-0	0-0	0-2	23.1	- 0.00
Mrs S Lamyman	3-41	0-4	3-22	0-7	0-2	0-1	0-0	0-0	0-5	7.3	- 20.50
M Bradstock	3-6	0-0	1-2	0-0	0-1	2-3	0-0	0-0	0-0	50.0	+ 9.88
J S Smith	3-11	0-3	1-2	0-0	0-1	2-5	0-0	0-0	0-0	27.3	+ 5.50
J M Turner	3-26	0-0	0-0	0-0	0-0	0-0	0-0	3-26	0-0	11.5	- 13.25
J R Cornwall	3-36	0-1	0-3	0-1	1-7	2-23	0-1	0-0	0-0	8.3	- 17.50
Mrs J R Buckley	3-11	0-2	0-0	0-0	0-0	3-8	0-0	0-0	0-1	27.3	+ 16.17
K F Clutterbuck	3-32	0-5	2-13	0-3	0-1	0-5	1-2	0-0	0-3	9.4	+ 21.00
D E Cantillon	3-8	2-4	0-0	0-3	0-0	1-1	0-0	0-0	0-0	37.5	+ 18.60

LEADING JUMPS TRAINERS AT FOLKSTONE

	Total W-R	Nov Hdle	H'cap Hdle	Other Hdle	Nov Chase	H'cap Chase	Other Chase	Hunter Chase	N.H. Flat	Per£1 Level centstake	
N J Henderson	14-32	3-7	2-3	2-9	2-2	0-1	1-3	0-0	4-7	43.8	+ 17.88
P F Nicholls	13-40	1-5	1-2	4-12	2-7	0-3	2-4	2-3	1-4	32.5	- 7.37
Miss Venetia Williams	13-58	3-15	2-3	1-8	1-9	2-15	2-3	0-0	2-5	22.4	- 6.75
R Rowe	12-97	2-28	3-13	0-3	5-15	2-29	0-3	0-0	0-6	12.4	+ 2.25
M Pitman	12-57	6-22	0-1	3-9	0-2	1-7	1-4	0-0	1-12	21.1	- 6.72
M C Pipe	11-36	3-17	4-5	3-8	0-1	0-2	0-1	0-0	1-2	30.6	- 3.76
G L Moore	10-92	4-20	0-16	3-18	1-11	1-15	1-9	0-0	0-3	10.9	- 26.88
Miss A M N'ton-Smith	9-67	0-10	2-12	2-10	0-7	4-22	0-2	1-2	0-2	13.4	+ 34.00
R H Alner	8-62	2-10	0-6	1-4	3-9	1-15	0-8	1-3	0-7	12.9	- 25.94
O Sherwood	6-29	0-5	1-3	1-2	0-1	0-7	1-5	0-0	3-6	20.7	+ 8.38
R T Phillips	6-32	2-8	1-2	0-9	0-2	1-4	0-3	0-1	2-3	18.8	- 0.52
Miss E C Lavelle	6-23	0-7	3-6	1-1	1-2	1-4	0-1	0-0	0-2	26.1	- 0.50
C J Mann	5-27	0-5	1-4	2-8	0-1	1-5	1-2	0-0	0-2	18.5	- 6.17
L Wells	5-40	2-10	0-7	0-3	0-5	2-9	1-3	0-0	0-3	12.5	+ 45.55
J S King	4-15	0-1	0-1	0-0	1-4	3-8	0-1	0-0	0-0	26.7	+ 0.58
Jonjo O'Neill	4-31	0-7	1-3	1-6	1-2	0-6	1-3	0-0	0-4	12.9	+ 2.73
D M Grissell	4-46	2-14	0-5	0-7	1-4	0-4	0-0	1-7	0-5	8.7	+ 70.37
Noel T Chance	4-27	1-9	0-3	2-6	0-0	0-1	0-0	0-0	1-8	14.8	- 9.00
P R Chamings	4-14	0-1	0-1	0-0	0-3	4-7	0-2	0-0	0-0	28.6	+ 3.50
J W Mullins	4-60	1-10	0-4	0-5	0-8	1-10	2-8	0-1	0-14	6.7	- 32.75
A King	4-24	1-7	0-1	0-3	0-2	0-2	1-3	0-0	2-6	16.7	- 9.46
A M Hales	4-18	1-7	1-3	0-2	0-2	2-4	0-0	0-0	0-0	22.2	+ 9.00
N J Gifford	4-17	2-6	0-0	0-0	0-0	0-2	0-4	2-5	0-0	23.5	+ 3.72
M J Hogan	4-12	0-0	4-7	0-0	0-3	0-1	0-1	0-0	0-0	33.3	+ 8.75
D J Wintle	3-35	0-9	1-10	0-7	1-2	0-5	0-0	0-0	1-2	8.6	- 7.00
D L Williams	3-16	0-3	0-1	0-0	0-2	1-5	0-0	2-5	0-0	18.8	- 3.00
J A B Old	3-21	0-3	0-4	0-2	0-1	2-5	0-0	0-0	1-6	14.3	- 3.00
T P McGovern	3-22	0-4	0-4	1-3	1-3	1-4	0-3	0-1	0-0	13.6	- 9.31
P Bowen	3-8	0-1	1-1	0-1	0-0	2-3	0-1	0-0	0-1	37.5	+ 11.00
M F Harris	3-21	0-6	2-5	0-2	0-2	0-2	0-1	1-2	0-1	14.3	- 8.75
Ferdy Murphy	3-18	0-3	0-2	0-1	0-2	1-5	1-4	0-0	1-1	16.7	+ 1.25

LEADING JUMPS TRAINERS AT FONTWELL

	Total W-R	Nov Hdle	H'cap Hdle	Other Hdle	Nov Chase	H'cap Chase	Other Chase	Hunter Chase	N.H. Flat	Per£1 Level centstake	
G L Moore	57-266	10-60	18-78	13-43	2-18	6-44	7-16	0-0	1-7	21.4	+ 18.76
M C Pipe	45-182	15-43	9-58	8-37	4-16	3-13	1-6	0-0	5-9	24.7	- 26.95
P F Nicholls	39-150	5-25	5-15	4-22	13-30	3-27	3-11	3-5	3-15	26.0	- 20.35
B G Powell	22-149	8-35	1-36	5-29	2-10	2-20	4-9	0-0	0-10	14.8	+ 146.74
R Rowe	20-164	1-30	8-39	3-18	2-16	6-51	0-3	0-0	0-7	12.2	+ 13.50
P J Hobbs	17-97	3-18	2-19	2-16	4-11	5-21	1-6	0-0	0-6	17.5	- 30.14
C L Tizzard	15-94	0-5	0-7	2-5	5-16	6-37	0-12	0-0	2-12	16.0	- 18.39
N J Henderson	13-71	3-21	2-10	2-18	2-5	1-4	1-2	0-0	2-11	18.3	- 11.21
Miss Venetia Williams	13-92	0-6	3-19	0-13	5-18	1-24	4-7	0-0	0-5	14.1	- 20.28
L Wells	11-95	2-17	1-21	0-10	1-8	6-19	0-7	1-1	0-12	11.6	- 31.32
P Bowen	10-50	0-7	2-19	1-3	1-3	6-14	0-1	0-0	0-3	20.0	+ 19.33
J W Mullins	10-110	2-24	1-18	1-16	2-8	0-13	1-8	2-4	1-19	9.1	- 9.04
C J Mann	10-74	3-24	4-18	1-16	0-3	2-9	0-2	0-0	0-2	13.5	- 8.09
A King	9-53	6-16	1-14	1-13	0-1	0-1	0-1	0-0	1-7	17.0	+ 1.86

S Dow	8-30	4-15	2-5	0-5	2-3	0-1	0-0	0-0	0-1	26.7	-	0.02
Miss H C Knight	8-35	5-16	0-0	1-7	1-3	0-5	1-3	0-0	0-1	22.9	+	15.73
A Ennis	8-54	0-11	0-1	0-5	1-2	7-27	0-4	0-0	0-4	14.8	+	18.50
Ian Williams	8-30	3-7	0-2	3-11	0-2	1-4	1-3	0-0	0-1	26.7	-	6.60
N J Gifford	8-46	3-8	1-8	0-7	0-2	3-12	0-2	0-2	1-5	17.4	+	14.00
R H Buckler	7-88	0-16	1-15	0-7	2-10	3-28	0-6	0-0	1-6	8.0	-	40.25
R H Alner	7-84	1-11	1-10	0-10	1-7	2-32	2-6	0-0	0-8	8.3	-	60.30
V R A Dartnall	7-28	1-6	1-7	1-2	0-0	2-7	0-1	0-0	2-5	25.0	+	12.70
Dr P Pritchard	6-68	0-4	1-15	0-6	0-10	5-30	0-3	0-0	0-0	8.8	-	32.75
B J Llewellyn	6-34	1-6	3-13	2-11	0-1	0-1	0-0	0-0	0-2	17.6	+	32.33
Miss Sheena West	6-32	1-10	2-12	3-8	0-0	0-1	0-0	0-0	0-1	18.8	+	57.75
M Pitman	6-38	1-11	0-8	0-4	2-6	1-5	0-0	0-0	2-4	15.8	-	5.37
O Sherwood	5-63	1-19	1-10	1-11	0-3	1-5	0-5	0-0	1-10	7.9	-	35.13
Jonjo O'Neill	5-47	0-14	1-10	1-6	1-5	1-7	1-2	0-0	0-3	10.6	-	27.13
G Wareham	5-16	0-1	2-7	0-1	2-2	1-5	0-0	0-0	0-0	31.3	+	12.10
P R Hedger	5-51	0-8	2-22	1-10	0-4	2-5	0-1	0-0	0-1	9.8	-	24.50
C R Egerton	5-14	1-1	1-4	0-3	1-1	0-0	0-0	0-0	2-5	35.7	+	6.13

LEADING JUMPS TRAINERS AT HAYDOCK

	Total W-R	Nov Hdle	H'cap Hdle	Other Hdle	Nov Chase	H'cap Chase	Other Chase	Hunter Chase	N.H. Flat	Per£1 Level centstake		
Jonjo O'Neill	30-140	8-41	12-48	2-10	1-9	0-15	2-3	0-0	5-14	21.4	-	23.46
Mrs S J Smith	29-160	5-47	5-26	4-13	6-20	8-42	1-1	0-0	0-11	18.1	+	71.81
M C Pipe	18-136	2-19	4-61	1-10	6-12	4-28	0-2	0-0	1-4	13.2	-	34.73
Miss Venetia Williams	17-86	3-11	4-27	0-0	7-16	3-30	0-0	0-0	0-2	19.8	+	1.16
P J Hobbs	13-74	3-20	3-22	1-1	2-5	4-21	0-0	0-0	0-5	17.6	-	14.67
N A Twiston Davies	13-95	4-23	3-21	1-3	1-13	1-24	0-2	0-0	3-9	13.7	+	6.71
Mrs M Reveley	12-92	3-23	6-41	2-11	0-2	1-11	0-0	0-0	0-4	13.0	+	1.00
D McCain	11-97	5-22	2-15	0-3	2-23	2-24	0-0	0-0	0-10	11.3	+	28.75
J Howard Johnson	10-31	5-11	1-7	2-4	0-1	2-8	0-0	0-0	0-0	32.3	+	14.02
A King	9-48	3-11	3-16	0-2	0-1	1-7	0-0	0-0	2-11	18.8	+	34.25
N J Henderson	8-44	2-10	0-8	1-1	3-7	0-9	0-0	0-0	2-9	18.2	-	19.61
Ferdy Murphy	7-81	3-28	0-9	0-4	2-8	1-16	0-4	0-0	1-12	8.6	-	48.79
T R George	7-45	2-9	2-11	1-7	2-7	0-10	0-0	0-0	0-1	15.6	+	4.00
J M Jefferson	6-53	2-19	1-14	0-1	0-1	1-8	0-0	0-0	2-10	11.3	-	18.50
S A Brookshaw	6-64	2-21	2-10	0-3	0-11	2-12	0-0	0-0	0-7	9.4	+	59.00
P R Webber	6-23	1-5	0-3	0-0	2-5	2-5	0-0	0-0	1-5	26.1	+	24.30
N G Richards	6-55	1-14	4-24	0-9	1-2	0-0	0-0	0-0	0-6	10.9	-	28.97
K C Bailey	5-35	0-15	0-0	1-5	0-3	4-9	0-0	0-0	0-3	14.3	-	6.50
L Lungo	5-81	1-18	1-38	1-2	0-6	0-7	0-0	0-0	2-10	6.2	-	60.63
H D Daly	5-71	0-22	0-7	0-4	3-8	2-13	0-1	0-1	0-15	7.0	-	19.58
R H Alner	4-28	1-6	0-0	1-1	1-4	0-8	1-2	0-0	0-1	14.3	+	6.75
M Todhunter	4-32	1-8	1-7	0-0	0-3	2-8	0-3	0-0	0-3	12.5	I	2.46
T D Easterby	4-52	1-19	1-7	0-2	1-4	1-17	0-0	0-0	0-3	7.7	-	25.25
C Grant	4-21	2-7	1-8	0-0	0-0	0-2	0-0	1-3	0-1	19.0	+	14.50
G M Moore	3-46	0-9	1-5	0-3	0-7	2-18	0-0	0-0	0-4	6.5	-	31.50
R Lee	3-29	0-1	0-10	1-3	1-5	1-8	0-0	0-1	0-1	10.3	-	4.00
J Mackie	3-34	0-10	3-16	0-1	0-0	0-0	0-0	0-0	0-7	8.8	-	12.00
M Scudamore	3-24	0-7	0-3	1-4	0-2	1-4	0-0	0-0	1-4	12.5	-	0.87
P C Haslam	3-16	2-7	0-3	0-0	0-1	0-3	0-0	0-0	1-2	18.8	+	4.20
John R Upson	3-21	0-6	0-2	0-0	0-0	3-12	0-0	0-0	0-0	14.3	-	2.75
P F Nicholls	3-36	1-4	0-11	0-0	1-7	1-10	0-1	0-3	0-0	8.3	-	22.09

LEADING JUMPS TRAINERS AT HEREFORD

	Total W-R	Nov Hdle	H'cap Hdle	Other Hdle	Nov Chase	H'cap Chase	Other Chase	Hunter Chase	N.H. Flat	Per£1 Level centstake	
M C Pipe	31-111	9-35	4-19	9-31	4-8	2-6	3-8	0-0	0-4	27.9	- 9.13
P J Hobbs	26-116	9-31	4-24	2-6	3-19	1-20	5-11	0-0	2-5	22.4	- 21.70
A King	19-82	8-29	2-14	4-12	2-8	2-6	1-4	0-0	0-9	23.2	+ 44.87
N A Twiston-Davies	17-139	1-29	2-17	4-22	1-19	6-31	0-6	0-0	3-15	12.2	- 26.41
N J Henderson	16-57	6-16	1-8	3-6	1-5	1-4	1-7	1-1	2-10	28.1	+ 24.95
P F Nicholls	15-60	7-20	1-3	2-10	1-8	1-4	3-7	0-0	0-8	25.0	- 19.82
Ian Williams	14-105	4-27	2-19	2-8	0-10	6-32	0-6	0-0	0-3	13.3	- 21.75
H D Daly	14-86	3-30	2-8	2-13	1-12	2-14	2-3	2-2	0-4	16.3	- 10.35
T R George	13-63	3-12	3-12	2-7	2-11	2-13	0-4	0-0	1-4	20.6	+ 29.00
Miss H C Knight	12-68	4-26	0-3	1-6	3-12	1-2	0-6	0-1	3-12	17.6	- 12.12
Miss Venetia Williams	11-91	3-26	2-12	0-8	1-10	2-17	1-10	0-0	2-8	12.1	- 42.09
R Lee	9-72	1-7	3-15	0-4	2-9	1-26	0-7	2-3	0-1	12.5	- 15.25
J W Mullins	9-58	1-14	0-5	1-4	2-8	2-13	1-4	0-1	2-9	15.5	+ 5.13
B G Powell	9-59	3-13	1-2	0-9	1-7	1 14	1-6	0-1	2-7	15.3	+ 6.61
R Dickin	8-119	4-24	0-14	1-18	3-21	0-26	0-8	0-0	0-8	6.7	- 61.88
Ferdy Murphy	8-42	0-8	1-4	1-7	2-6	2-14	2-3	0-0	0-0	19.0	- 17.75
D Burchell	7-78	0-23	5-33	0-4	0-2	2-14	0-1	0-0	0-1	9.0	+ 39.33
C J Down	7-53	2-15	1-6	0-9	0-2	3-11	0-4	1-2	0-4	13.2	+ 41.00
B J M Ryall	6-25	0-4	0-0	0-0	2-5	4-15	0-1	0-0	0-0	24.0	+ 67.00
O Sherwood	6-31	3-12	0-2	1-3	0-2	0-6	1-1	0-1	1-4	19.4	- 11.06
K C Bailey	6-62	1-15	0-9	1-8	1-6	2-14	0-4	0-0	1-6	9.7	- 20.75
C R Egerton	6-21	1-4	1-3	1-3	0-1	0-2	1-2	0-0	2-6	28.6	+ 3.28
Heather Dalton	6-54	1-9	0-7	0-7	2-8	2-13	0-2	0-1	1-7	11.1	+ 7.10
Miss E C Lavelle	6-32	1-10	0-3	0-2	1-3	2-7	0-2	0-0	2-5	18.8	+ 2.50
Evan Williams	6-59	1-18	1-9	0-4	2-9	2-11	0-3	0-1	0-4	10.2	- 0.67
W K Goldsworthy	6-22	0-6	0-4	1-3	0-1	1-1	0-0	4-7	0-0	27.3	+ 14.08
Miss S J Wilton	5-38	0-14	3-10	1-9	0-1	1-4	0-0	0-0	0-0	13.2	+ 35.00
M Sheppard	5-84	1-15	0-9	1-6	0-14	2-28	1-11	0-1	0-0	6.0	- 29.50
J Mackie	4-27	1-6	3-13	0-5	0-2	0-0	0-0	0-0	0-1	14.8	- 9.42
D J Wintle	4-54	0-20	1-7	0-10	1-6	2-8	0-1	0-0	0-2	7.4	- 25.50
Jonjo O'Neill	4-33	0-7	1-4	1-3	0-3	1-7	0-1	0-0	1-8	12.1	- 0.25

LEADING JUMPS TRAINERS AT HEXHAM

	Total W-R	Nov Hdle	H'cap Hdle	Other Hdle	Nov Chase	H'cap Chase	Other Chase	Hunter Chase	N.H. Flat	Per£1 Level centstake	
L Lungo	26-116	7-36	6-34	4-10	2-12	3-10	2-4	0-0	2-10	22.4	- 9.04
Ferdy Murphy	19-148	5-37	3-21	1-14	1-22	5-29	3-12	0-0	1-13	12.8	- 62.33
Mrs S J Smith	16-96	5-31	2-11	1-7	4-16	3-18	0-3	0-0	1-10	16.7	+ 13.60
R C Guest	15-104	1-17	5-24	0-8	5-17	1-28	3-5	0-0	0-5	14.4	+ 5.98
J Howard Johnson	13-84	6-31	4-23	1-10	0-4	1-5	0-3	0-0	1-8	15.5	- 28.27
M Todhunter	13-68	4-21	3-13	1-5	1-7	4-14	0-3	0-0	0-5	19.1	+ 51.18
N G Richards	13-52	3-14	3-14	0-2	4-8	1-4	1-3	0-0	1-7	25.0	+ 8.67
M W Easterby	11-81	3-23	2-17	0-6	1-5	0-7	1-6	0-1	4-16	13.6	- 45.99
J M Jefferson	10-66	6-24	0-14	0-4	1-6	0-4	1-1	0-0	2-13	15.2	+ 26.54
P Monteith	9-65	0-9	0-14	0-2	2-9	6-22	1-9	0-0	0-0	13.8	- 10.92
Miss Kate Milligan	8-85	0-7	2-16	0-6	1-14	4-31	1-7	0-0	0-4	9.4	+ 9.00
G M Moore	7-85	2-34	1-12	0-8	2-13	2-9	0-2	0-0	0-7	8.2	- 60.70
M D Hammond	7-39	2-11	2-6	0-1	1-7	1-9	1-2	0-0	0-3	17.9	- 15.59
Miss Lucinda V Russell	7-86	2-19	0-15	1-7	1-14	3-20	0-6	0-0	0-5	8.1	- 17.97

G A Swinbank	7-37	1-10	0-6	0-8	0-0	0-1	0-0	0-0	6-12	18.9	-	18.35
R Johnson	6-78	0-17	2-25	2-6	1-11	1-11	0-3	0-1	0-4	7.7	+	54.75
Mrs H O Graham	6-27	0-2	4-8	0-2	0-0	2-7	0-0	0-1	0-7	22.2	+	32.50
Miss L C Siddall	5-37	0-3	1-12	0-0	2-10	2-8	0-0	0-2	0-2	13.5	+	11.50
P C Haslam	5-16	2-5	1-6	0-2	1-1	1-2	0-0	0-0	0-0	31.3	-	0.75
A Parker	5-37	1-8	1-6	0-0	1-6	2-11	0-1	0-1	0-4	13.5	-	14.50
M A Barnes	5-79	0-17	2-18	0-9	0-10	2-14	1-6	0-0	0-5	6.3	-	20.75
J J Quinn	5-15	2-8	0-4	1-1	0-0	1-1	0-0	0-0	1-1	33.3	+	13.63
W S Coltherd	5-36	1-7	1-4	1-3	0-4	2-13	0-0	0-0	0-5	13.9	+	60.00
Mrs E Slack	4-50	0-11	2-21	0-0	0-3	1-12	0-1	0-0	1-2	8.0	-	28.25
R A Fahey	4-19	2-9	0-4	0-0	0-0	0-0	1-3	0-0	1-3	21.1	-	7.50
A Crook	4-30	0-3	1-6	0-3	1-4	2-9	0-1	0-0	0-4	13.3	+	2.75
P R Webber	4-5	4-4	0-0	0-1	0-0	0-0	0-0	0-0	0-0	80.0	+	3.57
G A Harker	4-23	0-2	0-2	0-1	0-3	0-3	0-2	0-0	4-10	17.4	+	0.50
Mrs M Reveley	3-22	1-5	0-6	0-2	1-3	0-4	0-0	0-0	1-2	13.6	-	13.62
P Beaumont	3-41	0-12	0-3	1-2	1-9	0-7	1-2	0-0	0-6	7.3	+	41.00
D McCain	3-39	1-9	2-13	0-4	0-3	0-4	0-3	0-0	0-3	7.7	+	0.75

LEADING JUMPS TRAINERS AT HUNTINGDON

	Total W-R	Nov Hdle	H'cap Hdle	Other Hdle	Nov Chase	H'cap Chase	Other Chase	Hunter Chase	N.H. Flat	Per£1 Level centstake		
N J Henderson	25-94	6-22	7-12	4-21	2-13	2-8	0-5	0-0	4-13	26.6	+	5.17
Jonjo O'Neill	25-130	6-27	6-32	0-14	7-21	3-16	0-2	1-1	2-17	19.2	-	15.86
Ian Williams	23-140	3-20	7-40	4-22	2-16	6-28	0-1	0-0	1-13	16.4	-	15.87
Miss H C Knight	18-109	1-16	0-7	1-13	4-29	4-15	4-11	0-1	4-17	16.5	-	8.49
A King	17-86	3-14	3-14	2-5	2-19	4-19	0-1	0-0	3-14	19.8	+	26.56
K C Bailey	15-131	0-17	5-34	3-14	2-23	4-30	0-1	0-0	1-12	11.5	-	27.25
Miss Venetia Williams	15-66	2-10	2-9	2-7	1-14	7-19	1-3	0-0	0-3	23.1	+	25.16
H D Daly	15-80	0-8	0-3	3-16	7-20	3-14	0-5	0-1	2-13	18.8	+	6.44
T R George	14-67	1-5	2-15	2-6	4-18	3-17	1-1	0-0	1-5	20.9	+	56.76
P J Hobbs	13-59	2-9	0-8	5-8	3-10	2-15	1-5	0-1	0-3	22.0	-	2.37
G L Moore	13-101	3-17	2-33	2-14	6-14	0-21	0-1	0-1	0-0	12.9	-	29.06
P R Webber	13-60	2-13	2-7	0-7	2-7	4-13	2-3	0-0	1-10	21.7	+	75.36
K G Reveley	11-38	1-1	5-15	0-2	1-6	0-6	1-1	0-0	3-7	28.9	+	17.93
Miss E C Lavelle	11-66	1-9	3-15	0-10	4-11	3-17	0-0	0-0	0-4	16.7	+	0.58
R Lee	9-46	0-3	0-10	0-4	3-7	5-21	1-1	0-0	0-0	19.6	+	19.08
D E Cantillon	9-25	4-8	1-1	3-7	0-2	0-1	0-1	0-0	1-5	36.0	+	31.92
C J Mann	8-49	1-12	2-12	3-6	0-3	0-11	1-3	0-0	1-2	16.3	-	6.95
M C Pipe	7-53	1-8	3-18	0-8	1-4	0-8	1-4	1-1	0-2	13.2	-	32.87
N A Twiston-Davies	7-80	2-14	2-23	0-4	1-11	0-16	0-1	0-0	2-11	8.8	-	35.65
Mrs P Sly	7-62	2-7	1-17	1-9	1-13	2-10	0-1	0-0	0-5	11.3	+	35.25
C R Egerton	7-18	3-3	2-6	1-6	1-1	0-1	0-0	0-0	0-1	38.9	+	26.00
M Pitman	7-48	0-7	2-15	2-8	0-4	1-3	0-3	0-0	2-8	14.6	-	18.20
B G Powell	7-91	0-15	1-17	0-14	0-10	4-21	0-1	0-2	2-11	7.7	-	30.50
J Mackie	6-42	2-4	3-24	0-6	1-3	0-1	0-0	0-0	0-4	14.3	+	38.50
Heather Dalton	6-48	0-7	2-8	0-9	1-6	1-7	1-1	0-0	1-10	12.5	-	10.29
J S King	5-36	0-6	0-3	0-3	1-7	3-14	1-2	0-0	0-1	13.9	-	4.39
O Sherwood	5-51	1-9	1-9	0-4	1-14	1-7	0-1	0-1	1-6	9.8	-	15.50
D L Williams	5-27	1-4	1-4	0-3	0-1	2-11	0-1	1-2	0-1	18.5	+	2.22
Ferdy Murphy	5-101	1-15	2-15	1-17	1-13	0-25	0-3	0-0	0-13	5.0	-	80.25
P F Nicholls	5-29	2-6	1-2	0-0	0-6	0-8	2-7	0-0	0-0	17.2	-	14.53
R Ford	5-20	0-1	4-8	0-3	1-2	0-5	0-0	0-0	0-1	25.0	+	17.00

LEADING JUMPS TRAINERS AT KELSO

	Total W-R	Nov Hdle	H'cap Hdle	Other Hdle	Nov Chase	H'cap Chase	Other Chase	Hunter Chase	N.H. Flat	Per£1 Level centstake	
L Lungo	36-172	11-51	9-65	7-21	3-10	3-18	1-2	1-3	1-2	20.9	- 12.89
N G Richards	27-100	12-36	9-32	2-15	1-6	2-5	0-1	1-3	0-2	27.0	- 8.79
P Monteith	21-152	7-41	8-50	2-19	0-8	3-27	0-4	1-2	0-1	13.8	- 26.68
Miss Lucinda V Russell	12-138	3-31	1-20	0-14	2-29	4-32	2-10	0-1	0-1	8.7	- 5.67
R C Guest	12-106	2-21	1-23	1-15	3-10	4-34	1-2	0-1	0-0	11.3	+ 64.48
Mrs M Reveley	11-85	4-17	2-26	2-6	0-5	1-27	1-3	0-0	1-1	12.9	- 9.11
Ferdy Murphy	11-81	3-18	0-8	3-7	1-14	3-30	1-3	0-0	0-1	13.6	- 43.49
Mrs S J Smith	10-35	3-6	2-7	0-1	1-5	2-12	2-4	0-0	0-0	28.6	+ 6.34
J M Jefferson	9-49	3-11	1-13	2-5	3-7	0-9	0-3	0-0	0-1	18.4	- 14.44
Mrs S C Bradburne	8-110	0-18	2-36	1-11	1-19	3-18	1-7	0-0	0-1	7.3	- 51.75
A C Whillans	8-92	0-24	5-30	0-12	0-4	3-18	0-1	0-0	0-3	8.7	- 48.75
A Parker	7-72	0-18	2-14	0-3	1-3	3-31	0-0	1-2	0-1	9.7	- 37.50
S J Marshall	7-23	0-2	1-2	0-3	0-1	3-10	0-1	3-4	0-0	30.4	+ 73.00
K G Reveley	6-28	2-10	0-8	1-1	1-3	2-5	0-1	0-0	0-0	21.4	1.87
M Todhunter	6-43	2-12	2-8	0-4	1-5	1-11	0-3	0-0	0-0	14.0	- 6.28
I D Easterby	6-27	0-3	1-5	1-4	3-7	1-8	0-0	0-0	0-0	22.2	- 2.75
W Storey	5-60	1-23	0-17	0-5	0-1	4-14	0-0	0-0	0-0	8.3	+ 26.50
M W Easterby	5-32	0-9	0-6	0-3	2-4	2-7	0-1	0-1	1-1	15.6	+ 6.00
R Allan	5-61	2-24	3-20	0-7	0-5	0-5	0-0	0-0	0-0	8.2	- 17.00
J I A Charlton	5-46	1-10	3-19	0-7	1-5	0-3	0-1	0-0	0-1	10.9	- 7.67
P C Haslam	5-21	4-13	0-2	0-1	1-2	0-2	0-1	0-0	0-0	23.8	+ 6.70
Mrs H O Graham	5-59	1-15	4-23	0-8	0-5	0-4	0-1	0-3	0-0	8.5	+ 16.50
J S Goldie	5-32	0-4	3-18	1-1	1-2	0-6	0-1	0-0	0-0	15.6	+ 12.75
Miss S E Forster	5-104	0-27	1-25	0-9	2-17	2-20	0-2	0-3	0-1	4.8	- 68.00
P Beaumont	4-40	1-12	0-1	0-9	0-4	1-11	2-3	0-0	0-0	10.0	- 13.00
Mrs A Hamilton	4-23	0-1	1-7	1-2	0-1	2-7	0-0	0-5	0-1	17.4	+ 7.87
R Ford	4-13	0-4	0-0	1-3	1-1	1-4	1-1	0-0	0-0	30.8	- 1.25
J Howard Johnson	4-66	2-27	2-12	0-8	0-4	0-12	0-2	0-1	0-0	6.1	- 53.20
Noel T Chance	4-5	2-3	0-0	1-1	1-1	0-0	0-0	0-0	0-0	80.0	+ 3.53
Mrs B K Thomson	4-28	0-2	0-4	0-1	0-1	4-17	0-2	0-1	0-0	14.3	+ 2.00
G T Bewley	4-10	0-0	0-0	0-0	0-0	0-0	0-0	4-10	0-0	40.0	+ 18.10

LEADING JUMPS TRAINERS AT KEMPTON

	Total W-R	Nov Hdle	H'cap Hdle	Other Hdle	Nov Chase	H'cap Chase	Other Chase	Hunter Chase	N.H. Flat	Per£1 Level centstake	
N J Henderson	30-156	6-39	5-37	2-4	9-29	4-22	0-10	0-0	4-15	19.2	+ 1.42
P J Hobbs	26-132	8-35	2-22	2-10	3-16	10-38	1-5	0-0	0-6	19.7	- 12.08
P F Nicholls	18-88	3-13	1-12	4-11	4-19	3-25	3-8	0-0	0-0	20.5	+ 6.23
Miss H C Knight	15-87	1-15	0-7	1-5	5-23	3-18	2-7	1-1	2-11	17.2	+ 9.87
M C Pipe	14-141	5-25	0-38	1-7	5-17	3-42	0-9	0-0	0-3	9.9	- 69.12
Miss Venetia Williams	13-76	1-12	3-18	1-3	4-7	4-32	0-1	0-0	0-3	17.1	+ 22.13
A King	13-69	4-23	2-13	3-9	1-7	1-8	0-0	0-0	2-9	18.8	+ 17.71
Jonjo O'Neill	12-66	3-22	5-14	2-3	1-11	0-10	0-1	0-0	1-5	18.2	- 18.92
N A Twiston-Davies	9-58	3-15	4-13	0-2	1-5	1-12	0-1	0-0	0-10	15.5	- 9.13
P R Webber	8-50	1-17	1-4	0-5	1-9	4-9	0-1	0-0	1-5	16.0	- 5.75
R H Alner	6-80	1-14	1-7	0-2	3-19	1-27	0-3	0-0	0-8	7.5	- 24.70
C J Mann	6-72	3-23	2-20	0-3	1-5	0-13	0-1	0-0	0-7	8.3	+ 18.00
F Doumen	5-23	3-8	0-2	1-3	0-2	1-3	0-3	0-0	0-2	21.7	+ 3.83
G Macaire	5-13	2-5	0-0	0-1	3-5	0-0	0-2	0-0	0-0	38.5	+ 0.88

P Bowen	4-14	0-2	3-8	0-0	0-2	1-1	0-1	0-0	0-0	28.6	+	7.83
R T Phillips	4-24	1-8	0-4	0-1	1-1	1-5	0-1	0-0	1-4	16.7	-	0.50
Ian Williams	4-31	1-4	1-13	0-1	2-2	0-9	0-0	0-0	0-2	12.9	+	19.50
Mrs M Reveley	3-27	0-3	3-14	0-3	0-2	0-4	0-0	0-0	0-1	11.1	-	4.75
G B Balding	3-23	0-4	2-8	0-1	0-5	1-5	0-0	0-0	0-0	13.0	-	7.50
Ferdy Murphy	3-25	0-2	0-5	0-0	2-7	1-9	0-1	0-0	0-1	12.0	+	5.33
R Rowe	3-42	1-16	0-8	0-0	2-7	0-8	0-0	0-0	0-3	7.1	-	7.50
T R George	3-29	1-7	1-10	0-0	0-3	1-8	0-0	0-0	0-1	10.3	+	10.00
V R A Dartnall	3 14	2-4	0-6	0-0	1-1	0-0	0-1	0-0	0-2	21.4	-	8.34
C L Tizzard	3-10	0-3	1-2	0-0	0-1	1-2	0-1	0-0	1-1	30.0	+	48.00
M Pitman	3-48	1-11	0-6	0-2	2-9	0-8	0-1	0-0	0-11	6.3	-	15.38
H D Daly	3-26	0-9	0-1	0-0	1-5	1-9	1-1	0-0	0-1	11.5	-	9.00
B G Powell	3-39	2-15	0-10	0-0	0-1	0-8	0-0	0-0	1-5	7.7	-	8.75
O Sherwood	2-17	1-4	0-2	0-0	1-6	0-3	0-1	0-0	0-1	11.8	-	13.93
R Dickin	2-20	0-7	0-0	0-1	1-4	1-6	0-0	0-0	0-2	10.0	+	2.00
C Tinkler	2-4	0-1	2-3	0-0	0-0	0-0	0-0	0-0	0-0	50.0	+	16.00
H J Manners	2-7	1-2	1-2	0-0	0-1	0-0	0-0	0-0	0-2	28.6	+	8.00

LEADING JUMPS TRAINERS AT LEICESTER

	Total W-R	Nov Hdle	H'cap Hdle	Other Hdle	Nov Chase	H'cap Chase	Other Chase	Hunter Chase	N.H. Flat	Per£1 Level centstake		
M C Pipe	16-68	5-19	3-19	5-15	0-4	2-8	1-3	0-0	0 0	23.5	+	4.91
Miss Venetia Williams	16-62	5-18	0-9	0-0	3-6	6-22	2-7	0-0	0-0	25.8	-	9.29
R H Alner	11-41	1-9	1-1	0-0	5-13	4-16	0-2	0-0	0-0	26.8	+	10.86
R Dickin	8-62	0-3	0-5	0-1	2-12	6-32	0-9	0-0	0-0	12.9	+	7.50
A King	8-36	2-10	4-8	0-1	2-9	0-6	0-2	0-0	0-0	22.2	-	1.92
N A Twiston-Davies	7-30	3-13	0-2	0-0	1-4	1-6	2-5	0-0	0-0	23.3	-	2.49
Jonjo O'Neill	7-47	1-16	1-5	0-1	3-9	2-13	0-3	0-0	0-0	14.9	-	9.55
P R Webber	7-36	0-7	0-2	1-2	4-14	1-7	1-4	0-0	0-0	19.4	I	5.51
P F Nicholls	6-14	1-2	0-0	1-2	0-2	1-2	3-6	0-0	0-0	42.9	+	1.53
Ian Williams	6-41	1-12	1-3	2-4	0-6	1-13	1-3	0-0	0-0	14.6	+	35.50
O Sherwood	5-19	3-5	0-2	1-2	1-5	0-3	0-2	0-0	0-0	26.3	+	11.33
N J Henderson	5-32	0-3	0-0	0-1	4-11	0-7	1-10	0-0	0-0	15.6	-	19.52
J A B Old	5-27	0-5	3-7	0-0	1-4	0-6	1-5	0-0	0-0	18.5	+	2.27
Heather Dalton	5-26	0-4	0-3	0-1	2-4	3-9	0-4	0-1	0-0	19.2	+	23.88
P J Hobbs	4-30	2-9	0-3	0-1	1-7	1-6	0-4	0-0	0-0	13.3	-	20.53
J Mackie	4-30	0-5	4-18	0-3	0-2	0-1	0-1	0-0	0-0	13.3	+	2.00
D J Wintle	4-32	1-8	1-14	1-5	1-1	0-4	0-0	0-0	0-0	12.5	-	9.25
W G M Turner	4-12	1-3	2-3	1-5	0-0	0-0	0-1	0-0	0-0	33.3	+	13.83
Mrs P Robeson	4-15	1-4	1-3	0-0	1-1	1-7	0-0	0-0	0-0	26.7	+	33.50
R T Phillips	4-25	2-12	0-2	0-0	1-2	1-8	0-1	0-0	0-0	16.0	-	6.80
S T Lewis	4-17	0-4	2-9	0-1	0-1	1-1	1-1	0-0	0-0	23.5	+	39.25
H D Daly	4-28	1-8	0-3	0-0	2-9	0-0	1-2	0 0	0 0	14.3		10.90
R C Guest	4-25	0-3	0-4	0-1	2-5	2-10	0-1	0-1	0-0	16.0	-	5.00
G M Moore	3-11	0-5	0-2	0-1	2-2	1-1	0-0	0-0	0-0	27.3	-	1.64
N A Gaselee	3-9	0-0	0-1	0-0	0-2	0-3	3-3	0-0	0-0	33.3	+	2.75
R Lee	3-32	1-3	0-4	0-1	1-6	1-12	0-6	0-0	0-0	9.4	+	9.50
K Bishop	3-7	0-0	0-1	0-1	0-0	3-5	0-0	0-0	0-0	42.9	+	94.50
David Pearson	3-17	0-0	0-1	0-1	0-2	2-10	0-1	1-2	0-0	17.6	-	1.50
Ferdy Murphy	3-25	0-7	0-2	0-0	0-2	2-7	1-7	0-0	0-0	12.0	-	4.50
B J Llewellyn	3-17	0-4	2-8	1-4	0-1	0-0	0-0	0-0	0-0	17.6	+	1.50
C R Egerton	3-6	1-2	1-1	0-0	0-1	0-1	1-1	0-0	0-0	50.0	+	2.00

LEADING JUMPS TRAINERS AT LINGFIELD

	Total W-R	Nov Hdle	H'cap Hdle	Other Hdle	Nov Chase	H'cap Chase	Other Chase	Hunter Chase	N.H. Flat	Per£1 Level centstake	
R H Alner	8-32	3-4	2-4	0-4	1-6	2-11	0-3	0-0	0-0	25.0	+ 26.33
M C Pipe	7-22	0-8	1-3	0-0	1-3	2-2	3-6	0-0	0-0	31.8	+ 20.94
P F Nicholls	6-23	2-4	0-3	0-1	0-4	3-6	1-5	0-0	0-0	26.1	+ 9.62
G L Moore	6-47	1-17	1-11	1-4	1-5	2-6	0-4	0-0	0-0	12.8	+ 20.83
N J Henderson	5-21	0-4	1-6	1-2	1-3	0-3	2-3	0-0	0-0	23.8	- 4.42
T R George	4-14	1-2	0-2	0-0	1-2	2-8	0-0	0-0	0-0	28.6	+ 4.19
O Sherwood	3-9	0-1	1-1	1-1	0-0	1-5	0-1	0-0	0-0	33.3	+ 10.40
Jonjo O'Neill	3-20	0-5	2-3	0-1	0-1	1-7	0-3	0-0	0-0	15.0	+ 1.50
N A Twiston-Davies	2-13	0-3	0-1	0-2	1-2	1-2	0-3	0-0	0-0	15.4	- 1.50
K Bishop	2-5	0-1	0-0	0-0	0-0	1-3	1-1	0-0	0-0	40.0	+ 7.40
C Tinkler	2-4	1-3	0-0	0-0	0-0	1-1	0-0	0-0	0-0	50.0	+ 7.75
F Doumen	2-2	1-1	0-0	0-0	1-1	0-0	0-0	0-0	0-0	100.0	+ 15.25
Mrs L C Taylor	2-9	0-1	1-5	0-0	1-1	0-2	0-0	0-0	0-0	22.2	+ 4.25
R Rowe	2-16	1-6	0-2	0-2	0-0	1-6	0-0	0-0	0-0	12.5	+ 5.00
Jamie Poulton	2-10	0-3	0-0	1-1	0-2	1-4	0-0	0-0	0-0	20.0	+ 1.00
J W Mullins	2-12	0-3	0-1	1-4	0-2	1-2	0-0	0-0	0-0	16.7	- 0.00
P R Webber	2-15	1-6	0-0	0-2	1-1	0-5	0-1	0-0	0-0	13.3	- 4.75
Miss Venetia Williams	2-15	0-1	2-5	0-1	0-1	0-7	0-0	0-0	0-0	13.3	+ 1.75
C L Tizzard	2-15	1-3	0-2	0-0	1-4	0-4	0-2	0-0	0-0	13.3	- 6.50
Nick Williams	2-3	0-0	2-2	0-0	0-1	0-0	0-0	0-0	0-0	66.7	+ 5.50
A King	2-8	2-5	0-0	0-0	0-0	0-2	0-1	0-0	0-0	25.0	+ 5.50
P J Hobbs	1-12	1-1	0-1	0-1	0-0	0-7	0-2	0-0	0-0	8.3	- 6.50
R J Hodges	1-6	0-3	1-2	0-0	0-0	0-1	0-0	0-0	0-0	16.7	+ 2.00
R Dickin	1-6	0-1	0-0	0-1	0-1	0-2	1-1	0-0	0-0	16.7	- 4.47
M Scudamore	1-3	0-1	0-0	1-1	0-0	0-0	0-1	0-0	0-0	33.3	- 1.56
D L Williams	1-1	0-0	0-0	0-0	0-0	1-1	0-0	0-0	0-0	100.0	+ 14.00
D R Gandolfo	1-5	1-5	0-0	0-0	0-0	0-0	0-0	0-0	0-0	20.0	- 0.50
J A B Old	1-7	0-3	0-2	0-0	0-1	1-1	0-0	0-0	0-0	14.3	- 2.50
P Bowen	1-7	1-1	0-2	0-1	0-2	0-0	0-1	0-0	0-0	14.3	- 2.00
M F Harris	1-7	0-1	0-1	1-2	0-1	0-2	0-0	0-0	0-0	14.3	- 4.13
J Akehurst	1-4	0-0	0-1	0-0	0-0	1-3	0-0	0-0	0-0	25.0	+ 2.00

LEADING JUMPS TRAINERS AT LUDLOW

	Total W-R	Nov Hdle	H'cap Hdle	Other Hdle	Nov Chase	H'cap Chase	Other Chase	Hunter Chase	N.H. Flat	Per£1 Level centstake	
P J Hobbs	27-123	7-28	3-22	2-15	9-19	4-20	1-4	0-2	1-13	22.0	- 37.21
Miss H C Knight	26-147	4-38	1-4	3-21	7-31	2-16	0-5	0-0	9-32	17.7	- 20.67
M C Pipe	25-132	9-24	2-26	8-46	3-15	2-11	1-6	0-1	0-3	18.9	- 46.64
N J Henderson	24-88	5-18	6-17	2-17	2-11	0-4	2-3	0-0	7-18	27.3	+ 34.51
H D Daly	20-140	2-28	1-9	3-19	5-23	6-38	3-6	0-2	0-15	14.3	- 40.38
Ian Williams	17-107	4-21	2-17	4-12	3-25	2-23	1-3	0-1	1-5	15.9	+ 87.73
N A Twiston-Davies	16-128	4-23	0-20	1-19	3-13	5-34	0-3	0-0	3-16	12.5	- 29.66
P F Nicholls	16-72	0-10	3-8	0-8	3-10	6-20	1-4	1-4	2-8	22.2	+ 4.55
Miss Venetia Williams	16-110	3-18	5-20	3-13	1-10	4-39	0-3	0-0	0-7	14.5	+ 7.60
Jonjo O'Neill	13-65	3-16	2-11	1-9	3-11	3-12	0-3	0-0	1-3	20.0	- 3.23
O Sherwood	11-63	2-12	1-8	1-12	2-10	3-9	0-1	0-1	2-10	17.5	- 16.00
K C Bailey	11-84	0-13	2-16	2-10	3-11	3-23	1-3	0-0	0-8	13.1	- 1.42
Evan Williams	11-52	2-6	3-10	2-4	1-6	2-16	0-4	0-1	1-5	21.2	+ 6.57
S A Brookshaw	8-106	1-17	1-15	0-5	2-23	3-25	0-3	1-2	0-16	7.5	- 20.13

Name	Total	Nov Hdle	H'cap Hdle	Other Hdle	Nov Chase	H'cap Chase	Other Chase	Hunter Chase	N.H. Flat	Per£1 cent	Level stake
T R George	8-56	1-8	1-6	0-8	4-14	2-10	0-0	0-2	0-8	14.3	+ 19.53
P R Webber	7-54	1-10	1-2	0-9	0-7	0-2	0-5	0-0	5-19	13.0	- 25.58
J S King	6-48	0-10	1-5	0-3	1-11	4-15	0-2	0-0	0-2	12.5	- 5.87
R Lee	6-59	1-12	0-4	0-9	2-11	3-18	0-2	0-2	0-1	10.2	- 12.75
C Tinkler	6-17	0-2	2-4	0-5	0-0	0-0	0-1	0-0	4-5	35.3	+ 11.75
C J Mann	6-37	2-11	2-7	2-8	0-2	0-5	0-1	0-0	0-3	16.2	+ 39.25
A W Carroll	6-53	2-7	0-8	2-11	0-5	2-15	0-2	0-0	0-5	11.3	- 10.25
Heather Dalton	6-30	2-3	0-6	3-4	1-5	0-5	0-0	0-1	0-6	20.0	+ 46.66
W G M Turner	5-44	2-10	0-9	1-17	0-1	1-3	1-2	0-0	0-2	11.4	+ 57.00
R J Hodges	4-56	1-7	1-12	0-10	0-5	2-13	0-1	0-0	0-8	7.1	- 22.00
R Hollinshead	4-40	0-9	1-13	2-12	0-2	0-3	1-1	0-0	0-0	10.0	+ 10.58
G B Balding	4-21	1-3	2-3	0-3	1-2	0-4	0-1	0-0	0-5	19.0	+ 3.13
R T Phillips	4-30	1-7	1-5	1-4	0-3	0-3	0-0	0-0	1-8	13.3	- 3.87
W M Brisbourne	4-50	0-7	0-4	2-19	0-0	0-0	0-1	0-0	2-19	8.0	- 32.38
C J Price	4-30	0-2	1-8	0-5	0-1	2-6	0-2	0-0	1-6	13.3	+ 32.50
Mrs L Williamson	4-29	0-6	0-1	0-6	2-6	2-5	0-1	0-0	0-4	13.8	- 5.75
M Sheppard	4-61	0-10	1-7	0-9	0-12	2-15	1-6	0-0	0-2	6.6	- 42.60

LEADING JUMPS TRAINERS AT MARKET RASEN

	Total W-R	Nov Hdle	H'cap Hdle	Other Hdle	Nov Chase	H'cap Chase	Other Chase	Hunter Chase	N.H. Flat	Per£1 centstake	Level
M C Pipe	33-128	9 25	9-39	1-10	7-14	5-35	1-3	1-1	0-1	25.8	+ 12.00
Jonjo O'Neill	33-173	8-42	9-48	1-9	6-20	4-35	1-6	0-0	4-13	19.1	- 56.59
Mrs S J Smith	31-177	3-36	6-38	1-16	9-22	10-47	0-6	0-0	2-12	17.5	+ 7.26
P Bowen	20-55	5-10	5-17	0-3	4-5	4 14	2-3	0-0	0-3	36.4	+ 32.02
Ian Williams	14-99	1-24	5-18	3-13	0-7	3-24	2-5	0-0	0-8	14.1	- 2.89
M W Easterby	13-139	3-37	1-19	0-15	0-16	2-18	0-3	0-0	7-31	9.4	- 41.25
R C Guest	13-108	2-22	3-36	1-7	2-5	5-32	0-3	0-0	0-3	12.0	+ 17.38
C J Mann	12-57	3-12	5-17	0-0	0-0	4 12	0 2	0 0	0 0	21.1	+ 17.85
Mrs L Wadham	11-46	3-18	5-16	0-7	0-0	0-2	2-2	0-0	1-1	23.9	+ 3.54
C C Bealby	10-87	1-17	0-15	2-10	1-10	4-21	0-1	1-2	1-11	11.5	+ 41.50
Miss Venetia Williams	10-54	1-11	2-10	1-3	2-7	2-17	0-4	0-0	2-2	18.5	- 13.09
J Howard Johnson	9-45	1-12	3-8	1-7	0-4	2-7	1-2	0-0	1-5	20.0	+ 2.57
P J Hobbs	8-46	3-6	3-19	0-2	1-5	1-14	0-0	0-0	0-0	17.4	- 6.27
M C Chapman	8-201	0-49	5-82	0-20	1-14	2-29	0-3	0-0	0-4	4.0	- 124.75
J M Jefferson	8-58	2-8	1-9	1-6	0-8	3-14	0-3	0-0	1-10	13.8	- 28.16
B Ellison	8-60	0-15	0-18	0-2	0-7	8-18	0-0	0-0	0-0	13.3	+ 9.75
Ferdy Murphy	8-50	2-10	1-6	0-3	4-10	1-17	0-2	0-0	0-2	16.0	- 17.30
Mrs M Reveley	7-96	0-14	2-36	2-6	0-7	2-25	0-3	0-0	1-5	7.3	- 60.76
R Dickin	7-49	2-7	0-6	1-4	2-9	2-16	0-6	0-1	0-0	14.3	+ 14.83
N A Twiston-Davies	7-30	0-7	1-5	2-6	0-1	2-7	0-0	0-0	2-4	23.3	+ 32.50
P F Nicholls	7-34	0-3	0-5	1-2	5-9	1-14	0-0	0-0	0-1	20.6	- 7.89
C R Egerton	7-23	4-11	0-3	1-3	2-4	0-0	0-0	0-0	0-2	30.4	- 6.07
S Gollings	7-87	0-17	2-26	1-7	0-6	3-12	1-3	0-0	0-16	8.0	- 31.00
T R George	7-42	3-10	0-5	1-4	0-4	3-18	0-0	0-0	0-1	16.7	- 21.91
A King	7-18	3-8	1-2	0-0	2-3	0-1	1-1	0-0	0-3	38.9	+ 8.38
Mrs S Lamyman	6-94	0-19	5-56	1-6	0-3	0-2	0-0	0-0	0-8	6.4	- 45.50
P R Webber	6-40	1-4	0-2	0-0	3-10	2-16	0-4	0-0	0-4	15.0	- 25.44
H D Daly	6-23	1-6	0-0	2-5	1-2	1-6	0-1	1-2	0-1	26.1	+ 17.98
O Sherwood	5-30	2-7	0-6	0-4	0-2	1-7	0-0	0-0	2-4	16.7	- 8.54
D L Williams	5-36	2-8	0-6	0-2	0-5	2-13	1-1	0-1	0-0	13.9	- 1.83
J R Cornwall	5-70	0-2	0-6	0-2	0-21	4-35	1-4	0-0	0-0	7.1	- 10.12

LEADING JUMPS TRAINERS AT MUSSELBURGH

	Total W-R	Nov Hdle	H'cap Hdle	Other Hdle	Nov Chase	H'cap Chase	Other Chase	Hunter Chase	N.H. Flat	Per£1 Level centstake	
J Howard Johnson	25-128	8-47	7-34	5-19	3-8	0-7	0-1	0-0	2-12	19.5	- 23.23
L Lungo	23-85	8-21	5-19	1-5	4-11	4-12	0-2	0-0	1-15	27.1	+ 1.26
Mrs M Reveley	13-67	1-16	4-18	2-7	4-9	0-5	0-0	0-0	2-12	19.4	- 4.12
Mrs S C Bradburne	12-110	3-14	3-35	1-9	1-24	3-18	0-2	0-0	1-8	10.9	- 26.75
Ferdy Murphy	10-90	3-22	1-20	0-8	1-16	4-21	1-2	0-0	0-1	11.1	- 34.26
K G Reveley	8-38	3-7	1-10	0-4	1-6	2-4	0-1	0-0	1-6	21.1	+ 30.40
N G Richards	8-42	4-17	0-10	2-2	0-6	2-2	0-0	0-0	0-5	19.0	- 12.29
B Ellison	7-47	2-19	0-13	1-5	4-5	0-2	0-0	0-0	0-3	14.9	- 30.94
R A Fahey	7-35	1-6	3-13	0-2	0-2	0-1	0-0	0-0	3-11	20.0	+ 2.00
G A Swinbank	6-25	2-6	1-6	1-2	0-0	0-2	0-0	0-0	2-9	24.0	+ 8.30
S Donohoe	5-17	0-2	2-5	1-1	1-3	0-0	0-0	0-0	1-6	29.4	+ 9.25
R C Guest	5-49	0-10	1-13	1-7	1-6	0-9	1-1	0-0	1-3	10.2	- 9.45
D McCain	4-12	1-3	0-1	0-1	2-4	1-2	0-1	0-0	0-0	33.3	+ 13.00
A Parker	4-35	0-4	0-3	0-2	1-6	2-15	1-1	0-0	0-4	11.4	- 15.85
E W Tuer	4-22	0-6	1-7	0-1	0-0	0-1	0-1	2-4	1-2	18.2	- 7.58
J M Jefferson	3-58	0-14	1-17	0-2	1-7	1-9	0-1	0-0	0-8	5.2	- 36.75
P Monteith	3-76	0-24	0-17	1-9	0-7	2-13	0-1	0-0	0-5	3.9	- 58.69
M W Easterby	3-19	1-7	1-1	0-2	0-1	0-1	0-0	0-0	1-7	15.8	- 5.00
J I A Charlton	3-31	0-6	0-2	0-3	0-5	3-9	0-1	0-0	0-5	9.7	+ 13.75
K A Ryan	3-6	0-1	0-2	0-0	1-1	0-0	0-0	0-0	2-2	50.0	+ 3.87
D W Whillans	3-24	1-5	1-9	0-3	0-0	0-0	0-0	0-0	1-7	12.5	+ 44.75
R Ford	3-21	1-3	1-6	0-1	1-3	0-6	0-1	0-0	0-1	14.3	- 4.00
T D Easterby	3-16	0-4	0-2	1-2	0-0	1-6	0-0	0-0	1-2	18.8	+ 3.00
Mrs D Thomson	2-30	0-8	1-10	0-3	0-3	1-6	0-0	0-0	0-0	6.7	+ 47.00
T D Walford	2-10	0-2	0-1	0-0	0-0	0-1	0-0	1-1	1-5	20.0	+ 5.63
M C Pipe	2-9	1-1	0-3	1-2	0-1	0-1	0-1	0-0	0-0	22.2	- 6.69
W Storey	2-22	0-7	1-5	0-3	0-2	0-2	0-0	0-0	1-3	9.1	+ 80.80
N B Mason	2-21	0-6	0-5	0-1	1-2	1-7	0-0	0-0	0-0	9.5	- 13.50
D E Cantillon	2-3	2-2	0-1	0-0	0-0	0-0	0-0	0-0	0-0	66.7	+ 2.25
W Amos	2-13	0-4	0-1	1-2	0-0	0-2	1-1	0-1	0-2	15.4	- 3.00
Mrs K Walton	2-11	1-3	1-3	0-1	0-0	0-4	0-0	0-0	0-0	18.2	+ 13.75

LEADING JUMPS TRAINERS AT NEWBURY

	Total W-R	Nov Hdle	H'cap Hdle	Other Hdle	Nov Chase	H'cap Chase	Other Chase	Hunter Chase	N.H. Flat	Per£1 Level centstake	
N J Henderson	47-254	15-78	11-61	6-33	3-19	8-37	1-5	0-0	3-30	18.5	+ 8.18
P F Nicholls	37-160	10-32	1-14	2-14	9-27	6-48	6-16	1-3	2-10	23.1	+ 7.27
M C Pipe	33-246	7-48	5-64	3-26	4-25	7-53	2-10	1-1	4-22	13.4	- 105.78
P J Hobbs	24-178	7-38	5-31	1-17	4-21	5-53	1-2	0-0	1-17	13.5	+ 18.83
Jonjo O'Neill	16-135	2-41	3-28	3-14	2-18	2-25	0-2	0-1	5-11	11.9	- 51.91
N A Twiston-Davies	10-119	2-28	1-19	1-6	4-16	3-32	0-2	0-0	0-18	8.4	- 32.00
Miss Venetia Williams	10-94	3-19	1-24	0-8	0-6	6-35	0-0	0-0	0-7	10.6	- 38.63
P R Webber	7-76	1-16	0-7	1-10	3-11	1-17	0-1	0-0	1-14	9.2	- 24.75
A King	7-84	1-29	1-10	1-14	0-4	2-11	0-2	0-0	2-16	8.3	- 44.88
Noel T Chance	6-54	2-19	1-7	0-5	0-3	0-3	0-2	0-0	3-15	11.1	+ 13.00
Miss H C Knight	6-94	1-22	1-10	2-21	1-9	1-15	0-1	0-1	1-21	6.4	- 36.25
R H Alner	6-79	2-12	0-4	1-8	3-12	0-31	0-2	0-0	0-11	7.6	- 47.00
C R Egerton	6-31	1-3	1-9	0-6	2-3	2-6	0-0	0-0	0-6	19.4	+ 6.53
J W Mullins	6-64	1-19	0-7	3-14	1-9	0-8	0-0	0-1	1-10	9.4	+ 70.00

	Total W-R									Per£1	Level centstake
H Morrison	6-30	0-7	4-12	0-3	0-2	0-1	0-0	0-0	2-5	20.0	+ 12.00
Miss E C Lavelle	6-55	2-15	2-5	0-7	0-6	2-12	0-1	0-0	0-9	10.9	+ 5.17
Mrs M Reveley	5-41	1-3	0-16	0-3	0-2	3-8	1-1	0-0	0-10	12.2	- 15.50
C J Mann	5-87	2-28	0-19	0-9	2-11	1-16	0-1	0-0	0-4	5.7	- 26.92
T R George	5-55	0-12	0-6	1-5	2-10	2-17	0-1	0-0	0-4	9.1	- 13.00
M Pitman	5-56	0-15	1-6	0-3	2-9	1-6	0-0	0-1	1-16	8.9	+ 16.00
H D Daly	5-40	1-8	1-6	0-0	2-5	1-18	0-1	0-0	0-2	12.5	- 2.50
G L Moore	4-89	0-42	4-26	0-12	0-0	0-6	0-0	0-0	0-8	4.5	- 57.00
V R A Dartnall	4-21	1-5	1-5	0-1	0-2	0-2	0-0	0-0	2-6	19.0	+ 3.13
B G Powell	4-74	1-29	0-8	0-11	2-10	1-9	0-0	0-1	0-7	5.4	- 40.25
A M Balding	4-18	1-5	1-1	2-2	0-0	1-10	0-0	0-0	0-1	22.2	- 5.45
J Mackie	3-18	1-2	2-15	0-0	0-1	0-0	0-0	0-0	0-0	16.7	+ 1.00
D R Gandolfo	3-27	0-3	1-11	1-3	1-4	0-5	0-0	0-0	0-2	11.1	+ 30.00
J A B Old	3-52	1-15	0-9	0-11	0-2	2-8	0-0	0-0	0-9	5.8	- 35.00
F Doumen	3-19	0-4	1-1	3-6	0-3	0-4	0-1	0-0	0-1	15.8	- 1.12
R M Stronge	3-19	0-1	1-4	0-1	1 2	1-10	0-0	0-0	0-1	15.8	+ 26.00
Ian Williams	3-59	1-14	1-25	1-4	0-4	0-10	0-0	0-0	0-4	5.1	- 39.00

LEADING JUMPS TRAINERS AT NEWCASTLE

	Total W-R	Nov Hdle	H'cap Hdle	Other Hdle	Nov Chase	H'cap Chase	Other Chase	Hunter Chase	N.H. Flat	Per£1 centstake	Level
Mrs M Reveley	20-143	3-39	4-36	1-6	6-12	5-28	0-2	0-0	1-20	14.0	- 67.05
M W Easterby	14-85	2-30	4-14	2-11	2-5	1-13	0-1	0-0	3-11	16.5	+ 11.63
L Lungo	14-117	5-35	4-45	0-7	1-8	0-6	2-6	0-0	2-10	12.0	- 79.56
N G Richards	14-68	4-20	2-17	2-14	1 6	2-4	0-1	0-0	3-6	20.6	+ 10.10
Ferdy Murphy	13-138	5-36	1-15	1-12	2-20	3-36	1-8	0-0	0-11	9.4	- 81.45
R Johnson	12-117	0-27	3-16	0-8	0-24	9-34	0-1	0-1	0-6	10.3	+ 8.88
J Howard Johnson	10-87	5-38	2-12	2-12	1-4	0-17	0-0	0-0	0-4	11.5	- 23.87
N B Mason	10-40	1-8	1-7	0-3	3 4	6 15	0-0	0-1	0-2	25.0	+ 34.50
T D Easterby	10-60	5-23	0-5	0-6	4-8	1-11	0-0	0-0	0-7	16.7	- 21.10
Mrs S J Smith	9-71	1-21	1-10	0-2	2-10	4-21	0-1	0-0	1-6	12.7	- 16.84
M Todhunter	8-39	0-12	2-6	1-5	1-5	4-7	0-0	0-0	0-4	20.5	+ 27.62
R C Guest	8-71	0-12	2-24	0-8	2-4	4-20	0-0	0-0	0-3	11.3	+ 2.50
T P Tate	7-8	1-1	0-1	1-1	0-0	0-0	0-0	3-3	2-2	87.5	+ 19.19
R T Phillips	7-21	2-6	1-4	1-3	1-2	1-3	0-0	0-0	1-3	33.3	+ 1.02
K G Reveley	7-43	1-10	3-12	0-3	0-2	1-9	1-3	0-0	1-4	16.3	- 12.40
P Monteith	6-60	0-13	1-16	2-7	0-7	2-12	0-1	0-0	1-4	10.0	- 23.17
P C Haslam	6-23	4-11	0-4	0-2	2-4	0-1	0-1	0-0	0-0	26.1	+ 18.50
Mrs K Walton	6-35	0-6	2-10	0-3	0-0	4-12	0-0	0-0	0-4	17.1	+ 27.50
H P Hogarth	6-13	0-3	0-0	0-0	4-5	1-3	1-1	0-1	0-0	46.2	+ 33.62
J M Jefferson	5-57	1-19	0-6	1-6	1-6	1-4	0-1	0-0	1-15	8.8	- 37.36
Jonjo O'Neill	5-24	2-5	1-5	1-6	0-1	1-6	0-0	0-0	0-1	20.8	+ 28.60
Mrs A Hamilton	5-13	2 3	1 1	0-0	0-1	1-3	1-1	0-0	0-1	38.5	+ 23.75
N A Twiston-Davies	4-11	3-4	1-1	0-0	0-0	0-5	0-1	0-0	0-0	36.4	+ 7.74
Mrs S C Bradburne	4-37	1-6	0-4	0-2	2-3	1-20	0-1	0-0	0-1	10.8	+ 11.50
M A Barnes	4-19	0-4	4-9	0-2	0-1	0-3	0-0	0-0	0-0	21.1	+ 49.00
A C Whillans	4-42	0-6	3-18	0-2	0-3	0-9	1-1	0-0	0-3	9.5	- 13.75
B Ellison	4-28	3-14	0-8	0-2	1-2	0-0	0-0	0-0	0-2	14.3	- 9.58
D W Whillans	4-16	2-5	1-7	0-0	0-0	0-1	0-0	0-0	1-3	25.0	+ 25.50
R Ford	4-15	0-1	1-6	0-0	1-3	2-4	0-1	0-0	0-0	26.7	+ 13.50
P Beaumont	3-40	1-17	1-4	0-1	0-3	1-8	0-0	0-0	0-7	7.5	- 2.00
F Kirby	3-14	1-4	0-1	0-1	0-2	2-5	0-0	0-0	0-1	21.4	+ 48.00

LEADING JUMPS TRAINERS AT NEWTON ABBOT

	Total W-R	Nov Hdle	H'cap Hdle	Other Hdle	Nov Chase	H'cap Chase	Other Chase	Hunter Chase	N.H. Flat	Per£1 Level centstake	
M C Pipe	98-470	22-94	23-150	12-67	20-50	9-77	6-12	0-1	6-19	20.9	- 139.55
P J Hobbs	58-250	14-44	7-79	3-15	11-34	17-60	3-7	0-0	3-11	23.2	+ 1.99
P F Nicholls	36-138	6-18	2-15	2-14	7-23	12-41	3-8	1-2	3-17	26.1	+ 10.64
J D Frost	21-189	3-39	7-60	6-33	2-18	3-20	0-4	0-0	0-15	11.1	- 78.28
Jonjo O'Neill	19-80	3-13	8-30	1-2	2-9	1-16	0-0	0-0	4-10	23.8	- 4.55
C L Tizzard	15-110	2-10	0-11	1-15	3-18	7-42	2-6	0-0	0-8	13.6	- 21.30
P Bowen	12-50	1-7	1-13	1-6	2-3	6-16	1-1	0-0	0-4	24.0	+ 15.00
J W Mullins	12-112	1-19	2-22	1-21	1-15	3-17	1-6	0-1	3-11	10.7	+ 27.25
C J Mann	9-49	2-12	1-12	3-8	1-4	2-12	0-1	0-0	0-0	18.4	- 4.30
T R George	9-59	4-12	2-12	0-4	1-11	0-14	1-4	0-0	1-2	15.3	- 8.37
R Lee	8-32	0-2	4-6	1-3	0-5	3-15	0-1	0-0	0-0	25.0	+ 4.25
Nick Williams	8-46	2-13	3-11	0-3	1-3	2-16	0-0	0-0	0-0	17.4	+ 26.75
R G Frost	7-63	0-16	3-19	1-6	1-8	1-11	0-1	0-0	1-2	11.1	- 16.50
R J Hodges	6-81	0-9	1-13	3-16	0-6	2-28	0-4	0-0	0-5	7.4	- 29.25
N J Henderson	6-21	1-4	0-3	2-6	1-3	1-1	0 0	0-0	1-4	28.6	+ 3.44
K Bishop	6-39	1-3	1-15	1-6	1-2	1-7	0-1	0-0	1-5	15.4	+ 115.74
R H Buckler	6-57	1-8	0-9	0-3	2-10	2-22	0-1	0-0	1-4	10.5	+ 5.50
C J Down	6-64	1-20	0-9	1-13	0-2	0-7	3-5	0-2	1-6	9.4	- 10.75
Miss Venetia Williams	6-55	1-12	1-12	0-5	2-5	2-14	0-3	0-0	0-4	10.9	- 34.04
Ian Williams	6-36	0-6	1-8	1-4	0-0	3-16	0-1	0-0	1-1	16.7	- 4.25
Mrs A M Thorpe	6-54	1-9	2-14	0-6	0-4	3-15	0-3	0-0	0-3	11.1	+ 48.50
Noel T Chance	5-14	1-2	2-4	0-1	2-2	0-0	0-0	0-0	0-5	35.7	+ 5.45
R H Alner	5-63	0-15	1-7	0-1	2-13	2-22	0-1	0-0	0-4	7.9	- 20.75
G L Moore	5-33	3-8	0-10	1-1	0-3	1-8	0-0	0-0	0-3	15.2	- 10.75
R T Phillips	5-33	1-1	1-16	2-8	0-0	0-6	1-1	0-0	0-1	15.2	+ 9.00
P C Ritchens	5-24	0-2	0-3	1-3	1-4	3-12	0-0	0-0	0-0	20.8	+ 2.25
A King	5-34	2-5	0-5	0-4	0-2	1-9	0-0	0-0	2-9	14.7	- 6.81
A E Jones	5-48	0-10	2-11	1-8	0-3	2-11	0-1	0-0	0-4	10.4	- 0.50
G B Balding	4-16	1-1	2-7	0-0	0-1	0-3	0-1	0-0	1-3	25.0	+ 12.75
D Burchell	4-32	1-4	3-15	0-2	0-1	0-8	0-1	0-0	0-1	12.5	+ 9.83
R J Baker	4-78	2-14	1-24	1-20	0-5	0-7	0-3	0-0	0-5	5.1	- 41.50

LEADING JUMPS TRAINERS AT PERTH

	Total W-R	Nov Hdle	H'cap Hdle	Other Hdle	Nov Chase	H'cap Chase	Other Chase	Hunter Chase	N.H. Flat	Per£1 Level centstake	
N G Richards	31-123	5-25	10-40	6-25	3-10	6-19	0-0	0-0	1-4	25.2	+ 27.87
N A Twiston-Davies	22-74	6-16	4-16	5-15	1-5	3-17	1-2	0-0	2-3	29.7	+ 30.67
Jonjo O'Neill	19-74	5-10	3-25	1-3	3-12	4-17	0-1	0-0	3-6	25.7	- 0.21
T R George	19-60	2-9	4-15	2-8	4-7	4-13	2-5	0-0	1-3	31.7	+ 41.14
L Lungo	18-105	6-25	3-33	4-18	1-6	2-8	1-3	0-0	1-12	17.1	- 54.48
J S Goldie	15-61	1-6	7-30	1-6	4-7	2-10	0-0	0-0	0-2	24.6	+ 16.36
Ferdy Murphy	13-77	3-9	4-17	3-14	0-5	3-25	0-2	0-0	0-5	16.9	+ 46.90
M Todhunter	13-49	5-11	4-15	3-9	0-4	1-8	0-0	0-0	0-2	26.5	+ 29.51
P J Hobbs	11-48	1-8	1-6	5-13	4-9	0-12	0-0	0-0	0-0	22.9	- 18.30
P F Nicholls	11-33	2-3	0-3	0-2	4-8	3-12	0-0	1-4	1-1	33.3	+ 9.24
Miss Lucinda V Russell	11-198	2-42	2-39	0-28	2-33	4-38	1-8	0-0	0-10	5.6	- 120.25
Miss Venetia Williams	11-61	2-8	1-8	0-8	2-5	4-24	1-5	1-1	0-2	18.0	+ 0.66
P Monteith	9-116	1-19	1-26	3-21	1-17	2-23	1-3	0-1	0-6	7.8	- 21.92
G M Moore	8-29	3-11	1-5	2-3	0-5	2-4	0-0	0-0	0-1	27.6	+ 22.25

	Total W-R									Per£1		
Mrs S C Bradburne	8-141	2-22	1-50	0-18	0-11	3-29	1-3	0-0	1-8	5.7	-	75.00
G A Harker	8-19	1-2	3-7	1-4	1-3	0-0	0-0	0-0	2-3	42.1	+	38.58
Mrs L B Normile	8-101	0-17	1-14	3-29	2-12	1-13	0-4	0-2	1-10	7.9	+	40.40
Mrs M Reveley	7-28	2-3	1-3	3-10	1-4	0-6	0-1	0-0	0-1	25.0	+	16.87
P Bowen	7-13	1-3	1-2	1-3	2-2	2-2	0-0	0-0	0-1	53.8	+	11.20
R Ford	7-46	1-5	3-14	0-5	0-5	3-16	0-0	0-1	0-0	15.2	-	5.77
P Beaumont	6-44	0-7	0-3	0-11	0-5	3-13	2-4	0-0	1-1	13.6	+	5.00
M C Pipe	6-32	1-6	3-9	0-3	1-8	1-6	0-0	0-0	0-0	18.8	-	6.40
A Parker	5-38	0-5	2-13	0-5	1-2	2-11	0-0	0-0	0-2	13.2	+	22.50
J J Lambe	5-95	0-29	2-18	1-14	1-9	1-14	0-5	0-1	0-5	5.3	-	51.50
J M Jefferson	4-45	1-4	2-9	0-6	0-9	1-8	0-0	0-0	0-9	8.9	-	19.93
A C Whillans	4-65	0-10	1-19	1-13	1-3	1-17	0-1	0-0	0-2	6.2	-	41.75
B Ellison	4-22	0-2	1-9	1-4	0-3	2-3	0-0	0-0	0-1	18.2	-	10.63
Mrs S J Smith	4-18	0-2	0-5	0-0	2-4	2-6	0-0	0-0	0-1	22.2	+	29.00
R A Fahey	4-18	1-3	1-6	0-1	0-1	0-2	0-0	0-0	2-5	22.2	-	5.68
Mrs D Thomson	3-53	0-10	3-16	0-5	0-10	0-6	0-5	0-0	0-1	5.7	-	33.50
Mrs A Hamilton	3-13	1-1	0-5	0-0	1-2	1-4	0-1	0-0	0-0	23.1	-	3.70

LEADING JUMPS TRAINERS AT PLUMPTON

	Total W-R	Nov Hdle	H'cap Hdle	Other Hdle	Nov Chase	H'cap Chase	Other Chase	Hunter Chase	N.H. Flat	Per£1 Level centstake		
G L Moore	49-226	18-78	11-67	10-34	4-16	3-18	0-7	0-0	3-6	21.7	+	74.94
M C Pipe	38-155	13-46	6-32	10-41	2-12	1-13	2-4	0-0	4-7	24.5	-	33.94
P F Nicholls	25-82	5 10	0-6	1-12	9-20	6-20	1-3	2-2	1-9	30.5	-	8.30
N J Henderson	17-52	6-19	1-6	4-9	3-8	0 4	2-4	0-0	1-2	32.7	+	1.27
R H Alner	15-89	6-17	1-11	2-9	2-17	4-28	0-2	0-0	0-5	16.9	+	26.63
Miss Venetia Williams	15-88	1-21	0-12	0-6	6-15	5-21	1-4	0-0	2-9	17.0	-	39.67
P J Hobbs	11-43	3-13	2-6	2-6	3-5	1-9	0-3	0-0	0-1	25.6	-	6.34
C L Tizzard	10-67	1-9	0-5	1-8	3-18	4-22	1-2	0-0	0-3	14.9	+	8.00
Miss E C Lavelle	10-32	5-8	1-3	1-3	1-7	2-6	0-0	0-0	0-5	31.3	+	52.83
C J Mann	9-55	2-12	1-7	2-8	0-2	3-18	1-5	0-0	0-3	16.4	-	17.90
Mrs N Smith	8-35	3-8	2-7	1-2	2-11	0-3	0-3	0-0	0-1	22.9	+	32.30
R H Buckler	8-85	1-19	1-8	0-9	2-10	2-28	2-6	0-0	0-5	9.4	-	10.52
P Winkworth	8-65	1-13	1-11	2-15	0-5	3-14	0-2	0-0	1-5	12.3	-	13.00
L Wells	8-71	3-20	2-12	0-8	0-4	1-12	0-4	0-1	2-10	11.3	+	0.88
Mrs L C Taylor	7-34	0-4	3-6	0-1	0-10	3-12	1-1	0-0	0-0	20.6	+	15.33
J W Mullins	7-88	1-21	0-6	0-7	1-19	5-27	0-2	0-0	0-6	8.0	-	31.42
Mrs A M Thorpe	7-27	1-4	4-10	0-2	0-1	2-9	0-0	0-0	0-1	25.9	+	8.75
D P Keane	7-28	0-8	2-4	0-2	3-4	2-7	0-0	0-2	0-1	25.0	+	18.43
Jamie Poulton	6-65	1-13	0-11	0-13	1-5	4-19	0-4	0-0	0-0	9.2	-	26.50
B J Llewellyn	6-33	2-5	4-15	0-7	0-1	0-3	0-1	0-0	0-1	18.2	+	16.00
R Rowe	6 81	0-20	3-18	0-7	3-12	0-20	0-1	0-0	0-3	7.4	-	47.30
M Pitman	6-52	1-17	1-7	2-6	0-5	0-5	1-3	0-0	1-0	11.6	-	19 00
Ian Williams	6-24	0-7	1-4	0-2	2-5	2-5	1-1	0-0	0-0	25.0	+	6.38
Jonjo O'Neill	5-46	3-14	1-6	0-6	0-4	0-10	0-1	0-0	1-5	10.9	+	28.38
M Scudamore	5-29	1-6	1-6	0-5	0-4	2-4	1-3	0-0	0-1	17.2	+	14.25
Noel T Chance	5-25	1-12	0-2	0-3	1-2	0-0	1-3	0-0	2-3	20.0	+	1.78
C R Egerton	5-19	2-7	1-2	1-3	0-2	0-0	0-2	0-0	1-3	26.3	-	6.68
Miss A M N'ton-Smith	5-104	1-19	4-35	0-13	0-11	0-22	0-4	0-0	0-0	4.8	-	62.00
A King	5-30	1-10	0-4	1-5	2-3	1-2	0-1	0-0	0-5	16.7	-	17.65
N J Gifford	5-30	1-9	0-5	2-6	0-1	0-4	0-1	0-0	2-4	16.7	+	18.00
D B Feek	5-49	3-23	0-7	1-8	1-4	0-5	0-0	0-0	0-2	10.2	-	29.09

LEADING JUMPS TRAINERS AT SANDOWN

	Total W-R	Nov Hdle	H'cap Hdle	Other Hdle	Nov Chase	H'cap Chase	Other Chase	Hunter Chase	N.H. Flat	Per£1 Level centstake	
N J Henderson	37-157	10-38	6-40	1-21	4-12	6-27	4-14	2-3	4-13	23.6	+ 25.27
P F Nicholls	37-183	3-16	1-23	3-23	10-23	10-64	11-38	0-2	0-1	20.2	- 21.60
M C Pipe	32-241	9-28	11-97	6-52	2-11	5-64	2-18	0-0	0-3	13.3	- 19.61
P J Hobbs	16-135	2-25	1-34	3-15	3-10	5-42	2-11	0-0	0-5	11.9	- 69.69
Jonjo O'Neill	15-110	4-29	6-38	4-17	0-5	0-18	0-1	0-0	1-8	13.6	- 22.81
Miss H C Knight	15-79	2-16	0-8	0-2	8-17	2-15	3-11	0-0	0-10	19.0	- 4.50
Miss Venetia Williams	11-108	3-11	2-30	0-8	2-9	4-45	0-8	0-0	0-3	10.2	+ 19.08
G L Moore	9-93	2-40	5-34	3-14	0-5	1-7	0-1	0-0	0-3	9.7	+ 31.00
F Doumen	7-34	0-9	1-6	3-7	0-0	2-10	0-2	0-0	1-1	20.6	- 7.09
P R Chamings	7-19	0-2	0-2	1-3	0-0	3-6	3-6	0-0	0-1	36.8	+ 54.50
J Howard Johnson	6-35	2-5	1-7	0-11	0-2	3-12	0-1	0-0	0-1	17.1	+ 7.00
P R Webber	6-51	0-13	1-6	0-0	2-5	1-18	0-3	0-0	2-6	11.8	- 10.75
R H Alner	5-41	2-6	2-10	0-0	0-4	1-15	0-4	0-0	0-2	12.2	+ 2.50
V R A Dartnall	5-15	2-2	0-6	0-2	0-0	0-1	0-1	0-0	3 6	33.3	+ 17.25
N A Twiston-Davies	4-54	1-14	1-12	0-4	0-3	2-11	0-4	0-0	0-8	7.4	- 29.00
C R Egerton	4-23	0-7	0-2	1-6	1-2	2-5	0-1	0-0	0-0	17.4	- 1.37
M Pitman	4-41	0-9	0-6	0-1	1-6	2-10	1-3	0-0	0-7	9.8	- 15.75
A King	4-43	2-9	0-11	1-11	0-3	1-10	0-2	0-0	0-3	9.3	- 19.75
A M Balding	4-7	1-1	1-4	0-2	0-0	0-0	1-1	1-1	0-0	57.1	+ 19.70
J Mackie	3-10	0-0	3-9	0-0	0-0	0-0	0-0	0-0	0-1	30.0	+ 5.25
Mrs John Harrington	3-8	0-1	1-2	1-2	0-0	0-0	2-5	0-0	0-0	37.5	+ 3.00
R Rowe	3-42	0-13	1-11	0-1	2-11	0-6	0-0	0-0	0-0	7.1	- 24.00
R T Phillips	3-19	0-1	2-11	0-1	0-1	1-2	0-1	0-0	0-2	15.8	- 2.12
A W Carroll	3-33	1-12	2-8	0-2	0-6	0-5	0-0	0-0	0-0	9.1	+ 25.20
N J Gifford	3-16	1-5	1-4	0-0	0-0	1-5	0-1	0-1	0-0	18.8	+ 8.50
B G Powell	3-23	0-8	0-10	0-0	1-1	1-2	1-1	0-1	0-0	13.0	- 6.75
R J Hodges	2-23	1-2	0-8	0-1	1-3	0-5	0-3	0-0	0-1	8.7	+ 9.00
D McCain	2-8	1-2	0-0	0-1	0-1	1-2	0-2	0-0	0-0	25.0	+ 5.50
C Sporborg	2-3	0-0	0-0	0-0	0-0	0-0	0-0	2-3	0-0	66.7	+ 8.00
G B Balding	2-18	1-6	0-2	0-0	1-2	0-6	0-0	0-0	0-2	11.1	+ 1.62
D M Grissell	2-13	0-3	0-1	0-0	1-3	1-5	0-0	0-0	0-1	15.4	+ 4.33

LEADING JUMPS TRAINERS AT SEDGEFIELD

	Total W-R	Nov Hdle	H'cap Hdle	Other Hdle	Nov Chase	H'cap Chase	Other Chase	Hunter Chase	N.H. Flat	Per£1 Level centstake	
J Howard Johnson	42-197	11-68	10-48	5-11	3-16	7-28	6-15	0-1	0-10	21.3	- 19.52
Ferdy Murphy	41-249	9-47	4-55	2-16	6-31	12-66	7-29	0-1	1-4	16.5	+ 16.22
Mrs S J Smith	25-135	5-24	4-21	0-6	4-19	8-37	3-19	0-0	1-9	18.5	- 6.97
B Ellison	21-117	7-41	6-41	1-8	3-10	1-11	3-6	0-0	0-0	17.9	+ 2.99
L Lungo	20-83	6-26	4-21	1-5	1-3	4-16	2-4	0-0	2-8	24.1	+ 29.30
G M Moore	16-150	10-47	3-36	0-8	1-17	2-23	0-9	0-0	0-10	10.7	- 75.21
N G Richards	15-66	3-16	4-27	0-5	5-11	0-1	1-3	0-0	2-3	22.7	- 10.30
Mrs M Reveley	14-84	1-20	0-16	3-8	4-16	4-17	0-1	0-0	2-6	16.7	- 25.23
G A Swinbank	14-47	5-21	4-11	0-3	2-2	1-2	1-1	0-0	1-7	29.8	+ 44.85
M W Easterby	13-84	6-32	0-8	1-8	0-3	3-13	0-4	0-0	3-16	15.5	+ 8.73
R Johnson	12-117	1-22	8-41	0-7	1-16	2-23	0-7	0-0	0-1	10.3	+ 62.38
R C Guest	12-96	3-18	3-36	0-3	0-7	6-28	0-2	0-0	0-2	12.5	- 8.50
Mrs E Slack	11-86	1-18	4-35	0-4	0-1	5-22	1-1	0-0	0-5	12.8	- 30.01
M D Hammond	11-55	5-16	0-9	2-2	0-3	4-21	0-4	0-0	0-0	20.0	+ 38.31

D McCain	10-82	3-19	1-25	3-6	0-7	1-15	2-8	0-0	0-2	12.2	+ 28.91
J M Jefferson	9-61	2-11	5-23	0-4	0-4	1-5	0-4	0-0	1-10	14.8	- 21.62
T D Easterby	9-44	2-13	0-6	2-5	0-4	1-8	2-3	0-0	2-5	20.5	+ 21.91
Miss S E Forster	8-67	0-9	3-23	0-4	2-6	2-11	0-8	1-1	0-5	11.9	- 3.08
J J Lambe	8-82	2-18	4-32	0-5	1-5	1-14	0-7	0-0	0-1	9.8	+ 2.82
J Wade	7-89	0-27	1-10	0-2	0-12	5-19	0-8	0-0	1-11	7.9	- 25.57
P C Haslam	7-30	2-12	3-11	1-2	1-3	0-1	0-1	0-0	0-0	23.3	+ 10.16
Miss Kate Milligan	7-108	2-20	4 46	0-1	0-5	1-24	0-7	0-0	0-5	6.5	- 39.00
E W Tuer	7-49	2-11	3-24	1-3	0-3	0-2	0-0	0-0	1-6	14.3	+ 3.75
Jonjo O'Neill	6-17	2-5	3-5	0-0	0-0	0-5	0-1	1-1	0-0	35.3	+ 6.16
Mrs A Hamilton	6-22	2-8	0-4	0-0	2-3	1-2	1-2	0-2	0-1	27.3	+ 4.00
Mrs K Walton	6-33	0-8	2-9	0-2	3-6	1-6	0-0	0-0	0-2	18.2	+ 32.75
A Crook	6-65	0-10	0-14	0-2	2-7	4-27	0-3	0-0	0-2	9.2	- 25.84
M Todhunter	6-61	0-12	0-12	0-1	3-12	2-20	1-3	0-0	0-1	9.8	+ 6.00
G A Harker	6-47	1-12	2-14	1-3	0-1	0-3	0-4	0-1	2-9	12.8	+ 13.00
A Scott	6-30	3-17	3-9	0-1	0-2	0-0	0-0	0-0	0-1	20.0	+ 19.75
G Tuer	6-8	0-0	0-0	0-0	0-0	0-0	0-0	6-8	0-0	75.0	+ 8.48

LEADING JUMPS TRAINERS AT SOUTHWELL

	Total W-R	Nov Hdle	H'cap Hdle	Other Hdle	Nov Chase	H'cap Chase	Other Chase	Hunter Chase	N.H. Flat	Per£1 centstake	Level stake
Mrs S J Smith	20-148	0-29	10-34	1-12	3-10	6-47	0-9	0-0	0-7	13.5	- 42.88
Jonjo O'Neill	18-73	3-11	5-23	1-5	2-8	4-18	2-4	0-0	1-4	24.7	+ 0.34
M C Pipe	16-70	5-20	3-17	3-10	2-6	2-12	1-5	0-0	0-0	22.9	- 30.50
Miss Venetia Williams	12-43	3-8	1-12	3-5	2-4	2-11	0-1	0-0	1-2	27.9	4.34
Evan Williams	9-26	2-3	1-5	2-5	1-3	1-7	2-3	0-0	0-0	34.6	+ 13.34
A King	7-34	1-4	1-12	0-3	2-5	2-5	0-1	0-0	1-4	20.6	+ 11.11
R Lee	6-33	0-2	0-6	1-2	1-5	4 17	0-1	0-0	0-0	18.2	+ 0.25
P F Nicholls	6-10	3-4	1-2	0-0	1-1	1-2	0-1	0-0	0-0	60.0	I 11.18
C R Egerton	6-16	2-4	0-1	2-4	2-4	0-1	0-1	0-0	0-1	37.5	+ 19.99
P J Hobbs	5-15	2-3	2-5	1-2	0-3	0-1	0-1	0-0	0-0	33.3	+ 4.70
J W Mullins	5-13	1-1	0-1	0-0	0-2	2-4	2-5	0-0	0-0	38.5	+ 9.41
Miss Kate Milligan	5-30	1-6	1-6	2-6	0-1	1-11	0-0	0-0	0-0	16.7	- 6.37
Ian Williams	5-38	2-7	0-8	0-5	1-5	2-11	0-2	0-0	0-0	13.2	- 21.64
H D Daly	5-20	2-5	0-3	0-1	2-4	1-5	0-1	0-0	0-1	25.0	+ 4.58
R C Guest	5-47	0-4	0-8	0-6	1-7	4-20	0-0	0-0	0-2	10.6	- 13.50
J R Jenkins	4-37	0-9	4-21	0-1	0-1	0-0	0-3	0-0	0-2	10.8	- 13.67
N A Twiston-Davies	4-19	1-2	0-3	0-0	1-2	1-7	1-1	0-0	0-4	21.1	+ 14.12
M C Chapman	4-38	0-4	1-17	0-4	1-4	2-7	0-2	0-0	0-0	10.5	- 9.00
D J Wintle	4-15	0-2	1-6	2-2	0-2	1-2	0-0	0-0	0-1	26.7	+ 10.50
J L Spearing	4-15	2-5	0-5	0-0	2-2	0-1	0-0	0-0	0-2	26.7	+ 8.73
P Bowen	4-23	1-3	1-6	0-1	0-4	0-5	1-2	0-0	1-2	17.4	+ 16.75
R H Alner	4-13	1-3	0-0	0-0	2-6	1-4	0-0	0-0	0-0	30.8	+ 4.25
C C Bealby	4-26	0-5	0-0	0-3	1-6	3-8	0-2	0-0	0-2	15.4	+ 9.75
B G Powell	4-38	1-7	1-10	0-8	1-3	1-8	0-2	0-0	0-0	10.5	- 5.00
Mrs M Reveley	3-25	0-3	1-5	1-4	1-2	0-7	0-2	0-0	0-2	12.0	- 1.50
P Beaumont	3-13	0-2	0-0	0-0	3-5	0-5	0-0	0-0	0-1	23.1	+ 40.00
R Dickin	3-34	0-3	0-3	1-6	0-6	2-12	0-2	0-0	0-2	8.8	- 26.68
N J Henderson	3-21	0-5	0-6	0-0	0-0	1-5	1-2	0-0	1-3	14.3	- 13.02
P A Blockley	3-12	1-3	1-3	0-2	0-1	0-1	1-2	0-0	0-0	25.0	+ 13.00
J R Cornwall	3-30	0-0	1-4	0-1	0-7	2-17	0-1	0-0	0-0	10.0	- 2.00
C T Pogson	3-39	0-3	2-14	0-4	0-9	0-4	0-3	0-0	1-2	7.7	+ 50.00

LEADING JUMPS TRAINERS AT STRATFORD

	Total W-R	Nov Hdle	H'cap Hdle	Other Hdle	Nov Chase	H'cap Chase	Other Chase	Hunter Chase	N.H. Flat	Per£1 Level centstake	
P J Hobbs	49-151	11-33	12-38	3-7	6-20	15-43	2-7	0-0	0-3	32.5	+ 72.61
M C Pipe	36-179	15-47	5-49	7-21	2-11	4-38	0-4	2-6	1-3	20.1	- 34.91
Jonjo O'Neill	31-133	11-37	2-33	3-11	5-13	8-32	1-4	0-0	1-3	23.3	+ 15.23
P F Nicholls	17-74	4-10	2-10	0-5	4-9	4-28	1-5	2-7	0-0	23.0	+ 1.79
Ian Williams	13-115	3-30	3-32	2-13	1-5	2-31	2-2	0-0	0-2	11.3	- 50.62
P R Webber	10-41	1-10	1-5	1-3	1-5	4-14	1-3	0-0	1-1	24.4	+ 59.12
Miss Venetia Williams	10-62	2-14	1-11	3-6	1-1	2-27	0-0	0-0	1-3	16.1	- 7.22
N A Twiston-Davies	9-68	2-12	1-13	2-9	2-7	1-19	1-3	0-1	0-4	13.2	- 20.71
M Pitman	7-36	1-7	3-12	2-3	0-8	1-5	0-1	0-0	0-0	19 4	+ 17.50
H D Daly	7-56	1-10	0-4	0-5	2-10	3-20	0-3	0-0	1-4	12.5	- 26.75
Nick Williams	7-29	2-6	2-8	0-0	0-0	3-14	0-1	0-0	0-0	24.1	+ 16.75
A King	7-51	3-14	1-9	0-3	1-4	2-16	0-1	0-0	0-4	13.7	- 10.69
Miss H C Knight	6-34	1-9	0-1	0-4	2-11	3-5	0-1	0-0	0-3	17 6	7.75
C J Mann	6-53	2-14	1-14	1-5	0-4	2-14	0-1	0-0	0-1	11.3	- 19.88
Miss E C Lavelle	6-30	1-5	1-5	1-3	0-2	3-15	0-0	0-0	0-0	20.0	+ 21.00
C Tinkler	5-13	0-1	2-6	0-2	0-0	1-2	1-1	0-0	1-1	38.5	+ 25.75
J W Mullins	5-39	1-10	1-7	0-5	1-5	2-9	0-0	0-2	0-1	12.8	- 12.25
R Dickin	4-71	0-26	0-8	0-5	1-10	2-17	0-1	1-2	0-2	5.6	- 38.50
J M Jefferson	4-22	1-9	2-3	0-3	0-3	1-3	0-1	0-0	0-0	18.2	+ 14.00
J L Spearing	4-35	0-5	0-10	0-6	1-2	2-7	1-2	0-0	0-3	11.4	- 12.00
Mrs L C Taylor	4-21	0-4	0-2	0-1	0-2	4-11	0-1	0-0	0-0	19.0	- 4.62
M F Harris	4-63	2-18	1-18	0-8	1-4	0-7	0-3	0-3	0-2	6.3	- 29.13
Mrs S J Smith	4-19	1-4	0-3	0-1	1-2	2-9	0-0	0-0	0-0	21.1	- 0.00
B J Llewellyn	4-28	0-4	1-11	1-3	1-6	1-2	0-1	0-0	0-1	14.3	+ 4.91
Mrs D A Hamer	4-33	3-10	1-10	0-6	0-2	0-4	0-1	0-0	0-0	12.1	+ 7.33
T R George	4-32	1-7	1-10	0-1	2-4	0-8	0-1	0-1	0-0	12.5	- 15.00
B D Leavy	4-20	0-2	1-4	0-4	0-2	3-6	0-2	0-0	0-0	20.0	+ 22.50
Evan Williams	4-34	1-9	1-5	0-4	0-4	0-6	2-4	0-2	0-0	11.8	- 12.92
J D Frost	4-34	1-5	0-4	1-15	0-1	2-7	0-1	0-0	0-1	11.8	+ 4.00
F Jordan	3-31	1-14	2-8	0-6	0-1	0-0	0-1	0-0	0-1	9.7	+ 9.50
D R C Elsworth	3-8	0-0	1-3	0-1	2-2	0-1	0-0	0-0	0-1	37.5	+ 7.30

LEADING JUMPS TRAINERS AT TAUNTON

	Total W-R	Nov Hdle	H'cap Hdle	Other Hdle	Nov Chase	H'cap Chase	Other Chase	Hunter Chase	N.H. Flat	Per£1 Level centstake	
M C Pipe	60-359	22-106	15-146	14-59	4-16	2-20	2-7	0-0	1-5	16.7	- 98.48
P F Nicholls	50-200	15-51	6-27	4-25	11-31	5-26	5-17	0-3	4-20	25.0	- 21.01
P J Hobbs	40-201	8-44	10-52	9-30	4-25	5-33	3-8	0-1	1-8	19.9	- 13.94
R H Alner	13-111	1-23	2-22	2-14	3-15	4-30	1-4	0-0	0-3	11.7	- 1.30
R J Hodges	11-145	2-27	2-32	1-22	3-17	2-22	1-7	0-0	0-18	7.6	- 61.67
Miss Venetia Williams	11-74	3-20	0-8	0-14	4-14	3-13	0-0	0-0	1-5	14.9	- 28.05
Miss H C Knight	10-56	1-16	0-0	2-6	4-20	0-3	2-4	0-0	1-7	17.9	- 22.25
N J Henderson	9-45	4-15	1-8	0-8	0-3	1-2	1-2	0-0	2-7	20.0	- 9.46
G L Moore	8-37	4-14	0-9	1-7	0-2	2-4	1-1	0-0	0-0	21.6	+ 9.12
R T Phillips	7-29	2-8	1-9	1-4	1-3	1-4	1-1	0-0	0-0	24.1	+ 6.75
Miss E C Lavelle	7-33	1-12	1-7	0-3	1-2	4-6	0-0	0-0	0-3	21.2	+ 7.25
A King	6-33	3-14	0-6	1-3	1-3	0-3	0-0	0-0	1-4	18.2	+ 2.60
K Bishop	5-68	1-7	2-23	1-9	0-8	1-19	0-1	0-0	0-1	7.4	- 42.94
C L Tizzard	5-83	0-15	0-9	0-6	3-19	2-28	0-2	0-0	0-4	6.0	- 46.50

	W-R									%		Level
B G Powell	5-45	1-9	2-12	0-4	0-9	1-3	0-1	0-0	1-7	11.1	-	5.50
A E Jones	5-36	0-5	2-10	0-3	0-2	2-7	0-5	0-3	1-1	13.9	+	37.38
T R George	4-38	1-13	1-5	0-5	0-3	2-9	0-3	0-0	0-0	10.5	+	4.00
C J Gray	4-45	0-8	4-23	0-7	0-3	0-3	0-0	0-0	0-1	8.9	-	5.00
J D Frost	4-77	0-14	1-23	3-21	0-5	0-7	0-2	0-0	0-5	5.2	-	21.27
S C Burrough	4-59	0-12	2-12	0-9	1-6	0-10	0-3	0-0	1-7	6.8	-	20.00
N A Twiston-Davies	3-42	0-8	2-9	1-5	0-6	0-12	0-1	0-0	0-1	7.1	-	25.75
G B Balding	3-21	1-4	0-6	0-2	0-2	0-3	2-2	0-0	0-2	14.3	-	6.42
D Burchell	3-30	0-4	3-17	0-3	0-1	0-4	0-1	0-0	0-0	10.0	+	2.50
C L Popham	3-44	0-7	0-4	0-8	0-9	3-12	0-2	0-0	0-2	6.8	+	13.00
J L Spearing	3-20	0-10	2-5	0-0	1-2	0-2	0-0	0-0	0-1	15.0	+	14.25
J A B Old	3-32	0-9	0-4	0-6	0-1	1-5	0-1	0-0	2-6	9.4		19.67
M Bradstock	3-14	1-6	0-1	1-3	0-1	0-2	0-0	0-0	1-1	21.4	+	0.25
C J Down	3-35	0-4	2-11	0-4	0-5	0-4	0-2	0-1	1-4	8.6	-	13.00
J G M O'Shea	3-26	0-3	0-9	3-6	0-5	0-0	0-0	0-0	0-3	11.5	+	4.25
Karen George	3-79	0-18	1-31	1-14	0-6	0-7	1-1	0-0	0-2	3.8	-	4.50
C R Egerton	3-10	1-7	0-0	1-2	0-0	0-0	0-0	0-0	1-1	30.0	+	0.65

LEADING JUMPS TRAINERS AT TOWCESTER

	Total W-R	Nov Hdle	H'cap Hdle	Other Hdle	Nov Chase	H'cap Chase	Other Chase	Hunter Chase	N.H. Flat	Per£1 Level centstake		
Miss Venetia Williams	30-99	7-18	4-11	0-6	3-12	12-34	3-10	0-0	1-8	30.3	+	52.96
N A Twiston-Davies	16-95	5-27	2-16	0-6	0-7	4-25	2-3	0-0	3-11	16.8	-	3.47
R Dickin	11-108	3-26	2-22	0-3	1-7	5-43	0-4	0-0	0-3	10.2	+	14.60
M C Pipe	10-36	5-15	0-2	0-6	2-3	0-5	0-1	0-0	3-4	27.8	-	5.37
Jonjo O'Neill	10-47	6-14	1-12	1-4	1-7	0-5	1-3	0-0	0-2	21.3	-	20.91
K C Bailey	9-81	2-18	0-14	1-8	2-11	3-20	0-6	0-0	1-4	11.1	+	3.23
H D Daly	9-58	3-17	0-4	0-5	2-6	2-13	1-1	1-4	0-8	15.5	-	28.80
R H Buckler	7-45	2-12	2-3	0-3	1-4	1-14	0-4	0-0	1-5	15.6	-	1.57
J R Cornwall	7-38	0-1	0-2	0-0	1-5	5-29	1-1	0-0	0-0	18.4	+	3.00
John R Upson	7-83	0-18	2-21	0-5	0-1	3-29	2-5	0-0	0-4	8.4	-	38.00
Ferdy Murphy	7-36	0-3	0-4	2-6	2-5	1-10	0-2	0-0	2-6	19.4	-	0.52
J W Mullins	7-53	2-9	2-5	1-6	1-8	0-11	1-8	0-0	0-6	13.2	-	1.63
B G Powell	7-36	1-8	0-9	0-2	2-5	1-6	2-4	0-0	1-2	19.4	-	3.51
C R Egerton	6-12	4-5	0-1	1-3	0-0	0-0	0-1	0-0	1-2	50.0	+	6.11
Mrs L Wadham	6-21	0-3	3-9	2-2	0-2	1-3	0-1	0-0	0-1	28.6	+	8.50
R C Guest	6-28	0-3	1-8	2-3	2-2	1-11	0-0	0-0	0-1	21.4	-	5.62
P J Hobbs	5-30	1-11	0-2	0-0	1-6	2-5	1-4	0-0	0-2	16.7	-	11.17
D McCain	5-30	2-8	0-7	1-5	0-2	0-2	0-0	0-0	2-6	16.7	+	8.00
P A Pritchard	5-37	2-10	0-5	0-2	0-2	3-10	0-2	0-0	0-6	13.5	-	18.67
J A B Old	5-54	0-18	1-11	2-7	0-0	0-9	0-1	0-0	2-8	9.3	-	1.09
G L Moore	5-24	1-7	3-10	1-2	0-2	0-2	0-0	0-0	0-1	20.8	-	6.00
F Jordan	4-42	0-16	1-9	0-5	0-3	0-2	1-1	0-0	2-6	9.5	-	15.37
R J Hodges	4-11	1-2	1-4	1-2	1-2	0-0	0-0	0-0	0-1	36.4	+	15.75
O Sherwood	4-22	1-8	0-0	0-1	0-3	2-5	1-2	0-0	0-3	18.2	-	7.25
N J Henderson	4-18	1-5	0-0	0-3	0-1	0-2	1-3	0-0	2-4	22.2	-	3.62
P C Haslam	4-10	2-3	0-1	0-1	0-1	1-2	0-0	0-0	1-2	40.0	+	9.63
J G M O'Shea	4-19	1-3	1-6	2-4	0-0	0-1	0-2	0-0	0-3	21.1	+	0.50
N M Babbage	4-20	0-1	1-6	0-3	0-2	3-6	0-0	0-0	0-2	20.0	+	9.00
R T Phillips	4-34	1-8	0-5	1-3	0-2	0-4	1-4	0-0	1-8	11.8	-	12.92
Heather Dalton	4-20	1-6	0-2	0-2	0-0	2-4	0-3	0-0	1-3	20.0	+	7.57
Ian Williams	4-37	1-10	2-7	0-2	0-5	0-8	1-3	0-0	0-2	10.8	+	15.50

LEADING JUMPS TRAINERS AT UTTOXETER

	Total W-R	Nov Hdle	H'cap Hdle	Other Hdle	Nov Chase	H'cap Chase	Other Chase	Hunter Chase	N.H. Flat	Per£1 Level centstake	
M C Pipe	34-178	8-27	8-68	4-21	6-10	5-41	3-7	0-0	0-4	19.1	- 47.85
Jonjo O'Neill	34-160	12-39	5-42	2-16	5-17	7-28	1-6	0-0	2-12	21.3	- 29.46
P J Hobbs	20-81	4-15	6-19	2-8	5-10	3-27	0-1	0-0	0-1	24.7	+ 15.02
Miss Venetia Williams	19-103	4-20	2-19	4-11	2-12	6-34	1-4	0-0	0-3	18.4	- 37.21
N A Twiston-Davies	17-89	4-21	3-13	1-6	2-9	6-30	0-1	0-0	1-9	19.1	- 19.59
Mrs S J Smith	13-85	3-11	3-23	1-6	2-6	4-29	0-5	0-0	0-5	15.3	+ 24.62
P F Nicholls	13-74	3-8	1-9	1-4	3-11	2-33	1-3	2-4	0-2	17.6	- 22.80
H D Daly	13-79	3-27	1-10	0-4	3-7	2-16	1-1	0-0	3-14	16.5	- 15.24
Ian Williams	12-85	3-20	3-25	3-14	1-4	2-16	0-3	0-0	0-3	14.1	+ 9.75
D McCain	11-90	5-23	1-13	2-12	2-15	1-14	0-4	0-0	0-9	12.2	+ 47.00
K C Bailey	11-77	3-18	1-11	1-9	5-14	1-17	0-3	0-0	0-5	14.3	+ 7.33
J M Jefferson	9-41	4-11	4-11	1-4	0-4	0-3	0-2	0-0	0-6	22.0	+ 8.72
P Bowen	9-62	1-9	5-21	1-9	0-5	1-11	0-1	0-0	1-6	14.5	- 6.52
C J Mann	9-43	4-12	0-9	1-6	1-4	3-10	0-1	0-0	0-1	20.9	+ 23.76
T R George	9-75	0-15	0-9	0-6	5-14	3-26	0-3	0-0	1-2	12.0	- 10.33
Mrs K Waldron	9-77	1-9	3-33	1-11	0-2	4-16	0-1	0-1	0-4	11.7	- 18.77
Evan Williams	9-50	0-6	3-16	0-6	1-6	5-13	0-1	0-0	0-2	18.0	+ 9.83
Mrs M Reveley	8-37	2-3	2-10	0-5	2-6	2-11	0-1	0-0	0-1	21.6	+ 1.68
J Mackie	8-79	2-17	5-37	1-12	0-3	0-3	0-2	0-0	0-5	10.1	- 14.17
V R A Dartnall	8-21	3-5	0-4	2-3	0-2	1-2	1-1	0-0	1-4	38.1	+ 7.13
Ferdy Murphy	7-66	2-16	2-11	1-5	0-8	2-22	0-2	0-0	0-2	10.6	- 17.25
R T Phillips	7-39	3-12	2-11	0-7	0-1	0-1	0-2	0-0	2-5	17.9	- 9.23
D P Keane	7-38	0-9	3-5	2-7	0-2	0-6	0-1	0-0	2-8	18.4	+ 14.38
A King	6-71	2-20	2-18	1-6	0-7	0-12	0-3	0-0	1-5	8.5	- 44.70
R J Price	5-26	0-6	5-14	0-1	0-0	0-5	0-0	0-0	0-0	19.2	+ 51.00
N J Henderson	5-40	3-11	0-9	0-3	0-7	0-5	2-3	0-0	0-2	12.5	- 25.37
C C Bealby	5-54	1-14	1-4	2-7	1-9	0-9	0-1	0-0	0-10	9.3	- 10.50
D J Wintle	5-38	0-3	2-19	1-3	1-3	1-7	0-2	0-0	0-1	13.2	+ 61.10
R H Buckler	5-25	1-3	0-3	1-4	1-7	1-6	1-1	0-0	0-1	20.0	+ 4.95
R Ford	5-36	0-5	2-8	0-3	1-6	2-12	0-1	0-0	0-1	13.9	- 1.90
P R Webber	5-38	1-9	0-5	0-7	0-2	1-7	1-3	0-0	2-5	13.2	+ 4.25

LEADING JUMPS TRAINERS AT WARWICK

	Total W-R	Nov Hdle	H'cap Hdle	Other Hdle	Nov Chase	H'cap Chase	Other Chase	Hunter Chase	N.H. Flat	Per£1 Level centstake	
M C Pipe	24-145	6-39	5-41	0-8	9-22	2-25	1-3	0-0	1-7	16.6	- 64.04
P F Nicholls	23-82	2-14	2-10	0-4	9-21	5-21	4-7	1-3	0-2	28.0	- 5.00
R Dickin	15-131	1-27	3-28	0-8	4-15	6-36	0-1	0-0	1-16	11.5	+ 30.88
Jonjo O'Neill	15-87	5-26	2-18	1-5	1-12	1-14	0-1	1-1	4-10	17.2	- 15.30
A King	15-77	3-22	2-15	3-9	6-7	1-10	0-3	0-0	0-11	19.5	- 8.36
N A Twiston-Davies	12-111	4-26	2-15	2-13	0-11	4-29	0-1	0-0	0-16	10.8	- 9.93
Ian Williams	11-116	5-36	2-34	1-8	1-11	1-16	1-1	0-0	0-10	9.5	- 63.23
H D Daly	11-64	6-23	1-3	0-2	0-10	4-14	0-2	0-0	0-10	17.2	+ 4.54
N J Henderson	10-48	2-10	1-9	0-5	1-8	1-3	3-4	0-0	2-9	20.8	- 3.15
Miss Venetia Williams	10-59	1-10	3-11	0-7	1-5	3-20	0-1	0-0	2-5	16.9	- 15.50
P J Hobbs	8-78	3-25	3-8	1-5	0-7	1-24	0-0	0-0	0-9	10.3	- 26.38
Noel T Chance	8-26	2-8	2-4	0-0	1-1	0-2	0-1	0-0	3-10	30.8	+ 10.87
M Pitman	8-32	3-8	1-5	0-2	1-4	2-5	0-1	0-0	1-7	25.0	+ 28.12
C J Mann	7-29	2-6	0-2	0-4	1-2	2-9	0-2	0-0	2-4	24.1	+ 17.88

P R Webber	7-35	2-6	1-5	0-1	3-10	1-5	0-0	0-0	0-8	20.0	+ 1.30
R Lee	6-37	0-4	0-9	1-3	1-3	2-11	0-2	2-4	0-1	16.2	+ 19.05
R H Alner	6-35	3-11	1-7	1-3	0-2	1-10	0-0	0-0	0-2	17.1	- 8.25
P A Pritchard	5-34	1-12	2-6	0-1	0-1	2-6	0-1	0-0	0-7	14.7	+ 82.78
J A B Old	5-56	2-14	0-10	1-4	1-4	0-10	0-1	0-0	1-13	8.9	- 17.00
D J Wintle	4-51	0-9	3-24	0-5	0-3	0-4	0-1	0-0	1-5	7.8	- 5.00
John R Upson	4-20	1-4	0-1	0-4	0-0	3-10	0-0	0-0	0-1	20.0	+ 4.83
P Winkworth	4-20	0-2	2-9	0-1	1-2	1-3	0-1	0-0	0-2	20.0	+ 0.50
T R George	4-39	1-7	2-10	1-4	0-5	0-10	0-0	0-0	0-3	10.3	- 3.00
C Von Der Recke	4-9	2-5	0-1	1-1	1-2	0-0	0-0	0-0	0-0	44.4	+ 22.75
R J Hodges	3-22	0-3	1-3	0-2	0-2	2-5	0-2	0-0	0-5	13.6	- 11.00
O Sherwood	3-29	0-6	0-4	1-3	1-4	1-8	0-0	0-0	0-4	10.3	- 11.20
Mrs P Sly	3-21	0-10	1-7	1-2	0-0	0-0	0 0	0-0	1-2	14.3	+ 31.00
C Tinkler	3-21	2-6	0-4	0-4	0-1	0-2	0-1	0-0	1-3	14.3	- 9.00
J L Spearing	3-25	1-10	2-7	0-4	0-1	0-1	0-0	0-0	0-2	12.0	+ 8.50
J Howard Johnson	3-6	2-3	0-0	0-0	0-0	1-2	0-0	0-0	0-1	50.0	+ 0.49
M F Harris	3-39	0-7	1-16	2-2	0-4	0-8	0-0	0-0	0-2	7.7	- 14.00

LEADING JUMPS TRAINERS AT WETHERBY

	Total W-R	Nov Hdle	H'cap Hdle	Other Hdle	Nov Chase	H'cap Chase	Other Chase	Hunter Chase	N.H. Flat	Per£1 Level centstake	
Mrs S J Smith	41-245	3-40	13-53	0-25	7-34	12-61	5-14	0-0	1-18	16.7	- 37.23
Mrs M Reveley	33-232	5-52	8-68	4-17	7-25	7-47	0-4	0-0	2-19	14.2	- 37.55
Jonjo O'Neill	25-109	6-21	7-29	4-14	4-13	3-22	0-4	0-1	1-5	22.9	- 0.87
M W Easterby	23-223	3-50	7-49	2-27	2-20	6-39	2-2	0-1	1-35	10.3	- 86.67
T D Easterby	21-173	4-47	2-31	2-12	3-14	7-47	3-7	0-2	0-13	12.1	- 58.67
J Howard Johnson	19-100	7-27	5-27	3-11	0-8	0-13	4-7	0-0	0-7	19.0	+ 66.15
G M Moore	18-125	4-41	1-18	0-6	7-15	4-29	0-4	0-0	2-12	14.4	+ 10.23
L Lungo	17-100	0-21	6-45	1-7	1-7	4-9	1-2	0 0	4-9	17.0	- 21.92
M D Hammond	14-106	1-25	4-27	1-13	5-10	3-17	0-0	0-0	0-14	13.2	- 25.69
Ferdy Murphy	14-126	1-36	3-21	3-11	1-16	3-29	2-7	0-0	1-6	11.1	- 44.42
R C Guest	12-94	3-22	5-33	0-5	1-9	3-16	0-4	0-0	0-5	12.8	- 38.93
P F Nicholls	11-45	4-10	0-3	0-4	1-1	1-12	3-13	2-2	0-0	24.4	- 22.78
P Beaumont	8-91	1-22	0-9	1-8	4-15	1-13	0-5	0-1	1-18	8.8	- 6.50
N A Twiston-Davies	7-37	3-9	0-3	0-8	1-5	0-4	1-4	0-0	2-4	18.9	- 8.09
J M Jefferson	7-66	1-18	2-23	1-7	2-5	1-8	0-1	0-0	0-4	10.6	- 29.98
P C Haslam	7-36	4-16	0-7	3-10	0-2	0-1	0-0	0-0	0-0	19.4	- 7.48
N J Henderson	6-25	3-8	0-4	1-2	0-3	0-3	2-3	0-1	0-1	24.0	- 7.92
K A Ryan	6-24	0-6	3-8	1-3	0-1	1-4	0-0	0-0	1-2	25.0	+ 27.50
P R Webber	6-35	1-8	0-1	0-1	1-3	3-17	0-4	0-0	1-1	17.1	- 4.75
A W Carroll	6-22	3-4	2-9	0-3	1-4	0-1	0-0	0-0	0-1	27.3	+ 17.58
C Grant	6-73	0-25	1-11	0-10	2-6	2-8	0-2	1-4	0-7	8.2	- 42.33
Ian Williams	6-48	1-11	4-13	0-5	1-3	0-10	0-1	0-0	0-5	12.5	- 17.48
N G Richards	6-28	0-3	2-11	1-5	1-3	1-3	0-0	0-0	1-3	21.4	+ 13.25
J Wade	5-45	0-11	2-7	0-6	0-7	3-7	0-3	0-0	0-4	11.1	+ 15.50
R A Fahey	5-52	0-14	4-26	1-3	0-2	0-4	0-1	0-0	0-2	9.6	- 12.80
J J Quinn	5-21	2-11	3-0	0-1	0-0	0-1	0-0	0-0	0-0	23.8	+ 9.25
K G Reveley	5-70	1-19	0-21	3-10	0-3	0-5	0-2	0-0	1-10	7.1	- 49.99
M Todhunter	5-40	2-15	1-8	0-5	0-5	2-4	0-2	0-0	0-1	12.5	- 10.33
Miss Venetia Williams	5-39	3-7	1-11	0-2	0-1	0-14	1-4	0-0	0-0	12.8	- 19.14
Heather Dalton	5-35	0-6	1-4	0-6	2-3	0-4	1-2	0-0	1-10	14.3	- 9.67
A King	5-39	4-11	0-5	0-10	1-4	0-5	0-2	0-0	0-2	12.8	- 18.32

LEADING JUMPS TRAINERS AT WINCANTON

	Total W-R	Nov Hdle	H'cap Hdle	Other Hdle	Nov Chase	H'cap Chase	Other Chase	Hunter Chase	N.H. Flat	Per£1 Level centstake	
P F Nicholls	112-399	27-86	15-83	10-34	15-50	26-90	10-26	0-3	9-27	28.1	+ 0.51
P J Hobbs	36-233	10-54	11-52	1-14	3-20	6-73	1-6	0-0	4-14	15.5	- 64.67
M C Pipe	24-181	5-31	7-68	4-22	4-8	3-40	1-6	0-0	0-6	13.3	- 58.18
Miss H C Knight	22-111	5-39	2-10	1-10	6-14	4-17	4-7	0-1	0-13	19.8	- 11.74
A King	21-133	7-41	4-26	1-15	5-12	4-19	0-4	0-1	0-15	15.8	- 25.43
N J Henderson	20-69	3-16	0-18	4-9	3-5	2-8	3-5	0-0	5-8	29.0	+ 6.35
R J Hodges	14-154	1-31	4-37	0-10	3-18	5-40	1-6	0-0	0-12	9.1	- 78.38
R H Alner	14-185	4-46	2-39	0-15	2-14	5-58	1-5	0-1	0-7	7.6	- 94.38
Miss Venetia Williams	14-95	2-11	2-24	1-7	2-6	4-36	1-5	0-0	2-6	14.7	- 37.98
T R George	12-64	6-17	2-9	0-5	2-4	2-25	0-1	0-0	0-3	18.8	+ 24.00
J W Mullins	10-135	3-46	4-23	0-17	2-17	0-12	1-4	0-1	0-15	7.4	- 39.00
B G Powell	7-85	3-25	1-19	1-15	0-6	2-12	0-1	0-0	0-7	8.2	- 50.27
D P Keane	7-61	1-18	0-9	0-5	0-6	6-20	0-1	0-0	0-2	11.5	+ 92.00
Dr J R J Naylor	6-28	0-8	0-3	0-4	0-0	6-12	0-0	0-0	0-1	21.4	+ 16.00
P R Webber	5-43	2-12	1-5	0-4	0-5	2-11	0-2	0-1	0-3	11.6	+ 21.50
G B Balding	4-46	1-20	3-11	0-4	0-5	0-4	0-0	0-0	0-2	8.7	- 25.00
J A B Old	4-33	1-15	0-3	0-3	0-1	2-7	0-0	0-0	1-4	12.1	+ 18.50
G L Moore	4-34	1-13	2-14	0-0	1-3	0-3	0-0	0-0	0-1	11.8	- 16.77
C J Mann	4-47	3-20	0-11	0-4	0-0	1-7	0-4	0 0	0-1	8.5	- 27.88
M Pitman	4-34	2-11	2-5	0-6	0-3	0-5	0-1	0-0	0-3	11.8	- 17.50
J G Portman	4-22	0-2	1-3	0-0	0-2	3-13	0-1	0-0	0-1	18.2	- 4.50
N A Twiston-Davies	3-40	0-13	1-9	0-2	0-5	1-6	0-1	0-0	1-4	7.5	- 10.17
Jonjo O'Neill	3-55	1-14	0-16	1-7	0-4	1-8	0-0	0-0	0-6	5.5	- 48.58
J L Spearing	3-13	0-4	2-2	0-1	1-3	0-0	0-1	0-0	0-2	23.1	+ 10.00
R H Buckler	3-73	1-17	0-13	0-5	0-10	2-19	0-2	0-0	0-7	4.1	- 57.00
P Bowen	3-30	0-10	0-8	0-0	0-1	3-8	0-1	0-0	0-2	10.0	- 10.20
Andrew Turnell	3-21	0-5	1-5	0-1	0-2	2-7	0-0	0-0	0-1	14.3	- 10.92
Noel T Chance	3-22	1-6	0-4	0-0	0-1	0-2	1-1	0-0	1-8	13.6	- 11.50
R Rowe	3-20	0-5	0-4	0-0	1-3	2-7	0-0	0-0	0-1	15.0	+ 25.00
C R Egerton	3-18	1-10	1-1	0-5	0-0	0-0	0-0	0-0	1-2	16.7	+ 2.00
C St V Fox	3-4	0-0	0-0	0-0	0-0	0-0	0-0	3-4	0-0	75.0	+ 4.69

LEADING JUMPS TRAINERS AT WINDSOR

	Total W-R	Nov Hdle	H'cap Hdle	Other Hdle	Nov Chase	H'cap Chase	Other Chase	Hunter Chase	N.H. Flat	Per£1 Level centstake	
M C Pipe	3-14	1-1	2-4	0-4	0-0	0-4	0-0	0-0	0-1	21.4	- 0.34
Miss Venetia Williams	3-11	0-0	0-5	0-0	2-2	1-4	0-0	0-0	0-0	27.3	- 3.15
A King	3-10	0-2	1-1	0-4	0-0	2-2	0-0	0-0	0-1	30.0	+ 0.38
O Sherwood	2-7	0-1	0-2	0-2	0-0	2-2	0-0	0-0	0-0	28.6	+ 0.83
C Tinkler	2-3	1-1	0-0	0-1	0-0	0-0	0-0	0-0	1-1	66.7	+ 2.79
R H Alner	2-8	0-1	0-1	0-1	1-2	1-3	0-0	0-0	0-0	25.0	+ 3.25
V R A Dartnall	2-5	0-1	1-1	0-1	0-1	0-0	0-0	0-0	1-1	40.0	+ 8.00
P J Hobbs	1-10	0-0	1-4	0-4	0-1	0-1	0-0	0-0	0-0	10.0	- 7.63
M J Ryan	1-2	0-0	0-1	1-1	0-0	0-0	0-0	0-0	0-0	50.0	+ 49.00
N J Henderson	1-11	0-1	0-1	0-4	0-1	1-4	0-0	0-0	0-0	9.1	- 9.00
Jonjo O'Neill	1-17	0-6	0-3	0-2	1-2	0-2	0-0	0-0	0-2	5.9	- 9.50
M Madgwick	1-3	1-1	0-1	0-0	0-0	0-0	0-0	0-0	0-1	33.3	+ 1.50
J A B Old	1-1	1-1	0-0	0-0	0-0	0-0	0-0	0-0	0-0	100.0	+ 14.00
F Doumen	1-4	0-1	0-0	1-2	0-0	0-0	0-0	0-0	0-1	25.0	- 2.38

	Total W-R	Nov Hdle	H'cap Hdle	Other Hdle	Nov Chase	H'cap Chase	Other Chase	Hunter Chase	N.H. Flat	Per£1 Level		centstake
J Howard Johnson	1-1	0-0	0-0	1-1	0-0	0-0	0-0	0-0	0-0	100.0	+	1.75
Miss H C Knight	1-13	1-3	0-0	0-5	0-1	0-1	0-0	0-0	0-3	7.7	-	9.00
J R Fanshawe	1-1	1-1	0-0	0-0	0-0	0-0	0-0	0-0	0-0	100.0	+	2.75
P F Nicholls	1-13	0-1	0-4	1-3	0-2	0-2	0-0	0-0	0-1	7.7	-	10.25
J W Mullins	1-3	0-0	0-0	0-0	1-3	0-0	0-0	0-0	0-0	33.3	+	4.50
R T Phillips	1-5	0-1	0-2	1-1	0-1	0-0	0-0	0-0	0-0	20.0	+	2.50
B De Haan	1-3	0-0	0-0	0-1	0-0	1-1	0-0	0-0	0-1	33.3	+	0.50
T R George	1-5	0-1	0-0	0-1	0-1	1-2	0-0	0-0	0-0	20.0	-	2.90
Mrs L Williamson	1-1	0-0	0-0	0-0	1-1	0-0	0-0	0-0	0-0	100.0	+	1.10
H Morrison	1-2	1-1	0-0	0-1	0-0	0-0	0-0	0-0	0-0	50.0	+	1.00
H D Daly	1-2	0-0	0-0	1-1	0-0	0-1	0-0	0-0	0-0	50.0	+	6.50
Miss E C Lavelle	1-4	0-0	1-3	0-1	0-0	0-0	0-0	0-0	0-0	25.0	+	7.00
N G Richards	1-1	0-0	0-0	1-1	0-0	0-0	0-0	0-0	0-0	100.0	+	2.75
J Joseph	0-1	0-0	0-1	0-0	0-0	0-0	0-0	0-0	0-0	0.0	-	1.00
A M Hales	1-2	0-0	1-1	0-0	0-1	0-0	0-0	0-0	0-0	50.0	+	15.00
K O Cunn'ham-Brown	0-1	0-1	0-0	0-0	0-0	0-0	0-0	0-0	0-0	0.0	-	1.00
J S King	0-1	0-1	0-0	0-0	0-0	0-0	0-0	0-0	0-0	0.0	-	1.00

LEADING JUMPS TRAINERS AT WORCESTER

	Total W-R	Nov Hdle	H'cap Hdle	Other Hdle	Nov Chase	H'cap Chase	Other Chase	Hunter Chase	N.H. Flat	Per£1 Level		centstake
M C Pipe	42-177	7-31	10-64	9-32	7-15	5-21	1-6	0-0	3-8	23.7	+	31.70
P J Hobbs	33-177	9-27	6-60	4-16	7-24	1-35	4-7	0-0	2-8	18.6	-	57.71
Jonjo O'Neill	24-165	4-33	4-53	4-19	2-12	2-21	0-7	0-0	8-20	14.5	-	73.46
P Bowen	19-101	1-10	7-25	2-17	3-11	4-17	2-6	0-0	0-15	18.8	-	11.23
Mrs S J Smith	19-116	4-20	3-22	1-14	5-9	5-25	1-9	0-0	0-17	16.4	+	10.93
P F Nicholls	18-58	3-7	1-8	3-5	2-6	5-14	0-5	0-0	4 13	31.0	+	42.25
N A Twiston-Davies	16-102	5-25	5-22	1-14	1-6	3-19	0-2	0-0	1-14	15.7	-	9.95
Ian Williams	12-101	1-9	5-34	2-12	1-12	3-23	0-1	0-0	0-10	11.9	-	12.77
N J Henderson	11-50	1-8	1-5	1-10	3-5	0-3	0-2	0-0	5-17	22.0	-	13.22
Miss Venetia Williams	10-48	3-11	1-8	3-11	0-2	2-11	1-2	0-0	0-3	20.8	-	7.38
B G Powell	10-91	3-21	1-20	0-8	1-13	2-14	1-6	0-0	2-9	11.0	+	4.50
Evan Williams	9-56	3-13	1-11	0-9	2-9	1-5	1-6	0-0	1-3	16.1	+	17.62
Heather Dalton	8-74	1-20	2-10	0-9	3-7	2-12	0-0	0-0	0-16	10.8	-	26.50
R Lee	7-50	0-6	2-10	0-2	0-6	4-20	1-4	0-0	0-2	14.0	+	13.50
R Dickin	7-76	0-11	1-8	0-11	2-19	4-22	0-2	0-0	0-3	9.2	+	18.08
H D Daly	7-49	2-11	0-2	1-9	0-6	1-10	0-3	0-0	3-8	14.3	+	2.50
D J Wintle	6-59	1-9	0-20	2-9	1-7	2-11	0-1	0-0	0-2	10.2	-	18.67
C J Mann	6-47	3-15	1-12	2-9	0-4	0-4	0-2	0-0	0-1	12.8	-	8.47
T R George	6-40	1-5	0-5	1-6	0-5	0-9	2-3	0-0	2-7	15.0	-	21.78
P R Webber	6-41	1-6	0-4	2-13	0-2	1-7	1-2	0-0	1-7	14.6	-	13.37
O Sherwood	5-27	1-5	1-3	0-5	0-2	0-5	1-1	0-0	2-6	18.5	-	3.79
R J Price	5-65	1-11	3-20	0-14	0-5	1-7	0-0	0-0	0-8	7.7	-	24.50
M Scudamore	5-36	0-6	1-11	0-3	2-4	1-6	0-1	0-0	1-5	13.9	-	10.00
D Burchell	5-51	1-9	2-19	1-6	1-7	0-6	0-1	0-0	0-3	9.8	-	6.00
J A B Old	5-31	2-13	1-6	1-3	0-2	0-4	1-2	0-0	0-1	16.1	+	12.50
Mrs D A Hamer	5-48	0-14	2-9	1-12	0-3	1-2	0-2	0-0	1-7	10.4	+	88.00
J W Mullins	5-57	0-8	0-8	0-4	3-12	1-13	0-6	0-0	1-6	8.8	-	2.00
M Sheppard	5-48	1-8	0-10	1-8	0-7	3-13	0-2	0-0	0-0	10.4	-	11.88
Mrs L Wadham	5-17	1-5	1-3	2-4	0-2	0-1	0-0	0-0	1-2	29.4	+	56.90
L A Dace	5-25	1-11	4-11	0-0	0-0	0-1	0-0	0-0	0-2	20.0	+	11.25
R C Guest	5-62	2-5	1-19	0-5	0-11	1-19	1-1	0-0	0-2	8.1	-	30.50

LEADING PRIZEMONEY WINNERS 2005–2006

NAME	WINS-RUNS	2nd	3rd	4th	WIN £	TOTAL £	£1STK
P F Nicholls	148-651 (23%)	103	71	68	1,565,591	2,404,288	-113.02
P J Hobbs	112-659 (17%)	82	79	66	1,058,393	1,631,939	-107.95
M C Pipe	112-880 (13%)	107	84	77	1,083,999	1,578,888	-287.58
Jonjo O'Neill	105-711 (15%)	88	65	60	759,693	1,194,883	-176.52
N J Henderson	85-390 (22%)	44	43	36	791,736	1,058,137	+43.42
A King	63-415 (15%)	61	43	41	616,152	967,442	-1.45
Mrs S J Smith	60-412 (15%)	45	42	35	484,000	713,556	-20.64
Miss V Williams	77-475 (16%)	67	42	41	432,630	662,814	-43.79
J H Johnson	58-331 (18%)	35	22	25	420,916	568,327	-46.71
N G Richards	59-277 (21%)	41	31	19	322,242	566,026	-16.86
G L Moore	63-452 (14%)	51	56	35	324,062	495,213	+17.04
R H Alner	38-352 (11%)	44	39	44	309,879	494,239	-94.13
N A T'stn-Davies	59-472 (13%)	36	36	46	327,147	486,192	-83.27
P Bowen	41-314 (13%)	38	33	27	286,603	485,662	-112.63
Ferdy Murphy	45-384 (12%)	48	34	31	300,373	461,267	-84.13
R C Guest	55-515 (11%)	49	48	60	311,995	451,180	-99.39
Martin Brassil	1-1 (100%)	0	0	0	399,140	399,140	+11.01
H D Daly	35-272 (13%)	36	23	40	242,077	390,951	-103.71
Evan Williams	56-340 (16%)	43	28	27	296,385	390,330	+97.90
Miss H C Knight	28-245 (11%)	18	23	26	243,018	359,087	-96.80
M F Morris	1-3 (33%)	2	0	0	228,080	322,598	+5.51
T R George	34-262 (13%)	31	33	33	166,938	321,740	-61.62
C R Egerton	21-85 (25%)	13	11	12	213,249	281,999	+72.45
K G Reveley	32-269 (12%)	28	26	32	169,577	272,987	-75.53
D McCain	35-300 (12%)	25	39	38	190,164	262,554	+92.04
C A Murphy	2-2 (100%)	0	0	0	259,703	259,703	+3.26
Miss E C Lavelle	30-197 (15%)	22	23	20	166,752	258,913	-15.42
W P Mullins	0-23	2	1	4	0	256,771	-23.00
C J Mann	23-181 (13%)	23	28	9	161,301	255,179	-16.91
F Doumen	4-39 (10%)	7	4	5	107,600	251,499	-14.75
Ian Williams	28-336 (8%)	40	36	33	144,657	246,320	-56.44
J L Spearing	14-113 (12%)	19	10	8	164,440	223,256	+5.51
O Sherwood	20-183 (11%)	22	21	20	117,097	218,161	-50.42
C L Tizzard	24-198 (12%)	26	26	22	113,425	211,509	-25.38
J W Mullins	22-300 (7%)	42	31	36	101,819	209,651	-84.47
B G Powell	32-330 (10%)	33	30	31	125,678	203,666	-103.27
Noel Meade	3-23 (13%)	1	0	3	162,507	203,036	+5.42
L Lungo	27-227 (12%)	18	20	19	129,896	188,239	-112.76
P C Haslam	28-157 (18%)	19	17	12	108,056	188,174	-10.76
S Gollings	13-124 (10%)	16	13	9	101,551	187,012	-28.90
Nick Williams	11-80 (14%)	5	12	6	137,918	182,473	+12.09
J M Jefferson	28-191 (15%)	17	16	18	126,739	180,933	-11.45
P R Webber	23-157 (15%)	12	21	13	109,300	168,361	+6.83
John J Murphy	1-5 (20%)	0	0	0	165,358	167,368	+12.01
M Pitman	19-133 (14%)	19	16	8	97,808	162,788	+14.26
N J Gifford	14-89 (16%)	6	10	8	115,860	155,325	+26.48